National Intelligencer Newspaper Abstracts 1848

Joan M. Dixon

HERITAGE BOOKS
2007

HERITAGE BOOKS
AN IMPRINT OF HERITAGE BOOKS, INC.

Books, CDs, and more—Worldwide

For our listing of thousands of titles see our website at
www.HeritageBooks.com

Published 2007 by
HERITAGE BOOKS, INC.
Publishing Division
65 East Main Street
Westminster, Maryland 21157-5026

Copyright © 2007 Joan M. Dixon

All rights reserved. No part of this book may be reproduced or transmitted in any form or by any means, electronic or mechanical, including photocopying, recording or by any information storage and retrieval system without written permission from the author, except for the inclusion of brief quotations in a review.

International Standard Book Number: 978-0-7884-4476-0

NATIONAL INTELLIGENCER NEWSPAPER
WASHINGTON, D C
1848

TABLE OF CONTENTS

Daily National Intelligencer
  Washington, D C, 1848: pg 1
Army deaths-Mexico-attached to D C & Md Regt: 73
Army deaths-Hospital at Perote: 49-50
Army ofcrs wounded and sick, city of Mexico: 44
Army-Mexico: 115-116
Army promotions: 173-174; 275-283; 288-289; 310-323; 338-346
Kosciusko's Estate: 363-365
Commencements: Columbian College: 254
                Gtwn College, D C: 264-265 & 267
                Visitation Academy: 267
                St Mary's, Chas Co, Md: 287
Harvard College: 331
Licenses issued in Wash, D C: 153-162; 243-248; 368-369
Life of John Fillmore: 296; 365; 377
Marine Corps-promotions: 292
Deaths in Military Hosp-city of Mexico: 31-33
New States: 360-361
Presidential elections: 419-420
Rock Creek/Kolarama: 384-385
Sir Lawrence Washington's tomb: 356
Sold for taxes-Alleghany Co, Md: 148-152
Wash City lots to be sold for taxes: 304-308
Wash Nat'l Monument-inside the corner stone: 237-239; & 242

Index: pg 455

PREFACE
Daily National Intelligencer Newspaper Abstracts
1848
Joan M Dixon

The National Intelligencer & Washington Advertiser is hereafter the Daily National Intelligencer. It was the first newspaper printed in Washington, D C; Samuel H Smith, the originator. The same was transferred to Jos Gales, jr on Aug 31, 1810; on Nov 1, 1812, the paper was under the firm of Jos Gales, sr, & Wm W Seaton. The Library of Congress has microfilm of the paper from the first issue of Oct 31, 1800 thru Jan 8, 1870, the final paper. The Evening Star Newspaper of Jan 10, 1870 reports: The Intelligencer is discontinued: the proprietor, Mr Alex Delmar, says that having lost several thousand dollars, & being in poor health, he has resolved to discontinue its publication.

Included in the abstracts are advertisements; appointments by the President; Hse o/Rep petitions; passed Acts; legal notices; marriages; deaths; mscl notices; social events; tax lists; military promotions; court cases; deaths by accident; prisoners; & maritime information-crews. Items or events which might be a clue as to the location, age or relationship of an individual are copied.

No attempt has been made to correct the spelling. Due to the length of some articles, it was necessary to present only the highlights of same. Chancery and Equity records are copied as written.

The index contains all surnames and *tracts of lands/places*. **Maritime vessels** are found under barge, boat, brig, frig, schn'r, ship, sloop, steamboat, tugboat, yacht or vessel.

ABBREVIATIONS:

AA CO	ANNE ARUNDEL COUNTY
CO	COMPANY/COUNTY
CMDER	COMMANDER
CMDOR	COMMODOR
D C	DISTRICT OF COLUMBIA
ELIZ	ELIZABETH
ELIZA	ELIZA
MONTG CO	MONTGOMERY COUNTY
PG CO	PRINCE GEORGES CO
WASH	WASHINGTON
WASH, D C	WASHINGTON, DISTRICT OF COLUMBIA

BOOKS IN THE NATIONAL INTELLIGENCER NEWSPAPER SERIES: 1800-1805/1806-1810/1811-1813/1814-1817/1818-1820/1821-1823/1824-1826/1827-1829/1830-1831/1832-1833/1834-1835/1836-1837/1838-1839/1840/1841/1842/1843/1844/1845/1846/1847/1848/SPECIAL: CIVIL WAR 2 VOLS, 1861-1865

Dedicated to the memory of my G G Grandparents:
Benedict Neff: b Feb 2, 1815-Germany; died Apr 10, 1879-Wash, D C
Mrd: Oct 2, 1840-Wash, D C
Mary Catherine Grimes: b Oct 20, 1825, Germany; died Sep 21, 1892-Wash, D C

DAILY NATIONAL INTELLIGENCER
WASHINGTON, D C
1848

SAT JAN 1, 1848
Great loss of life at Clermont, Ohio, by the flood, on Wed. A just completed bldg, near the river, fell in a heap of ruins, owing to the great weight of snow upon its roof & the pressure of the waters. Those in the bldg killed were: Moses J Cornell, wife & 2 children; the family of Mr Ransom, [except himself & an infant,] viz. Mr Ranson, Henry Ransom, & Eliz Ransom, a dght grown up; Alonzo Guernsey, John Hemple, Charlotte Hemple, John P Schroeder, Jas A Mackinson, from Scotland; Chas R Kenan, Ireland; John Woodson, a colored man; Mrs Hannah Lee, Chas Lee & Ann Madison, also colored.

A Sgt of the Marines, John B Wetherell, who recently returned to N Y C from Monterey, felt unwell on Sat, & sent for some tartar emetic, which he took 3 doses of, without producing any apparent effect, & on Sunday he expired. The coroner said the tarter emetic killed him.

Mrd: on Dec 29, by Rev Levi R Reese, Mr Jas B Ager to Miss Susan E, daughter of Mr Wm Drake, both of Wash City.

Mrd: on Dec 23, by Rev J B Donelan, Louis L Brunet to Mary Jane King, both of Wash City.

Mrd: on Dec 22, at Strawberry, near Wilmington, N C, by Rev Dr Drane, Lariston B Hardin, of Wash City, to Augusta, daughter of Levin Lane.

Mrd: on Dec 14, in Cambridge, Md, by Rev T J Wyatt, Dr Jas A Muse, of Talbot Co, Md, to Miss Mary S Sulivane, of the former place.

Mrd: on Thu, by Rev John C Smith, Mr Chas J Columbus to Miss Martha R Sheid, all of Wash City.

Died: on Dec 23, in Gtwn, suddenly, of disease of the heart, Mrs Mary Davis, consort of Richd Davis, in her 70th year.

Died: yesterday, after a lingering & painful illness, Wm Croggon, in his 40th year. His funeral will take place from his late residence, on 6th st, between F & G sts, on Jan 2, at 2 o'clock. [I am directed by the W Patriarch of Northern Liberty Division, 12, of the Sons of Temperance, of which Bro Croggon was a member, to notify the members to attend the meeting on Sunday to make arrangements preparatory to his funeral.
–B F Pleasants, R S N L D, 12, S of T]

Orphans Court of Wash Co, D C. Letters of administration on the personal estate of Joanna M Ruff, late of said county, deceased. —Geo R Ruff, John A Ruff, excs

On Sat, Miss Frances Ann Baker was walking in the attic of her father's store in Utica st, she made a misstep & fell through the scuttle, a distance of 35 feet, to the lower floor. She was 18 years of age, & survived but 2 hours. —Boston Journal

New Haven Paladium: the late Hon Timothy Pitkin, aged 82, died at the house of his son, in this city, on Dec 18. He was a native of Farmington, & son of the Rev Timothy Pitkin, the Congregational minister of that town. He graduated at Yale College in 1785: the law was his profession: elected a Rep in the Congress of the U S in 1805 till 1819.

Memoir of Miss Margaret Mercer, by Casper Morris, M D. Phil: Lindsay & Blackiston. Of Mgt Mercer, of Md, then in the heyday of youth & fortune, it was often our fortune to hear from her only brother, than an ofcr of the U S army & aid-de-camp to Gen Scott. In the volume now before us we find a record that, confirming all a brother's praises, adds to them the testimony of her own acts & words, to show how wide the sphere, how admirable the workings of the good influence of a true energetic, disinterested Christian woman. —North American

Ladies with letters in the Wash Post Ofc, Jan 1, 1848. [Abbreviations copied as the post ofc listed them.]

Brooks, Miss B E
Brown, Mrs Louisa
Bright, Mrs Mary
Boothe, Mrs Ellen
Bryles, Miss Mary
Barrett, Miss Julia D
Burgan, Kate
Brodie, Mrs L A
Bailey, Mrs J
Burch, Miss Caor E
Blackson, Mary J
Barea, Miss M
Bowman, Mrs El'h
Barrett, Mrs Laura
Brenner, Miss Ju A
Bridgman, Miss M W
Boudinot, Miss Mary
Chase, Mrs Diana
Cooke, Mrs M
Cobb, Mrs Aug'a-2
Clements, Miss Kate
Cooper, Miss M F
Carter, Mrs J F
Douglas, Mrs M A

Dunlop, Mrs Jane
Denison, Mrs
Dulany, Mrs Ann
Dermott, Miss A R
David, Mrs Melinda
Edwards, Miss G A
Frances, Miss Aman
Fraiser, Mrs Rebecca
Gates, Mrs Mary A
Graham, Mrs Danl
Giveney, Mrs Ellen
Hill, Miss Maria L
Hughes, Miss M F
Hastie, Mrs Clau M
Joyce, Mgt
Johnson, Mrs H
Jackson, Maria L
Jackson, Mrs Ma'y A
Jackson, Miss A F
King, Mrs Sarah S-3
Lee, Miss Lucy Ann
Lewis, Eliz
Lanham, Miss Caro
Miller, Miss Maria

Morse, Mary C
More, Miss Jane
Mills, Mrs Lou's M
Middleton, Miss Ro
Miller, Mrs Jane S
Manly, Miss Hannah
Murphy, Miss J E
Martin, Miss Ma R
Mardus, Miss Jane
Marshall, Miss Mary
Macgregor, Mrs Su
McKenny, Miss M L
Nettleton, Mrs Ju'a
Nusby, Miss Caro
Newton, Miss M L-2
Pope, Mrs Eliza
Plowman, Miss M'n
Powell, Miss M A V
Parker, Mrs Ellen
Powers, Miss Ann J
Queen, Mrs M E
Queen, Mrs Abba
Queen, Miss Mary
Queen, Miss Henri A

Ready, Mrs Marg L
Renshaw, Miss Va
Robinson, Mrs Sarah
Rentzel, Miss E-2
Smith, Miss Ros M
Shaw, Mrs Mary
Scott, Mrs Betsy
Smith, Miss Char'e
Schutt, Mrs Nancy
Savoy, Mrs E-3
Smith, Miss Eliza
Sefton, Miss Sarah
Seymour, Miss Cath

Schureman, Miss La
Seger, Ann Francis
Summers, Miss A E
Summers, Mrs Sus'h
Spellman, Mrs Ra'l
Somers, Miss Eliza
Thompson, Mrs A
Thompson, Mrs E
Tyler, Mrs John W
Van Metre, Miss Isabella
Wright, Mrs El'h
White, Mrs Martha

Ward, Mrs Char'e
Williams, Mrs Eliza
Wood, Mrs Phoebe
Walker, Miss Ma'a
Whitney, Mrs Eli
Wiley, Miss Va A
Wilkinson, Miss A M
Williams, Miss M'a
Wilson, Sarah A
Williams, Mrs Sarah

MON JAN 3, 1848
The subscriber wishes to employ a gentleman of experience as a teacher in his family. Salary of $300 & board will be given. Address Salem, Fauquier Co, Va. –W J Morgan

Yesterday a fire destroyed the interior of the bldg in which Mr Jas Williams' cabinet & chair factory, on 7th st, was located. The barber shop on the first floor was partially destroyed. In the confusion of the fire some villain entered the tin & stove warehouse of Mr C Schussler, & stole from his desk $36 in bank notes.

The jury in the case of the U S vs Edw Leeds, have rendered a verdict of guilty, & Leeds was sentenced to be imprisoned 4 years in the penitentiary.

Henry Thorne returns his sincere thanks to the Fire Companies & the citizens for their exertions in saving his property from destruction by fire on yesterday.

Having discontinued business in Wash City, I have appointed Mr S E Douglass as my agent. –Thos P Morgan

For rent: the fine corner store under Gadsby's Hotel. –R W Latham, agent of Jno Withers

Chas Stott has this day associated Saml B Waite with him in business. It will be conducted under the name of Chas Stott & Co.

TUE JAN 4, 1848
House of Reps: 1-Cmte on Invalid Pensions: to inquire into placing the names of Alex'r McClean, Peter Myers, & Jos Taylor, soldiers of the late war, on the invalid pension list. 2-The ptn & papers relating to the claim of the heirs of Col Archibald Laughery, who was killed by the Indians in 1781, while in the service of the U S, praying for the military bounty lands to which their ancestor was entitled, be taken from the files of the House & referred to the Cmte on Public Lands.

Mrd: on Sabbath evening, by Rev John C Smith, Mr Aquila R Allen to Miss Mary Ann Johnson, all of Wash City.

Senate: 1-Ptn from Geo L Brent & Jos L Graham, asking compensation for services as special agents to Paraguay. 2-Ptn from Thos M Corley, asking indemnity for French spoliations prior to 1800. 3-Cmte on Finance: asking to be discharged from the further consideration of the memorial of J Kearsley, & that it be referred to the Cmte on Public Lands. Same cmte: asking to be discharged from the further consideration of the memorial of Jos Bouchard, & that it be referred to the Cmte on the Judiciary. 4-Cmte on the Judiciary: bill for the relief of Peter Capello, adm of Andrew Capello, deceased; & for the relief of John Capo & Hannah Petry & her husband, heirs of John Bearden, accompanied by a report, which was ordered to be printed. 5-Cmte on the Territories: bill for the relief of Wm B Slaughter. 6-Bill for the relief of Jos Wilson was ordered to be engrossed for a third reading. 6-Bill for the relief of the admx of Elisha L Keen was considered in Cmte of the Whole, & was ordered to be printed.

Died: on Dec 23, at Old Point Comfort, Va, Capt Timothy Green, of the U S Army, aged 65 years.

Died: on Fri last, in Wash City, suddenly, Fanny Shorter, for many years an eminent & faithful Nurse, & well known as such in many families in this city.

Iron Works for sale: by decree of the Court of Equity of Lincoln Co, N C, will be offered at public outcry, on Feb 18, at Vesuvius Furnace, all the interest of Jas Franklin Graham, being an undivided half in the said furnace & its appurtenances. Also, a large body of valuable land at & around the Furnace, with dwlg houses, & all necessary outbldgs. Household & kitchen furniture, horses, mules, oxen, & cows; entire property in several valuable negroes; the interest of said Jas F Graham in the celebrated Ore Bank & Limestone Quarry. –W Williamson, C & M E [I am further authorized & requested by Jos M Graham, to make known that he will at the same time & place offer for sale his undivided half of the said real estate.]

WED JAN 5, 1848
Wash Corp: 1-Ptn from Moses Lazarus, for the remission of a fine: referred to the Cmte of Claims. 2-Ptn from H B Sawyer, for the remission of a fine: referred to the Cmte of Claims. 3-Cmte of Claims: bill for the relief of Wm Quigley: passed. 4-Cmte on Public Schools: bill entitled "An act to remunerate Emma D E Southworth for services as assistant teacher in the 4th Public School;" was ordered to lie on the table. 5-Cmte of Claims: asked to be discharged from the further consideration of the ptn of Messrs Maxwell & Sears: discharged accordingly. 6-Ptn of Wm Fleming, praying remission of a fine: referred to the Cmte of Claims. 7-Ptn of Thos McDonnell, praying remission of a fine: referred to the Cmte of Claims. 8-Cmte of Claims: payment of the claim of Wm Dalton & J Beasley, was passed. 9-Bill for the relief of I Howe, police ofcr of the 6th Ward: referred to the Cmte on Police. 10-Bill for the relief of Wm Bush was indefinitely postponed.

Senate: 1-Ptn from Herrick Aiken, asking an extension of his patent for an improvement in the "saw set." 2-Ptn from Betsey McIntosh, asking payment of money awarded her under the treaty of 1815 with the Cherokees. 3-Cmte on Naval Affairs: bill for the relief of Chas L Bell. 4-Bills passed: relief of Jos Wilson; payment of the claim of Walter R Johnson against the U S; relief of the admx of Elisha L Keen, deceased; joint resolution in favor of David Shaw & Solomon T Corser. 5-The bill for the relief of Henry Rhodes was considered in the Cmte of the Whole, & ordered to a 3rd reading.

For rent: a 2 story brick house on G st, between 12th & 13th sts. Inquire of Thos Baker, or Mr Joyce, corner of F & 13th sts.

Orphans Court of Wash Co, D C. Letters of administration on the personal estate of Adrian Hope, late of Hosley st, England, deceased. —Walter D Davidge, adm

House of Reps: 1-Cmte on Naval Affairs: adverse report on the ptn of Catharine Clark, widow of Jos Clark: laid on the table. Same cmte, reported a bill for the relief of Edw Quinn: committed. 2-Cmte on Revolutionary Pensions: adverse report on the ptn of Mary Patton: laid on the table. 3-Cmte on Revolutionary Pensions: adverse reports on the ptns of Catharine Abel, Sarah Nixon, & Eunice Goodell: laid on the table. Same cmte: adverse reports on the ptns of Alex'r Wallace & Mary Corwin: laid on the table. 4-Cmte on Invalid Pensions: bills for the benefit of Harriet Barney, widow of Joshua Barney; for the relief of Anthony Walton Bayard; & for the relief of Geo Newton: committed. Same cmte: bill for the relief of Russell Goss: committed. Same cmte: adverse reports on the ptns of Jos Coberly & Peter Coville: laid on the table. 5-Cmte on Patents: bill to provide for additional examiners at the Patent Ofc; for the relief of Capt Henry M Shreve; & for the relif of Calvin ___: read & committed. 6-Cmte on Patents: bills for the relief of John J Adams & for the relief of E Goodrich Smith: read & committed. 7-Cmte on Naval Affairs: bill for the relief of David Myerle: committed. 8-Ptn of Nathl Harrison, praying for a pension. 9-Ptn of Jas Burns, of Newburyport, Mass, praying for pecuniary aid in consideration of wounds received while on board the frig **Constitution** in her conflict with a French ship of war. 10-Ptn of John Jennings & others, citizens of Trumbull Co, praying for peace with Mexico. 11-Memorial of Lewis Roberts, praying Congress to grant him pay for services rendered during the last war with Great Britain as artificer. 12-Ptn in behalf of Thos A Boyd & others, legal reps of Col Geo Boyd, deceased, late sub Inidan agent at Green Bay, Wisconsin, praying for the just settlement of his accounts. 13-Ptn of Bersheba McDaniel, a Revolutionary pensioner, praying for a continuance of her pension. 14-Ptn of Dolly Tracy, widow of Solomon Tracy, a soldier of the Revolution, praying for a pension. 15-Memorial of John Ambrozine, praying to surrender the bounty land to him patented, be taken from the files of the House & referred to the Cmte on Public Lands. 16-Ptn of Elemuel Robinett, praying an extension of his pension, on account of his disability resulting from wounds & injuries received during the war of 1812, while in the service of the U S. 17-Ptn of Isaac Porter, asking Congress to redeem $275 of Continental money, according to the resolution of Congress under which the same was issued; said money having been received by petitioner's father for medical services rendered during the war of the Revolution.

A petition has been presented to the Legislature of Alabama that Chas Fred'k Kollessinsti Von Poniatowski la Poggealt de la Ferrassee de la Pooquellairiee Nommen Pavilion may be permitted to change his name to Francis Duncan.

Dr Negroes, an old & respectable citizen of St Louis Co, left St Louis on Fri last for his home on the Merrimac; before reaching it, he was thrown from his horse, his foot hanging in the stirrup, & dragged a considerable distance. He died on the following day. –St Louis Era, Dec 22.

Mrd: on Jan 1, by Rev J H Allan, Arthur H Fletcher to Eliz J, daughter of Moses Poor.

House for rent: on D st, between 2nd & 3rd sts. Inquire of A Baldwin, next door.

For rent: fine 3 story brick dwlg on Pa ave, between 13th & 14th sts. Apply to Balaam Burch, corner of D & 18th sts, or at his dwlg, 14th st, near G, for the key or further information.

On Dec 29, the steamboat **A N Johnson**, of Wheeling, in her upward passage from Cincinnati, landed near Maysville to put out a passenger. At the moment of leaving the shore her boilers bursted. List of the sufferers: Redman, flatboat pilot, killed; S S Sanders, Cincinnati, badly scalded; J Kirkpatrick, Massillon, Ohio, scalded; Wm Everhart & son, Pa, do; G L Weatherby, Phil, do; D Rutlidge, Ohio, do; N Wheat, Balt, do; Saml Fisher, Warren, Ohio, do; Saml Pilson, Balt, Ohio, do; Henry Shane, Cincinnati; Arthur Foal, Pittsburg; A N Johnston, wife & child, Wheelings; ___ Conway, Graham's Station; Cyrus Rollan, Letart Falls; Jacob Shafer, Ohio, scalded; Alex'r Baily, Ohio, badly scalded; Robt Russell, Ohio; John Clancy, Cincinnati; John Hardy, Cincinnati, John Kenline, Ohio; H J Bonner, Hanover, Indiana; C Harden, Guyandotte, Va; John Boyd, Warren, Ohio; Wm Beard, St Louis, Mo; F Platter, Ohio; S Cunningham, Cumberland, Md; J Swagart, Belle Air, Ohio; J Barnett, Dayton, Ohio; T McDonald, Pitts, Indiana; Wm Knight, Va; John Fowler, Ohio; Wm Miller, Cincinnati; M R Hayden; Jas Wickersham, Pittsburg; F A Horn, O; Jas M Lissam, O; Red Hinckson, Cin; Augustus Marsh, slightly scalded; Henry Ladd, Randolph, Ohio; Wm Ladd, Randolph, Ohio; John Borum, Clarington, Ohio; Wm Parker, Dilley's Bottom, Ohio; H Davis, Captine, Ohio; ___ Tiger, Parkersburg, Va; McColough, do; Lamb, do; All, do; Jas Brandon, Belle Air, Ohio; Edmond Swagart, do; John Gilbreath, Pittsburg, badly scaled; Hamilton Bearbout, Warren, Ohio; John Williams, do; Jas Sprouts, do; A Bacon, do; Wm Allen, Wheeling, Va; Anderson Bonum, Cincinnati, Ohio; Benj Bonum, do; G Baker, Pittsburg; C Weaver, Wheeling, Va; Jas Henderson, Belmont Co; E T Cole, Athens Co, Ohio; John R Dearey, do; Paulser Flesher, Doddridge Co, Va; Jacob Shoewalter, Warren Co, Ohio; A Fairchild, Wheeling, 1st clerk, dead; Jacob Johnson, 2nd clerk, missing; Jas Bellsville, carpenter, missing; John Lyle, 2nd engineer, dead; 2 found dead-names not known.

For sale: a Newfoundland Dog, of great beauty & symmetry. For particulars apply to the bar of Mr Jas Maher's Globe Hotel.

THU JAN 6, 1847
Wm Lingan Gaither, of Montg Co, & Wm Matthews, of Chas Co, have been appointed Brig Gens of Militia of the State of Md.

Great Robbery-$5,000 reward. The President of the Bank of Chester Co was robbed on Dec 23, at the West Chester Railroad Depot, near Broad & Race sts, Phil, of his trunk or valise, containing upwards of $50,000. –Wm Darlington, Pres of the Bank of Chester Co. -David Townsend, Cashier

Senate: 1-Ptn from the children of Jos White, deceased, asking arrears of pension. 2-Additional documents relating to the claim of John L Graham. 3-Ptn from the widow & legal reps of Reuben Lassiter, asking indemnity for property destroyed by the U S troops in Florida. 4-Documents relating to the claim of Hugh W Dobbin: presented. 5-Ptn from Susan C Randall, excx of Judge Randall, asking some allowance for the arduous & increased duties of her late husband, in consequence of the decease of Judge Balum. 6-Ptn from Mary Morris Foot, widow of a surgeon of the U S army, asking a pension. 7-Ptn from Marvin W Fisher, asking compensation for the use by the U S of his invention for charging percussion caps. 8-Ptn from Albert Pike, asking indemnity for horses lost by a company of Arkansas cavalry, commanded by him in Mexico. 9-Ptn from Wm Woodbridge & Henry Chipman, late U S Judges in the Territory of Michigan, asking compensation for services performed which did not properly belong to them. 10-Cmte on Revolutionary Claims: a resolution directing the Sec of the Senate to send the ptn of Thos N Welsh, administrator of C Gibbs, to the Sec of War for settlement. 11-Cmte of Claims: adverse report on the report of Geo Hervey. 12-Cmte on the Judiciary: bill for the relief of Richd S Coxe. 13-Bill introduced on leave: bill for the relief of the legal reps of Martin Fenwick. 14-Bill for the relief of Thos Rhodes: passed. 15-Bill for the relief of Wm B Slaughter, late Sec of the State of Wisconsin; bill for the relief of Capt Foxall A Parker; bill for the relief of Wm A Christian; & bill for the relief of the heirs of Andrew D Crosby: laid on the table for the present for further explanation.

Trustee's sale of valuable property at auction: by decree of the Circuit Court of Wash Co, D C, in Chancery, in the case of Scholfield & others against Scholfield & others, the subscriber, as trustee, will sell at public auction, at the risk & cost of the first purchaser, who has failed to comply with the terms of a previous sale, made on Dec 11, 1847, on the premises, on Jan 11, the whole of square 863, on Md ave, between 6th & 7th sts, with a good cottage house thereon. –Jos Scholfield, trustee -A Green, auctioneer

Died: on Jan 4, Jas Beverly, only son of Wm B & Caroline M Waugh, aged 9 months & 9 days. His funeral will take place at the residence of his parents, on Mass ave, tomorrow, at 2 o'clock.

David P Page, Principal of the State Normal School of N Y, died on New Year's morning, aged 37 years.

The Fitchville Cotton Factory, the property of Asa Fitch, at Norwich, Conn, was destroyed by fire on Thu. [Jan 10th newspaper: Mr Austin, the watchman, was so much shocked by the fire that he fell into a fit, & died after suffering another fit.]

Valuable real estate at public vendue: by an order of Montg Co Court, as Court of Equity, in the case of Chas Offutt & others vs Horatio Beall & others, the undersigned Com'rs will offer, on Jan 10, at the late residence of Aaron Offutt, deceased, all the real estate of which he died seized, lying in said county, & divided into 4 lots. Lot 1-part of the *Mansion-House Farm*, containing 292 acs of land, about 2 miles from F C Clopper's mill. Lot 2-part of the *Mansion-House Farm*, containing 369 acres of land, & adjoins lot 1. Lot 3-containing 83 acres, on the public road leading from Rockville to Darnestown. Lot 1 & 2: improvements are a large 2 story brick dwlg-house, 30 by 40 feet. Lot 4 contains 3/4ths of an acre. –Otho Magruder, F C Clopper, Lemuel Clements, Jno T Desellum, Com'rs

The New Orleans Picayune furnishes accounts from Vera Cruz to Dec 24, brought to that city by the steamship **New Orleans**. The **New Orleans** brought over the following passengers: Gen Pierce, U S A; Dr Jackson, U S N; Capt Magruder, light artl; Capt J M Scantland, 14th Infty; Capt Pemberton, U S A; Capt Prince, U S A; Capt P W Gushire, 11th Infty; Capt L Ford, 3rd Dragoons; Capt W Blanding, S C Regt; Capt F Sumter, do; Capt McComas, 11th Infty; Capt Jones, 15th Infty; Capt W A Nichols, 2nd Artl; Dr Barton, U S A; Dr L W Jordan, 14th Infty; Dr Scott, 3rd Dragoons; Col Wm M Smyth, bearer of dispatches; Col Wm Trousdale, 14th Infty; Maj Talcott, 1st voltigeurs; Lt McLain, Lt Lincoln, Lt McCowan, U S A; Lt Love, 14th Infty; Lt Williams, 3rd Dragoons; Lt H C Murray, 14th Infty; Lt Thos Smith, 14th Infty; Lt L D Pitcher, voltigeurs; Lt A Steen, 12th Infty; Lt C McClung, 13th Infty; Lt Briceland, U S N; Lt Bradford, 13th Infty; Lt T P Pierce, 9th Infty; Lt L Woodhouse, 9th Infty; Lt Cantwell, 12th Infty. Also, the remains of Col Butler; Lt Col Dickinson; Col Martin Scott; Col T B Ransom; Lt Col Graham; Capts Thompson & Taylor; Lts Williams, Clark, & Adams; Sgt Madison; Dr Slade; Privates Trezvant & Kennedy.

Furnished rooms: Mrs C Buckingham: E st, between 9th & 10th sts.

FRI JAN 7, 1848
Tutor Goodrich, at New Haven, is still living, & is considered nearly out of danger. Fears are entertained that his mind may permanently suffer from the severe injury he received. The two students who perpetrated the outrage, [Towar, of Phil, & Ewing, of Tenn,] are still in prison.

From Gen Wool's Army: the U S steamship **Telegraph** arrived at New Orleans on Dec 28, from Brasos. She brought over Messrs Stephenson & Shaw, [with the remains of the late Capt Stephenson,] Dr Haley, wife, & child, & Messrs Geo Judkins, J Mauran, & Coudas, Capts Dubs & Stotesbury.

Household & kitchen furniture at auction: on Jan 11, by order of the Orphans Court of Wash Co, D C, in front of the Centre Market. Also, a valuable young negro woman, a slave for life, belonging to the estate of Mary Clements, deceased. -A Green, auctioneer

Headquarters Army of Occupation, Monterey, Dec 9, 1847. The following ofcrs are announced as chiefs of the staff attached to the Army of Occupation:
Brevet Capt Irvin McDowell, Assist Adj Gen at headquarters
Capt W D Fraser, Chief of Engineers & Aid de-Camp.
Maj Lewis Cass, jr, 3rd Dragoons, Acting Inspector Gen.
Maj I M Washington, 3rd Artl, Chief of Artl at Saltillo.
Capt G D Ramsay, ordnance dept, Chief of Ordnance at headquarter.
Col Henry Whiting, Assist Quartermaster Gen, Chief of the Quartermaster's Dept at Matamoros.
Capt E S Sibley, Assist Quartermaster at headquarters.
Capt T B Linnard, Chief of the Topographical Corps at Saltillo.
Lt L Sitgreaves, Corps of Topographical Engineers at headquarters.
Capt A B Eaton, Commissary of Subsistence, Chief of the Commissary Dept at Brasos.
Capt J C Casey, Commissary of Subsistence at headquarters.
Surgeon N S Jarvis, Chief of the Medical Dept at headquarters.
Maj D Hunter, Chief of the Pay Dept at Matamoros.
Maj W A Spark, Paymaster at headquarters.

Mrd: on Dec 21, by Rev Jas Hervey Otey, D D, Bishop of Tennessee, John Seay, M D, of Alabama, to Salina Patten, daughter of Rev J T Welat, D C, Rector of Christ Church, Nashville.

Mrd: on Jan 4, in Gtwn, by the Most Rev Archbishop of Balt, Rice W Payne, of Va, to Miss America, daughter of the late Raphael Semmes.

Died: on Jan 1, at the residence of Richd Beckett, in Calvert Co, Md, Mrs Sarah Waters, in her 69th year. Her death, like her life, was peaceful & happy.

Senate: 1-From the Legislature of Ohio, in favor of placing the name of Henry Johnson on the pension roll. Johnson, of Washington Co, Ohio, was one of the heroic Johnson boys who delivered themselves from savage captivity & the prospect of a horrid death, by killing 2 Delaware Indians, after having spent a youth of hardship as a ranger on the frontier, enduring the severest privations, with the most inadequate compensation, is now passing through the old age of indigence; that it is right & proper that acts of noble daring should receive some reward from a grateful & admiring county. 2-Ptn from Patrick Marantette, asking compensation for provisions & clothing furnished to the Pottawatamie Indians.

Cold blooded murder at Sparta, Tenn, a few days since, upon Wm Little, the Clerk of the County Court there, by Richd B Jones, a saddler. Jones placed himself in a grocery, & shot & killed the former as he passed with a rifle. Jones was immediately arrested.

SAT JAN 8, 1848
Annapolis Republican: We are pained to learn the death of Robt W Bowie, of PG Co. He died in the meridian of life, deeply regretted by a large circle of friends throughout the State. He was a fearless & consistent politician, always seeking the approval of his conscience rather than the popular applause.

The death of Lt H Ridgely is confirmed by letters from Vera Cruz, dated Dec 24. It states that he was killed in action with the Mexicans about Nov 23, at a small town called Matamoros, about 50 miles from Puebla. He was serving as Adj Gen to Gen Lane, & when he fell was displaying the gallantry of his name & race, in leading a charge against the enemy, in which he sustained the honor of his ancestors & proved himself worthy of his comrades. Lt Ridgely leaves a wife & 3 children to mourn the loss of a most affectionate husband & parent. –Balt Patriot

The New Orleans papers announce the death of Benj Story, long Pres of the Bank of Louisiana, at an advanced age. The estate of the deceased was estimated at $500,000, & $1,000,000.

Orphans Court of Wash Co, D C. Letters testamentary on the personal estate of Geo Oyster, late of said county, deceased. –Geo M Oyster, Thos Parker, excs

Appointments by the Pres, by & with the consent & advice of the Senate.
Seth Barton, of Louisiana, Charge d'Affaires to the Republic of Chili, [appointed in the recess.]
John W Davis, of Indiana, Com'r to China, vice A H Everett, deceased.
John Rowan, of Ky, Charge d'Affaires to Naples, vice Wm H Polk, recalled at his own request.
Nathl Niles, of Vt, Charge d'Affaires to Sardinia, vice Robt Wickliffe, jr, resigned.
Thos J Morgan, of Ohio, Sec of Legation to Brazil, vice R Walsh, recalled.
Wm J Staples, of N Y, Consul at Havre, in place of Mr Beasley, deceased.
Chas Huffnagle, of Pa, Consul at the port of Calcutta, vice Jas B Higginson, recalled.
Hugh Keenan, of Pa, Consul at the port of Dublin, vice Thos Wilson, recalled.
John McPherson, of Va, Consul at the port of Genoa, vice C E Lester, recalled.
Geo J Fairfield, of Maine, Consul at the port of Buenos Ayres, vice Thaddeus Sanford, declined, & who was vice W Greenhow, declined.
Adolphe Renard, Recorder of Land Titles at St Louis, Mo, vice L Spencer, deceased.
Robt W Pooler, Surveyor at Savannah, Ga, from Jul 1, 1847.
Eleazer P Kendrick, of Ohio, Surveyor of Va military district in Ohio, vice Wm M Anderson, resigned.
Abel M Bryant, Collector at Kennebunk, Maine, vice Jas Osborne, removed.
Wm P Porter, Surveyor at City Point, Va.
Alex'r Somerville, Collector at Saluria, Texas.
Edw Fitzgerald, Surveyor of the Customs at Corpus Christi, vice Geo W Collingsworth, resigned.
Henry P Norton, Surveyor of the Customs at Copano, Texas, vice John F Stephens, resigned.

The Maysville Eagle of Jan 1: of the wounded who were taken to Maysville the following have died, viz: Messrs A Richardson & P Long, of Wheeling, Va; Robt McGowan, of Zanesville, Ohio; & Dr Alex'r C Gillespie, of New Orleans.

The Charlestown [Va] Free Press announced the sudden death on Mon last of Alex'r S Tidball, of Winchester, Va.

Died: on Jan 6, Mary Jane, only daughter of Uriah & Mary Heeter, in her 16th year. Her funeral is from the residence of her father, on I st, this morning, at 9 o'clock.

Extensive sale of Wash Co [Md] Lands: by a decree of the Wash Co Court, as Court of Equity, dated Nov 18 last, I will offer at public sale, in Hagerstown, on Feb 8 & 9 next, the entire real estate of which the late Col Frisby Tilghman died seized & possessed, containing upwards of 1,100 acs of prime limestone land-250 acs of wood. Improvements are elegant & extensive: every necessary bldg has been provided.
–W B Clarke, trustee [Thos E Tilghman & Wm Koontz, residing on the premises, will point out the lines of the estate.]

By virtue of 3 writs of fieri facias: I shall expose to public sale, on Jan 18, on the wharf near N J ave, Wash City, all the right, title & interest of Zachariah Hazel in & to one wooden bldg & fixtures, seized & taken as the property of the said Zachariah Hazel, & will be sold to satisfy 3 judgments in favor of John Grinder. -R R Burr, constable

MON JAN 10, 1848
House of Reps: 1-Ptn of Skelton Felton, praying for a pension for wounds received while in the service of the U S, during the late war with Great Britain. 2-Ptn of Wm C Mallicoat, & 124 other citizens of Grainger Co, Tenn, praying Congress to establish a post route from Thorn Hill, in said county, to Blain's Cross Roads. 3-Ptn & other papers of Capt Thos Dewar, asking pay for money advanced while in the service of the U S, in the last war with Great Britain. 4-Ptn of Mrs Catharine Hoffman, widow of the late Lt Col Wm Hoffman, for a pension. 5-Ptn of Lewis McKenzie, praying to be paid money advanced for transportation of troops. 6-Ptn of Thos Scott, late Register of the Land Ofc at Chillicothe, Ohio, praying compensation for extra services connected with the duties of his ofc; heretofore presented, Apr 1, 1844. 7-Ptn of Saml Reed, of Pike Co, Ohio, praying payment for part of a tract of land, purchased of the U S, the title to which has not been maintained; heretofore presented, Jan 21, 1846. 8-Ptn of Geo of De la Roche & Wm P Sanger, praying compensation for services rendered in the Navy Dept. 9-Ptn of Horatio Sprague; heretofore presented. 10-Ptn of Valery Gainnie, praying for the correction of an error in an act of confirmation of land. 11-Ptn & papers of Wm Queen be taken from the files & referred to the Cmte of Claims. 12-Ptn of Saml Jones be taken from the files of the House & referred to the Cmte on Revolutionary Claims. 13-Ptn of Saml Butler, praying to be placed upon the list of invalid pensioners.

Piano Forte Tuning: J B Woodruff: apply at Odd Fellows' Hall, 7th st, or by leaving orders at Piano Forte & Music Store of Mrs G Anderson, Pa ave, between 11th & 12th sts.

Mr Andrew Kennedy, formerly a Rep in Congress from the State of Indiana, died at Indianapolis, in that State, on Dec 31. He was seized with the smallpox while performing his duties as a member of the Legislature. The State Journal of Jan 3 states that no other case of the disease had occurred in that town.

City Ordinances-Wash: 1-Act for the relief of Isaac Selvey: sum of $2 be paid to him, said Selvey having deposited that sum in the Bank of Wash to the credit of the corp by mistake. 2-Act granting a special license to Messrs Brown & Nichols, for theatrical & other performances at the bldg known as the Adelphi, for the sum of $9 per week, payable in advance to commence from Dec 20, 1847.

Valuable real estate at auction: by a deed of trust executed by Sylvanus Holmes, on Nov 14, 1846, recorded in the ofc of the Clerk for Wash Co, D C: sale on Jan 14, all of that piece or parcel of land in Wash City, D C, consisting of portions of lots 4 & 5 in square 369, fronting on L st, between 9th & 10th sts. –John H Saunders, Trustee
-A Green, auctioneer

Sale of Gtwn Ironworks: by deed of trust, executed to the subscriber as Trustee, by John Rynes, dated Jun 16, 1846, recorded in Liber W B 126, folio 272, of the land records for Wash Co, D C: sale on Feb 21, of the following premises, together with all the improvements, bldgs, & fixtures erected thereon, to wit: All those parts of lots 2 & 3 in Peter, Beatty, & Threlkald, & Deakins' Additions to Gtwn, D C, which lie between the Chesapeake & Ohio Canal & Water st, fronting 126 feet 8 inches on the north side of Water st. Also, all that parcel of ground in front of said lots 2 & 3, lying between Water st & the channel of the river Potomac, fronting 126 feet 8 inches on the south side of Water st. Also all that parcel of ground lying in front of lot 4, in said additions, being part of the wharf attached, surveyed to Francis Dodge by deed dated Jul 20, 1830. The improvements are a large Iron Manufacturing Establishment.
–Robt Ould, Trustee -Edw S Wright, auctioneer

Real Estate, household furniture, & negroes at auction: under 3 deeds of trust from John W Bronaugh, made to the subscribers separately: sale on Jan 12: one undivided third part of the dwlg-house & lot, part of lot 30, at the corner of Prospect & Fred'k sts, in Gtwn, now occupied by Mr Bronaugh. All his household furniture. The following negroes: Christian, about 31, & 2 children; Julia, about 18; Maria, about 42; Jas, about 13; Eliz, about 8; & Abraham, about 37. –John M Brodhead, Trustee of first deed. Henry Trunnell, Trustee of 2nd deed. Robt Ould, Trustee of 3rd deed. [The servants above named have been raised about the house, are most capable, & strictly honest, & would be particularly desirable to any person wishing family servants. They can be seen on application to the auctioneer. –John W Bronaugh -Edw S Wright, auct]

The Worcester [Md] Shield states that a man named Hillary Warren, at Whaleysville, in the upper part of Worcester Co, was burnt alive in his own house on Dec 26. Endeavoring to save some of his property from his dwlg, which was on fire, he was caught by the falling of a portion of the bldg, & perished in the flames.

J B Carter committed suicide at New Orleans, on Dec 28, by drowning himself in the river. He was about 50 years of age, & has recently resided in Arkansas.

Miss A McDonnell, Dress maker & Milliner: 10th st, near Pa ave, Wash. [Ad]

Appointments by the Pres:
Ransom H Gillet, of N Y, to be Solicitor of the Treasury of the U S, in place of Seth Barton, resigned.
Geo W Clinton, of N Y, to be U S Atty for the northern district of N Y, in place of Wm F Allen, resigned.
Josiah Minot, of N H, to be U S Atty for the district of N H, in place of Franklin Pierce, resigned.
Thos M Griffin, of Ga, to be U S Marshal for the district of Ga, in place of Henderson Willingham, resigned.
Jas H Cocke, of Texas, to be U S Marshal for the district of Texas, in place of John M Allen, deceased.
Arnold Plumer, of Pa, to be U S Marshal for the western district of Pa, in place of Saml Hays, resigned.
Wm H Rogers, to be U S Atty, for the district of Delaware, from & after Jan 16 next, when his present commission will expire.
Geo M Keim, to be U S Marshal for the eastern district of Pa, from & after Jan 16 next, when his present commission will expire.
Edmund Christian, to be U S Marshal for the Eastern district of Va, from & after Jan 16 next, when his present commission will expire.
Jas Points to be U S Marshal for the Western district of Va, from & after Jan 16 next, when his present commission will expire.
Alex'r G Penn, to be Deputy Postmaster at New Orleans, La, his present commission having expired.
Wm H Stevenson, to be Register of the Land Ofc at Little Rock, Ark.
Danl J Chapman, to be Receiver of Public Moneys at Batesville, Ark.

Mrd: on Jan 4, by Rev Mr Finckel, Mr August Schneider to Miss Sarah Rheem, all of Wash City.

Mrd: on Jan 4, by Rev J B Donelan, Mr Benj R Bohrer, of Gtwn, to Miss Mgt L, daughter of Jeremiah Sullivan, of Wash City.

Mrd: on Jan 6, by Rev Jas Laurie, D C, the Hon Richd Coke, of Va, to Eglantine, daughter of the late Alex'r Cochran, of Wash City.

Died: on Nov 26 last, Margaret P Espy, in her 22nd year, daughter of Jas S Espy, of Harrisburg, Pa, & adopted daughter of Prof Jas P Espy, of Phil.

Died: on Jan 9, at the residence of his mother, Mrs Pilling, on the corner of Md ave & 4½ sts, of consumption, Theodore Dalton, in his 21st year. His funeral will take place this afternoon, at 2 o'clock.

Died: on Dec 31, at Middleburg, Va, Jas Bradshaw, son of Robt Beverley, of Avinelle, Fauquier Co, Va, aged about 2 years.

Died: on Jan 9, in Gtwn, Frances Rebecca Marll, eldest daughter of John S & Ursula Aloysius Marll, aged 2 years, 3 months & 27 days.

Died: on Jan 4, at Aldie, Va, Betty Burwell, only daughter of Edmund Berkeley, aged 2 years & 1 month.

Cazenova for rent: that eligibly situated town & country residence *Cazenova*, within the limits of the Corporation. For particulars, apply to H G Wilson, High st, Gtwn.

TUE JAN 11, 1848
St Joseph's Academy for Young Ladies, under the charge of the Sisters of Charity, has been removed from E st, near 7th, to F st, corner of 10th, in the house formerly occupied by D Claggett, where it will be opened this morning at the usual hour. Prospectuses may be had on application at the Seminary.

Died: on Jan 9, after a brief illness, Henrietta Maria, aged 2 years & 7 months, daughter of Wm B & Caroline M Waugh. Her funeral will take place at the residence of her parents, on Mass ave, today at 2 o'clock.

Grand Divison Sons of Temperance of D C meeting on Tue at 7 o'clock.
–R Gray Campbell, G Scribe

Navy Yard Bridge Co: a dividend of 1½% has been declared our the profits of the last 3 months, payable on demand at the Bank of Wash. –Wm Gunton, President

WED JAN 12, 1848
Senate: 1-Ptn from John Olive Means, asking the settlement of his accounts as acting purser of the U S brig **Dolphin**. 2-Memorial from Thos Jefferson Randolph, offering to Congress certain manuscript papers, late the property of Thos Jefferson, deceased. 3-Ptn from J C Montague & other citizens of Memphis, Tenn, asking that bounty land may be granted to those soldiers of the regular army who were present at the battles of Palo Alto, Resaca de la Palma, & Monterey. 4-Cmte of Claims: bill for the relief of the legal reps of Geo Fisher, deceased. 5-Cmte on the Post Ofc & Post Roads: bill for the relief of Jones & Boker. 6-Cmte on Military Affairs: asking to be discharged from the further consideration of the ptn of Isaac Barnes, & that it be referred to the Cmte of Claims. 7-Bill for the relief of Creed Taylor: introduced. 8-Bill for the relief of Mary McRae, widow of Lt Col McRae, late of the U S Army: laid on the table. 9-Ptn from Chas Findlay, rep of P Chouteau & Co, asking the payment of a draft of the headmen of the Shawnee Indians on the Com'r of Indian Affairs. 10-Ptn from Catharine Hoffman for a pension. 11-Ptn from Aaron Carman, asking that letters patent may issue to him for an improvement in the plough. 12-Ptn from John Brognerd, attached to the allied corps of French troops during the Revolution, asking a pension. 13-Ptn from John H Kinzie & others, asking the relinquishment of the reversionary interest of the U S to certain lands

purchased. 14-Ptn from Archibald Williams & Chas Griffen, asking compensation for supplies furnished the Florida militia during the Seminole war. 15-Ptn from Leroy Hammond, asking pay for the use of his team during the last war with Great Britain. 16-Ptn from John H Williams, asking to be allowed the bounty granted by the act of 1833 on his enlistment in the marine corps. 17-Ptn from Abel Gregg, asking compensation for services while a sgt in the marine Corps. 18-Ptn from Mary Conelly, widow of a Revolutionary soldier, asking that a pension may be continued to her during her life. 19-Ptn from Don Carlos Buell, asking compensation for a horse lost in the service of the U S. 20-Ptn from John Stanert, asking compensation for services performed during the last war. 21-Cmte of Claims: asking to be discharged from the further consideration of the ptn of Martin Fenwick, & that it be referred to the Cmte on Private Land Claims. 22-Cmte on Private Land Claims: bill for the relief of Nathl Hoggat. 23-Cmte on Pensions: asking to be discharged from the further consideration of the memorial of Anna J Hassler, & that it be referred to the Cmte on Naval Affairs. 24-Cmte on Military Affairs: asking to be discharged from the further consideration of the ptn of Chas M Gibson, & that it be referred to the Cmte of Claims. Same cmte: asking to be discharged from the further consideration of the memorial of A H Cole, of Florida, & that it be referred to the Cmte of Claims. Also, from the same cmte: bill for the relief of Walter Loomis & Abel Gay. 25-Cmte of Claims: bill to authorize the settlement of the account of Jos Nourse, deceased, with a report. Same cmte: bill for the relief of Edw Bolen, with a report. Same cmte: adverse report on the ptn of Jos Watson. 26-Cmte on Private Land Claims: bill for the relief of Wm Marvin. 27-Cmte on Indian Affairs: adverse report on the ptn of Geo S Gaines.

By virtue of 3 writs of fieri facias, against the goods & chattels, lands & tenements, rights & credits of Abel Griggs, Aquila Rickets, & Stephen Gould, superseder, & to me directed, I will sell one frame dwlg house, & lot 6 in square 942, for cash, on the premises, on Feb 10 next, the said property, to satisfy judgments in favor of Murray & Simms & L Harbaugh. –Thos Plumsell, Constable

A Board of Naval Surgeons assembled at the Naval Asylum in Phil on Monday for the examination of assist Surgeons in the Navy for promotion. The Board consists of Surgeon J M Green, Pres; & Surgeons W S W Ruschenberger, Robt J Dodd, Thos L Smith, Wm Maxwell Wood, members.

An 8 year old son of Lawrence Hogan, of Waterford, was killed by the gravel train on the Worcester road, between Blackstone & Waterford, yesterday. The boy was walking on the track on a bridge, & had no where to go when he was hit. –Newport Herald

Jos Caldwell has resigned the Presidency of the Merchants' & Mechanics' Bank of Wheeling, a post which he has filled for the last 10 years.

Edw McCubbin, Barber & Hair-dresser: Temple of Fashion, #1, 8th st, near Pa ave. He has secured the services of that well-known & finished operator in the Art, Jas Jefferson. He continues the old prices: Hairdressing, 12½ cents; Shaving, 6½ cents.

House of Reps: 1-Cmte of Claims: bills for the relief of Jacob Gideon; for the relief of Bent, St Vrain & Co; & for the relief of J Throckmorton: committed. 2-Cmte of Claims: bills for the relief of John Anderson, of Missouri; for the relief of Jos C Doxey; for the relief of S Morris Waln; & for the relief of Alborne Allen: committed. Same cmte: adverse reports on the ptns of John O Dickey, Roswell Fitch, & Geo Reeder: laid on the table. 3-Cmte on Naval Affairs: be discharged from the further consideration of the ptn of Thos M Newell, & that it be referred to the Cmte of Claims. 4-Ptn of Levi Nicholas & others, citizens of Warren, Trumbull Co, Ohio, for a further reduction of postage. 5-Ptn of John P Converse, praying an allowance of his expenses whilst acting as special agent for the Post Ofc Dept, in settling the claims of certain toll-bridges against Converse & Reese, mail contractors from Sandusky to Detroit. 6-Ptn from the heirs of John B Beaugrand, praying Congress to carry into effect the provisions of the 6th article of the treaty of Mar 17, 1842, with the Wyandott Indians. 7-Ptn of John Morrison, of Geneva, N Y, as soldier in the war of 1812, for an increase of pension. 8-Ptn of Solomon Hersey, praying compensation for property destroyed in the late war with Great Britain. 9-Ptn of Sol Frazier & others, praying the establishment of a post route from Brunswick, via Utica, to Gallatin, Missouri. 10-Ptn of Jas Bernard & 180 others, praying for a mail route from Dixon, Ill, to Rock Island. 11-Ptn of Geo F Bloom & Henry S Bloom, of Will Co, Ill, for a preemption. 12-Ptn & accompanying papers in the case of Benj Holland, on file in the Clerk's ofc, be referred to the Cmte on Invalid Pensions.

Mrd: on Jan 8, at the Church of the Ascension, in N Y C, by Rev G T Bedell, John H Beeckman to Margaret M Gardiner, youngest daughter of the late Hon David Gardiner.

Mrd: on Nov 23 last, by Rev Mr Moon, John W Boarman to Miss Eliz, the eldest daughter of Alexius Lancaster, both of Chas Co, Md.

Died: on Jan 10, of consumption, in his 59th year, in the triumphs of Christianity, Mr Danl Turner, stonecutter. His funeral is today at 2 o'clock, from his late residence, on Md ave, near the Capitol gate.

Died: on Nov 2 last, at *Fort Leavenworth*, Virginia Theodocia, daughter of the late Lt Theodorick H Porter, U S Army, aged 21 months.

THU JAN 13, 1848
Senate: 1-Ptn from Elia A Mellon, widow of the late Capt Chas Mellon, killed by the Seminole Indians in 1837. The petitioner tells Congress that 'the trifling pittance of 5 years' pension is but a poor remuneration for the loss to his family in a pecuniary point of view, to say nothing of the fireside & domestic circle made desolate by the bereavement," & earnestly asks Congress to take immediate & efficient steps in the premises.
2-Additional papers in the case of Isaac Varnes: presented. 3-Cmte on Private Land Claims: bill for the relief of the legal reps of Jacques Moulon. Same cmte: bill for the relief of Jesse Turner. 4-Cmte on the Judiciary: bill for the relief of Richd Bloss & others. Same cmte: asking to be discharged from the further consideration of the ptn of the heirs of Abner L Duncan. 5-Cmte on Pensions: bill for the relief of Ferdinand Fellany; relief of Eliz Pistole, widow of Chas Pistole; relief of Peter Engels, sen; adverse

report on the ptn of Geo Petty. Same cmte: asking to be discharged from the further consideration of the memorial of Mary D Wade, & that it be referred to the Cmte on Naval Affairs. 6-Cmte on the Judiciary: asking to be discharged from the further consideration of the memorial of Gen Lee & other members of the bar of the western district of Va. 7-Cmte on Naval Affairs: bill for the relief of the legal reps of Capt Jesse D Elliot. Same cmte: bill directing the Sec of Navy to purchase from Dr J P Espy his patent right for the conical ventilator for the use of the U S. Same cmte: asking to be discharged from the further consideration of the ptn of Cmder Wm M Glendy. 8-Bill for the relief of Wm B Slaughter, late Sec of the State of the Territory of Michigan: passed.

House of Reps: 1-Cmte of Claims: adverse report on the ptn of Geo Hix: laid on the table. Same cmte: bill for the relief of Wm Hogan, administrator of Michl Hogan, deceased: committed. Same cmte: bills for the relief of the securities of Elijah J Weed, late Quartermaster of the Marines, deceased; for the relief of Aurelia Brereton; for the relief of the legal heirs of John Snyder, deceased; & for the relief of Thos Scott: read & committed. 2-Cmte of Claims: adverse reports on the ptns of Wm Harris, Chas Foreman, Eli Ackley, Martin L Patterson, Saml Reed, Wm Greer: laid on the table. Same cmte: adverse reports on the ptns of Danl Brown, A R S Hunter, & Martin Thomas: laid on the table. Same cmte: bills for the relief of Reginald alias Nick Hillary, & for the relief of Jas McAvoy: read & committed. Same cmte: bill for the relief of the legal heirs & rep of Nathl Cox, deceased, formerly naval agent at New Orleans: read & committed. 3-Cmte of Claims: bills for the relief of Wm Ralston; for the relief of Chas Benns; for the relief of John W Hockett; & for the relief of the heirs of Matthew Stewart: committed. 4-Cmte on Public Lands: asked to be discharged from the consideration of the papers of Jacob Keer, & that they be referred to the Cmte on Private Land Claims: agreed to. Same cmte: bill for the relief of Amzy Judd: committed. Same cmte: asking to be discharged from the consideration of the ptn of Jas Vangorden, & that it lie on the table: agreed to. 5-Cmte on Revolutionary Claims: asked to be discharged from the consideration of the ptn of Isaac Beall, & that the petitioner have leave to withdraw his papers: agreed to. 6-Cmte on Revolutionary Claims: be discharged from the consideration of the ptn of ___ Welsh, administrator of Churchill Gibbs, & that it be referred to the Sec of War: agreed to. 7-Cmte on Private Land Claims: adverse report on the ptn of Thos Jenne: laid on the table. 8-Cmte on Indian Affairs: adverse report on the ptn of Jno A Bryan: laid on the table. Same cmte: bill for the relief of Jos & Lindsley Ward: committed. 9-Cmte on Naval Affairs: bill for the relief of Ann W Angus: committed. Same cmte: bill for the relief of Eliz Mays; & bill for the relief of Nancy Tompkins: committed. Same cmte: joint resolution for the relief of Jas Glynn & others; & for the relief of Jas H Conley: committed. 10-Cmte on Foreign Affairs: bill for settling the claims of the heirs of Richd W Meade, deceased: committed. Same cmte: bill for the relief of the legal reps of Benj Hodges, & a bill for the relief of the legal reps of Cornelius Manning: committed. 11-Cmte on Revolutionary Pensions: adverse report on the ptn of Anna Smith & others: laid on the table. Same cmte: adverse report on the ptn of Jas Hillman: laid on the table. Same cmte: asked to be discharged from the ptns of Peter Rife & Silvia Pond, widow of Beriah Pond: laid on the table. Adverse report on the ptn of Esther Scolley: laid on the table. Same cmte: adverse reports on the ptns of Jos Carter & Benj Johnson: laid on the table. Cmte asked to be discharged from the resolution of the House relative to the expediency of allowing a pension to Artemas Conant, & that it be referred to the Cmte on Invalid Pensions: agreed to. 12-Cmte on Invalid Pensions: bill for the relief of John Mitchell; bill for the relief of Jesse Young; & a bill for the relief of Silas Waterman: committed. 13-Bills from the Senate were taken up & referred: bill for the relief of Jos Wilson; relief of the administrator of Elisha L Keen, deceased; payment of the claim of Walter R Johnson against the U S; relief of Thos Rhodes; resolution in favor of David Shaw & Solomon T Corser; to provide for the purchase of the manuscript papers of the late Jas Madison, former Pres of the U S.

One dollar reward for return of a Pocket-book containing a note of the German Benevolent Society, dated Oct, 1846, payable Jul 7, 1848. –Henry Bergman, 6th & N sts

The late Lt Levi Gantt was killed in the attack of the Castle of Chapultepec. This young ofcr, a graduate of West Point, took part in every battle fought during the present war by Gens Scott & Taylor, excepting that of Buena Vista. At Monterey, while clambering up the steep asent a cannon ball fired at his party came within a foot of his head, covering his face with sand & gravel. He was among the first to enter the Mexican fortifications on the summit of Cerro Gordo. It is believed that the only ofcr in advance of him was his cousin, Lt Thos Ewell, of the rifle regt, who died on the field the next day from the effects of a wound. Lt Gantt was a volunteer from his own gallant regt, the 7th Infty. He was struck in the middle of the breast by a musket ball, & expired in a few minutes. He was buried the next day in the church yard in Tacubaya. Lt Gantt was a grandson of the late Benj Stoddert, of Md, Sec of the Navy under the Administration of the Elder Adams, & was of the numerous & respectable family of Gantts of PG Co, Md. He was a native of Gtwn, D C, but moved at an early age to PG Co, where, till he entered West Point, he resided.

FRI JAN 14, 1848
Senate: 1-Ptn from Geo C Mitchell, asking that a certain sum of money improperly collected from him may be refunded. 2-Ptn from Henry V Keep, of Vicksburg, asking compensation & allowances for services in the army of invasion in Mexico. 3-Ptn from Fred'k Dawson, Jas Scholl, & Elisha Dana Whitney, asking payment for the certain vessels furnished Texas, & given up by that Republic on her annexation to the U S. 4-Cmte on Foreign Relations: a bill for the relief of John Black, late Consul at Mexico. 5-Cmte on the Post Ofc & Post Roads: bill for the relief of Jos Caldwell. Same cmte: bill for the relief of Creed Taylor. 6-Cmte on Military Affairs: asking to be discharged from the further consideration of the ptn of Geo Center, & that it be referred to the Cmte of Claims.

Died: on Jan 1, in Nashville, Tenn, Robt W Hinton, of Wash City, in his 32nd year, leaving a wife & 2 children to mourn his early death.

Carusi's Saloon, for 9 nights commencing Jan 6, 1848: the celebrated Ethiopian Serenaders, Messrs Germon, Stanwood, Harrington, Pell, White & Howard, since their return from Europe. Under the direction of Mr J A Dumbolton. Admission 25 cents. Concert to commence at 7½ p m.

Mrd: on Tue, at the residence of the Russian Minister, in Gtwn, by Rev Mr Gassaway, Brooke Williams to Carolina De Bodisco.

Mrd: on Jan 13, by Rev John C Smith, John Lowry, of St Louis, Mo, to Ann Louisa, youngest daughter of Edw Deeble, of Wash City.

SAT JAN 15, 1848

Groceries & liquors at auction: by deed of trust, executed by Richd M Beall to the subscriber: public auction on Jan 19, at the store now occupied by Mr Beall, on Pa ave, south side, between 4½ & 6th sts. —Stanislaus Murray, Trustee -R W Dyer, auct

House of Reps: 1-Cmte of Claims: bill for the relief of the admistratrix of Elisha L Keen, deceased: committed. Same cmte: ptns of Danl Brown & A Conkling: laid on the table. 2-Cmte on Naval Affairs: bill for the relief of Stephen Champlin: committed. Same cmte: to inquire into continuing the pension of Martha L Downs 5 years from Mar 20, 1847, & report by bill or otherwise. 3-Cmte on Invalid Pensions: asking to be discharged from the further consideration of the ptn of Levi M Roberts, & that it lie on the table: agreed to. 4-Bill introduced for the relief of N C Orear: read & referred. 5-Bill for the relief of Robt Roberts, & the bill for the relief of Phineas Capen, legal administrator of John Cox, deceased, of Boston, laid aside. 6-Bill for the relief of Mary Brown, widow of Jacob Brown. This bill provides for the granting a pension to Mrs Brown, of Clarksburg, Mass, at the rate of $20 per month, to commence Jan 1, 1847, to continue during her natural life. The petitioner is the stepmother of Maj Jacob Brown, who was killed while conducting the military operations at **Fort Brown**, on the Rio Grande, & the widow of Jacob Brown, sen, a soldier of the Revolutionary war, who died in Oct last, in his 83rd year. She is now 74 years of age, &, by the death of her husband, & the more recent death of her son, she is deprived of the means of support which she heretofore enjoyed, of which a revolutionary pension of $24, received by her husband, was a part. To her husband she was married more than 40 years ago, which did not bring her within the provisions of the general pension law; but all the circumstances furnished a case which appealed to the sympathies of the House. For the last 13 years of the life of her husband he was very infirm, & suffered extremely by sickness, by which their means were limited, & now she is entirely destitute. A provision in the bill put this pension on the ground of the services of her step-son, but it was opposed by several gentlemen as the introduction of a principle that might lead to invidious distinctions, & very objectionable as a precedent in the bestowal of the bounties of the Govn't in the shape of pensions, however much they might sympathize with the applicant. The cmte reported progress on the bill for the relief of Mary Brown, widow of Jacob Brown. 7-Bills for the relief of Robt Roberts & of Phineas Capen: were reported on.

Assistant Surgeon Suter died in the city of Mexico on Dec 15. Full military honors were paid to his remains.

On Thu night the stable of M de Figaniere, the Portuguese Minister, in the rear of the Six Bldgs, was destroyed by fire. The cause has not yet been ascertained.

Galipolis Journal: explosion of the steamer **Blue Ridge**, a few days ago: among the killed & missing: Wm F Whittaker, dead; mother-in-law of Mr Stewart, missing; Mr Overshiner, missing; Jos Brulon, missing; F J Sanns, dead; Geo Beard, dead; Jos Miller, missing; P Carpenter, missing; & F Scott, missing.

For rent: the commodious 2 story brick dwlg owned by Jacob B Moore, on 8th st, near F, between the Patent Ofc & the Genr'l Post Ofc. Inquire of Dr A H Lee, 7th st, or to A Green, auctioneer

MON JAN 17, 1848

Annual meeting of the Wash City Orphan Asylum on Jan 11. The following ladies were re-elected Managers for the ensuing year:

Mrs Hawley, 1st Directress
Mrs Laurie, 2nd Directress

Miss Ann Smith, Treasurer
Miss Taylor, Secretary

Managers:
Mrs Lear
Mrs R S Coxe
Mrs Shubrick
Mrs Stone
Mrs Tucker

Mrs Brown
Miss Bingham
Mrs Henderson
Mrs Washington
Mrs Richd Smith

Mrs Geo Totten
Mrs Gilliss
Mrs Luce

Wash Corp: 1-Nomination of J F Wannall as police ofcr of the 2nd Ward, in the place of J W Dexter, deceased. 2-Ptn of Michl Keller; ptn of Louisa Collins; & ptn of Chas Middleton: each for remission of a fine: referred to the Cmte of Claims. 3-Bill for the relief of E D Southworth was referred to the Cmte on Public Schools. 4-Bill for the relief of John Seitz: indefinitely postponed. 5-Bill for the relief of S Cunningham: indefinitely postponed.

On Dec 24, Miss Elmira Brewer, a young lady who resided with a relative, about a mile from White Plains, in that county, was shot by a young man named Rooney, & severely wounded. It appears Rooney prepared himself with 2 pistols, went to a cotton field, where the young lady was alone, & immediately on declaring his intention shot her down with one pistol, & then fired the other after she fell. He had desired to marry the girl, but she would not have him. He pleaded guilty before the committing magistrate, & said he desired to be hung. –Jacksonville [Ala] Republican

Mrd: on Jan 13, in Wash City, by Rev Henry Slicer, Mr John T Evans, jr, to Miss Mary J Henderson, all of Alexandria, Va.

Mrd: at Brentwood, by Rev Smith Pyne, Peter Augustus Jay, of N Y, to Josephine, youngest daughter of the late Jos Pearson. [No date-current item.]

Died: on Jan 11, in Gtwn, Jas Edw, youngest son of Rev John Poisal, in his 3rd year. [N Y papers please copy.]

On Sat week, whilst with a party of boys gunning, Wm L Sumpter, a fine youth about 10 years of age, the oldest daughter of Mr Benj E Sumpter, of Lynchburg, Va, was killed by the accidental discharge of the fowling piece of one of the party.

TUE JAN 18, 1848
Senate: 1-Mr Wyman D S Moor was appointed by the Govn'r of Maine to fill the vacancy occasioned by the death of Mr Fairfield. Mr Moor was duly qualified & took his seat. 2-Cmte on Post Ofc & Post Roads: bill for the relief of Nathl Kuykendall. 3-Cmte on Public Lands: bill to provide for the compensation of Saml Leech for services in the investigation of the suspended sales in the Mineral Point district, Wisconsin. 4-Cmte on Pensions: bill granting a pension to Abigail Garland, widow of David Garland, deceased. 5-Cmte on Naval Affairs: bill for the relief of Thos Brownell. 6-Cmte of Claims: asking to be discharged from the further consideration of the ptn of Amos Holton.

Com'r Bernard's Ofc, Petersburg, Dec 24, 1847: in Chancery. Walter Evans & others against Jos Cockerille & others. By a decree of the Circuit Superior Court of Law & Chancery for Petersburg, Va, rendered in the above cause at Nov term, 1847, the undersigned was to inquire who were the kindred of Eliza Emanda Evans, deceased, on the part of her father, Alex'r Evans, deceased, late of Petersburg, at the time of her death, viz, on Oct 8, 1843, & who are the parties now representing such kindred, & as such entitled to a portion of the real estate of which said Alex'r Evans died seized. The kindred referred to consist of the brothers & sisters of said Alex'r Evans, deceased, & their reps. It is represented that he had 4 sisters of the whole blood, viz: 1-Mary, who is to have married Jos Harper & removed to the State of Tenn, where it is said that she & her husband both died many years ago. It is said she left a son, Geo Harper, but that he is believed to have died many years without issue & intestate. 2-Nancy, whose children are known. 3-Sally, who is said to have died some 30 years ago, in Ky, intestate, unmarried, & without issue. 4-Ellen, who is said to have twice married, first to John Hummer, & afterwards to Saml Walker. It is said that she died childless, & that her last husband is also dead. The said Alex'r Evans had 2 sister & a brother of the half blood, in respect to whom no inquiry is necessary. The undersigned desires that any person who may be able to give information respecting Mary Evans, who married Harper, or her husband or son, Sally Evans, & Ellen Evans, or either of her husbands, or neither of them, will communicate the same to him at Petersburg, Va, by Apr 1, 1848; & if any of these parties be living, he desires that they or some others will communicate the fact to him by the same time, that he may comply with the order of the Court. –D M Bernard, Com'r

Household furniture, slaves, buggies, & liquors at auction: on Jan 28, by order of the Orphans Court of Wash Co, D C: the personal effects of the late Patrick Moran, at his late residence at the corner of 8th & D sts. -R W Dyer, auct

WED JAN 19, 1848
Annual meeting of the Topographical Society-Jan 1, 1848: following were re-elected for the ensuing year: Chas F Lowrey, Pres

Patr'k H Brooks, V Pres	Thos W Howard, Corr Sec	Thos Rice, Recording Sec
Michl Caton, Treas		

Senate: 1-Cmte on Pensions: bill for the relief of Eliz Jones & the other children, if any, of John Carr. Same cmte: bill for the relief of Thompson Hutchinson. 2-Cmte of Claims: adverse report on the ptn of Hugh Munro McLean. Same cmte: asking to be discharged from the further consideration of the ptn of John Stanert, & that it be referred to the Cmte on Pensions. 3-Ptn from Mrs Susan Decatur, widow of the late Com Decatur, asking for a renewal of her pension. 4-Ptn from Asa Whitney, asking a grant of land to enable him to construct a railroad from Lake Michigan to the Pacific Ocean. 5-Ptn from Abraham Edwards, register of the land ofc at Kalamazoo, Michigan, asking to be allowed expenses incurred in clerk hire. 6-Ptn from Chas Richmond, asking compensation for aiding the U S marshal to preserve the neutral relations of the U S with the provinces of Upper & Lower Canada. 7-Ptn of Robt Pyatt, only surviving son of Maj Danl Pyatt, asking the 7 year's half-pay allowed under the resolution of Congress of the year 1780. Also, from the same, asking the final settlement of his accounts as deputy purchasing commissary. 8-Ptn from Jas Wilkins, asking payment for cattle destroyed by a band of Seminole Indians. 9-Ptn from Mary Telfair, asking that the claim of her late husband against the U S for final settlement certificates may be granted. 10-Ptn from Richd M Martin, asking that Congress will extend to him the law granting land bounty to those who served in the war with Mexico. 11-Bill for the relief of Wm DeBuys, late postmaster at New Orleans: introduced. 12-Bill for the relief of the heirs of Matthew Rea, a Lt in the Revolutionary war: introduced.

The Albany Argus announces the death of Judge Coon, a prominent member of the bar, formerly of Rensselaer Co, but for several years a resident of Albany, & whose death is regarded as the immediate or proximate effect of injuries received in a personal encounter with Mr Hayden, of the Rensselaer bar, in the course of a hearing on a motion before the Rensselaer county judge.

House of Reps: 1-Ptn of Horatio Dyer, legal rep of Chas Smith, a captain in the Md line, for Revolutionary services. 2-Ptn of John & Eliz Bellinger, praying Congress to grant them a pension. 3-Ptns of Esther Alexander, Isabel Bugbee, Mary Bemis, Pheba Cobb, Martha Chapman, Mary Chase, Abigail Coburn, Marcey Howard, Charity Harlon, Susannah Knight, L Roberts, Sarah Strickney, Marcy Wood, & Anna Watson, for an extension of the widows' pension act of Jun 17, 1844. 4-Memorial of E B Cogswell, praying for payment of services as armorer to Texas Indians. 5-Memorial of G W Crawford, praying for payment of supplies furnished to volunteers on the way to Mexico. Original papers lost in the steamer New York. 6-Ptn of Patrick Marsutette, of St Joseph Co, Mich, that his claim against the Pottawattamies of the Nollawasepe, as audited by Gen Mitchell, U S Com'r of Indian Claims, may be allowed & paid to him. 7-Ptn of John Pyatt, asking the comfirmation of a land claim in the State of Missouri. 8-Ptn of Lt A Garland, of the marine corps, for compensation for services rendered as a purser on board the frig **Brandywine** in 1840-41. 9-Ptn & papers of Wm Triplett, applying for the confirmation of a land entry, be taken from the files of the Clerk's Ofc & referred to the Cmte on Private Land Claims. 10-Ptn of the heirs of Micah Whitmarsh, for commutation. 11-Ptn of Nathan Beard, praying Congress to grant a pension. 12-Ptn of Patience Corbin, praying to be place on the pension roll. 13-Ptn of Benj P Smith, praying the passage of a law granting a pension to the petitioner. 14-Pt of Geo Read & others, of

Deep Creek, Conn, for an alteration of postage & absolution of the franking privilege. 15-Ptn of J T Roper, Collector of the Customs at Petersburg, Va, for an increase of salary. 16-Ptn of Stephen Bowerman, of Michigan, praying the House to adopt a Legislative Telegraph of his invention, for taking the yeas & nays. 17-Ptn of F F Backus & other physicians of Rochester, N Y, asking Congress to pass a law to prevent the importation of spurious & adulterated medicines. 18-Resolved, that Wm A Poor, of Md, have leave to withdraw his ptn & papers from the files of this House, & be used by the petitioner in prosecuting his claim at the Executive Depts. 19-Sec of War directed to furnish the Cmte on Invalid Pensions with the papers of Arthur Wilson, an invalid pensioner; also, the Cmte on Revolutionary Pensions with the papers of Saml Pool, an applicant for pension. 20-Com'r of Pensions to deliver to this House the papers on file relating to the application of Sarah Dunham for a pension, & that they be referred to the Cmte on Revolutionary Pensions. 21-The papers in relation to the application of Jas Hillman, of Ohio, for a pension, be taken from the files, & be referred to the standing Cmte on Revolutionary Pensions. 22-The papers in the case of Bryan Manypenny & Co, be taken from the files & referred to the Cmte on the Post Ofc & Post Roads.

Mrd: on Jan 13, by Rev H H Bean, Jas Hubard Bowyer, of Lexington, Va, to Aurelia, daughter of the late John G McDonald, of Wash City.

Mrd: on Jan 11, at the residence of Mr Wm P Taylor, in Caroline, Va, by Rev Mr Friend, Williams C Wickham, of Hanover, to Miss Lucy P, eldest daughter of the late Henry Taylor, of Spottsylvania.

Died: on Jan 11, John Scott, of Fredericksburg, Va, leaving a wife & a numerous family of children & grandchildren, & most extensive circle of friends, who mourn his irreparable loss. The deceased was born at Greenock, in Scotland, on Jul 22, 1772, & had for more than half a century been one of the principal merchants in Fredericksburg, engaged in extensive business & in agencies from abroad of high responsibility.

Household & kitchen furniture at auction: on Jan 26, at the residence of Mrs Potter, on G st, nearly opposite the State Dept. -R W Dyer, auct

Governess wanted: a French lady, who has some experience, desires a situation as a Governess in a private family. Address to Mrs Amanda Arnett, at Mrs Burrows', on D st, near 7th st, will meet with attention.

Appointments by the Pres: To be Register of the Land Ofc:
Jas B Hunt, at Sault de Ste Marie, Michigan.
Saml Holmes, at Quincy, Ill, vice Wm G Flood, resigned.
John Miller, at Batesville, Ark, vice Henry Neil, removed.
To be Receiver of Public Moneys:
Mich A Patterson, of Sault de Ste Marie, Michigan.
Theodore H Gillaspie, at Greensburg, La, vice Peter H Kemp, resigned.
Purdy McElvaine, at Upper Sandusky, Ohio, vice Christian Huber, removed.

In the Navy:
Saml Chas Barney, now a master, to be a lt in the navy, from Nov 12, 1847, vice Lt Theodore B Barrett, deceased.
Benj F B Hunter, now a master, to be a lt in the navy, from Nov 28, 1847, vice Lt John M Gardner, deceased.
In the Marine Corps:
Wm Dulany, now a capt, to Major in the marine corps, from Nov 17,1847, vice Maj Saml W Watson, deceased.
Archibald H Gillespie, now a 1st lt, to captain in the marine corps, from Nov 17, 1847, vice Capt Wm Dulany, promoted.
Danl J Sutherland, now a 2nd lt, to be a 1st lt in the marine corps, from Nov 17, 1847, vice 1st Lt Archibald H Gillespie, promoted.
John Lloyd Broome to be a 2nd lt in the marine corps, vice 2nd Lt Danl J Sutherland, promoted.
Wm Stokes Boyd to be a 2nd lt in the marine corps, vice 2nd Lt Henry Walsh, deceased.

THU JAN 20, 1848
Senate: 1-Cmte on the Judiciary: a bill for the relief of Mormon Douglass, late U S Atty in East Florida. Same cmte: asking to be discharged from the further consideration of the ptn of Leslie Combs, & that it be referred to the Cmte of Claims. 2-Cmte on Pensions: adverse report on the ptn of John Searing: ordered to be printed. 3-Cmte of Claims: asking to be discharged from the further consideration of the memorial of Gad Humphreys, & that it be referred to the Cmte of Claims. 4-Ordered, that the memorial of John Hagan, E Lackett, & Sherman Johnson, owners of the slaves compelled by mutiny on board the ship **Creole** to enter the port of Nassau, & liberated by the authorities of that place, be taken from the files & referred to the Cmte of Claims. 5-Vote confirming the adverse report in the case of Amos Holden was reconsidered, & the papers with additional evidence referred to the Cmte of Claims.

House of Reps: 1-Cmte of Claims: bill for the relief of John P Converse: committed. Same cmte: adverse report upon the ptn of Wm B Norris: laid on the table. Same cmte: adverse report on the ptn of A H Hughes: laid on the table. 2-Cmte on the Post Ofc & Post Roads: bill for the relief of Wm Fuller & Orlando Saltmarsh: committed. Same cmte: joint resolution for the relief of Geo R Smith: committed. Same cmte: be discharged from the further consideration of the ptn of Landon G Chambers, of Va, asking to have refunded to him certain money lost in its passage through the mail. 3-Cmte on the Judiciary: adverse report on the ptn of J H Overstreet & Geo B Didlake: laid on the table. 4-Cmte on Naval Affairs: bills from the Senate for the relief of Jos Wilson; & providing for the payment of the claim of Walter R Johnson against the U S: committed. Same cmte: bill for the relief of H D Johnson: committed. 5-Francis Harper died on Mar 18, 1837, after his election from the 3rd district of Pa to be a member of the House of Reps, & his death was omitted to be announced to the House as usual during the 25th Congress. Therefore, the Clerk will cause the usual monument to be erected in the Congressional Burying ground to the memory of the said Francis Harper. 6-Cmte on Revolutionary Pensions: bill for the relief of John Manly & for the relief of Sarah Stokes: committed. Same cmte: adverse report on the ptn of T Campbell: laid on the table. Same cmte: bill for the relief of Esther Russell: commited. 7-Cmte on Invalid Pensions: adverse report on the ptn of Wm B Edwards: laid on the table. 8-Cmte on Patents: adverse report on the ptn of Jos Nock: laid on the table.

Mortality in the 9th Regt: a letter received by Benj Wade, of Bangor, a few days since, from his son in Mexico, who belongs to the 9th Regt, which states that when they left Newport, R I, it numbered 800 strong, but that it had been reduced to 265.

Naval: 1-Ofcrs attached to the U S brig **Porpoise**, destined for the coast of Africa: Lt Commanding, A G Gordon; Lts, B F Sands & A D Harrel; Passed Assist Surgeon, Lewis J Williams; Acting Master, Jas H Somerville; Passed Midshipman, F P Wheelock; Cmder's Clerk, Chas A Sands; Acting Midshipmen, Edw A Burke & Geo A Belknap; Acting Master's Mate, John Belknap.
2-The basque **Kirkland** arrived at N Y on Fri from Rio de Janeiro, having on board, as passenger, Capt S H Stringham, who took the ship-of-the-line **Ohio** to Rio Janeiro, & there resigned the command into the hands of Capt Taylor on Nov 25.

On Monday of last week 4 companies of the Michigan volunteers, under command of Col T B W Stockton, arrived at New Orleans on their way to the seat of war in Mexico. These companies are commanded by Capts Curtenius, Gernsel, Rowland, & Witenmyer.

Fairfax Co land for sale: by deed of trust from Saml Whitall to the subscriber: public auction on Mar 22: 6 lots or farms of 100 acs each, part of the tract in said county, called "*the Union Tract*," which was all allotted to Bushrod C Washington in the division between him & Geo C Washington, & which was sold by Edw C Cooke, com'r, on Apr 20, 1840, & purchased by said Saml Whitall. This land adjoins the **Mount Vernon** tract, & has, for the purposes of this sale, been divided into convenient farms of 100 acres each. Sale at the auction room of A J Fleming, Alexandria. –Evan Lyons, Trustee
-A J Fleming, Auctioneer

A Great Bargain: 200,000 acres of land for sale: the subscriber wishes to dispose of all his lands in Texas: composed of different tracts in the counties of Harris, Liberty, Polk, Tyler, Jasper, & Jackson. The residence of the subscriber is on a 6,000 acre tract. He is aware of the sacrifice he is making in selling his lands at these prices; but he has no family, & intends leaving Texas as soon as he can dispose of his lands.
-J Morgan, New Washington, Galveston Bay, Texas

Mrd: on Dec 16, 1847, in St Luke's Church, in Lincolnton, N C, by Rev Mr Husks, V A McBee to Miss Mary E Sumner, daughter of Benj Sumner, late of Gates Co, N C.

FRI JAN 21, 1848
Senate: 1-Cmte on Indian Affairs: bill for the relief of Saml W Bell, late of the Cherokee nation. 2-Cmte on Military Affairs: asking to be discharged from the further consideration of the ptn of Eugene Van Ness & John M Brush, executors of Nehemiah Brush, & that it be referred to the Cmte of Claims: 3-Cmte of Claims: adverse report on the ptn of David Whelpley.

House of Reps: 1-The late John W Hornbeck was a native of N J, a graduate of Union College, at Schenectady, N Y: removed to Pa, & the study of law; elected a member of the present Congress in that patriotic district composed of the counties of Lehigh & Bucks. He died in the midst of his family & friends, & had the consoling presence of the partner of his bosom in his dying hour. His wife, his devoted wife & children, have lost a kind husband & father, & the country an intelligent & patriotic representative. He died at his residence, in Allentown, Pa, on Jan 16. 2-Ptn of Ann Kelly, widow of Danl Kelly, a gunner in the navy, for a pension. 3-Additional documents relating to the ptn of Hugh Wallace Wormly. 4-Ptn from Wm Darby, author of the map of Louisiana now known as Melish's map, asking remuneration for money & time spent in the survey of the Saline. 5-Ptn from Wm R Stokes, surviving partner of the firm of Stockton & Stokes, asking compensation for services in carrying the U S mail. 6-Ptn from Edw Mills, asking to be restored to the rights & benefits of a contract made with the Post Ofc Dept for carrying the mail from N Y to Bremen, which contract was transferred without his assent to the Ocean Steam Navigation Co. 6-Ptn of David Williamson, asking to be compensated for the benefits which the Gov't has derived from the use of his invention. [The inventor is now poor, & sought some compensation for the benefits from his efforts.]
7-Ptn of Sarah Mendeville, praying to be placed on the pension roll. 8-Ptn of the heirs of Nehemiah Stokely, who was a captain in the Revolutionary war, for commutation pay. 9-Ptn of the heirs of Robt Laughlin, late of Westmoreland Co, Pa, deceased, praying compensation for property destroyed during the Revolutionary war. 10-Ptn of legal reps of Jas Green, a soldier of the Revolutionary war, for a pension. 11-Ptn of Wm Harding, master of the schnr **Albatross**, for the remission of a penalty under the revenue laws. 12-Memorial of C H Pix, for payment of rent of bldgs occupied by Judge of the Admiralty Court, at Galveston, Texas.

Nat'l Hotel: I have this day purchased out the interest of Saml S Coleman in this establishment & it will hereafter be conducted by me on my own account.
–C W Blackwell

Great bargain in a farm of 120 acres, lately occupied by F G Skinner, who has removed to Va. It is situated in PG Co, Md, about 10 miles from Wash. When last sold, in 1842, it brought at public auction, including the dower, $63 an acre. It has been supplied with a commodious dwlg, 2 stories high, with 4 rooms on each floor, ice house, & all requisite out-bldgs. –T F Bowie, Upper Marlborough, Md

Official: the remains of the gallant Lt Col Wm M Graham, late of the 11th U S Infty, who fell at the head of his regt in the battle of Molino del Rey, having reached this city, the Ofcrs of the Army & Navy present are respectfully invited to attend [in uniform] his funeral, which will take place from St John's Church at 12 o'clock on Jan 22.
–R Jones, Adj Gen

Col Thos M Bondurant has disposed of his interest in the Richmond Whig to Alex'r Moseley, & the proprietors of that journal now are W M Elliott, Richd H Toles, & A Moseley.

Capt John Butler, of the 3rd Regt, died at Brasos in the early part of this month.

On Wed last an infant child of Thos Glancy was killed by the administration of croton oil instead of castor oil. The child was dead in an instant after swallowing it.
–Boston Traveller

Mrd: on Jan 20, by Rev Mr Brown, Mr Blanchard P Paige, formerly of N H, to Miss Mary Ann Tate, of Wash City.

Mrd: on Jan 11, by Rev Mr Morgan, Henry C Mitchell, of Wash City, to Miss Ann E Ennis, of Prince Wm Co, Va.

Died: on Jan 1, after a short illness, in Yazoo Co, Miss, Mrs Margaret Ellen Ingersoll, consort of John Ingersoll, formerly of New Orleans, & daughter of Dennis A Smith, of Balt, Md.

SAT JAN 22, 1848
For rent: the house at present occupied by Mrs Wells as a boarding-house, will be for rent on Feb 16 next. It is over the store of the subscribers. Apply to Wm Egan & Son, south side Pa ave, between 6th & 7th sts.

House of Reps: 1-Bill for the relief of Milledge Galplin, exc of Geo Galphin, deceased, was referred to the Cmte on the Judiciary. 2-Bill for the relief of Thos Talbot & others: referred to the Cmte on Indian Affairs. 3-Bill for the relief of Robt Roberts: recommitted to the Cmte of Claims. 4-Bill for the relief of Phineas Capen, legal administrator of John Cox, deceased, of Boston: returned to the Senate.

The remains of the gallant soldier, the lamented Capt W H Churchill, were yesterday received by the brig **John Enders**, from New Orleans. After receiving a brevet for his gallantry on the fields of Palo Alto & Resaca, it was the fate of this accomplished ofcr to perish, after a brief illness, in a foreign land, far from family & kindred. The usual military honors having been paid to Capt Churchill, at *Point Isabel*, his remains will, we learn, be interred here in a private manner, in accordance with the desire of the members of his family, who decline any military escort. –Savannah Georgian of Jan 15.

Trustee's sale: by virtue of a deed of trust from Andrew R Carroll & wife, dated Aug 14, 1845, recorded in Liber W B 120, folios 105 & 106, of the land records of Wash Co, D C: sale for cash, on Feb 2, all the right, title, interest, & estate of said Carroll & wife in lot 7, in square 17, in Wash City. -R W Dyer, auct

Wash Corp: 1-Ptn of Richd B Posey, asking that the sale of certain property for taxes be set aside: referred to the Cmte on Finances. 2-Ptn of Jos B Ellis, for the remission of a fine: referred to the Cmte on Police. 3-Cmte of Claims: joint resolution authorizing the payment of Wm Dalton & J Beasely: passed.

The Cecil Co Advocate announces the death of Dr A Evans, the venerable father of the Hon A Evans, member of Congress.

MON JAN 24, 1848

The American Colonization Society was organized 31 years ago; 25 years ago the first emigrants landed on Cape Missurado to seek a home for themselves & their children; 6 months ago the citizens of the Colony organized the Republic of Liberia, & announced their independence to the world.

The funeral ceremonies in honor of Col Butler & Lt Col Dickinson, of S C, who fell in battle in Mexico, took place at Columbia, the capital of the State, on Tue last. The remains of Col Butler were entombed in the cemetery of Grace Church, at Columbia, & those of Lt Col Dickinson were placed in charge of a deputation to be conveyed to Camden.

On Fri last the barque **Margaret Hugg** sailed from *Fort McHenry* [Balt] for Vera Cruz, with 108 voltigeurs, detached recruits, for the regt in Mexico; 129 for the 11th Infty, & 30 volunteers for 2nd Pa Regt. Capt Campbell commands the detachment; Lt Kerner, Acting Commissary; M H Hooper, Acting Quartermaster; Dr Hammond, Surgeon.

The funeral obsequies of the late Col Wm M Graham, whose remains had reached here from Mexico, were celebrated on Sat, at St John's Church, Wash City, with impressive solemnity. The body had been brought from the lodgings of his relatives, where it had been temporarily deposited; it was received by the Pastor, Rev Mr Pyne, accompanied by the Pastor, Rev Mr French. The Funeral service prescribed by the Episcopal ritual. The President of the U S & his cabinet were present. The procession moved towards the Congressional Cemetery, where these honored remains were to find their last earthly resting place, in the family burial ground of a surviving & devoted brother.

Mrd: on Jan 17, in Wash City, by Rev Mr French, Mr Richd T Jacob, of Louisville, to Miss Sarah McDowell Benton, 3rd daughter of the Hon Thos H Benton, of Missouri.

Mrd: Jan 20, by Rev C M Butler, Raymond W Burche to Kate, youngest daughter of the late Wm Hewitt, all of Wash City.

Mrd: on Dec 29, in Accomac, by Rev John Ufford, Mr John W H Parker to Miss Sarah, only daughter of Nathl Ropping.

Mrd: on Dec 14, at Cambridge, Md, by Rev Dr T J Wyatt, Dr Jas A Muse, of Talbot Co, Md, to Miss Mary S Sulivan, of the former place.

Mrd: on Jan 12, in Newbern, N C, by Rev Mr Hawks, John N Washington to Miss Sally Vail, daughter of the late Thos J Emery.

Mrd: on Jan 18, at **Bloomsbury**, Fred'k Co, Md, by Rev J Peterkin, Wm Richardson to Eliz R, daughter of Dr Jas T Johnson, all of the above county.

Died: recently, in Richmond, Va, after a prolonged illness, Mrs Sarah C Stevenson, the excellent & esteemed wife of the Hon Andrew Stevenson.

Died: on Jan 20, after a lingering illness of several months, Mary Jane Sandy, aged 18 years & 6 months.

Gtwn Assemblies announce that the 2nd Assembly will be held at the Union Hotel, on Jan 25. Managers:

Col G C Washington	John Appleton	Wm D Beall
Wm S Nichols	Peter F Wilson	A H Pickrell
Dr O M Linthicum	F W Risque	Jas M Ramsey
Geo Poe, jr	Henry Brewer	Robt Ould
Dr Wm Plater	Edgar Patterson	Thos Sims
J R McCorkle	O S X Peck	Robt Dick
S G Davidson	Edw Chapman	J M Belt
Stephen Gough	Watkins Addison	Dr A Matthews
C Morton	Chas Dodge	
Jas Cassin	Francis Dodge, jr	

The establishment of the Columbian Fountain for sale: the present proprietor finds his duties as a Minister of the Gospel at Phil, will prevent him from devoting his attention to the publication of a newspaper in this city, & has determined to offer it for sale, along with the printing materials. Apply to Ulysses Ward, Wash

TUE JAN 25, 1848
Mrd: on Jan 20, by Rev Mr Balantine, Hon T Purrington, formerly of Maine, to Miss Amelia Josephine Archer, of Wash, daughter of Wm Archer.

Died: on Dec 24, of consumption, Miss Debroah Kendall Greer, aged 17 years & 6 months, daughter of Wm & Susan Greer. Her funeral is this afternoon, at 3 o'clock, from her father's residence on 10th st, near F.

Died: on Jan 22, at the residence of her son-in-law, Mr Wm C Greenleaf, Mrs Ruth Owen, in her 76th year, relict of the late Col Washington Owen, of Montg Co, Md.

The partnership existing between John Warring & L C Brown was dissolved by mutual consent on Dec 15 last, the said L C Brown withdrawing from the firm, & assigning all his interest to John Warring. –John Warring, L C Brown

Appointment by the Pres: John Robb, of Md, to be Principal Clerk of the Public Lands in the Genr'l Land Ofc, vice Jas H Piper, resigned.

WED JAN 26, 1848
On Monday last Mr Wm Perry, an old & respectable citizen of Clarkson, was instantly killed by the falling of a tree. On Tue another highly esteemed citizen, Mr John Blodgett, lost his life in a similar manner. -Rochester Democrat

Senate: 1-Ptn of S J Bowen, praying remuneration for services in the ofc of the 2nd Auditor of the Treasury. 2-Ptns from citizens of Charlestown, Mass, praying for the repeal of a patent granted to Wm W Woodworth. 3-Ptn from Peter Godfrey, praying for leave to locate a new section of land in lieu of one of which he has been deprived. 4-Ptn from Peter W Knaggs, praying leave to locate a new section of land under similar circumstances. 5-Cmte on Public Lands: bill for the relief of Henry Washington.

House of Reps: 1-Mr Albert G Brown, a representative from the State of Mississippi, appeared this day, was qualified according to law, & took his seat in the House. 2-Cmte of Claims: bill for the relief of Stalker & Hill: committed. Same cmte: bill for the relief of Reuben Perry & Thos P Ligon: committed. Same cmte: adverse report on the ptn of the administrators of Saml Holgate: laid on the table. Same cmte: bill for the relief of Jos Girard. 3-Cmte on Commerce: adverse report on the ptn of Ferdinand N Clarke. 4-Cmte on Public Lands: adverse report on the ptn of Jas Chapman: laid on the table. Same cmte: bill for the relief of Benj White: committed. Same cmte: adverse reports on the ptns of Jas Dossett & Edw Keating, mayor of Alton: laid on the table. 5-Cmte on the Post Ofc & Post Roads: bill for the relief of Thos Rhodes: laid on the table. 6-Cmte on Private Land Claims: bill for the relief of Lewis Benedict: commited. Same cmte: bill for the relief of Anthony Bessee: committed. 7-Cmte on Indian Affairs: bill for the relief of Jos Perry, a Choctaw Indian: committed. 8-Cmte on Naval Affairs: bill for the relief of G F De La Rache & W P S Sanger: committed. 9-Cmte on Revolutionary Pensions: bill for the relief of Jonathan Moore, of the State of Mass. Same cmte: bill for the relief of Robt Ellis: committed. Same cmte: adverse report on the ptn of Jedediah Morse: laid on the table. Same cmte: bill for the relief of Catharine Fulton, widow of Saml Fulton: committed. Same cmte: adverse reports on the ptns of Wm Sparks; Geo Taylor; & Marshal Gentry: laid on the table. Same cmte: bill for the relief of Rilpha White; also, bill for the relief of Anna Yarrington: committed. 10-Resolved: to pay Mrs Ellen S Bradley, widow of the Hon Edw Bradley, late of Michigan, deceased, his mileage, as allowed by the Cmte of Meleage, from Marshall, his place of residence in Mich, to N Y C, where, on his journey to Washington to take his seat as a member of the House, he died. 11-Ptn of N J Knight, & others, of Truro, Mass, asking that a lighthouse & buoys may be established at Parmot river. 12-Ptn that the papers of widow Mary Stunton, presented at a previous session, be taken from the files & again committed to the Cmte on Revolutionary Pensions. 13-Ptn of Saml J Finch & others, praying the discharge of all the married men in the N C regt after 12 months service. 14-Memorial of A Hunter, marshal of D C, praying that provision may be made for maintaining in jail persons committed to his keeping as marshal. 15-Ptn of March Farrington, of Duchess Co, N Y, for a pension. 16-Ptn of Geo Bock, praying for a pension. 17-Ptn of Alex'r Scott, of Canfield, Mahoning Co, Ohio, for relief. 18-Ptn of Stephen G Hogan, of Balt city, for a pension. 19-Ptn of Richd Mackall for compensation for property destroyed by the enemy in the war of 1812. 20-Memorial of Mrs Eliza A Mellow, widow of Capt Chas Mellow, late of the U S army, praying for a continuance of pension. 21-Ptn & documents of John Morrison, of Pa, a Revolutionary soldier, & a soldier under Gen Wayne, from 1791 to 1794, until after the treaty of **Fort Grenville**, praying for a pension, being at present 98 years of age. 22-Ptn of Mrs Sally Ketchum, asking to be placed on the pension roll. 23-Ptn of H P Daniels & 168 others, inhabitants of Lowensworth, N H, praying that measures may be adopted to close the Mexican war. 24-Ptn of Mehitable Marble, for a pension. 25-The ptn of Levi Nichols to be taken from the files of the House & referred to the Cmte on Revolutionary Claims. 26-Ptn & papers of Jas Monroe, in relation to the loss of certain horses in the war of 1812: referred to the Cmte of Claims.

London Dec 31, 1847. Foreign News: The Arch-Duchess Maria Louisa, widow of Napoleon, died on Dec 17. This event was long expected. She was Duchess of Parma & Placenza, in Italy. Chas Louis, of Bourbon, late Duke of Lucca, succeeds to her dignities.

Mr John Hildebrand died at the residence of his son, Mr David Hildebrand, near this place, on Jan 20. Mr John Hildebrand, was one of the oldest men in the Nation. He was born on Feb 12, 1755, & was aged at the time of his death, 92 years, 10 months & 8 days. He came among the Cherokees east of the Mississippi more than 50 years ago, among whom he intermarried. He has left more than 100 lineal descendants, a majority of whom are now residing among the Cherokees. –Cherokee Advocate

On Thu night the house of Mr Thos Franklin, of Old Point, Va, was entirely consumed by fire, & 2 of his children, a little girl about 6, & a boy about 4 years of age, perished in the flames. –Portsmouth Chronicle

Dr John Snowden, the Physician & Superintendent of the Institution of the Com'rs of Emigration at Ward's Island, N Y, has fallen victim to the ship fever. He died a martyr. [No date-current news.]

Lists of deaths in the Military Hospital in the city of Mexico for the month of Oct, 1847.

2nd Dragoons:
Lenze	Haberstein	Miller	Reyno
Hill	Durham	Frederick	Cpl Dougherty
Spenser	Cain	Spear	Dugan
Varpes	Waldron	Cohen	Zink
Eldred	Leggett	Forbes	Ginters

3rd Dragoons:
Royce	Bernard	Williams	Fassett
Hall	Harmon	Baker	Cornice
Delshy	Horton	Adains	

1st Artl:
Irons	Thompson	Meade	Shadd
Lesenfalt	Leigh	Dingle	Collins
Myers	Lewis	Short	Wilson

2nd Artl:
Hoover	McWade	Putnam	Ross
Tiernan	Buchanan	Hainman	Watson

1st Lt Shackelford	Capt S Mckenzie	Page	1st Lt C B Daniels
Sgt Douglass	Connors	Serg Beard Ormas	

3rd Artl:
Setzer	Devitte	Clement	
Finch	Watson	Artificer	
Walsh	Whittaker	Kingsbury	

4th Artl:
Johnson	Tracy	Elkins	

Voltigeurs:
McCorgan	Delacey	Herchy	Miller
McGava	Haughrey	Cpl Mager	Wimp
Bird	Cpl Bryan	Pryer	Barnheart
Vogel	Dinas	Brauguard	

2nd Infty:
Gordon	Wilson	McKoun	Cpl Hood
Pearson	Smith, 2nd	Kubanks	Carl
Stuart	Palmer	Keniford	Force
Salisbury	Pickett	Hatfield	Knepper
Brooks	Brenan	Fitzpatrick	

3rd Infty:
Dale	Smith	Bayles	Ruth
Schofield	Ser Simmons	Davis	Cpl Patterson
Anderson	Serg Williams	Stanton	
Upton	Serg Allen	Smith	
Door	Trowbridge	Parhall	

4th Infty:
Lauless	Smallbeck	Loomis	Wiernett
Heskinson	Dehart	Barton	Woods
Wilson	Carmichael	Sparks	
Crofoot	Oliver	Buel	

5th Infty:
Sgt McClelland	Cpl Green	O'Neil	Volly
Camon	Clarks	Lindon	Carlin
Coglan	King	Cpl Ballard	
McElroy	McCary	Powers	

6th Infty:
1st Lt Bacon	Rupert	Fernando	Edwards

| Mathias | Smith | Schyder | Cooke |
| Francis | Tibbets | Morrison | |

7th Infty
Butler Byrnes   Janpear

8th Infty:
Chappel	Hess	Everson	Hopkins
Silver	McCormack	Buckland	Landis
Cain	Holt	Lesban	Henner

11th Infty: Disbrow

Serg Peath, Ord

Rifles:
Raymond   Ser Brooks   Debaugh

South Carolina Regt:
Hallstead   Tillman   Loupean   Rodgers

Died: on Dec 27 last, at her seat, ***Rose Hall***, near Glasgow, Scotland, aged about 80 years, Mrs Catharine Douglas, relict of the late Gen Pye Douglas, of the British Army. Born in the State of Virginia, she was carried to Scotland, together with her brother & sister, long since deceased, by their widowed mother, by the invitation of the Duchess of Douglas, their aunt. Mrs Douglas has numerous relations in this city & vicinity & others whose residences are remote, & it is for their information this notice is published.

$25 reward for the apprehension of 2 horses stolen from my stable, one mile beyond Beall's Bridge. –Hillary S Williams

By virtue of an order for distress, to me directed, I shall expose to public sale for cash, on square 409, in Wash City, on Jan 31: one lot of celery, one lot of kale & spinach, one lot of carrots, 14 rows of cabbage plants, one lot of parsnips, seized & taken as for rent due in arrears by Wm Murray to Henry Haw, & will be sold to satisfy the same.
–R R Burr, Bailiff

THU JAN 27, 1848
Senate: 1-Ptn from the Pres of <u>Wm & Mary College</u>, Va, praying compensation for the use of & damage done to the College bldgs by the French troops in the Revolutionary war: referred to the Cmte on Revolutionary Claims. 2-Cmte on Patents: bill to further extend the patent of Jethro Wood: read a first time.

Mrd: on Dec 10, in the Calvary Church, N Y C, by Rev Saml L Southard, H Augustus Taylor to Kate Augusta, daughter of the late Wm Osborn, all of said city.

Died: on Dec 30, at Hudson, N H, after a long & painful pulmonary disease, which was borne with resignation, Chas Fulton, in his 27th year.

Died: at ***Prospect Hill***, PG Co, Md, the residence of Mr John M Brown, in his 25th year, Mr Thos C Boarman. He had been married only 6 weeks prior to his death, & leaves a large circle of friends to sympathize with his devoted wife for her untimely loss. His funeral is this morning at 11 o'clock, from the residence of Mr Brown. [No death date given.]

FRI JAN 28, 1848
Fine beef at the West Market on Jan 28, 1848: beef is superior, & was grazed & fed by Mr Elijah James, Va. –Wm Linkins, stall #9

Mrs & Miss Cady: Plain & Fancy Dressmakers. Have taken rooms on 14th st, exactly opposite Willard's City Hotel, where the above business will be carried on in all its various branches.

Fat beef, & no mistake: purchased of Mr John Lasby: will exhibit for sale on Sat at stalls 43 & 45 in the new Centre Market. Come & see it. –Geo W Emerson

Lost, between Mr Wm Greer's residence, on 10th st, & A Carothers' grocery store, 11th & F sts, a lady's Breastpin, of oval shape, with tapaz set, large size. Reward for leaving it at this ofc.

We announce the death of Capt John Butler, who left this city but a few months since at the head of, as gallant a company as has been mustered into the service during the present war. His high merits as a soldier secured him the command of the Revolutionary first troop, the holy guard of Washington. The war with Mexico called him into a sphere of more active service; he left a large fortune, to rush into the ranks of those who gathered under the flag. He died by the pestilence of the climate. –North American
[See newspaper of Jan 21, 1848-he died the early part of Jan, 1848.]

Supreme Court of the U S: Jan 23, 1848. #145: Mary Ann Van Ness vs Cornelius P Van Ness, administrator of John P Van Ness. In error to the Circuit Court U S for Washington. Mr Chief Justice Taney delivered the opinion of the Court, dismissing the case for the want of jurisdiction.

Com Kearny, at his own request, on account of the delicate health of some of the members of his family, has been relieved of the command of the Gosport Navy Yard, & he will be succeeded by Com Sloat. –Portsmouth Chronicle

Senate: 1-Cmte on the Judiciary: bill for the relief of Reynolds May, accompanied by a report: ordered to be printed. 2-Cmte on Naval Affairs: bill for the relief of Purser Benj J Cahoone.

House of Reps: 1-Cmte of Claims: bills for the relief of Archibald Bull & Lemuel S Finch; of B O Taylor; of the legal reps of David Gardner, of Southborough, Mass; & of Medford Caffey: all committed. Adverse report on the ptn of Wm Darby: laid on the table. 2-Ptn of Edwin Porter, of Va, praying for a settlement of his Post Ofc Dept accounts. 3-Ptn of the heirs of Jas Conway.

City News: Wm Athery, about 12 years of age, fell yesterday from the roof of the City Hall & broke his arm a little above the wrist. Strange to say, the lad fell headforemost to the ground. He was in the employment of Mr F Y Naylor, tinner, & was engaged in repairing a spout when he fell.

Died: on Jan 24, at Gtwn, at the residence of Chas Dean, Hanson Page, aged 16 months, youngest child of Henry & Mary E Barron, of PG Co, Md.

From Mexico. The steamship **New Orleans** arrived Jan 18 from Vera Cruz, having sailed on Jan 14. She brought the following passengers:

Lt B F McDonald	Lt C C Robbins	Dr J W Richardson
Lt Fairfax	Lt G W Walker	Capt John Bristow
Lt J B Moeler	Capt Rice	Capt D B Berry
Lt Gansevoort	Lt Elder	Lt T G Andrews
Capt J C Huffington	Capt W Norfleet	Assist Surgeon N Hall
Maj A G Johnson	Lt Lyman Andrews	Lt J M Richardson
Lt J M Dye	Lt C S Dickson	

Horace Wells, about 35, was committed to prison on Sat last, on a charge of having thrown vitriol upon 2 females in Broadway, & was found dead in his cell, having committed suicide by cutting the main arteries of his left thigh with a razor. In a note he writes: Oh! My dear wife & child, whom I leave destitute of the means of support-I would still live & work for you, but I cannot; for I should become a maniac. Another note: Please write to Mr T W Storrow, 19 Run du Faubourg, Possonier, Paris, & tell him of my death.

SAT JAN 29, 1848
Trustee's sale: by deed of trust from Jos Whipple to me, dated Oct 14, 1842, recorded in Liber W B 99, folios 95 through 98, of the land records of Wash Co: auction on Feb 17, all the right, title, & estate of said Whipple in the south part of lot 12 in square 904, in Wash City, fronting on 7th st east. –John Wilson, trustee -R W Dyer, auct

Senate: 1-Paper of Welcome Parmanter taken from the files & referred to the Cmte on Pensions. 2-Papers of Bancroft Woodcock taken from the files & referred to the Cmte on Patents. 3-Cmte on the Library: bill to authorize the purchase of the papers of the late Alex'r Hamilton. 4-Bill for the settlement of the account of Jos Nourse, deceased: passed. 5-Bill for the relief of Richd Bloss & others: passed.

Died: on Thu, at her residence, in Wash Co, D C, after a brief illness, Mrs Nancy Beall, wife of Robt L Beall.

Died: yesterday, at his residence, in Gtwn, Clement Cox, in his 45th year. The suddenness of this event & the loss of a life so valuable & useful have spread a gloom over the community in which he lived & was loved. His bereaved & afflicted family mourn his loss. His funeral is on Sat at half past 3 o'clock.

House of Reps: 1-Bills taken up, considered, laid aside to be reported to the House: relief
Of reps of Jas Brown   Of Geo Newton   Of Alborne Allen
Of Edw Quinn   Of Russell Goss
Bills taken up, &, being objected to, were laid aside:
Relief of Mary Brown, widow of Jacob Brown
Heirs of John Paul Jones
Settle claims of Chas G Ridgley
Wm Hogan, adm of Mich Hogan, deceased
Legal reps of John Suyder, deceased
Heirs & legal reps of Regnal, alias Nick Hillary
Barclay & Livingston, & Smith, Thruger & Co
Legal heirs & reps of Nathl Cox, deceased, formerly navy agent at New Orleans
Relief of :
Wm Culver   Anthony Walton Bayard   Jas McAvoy
Danl Robinson   Calvin Emmons   Chas Benns
Eliz Clapper   Henry M Shreve   John W Heckett
Mrs Harriet Barney   John Anderson, of Mo   Wm Ralston
2-Ptn of Col H W Dobbin & many of the general ofcrs under whom he served in the late war with Great Britain, praying Congress to grant him a pension for his services in the late war with Great Britain. 3-Bill to provide for the compensation of Saml Leech for services in the investigation of suspended sales in the Mineral Point District, Wisconsin, was referred to the Cmte on Public Lands.

Mrd: on Thu, by Rev John C Smith, Mr Jas W Allen to Miss Matilda E Smith, all of Wash City.

Mrd: on Jan 20, at St Matthew's Church, by Rev J B Donelan, Dr J B Edelin, of Wash City, to Agnes Cecilia, daughter of the late Jas Abercrombie, of Balt.

The steamboat **Yallabusha**, on her way from Red River to New Orleans, was entirely destroyed by fire on Jan 18. Judge Mills, of Texas, lost a child about 4 years of age & a servant. The judge, having his wife & 2 children on board, took a child in each hand, & in leaping overboard received a blow on one arm from a falling timber, causing him to relax his hold on one of the children, which was lost. Mrs Mills leaped overboard with her husband, & was saved by the efforts of Maj Yancy, of Natchitoches. Mr Johnson, one of the passengers, lost 3 children & one grandchild-all supposed to be burnt. Mr A M Alexander, formerly of Ky, lost 2 children, both girls; himself & wife were saved by swimming ashore. A brother of Mr Alexander & his wife, & Dr John D Wall, of Harrison Co, Texas, & his wife, were saved by swimming ashore. The Rev Mr Page, Episcopal minister, & 2 of his children, were lost. He was lost in attempting to save his family. Mrs Page was saved.

Mr John Long, a farmer near Cumberland, Md, while felling a tree on Fri last, was caught under it and seriously injured, his back being broken. His recovery is doubtful.

MON JAN 31, 1848
City Ordinances-Wash. 1-Resolution authorizing the payment of Wm Dalton & Jos Beasley the sum of $8, for services rendered in celebrating the late victories in Mexico.

New Orleans papers announce the death of Judge John Francis Canonge, aged 64: a native of St Domingo, but had long resided in Louisiana.

Obit-died: on Aug 17, 1847, aged 22 years, Colville J Minor, youngest son of Col Wm Minor, of Fairfax Co, Va. He was appointed a cadet at West Point in Jul, 1842, & graduated in Jul, *1486, with high honors. He was ordered to Mexico; he was seized, while at Monterey, in Upper Calif, with a malignant fever, & taken to the house of La Senora Dona Augustia de la Guena, the best & kindest lady in Monterey; all that could have been done for him was done to save his life. He was buried with military honors- every company at the post & every ship's crew in the harbor swelling the procession. His remains rest in a quiet grave, at the hill behind the fort, enclosed in metal for removal, if desired; but he has left a name behind which will keep his tomb sacred to all for many long years to come. [*Must be a typo in the newspaper.]

House of Reps: 1-Bill for the relief of Mary Brown, widow of Jacob Brown: amendment to read: after the word <u>Massachusetts</u>, the words aged 74 years, & born before the close of the Revolutionary war: agreed to. Mr Ficklin moved to amend the bill by adding: this pension is granted in consideration of the gallantry & death of Maj Jacob Brown, [her step-son.] Mr Smith, of Ill, moved to amend the bill by striking out $20 per month & inserting $8 per month: agreed to. Bill was ordered to be engrossed. 2-Ptn of Hannah Wightman, formerly widow of John Hart, deceased, for a pension. 3-Memorial of Jean Baptiste Grange, praying permission to locate a tract of land. 4-The papers & ptn of Cornelius Washburn & others, of Missouri, on the files of the House, were referred to the Cmte on Public Lands. 5-Papers relating to the claims of Reuben Gentry & others, for Indian depredations, were referred to the Cmte on Indian Affairs.

Third Annual Ball of the Vigilant Firemen of Gtwn, D C: Cmte of Invitation & Reception:

P H Donelan	Saml Fearson	Wm E Mastin
Wm S Jones	Wm Donaldson	Wm E Hilton
Albert Palmer	John Clements	John W Gross
Obadiah B Ritter	Wm W Waugh	John B Conway

Wash Corp: 1-Ptn of Noel Penot, for the remission of a fine: referred to the Cmte of Claims. 2-Nomination of Andrew Rothwell, as Collector of Taxes, for the ensuing year: confirmed. 3-Cmte of Claims: asking to be discharged from the further consideration of the ptn of Jas Cuthbert: to lie on the table. 4-Bill for the relief of Jonas B Ellis: passed. 5-Ptn from P C Peetach, for the remission of a fine: referred to the Cmte of Claims.

6-Cmte of Claims: asking to be discharged from the further consideration of the ptn of Timothy K Buckley: discharged accordingly. 7-Bill for the relief of Wm Bush: recommitted to the Cmte of Claims. 8-Bill for the relief of Augustus Ross: passed.

Leather Dealers, & Curriers: J M Tunbridge, corner of Beaver & St John sts, Phil.

TUE FEB 1, 1848
The Metropolitan Club will hold their second ball on Feb 14, St Valentine's Night, at Carusi's Saloon.
Cmte of invitation & reception:

Thos Caton	W G Newton	Jas Owner	S H Lamborn
Jas McDermott	Louis L Brunet	J M Judge	T H Phillips
W A Flaherty	W M Payne	W M Belt	T A Stephens

For rent: 2 story brick dwlg house on 10th st, & Pa ave: for a number of years in the occupancy of the late Geo McDuell. Apply to M Delany, 4½ st & Pa ave, or to the subscriber, in Gtwn. –S H L Villard

House of Reps: 1-Memorial of the children of Eli Whitney, the inventor of the cotton-gin, & moved its reference to a select cmte of 9 members. 2-Sec of War is to transmit to the Clerk of this House the papers in the cases of Jos Graham & Geo Kirk, applicants for pensions under the act of Jun 7, 1832, & that they be referred to the Cmte on Revolutionary Pensions. 3-Cmte of Claims: to inquire into the justice of causing to be paid to the ofcrs & seamen who, in 1804, volunteered their services under Capt Stephen Decatur, to recapture or destroy the brig **Philadelphia**, then lying in the harbor of Tripoli, the value of said vessel, which was, by the cmder of the squadron, promised to said ofcrs & men as a reward for their courage & enterprise, but which has never been paid to them. Resolved: That the Cmte on Revolutionary Pensions be instructed to inquire into the justice of causing the names of the surviving ofcrs & seamen, & the widows of such as may have died, who, in 1804, volunteered under Capt Stephen Decatur to recapture or destroy the brig **Philadelphia**, & that said cmte report by bill or otherwise. 4-Cmte on Revolutionary Pensions: to inquire into granting a pension to Eliz Wright, of N C. Cmte on Accounts: to inquire into allowing to John Lee, hostler to the House of Reps, the same amount of extra compensation as was allowed to the hostler to the Senate & the messengers of the House for the last Congress, as he has been accustomed to receive in common with said persons. 5-Resolved: that leave be given to withdraw from the files of the Pension Ofc the papers of Eliz Williamson, of Eliz Simpson, of Sarah Victor, of Ann Hancock, Susan Oglesby, & that they be severally referred to the Cmte on Revolutionary Pensions; also, that leave be given to withdraw from the House, the papers presented in the case of Chas Lewis. 6-Ptn of John Scholfield, for a pre-emption right. 7-Ptn of John Tucker, of Franklin Co, Ill, praying Congress to pass a law authorizing him to locate a land warrant. 8-Memorial of Collins Stevens & others, praying that they may be protected against a foreign infraction of their patent. 9-Ptn & papers of B M Bonton, asking compensation for the use of his invention & machines in making percussion caps, used by the army of the U S. 10-Bill for the relief of Shadrach Gillet & others: referred. 11-Bill for the relief of the heirs of Matthew Rea, a lt in the Revolutionary war: referred.

12-Ptn of E H Field & others, of Franklin, Ohio, praying for a reduction on newspaper postage. 13-Ptn of Eunice Grossman, of Sheldon, N Y, the widow of a Revolutionary ofcr, praying to be placed on the pension roll. 14-Ptn of Geo Kirk, of Greene Co, Tenn, a soldier of the Revolution, praying Congress to grant him a pension. 15-Ptn of Chas B Collins for a railroad across the American continent to the Pacific.

Ky Military Institute: located at the Franklin Springs, 6 miles from Frankfort, Ky. The Superintendent, Col R T P Allen, a graduate of the U S Military Academy, is assisted by 8 Professors. Spring terem will commence on Mar 1. -P Dudley, Adj Gen, & Pres of the Board. Franklin Co, Ky.

Senate: 1-Ptn from Priscilla Decatur Twiggs, widow of Maj Twiggs, who fell at the storming of Chapultepec, & mother of Gen Decatur Twiggs, who fell at the engagement at the Nat'l Bridge. She asks that some provision may be made for her relief & that of her dghts, leaving the principles upon which it may be granted, & the extent & mode in which it may be accomplished, to the wisdom & justice of Congress. 2-Ptn from Jas M Kibben, asking the release of certain reversionary interest of the U S in certain reservations. 3-Ptn from John Baldwin, asking that the U S will pay such portions of the award made in his favor by the Mexican Commission as have not been paid. [Mr Benton explained the object of the memorialist, stating the grounds on which he sought redress; one of which was that under the treaty of 1843 certain revenues were set apart by Mexico for the payment of her indebtedness to the U S, which revenues had been seized upon by the order of the U S Gov't, & were now collected by the military & naval forces of the nation.] 4-Cmte on Revolutionary Claims: adverse report on the ptn of Maria Caldwell Robertson. 5-Cmte of Claims: bill for the relief of Wm H Prentiss.

Died: on Jan 31, in her 88th year, Mrs Rebecca Burche, wife of the late Capt Benj Burche, & mother of the late Saml Burche. Mrs Burche was in the communion of the Catholic Church; in the confidence of a certain faith, & in perfect charity with all. Her funeral is 3 o'clock today, from her late residence on Capitol Hill.

Died: on Jan 7, at his residence on Deer Creek, Wash Co, Miss, Mr Saml W Adams, in his 60th year. He was a native of Md, & removed to Wash Co a stranger about 13 years ago. By industry & uprightness of character he gained an independence, & was much esteemed.

Died: yesterday, at the residence of his son, Wm M Addison, in Balt, Rev Walter D Addison, in his 79th year. The body of the deceased will be brought to Wash this morning, at 11 o'clock, by the railroad cars, & will be carried thence for interment to the family burial ground at *Oxen Hill*, Md, opposite Alexandria.

Geo A Dwight died in N Y on Sat at the Croton Hotel. He had for several years been connected with the N Y Express, & was much esteemed in a large circle of acquaintances. [Feb 2nd newspaper: Mr Dwight was a native of Northampton, a nephew of the late Pres Dr Dwight, & a great-grandson of Pres Edwards. He died after a protracted illness.]

On Jan 7 a son & dght of Mr Harvy Tryon, of Glaftenbury, came into their father's house from school, when the boy saw a gun in the room. Not thinking it was loaded, he took it up & pointed it at his little sister. The gun discharged and the little girl died instantly. The lad was 11 years of age & the girl 9. -Hartford Times

WED FEB 2, 1848
Another veteran Jerseyman of the Revolution, Aaron Chamberlain, of Monmouth Co, died on Jan 21, aged near 100 years. His brother, also a soldier of the Revolution, died at Manasquan, in the same county, a few years since, aged over 100 years.
–Newark Advertiser

Capt Kennally, of Cincinnati, killed himself at Rio Frio, by placing the hilt of his sword upon the ground & throwing himself upon the blade. He had command of one of the volunteer companies of Ohio.

The Hon John W Jones, formerly Speaker of the House of Reps, & who recently resigned his seat in the Va House of Delegates, of which he was also Speaker, died at his residence in Chesterfield last week.

Household furniture at auction: on Feb 5, by order of the Orphans' Court, the personal effects of the late Catharine Campbell, in front of the Centre Market.
–T M & B Milburn, auctioneers

For rent: the house lately occupied by Capt Chauncey, in Granite Row. Apply to Mrs Gadsby, or at the store of J H McBlair.

Household furniture at auction: on Feb 3, at the Mansion house, on Pa ave, between 14th & 15th sts, recently kept by Mr Hand. -R W Dyer, auct

House of Reps: 1-Ptn of Jane Lynn, of Union Co, Pa, widow of a Revolutionary soldier, praying for a pension. 2-Ptn of David Jackson & 127 others, citizens of Ohio, for the abolition of slavery in D C.

Orphans Court of Wash Co, D C. Letters of administration de bonis non with the will annexed on the personal estate of Bernard Kelley, late of said county, deceased.

THU FEB 3, 1848
Senate: 1-Ptn from Philo B Johnson, asking indemnity for injuries done his person & property by the Mexican citizens. Capt Johnson, it appears, was compelled, at the point of the bayonet, to aid in the civil war going on in the country, first on one side & then on the other, & his vessel alternately used as either party happened to triumph. 2-Cmte of Claims: report a memorial of A F Frasier & Alvin Baker, owners of the brig **Douglas**: referred the matter to the Sec of State. 3-Cmte on the Judiciary: bill for the relief of the legal reps of Francis Cazeau, late merchant at Montreal. 4-Cmte on Pensions: adverse report on the memorial of Francis O & Andrew C Dorr.

Walter S Cox, Atty at Law, having been associated in the practice of law with the late Clement Cox for some months before his decease, will proceed with the unfinished business in his hands. —W S Cox

FRI FEB 4, 1848
Mrd: on Feb 1, by Rev O B Brown, Mr Chas Fred'k L Emmerich to Miss Kate, daughter of Mr Thos Sanderson, all of Wash City.

Mrd: on Feb 1, by Rev Wm Hamilton, Mr Jos Prather to Miss Martha Jane Belt, all of Wash City.

Died: on Feb 2, Mrs Susan C Knott, wife of Ignatius M Knott, & daughter of the late Mr Chas Bell, in her 28th year. Her funeral is at 2 o'clock this afternoon.

G E Divernois, who has been head cook at Mr S S Coleman's Hotel for 3 years, & whose employment ceased on Feb 1 on account of a change of proprietors, offers his services to the public in general as cook, for parties, dinners, or single dishes. Residence on 13th st, between Pa ave & E st.

Senate: 1-Cmte on Pensions: bill to allow arrearages of pension to Hugh W Dobbin, an ofcr in the late war, accompanied by a report. 2-Cmte on Naval Affairs: bill for the relief of Anna J Hassler, accompanied with a report. 3-Cmte on the Judiciary: adverse report on the memorial of Jos Bouchard. 4-Bills for the relief of Chas L Dell; of Richd S Coxe; relief of Peter Capella, adm of Andrew Capella; relief of John Capa; & relief of Elijah Pettit & Hannah Pettit, his wife, heirs of John Beardon, deceased.

For sale or rent: the house now occupied by the subscriber, on B st south, Capitol Hill, one square from the Capitol. —Simon Brown

House of Reps: 1-Cmte of Claims: bills for the relief of Joshua Kennedy, deceased; for the relief of G DeLirac; relief of the legal reps of Capt Geo R Shoemaker, deceased; & relief of Chas Waldron: all committed. Same cmte: bill for the relief of Lyon & Howard: committed. Same cmte: adverse report on the ptns of Geo Cochran; on ptn of Jas Little; of Thos A Williams; of Jas Graham; of Michl Hogan; & on the legal reps of Isaac D Taulbee: laid on the table. Same cmte: bills for the relief of Elisha F Richards; relief of Jeremiah Moor; relief of Col Robt Wallace, aid-de-camp to Gen Wm Hull; & bill for the legal reps of Nimrod Farrow & Richd Harris: committed. 2-Ptn of Abram Brinker, of Butler Co, Pa, for amount due from Gov't on certificate for services in the Revolutionary war. 3-Ptn of Barbary Lancaster, of Westmoreland Co, Pa, formerly widow of Hugh Greer, who was a soldier in the war of 1812, & died in service, for his bounty lands. 4-Ptn of Edw Clark & others, of Sally Taylor, of Abigail Goodwin, of Lewis Goodwin & others, of Saml Stacy & others, for their proportions of the Bergen prizes taken by the squadron of the John Paul Jones. 5-Ptn of Eunice Crossman, the widow of a Revolutionary ofcr, praying to be placed on the pension list. 6-Ptn & papers of Mgt G Leverett, widow of Thos Leverett, for a pension. 7-Ptn of S H Zink, of Ohio, for pay for subsisting volunteers. 8-Ptn of Capt C M Clay, for property lost in Mexico.

Selling off cheap: our winter goods. Also, table damask, linen sheetings, Irish linens, Birdeye Diaper, & toweling. –W M Shuster & Co, Pa ave, 4 doors west of 4½ st.
Two weeks from Europe: the Princess Adelaide, sister of the King of the French, is dead.

Passengers by the steamship **Acadia** from Liverpool: Mr Reynolds, Mrs Reynolds, Mr L H Gostenhoffer, Miss Reynolds, Miss Sarah Miller, Mrs Jane Watson, Mr Jos Reid, Mr H B Break, Stephen Howell, Thos Dorby, Wm Knight, John Connolly, Mrs Delmotte, Mr N Habs, Mr P Harrison, Mr Chas Lawson, Mr Weller, G Newsman, Benj Thornton, Mr Sarint, Mr Jos Green, Hitchcock Bryden, J McMasters, Jo Kay, H W Mead, Mr Lynde, Mr Osborne, Mr Louisen, Mr C R Matthews, Mr Bentley, Mr Muller, C D Kenney, Rev S H Gloscester, Etherington, W J Clarke, Robt Fotherill, Mr J G Miller. Five from Liverpool to Halifax, & six from Halifax to Boston.

SAT FEB 5, 1848
Senate: 1-Ptn of Orville B Dibble & Geo C Bates, praying the grant of right of way & a portion of the public lands for construction of a canal around the falls of St Mary's river, Michigan. 2-Cmte of Claims: bill for the relief of Jas Southron, accompanied by a report.

Henry Janney, 8th st, near the Gen Post Ofc: having enlarged his premises & doubled his force, is determined to give even greater satisfaction in the manufacture of his beautiful & comfortable boots.

House of Reps: 1-Bills objected to & laid aside-ptns for the relief of: the heirs of John Paul Jones; of Anthony Walton Bayard; of Calvin Emmons; of Henry M Shreve; of E G Smith; of David Myerle; of Jacob Gideon; of Bent, St Vrain & Co; of J Throckmorton; of Wm Hogan, adm of Michl Hogan, deceased; of the securities of Elijah H Weed, late quartermaster of marines, deceased; of Thos Scott; of the heirs & legal reps of Regnal, alias Nick Hilliary; of Jas McAvey; of Chas Beans; of John W Hockett; of Wm Ralston; of Nancy Tompkins; of Jas Glynn & others; of J Melville Gilliss & others; of Jas H Conley; of Chas Reeder, Walter R Johnson, & Thos P Jones; of the legal reps of Cornelius Manning; of John Mitchell. Also, the claim of the legal reps of Richd W Meade, deceased; mode of settling the claims of Chas G Ridgley; & to extend John J Adam's patent for flattening cylinder window glass. 2-Following bills were ordered to be reported to the House-relief of: Wm Culver; Danl Robinson; Eliz Clapper; Mrs Harriet Barney; John Anderson, of Mo; Jos C Doxey; of S Morris Waln; of the legal reps of John Snyder, deceased; of Amzy Judd; of the heirs of Mathew Stewart; of Jos & Lindley Ward; of Mrs Anne W Angus; of Eliz Mays; of Jas H Conley; of Jesse Young; & of Silas Waterman. 3-Bill for the relief of Amelia Brereton was amended by inserting before the words Amelia Brereton the words legal reps of Amelia Brereton. 4-The bill for the relief of the legal heirs & reps of Nathl Cox, deceased, formerly navy agent at New Orleans, was recommended that it be recommitted to the Cmte of Claims. 5-Bills from the Senate appropriately referred: bill for the relief of Richd Bloss & others; act to pay Jafnes Crutchett $2,000 for lighting the Capitol & Capitol grounds; & act to further extend the patent of Jethro Wood. 6-Com'r of Pensions to deliver the papers of David H Warren on his application for a pension to any member of the Cmte on Invalid or Revolutionary Pensions, such member giving his receipt for the same.

Wash Corp: 1-Payment of the claims of Wm H Padgett was passed. 2-Bill for the relief of Augustus Ross was referred to the Cmte of Claims. 3-Cmte of Claims: ptn of Moses Lazarus for relief was passed. 4-Ptn of Wm Jasper, praying remission of a fine: referred to the Cmte of Claims. 5-Cmte of Claims: relief of Louisa Collins: laid on the table.

Died: on Jan 28, at his late residence near Trenton, N J, Wm Welling, in his 67th year. His life was an illustration of the virtues which adorn the Christian character.

Private Teacher Wanted: to take charge of the tuition of 8 or 10 boys in a private family. Apply to the Hon R L T Beale, member of Congress.

Furniture & Fancy goods at auction: Mon, at W B Lewis' store, Pa ave, near 11th st. –John McDevitt, auct

Cmdor Ridgely, U S Navy, died last night at Barnum's Hotel, in the city of Balt, after a lingering illness.

MON FEB 7, 1848

The ferry-boat, while crossing the Illinois river at Ottawa on Jan 5, was swamped & the following passengers in it were drowned: Mr Wheatland, John Law, & a young man named McGraw. Mr Keeler, Mr Boles, & Mr G Burr were saved. Mr Wheatland leaves a young wife to mourn his loss, having been married but 4 weeks.

The venerable widow of the late Matthew B Whittlesey, lately came to a sudden & shocking death in Danbury, Conn, when her night clothes took fire. [No death date given-current news item.]

Died: on Sat last, of small pox, at his house in Lispenard st, N Y, Mr Henry B Costard, eldest son of Madame Josephine Villagrund, now of this city. He was born on Jan 3, 1795, the son of a family of planters in San Domingo, then wealthy as they were well descended; but soon after ruined & driven to this country as refugees by the servile revolt in that island in which his father & all his mother's family except herself & one brother perished. This son was put to a trade & was deservedly successful, amassing at one time a considerable fortune. This was entirely swept away in 1837, fatal to so many of the N Y men of business. He began afresh & again rapidly founded a fortune. The casual contagion of a malady from which he was thought to be perfectly secured by the having been made to take it artificially in the country of his birth, came to terminate, within only some 9 days, his useful life.

By order of distrain for rent due to Henry Haw by Wm Murray, I will expose at public sale on the premises occupied by said Murray, on Md ave, between 8th & 9th sts, known as **Brown's Garden**, sundry articles of said Wm Murray. -Horatio R Maryman, Bailiff for H Haw

Tavern for rent: the Farmer's Hotel, 8th & D sts. Inquire of Owen Connolly.

In the case of Elisha H Hale vs the city of Boston, the jury rendered a verdict in favor of the plntf, assessing damages at $4,416.66. He was injured when he fell into a hole, [which should have been covered by a grating] in Pearl st. His injuries are permanent & incapacitate him for active business.

The public are cautioned against taking a note drawn by John Scott Cunningham for $33.81, payable Jun 1, 1848, in the order of D Jones, as said note belongs to me, & will not be paid to any other person. The above note was not given for his benefit.
–J A Lenman

Ranaway from the subscriber, on Jan 8, a negro woman named Rachael Meekins, formerly the property of Mr Chas Vinson, of Montg Co, Md. She is about 40 years of age, & took her child with her, aged between 3 & 4 years. $10 reward for either of them.
–Francis A Dickins

New Orleans Delta of Jan 29. The steamship **Edith**, which left Vera Cruz on Jan 20, brought the bodies of the following deceased ofcrs; also, 40 sick & discharged soldiers, two of whom died on the passage: Brevet Col J S McIntosh, Capt Whipple, Lts W S Burwell & Lt Smith, 5th Infty; Capt S B Thornton, 2nd Dragoons; Capt G Hanson, 7th Infty; Capt Capron; Capt Burke; Capt McKenzie, 2nd Artl; Capt M E Merrill, 3rd Infty; Capt E K Smith, 1st Infty; Capt J W Anderson, 2nd Infty; 1st Lts C B Daniels & Wm Armstrong, 2nd Artl; Lt Johnson; Lt J F Irons; Lt Hoffman; Lt J D Bacon, 6th Infty; Lt J J Burbank, 8th Infty; Lt Sidney Smith, 4th Infty; Lt E B Strong; J F Fairy; G W Ayres, 3rd Artl; T Cosley.

Capt Chas Boarman has been appointed to the command of the U S frig **Brandywine**, on the Brazil station.

Headquarters of the Army, Mexico, Jan 11, 1848. Genr'l Orders #14. The following named ofcrs, sick, wounded, or reported supernumerary in compliance with Gen Orders 382 of the last year, will proceed to their respective homes, & on arriving at New Orleans report, by letter to the Adj Genl's ofc, Wash, for [if able] the recruiting ofc.

1-Maj E B Sumner, 2nd Dragoons
2-Maj C A Waite, 8th Infty
3-Capt W J Hardee, 2nd Dragoons
4-1st Lt L G Arnold, 2nd Artl
5-1st Lt Arnold Elzey, 2nd Artl
6-1st Lt C J Emery, Mass Regt
7-1st Lt J Ward Henry, N Y Volunteers
8-2nd Lt H F Clarke, 2nd Artl
9-2nd Lt W C Wagley, 3rd Dragoons
10-2nd P A Farrelly, 5th Infty
11-2nd Lt H B Clitz, 3rd Infty
12-2nd Lt Geo Wainwright, 8th Infty
13-2nd Lt J G Fitzgerald, 14th Infty
14-2nd Lt L W Templeton, 15th Infty
15-2nd Lt J E Slaughter, Voltigeurs
16-Capt J R Smith, 2nd Infty

By order of Maj Gen Scott: H L Scott, A A A G

Today the funeral of Capt Irwin took place. He was followed to the grave by a long line of mourning friends. The Rifle Regt paid the military honors to his remains, but it was no one corps that grieved at his death. When he died the army wept.

The Buffalo Republican of Jan 27 announces the death of Geo P Barker, one time a member of the House of Assembly of N Y, for Erie Co, & at a later period Atty Gen of the State, a post which he filled with eminent credit. [No death date given-recent news item.]

Dr Green lately died at West Newtown, Pa, from poisonous humor supposed to have been caught from a slight wound by the dissecting knife.

At Brooklyn, N Y, on Tue last, Bridget Pense, about 16 years of age, came to a sudden & violent death by the hand of her little brother. He took up a gun he did not think was loaded, & discharged it at his sister.

WED FEB 8, 1848

Senate: 1-Ptn from Wm W Wynn, asking to be allowed pre-emption right to certain lands House of Reps: 1-Ptn of of J Gibbs & 71 others, praying for a post route from Mount Lebanon to Alexandria, La. 2-Ptn of Jesse Gordon, a Revolutionary soldier, in his 93rd year, praying an increase of pension. 3-Ptn of John Hamilton, of Alton, Ill, praying remuneration for moneys paid by him for the U S Gov't during the late war with Great Britain. 4-Ptn of Ephraim Finch & others, in behalf of Thos Duer, for money expended while in the service of the U S during the last war with Great Britian. 5-Ptn of Lowry Williams, an Indian countryman, entitled to all the privileges of a Cherokee Indian, praying that Congress may provide for the payment of one-half the value of his improvements, as assessed by the valuing agents, & which have been withheld from him illegally. 6-Memorial & papers of the heirs of Israel Cryder for claims against the U S for provisions purchased for the army during the Revolution.

Mrd: yesterday, in Wash City, in the Church of the Epiphany, by Rev Mr French, Hon Dennis Condry, of Newburyport, Mass, to Miss Catharine Rebecca Browne, of Wash City.

Senate: 1-Ptn from Wm W Wynn, asking to be allowed pre-emption right to certain lands in Arkansas. 2-Ptn from Obed Hussey, asking to be allowed a renewal of his patent for a reaping machine. 3-Cmte on Indian Affairs: joint resolution for the relief of Betsy McIntosh. 4-Bills passed: bill in addition to an act for the relief of Walter Loomis & Abel Gay, approved Jul 2, 1836. Bill for the relief of Edw Bolon.

Balt, Feb 7. The funeral of Cmdor Ridgely was largely attended yesterday afternoon. The deceased was in his 63rd year.

Male teacher wanted: the subscribers, living near Pactolus Post Ofc, Pitt Co, N C, wish to hire a competent gentleman to instruct a small school. –Godfrey Langley, Henry I Toole, C Perkins, L S Jordan, Ben Daniel

Household furniture at auction: on Feb 8, at the residence of C Hogmire, on Bridge st, near the market. -E S Wright, auctioneer

WED FEB 9, 1848
Wash Corp: 1-Ptn from John Hitz: referred to the Cmte of Claims. 2-Ptn from Thos Mustin: referred to the Cmte of Claims. 3-Bill for the relief of John Simmons: referred to the Cmte of Claims. 4-Cmte of Claims asking to be discharged from the further consideration of the ptn of John Waters: laid on the table. 5-Ptn of Mary Gumaer, widow of Elias Gumaer, praying a settlement of her late husband's claim for loss on stock received in lieu of money for work done on the Washington Canal. 6-Act for the relief of Michl Shanks: passed. 7-Cmte on Police: bill for the relief of E D E Southworth: no further compensation shall be made to Mrs Southworth for services rendered or to be rendered, excepting such compensation as is provided for in the 10th section of the act approved Dec 5, 1845. 8-The sum of $86.96 be paid to Mrs J L Henshaw, the assist teacher, which is the difference between the salary she had received for the last 2 years & the maximum allowed by the trustees. 9-Bill for the relief of Moses Lazarus, & for the relief of J C Peetch: referred to the Cmte of Claims. 10-Bill for the relief of Michl Shanks: referred to the Cmte of Ways & Means. 11-Bill granting a special license to T Buckley: referred to the Cmte on Police. 12-Gentlemen to superintend the polls:

Chas A Davis	John Boyle	Andrew Coyle	Wm M Ellis
Wm Wilson	Valentine	Simon Brown	Joel W Jones
Wm H Perkins	Harbaugh	Geo M Dove	John W Martin
Willard Drake	Geo Crandell	Danl Homans	Peter Hepburn
Elexius Simms	Saml Wroe	Noble Young	
Wm Fischer	David Saunders	Jas Crandell	

Gov Young, of N Y, has pardoned Pollock, the Midshipman who attempted to kill Mr Jewett, of the Buffalo Commercial, a few months since, by firing 3 balls into him, & was sentenced to the State Prison for 2 years.

Senate: 1-Mr Bright presented: from the Legislature of Indiana in favor of providing for the settlement of the claim of Col Francis Vigo, a citizen of that State. 2-Ptn from the Right Rev Benedict Madeore, vicar genr'l of Florida, & pastor of St Augustine Church, & also other citizens of Florida, claiming as private property the St Augustine Church, the convent of St Francis, the Bishop's house, & the Church of Our Lady of the Milk, for the uses of the Catholic religion, & which were intended to be secured to the Catholics of Florida, & which had been improperly conveyed to the U S at the cession of Florida. 3-Ptn from Alfred Marshall, asking a salary to the collector of the district of Belfast, in Maine. 4-Ptn from Saml Blake, asking that certain allowances may be made for his services in taking the 6th census. 5-Ptn from Thos L Brent, asking to be allowed the usual outfit for acting as charge d'affaires to Spain. 6-Ptn from C H McCormick, remonstrating against the extension of Obed Hussey's patent. 7-Ptn from Jos Nock, asking the extension of his patent for padlocks for desks, chests, & trunk locks. 8-Memorial from John Golder, who states that in 1835 he discovered & invented an improvement in the art & science of public finance, for which he purchased the patent right. Asks to be remuneration for the injury he has sustained by infringement. 9-Ptn from John W Leucks, asking indemnity for the seizure of certain goods by the customhouse ofcrs at N Y. 10-Ptn from John P Baldwin, asking that a register may be issued for the schnr **Robt Henry**.

Trustee's sale of Valuable Real Estate: under a decree of the PG Co Court, in Chancery, made in a cause wherein Tresa Brooks et al are cmplnts & Geo W Dunlop, ex'r, et al, are dfndnts. Sale on Mar 2 next, that tract of land in said county on the road leading from Wash to Upper Marlborough, know as *Long Old Fields*, formerly owned by Jos Dunlop, deceased, & for many years used by him as a tavern: tract contains 60½ acs, more or less, with a good 2 story & attic frame house, & stables. –S S Williams, trustee

Salem Advertiser: Mr Zebulon Paine, of Conway, sentenced for 8 years in Nov, 1846, has been pardoned by the Govn'r of N H. He was convicted of hiring a boy, age 15, to burn a barn. His complete innocence was recently established by the confession of the boy who bore false witness, &, after 14 months confinement, has been restored to his family

Two boys, sons of Capt David Cain, of Clinton, Me, were recently drowned while skating on a pond.

Fatal mistake in medicine: carelessness of an apothecary at Alleghany City: Mr Van Winkle went to purchase pulverized rhubard. Both unlabelled on the counter, he picked up pulverized opium & administered the medicine to his children, causing the death of one of them, a child of 2 or 3 years.

Household & kitchen furniture at auction: on Feb 16, at the residence of Mr Gordon, on I st, between 23rd & 24th sts, immediately in the rear of the residence of the late Mr Fox. -R W Dyer, auct

City of Mexico, Jan 10, 1848. Capt Jas R Irwin, Acting Quartermaster Genr'l, died after a few days' illness from pneumonia. Peace to his ashes-eternal honor to his memory. –Corr New Orleans Delta [No date]

Died: on Feb 7, Ellen Ann, aged 27 years, consort of Chas W Haydon, & youngest daughter of the late Edw Toole, of Petersburg, Va. Her funeral is Feb 10, at 10 o'clock, from the residence of her husband, Pa ave, between 4½ & 6th sts.

Died: on Jan 4 last, at Belfast, Ireland, Thos W Gilpin, for many years Consul of the U S at that port. He was a native of Phil, where he resided previous to his appointment. His funeral was attended by a large number of the most eminent citizens & merchants of Belfast.

House of Reps: 1-Cmte on Commerce: bill for the relief of Elisha H Willis; bill to authorize the issue of a register to the barque **Wilhamet**: committed. 2-Cmte on Public Lands: adverse report upon the ptn of Wm W Gitt: laid on the table. 3-Cmte on the Judiciary: bill for the relief of John P Skinner & the legal rep of Isaac Green: committed. Same cmte: bill for the relief of the legal reps of Wm McKenzie, late a seaman on board the U S ship **Vincennes**: committed. 4-Cmte on Revolutionary Claims: bill for the relief of the grandchildren of Maj Gen Baron de Kalb: committed. Same cmte: bill for the relief of the legal reps of Lt Francis Ware: committed. Adverse report upon the ptn of Isaac Porter: laid on the table. 5-Cmte on Private Land Claims: bill for the relief of Jas B

Davenport: committed. Same cmte: bill for the relief of Fred'k Durrire, & a bill for the relief of Elisha Thomasson: committed. Same cmte: bill for the relief of Jas B Sexton; bill to confirm Eliz Burriss, her heirs & assigns, in their title to a tract of land; bill for the relief of the heirs & widow of Francis Gramillion: committed. Same cmte: reported a bill for the relief of Wm Triplett; relief of Simon Rodrigues; relief of Marcus Fulton Johnson. Adverse report on the ptns of Jas Swan & Adino Goodenough: laid on the table. Same cmte: adverse report on the ptn of Henry Reeks: laid on the table. 6-Senate bills taken up & referred: relief of Peter Capella, adm of Andrew Capella, deceased, & for the relief of John Capo, & relief of Elijah Petty & Hannah Petty, his wife, heirs of John Beardon, deceased. Acts for the relief of Chas L Dell; of Richd S Coxe; of Nathl Hoggatt. Act for the relief of Walter Loomis & Abel Gay, approved Jul 2, 1836. Act for the relief of Edw Bolon. 7-Presented: two ptns of Nathl & Catharine Lawrence, of N Y, parents of Lt N C Lawrence, & of John C Lawrence, of the U S Navy, deceased, praying for pensions. 8-Presented: ptn & papers of Ruth Freeman, widow of Capt Thos Freeman, of Ohio, praying compensation for extraordinary services rendered in the war of 1812-15, & for reimbursement of moneys advanced to the soldiers under his command, withdrawn from the files. 9-Presented: ptn of Catharine Rinker, of Phil, widow of Saml Rinker, who was a sailingmaster in the U S Navy during the war of the Revolution, praying for a pension or compensation.

$50 reward for runaway negro boy Travers, about 18. Ran away from *Windsor*, the plantation of John Tayloe, in King Geo, Va, on Jan 24. Address letters to Wm Hudson, Overseer at *Windsor*, Hampstead Post Ofc, King Geo, Va.

THU FEB 10, 1848

Senate: 1-Ptn from the heirs of Nicholas Jarrot, asking to be allowed to locate 600 acs of land in lieu of certain lands claimed & sold by the U S. 2-Ptn from the heirs of Timothy P Anderson, for an extension of a patent. 3-Ptn from Justus Powers, asking arrears of pension. 4-Cmte on Commerce: bill to authorize the issuing of a register or enrollment to the schnr **Robert Henry**. 5-Cmte on Pensions: bill for the relief of Welcome Parmenter. Same cmte: bill for the relief of David Currier. Bill for the relief of Alborne Allen: referred to the Cmte of Claims. 6-Cmte on Revolutionary Claims: bill for the relief of the heirs & legal reps of Col Wm Grayson. 7-Cmte on Pensions: bills for the relief of Geo Newton; of Russel Goss; of Mary Browne; of Harriet Barney, & of Jesse Young. 8-Bill for the relief of Wm Marvin: passed. 9-Cmte on Military Affairs: bill for the relief of the legal reps of Antonie Pacheco: adverse report. 10-Cmte on Naval Affairs: bill for the relief of Purser Jos Bryan: committed. Same cmte: bill for the relief of John W Simonton & others: committed. Same cmte: bills for the relief of the widow & heirs at law of Silas Duncan, deceased, late of the U S Navy; & a joint resolution for the relief of Wm Speiden, purser U S Navy: both committed. 11-Cmte on Revolutionary Pensions: adverse reports on the ptns of Lucy Johnson, John Young, Saml Pool, Caroline W Cone, John Murcheson, Anna Hamilton, & Charlotee McCam: laid on the table. Same cmte: adverse report on the ptn of Saml Gregory: laid on the table. Same cmte: adverse reports on the ptns of the heirs of Prudent La Jeunesse, Jacob Olinger, & Bersheba McDaniel: laid on the table. Same cmte: adverse reports on the ptns of Sarah May, widow of John May, & of Francis G De Liessielin: laid on the table. Same cmte: adverse reports on the ptns of Phebe Brown, Mehitabel Marble, Phineas Raymond, & Hugh W Dobin: laid on the table. 12-Cmte on Invalid Pensions: bills for the relief of Wm Blake, for the relief of Jonathan Fitzwater, & relief of Mrs Sarah Hildreth: all committed. Same cmte: bills for the relief of Wm Pool; of Aaron Tucker; heirs of Wm Evans; of W P Brady; of Hervey Jones; & relief of Saml Cony: committed. Same cmte: adverse report on the ptn of John Morrison: laid on the table. 13-Cmte on Patents: adverse report on the ptn of Stephen Bowerman: laid on the table. 14-Cmte of Claims: adverse report on the report of Lewis Roberts: laid on the table. Same cmte: bills for the relief of Wm T Holland; of Mary B Renner, widow of David Renner; & a bill for the relief of Noah A Phelps: committed. Same cmte: adverse reports on the ptns of Wm Stocks, of Ala, of John Martin; & Jas Monroe: laid on the table. Same cmte: bills for the relief of Peter Shaffer; of the legal reps of Col Francis Vigo: committed. 15-Cmte on Foreign Affairs: adverse report on the ptn of Horace Sprague: laid on the table.

Died: on Jan 10, at his residence, Montg Co, Md, Mr Benj Perry, in his 70th year, an old & much respected citizen of said county.

Died: on Feb 8, Wm Alfred, 2nd son of John & Maria France, aged 3 years & 6 months. His funeral is today at 11 o'clock.

Dr Isaac Hamberlin, of Mississippi, a few days ago died from the effects of injuries received in a conflict with a bear.

FRI FEB 11, 1848
Senate: 1-Cmte on Revolutionary Claims: adverse report on the memorial of Mary M Telfair. 2-Cmte on Pensions: bill for the relief of David N Smith was ordered to be printed. 3-Cmte on Indian Affairs: House bill for the relief of Jos & Lindley Ward: passed. 4-The bill granting compensation to J N Moore was passed. 5-Bills passed: relief of Susan E Gordon; relief of Jones & Boker.

The Hon Albert G Marchand, formerly a Rep in Congress from the Westmoreland district of Pa, died at his residence in Greensburg last Sat.

Deaths at Perote: in the Army Hospital at Perote, Mexico, for the two months from Oct 31 to Dec 31 last.

A Barney	Augustus	Jos Rudersell	John A Smart
Lucius Bryand	Harlon	Jos Haige	Jacob Baner
Jas Dincan	Henry Stodherd	Moses Connor	John Lindsey
Edw Jones	Henry H Dunne	Isaac Westons	D W Miller
Edw Carper	Jefferson	Wm Martin	R M Pratt
Andrew Harman	Almond	Alex'r Grady	Wm H Cobb
Jas White	Robt M Jones	Geo Reniger	Wm Patterson
Jas McDonald	A Andorff	Jacob Dewey	Wm Chuston
Jas McGuire	John W Hames	John Suedly	Danford Avery
Wm E Hopkins	Wm Kirtz	Jas Spaier	Wesley
Jas McConkey	R B Ennis	Jacob Jennings	Richards

J B Murray	D Miller	Levi Keeler	Mitchell Sloam
Robt Mathews	D Chatman	Wm Ricker	J B Warrick
Thos Hansell	Wm Childers	Saml F Main	Henry Moro
J J Stevens	Green Corder	Lewis Stiles	Saml
F Turner	Wm F Hutton	Wm Balner	Yarlborough
Levi J Bruss	Wm Shran	Nathl Smith	Wayne
Thos O'Neil	Robt Merean	Fred'k Satinere	Whitecotton
Christian	Parnel Herron	Jas Hamilton	
Barthon	John Dedman	E W Richardson	

The N Y papers announce the decease, from small-pox, of Mr Costar, of the firm of Beebe & Costar, of that city & Phil. He died on Feb 6.

Death of a Sister of Charity. Sister Mary Dennis died in New Orleans on Feb 1, in the Charity Hospital, where she had been a zealous & devoted attendant upon the sick & destitute for the last 15 years. She fell a victim to that dreadful scourge, the ship fever. Her name was Catharine Trgy, & she was born in the county Waterford, Ireland, & died in her 55th year.

Arkansas Intelligencer, Jan 22. By a letter from a friend at **Fort Gibson** we have learned the painful news of the death of our worthy fellow-citizen, Col Jas McKizzick, Cherokee Agent, on Jan 12. He was a native of Tenn, & emigrated to this State at an early day. His decease will be lamented by a numerous connexion & an extensive circle of friends.

Fruits of Intemperance. 1-On Sunday last Jacob Garret was mortally stabbed by a young man named Bertach. 2-Sarah Farrell died at the almshouse in Boston on Sunday from the effects of wounds received from an assault upon her by her son. 3-Boonstown, Morris Co, N J: Mahlon Taylor, after a drunken frolic, fell from the canal bridge on his way home, & was killed. 4-At Millersburg, Ohio, on Sunday a week, a young man named Rankin killed Mr Miller, his own nephew, by cutting his throat. Both were drunk.

House of Reps: 1-Ptn of D Plimpton & others, for reduction of postage on newspapers. 2-Ptn & papers of Jas Sloan, of Erie Co, N Y, praying for prize-money as one of the captors of the brig **Caledonia** & the brig **Adams**, near **Fort Erie**, in the war of 1812. 3-Ptn of R C Stockton, tutor of the minor Octave de la Houssaye, praying for an amendment to an act confirming the heirs of De la Houssaye to a track ot land. 4-Ptn & papers of Mrs Boyd, of Pa, widow of Col John Boyd, a Revolutionary ofcr, taken from the files of the House. 5-Ptn & papers of John P Schuyler, of Muney, Pa. 6-Three memorials from citizens of Pa, against the further renewal of the patent of Jethro Wood's cast iron plough in favor of his heirs.

Mrd: on Tue, in Wash City, by Rev Mr Cushman, Wm H Williams to Violet A, daughter of the late Geo Milburn.

Died: suddenly, Mr Catherine Metcalf. Her funeral is this afternoon at 3 o'clock, at the residence of Mrs Jane Hawly. [No death date given.]

By writ of fieri facias, at the suit of John B Wilkerson, against the goods & chattels, lands & tenements, of John L Maddox & Danl G Hickey, I will sell for cash, at public auction, part of lot 14 in square 770, in Wash City, on Mar 14, in front of the premises on 3rd st. —Wm Cox, Constable

SAT FEB 12, 1848
Senate: 1-Memorial from Hezekiah L Thistles, remonstrating against the injustice done him by the Com'rs of Patents in granting to a subsequent applicant a patent for an invention claimed by him & asking that the said Com'r may be directed by law to issue a patent to him for his invention. 2-Ptn from Midshipman Rodgers, asking the reimbursement of expenses incurred by him during his captivity in Mexico & in effecting his escape, & indemnity for the loss of his property by the foundering of the U S brig **Somers**. 3-Cmte on Military Affairs: bill for the relief of John Caldwell. 4-Cmte of Claims: bill for the relief of John P Baldwin.

House of Reps: 1-Act to compensate John M Moore: referred. 2-Relief of the legal reps of Geo Fisher, deceased: referred. 3-Act for the relief of Wm Marvin in confirming the title to a tract of land in Florida, granted by the Spanish Gov't to Bernardo Segui on Dec 20, 1815. 4-Bill for the relief of Betsy McIntosh. 5-Bill from the Senate for the relief of the heirs of John Paul Jones, to which an amendment reported by the Cmte of Claims was pending.

Ofc of the Wash Coal Co: meeting this day in Wash City: following Directors were elected:
J Washington Tyson-Pres   Edwin P Hewlings-Sec
Wm A Bradley   John F Ehlen
C M Thruston

Miss Julia Turnbull, the celebrated danseuse has afforded much entertainment at the Adelphi Theatre for several nights.

The undersigned, being anxious to curtail their farm, offer for sale about 200 acres of land in PG Co, Md, within 6 miles of the Centre Market. —Norah Digges, Geo A Digges

By virtue of 3 writs of fieri facias, at the suits of C Bradshaw, R M Coombs, W Watson, use of N Callan, & R A C Magruder, use of Stephen Blumer, against the goods & chattels, lands & tenements, rights & credits of John L Maddox: sale of part of lot 14 in square 770 in Wash City, with a 2 story frame dwlg house: auction on Mar 14, in front of the premises on 3rd st. —Thos Plumsell, Constable

Obit-died: among those lost by the explosion of the steamer **Blue Ridge**, on the Ohio, on Jan 8, 1848, was Jos Miller, of Mason Co, Va. He was in his 25th year, had been married but a few months, & was returning home with his wife from a visit to his brother in Charleston, Kanawha, where the accident occurred. His wife was saved from the wreck after the explosion. Nothing could exceed the deep love he bore to his parents: their loss is indeed irreparable.

Died: on Feb 1, at Glenocher, his residence, in Fauquier Co, Va, after an illness of 4 days, in his 83rd year, Rev Wm Williamson. He was a native of Scotland, came to this country in early life, & settled in Va, where he continued up to the day of his death. His ministerial labors in the Presbyterian Church continued for upwards of 50 years. He has left a widow & a large family of children & connexions, & many friends.

Died: on Jan 27, in Balt, in her 17th year, Margaret Sheppard Woodside, daughter of Wm S Woodside, of that city.

Mr Saml W Whittlesey, of Saybrook, Conn, was killed on Thu, at Lyme Ferry, by an enraged ox. He was one of the oldest inhabitants of Saybrook, being between 80 & 90 years of age, & greatly beloved & respected by all who knew him.

MON FEB 14, 1848

Supreme Court of Pa last week Judge Coulter delivered the opinion of the Court upon the habeas corpus directed to Sgt Fox, of the army, & which was issued to procure the discharge of Thos Gilbert Webster, a minor, who had deserted, & was arrested after such desertion. The contract of enlistment made by a minor, without the consent of his father, master, or guardian, is void. The enlistment was not binding, & the minor might leave. The Court, therefore, order that the boy be discharged.

Another skillful physician, Dr Zabriskie, of the Almshouse at Flatbush, N Y, has fallen to the ship-fever.

The author of The Curiosities of Literature, Senior D'Israeli, died of the prevailing epidemic, on Jan 19, at his residence in Buckinghamshire, at age 82 years. He died a widower, having lost his wife, to whom he had been united for more than 40 years, in the spring of 1847. He has left one dght & 3 sons, the eldest of whom is the member for Buckingham.

The Phil Ledger says that a new rule has been adopted by the officiating priests in the Roman Catholic Church, which requires persons from the old country who wish to enter into the marriage state to have the fact announced in church some time before the ceremony takes place.

Mr Chas McCormick, a wealthy & respectable citizen of Clarke Co, Va, met with an accident on Thu week, which terminated in his death a week afterwards. Being advanced in years, & quite feeble, he was walking near his fire-place, when he slipped into the fire, & was burnt in a most shocking manner.

Died: on Feb 3, at Carlisle, Indiana, Mr Saml Francis Davis, aged 23 years. He was the eldest son of Hon J W Davis. He proceeded with friends to witness the process of turning a flat-boat, he was instantly killed by a falling piece of timber. Dr Davis has been a short time in this city preparatory to his departure on his mission to China.

Died: on Jan 27, at Millfield, Southampton Co, Va, the residence of his family in his 38th year, Capt Wm O Kello, of the 8th Regt of Infty, U S A. He was educated at West Point, & entered the army as a brevet 2nd Lt. About the commencement of the war with Mexico, his health, which had been gradually giving way for 2 or 3 years, became so seriously impaired as to disqualify him for further service.

Cmdor Chas G Ridgely was born in Balt, Md, on Jul 2, 1784, & entered the navy on Oct 17, 1799. He was the first midshipman appointed from the city of Balt. He was with Cmdor Preble at the battle of Tripoli. He was rated Post Capt on Feb 28, 1815, & appointed to the command of the sloop-of-war **Erie**, [which vessel was built under his supervision at Balt,] but could not get to sea in her, being blockaded by the British squadron in the Chesapeake Bay; he consequently started by land, with his command of sailors, to join Com Chauncey on the lakes. In 1820 he was appointed to the command of the Pacific squadron, & sailed in the frig **Constellation** as his flag-ship. In 1825 appointed to command of the navy yard & station at Kittery, Maine. In 1828 command of the West India station & navy yard at Pensacola, Fla, until winter of 1830. In 1833 to the command of the navy yard at N Y, until Nov, 1839: then to command of the U S naval forces on the coast of Brazil & in the Rio de la Plata, & returned to the U S in the frig **Constitution** in Nov, 1841. He was twice in command of the Balt station, & had been over 48 years in the service, & was the 7th on the list of post captains.
–N Y Com Adv

Died: on Feb 9, in Wash City, Christina, only daughter of Nicholas & Christina Callan, aged 6 days.

City Ordinance-Wash: Act of the relief of Wm Quigly: that the fine imposed for an alleged violation of an order relative to grocery licenses, be remitted.

Household & kitchen furniture at auction: on Feb 19, at the residence & furniture store of L S Beck, on E st, near 9th st. -A Green, auctioneer

Orphans Court of Wash Co, D C. Letters testamentary on the personal estate of Jas Owner, late of said county, deceased. –Jas Owner, Hannah Allen, excs

THU FEB 15, 1848
Senate: 1-Ptn from Mrs M Rodgers, widow of Com Rodgers asking to be allowed the amount of an account which she alleges to be due her late huband: referred. 2-Additional documents in favor of the claim of Geo Poindexter: referred. 3-Ptn from Jos Newell, asking to be allowed to locate a certain section of land: referred. 4-Ptn from Henry B Gaither, asking compensation for services rendered the superintendent of Indian affairs west of Arkansas in 1841: referred. 5-Ptn from the exc of Cowal Ten Eyck, late U S Marshal, asking payment of a balance due him. 6-Ptn from Rebecca M Gibbs, for a pension: referred. 7-Additional documents in favor of Maj Larabee & of Asabel Kingsley.

Public sale of valuable real & personal property in PG Co, by virtue of the last will & testament of Robt W Bowie, deceased, the undersigned will offer at public sale, at the late residence of the deceased, on Mar 1, all that portion of real estate which lies south of Mattaponi Branch, known as ***Connick Farm***, except about ½ an acre devised to him by the late Gen Robt Bowie. This estate contains about 400 acres: about 2 miles from ***Nottingham***; improvements are 3 new & very large houses, & overseer's house & quarters for the use of the farm. –Wm H Tuck, exc of Robt W Bowie

Rev Mr Mandeville, the blind preacher, preached on Sabbath in the 4th Presbyterian Church to a crowded house. He is a licentiate of a Congregational association in Massachusetts. –J C S

Died: on Jan 18, at his residence, in the township of Markham, Home District, Canada West, the Rev John Dietrich Peterson, late pastor of the German Lutheran congregations in the townships of Markham & Vaughan, in said district, at the advanced age of 91 years. He was born in Bremen, Germany, on Nov 23, 1756; arrived in America in 1795; took charge of the Lutheran Church in Harrisburg, Pa, in 1803; removed to Upper Canada in 1819, being one of the first pioneers, if not the first, to the German Church in the wilderness of Markhan & Vaughan.

Died: on Sunday, at the residence of her mother, Mrs Macdaniel, on 4½ st, Sarah A, wife of Dr Vere Burn, in her 34th year. Her funeral is this morning at half past 9 o'clock.

Died: on Feb 13, Mrs Josephine L Blake, wife of Dr John B Blake, & daughter of the late Hon E Tucker, of N J. Her funeral is tomorrow, at 10 o'clock.

WED FEB 16, 1848
A few days since, Mr Addison Spaulding, of Dracut, Mass, was pinned under his cart a distance from his house and when he finally succeeded in freeing himself, his leg was much injured. It had to be amputated on Thu, by Dr Kimball, of this city. Chloroform was used in the operation. –Lowell Corp

Senate: 1-Ptn from Mary Cassin, widow of Lt Cassin, of the U S Navy, for a pension. 2-Ptn from Polly Taylor, asking for a pension. She states she was married to John Taylor in Mecklenburg Co, Va, in 1792, & had made application for her pension under the act of Jul 7, 1838, but because her first child was not born until 1796, it is inferred by the Com'r of Pensions that her marriage could not have taken place, & not being able to obtain her claim from the Dept of War, she asks Congress to examine her proofs & place on the pension roll. 3-Ptn from Jas Hardy, for extension of patent. 4-Papers in the case of John P Douglass, with additional documents in favor of the heirs, [Mr Douglas being dead,] to be referred to the Cmte on Public Lands. 5-Cmte on Pensions: bill granting a pension to John Clarke. Same cmte: House bill for the relief of Silas Waterman, without amendment. Same cmte: adverse report on the ptn of John Davenport. 6-Cmte on the Judiciary: bill for the relief of Wm Woodbridge & Henry Chipman. 7-Cmte on Private Land Claims: bill for the relief of the heirs of Jean F Perry, Josiah Bleakley, Nicholas Jarrot, & Robt Morison. 8-Cmte of Claims: bill for the relief of John Devlin.

9-Introduced: bill for the relief of Benj Adams & Co & others. 10-Bill for the relief of the heirs of Francis Caneau: referred to the Cmte of the Judiciary.

House of Reps: 1-Ptn of Solomon Davis & 60 other citizens of Oregon Co, Mo, praying a change of the entry of a small tract of land which by mistake was located upon barren hills, entirely unfit for cultivation or any other purpose, instead of his home, which he designed to enter. 2-Ptn of Abigail Stafford, for a pension for services of her husband in the Revolutionary war. 3-Papers in the case of Capt John Percival, U S Navy, praying for the allowance of money paid for a naturalist on board the frig **Constitution**. 4-Ptn of the heirs of J Mountjoy. 5-Ptn of C Ordendorff. 6-Memorial of W A Bradley & others, citizens of D C, asking for a charter for a steamboat company. 7-Ptn of Robt Ramsay, for a pension. 8-Ptn & papers of Wesley Leake, relating to his claim for a horse & gun pressed into the service during the late Seminole war. 9-Ptn of Wm Sampson & 90 others, praying for a mail route from Peru to Como & Mount Carroll, in the State of Illinois. 10-Memorial of Peleg B Phelps, of the city of Lafayette, asking for additional compensation as surveyor & inspector of the revenue for the port of the city of Lafayette, La. 11-Memorial of Lewis B Willis, late of the city of New Orleans, & late paymaster in the army, praying for the payment of a balance due him. 12-Ptn & papers of Jos R Brown, of **Fort Snelling**, Wisc, praying indemnity for expenses incurred in the arrest & surrender to the U S ofcrs of certain Indian offenders. 13-Ptn of Capt Zantzinger, of the U S Navy. 14-Ptn of Martin Davey for the payment & continuance of his pension. 15-Ptn of Solsberry Wheeler for an increase & the payment of the balance of his pension under the act of Jun 7, 1832.

On Fri last, Felix Renick, came to a violent death. While waiting for the boat at Paint Creek Ferry, a piece of hewn timber fell upon him as he sat in his carriage, & so crushed him as to cause instant death. He was 27 years old, & a great friend to internal improvement. –Scioto [Ohio] Gazette

Died: on Feb 15, Catherine Eliz, eldest child of John T & Susan B Towers, aged 12 years. Her funeral is tomorrow at 2 o'clock.

Information of the "Whites." One Mr ___ White, supposed to live in either western Va, or western Pa, or eastern Ohio, is said to be the owner of a tract of **Mountain Island** in Augusta Co, Va. The subscriber is desirous to hear from the owner the quantity, situation, & who was the original patantee. Any information communicated to Thos P Ladd, Staunton, Va, [post paid,] will be attended to. –Thos P Ladd

Coroner's inquest was held on a white boy, John Wm Marr, age 16 years, who died suddenly on Feb 14. Verdict: he died suddenly, but not from the effect of blows or any injury received in a fight that night.

Elias Lomax, free negro, was fully committed for trial, under the charge of maliciously & willfully setting on fire a stable occupied by Wm Grayson, in an alley between 3rd & $4\frac{1}{2}$ sts.

Valuable property at auction: Monday, in front of the premises: 3 story brick house & lot on south side of Pa ave, between 9th & 10th sts, occupied by Mr Haslup as a second-hand furniture store. -R W Dyer, auct

THU FEB 17, 1848
Senate: 1-Ptn from Amaziah Goodwin, asking an increase of pension.

Wash Corp: 1-Cmte of Claims: bill for the relief of Thos Mustin: passed. 2-Cmte of Claims: bill for the relief of Richd Cruit: passed. 3-Bill for the relief of Wm Bush was taken into consideration & concurred in. Same for the bill of Emma D E Southworth. 4-Ptn of Wm Begnam: referred to the Cmte of Claims. 5-Cmte of Claims: bills for the relief of John Bohlayer, jr; & relief of John Burch: both passed. 5-Ptn of Albert Hart, praying the remission of a fine: referred to the Cmte of Claims. 6-Ptn of Michl H Grimes, praying remission of a fine: referred to the Cmte of Claims. 7-Cmte of Claims: bill for the relief of Jonas B Elli: passed.

Household & kitchen furniture at auction: on Feb 18, by virtue of a bill of sale to W H Ward from C C Berry, at the residence of said Berry, on C st, near 9th, an excellent assortment of furniture. -A Green, auct

Mrs Lanman, of Norwich, Conn, widow of the late Judge Lanman, was burnt to death on Feb 11 by her clothes taking fire at the grate. She was about 70 years of age.

From the seat of war: 1-The following gentlemen, all belonging to the navy, have lately arrived at New Orleans from Mexico: G J Van Brunt, cmder of the ship **Etna** & late Govn'r of Tabasco; Lt S W Gordon, late Govn'r of Laguna; Lts Gray, J M Berrien, L G Sartori, & H J Hartstene; Midshipmen C L Smith & W C Wheeler. 2-The train which left the city of Mexico on Jan 14 arrived at Vera Cruz on Jan 27, comprised of about 200 wagons, with the following escort, under Maj Caldwell, of the Voltigeurs: one squadron of cavalry, companies B & G, 2nd Dragoons, commanded by Capt H W Merrill, with Lts Bicknell & Armstrong; one btln of Infty, commanded by Capt Ruggles, 5th Infty, comprising Co A, 5th Infty, 2nd Lt Hendershot, commanding; Co C, 4th Infty, 1st Lt O F Haller, cavalry, commanding; Co I, 2nd Infty, Lt Davis, commanding; one company of Voltigeurs, 1st Lt Titton, commanding, with Lts Cochran & Swan. The mountain howitzer battery, 6 pieces, 1st Lt Reno commanding, with Lt Walker, Voltiguers. Dr Barnes, U S A, attending surgeon; Capt O'Donnell & Bishop, assist quartermaster; Capt Hoyt, commissary. 3-The Vera Cruz Free American gives the following list of the ofcrs who came down with the train: Maj Sumner, 2nd Dragoons; Maj Waite & Col Howard, Infty; Capt Hardee & Lt Hawes, 2nd Dragoons; Lt Haggler, 3rd Dragoons; Lts Arnold & Elzy, Artl; Capt Roberts, Rifles; Lt Russell; Capts Smith, Haille, & Simmons, [to remain in Vera Cruz,] Infty; Lts Clitz, Wainwright, Farrell, & Wilcox, Infty; Lt Slaughter, Voltigeurs; Lt Shubrick, navy; Capt Henry & Hall, & Lt Floyd, N Y volunteers; Lt Robertson, S C volunteers; Lt Whipple, volunteers; Capt Benham, Ohio volunteers; & Lt Phelps, volunteer aid-de-camp to Gen Lale.

FRI FEB 18, 1848
On Feb 10, in Raleigh city, the Hon Jos J Daniel, one of the Judges of the Supreme Court of the State of N C, departed this life, whilst in the midst of his judicial labors. He had been in feeble health for some time past, but was confined to his room but a week or two before his death. He was about 70 years old, & for more than 30 years past has been constantly in the service of the State as Superior or Supreme Court Judge.

Senate: 1-Cmte on Pensions: bill for the relief of Patrick Walker.

House of Reps: 1-Cmte on Printing: to which was referred the report & maps of Lt Emory, containing the report of Capt Cook, the report & maps of Lt Abert, & the journal of Capt Johnson: 10,000 extra copies of each of said reports to be printed for the use of the House; & that of said number 250 copies be furnished for the use of Emory, Cook, & Abert. 2-Memorial of Jas H Chezum for payment for work done for the Gov't. 3-Memorial of Saml J Bayard, late receiver at Fairfield, Iowa. 4-Ptn of the heirs of Jacob Cohen. 5-Ptn of Mary M Talfair, praying for balance due her father, Israel Pearce, for final settlement certificates.

Died: on Feb 12, in Wash City, after a lingering & painful illness, Martha M, wife of Jos H Waring, of the Treasury Dept, & daughter of the late Capt Hugh Minor, of Fairfax Co, Va, aged 30 years.

Died: on Feb 14, Jas Eugena, 2nd son of Jas T & Deborah Boineau, aged 3 years & 4 months.

Died: on Jan 10, at Jalapa, Mexico, B Franklin Bogan, late of this city, in his 25th year. A few months since he was residing on a farm in Jefferson Co, Ill, & when a call was made for volunteers he, with a number of his young friends, offered their services, & were accepted. He went to Mexico as Sgt of Capt Bowman's company, & now his remains lie in Jalapa, with those of all the commissioned ofcrs, 3 sgts, 2 cpls, & 46 rank & file of his company. He was moral; more, he was religious.

Died: on Feb 15, at his residence in Wash Co, D C, Michl Downey, a native of Ballinasloe, county of Rosscommon, Ireland, aged 40 years, leaving a wife & 3 small children to lament their loss, & the circle of his friends to deplore the loss of an industrous & enterprising citizen & an honest man. –Balt Sun

Phil Nisi Prius, Feb 15. Wm Suddards vs the Excs of Eliz Greenfield, deceased. A single bill was executed by Mrs Greenfield to Mr Suddards for $6,000 in 1835. The defence was that there was no consideration. It appeared that the plntf, who is a clergyman, had for many years, in the exercise of his profession, acted as the spiritual & confidential friend of Mrs Greenfield & her family: Mrs Greenfield was a lady of wealth: she voluntarily executed the instrument sued upon & presented it to Mr Suddards. He never demanded the amount until after her death, the excs refusing to pay it. The Judge charged the jury that the services rendered by Mr Suddards constituted a sufficient consideration, & the jury found for the plntf $10,640. -Ledger

Fire at Nottingham, PG Co, Md, on Fri, destroyed the dwlg of Mrs Mgt Fowler; the Quynn's meat house; & Dr Taylor's stable with a buggy & 100 bushels of oats. It extended to Rollin's old house, but was extinguished before much damage had been done. –Balt Sun

Pittsburgh, Feb 14. Mrs Sharp, a vocalist of some note, fell from the steamer **Fashion** on Sat last, & was drowned. The accident occurred below Rising Sun, Indiana. She, Miss Bruce, & Mr Kneads were going to Louisville. [Feb 21st newspaper: Mrs Sharpe was married a few days since to Mr Kneads, the vocalist, & it was he who was with her when she fell off the boat. They were ascending the step over the wheel-house leading to the hurricane deck. The banister or railing broke, & both fell, Mrs Sharpe into the river, & Mr Kneads on the guard of the boat. Mrs Sharpe was so badly hurt in the fall that she sank immediately. –Public Journal]

The Livingston [N Y] Union mentions the death, by hanging, of Saml Trist, of Nunda, aged 16 years. It is supposed he was trying the experiment of hanging by the neck, & could not disengage himself.

Bloomsbury at public auction: on Mar 1, this valuable estate is 7 miles from Balt, 4 from Ellicott's Mills; & adjoins the farm of John Glenn. The dwlg is of brick, rough-cast, 80 feet front by 40 feet deep, with porticos in front & rear. St Timothy's Church is within one mile. –W T Somerville, on the property, or #83 Fayette st, Balt. Cannon & Bennett, auctioneers, Balt, Md.

Music teacher wanted: a gentleman in Va wishes to employ a Music Teacher for his own children & a few neighboring pupils. Apply to the Hon T S Flournoy.

SAT FEB 19, 1848
For rent: the store & dwlg lately occupied by John C Rodgers, on the s w corner of Md ave & 12th st west. –Edw Mattingly, near the Navy Yard, Wash

Mr Francis Markoe, long known as a highly respected merchant of N Y C, died on Wed, in his 74th year.

The U S ship **Germantown**, Cmder Buchanan, arrived at Hampton Roads on Tue from Vera Cruz, whence she sailed on Jan 15; touched at Havana on Jan 29 for water, & left Norfolk on Feb 1. Her ofcrs: Franklin Buchanan, Cmder; Lts A L Cass, A A Holcomb; Surgeon, N Pickney; Purser, J O Bradford; Acting Master, J Pringle; Passed Midshipman, A L Dance; Lt Marines, M R Kintzing; Midshipmen, F Grandy & T H Locker; Capt's Clerk, J L Breeze; Boatswain, W Black; Gunner, W C Thompson; Carpenter, J O Butler; Sailmaker, J Parker. The **Germantown** has brought the remains of the following ofcrs of the Army & Navy, who fell in battle, or from the effects of disease: Lt C W Chauncey, Dr J A Kearney, Passed Assist Surgeons J H Smith & C P Bates, Midshipman R T Carmichael, Lt Col S E Watson, Maj Levi Twiggs, Lt C F Morris, Lt A P Rogers. The 3 last named were killed in the battle of Churubusco.

Liberal reward for the recovery of the freedom papers of Wm Spense Robinson & Mary Spence Robinson, which were stolen from their residence, near the steamboat wharf, on Feb 15.

The Matamoros Flag states that a duel at Camargo, between Capt Joshua Collet & Capt Alex'r Wilkins, both of the 10th Infty, now stationed at that place, in which the former was killed. The meeting arose our of a dispute between Capt Wilkins & Capt Postley, of the same regt, of which Capt Collet acted as the friend of the latter.

Household & kitchen furniture at auction: on Feb 22, at the residence of Mrs Wells, on Pa ave, near 7th st, south side, over Mr Egan's dry goods store: a lot of good furniture. -A Green, auctioneer

MON FEB 21, 1848

Mr John B Thorne, a skillful dentist of Newark, N J, committed suicide a few days since, while laboring under mental derangement, by drinking sulphuric acid. He was a native of Devonshire, England, & had been in this country only a few months.

Mrd: on Feb 17, in Wash City, by Rev John Robb, Gerard Stith, of New Orleans, to Miss Clara S, daughter of Benj K Morsell, of Wash City.

Gardener wanted: the Com'rs of the Wash Asylum are desirous of employing an experienced Gardener. -C A Davis, Jas Marshall, T Wheeler, Com'rs

Senate: 1-Ptn from Jos Barclay, a soldier in the last war with Great Britain, asking to be allowed bounty land. 2-Cmte on Pensions: asking to be discharged from the further consideration of the ptn of Mary Cassin, & that it be referred to the Cmte on Naval Affairs. 3-Cmte on Patents: an adverse report on the ptn of Aaron Carman for a patent. 4-Cmte of Claims: House bill, without amendment, for the relief of Phineas Capen, legal administrator of John Cox, deceased, of Boston. 5-Cmte of Claims: without amendment, the following House bills: relief of the legal reps of John Snyder; relief of S Morris Waln; & relief of the heirs of Jas Brown. Same cmte: adverse report on the claim of the legal reps of Francis Cazeau. 6-Senate proceeded to the consideration of the bill for the relief of Mary MacRae, widow of Lt Col Wm MacRae, late of the U S Army. This bill having been amended so as to give half pay for 5 years, in semi-annual instalments dating from 1846, was ordered to be engrossed, &, by general consent, was passed. 7-Bill for the relief of John Black, last consul of the U S for Mexico: passed.

City Ordinances-Wash. 1-Act for the relief of Wm Bush: the sum of $32.69 be paid in full satisfaction for filling up 525 yards of space for a foot pavement on Pa ave. 2-Act for the relief of Richd Cruit: the fine imposed for a violation of law relative to hucksters' license, is remitted: provided Cruit pay the costs of prosecution. 3-Act for the relief of Jonas B Ellis: the fine imposed for a violation relative to dogs, be remitted: provided Ellis pay the costs of prosecution. 4-Act for the relief of Mrs D E Southworth: to pay her any balance due for her services as assistant teacher up to Dec 31, 1847, not exceeding $146.72.

House of Reps: 1-Ptn & application of John F Staser, for a military land warrant under the act of Congress of Feb 11, 1847. 2-Ptn of Jas McLaughlin & 48 other citizens of Morgan Co, Ohio, regarding the cost of the postage on newspapers. 3-Ptn of the heirs of John Paul Jones: Mr Bowlin moved to amend the bill by striking out all after the enacting clause & inserting a substitute authorizing the Sec of the Treasury to pay to the legal heirs of John Paul Jones the sum of $24,421.78, the value of the prizes captured by said Jones & carried into the port of Bergen, in Norway, & by Denmark delivered up to Great Britain in 1779: rejected.

Appointments by the Pres, by & with the advice & consent of the Senate. Postmasters:
Saml Medary, Columbus, Ohio
Luke Baldwin, Ogdensburgh, N Y
Isaac G McKinley, Harrisburgh, Pa
Phineas Allen, jr, Pittsfield, Mass
Bowen C Green, Saco, Maine
Robt D Johnson, Galveston, Texas
Jacob Walker, Lafayette, Indiana

Rolly Doolittle, Madison, Indiana
Thos Eaton, Bath, Maine
Jas B Glass, Columbia, S C
Levi J Cooley, Elmira, N Y
Jos Ficklin, Lexington, Ky
Jas M Bouck, Schenectady, N Y
Jos Justice, Trenton, N J

Decisions of the Court Martial & by the Pres of the U S in the case of Lt Col Fremont: on charges I, II, & III, guilty. Sentence: And the Court does therefore sentence the said Lt Col John C Fremont, of the Regt of Mounted Riflemen, U S Army, to be dismissed the service. The Court deems it proper, in view of the mass of evidence on the record, to remark that the Court has been unwilling to confine the accused to a strict legal defence, which appeared to lie within narrow limits.
The President's decision & orders in the case. Wash, Feb 16, 1848. I have carefully considered the record of proceedings of the Gen Court Martial in the case of Lt Col John C Fremont, which convened at Washington Arsenal, in D C, on Nov 2, 1847, & of which Brevet Brig Gen Geo M Brooke was Pres.
The Court find Lt Col Fremont guilty of the following charges, viz:
1-Mutiny 2-Disobedience of the lawful commands of his superior ofcr; 3rd: Conduct to the prejudice of good order & military discipline-& sentence him-to be dismissed the service. –Geo M Brooke, Brevet Brig Gen U S Army. -Thos F Hunt, Lt Col & Dep Quartermaster Genr'l. -J P Taylor, Lt Col & Assist Com Gen of Sub. -R L Baker, Major Ordnance Dept.
Three other members of the Court append to the record of their proceedings the following, viz: under all the circumstances of this case, & in consideration of the distinguished professional services of the accused previous to the transactions for which he has now been tried, the undersigned beg leave to recommend him to the clemency of the Pres of the U S. –S H Long, Lt Col Topogrpahical Engineers. –Richd Delafield, Major of Engineers. –E W Morgan, Lt Col 13th Infty
Upon an inspection fot the record, I am not satisfied that the facts proved in this case constitute the military crime of "mutiny." I am of opinion that the 2nd & 3rd charges are sustained by the proofs, & that the conviction upon these charges warrant the sentence of the Court. The sentence of the Court is, therefore, approved; but in consideration of the peculiar circumstances of the case; of the previous meritorious & valuable services of Lt Col Fremont, & of the foregoing recommendations of a majority of the members of the

Court, the penalty of dimissal from the service is remitted. Lt Col Fremont will accordingly be released from arrest, & will resume his sword & report for duty.
–Jas K Polk

Lt Col Fremont, of the Mounted Rifle Regt, is accordingly released from arrest, & will join his regt in Mexico. The Gen Court Martial of which Brevet Brig Gen Geo M Brooke is Pres is hereby dissolved. By order: R Jones, Adj Gen

TUE FEB 22, 1848
Senate: 1-Mr Benton rose to make a painful announcement to the Senate. He had just been informed that the House of Reps had adjourned under the most afflicting circumstance-a calamitous visitation to its oldest & most venerable member-one who had been Pres of the U S, & whose character inspired universal respect & esteem. He spoke of Mr Adams, who had just sunk down in his chair, & had been carried into an adjoining room, & might at this moment be passing from this world under the very roof which covers us, & almost in our presence. Under such circumstances the whole Senate will feel alike, & find itself utterly unable to attend to any business. He therefore moved the immediate adjournment of the Senate. Agreed.

A young lady named Eliza Vance, who, with her 3 sisters, was eating supper at their house in Prince st, Boston, on Tue, became choked by a piece of meat lodging in her throat. She died soon after.

Anniversary of the Birthday of Geo Washington: Feb 22, 1848. The "Resignation of the Commission", was on Dec 12, 1783, at Annapolis. After a long absence, the retired Genr'l returned to **Mount Vernon**: his landed estate, comprising 8,000 acres, underwent many changes & improvements. It was divided into farms, with suitable enclosures; hedges were planted, & farm bldgs were erected, from European models. On leaving Annapolis the Genr'l was accompanied by 2 of the ofcrs of his former staff, Cols Humphreys & Smith, who remained for several years at **Mount Vernon**, engaged in arranging the vast mass of papers & documents that had accumulated during the war of Independence. At a short distance from the mansion house, in a pleasant & sheltered situation, rose the homsestead of Bishop, the old body-servant. Thos Bishop, born in England, attended Gen Braddock to the Continent during the Seven Years' War, & afterwards embarked with that brave & unfortunate cmder for America in 1755. On the morning of Jul 9, the day of the memorable battle of the Monongahela-Bishop was present when Col Washington urged upon the English Genr'l for the last time the propriety of permitting him [the Col] to advance with the Va woodsmen & a band of friendly Indians, & open the way to **Fort Duquesne**. Braddock treated the proposal with scorn; but, turning to his faithful follower, observed: Bishop, this young man is determined to go into action today, although he is really too much weakened by illness for any such purpose. Have an eye to him, & render him any assistance that may be necessary. Bishop had only time to reply, Your honor's orders shall be obeyed, when the troops were in motion & the action soon after commenced. 64 British ofcrs were killed or wounded, & Washington was the only mounted ofcr on the field. His horse being shot, Bishop was promptly at hand to offer him a second; & so exhausted with the youthful hero from his previous illness, that he was with difficulty extricated from his dying charger, & was actually lifted by the strong arms of Bishop into the saddle of the second horse. His second horse having fallen, the provincial colonel made his way to the commanding general, though mortally stricken, raging like a wounded lion, & yet breathing defiance to the foe, was supported in the arms of Bishop. Braddock grasped the hand of Washington, exclaiming, Oh, my dear colonel, had I been governed by your advice, we never should have come to this. The British general called his friend to his side, & said, "Bishop, you are getting too old for war; I advise you to remain in America & go into the service of Col Washington. Be but as faithful to him as you have been to me, & rely upon it the remainder of your days will be prosperous & happy." Bishop took the advice of his old master, & at the close of the campaign returned with the colonel to **Mount Vernon**. As a body servant, Bishop attended Col Washington at the time of his marriage, & was installed as chief of the stables & the equipage in Williamsburg, in the bright & palmy days of that ancient capital. Finally, Bishop settled on the banks of the Potomac, married, & was made oversee of one of the farms of the **Mount Vernon** estate. Upon the General's return after the peace of 1783 the ancient body servant had passed fourscore, had been relieved from all active service, &, having lost his wife, he, with his daughter & only child, was settled down in a comfortable homestead that had been built expressly as an asylum for his age.

By virtue of a writ of fieri facias, at suit of Nancy Sheehy, against Thos Joice, I have seized & taken in execution the north part of lot 9 in square 266, in Wash City, with the bldgs thereon: to be sold on Mar 30, on the premises. –John Waters, constable

House of Reps: 1-Several gentlemen, sprang from their seats to the assistance of the venerable John Quincy Adams, who was observed to be sinking from his seat in what appeared to be the agonies of death. Mr Adams was immediately borne to the Rotundo for the benefit of purer air, & afterwards to the Speaker's room, assiduously attended by many members of the House; & the House hastily adjourned.

Passengers by the U S steamship **New Orleans**. Maj Van Buren, U S A; Capt R Smith, 2nd Infty; W D Lee; Capts W I Haldee & C P Hervey, Ga btln; Lt Col J Howard, 15th Infty; Lt H N Owen, 4th Ky volunteers; Lt S Lockwood, U S N; Lt H D Grafton, 1st Artl; B E Wheat, Surgeon U S A; Lt W T Walker, 3rd Ky volunteers; Jos G Eastland; Lts L G Arnold, A Elzey, & H F Clark, 2nd Artl; W H Tyler, 7th Infty; H B Clitz, 3rd Infty; Geo W Chiney, 14th Infty; Calhoun Benham, 4th Ohio volunteers; Capt Geo B Hall, N Y volunteers; Lt R H Thompson, 4th Ohio volunteers; E S Estaureson, 2nd Pa volunteers; C J Emery, 1st Mass volunteers; C M Wilcox, 7th Infty; Geo Womught, 8th Infty; Assist Surgeons A E Highway & J H Barnes, U S A; Lts J M Hawes, 2nd Dragoons; R M Floyd & W Henry, N Y volunteers; Maj V E Prollett, Paymaster; Drs J B Porter, Surgeon U S A, & D L Scott; Victor Perra; Lt J E Slaughter, Voltigeurs; Mr Dusenbury, Quartermaster's Dept; Mr John Staples, Mr J B Crookes; Capt A Phelps, Aid to Gen Lane; Messrs F Gayon, Paymaster's Clerk, P Prindergart, Quartermaster's Clerk, Hart & Keller; Capt Dury; Messrs C Bradly, Cummisky, & Corson; Lt L F Robinson, Palmetto Regt; Capt J S Slocum, 9th Infty; Lt J G Fitzgerald, 14th Infty; Henry D'Olier, Prussian Consul, Vera Cruz; Lt H A Holbernan, 11th Infty; Mr Catipidam; W P Milby, J B Hewson, Subsistence Dept; R B Cheethan; Lt Fanelly, 5th Infty; W H Robinson, Geo W

Hopkins, Geo Walbridge, Jos H Hodge & Son, Chas Hernander, Prosper Molrudge; Capt C M Hale, 14th Infty; Lts J J Whipple, 9th Infty; W C Wagley, 3rd Dragoons; W W Rich, Ga cavalry; W W Blecker, U S N; Surgeon John Irwin, U S A; Lt Danl Nichols; Lt Andrews, 2nd Ohio volunteers. List of passengers on board the steamer **Fanny**, at New Orleans from Brasos Santiago: Capt J P O'Brian, U S A; Lt W P Morrison, Ohio volunteers; Lt R F Coleman, Va volunteers; Lt W McCormick; Mrs Brown, Mrs Burk, & 2 children; Messrs W Sibley, H Maston, Ed H Bierns, Thos Bucks, S A Caldin, L C Pyron, Capt McCerren, & 22 on deck.

Trustee's sale of valuable improved real estate: by power invested by a deed of trust, dated Mar 15, 1843, recorded in the land records of Wash Co, D C, in Liber W B 100: sale of one-half of lot 3 in aquare 219, beginning on north H st. Also, the western half of lot 4 in square 286, in Wash City, fronting on N Y ave. Sale on Mar 20th next.
–P M Pearson, trustee -R W Dyer, auct

The Hagerstown News states that Hezekiah Burhans, an old man who lately died in Balt, has left all his property, valued at $12,000, to a young lady, a school-mistress of that town, who, when the old gentleman visited Hagerstown a year ago, treated him with great kindness, when others, viewing him as beneath their notice, because of his shabby appearance, treated him with great coldness. The lady also introduced into her school the "Monotonical Speller," a work of which the deceased was the author. –Balt Clipper

Maj Edw Webster, of Mass Regt of volunteers, & son of Hon Danl Webster, died at St Angel, 8 miles from Mexico, the headquarters of Gen Cushing's brigade, on some day between Jan 20th & Jan 25th. His funeral was attended by the regt; remains will be sent home. One of his horses was sold in Mexico, & one retained. He died of a typhoid fever.

WED FEB 23, 1848
Wash Corp: 1-Mayor nominates W B Mitchell as Police Ofcr of the 2nd Ward, in place of J W Dexter, deceased, & withdrawing the nomination of J F Wannell for that ofc: confirmed. 2-Cmte of Claims: bill for the relief of Augustus Ross: passed. 3-Ptn from Jno Miller, referred to the Cmte of Claims. 4-Ptn from David Rich: referred to the Cmte of Claims. 5-Ptn of J Luechese, praying remission of a fine: referred to the Cmte of Claims. 6-Bill for the relief of John Burch; & bill for the relief of Thos Mustin: both referred to the Cmte of Claims.

House of Reps: 1-Papers of Jonathan Neff, Edw Taylor, & Cornelius Hughes, all applicants to be placed on the roll of invalid pensioners: referred. 2-Papers of Thos Richard, an applicant to be placed on the roll of Revolutionary pensioners: referred. 3-Ptn of W H Scott, for indemnity for loss sustained by the failure & refusal of the Postmaster Genr'l to give him a mail contract according to agreement. 4-Ptn of Jarvis Jackson, praying to be relieved from the payment of a judgment obtained against him as the security of Calvin Carter, late Postmaster at London, Ky. 5-Ptn of W S Rossiter, Jas Brown, jr, & other citizens of N Y, for the admission of Canadian produce free of duty.

Senate: Mr Davis, of Mass, was informed that the House had met & immediately adjourned in consequence of the continued & dangerous illness of Mr Adams, who still lay within these walls in a very perilous condition. The Senate agreed to adjourn. [Mr Adams was lying as in a profound sleep, breathing calmly, but obviously unconscious of all around him.]

The U S sloop-of-war **Saratoga** arrived at N Y on Sat from Pensacola, having on board 34 invalids from the Gulf squadron. A list of her ofcrs: D D Farragut, Cmder; W H Noland, Lt; F R Renshaw, Lt; L B Hunter, Surgeon; G H White, purser; J Wilkinson, master; J B Steel, Assist Surgeon; K R Breese, J Waters, Jas Packer, midshipmen; P Loyal, Capt's clerk.

Capt Martin Lund, a Dane by birth, well known in New Orleans, left there about 18 months ago in the schnr **Independence**, loaded with merchandise for a Mexican port. He went to the Rio Grande, sold his cargo, & again put to sea. His friends hearing no news from him, a rumor circulated that his vessel was lost with all on board. A succession was opened in the proper court, his property sold, & the proceeds paid over to the supposed widow. The wife, about 6 months ago, married a young lawyer of New Orleans. Three of 4 day since, to the wonder of everyone, the long lost but veritable Capt Lund returned to his former home, & found quite an alteration in his affairs, both pecuniary & domestic.

Montreal paper-yesterday: loss of a mail stage in the ice, was followed by the death of the driver, Mr Mudge, on its way back from Port St Claire to Lachine. Two passengers, Mr Ogden, of Quebec, & Mr Russell, of Ancaster, were saved.

$10 reward for a lost Gold Lever Watch. Reward will be paid on delivery of same to Chas Stott, Druggist, near the Market-house, or at my store, near the Steamboat wharf. –Henry A Clarke

Letter dated Mazatlan, Dec 1, 1847. At anchor in the harbor, razee **Independence**, Com Shubrick; ship **Congress**, Capt La Vallette, who, with 500 on shore, governs & commands Mazatlan, supported by well-appointed batteries & the frig **Cyane**, Com Dupont; & the frig **Portsmouth**, Com Montgomery, soon for home, all her crew being over their term of enlistment; brig **Caroline**, prize to the **Portsmouth**, Lt W A Bartlett, commanding, taken up the gulf, & I learn has been ransomed today for $10,000. The ship **Dale**, Com Selfridge, hold Guaymas, where she relieved the **Portsmouth** on Nov 9. Lt Haywood, U S N, with 3 ofcrs & 25 men, were posted by Com Shubrick at San Jose, near Capt St Lucas, early in Nov, to hold that port, some probability of a revolution appearing in the country. On the 18th the enemy attacked with 2 six-pounders & 150 to 200 men. Majores, the Mexican chief, was killed, & 20 to 30 of his men. Passed Midshipman McLanahan was slightly wounded. Thus ended the battle of San Jose. Mr Gillespie, an American merchant, distinguished himself in the command of the Calif residents.

Mrd: on Feb 20, by Rev J E Graeff, Mr Jas Foyles to Miss Caroline Smith, both of Wash City.

Died: on Feb 19, after a short & painful illness, Robt Kearon, the worthy messenger in the Library of Congress, aged 58 years, & long a respected resident of Gtwn & Wash City.

Died: on Feb 21, John D Thomas, aged 26 years, eldest son of the late Col Jas Thomas, of Wash City. His funeral is this morning, at 11 o'clock, from his late residence on 10th st, between D & E sts.

THU FEB 24, 1848
Information wanted of Thos Buchanan, [eldest son of Judge Thos Buchanan, deceased,] who left his father's residence in Wash Co, Md, in 1840. Information as to whether he be living or dead, & if living, where his residence is, & if dead, when & where he died.
–Geo Schley, Jas A Dall, excs of Thos Buchanan, deceased: Hagerstown, Md

Groceries, liquors, buggy & horse at auction: on Feb 28, by deed of trust to the subscribers, at the store of Mr John Waring, 6th & Pa ave. –Henry Brooke, John L Waring, trustees -R W Dyer, auct

Dr N H Ashe, a Surgeon in the U S Army, died at Memphis, Tenn, on Feb 7. He was on his return home from the army in Mexico.

Valuable lot at auction: on the last day of Feb, on the premises, desirable lot on 10th st, between I & K, near Franklin Row, adjoining the residence of Mr Lovejoy.
-A Green, auctioneer

The venerable Patriot & Statesman, John Quincy Adams, expired at the Capitol last evening a little after 7 o'clock. [The last person who conversed with Mr Adams on Monday was Mr Hilliard, of Ala.]

For rent: the house lately occupied by W W Corcoran, on H st, between 15th & 16th sts. Apply to J C Harkness or Saml Redfern.

FRI FEB 25, 1848
John Quincy Adams was born on Jul 11, 1767, in that part of *Braintree*, Mass, which was incorporated into a town by the name of Quincy, & hence was in the 81st year of his age.

Sale on Feb 29, of a beautiful lot on 12th st, between I & K sts, in square 285, belonging to Mr J P Keller. -A Green, auctioneer

Senate: 1-Ptn from Mary E D Blaney, admx of Geo Blaney, Brevet Major of the corps of Engineers, asking that certain moneys, the private property of her late husband, claimed & taken by the Gov't as public funds, may be paid to her. 2-Ptn from Isabella Cole, admx of Wm Cole, asking indemnity for injuries done to a vessel & cargo belonging to her late husband by the Peruvian authorities. 3-Cmte on Private Land Claims: asking to be discharged from the further consideration of the ptns of Issac C Elston & Jas M Kibben. 4-Cmte of Claims: bill for the relief of Chas Richmond.

Fresh groceries: J T Radcliff, 2nd door above Odd Fellows' Hall, on 7th st.

Gardening: the undersigned has made arrangements to commence the dressing & keeping of private gardens, either by day or by season. Orders can be left at the green-house near the Patent Ofc, or at the subscriber's residence, on 16th st, 4 squares north of the Pres' mansion. –Jas Watt

For rent: commodious 3 story dwlg & premises on West st, Gtwn. Being about to remove to my farm on Rock Creek, near town, I take this occasion to warn all gunners & huntsmen & others from trespassing or hunting on said farm, under penalty of the law. –W Morton

The Pres of the U S, with deep regret, announces the death of John Quincy Adams, our eminent & venerated fellow-citizen. He expired on Feb 23, without having been removed from the Capitol. The nation mourns his loss; I direct that all the Executive ofcs at Washington be placed in mourning, & that all business be suspended during this day & tomorrow. Jas K Polk, Wash, Feb 24, 1848

For rent: comfortable dwlg, in good repair. Now occupied by Lt Sands, of the Navy, situated on 6th st, one door above the residence of Gen Roger Jones. Apply on the premises, or at Dr Washington's opposite.

Funeral services of Hon John Quincy Adams will be on Sat next at 11 o'clock. Pall-Bearers:

Hon J J McKay, N C
Hon Linn Boyd, Ken
Hon John C Calhoun, S C
Chief Justice R B Taney
Gen Geo Gibson
Hon W W Seaton

Hon Truman Smith, Con
Hon J R Ingersoll, Pa
Hon Thos H Benton, Mo
Hon Justice J McLean
Com Chas Morris
Hon Thos H Crawford

A boy named Stewart, about 15 years of age, was killed on Pa ave, last Wed: there was a false alarm of fire, & the deceased, while engaged with other boys in hauling the hose reel, fell down, & the reel passing over him, caused such severe injury of his skull & body as to result in the poor lad's death in about 20 minutes.
+
Died: on Feb 23, suddenly, Chas J Stewart, the 2nd son of John C Stewart, in his 15th year. His funeral will take place from his father's residence on 12th st, near Md ave, this day, at 11 o'clock.

From Vera Cruz: ofcrs arrived at New Orleans on Feb 14 from Mexico: Maj E V Sumner, 2nd Dragoons, Maj C A Waite, 8th Infty; Capts J C Hughes, D G Jones, Hoagland, J M Anderson, & L Metcalf; Lts J Hettleson, C S French, J A Fell, H Harrendon, & L D Vanhook; Commissaries, J H Phelps & D E Adalt; Drs H Owen & J M Daniel, & 173 discharged soldiers & teamsters.

Died: on Dec 11 last, at Jalapa, Mexico, Edw Glover, 2nd sgt in Capt Barry's company of volunteers, of the District & Md btln.

SAT FEB 26, 1848
To join in the funeral of the late John Quincy Adams:
Columbia Fire Co: N M Iardella, Sec   Nat'l Blues: J Stoddard, O S
Northern Liberties Fire Co: J Y Bryant-   Temperance Men: P M Pearson, G W P
Pres   I O O F: Grand Lodge of D C: R J
Perserverance Fire Co: V Harbaugh, Sec   Roche, Grand Sec
Union Fire Co: Chas Calvert, Sec
Columbia Typographical Society: Patrick H Brook, Pres pro tem

Died: on Feb 10, at his residence in Claremont, N H, aged 79 years, the Hon Geo B Upham. He was a Rep in Congress more than 40 years ago, & was quite distinguished as a lawyer in his day, though he retired from the profession 20 years ago. He was supposed to be at the time of his death, one of the wealthiest men of the State.

Orphans Court of Wash Co, D C. Letters testamentary on the personal estate of Michl Downey, late of said county, deceased. –Mary Downey, excx

By an order for distress, I will sell, on Mar 4, one Dray, seized & taken for stable rent due in arrears by J Waring & L J Brown, trading under the firm of Waring & Brown, to Jacob Gideon, & will be sold to satisfy the same. –R R Burr, Bailiff

MON FEB 28, 1848
The Last Days of Mr Adams' Life. On Sunday, though the day was showery, Mr Adams visited the Capitol, & was an attentive listener to the discourse of Rev Dr Mathews. In the afternoon, with his dght-in-law, Mrs John Adams, he attended Rev Dr Pyne's church, & stood through the accustomed services. Mr Adams has been a member for many years of the Unitarian Church. On Monday as usual rode to the Capitol & was early in his seat.

The El Nationel, at Zacatlan, Mexico, announces the death of Gen Morales, one of those who fought with zeal for independence. [No death date given-current news item.]

Mrs Himes, a young married woman, was frozen to death in Leyden, Lewis Co, N Y. She lost her way on her return from church on Sunday, & was not found until Wed.

Mrs Henrietta Rogassi, well known in the theatrical circles as Miss Henrietta Blanchard, but for 3 weeks the wife of Veta Rogassi, a trombone player in the St Charles theatre, New Orleans, was mortally wounded by her husband in that city on Feb 10, by a stab in the side & another in the arm. She is the woman who, about 2 years since, shot a man in New Orleans named Pettipau, with a pistol, in resentment for a gross indignity committed upon her, & for which the jury acquitted her. Rogassi had fled.

Died: on Feb 18, in Wash City, at the residence of E Goodrich Smith, Mrs Alice Colden Wadsworth, of N Y C.

Funeral obsequies of Mr Adams: funeral ceremonies in the Hall of the House of Reps, shrouded in black and gave a very solemn appearance: the portraits of Washington & of Lafayette, were covered over with thin crape, casting a melancholy dimness over the features: Washington gave the deceased his first commission: The Chaplain of the House, Rev Mr Gurley, read an appropriate portion of Holy Writ. The lobbies & passages were densely crowded by hundreds of thousands who could not gain admittance to the Reps Hall, the scene being striking, from the vast multitude of orderly & well-dressed people of both sexes, which filled the great space in front of the Capitol: many stores & dwlgs hung with mourning drapery: the procession was under the direction of Jos H Bradley, as chief marshal, aided by the following assistant marshals: Mr Jas Scott, Mr E H Fuller, Mr G S Gideon, Mr W H Winter, Mr Wm Barker, Mr J R Queen, & Mr J W Martin. The Funeral car was built by Mr J F Harvey, & had a canopy covered with black velvet; surmounted with a spread eagle covered with cape; the car was drawn by 6 white horses: the coffin was made by Messrs Lee & Espy, & was covered with black velvet ornamented with silver lace: the silver breastplate, manufactured by Mr S Masi, presented the following inscription:
John Quincy Adams
Born
An Inhabitant of Massachusetts, July 11, 1767.
Died
A Citizen of the United States,
In the Captiol of Washington,
February 23, 1848;
Having served his Country for Half a Century
And
Enjoyed its Highest Honors.

Died: on Feb 26, in Wash City, Mr Jacob Durff, in his 64th year. He was a native of Fredericktown, Md; had resided many years in Phil, but for over the last 20 years was a resident of D C, where he had attached to himself many sincere friends, who will long cherish his memory.

Died: on Feb 20, at his residence near Port Tobacco, Chas Co, Md, after a short illness, Wm M Hodges, in his 41st year-a gentleman esteemed & respected wherer he was known.

Died: on Feb 6, at New Orleans, Dr Wm J Powell, Surgeon in the U S Navy. He was one of the surgeons attached to the squadron cruising for the last 4 years in the Pacific, & had gained the warm affection of his brother ofcrs by his frank & amiable manners, & courteous & gentlemanly deportment.

Died: on Feb 23, at Fredericksburg, Va, Lt Neil M Howison, of the U S Navy, in the 43rd year of his age. But a few days since, Lt Howison was in his usual health. He visited Washington upon official business, when he contracted a cold, which settled upon the heart, & terminated his earthly career the day after his arrival at home. The deceased had for upwards of 20 years been in the Navy. A native of this place, he has a large & respectable family connexion who mourn his death. –Fred News

TUE FEB 29, 1848
Senate: 1-Ptn from Levi Wells, a soldier of the last war with Great Britain, asking for a pension. 2-Cmte on Pensions: adverse report on the ptn of Asabel Kingsley. 3-Cmte on the Post Ofc & Post Roads: bill for the relief of Wm B Stokes. 4-Bill for the relief of Peter Engles, sen, was considered in the Cmte of the Whole: passed.

Mr Osma, the Peruvian Minister, is about to leave the U S. All persons having claims against him are notified to present them forthwith for payment.

House of Reps: 1-Be it enacted: that all letters & packets carried to & from Louisa Chatham Adams, widow of the late John Quincy Adams, be conveyed free of postage during her natural life. [Mrs Madison had been conferred the privilege of this hall, & the same mark of respect should be extended to Mrs Adams.] Bill was passed. 2-Bill for the relief of the legal reps of Abraham Hogeboom, deceased: introduced.

Caution: to all whom it may concern. Between 1835 & 1849 Gilbert L Thompson, for himself, &, as he alleges, trustee of the separate estate of the late Mrs Arietta M Thompson & her heirs, petitioned the Republic of Mexico to be allowed certain claims. On Jan 4, 1842, Thompson executed what purported to be an assignment in trust of said claims to Richd S Coxe. A portion of said claims were acted upon & allowed by the American Com'rs under a convention with Mexico. The said Thompson is not, & never was, the trustee of the heirs of the late Mrs Thompson, & neither can, nor ever could, made any valid assignment of their claims. The heirs are determined to assert & protect their rights, & the whole matter will indue time undergo a full judicial investigation & settlement. –Jas J Dickins, for himself, his wife, & other heirs of the late Mrs Arietta M Thompson.

The remains of Fleet Surgeon Kearney & Lt Chas W Chauncey, of the U S Navy, having arrived from Mexico, will be re-interred at the Congressional Burial ground. The funeral ceremonies will take place at the Episcopal Church, Rev Mr Bean, near the Navy Yard, on Mar 1, at 12 o'clock.

A private letter states that Lt Scholl, of Capt Peltzer's company, shot himself on Jan 24. The deceased was from Belleville, Illinois.

The trustees of Primary School #8 of the 3rd election district of St Mary's Co, Md, wish to employ a Teacher: compensation $200 or upwards. –Thos Loker, Thos Hebb, Edw Plater, Great Mills Post Ofc, Leonardtown, Md

Cincinnati, Feb 24. Mrs Simonds, wife of Mr Simonds, a planemaker, on 4th st, died yesterday while under the influence of choloroform, at Dr Meredith's, [dentist] ofc on 6th st. Mrs Simonds has left a youthful family of 4 children & an affectionate husband, inconsolable at her heart rending death. –Queen City

Mrd: on Feb 23, by Rt Rev Bishop Potter, E Coles Lambert, of Phil, to Sarah Eliz, daughter of Benj F French, of New Orleans. [New Orleans papers please copy.]

Died: on Feb 28, Caroline Matilda, wife of Wm B Waugh, in her 27th year. Her funeral will take place at the residence of the family, on Mass ave, this afternoon, at 4 o'clock.

Died: on Feb 17, at Nashville, Hon Geo W Campbell, a distinguished citizen of that State. He had reached 80 years of age.

Wanted: a man to make Cheese & take charge of 30 or more cows. Address T Kennerly, White Post, Clarke Co, Va.

WED MAR 1, 1848
The subscriber announces to his customers & the public in general, that he intends slaughtering a very fine Bear, which he will have on his stall on Sat next, & wishes that they will call & judge for themselves. -Henry Weaver

Wash Corp: 1-Special license to Thos Buckley: agreed to. 2-Bill for the payment of the claim of A C Kidwell: referred to the Cmte on Improvements. 3-Bill for the relief of Thos McDonnell: referred to the Cmte of Claims. 4-Ptn of A G Herold, praying remission of a fine: referred to the Cmte of Claims. 5-Cmte of Claims: bill for the relief of John Burche: reported the same without amendment.

Senate: 1-Ptn from Rockland Carlton, asking the reimbursement of a fine incurred by him through the mistake of a custom-house ofcr. 2-Ptn from the legal reps of Nathl A Haven & Eliphalet Ladd, asking the action of congress to indemnify them for spoliations made on our commerce prior to 1800. 3-Cmte on Public Lands: bill to confirm to the legal reps of Jos Dutaillis the location of a certain New Madrid certificate. 4-Cmte on Pensions: bill granting a pension to Bethiah Healey; accompanied by a report. 5-Bill granting franking privilege to Louisa Chatham Adams, widow of the late John Quincy Adams: passed.

House of Reps: 1-Cmte of Claims: bills for relief of Mathews, Wood & Hall; for relief of the legal reps of Wm D Cheever, deceased; & for relief of John Morgan: all committed. Same cmte: to which were referred the ptns of Jas Jones, Jas C Neely, Jas C Cooper, Caleb Neely, Saml Pigg, Jas Mahoney, Mary Carty, Catharine Ramey, & Thos E Thorp, praying compensation for horses lost in the war with Mexico: read & committed. Same cmte: adverse reports on the ptns of Jas F Megowan, Geo W Rumyon, Thos Bryan, & Geo W Bell: laid on the table. 2-Cmte of Claims: bill for relief of the legal reps of Jas Porterfield: committed. Adverse reports on the ptns of Allen Gorham, McKnight, Brent & Wood, & Henry W Andrews: laid on the table. Same cmte: bill for relief of Andrew A Jones & Caspar R Cooke & others: committed. Same cmte: reported bills for relief of Zachariah Lawrence, of Ohio, & for relief of Wm P Zantzinger: committed. Adverse report on ptn of Herman Loury: laid on the table. Same cmte: bills for relief of Danl Steenrod; relief of Gideon Walker; relief of Dr A G Henry, of Ill; relief of John B Rogers, of S C; relief of the legal reps of Bernard Todd; & for relief of the legal reps of Robt Dulton, deceased: committed. Same cmte: adverse report on the ptn of W J A Bradford: laid on the table. Same cmte: bill for relief of Geo Fisher: committed. Same cmte: bill for relief of the legal reps of Capt Wm Smallwood: committed. 3-Cmte on Commerce: bill to change the name of the steamboat **Charles Downing** to the steamboat **Calhoun**:

passed, & sent to the Senate for concurrence. Same cmte: adverse report on the ptn of Jas Foster: laid on the table. 4-Cmte on Public Lands: bill for the relief of John O'Siris: committed. Same cmte: adverse reports upon the ptns of John Tucker & Barbara Lancaster: laid on the table. 5-Cmte on the Post Ofc & Post Roads: relief of David Shaw & Solomon T Corser: committed. Same cmte: adverse report on the bill for the relief of Wm De Buys, late postmaster at New Orleans: committed. Adverse report on the ptn of Edwin Porter & Co: laid on the table. Same cmte: adverse reports on the ptns of Farley D Thompson, & of merchants & citizens of Mobile, Ala: laid on the table. 6-Cmte on the Judiciary: bills for the relief of Richd S Coxe; relief of Milledge Galphin, exc of Geo Galphin, deceased; & relief of Richd Bloss & others: committed. 7-Cmte on the Judiciary: bill for the relief of Wm Fuller: committed. Same cmte: bills for the relief of Susan C Randall & for the relief of Francois Cazean: committed. Same cmte: bill for the relief of Mr Cappella, adm of Andrew Capella, deceased, & for the relief of John Capo, & for the relief of Elijah Petty & Hannah Petty, his wife, heirs of John Beardon, deceased: committed. 8-Cmte on Revolutionary Claims: Bill for the relief of the heirs of Col David Hopkins: committed. Same cmte: bill for the relief of Eliz Converse: committed. Same cmte: adverse report on the ptn of the heirs of Susannah & Geo Stewart: laid on the table. 9-Cmte on Private Land Claims: bill for the relief of Chas Cappel, passed: sent to the Senate for concurrence. 10-Cmte on Indian Affairs: relief of Betsey McIntosh: read & agreed to. Same cmte: bill for the relief of Thos Talbot & others: committed. 11-Cmte on Military Affairs: bill for the relief of Chas L Dell: committed. 12-Cmte on Naval Affairs: adverse report on the ptn of Uriah Brown: laid on the table. Same cmte: bills for the relief of Thos Ap Catesby Jones & for the relief of Andrew C Armstrong: committed. Same cmte: bill for the relief of Capt John Percival: committed. 13-Cmte on Revolutionary Pensions: adverse reports on the ptns of the widow of Jonathan Weightman; the widow of Wm Wright; of Hannah Weightman, formerly widow of John Hart; & Sarah Miles, widow of Wm Miles: laid on the table. Same cmte: adverse report on the ptn of Saml Hutchinson: laid on the table. Bills for the relief of H Carrington, exc of Paulina Le Grand, deceased; & for the relief of Anna Griffin: committed. Same cmte: adverse reports on the ptns of John Morrison & Eliz Pool, deceased: laid on the table. Same cmte: adverse reports on the ptns of Tabitha Temple, of Clarinda Mix, of Agney Clark, of Mary M Foot, of Lucy Wright, of Eliz Martin, of John Gorman, & of Jane Lynn: laid on the table. Same cmte: bill for the relief of John Morrison, & a bill granting a pension to Ruth Hallenbeck: committed. 14-Cmte on Invalid Pensions: bills for the relief of Wm Butler; of Jesse Washington Jackson; of Saml Gray; of Jas Fugate; of Lizur B Canfield, & the relief of Artemas Conant: committed. Same cmte: bills for the relief of Richd Reynolds; of John Hibbert; of Danl H Warren; of John Campbell; of Nathl Shiflet; of Lewis Hastings; & of Skelton Felton: committed. 15-Cmte of Accounts: advance report upon the resolution of the House relative to extra compensation to John Lee: laid on the table. 16-Cmte on Patents: bill for the relief of Elisha H Holmes: committed. 17-Ptn of John McAllistar, for compensation for carrying the mail. 18-Ptn of Edw Armor for an increase of his pension. 19-Ptn of Almy Tifft, for compensation for her father's service in the Revolution. 20-Ptn of Maria Brown, widow of Joel Brown, a soldier in the late war with Great Britain, praying for a pension. 21-Ptn of John Harrigan, of Wash Co, Md, praying Congress to grant him a pension for wounds received at the bombardment of **Fort McHenry**, in the last war with

Great Britian. 22-Ptn of the heirs of John Kendrick, one of the first explorers of Oregon, asking for a confirmation of their titles to land in that Territory. 23-Ptn of Rebecca Bump, of Mount Morris, N Y, widow of John Bump, a Revolutionary soldier, praying for an extension of the laws granting pensions to widows of soldiers of the Revolution, with accompanying certificates of Hon Micah Brooks & others. 24-Ptn of Sarah Munger, the widow, & Mary Ann Lowell, the dght of Lt Wiseman, deceased, praying for a pension on account of the decease of said Wiseman from sickness contracted while in the service of the U S on the Niagara frontier in the war of 1812, with papers accompanying said ptn, & former papers on the same subject taken from the files. 25-Ptn of Messrs Koons & Dean, praying to be paid for advances made to Capt Fairfax's company of volunteers. 26-Mr Homan obtained leave to withdraw the papers in relation to the claim of the legal reps of Henry Hoffman, of Md, dec;d, & that the same be referred to the Cmte on Revolutionary Claims.

Letter from the city of Mexico of Jan 26, to the New Orleans Picayune: I am compelled to state the death of Maj Edw Webster, of the Mass volunteers, & youngest son of the Hon Danl Webster. H left his native State as the senior captain of the regt, & was chosen to the post which he held at the time of his death. He was buried on Tue, & the scene at the grave was deeply impressive. His interment here was but temporary, & his remains will be conveyed for the final sepulture to the land of his birth.

The last portrait of the Hon John Quincy Adams, late Ex-Pres of the U S, has been taken from life by our fellow-citizen, Mr Chas Frederich, before the departure of Mr Adams from our city for Boston last spring. The likeness is an admirable one, & can be seen in the Lobby in the House of Reps.

The subscriber announces to his customers & the public in general, that he intends slaughtering a very fine Bear, which he will have on his stall on Sat next, & wishes that they will call & judge for themselves. -Henry Weaver

$25 reward for lost pocket-book. Return the same to the Paint & Glass Store, Pa ave, between 12th & 13th sts. —Geo E Jillard

Valuable farm & water power for sale: 344 acs, at the s e extremity of Chas Co, Md, bounded by the Potomac river on the south, & on the east by the Wicomico river: with a comfortable dwlg-house, kitchen, quarters for servants, & necessary out bldgs.
–Jno Hamersley, Milton Hill P O, Chas Co, Md

Mrd: on Feb 27, by Rev Mr Prettyman, Geo Emmerich to Mary Ellen, daughter of Mr John Smith, all of Wash City.

Died: on Feb 29, Mr Jacob Kengla, in his 33rd year. His funeral is from his late residence, High st, Gtwn, at 9½ o'clock on Thu, whence the corpse will be borne to Trinity Church.

Died: on Feb 27, after an illness of 3 days, [of scarlet fever,] Emma Cornelia, youngest child of John Thomas & Eliza Clements, aged 2 years, 11 months & 11 days.

Died: on Feb 18, in Cincinnati, Mrs Clara Van Hamm, wife of Washington Van Hamm, & daughter of the late Saml N Smallwood, of Washington, aged 31 years.

THU MAR 2, 1848
Senate: Ptn of Manuel Ravens, asking compensation for the schnr **Franciscan**, seized by the U S Marshal at Galveston, & sold for the benefit of the U S.

Household & kitchen furniture at auction: on Mar 4, at the residence of Mr Wm Waugh, on Mass ave, between 6th & 7th sts, [Philip's Row.] -A Green, auctioneer

Died: on Feb 29, at his residence, *Pleasant Hill*, Chas Co, Md, Mr John M Spalding, in his 51st year.

Deaths in the District Regt: letter dated at Jalapa, Mexico, on Jan 20, give a correct list of those who have died in Mexico attached to the D C & Md Regt:
Co A, Capt Degges: Bartlett Gannon, Fred'k Hagadorn, Nicholas Schrack, John H Bean, Peter Finnegan, Capt Fred'k Seizd, Henry Brandy, Sgt Alex'r Berowski.
Co B, Capt Barry: Sgts P Myerhaffer, Chas White, Burrows, Edw Glover, Saulsbury; Cpl Jos Parsons; Pvts Jackson, Deer, Josiah Bean, Rowlett, Myers, Chrisman, Joff, Osbin, Tippett.
Co C, Capt Dolan: Jas Dolan, Benj F Kendig, B F Millis, Wm B Carey, Lemuel Beal, Lewis Roach, Nicholas Schoennewolf, John Richardson, John Snyder, Jos Krantz, missing.
Co D, Capt Henrie: Cpl Jos V Hughes, Auguste Gurner
Co E, Capt Brown: Saml Sliker, Jas Knight, John Kaumick
Co F, Capt Taylor: Wm Johnson, John Roberts, Frank Murray, Edw Thomas, missing, supposed to be killed y the guerrillas.
Co G, Capt Schaeffer: Basil Brown, John Brown
Artl, Capt Tilghman: John Tensfield, Cpl Nicholson, John Baers

At Mobile, on Feb 18, while in a fit of jealousy, Francis Conklin, an engineer, caught his wife by the head, & inflicted a deadly wound with a razor. He cut his throat & expired.

Money lost between Gtwn & the Centre Market-house. Finder will be liberally rewarded by leaving it at Mr Geo Sinclair's, opposite the Centre Market-House.
–Hendrick Mitchell

Died: on Feb 29, in Wash City, Mr Wm Henning, in his 28th year, after an illness of 3 months. His funeral is this afternoon, at 2 o'clock, from his late residence on 6th st, near East Capitol st. [Members of the Eastern Lodge #7 will attend the funeral of our late brother, Wm Henning.]

Died: on Feb 29, at his residence, *Pleasant Hill*, Chas Co, Md, Mr John M Spalding, in his 51st year.

FRI MAR 3, 1848
City Ordinances: 1-Act for the relief of Wm Cooper: to pay him $131.13, in full for the balance of his claim against this corp, for filling up 3,261 square yards on the s w corner of Centre-market space, in Oct, 1844; said work was done at the request of the clerk of said market, & with the knowledge & assent of the Mayor. 2-Act for the relief of Augustus Ross: the fine imposed for an alleged violation in regard to harboring dogs, is remitted: provided Ross pay the cost of prosecution. 3-Act for the relief of John Bohlayer, jr: to be refunded the sum of $5, being the amount of a fine paid by him.

Died: on Mar 1, in Wash City, Maj Satterlee Clarke, of Michigan, formerly a Paymaster in the U S Army, in his 65th year.

Died: on Feb 27, at the residence of his father, Wm S Wilson, near the Cross Roads, Montg Co, Md, Josiah S Wilson, in his 22nd year.

Appointments by the Pres, by & with the advice & consent of the Senate:
Seth B Forwell, Register of the land ofc at Dixon, Ill, vice Geo Mixter, removed.
Geo McHenry, Receiver of Public Moneys at Debuque, Iowa, vice Stephen Langworthy, removed. Geo Jefferies, reappointed Receiver of public moneys at Helena, Arkansas.

House of Reps: 1-Ptn of Moses D Hyams & others, for papers to change the name of the French brig **Bontemps** to **Palmetto**. 2-Ptn of Lewis D Offield, praying compensation for services of his sons, who marched to the place of rendezvous to be mustered into service, after having volunteered, & were not received into service. 3-Ptn of Edw Cole, of Frankfort, Maine, for increase of pension. 4-Ptn of James Co, praying for a pension. 5-Ptn of D Drake Henrie, praying indemnity for property lost & services rendered in the service of the U S in the war with Mexico. 6-Ptn of Sarah Sampson, widow of Peleg Sampson, a Revolutionary soldier, for a pension. 7-Ptn of Linchfield Sharp, praying compensation for services rendered & injuries received in the Indian war in 1793 & 1794, as well as in 1812. 8-Ptn of Priscilla Maxwell, of Charlemont, Mass, daughter of the late Lt Col Hugh Maxwell, of the Revolutionary army, for a pension.

Corp of Gtwn: following gentlemen were elected on Feb 28, for 1848:
Aldermen:
Evan Lyons	Jno Pickrell	Jos Libby
Francis Dodge, sen	Jno Dickson	

Councilmen:
Wm Mck Osborn	Chas E Mix	Robt White
Alex H Dodge	Richd Jones	Wm G Ridgely
Jas C Wilson	Wm D Beall	David English, jr
Bladen Forrest	Jeremiah Orme	

Washington's Birthday: to show that Feb 22 is not, since the year 1800, the true anniversary of the birthday of Wash; that, properly, that event should now be celebrated on the 23rd of the month; & that, consequently, the venerable John Quincy Adams died on the real & true anniversary of the birthday of the Father of his Country. The <u>Christian year</u>, [or Julian year,] arranged as we have shown, was 11' 11" too long, amounting to a day in nearly 129 years; & towards the close of the 16th century, the time of celebrating the Church festivals had advanced 10 days beyond the periods fixed by the Council of Nice in 325. It was in consequence ordered, by a bull of Gregory XIII, that 1582 should consist of only 355 days; which was effected by omitting 10 days in the month of Oct, viz, from the 5th to the 14th; & to prevent the recurrence of a like irregularity, it was also ordered that, in 3 centuries out of 4, that last year should be a common year, instead of a leap-year, as it would have been by the <u>Julian calendar</u>. The year 1600 remained a leap year, but 1700, 1800, & 1900, were to be common years. This amended mode was called the new style, & immediately adopted in all Catholic countries, while, the old style continued to be employed by other Christians. Gradually the new style was employed by Protestants also. The last 10 days of 1699 were omitted by the Protestants of Germany, who, in consequence, began the year 1700 with the new style; & in England the reformed calendar was adopted in 1752 by omitting 11 days, to which the difference between the styles then amounted. The alteration was effected in Sept; the day which would have been the 3rd being called the 14th. The Russians continued to use the old style till 1830, when they adopted the new.

To turn the <u>Old style</u> to the New.
Form the alteration of style to 28th Feb, 1700, add 10 days.
From the 1st Mar, 1700, to 28th Feb, 1800, add 11 days.
From the 1st Mar, 1800, to 28th Feb, 1900, add 12 days.
From the 1st Mar, 1900, to 29th Feb, 2000, add 13 days.
Examples:
The 17th Mar, 1801, O S, is the 29th Mar, 1801, N S
The 19th Feb, 1703, O S, is the 2nd Mar, 1703, N C
The 24th Dec, 1690, O S, is the 3rd Jan, 1691, N S
The 20th Dec, 1829, O S, is the 1st Jan, 1830, N S
Gen Washington was born Feb 11, 1732, before the alteration of the style in England or the Colonies; as during the present century an addition of 12 days is required to reduce the old style to the new; & Feb 23, 1848, was therefore the true anniversary.

Senate: 1-Cmte of Claims: bill for the relief of the heirs of John Paul Jones: recommending a concurrence in the amendment of the House. 2-Cmte on Patents: adverse report on the memorial of Hezekiah L Thistle: ordered to be printed. Same cmte: adverse report on the ptn of Herrick Aiken.

SAT MAR 4, 1848
Senate: Cmte on the Judiciary: asking to be discharged from the further consideration of the ptn of Alex'r Ladd.

Destructive fire at Albany, N Y, on Tue night, & loss of life: a young journeyman printer named Gillespie, of Engine Co #2, & a lad named O'Toole were killed.

House of Reps: 1-Bills referred: relief of the legal reps of Jaques Moulon; of Fernando Fellany; of Peter Enbels, sen; of Mary McRea, widow of Lt Col Wm McRea, late of the U S Army, deceased. Also, bills for the relief of John Black, late U S consul at the city of Mexico. 2-The claims of Chas G Ridgely taken up & amended: & sent to the Senate for concurrence. 3-Bills reported to the House, viz: relief of Calvin Emmons; of E G Smith; of Bent, St Vrain & Co; of J Throckmorton; of Wm Hogan, adm of Michl Hogan, deceased; of the heirs & legal reps of Regnal alias Nick Hilliary; of Jas McAvoy; of Chas Benns; of Wm Ralston; of Nancy Tompkins; of John Mitchell; of David Thomas; of Stephen Champlin; of Geo R Smith, of Mo; of Bennett M Dell; of John Manley; of Sarah Stokes; of Esther Russell; of Stalker & Hill; of Reuben Perry & Thos P Ligon; of Benj White; of Anthony Bessie; of G F de la Roche & W P S Sanger; of Jonathan Moore, of the State of Mass; of Robt Ellis; of Catharine Fulton, of Wash Co, Pa. 4-Senate bills for the relief of the admx of Elisha L Keen, deceased, & providing for the payment of the claim of Walter R Johnson against the U S, were ordered to be reported to the House.

Another Flash from the Lakes: Cincinnati, Mar 1, 1848. The whole line from Buffalo to Detroit by the lake is already completed, & by its means the telegraphic world has enlarged the area of its freedom, thus accomplishing the promise made by Mr O'Reilly. The first dispatch from Detroit to Cincinati was received by Mr O'Reilly about noon today.

Ofcrs attached to the U S frig **Brandywine**, at Rio Janeiro, Jan 15, 1848.
Geo W Storer, Cmdor; Thos Crabbe, Captain. Lts: John A Davis, Luther Stoddard, [Flag Lt,] Saml Larkin, Geo Wells, & John J Guthrie. John S Taylor, Master; Benj F Bache, Fleet Surgeon; John H Terry, Purser; John L Lenhart, Chaplain; Richd T Maxwell, Passed Assist Surgeon; Philip Lansdale, Assist Surgeon; J C Grayson, Lt of Marines; Jacob J Storer, Cmdor's Sec. Passed Midshipman: Jos M Bradford, Thos W Brodhead, W T Truston, T L Walker, S S Bassett, & John T Barrand. J M Wilder, Capt's Clerk; Wm H Parks, Purser's Clerk. Midshipmen: J G Sproston, R T Chapman, Wm Gwin, Chas B Smith, John P Baker, & B E Hand

By order of the Orphans' Court, I shall commence the auction of the valuable & extensive private library of Henry S Fox, deceased, late her Britannic Majesty's Minister to the U S. Sale at my room, 2nd door from 4 ½ st west, Pa ave. –W M Morrison, auct

Mrd: on Mar 2, by Rev Jas B Donelan, Mr Chas L Chapman, of South America, to Miss Anne E Miller, only daughter of C Miller, formerly of Balt.

Mrd: on Mar 2, in Wash City, by Rev Elisha Ballantine, Saml M Parsons, of N Y, to Miss Virginia, only daughter of the late John G Whitwell, of this place.

Died: on Feb 2, at Weverton, Md, Mary Josephine Wever, daughter of Mr C W Wever, in her 18th year, of an affection of the lungs. The was entirely resigned to God's will.

MON MAR 6, 1848
The U S ship of the line **Columbus**, Capt Wyman, bearing the broad pennant of Cmdor Biddle, anchored in Lynhaven Bay on Thu, from a long cruise on the East India & Pacific station, & last from Rio Janeiro-57 days passage. The following are her ofcrs: Cmdor, Jas Biddle; Capt, Thos W Wyman. Lts: Percival Drayton, Henry French, Wm L Maury, Wm Renshaw, Geo W Chapman; Acting Lts: Louis McLane, jr, Madison Rush Fleet Surgeon, Bensjah Ticknor; Passed Assist Surgeon, Chas F Guillow; Assist Surgeon, Danl L Bryan; Purser, Edw T Dunn; Chaplain, J W Newton; Acting Master, J M Wainwright; Prof Mathematics, M Yarnall; Cmdor's Sec, E St C Clarke; Capt's Clerk, Robt Harris; Cmdor's Clerk, J Lewis; Purser's Clerk, Wm H Needles; Cmder's Clerk, John L Keffer. Passed Midshipmen: A J Drake, John C Febiger, Maurice Simons Midshipmen: C W Stevenson, Edw A Seldon, John B Stewart, Chas R Graham, Nicholas H Van Zandt, Jonathan Young, Stephen B Luce, G Harrison, jr, D A McDermut, John G Whitaker, Elliott Johnston, Wm P Toler. Boatswain, V R Hall; Gunner, Thos Robertson; Carpenter, Jonas Dibble; Sailmaker, Robt C Rodman. Marine Ofcrs: Capt, Henry B Tyler; 1st Lt, Wm A T Maddox; 2nd Lt, John C Cash. Passengers: Mrs Morgan & child, Hon Wm Crump, Wm E Dow, Mr Richd Crump, Lt Carter B Poindexter, U S N.
–Norfolk Herald

Senate: 1-Cmte of Claims: adverse report on the memorial of Mary Ann Davis.

Death of a venerable lady. Died, in Balt, on Mar 2, aged 93 years, Mrs Chase, relict of Saml Chase, one of the signers of the Declaration of Independence.

For rent: commodious brick dwlg house & store , 7th & F sts: now occupied by Mrs M A Brereton.

Administration notice: I have taken letters of administration upon the estate of Miss Sally Crook, late of this county. Having settled up the estate, I am prepared to distribute the same to her heirs. She is a native of England, & I believe came from near London. She lived near 20 years in the family of the late Clark Robinson, of this county.
–Henry G Goodloe, Adm, Warren Co, N C

For hire, a colored boy, about 18 years of age, of unexceptionable character, & accustomed to house work. A private family would be preferred.
–Richd Davis, Music Store, Pa ave

For rent: 2 story brick dwlg house on Capitol Hill, recently occupied by Mr Graninger, & near the residence of J H Houston. Apply to J H Houston, or to Jas Larned, 13th st, for the owner.

For rent: 2 story brick house, the residence of Dr Worthington, on Prsopect st, Gtwn. Apply personally or by letter to N W Worthington, Brentwood, near Wash City.

Orphans Court of Wash Co, D C. Letters of administration on the personal estate of Chas King, late of Wash Co, deceased. –Walter S Cox, adm de bonis non

Dr John C Glenn was shot on Feb 7, at Williams' Billard room, Metamoros, by a man with whom he had had some difficulty, & died Feb 15, 1848. Dr Glenn was a man of fine attainments in his profession & his death is much regretted. The person was arrested & put under bonds for $2,000.

The Baton Rouge Gaz announces the death of Maj Saml Vail, a veteran of '14 & '15, aged 72 years. He was a captain during the late war with Great Britain in the 7th Regt of U S Infty, & was present at the battles of Dec 23, 1814, & Jan 8, 1815, where he gallantly did his duty. He died at his residence in East Baton Rouge on Feb 9.

Ira Bennett was found frozen to death in the ditch a few rods west of the depot yesterday, having probably fallen into the water whilst in a state of intoxication.
–Goshen Repub, Fri

Mrd: on Thu last, by Rev Levi R Reese, Geo H McDuell to Sarah Jane, eldest daughter of Wm Morrow, all of Wash City.

Died: yesterday, Mrs Alice Hepburn, in her 87th year. Her funeral is tomorrow at 10 o'clock, from the residence of Mr Jacob Kleiber, at the City Hall.

Died: on Feb 29, at Dayton, Ohio, Thos Jefferson Given, in his 19th year, youngest son of the late Thos Given, of Wash City.

Died: on Feb 26, of consumption, Mrs Mary Barrett, in her 46th year.

Died: on Mar 1, at the Convent of the Visitation in Balt, Sister Mary Agnes Spalding, eldest daughter of the late Zachariah Spalding, of St Mary's Co, Md.

Died: on Mar 4, Henry Jackson, son of the Hon Howell Cobb, of Georgia, aged 3 years, 9 months & 18 days. This is the second visitation of the kind which in a few months has pierced the hearts of the afflicted parents of this interesting child. In the short space of 2 months they have been called to mourn the loss of 2 lovely children.

House of Reps: 1-Ptn of Sarah A Wirt, praying compensation for 2 horses taken during the late war with Great Britain from her late husband for the use of the U S. 2-Ptn of Jas Abeel, asking Congress to increase the pay of military storekeepers. 3-Ptn of John J Young, a cmder in the U S Navy, praying for a pension. 4-Files of the House of the ptn & papers of Jos Brown, of Pa, a soldier of the Revolutionary war, asking arrears of pension: withdrawn. 4-Ptn of Jos J Watson, for an increase of pension.

TUE MAR 7, 1848
Ladies with letters in the Wash Post Ofc, Mar 1, 1848:

Allen, Mrs Eliz	Addams, Mrs Louisa	Bogue, Mrs Eliz
Adam, Miss	Arnold, Mrs S Edw	Ball, Miss Joann
Adams, Mrs Mtt	Aguiel, Miss Lou'a-3	Brooke, Miss E
Adams, Mrs Mary A	Boyd, Miss Eliz	Boswell, Miss Sus'h

Brisco, Miss Jane
Bryant, Mrs Mary
Bayne, Miss M A
Biscoe, Miss Sarah A
Butler, Miss Eliz
Braiden, Miss Eliz
Barton, Miss Char'te
Barrabino, Sar'n N C
Benjamin, Mrs Susan
Clark, Miss Eliz
Cook, Mrs Sarah
Chew, Mrs Charl'te
Clark, Mrs Maria
Clare, Bridget
Cecil, Mrs Emeline
Coventry, widow
Clements, Miss S
Crier, Miss Rebecca
Clifford, Miss Jane
Clifford, Mrs Han'h
Coffin, Miss Sar A H
Carter, Mrs Sarah A
Coxen, Miss Mar'a E
Driggs, Sarah
Dunn, Mrs Sarah
Dickson, Miss Em'a
Ellis, Mrs Mary M
Elliott, Mrs Mary
Evans, Miss M Ann
Ford, Miss Rose C
Franklin, Miss O
French, Miss Rosa C
Fairfield, Miss Eliz
Gibbs, Mrs Mary
Green, Eliz
Graham, Miss M R
Gates, Miss Adeline
Graeve, Mad Julie-2
Howard, Eliza
Holmes, Miss Lou'sa
Huntt, Miss E C
Hazelton, Miss Sarah
Hunton, Miss Amelia
-C K Gardner, P M

Henderson, Mrs Ann
Helevman, Mrs Ann
Handley, Miss Isabel
Juricks, Mrs Susan
Johnston, Mrs E
Johnson, Eliz
Joy, Miss Cornelia C
Jackson, Mrs Aranar
Jackson, Mrs Eliz
Keller, Miss Cornelia
Lee, Miss Lube
Lehman, Miss Paul
Lindsley, Mrs E E
Lewis, Miss Mgt C
Loats, Miss Cath'ne
Moore, Miss Sarah
Myers, Miss Susan
Morton, Mrs A B
Mason, Mrs Mary A
Markland, Ann
Murphy, Miss S L
Moore, Miss Marian
Mahue, Miss Mgt
Middleton, Mrs E R
Miller, Mrs Isabl N
Martin, Miss Cassy A
Middleton, Miss B E
McDonald, Miss A S
Newman, Susannah
Nored, Miss So C
Newton, Matilda
Owen, Mrs Sarah
Page, Mrs Eliza
Perry, Miss Susan
Powers, Mrs Mgt
Padgett, Mrs Hen'ta
Rand, Mrs Mary J
Roucard, Miss
Robinson, Dolly
Richardson, Mary
Roeris, Katharine
Rice, Miss Eliz A
Rogers, Miss Fanny

Roberts, Mrs Ang'e
Robertson, Miss E A
Roberts, Miss Fanny
Smith, Miss Eliz
Smith, Miss Lizzie
Smith, Miss Jane P
Simmes, Miss C
Smith, Miss Nancy
Smith, Miss Mary
Steward, Mrs G A
Sadler, Mrs S A
Sidway, Mrs Jona
Stevenson, Mrs E
Smoot, Miss Aram'a
Smith, Miss Char'te
Smith, Miss Marion
Semmes, Mis M O
Stinchecomb, Mrs S
Stroman, Miss Julia
Stroman, Miss Sarah
Simons, Catharine W
Solomon, Mrs Maria
Spillman, Mrs Mary
Thompson, Mrs L
Tolson, Mrs E B
Thorn, Mrs Mary A
Taylor, Miss Eml'e
Tibbats, Mrs M A
Tyler, Fanny
Vandeveer, Miss J W
Ward, Mrs Nancy
Wear, Miss Ann
Williams, Mrs E
Wilson, Miss M E
Whitney, Mrs H F-2
Wheeler, Mrs M A
West, Miss Cass'dra
Wood, Mrs Sarah F
Williams, Miss M V-2
Weatherburne, Miss Eliz
Wineberger, Miss J E

Senate: 1-Ptn from John Erickson, asking compensation for his services as engineer in planning & superintending the construction of the steam machinery of the U S steamer **Princeton**. 2-Ptn from the heirs of Col Jas Mayson, asking compensation for the services of said Mayson during the Revolutionary war. 3-Ptn from Luke Lea & David Shelton, asking for a grant of land in Mississippi for the purpose of experimenting on turpentine. 4-Ptn from Moses D Hyams & others, asking to be allowed to change the name of the vessel **Roger Bontemps** to **Palmetto**. 5-Ptn from Jas F Haliday & other printers of D C, asking the establishment of a national printing ofc at the seat of Gov't. 6-Cmte of Claims: bill for the relief of Saml Grice.

Died: on Mar 6, Sarah Ann, in her 33rd year, eldest daughter of Seth Hyatt. Her funeral is today, at 11 o'clock, from the residence of her father.

The Chicago Daily Tribune says that David Kennison, one of the survivors of the famous party who made a dish of tea in Boston harbor, is living in that city at the advanced aged of 114 years.

WED MAR 8, 1848
Criminal Court for D C: Hon Judge Crawford, presiding. Grand Jury during the present term: [Amos Holton was admitted an atty of the Court.]

R C Weightman- Foreman	Thos Thornley	Geo Thomas
Lewis Johnson	Geo W Young	John C Rives
Saml McKenney	Geo Sweeny	Jesse E Dow
Edw W Linthicum	Levi Sheriff	Benj f Middleton
Wm Doughty	Geo Watterston	Henry Addison
John Carter	Wm H Gunnell	Wm I Stone
Hamilton Luffborough	John P Ingle	
Robt White	Edw Simms	
	Geo Lowry	

Centre Market: Superior beef of Messrs Walker & Peck, & of Mr Saml Little. Mutton of an extraordinary quality at the stalls of Mr P Otterback & Mr Chas Miller. Mr Jas Rhodes had a ready sale for some superior mutton raised by Mr Carter, Loudoun Co, Va.

Corp of Wash: 1-Cmte of Claims: bill for the relief of John Miller: passed. 2-Ptn from John Skinner: referred to the Cmte of Claims. 3-Cmte on Finance: asking to be discharged from the further consideration of the ptn of Richd Posey: agreed. 4-Act for the relief of John Simmons, & act for the settlement of the claim of A C Kidwell: passed. 5-Ptn of Danl Harkness & others, for improvement of K st north: referred to the Cmte on Improvement. 6-Ptn of Dearborn Johnson & others, praying a modification of the law regulating the renting of fish stalls: referred to the Cmte on Police.

Mrd: on Jul 27 last, in Charleston, S C, by Rev Dr Post, Wm McCullough Forshaw, of Columbia, S C, to Harrietta Anne Grady, formerly of Wash City.

The remains of the late Capt Erastus A Capron, 1st Artl, who fell in the battle of Churubusco, Mexico, were received by the Bremen ship **Mississippi**, at Balt. They were brought to the railroad depot, in Wash City, on Feb 29, from whence they were conveyed to the Congressional Burying Ground, & interred-the funeral service being performed by the Rev S Pyne.

Maj Jos H Stokes, of Dalton, was killed on Feb 19 at Kingston, Ga, on the State Railroad in attempting to gain the car while it was in motion. His foot slipped, & he was caught between the passenger & baggage car, & in this manner was most horribly crushed & killed instantly. He was an old practitioner at the bar in the Cherokee Circuit.

At Indianapolis, on Feb 19, Eleazar Luse, an apprentice of H & E Gaston, coachmakers, was killed by Hiram Gaston, one of the firm. A scuffle ensued over some work of Mr Luse's, & Gaston struck Luse with a hammer on the head. The blow was fatal in a few minutes. Mr Gaston was held to bail.

Passengers in the steamer **Britannia**, from Liverpool for Boston. John Parker & lady, Mrs Bouion, Mr J D Bechtor, Mr McArthur, lady, & son, Mr Bell & lady, Mr Hyman & lady, Mr Simpson, Mr P Groshoby, Capt Wetherall, Thos Carlton, Commissary Gen Pennell, Master C Pennell, Alex Barrowman, Messrs Pardoe, Bulmocke, J Shoumo, jr, H J Ibottson, G L Sammi, J Renard, J Bishop, I M Mayo, jr, Petrie, John Moore, D Wichelhams, Steere, Edw Rogers, M Brooks, F Greenan, J Warburton, J Thompson. In the ship **Ivanhoe**, from N Y for Liverpool: Rev Mr T Ellis, Messrs Geo Merrill, J Heighan, Chas Wilmer, David J Warraner, Miss Sarah Jones.

House of Reps: 1-Cmte of Claims: adverse report on the ptn of Jos R Brown: laid on the table. 2-Cmte on Commerce: bill for the relief of Wm Harding; bill for the relief of Emanuel Berri & John M Keene: committed. 3-Cmte on Public Lands: adverse report on the ptn of Fred'k Hall: laid on the table. 4-Ptn Woodson Wren, of Natchez, Miss, praying for a modification of the post ofc laws increasing the compensation of postmasters.

Public sale of valuable fisheries & land on the Potomac river: by deed of trust from Richd Thompson & wife to Wm Prout, dated Oct 14, 1837, & as substituted trustee in the place of said Prout, deceased, by the decree of the Circuit Court of Fairfax Co, Va, will offer for sale, on Apr 11, all that tract or parcel of land in Fairfax Co, Va, which was purchased by the said Rich Thompson from Thomson F Mason, as trustee of Geo Mason, late of **Gunston**, Fairfax Co, deceased, being part of the **Gunston estate**, binding on the Potomac river, & embracing several valuable fisheries, among which are included Court's Point & Hallowing Point, which tract of land contains 1,081 be the same more or less.
–Cassius F Lee, trustee

Balt, Mar 7. The solemn funeral ceremonies of yesterday over the remains of Ex-Pres Adams were closed this morning by removing the body from the Rotundo of the Exchange to the Railroad Depot, en route for Phil, under charge of the Congressional Cmte & others, who accompanied them. It was a solemn scene.

Died: on Thu last, in Warrenton, Va, Mrs Eliz M, wife of Gen R Wallace. She was a lady of fine intelligence, distinguished for her highly cultivated taste & manners, as she was known for her Christian virtues.

Square & garden for sale: contains over 3 acres of ground, & has all the bldgs necessary for a gardener & laborers: valued at $3,000. Apply to Henry Douglas, Florist & Seedsman, opposite State Dept.

THU MAR 9, 1848
Senate: 1-Cmte on Commerce: bill to change the name of the steamboat **Chas Downing** to the steamboat **Calhoun**, without amendment.

Trustee's sale of house & lot: by deed of trust from Dollar Mullen, dated Sep 30, 1837, recorded in Liber W B 56, folios 421 thru 413, in the land records of Wash Co: sale on Apr 10, of part of lot 1 in square 343, fronting on 10th st-21 feet & 6 inches, by 95 feet in depth, with improvements thereon. -R W Dyer, auct

For rent: dwlg on K st, in Franklin Row, now occupied by Henry Johnson. Possession on Apr 1: rent will be $250. –Wm Orme, corner of E & 10th sts

By 2 writs of fieri facias, public sale, for cash, on East Capitol st, in Wash City, at the house of Jeremiah Kenny, sundry goods & chattels: seized & taken as the property of said Kenny, & will be sold to satisfy one judgment in favor of Middleton & Beall, & one judgment in favor of P H Hooe & Co, & will be sold to satisfy the same.
–Robt T Mills, Constable

Died: on Mar 7, of consumption, Miss Salome Rich, aged 24 years. Her funeral is this afternoon at 3 o'clock, from the McKendree Chapel.

The sloop-of-war **Plymouth**, Cmder Gedney, was expected to sail from Norfolk on Wed. Her destination is the East Indies, & she carries out as passengers the Hon John W Davis, U S Com'r to China, & R Oliver Gibbs, Attache to Legation. List of the ofcrs of the **Plymouth**: Cmder Thos R Gedney; Lts, Thos J Page, Thos T Hunter, Geo W Doty, Ed Donaldson; Acting Master, Gustivus V Fox; Fleet Surgeon for East India station, W S Ruschenberger; Purser, L Warrington, jr; Assist Surgeons, Wm Lowber, Owen Jones Wister; Passed Midshipmen, Clark H Wells, Geo P Welsh, Jno L Davis; Capt's Clerk, Geo R Goldsborough; Acting Midshipmen, Chas L O Hammond, Jas H Rowan, Andrew E K Benham, Chas L Haralson.

A fire at N Y last Sat, which consumed some 8 or 10 bldgs, Wm E G Welsh, aged 50 years, & his 3 children, all perished in the flames of their dwlg. Their mother, Mary Ann Welsh, was so badly burnt that she died the next day. This heartrending catastrophe was the result of a drunken quarrel.

Cmte of Arrangements for the funeral of the late Capt Chas Hanson, 7th Infty, U S A, are to meet on Friday. The remains of Capt Hanson are expected to arrive in Balt within a few days. —John Y Bryant, chrm

FRI MAR 10, 1848
Recently a man named Reed was hung in England, in front of the Castle at York, & thousands came to attend the execution. No execution has had so many spectators, except that of Eugene Aram for the murder of Danl Clark at Knaresborough, which was rendered famous by the polished pen of Bulwer.

Death of Capt Seth Thayer: Boston Journal of Mon: during the passage of his favorite boat on last Tue, Capt Seth Thayer was taken ill & upon landing at Stonington was taken to his residence. His age was not far from 55 years. He was the oldest person who traveled the Sound in the capacity of steamboat captain.

Orphans Court of Wash Co, D C. Letters of administration on the personal estate of Alex'r Begbie, late of London, deceased. —Jos E Nourse, adm

Passed Midshipman Robt Savage, U S Navy, died on Feb 8, at St John's, Porto Rico, after a protracted illness of several months.

House of Reps: 1-Ptn of C Evans, of Pittsburg, Pa, praying Congress to pass a law authorizing the Gov't to purchase his patent-right for the prevention of explosions of steam-boilers. 2-Ptn of John Dearment, of Hollidaysburg, Pa, praying for a law which shall empower the Postmaster Genr'l to make an allowance to Mr Dearment on his contract #1601. 3-Ptn of Fred'k Taylor, of Westmoreland Co, Pa, a soldier in the late war with England, praying for a pension. 4-Ptn of Henry Neely, of Westmoreland Co, Pa, a soldier in the late war with England, praying for a pension. 5-Ptn of Barton Ricketson, asking compensation for removing those wrecks from the harbor formed by the Delaware Breakwater. 6-Ptn of W H Cleveland, J A Talbot, N Holley, J R Nixon, & J Elmer, praying the change of the custom-house from Shieldsborough to Beloxi, Miss. 7-Ptn of D G Garnsey, praying Congress for pay for services during the war with Great Britain. 8-Ptn of Wm Gibson, asking pay for certain property lost while in the service of the U S. 9-Ptn of Jos Jesetr, a captured volunteer, paying relief. 10-Ptn of Jas S McGinnis, of Ross Co, Ohio, praying that he may be paid his account against the U S, for subsistence furnished for 93 men in the 2nd Regt of Ohio volunteers. 11-Cmte on Public Lands: adverse reports on the ptns of Geo F Bloom & Henry S Bloom, & of Martin Sled, Mary King, Tottenger Schnebel, Allen Sink, Jos Porterfield, & Henry Keeton: laid on the table. Same cmte: bill for the relief of John S Conger: committed. 12-Cmte on the Post Ofc & Post Roads, made an adverse report on the ptn of Mary Matthews Nowland: laid on the table. Same cmte: joint resolution for the relief of H M Barney: committed. 13-Cmte on the Judiciary: bill for the relief of Jones & Boker, without amendment: committed. Same cmte: joint resolution for the relief of Alex'r Hunter, marshal of D C: committed. 14-Cmte on Revolutionary Claims: bill for the relief of the legal reps of Capt Saml Jones, deceased: committed. Same cmte: bill for the relief of the legal reps of Jos Savage, deceased: committed. Same cmte: discharged from the further consideration of the ptn of

Wm Champlin: laid on the table. Same cmte: bills for the relief of Geo A Barnitz, husband of Mgt Barnitz, the only surviving heir of Lt Col David Grier, of the army of the Revolution, authorizing the Sec of War to issue a duplicate land warrant #1,469, which originally issued in favor of Adam Hart, Feb 2, 1829; which bills were severally read & committed. Same cmte: adverse report on the ptn of the legal reps of Lt Geo Brent: laid on the table. Same cmte: adverse report on the ptn of Nathan Beard: laid on the table. 15-Cmte on Private Land Claims: adverse report on the ptn of the heirs & legal reps of Wm Marshal: laid on the table. Same cmte: bill for the relief of Sarah D Caldwell, wife of Jas H Bingham; relief of Edna Hickman, wife of Alex'r D Peck; & relief of the heirs of John Wood, deceased: read & referred. Same cmte: bill for the legal reps of Wm McFarland, deceased: committed. 16-Cmte on Military Affairs: discharged from the ptn of Anthony Drane, late a captain of the U S Army: laid on the table. 17-Cmte on Naval Affairs: adverse report on the ptn of Thos Gregg: laid on the table. Same cmte: bill for the relief of John J Young, a cmder in the U S Navy: committed. 18-Cmte on Foreign Affairs: bill for the relief of Wm M Blackford, late charge d'affaires to New Grenada: committed. 19-Cmte on Revolutionary Pensions: bill for the relief of Francis Hutinach: committed. Same cmte: adverse report on the ptn of Dolly Tracy, widow of Solomon Tracy: laid on the table. 20-Cmte on Invalid Pensions: bills for the relief of Fernando Fellany, & for the relief of Peter Engils, sen: committed. Same cmte: bill for the relief of Eliza S Roberts, widow of Lt Moses A Roberts, deceased: committed. Same cmte: adverse reports on the ptns of John Whitmore, Jas Burns, Saml Dickson, & Rachel Salts: laid on the table. Same cmte: bill for the relief of Seth Morton, & for relief of Jos Johnson: committed. 21-Cmte on Patents: bill for the relief of Hamilton Hapham: committed. Same cmte: bill to authorize the Com'r of Patents to renew the patent of Cyrus McCormick for his horizontal plough: committed. 22-Cmte of Claims: bills for the relief of Elijah Milan; relief of Thos P Graham, for the payment of a debt due to the heirs of Antoine Peltier; relief of the heirs of Nicholas Lachance & others: committed. Adverse report on the ptn of Benj Sawyer. Same cmte: adverse reports on the ptns of John Harris, Capt W J Heady, Hiram Hall, & S H Zink: laid on the table. Same cmte: bill for the relief of Christopher H Pix, of Texas: committed. Adverse report on the ptn of Nathl Cox: laid on the table.

The late Capt Stevens T Mason, previous to his departure from Washington for Mexico, deposited or otherwise disposed of several pieces of silver plate; &, as nothing has been heard of them since, it is supposed [if deposited for safekeeping] that they may have been left in charge of one who does not know to whom such information should be given. The subscriber will esteem it a favor, if any person has information, to communicate such to him at Leesburt, Va. -Westwood T Mason, adm of C E Mason, deceased.

Mrd: on Mar 2, Wm J Stewart, of Chas Co, Md, to Miss Maria Supple, of Wash City.

I certify that Henry Miller, of Wash Co, D C, brought before me as an estray a dun colored Horse. -Thos C Donn, J P [Owner is to come forward, prove property, pay charges, & take him away. –Henry Miller, near Beall's bridge]

Criminal Court-Wash:
1-Patrick Magee, convicted of an assault & battery: guilty & fined $10 & costs. 2-Benj Suit & John Shelton: tried for assaulting Wm A Mulloy, a constable in the discharge of his duty: Suit-not guilty; Shelton-guilty. 3-Wm Mulloy, indicted for an assault & battery on John E Brown, was found guilty of the assault. 4-*Mordecai Carpenter & John Martin, indicted for grand larceny: jury had not agreed when the Court adjourned. 5-Henry Smith, free negro, guilty of grand larceny, & recommended to the mercy of the Court. 6-Moses Jennings, free negro, guilty for an assault on Jane E Finnegan. [*Mar 13th newspaper: Carpenter & Martin found guilty: sentenced to one year in the penitentiary.]

SAT MAR 11, 1848
Orphans Court of Wash Co, D C. Letters testamentary on the personal estate of Rebecca Burche, late of said county, deceased. –C H Wiltberger, exc

Furniture & clothing at auction: on Mar 15, at the store of W B Lewis, on Pa ave, between 10th & 11th sts, his entire stock of ready-made clothing; & furniture. -R W Dyer, auct

Wigs, Toupets, Braids, & Curls: Thos Quirk, 490 Broadway, N Y: has arrived to serve all requiring his artistic services in the way of an ornamental head of hair. Apply at his room, over Eagan & Son's store, Pa ave, where he will be found during his stay.

The Treaty of Peace & Cession concluded between the Com'rs of the U S & Mexico, which has been for 2 weeks under debate in the Senate, & was ratified by a vote of 38 yeas to 15 nays.

The following candidates for admission into the Navy as Assit Surgeons were examined & passed by the late Naval Medical Board which was convened in Phil:
*1-Saml H Stout   4-W D Harrison   7-Wm F Carrington
*2-A A F Hill   5-Albert Pearson   8-Chas Martin
*3-Owen Jones Wister   6-John Ward
*Confirmed by the Senate. -Union

Death of a Veteran. Stephen Brown, long & favorably known in Boston, & the country, as a stock & exchange broker, died on Sat last, in his 84th year. He has reported the bank dividends for the last 18 years for the Transcript, & has probably sold more stocks in his day than any other man in New England. –Boston Transcript

Charlestown [Mass] Aurora: Andrew W Oliver, who had his thigh crushed at a stone quarry in Medford, a few days ago, took chloroform for the purpose of having the limb amputated, & died in about an hour, without recovering his senses after inhaling it.

Senate: 1-Cmte of Claims: bill for the relief of Stalker & Hill. 2-Ptn from Wm W Wall, asking to have confirmed the sale of a tract of land in Mississippi. 3-Cmte on Indian Affairs: joint resolution for the relief of H B Gaither.

Mrd: on Mar 9, by Rev Chas A Davis, Mr Jas Westcott to Miss Virginia Lowe, all of Wash City.

Mrd: on Mar 9, by Rev F S Evans, Mr John Walker to Miss Martha A Fraser, daughter of the late Simon Fraser, all of Wash City.

Died: yesterday, suddenly, Mr Richd J Brown, in his 30th year. His funeral is tomorrow at 2 o'clock, from his late residence on 20th st, near F st.

MON MAR 13, 1848

Meeting of the Friends of Ireland, held on Mar 6, for the purpose of taking measures for the celebration of St Patrick's Day, E Stubbs called to the chair & Jas Maguire appointed secretary. Tickets can be procured from the members of the Cmte of Arrangements, viz: Jas Maguire, G Ennis, Wm P Faherty, & W E Stubbs. Also, at the bar of Mr Lakemeyer, & Mr John Foy-at Messrs Brooke & Shillington's bookstore, & at R S Patterson's drug store, until Mar 13. The Dinner will be provided by the Mansion House.

Criminal Court-Wash: 1-Mary Lafontaine, was acquitted by the jury on the indictment grand larceny. 2-Wm Garner, free negro, found guilty of assaulting Geo McNaughten, keeper of the Long Bridge: fined $3 and be imprisoned 10 days in the county jail. 3-Henry Keenan, found guilty of assault & battery on Thos Magill, watchman: fined $2 & 2 weeks in jail 4-Wm Thomas, free negro, was found guilty of assaulting with intent to kill Chas Brown, free negro. The prisoner was sentenced to 4 years in the penitentiary.

In 1753 there died in the s e part of Newton, according to the history of the town, Mrs Davis, at the advanced age of 117 years & 115 days. She buried 3 husbands, had 9 children, & at her death left 45 grandchildren, 200 great grandchildren, & 800 great-great-grandchildren. At age 100 she was able to preforma good day's work on her land. Gov Dudley visited her a few years before her death with a portrait painter, who took her likeness, which is supposed to be now in possession of the Mass Historical Society.

Two boys, aged 15 years each, belonging to the British ship **Speed**, lying in the Savannah harbor, were drowned on Sat week by the upsetting of a boat which was in tow of a steamer. Their names were James Gyles, of London, & F McGuire, of Liverpool.

Jas Sanders lost his life in Augusta, Ga, day before yesterday. He had placed his knife in his pocket, & when he fell from his wagon, the knife penetrated his thigh. Medical aid was called, but he died from the flow of blood in the course of some 8 or 10 hours.

The dwlg house of Mr Wm T Washington, of Jefferson Co, Va, was burnt down on Fri last.

Mr Marshall Johnson, a highly respectable citizen of Rappahannock Co, Va, was accidentally shot about 3 weeks since. Being dressed in a thick coat, he was mistaken for a bear, & fired upon by Mr Madison Fletcher.

Appointments by the Pres, by & with the advice & consent of the Senate.
Collectors of the Customs:
Nicholas Willes, reappointed at Oxford, Md
Wm C Bettincourt, at Wilmington, N C, vice Murphy V Jones, resigned.
Benj Cowell, at Providence, R I, vice Hezekiah Willard, deceased.
Surveyors of Ports:
Chas S Garrett, reappointed at Camden, N J
Thos W Hoye, reappointed at Nottingham, Md
Aloysius Thompson, reappointed at Llewellensburg, Md
Nicholas Tucker, at Marblehead, Mass, vice Benj Wormstead, resigned.
Treadwell L Ireland, at Greenport, N Y [new ofc]
Jacob C Hewlett, at Cold Spring, N Y [new ofc
Land Ofcrs:
Alanson Saltmarsh, Register at Cahaba, Ala, reappointed
Jas M B Tucker, Receiver at Natchitoches, vice Andrew J Isacks, resigned

Household & Kitchen furniture at auction: on Mar 16, at the house lately occupied by Lt Poor, in the Navy Yard. -A Green, auctioneer

Died: on Sat last, Dr Thos P Jones, of Wash City, formerly Superintendent of the Patent Ofc, & Editor of the Franklin Journal of Phil, aged 75 years. His funeral will take place from his late residence on F st, this day, at 4 o'clock.

TUE MAR 14, 1848

House of Reps: 1-The ptn & papers of Mrs Martha Gray, widow of Capt Gray, the discoverer of the Columbia river, taken from the files & referred to the Cmte on Public Lands. 2-Bill introduced: bill for the relief of John B Smith & Simeon Darden: referred to the Cmte of Claims. 3-Bill to refund to the N Y Indians the moneys withheld from them by Janus Stugker, sub-agent appointed for said Indians by the U S: introduced.

Five Mexicans were hung on Jan 19, in the public plaza at Saltillo, by order of Col Hamtramck, of the Va Regt, now in command of Buena Vista. They belonged to a party of guerilias, who had been found guilty of the murder & robbing of 3 discharged soldiers of the Mississippis Regt, who were returning on account of ill health.
–Lynchburg Virginian

Died: on Mar 12, John Hurley, aged 31 years, after a protracted & painful illness, leaving a wife & 2 children to mourn the loss of an affectionate husband & father. His funeral is today at 4 o'clock precisely, from his late residence, on Potomac st, Gtwn.

Died: on Thu, in Wash City, suddenly, though he had been in feeble health for months preceding, Shermont Smith, aged 51 years. He had been for many years employed as a porter & messenger in the Nat'l Intelligencer, & always proved himself faithful & trustworthy.

The extensive printing establishment of Messrs Damrell & Moore, [formerly S N Dickinson's,] on Washington st, Boston, was consumed by fire last Fri.

WED MAR 15, 1848
Found, a small sum of money, which the owner can recover on application to Wm Feeney, 7th st.

Senate: 1-Ptn from Capt Seneca G Simmons, asking to be released from certain liabilities for public money stolen from his possession in Mexico. 2-Ptn from Jos M Merriwether & 125 other citizens of Arkansas in favor of said Merriwether's claim to a pre-emption right. 3-Ptn from H N Depuison, asking payment of a draft drawn by Jas Reeside on the Post Ofc Dept. 4-Cmte on the Post Ofc & Post Roads: bill for the relief of Abel White. 5-Cmte on Finance: bill for the relief of Benj Adams & Co & others, without amendment. 6-Cmte on Finance: bill for the relief of Benj Adams & Co & others, without amendment. 7-Cmte of Claims: report, by resolution, on the ptn of Volney E Howard, & others. Same cmte, a report, by resolution, on the ptn of Isabella Cole, excx of Wm Cole.

Wash Corp: 1-Ptn from John J Joyce: referred to the Cmte of Claims. 2-Ptn from Thos Downey: referred to the Cmte of Claims. 3-Ptn of Richd Eaton, praying remission of a fine: referred to the Cmte of Claims. 4-Ptn of Chas Stewart, praying payment of a balance due him for certain work: referred to the Cmte on Improvement. 5-Cmte of Claims: act for the relief of Seth S Cole: passed. Same cmte: act for the relief of A G Herold: passed. Same cmte: bill for the relief of Albert Hart: passed.

House of Reps: 1-Ptn of John Christie. 2-Ptn of Wm Hudson, Geo W Bennett, David F Karmer, John J R Poole, & others, praying the appointment of a person to grant enrollments & licenses, to reside at Chesapeake city, Md. 3-Ptn of Robt R Emerson & others, citizens of Caroline Co, Md, praying the discontinuance of certain mail routes & establish others.

House of Reps: 1-Cmte of Claims: bill for the relief of Cassius M Clay; & relief of Thos Crown: committed. Same cmte: adverse report upon the ptn of John Hamilton; & the ptn of John Degroot; & ptn of Jarvis Jackson & Jeremiah Rushton: laid on the table. 2-Cmte on Commerce: ptn of Atkins Dyer: laid on the table. 3-Cmte on the Post Ofc & Post Roads: adverse report on the ptn of John Melton: laid on the table. 4-Cmte on the Judiciary: bill for the relief of Geo R Ward: committed. 5-Cmte on Revolutionary Claims: bill for the relief of Joshua Eddy, deceased: committed. 6-Cmte on Naval Affairs: joint resolution for the relief of Saml T Anderson: committed. 7-Cmte on Revolutionary Pensions: adverse reports on the ptns of Mary Woods, Rebecca Bump, Harriet McAlister, & Emily Hoyt: laid on the table. Same cmte: adverse reports on the ptns of Abigail Harris & Eliza Throop: laid on the table. Same cmte: adverse reports on the ptns of David Black, Hannah Hampton, the heirs of David Jewett, Ruth Loomis, Philena Phelps, Thankful Penly, & John Sutherland: laid on the table. 8-Cmte on Invalid Pensions: bill for the relief of Joel Thacker: committed.

From Mexico: A skirmish took place about Feb 18th or 20th, on the road between Vera Cruz & Orizaba, between a detachment of our troops, under command of Col Briscoe, & some 400 Mexican guerillas, at Mitagorda. The guerillas were dispersed, with what loss is not stated; but Lt Henderson & 4 Georgia volunteers were killed in the action. Gen Twiggs, being apprized by express of the interruption to the advance of Col Briscoe's command, sent to his aid several companies, which, not finding him, returned to Vera Cruz.

THU MAR 16, 1848
On Feb 19, at *Fort Smith*, Ark, Saml Edmondson killed Jesse Merritt by shooting him with a pistol. Edmondston was placed in custody.

One Cent Reward: for runaway, Wm H Lusby, on indented apprentice to the Coach Blacksmithing. Reward paid if returned to the subscriber, living on Pa ave, near 3rd st. –Michl McDermott

Cmte of Arrangements will meet at City Hall, on Fri, to make further arrangements for the funeral of the late Capt Hanson. –John Y Bryant, chrmn

Senate: 1-Ptn from Leonard Gray, a soldier of the war of 1812, asking to be allowed a pension. 2-Cmte on Pensions: House bill for the relief of John Manley; House bill for the relief of John Mitchell: both without amendment. 3-Cmte on the Judiciary: bill for the relief of Dawson Schott & ___ Whitney, holders of Texas bonds for vessels furnished to Texas & received by the U S. Same cmte: a resolution respecting the claim of Leslie Combs, a holder of Texas bonds. 4-Cmte of Claims: adverse report on the memorial of the widow & legal reps of Reuben Lassiter. 5-Bill introduced on leave: to pay to Jas Moore the same per diem compensation that is now allowed & paid to the boys assisting the mail carriers of the Senate, he having performed the same duties during the 28th Congress, without compensation. 6-Amendment made by the House of Reps to the bill for the relief of the heirs John Paul Jones: concurred in.

House of Reps: 1-Cmte on Invalid Pensions: bill for the relief of John Knight; bill for the relief of Thos Flanagan: committed. 2-Resolved: that the papers in the Pension Ofc relating the application of Tilly Hamilton & Carty Burnham for pensions, be taken from said ofc & referred to the Cmte on Revolutionary Pensions. 3-Cmte of Claims: discharged from the consideration of the ptn of Sam J Bayard, late receiver at Fairfield, Iowa: laid on the table. Same Cmte: adverse reports on the ptn of Levi Seakly; of John Walker; of Benj Perham, of Harry Richardson, of Darcus Jewell, of Jacob Yerty, & of Jos Hall: laid on the table. 4-Cmte of Claims: discharged from the consideration of the bill for the relief of N C Orear; also, the ptn of Peleg B Phelps, of La; also, from the resolution of the House of Jan 21st last, in relation to the expediency of paying to the ofcrs & seamen who, in 1804, volunteered under Capt Stephen Decatur to recapture or destroy the frig **Philadelphia**, then lying in the habor of Tripoli: laid on the table. 5-Cmte on Naval Affairs: discharged from the consideration of the ptns of H S Stellwagen & Wm R Ashards: laid on the table. 6-Cmte of Claims: bill for the relief of the legal reps of Geo W Milam: committed.

Death of 2 eminent citizens: Ambrose Spencer died at Lyons, N Y, on Monday; the Hon Henry Wheaton died at Roxbury, Mass, on Sat. Mr Wheaton returned not long ago from a diplomatic residence of many years in Europe, his last post of duty having been the capital of Prussia. The death of Chief Justice Spencer was not unexpected. He achieved a long term of eminent & useful service. [Mar 18th newspaper: Mr Wheaton was born in Providence in Nov, 1785; entered Brown Univ in 1798, & graduated in 1802 in the class with Henry Bowen, John Whipple, & Richd Waterman. He studied law in the ofc of Nathl Searle, & in 1804, while yet a student of law, went to France, where he engaged in the study of the French language & literature; on his return to R I he was admitted to the bar. In 1812 he removed to N Y, & became the editor of the Nat'l Advocate. In 1827 he was appointed by John Quincy Adams Charge d'Affaires to Copenhagen. In 1836 he was transferred to Berlin, & in 1837 raised to the rank of Minister Pleniplotentiary. In Prussia his services were long & eminent.]

Appointments by the Pres: by & with the advice & consent of the Senate:
Ambrose H Sevier, of the State of Arkansas, to be U S Com'r, with the rank of envoy extraordinary & minister plenipotentiary, to the Mexican republic.
Robt M Walsh, of the State of Pa, to be sec of the legation of the U S to the Mexican republic.

At a Military Review [of volunteer corps] at Charleston, S C, on Fri last Col Blum's horse reared & fell with him, by which he sustained some injury, though not seriously, by a fracture of his collar bone; & a member of one of the German companies, being also thrown from his horse, was so seriously hurt that he died on the following morning.

The ship **Arcole** & the ship **M Howes** sailed from N Y on Sat for Verz Cruz, with a btln of U S Marines, consisting of 360, rank & file, under command of Maj John Harris. List of the ofcrs attached to the btln: Maj John Harris, Commanding; Capt, N S Waldron; 1st Lt Josiah Watson; 1st Lt A S Taylor, Adj; 1st Lt W L Shuttleworth, A A Quartermaster; 2nd Lt ___ Jonas; 2nd Lt Geo R Lindsay; 2nd Lt Geo R Graham; 2nd Lt J R F Tatnall; 2nd Lt J L Broom; 2nd Lt W Stokes Boyd. Medical ofcrs: Surgeon, D S Edwards; Assist Surgeon, ___ Oakley.

Randall Hutchinson, the absconding defaulter to the U S Mint in Phil, returned to that city on Mon, & was immediately committed to jail in default of $28,000 bail. [Apr 21st newspaper: Court decided that, being merely a clerk, the acts of Congress against embezzlement did not extend to him. Indictment could not be sustained, & a nol pros was entered by the district atty.]

Passengers by the steamship **New Orleans**: Lt Isaac Wallace, Ga mounted volunteers; Lt John Donan, 4th Ky vols; Lt Wm D Gray, 13th Infty; Capt G A Buel, 1st Regt Michigan volunteers; Dr John Battee, U S A; Dr Wm S Patten, U S A; & Lt R W Young, 3rd Infty.

The house of Mr Wm White, at Old Tavern, Henrico Co, Va, was entered on Sat night, & he himself murdered with an axe, & Mrs White left insensible on the floor. Doubtful whether she will ever recover. The murderer then robbed the house. He has not been apprended as yet.

Petersburg [Va] Mar 15, 1848. Dandridge Epes, the murderer of Adolphus Muir, arrived today in this place from Texas, where he had been arrested. He was committed in Dinwiddie Co some 18 months ago, & is one of the most atrocious on record.

Died: on Feb 28, at Warsaw, Trenton Co, Missouri, of congestive fever, Mary Jane Rosell Handy, consort of Rev Isaac W K Handy, & daughter of Moses Purnell, of Worcester Co, Md.

New 2 story frame house & lot at auction: on Mar 19, part of lot 2 in square 246, fronting 20 feet on M st north, & running back to Mass ave. It is nearly in front of the residence of Mr C L Coltman, between 13th & 14th sts. -A Green, auctioneer

FRI MAR, 17, 1848
Criminal Court-Wash: the case of the U S vs Gaspard Tochman, charged with sending a challenge to fight a duel.

City Ordinances-Wash: 1-Act for the relief of Ignatius Howe, police ofcr of the 6th Ward: to be paid $40.50, being the balance due him for workhouse & other fees up to Jun 30, 1847. 2-Act for the relief of John Simmons: to pay him $6.50, to make good a deficiency in the appropriabion made by the act of May 28, 1847. 3-Act for the payment of the claim of A C Kidwell: to pay him the sum of $19.72, being a balance due him for laying a footway across N Y ave, & 15th st. 4-Act for the relief of Thos McDonnell: fine imposed in relation to obstructing streets & alleys: remitted. Provided he pay the costs of prosecution.

Trustee's sale of valuable furniture at auction: on Mar 20, by deed of trust from Cranstoun Laurie to Geo Barker, dated Nov 25, 1846, recorded in Liber W B #129, folios 496 thru 500, in the land records for Wash Co, D C, on north B st, between Delaware ave & 1st st east: desirable furniture. –Geo Barker, trustee -R M & B Milburn, aucts

Senate: 1-Ptn from Jas G Carson, asking confirmation of his land title. 2-Ptn from Lewis Kinchy & Henry Gaither & Co, asking to be allowed to erect sawmills on a certain tract of land belonging to the U S in Florida. 3-Resolved: that the Pres of the U S be requested to transmit to the Senate a copy of "a dispatch to the U S Consul at Monterey, T O Larkin, " forwarded in Nov, 1845, by Capt Gillespie, of the Marine corps, & which was by him destroyed before entering the port of Vera Cruz.

House of Reps: 1-Gen H A S Dearborn was on Monday re-elected Mayor of the city of Roxbury, in Mass.

The Phil Ledger says it has seen the original of the following curious paper: "My sweetheart as well as myself desire that thou wilt favor us with thy company at our marriage, which is intended to be at Burlington, the 4th of next month. I am thy respectful friend, Aaron Ashbridge. Oct 19, 1746"

Died: on Mar 10, at Fairview, King Geo Co, Va, after a short & painful illness, Dr Austin Smith, aged 44 years.

Thos S Ferral, living near Bladensburg, will sell 150 acres of prime land, being part of the farm on which he lives, at private sale, at any time between Mar 15 & Apr 30. Land is within 6 miles of Washington.

SAT MAR 18, 1848
Senate: 1-Cmte on Pensions: reported a bill for the relief of Sarah Stokes, widow of John Stokes. 2-Cmte of Claims: reported a bill for the relief of Chas M Gibson.

The Whigs of Pa: the following were nominated as Pres Electors in the various districts of the State, [embracing all of them except the 15th & 23rd, which are yet vacant.]

Jos G Clarkson	Jos K Schmucker	Thos R Davidson
John P Wetherill	Chas Snyder	Jos Markle
Jas M Davis	Wm G Hurley	John Allison
Thos W Duffield	Francis Tyler	A W Loomis
Danl O Hitner	Henry Johnson	Richd Irvine
Joshua Dungan	Wm Colder, sen	Saml A Purviance
John D Steele	Chas W Fisher	
John Landis	Andrew G Curtin	

A Cast-Steel Factory is projected at Jersey city to pursue the process recently invented by Mr Jos Dixon: use of the black lead crucibles of the inventor's own make, & anthracite coal instead of coke, which is used exclusively in Europe, with clay crucibles. Mr Dixon has also succeded in making pure iron in masses of any magnitude, a result never before effected.

Chief Justice Spencer died at Lyons on Mar 13, at the advanced age of 83. He was a bold & sagacious advocate & supporter of Madison & the war of 1812, opposing the claim of his brother-in-law, DeWitt Clinton, to the Presidency. One of his sons, Capt Ambrose Spencer, died bravely fighting for his country at the battle near Niagara Falls. Another of them, John C Spencer, who has since been member of Congress, Sec of State, & Speaker of Assembly in this state, & Sec of War, & of the Treasury in the U S, was an aid-de-camp to Gov Tompkins during the struggle. After the war, Judge Spencer & Gov'r Clinton were reconciled. We have heard that his first wife, the mother of John C & Ambrose Spencer, jr, was a native of Connecticut; he afterward married twice, & each time to a niece of Govn'r Geo Clinton & sister of DeWitt Clinton. In person he was tall & good-looking.

Groceries & furniture at auction: on Mar 22, at the store & residence of Mr Pancost, on north B st, Capitol Hill, in the rear of Mr Dowson's bldgs. -A Green, auctioneer

The funeral of Capt Chas K Hawson will be on Monday next, at 12 o'clock, at Trinity Church, with burial in the Congressional Burial Ground. The procession will move from 5th & La ave to the intersection of 7th st & Pa ave, thence to the Burial Ground. Messrs B B French & Jas Scott will act as Assist Marshals.

MON MAR 20, 1848

Died: on Mar 19, John Marshall Black, formerly of Frankfort, Ky, but for the last 7 years a resident of Wash City, leaving an affection wife & 2 small children to mourn his loss. His funeral will take place from the residence of his father-in-law, Isaac H Wailes, at 2:30 p m today. [Frankfort, Ky papers please copy.]

Paris, Thursday [By Telegraph.] Louis Philippe has abdicated in favor of his grandson, the Count de Paris, infant son of the late Duke of Orleans.

Appointment by the Pres: Nathan Clifford, to be Associate Com'r to Mexico, with the powers of Envoy Extraordinary & Minister Plenipotentiary.

Mr Custis, of Arlington, has presented to his son-in-law, Capt R E Lee, of the U S Engineers, [an ofcr whose brilliant services in the Mexican war have elicited the praise of all the Generals,] a sword, with the following inscriptions: "The gift of General Washington to George W P Custis, 10th of January, 1799." "Presented by George W P Custis to Capt Robert E Lee, U S A, on 22nd February, 1848." The ancient sabre is peculiarly venerable, from its being the only sword that Washington ever presented in his lifetime, & with his own hand, to a human being. When presented by the Chief to his adopted son, [then an ofcr of cavalry,] in 1799, it was attended with this injunction: "This sword, sir, you are never to draw but in a just cause, or in defence of your country." The Washington Sabre will remain a short time at Mr Keyworth's, who is executing the inscription.

TUE MAR 21, 1848

Senate: 1-Ptn from E P Hastings, asking compensation for his services as pension agent in the State of Michigan. 2-Cmte on Naval Affairs: bill for the relief of David Myerlee, accompanied by a report. 3-Cmte on Pensions: bill for the relief of the heirs of Moses White, accompanied by a report. 4-Cmte of Claims: bill for the relief of D A Watterston, accompanied by a report. Same cmte: bill for the relief of Columbus Alexander & Theodore Barnard. 5-Cmte on Private Land Claims: House bill for the relief of Chas Cappel, without amendment. Same cmte: bill for the relief of the heirs of John Wall, accompanied by a report.

Died: on Mar 19, in Wash City, Mrs Mary King, widow of the late Ezekiel King, aged 86 years. Her funeral is today at 3 p m, at the F st [Rev Dr Laurie's] Presbyterian Church. The friends of the family, & those of Lt Col Hunt, of the Army, are respectfull invited to attend, without further notice.

Funeral of Capt Chas Hanson: on Mar 20, 1848, in Wash City. The coffin of Capt Hanson was covered with dark blue velvet, & edged with silver lace. Two eagles of silver were on each side of it. The silver breastplate bore the following inscription: Captain Charles Hanson, 7th Infantry.
Born March 16, 1818.
Killed on the 19th day of August, 1847, at Contreras, Mexico.
In the languarge of the Commander-in-chief,
He was "not more distinguished for his gallantry than for modesty, morals, & piety."
The superb funeral car, manufactured by Mr J F Harvey, under the superintendence of Mr M W Winter, was canopied & covered with black velvet: on the canopy was a spread eagle shrouded with crape. The American flag was gracefully folded on each side of the car.

House of Reps: 1-Mr Tweedy, by leave, introduced a bill, of which previous notice was given, viz: A bill for the admission of the State of Wisconsin into the Union: referred to the Cmte on the Territories.

Mrd: on Sabbath afternoon, by Rev John C Smith, Mr Jas A Riddle, of Balt, to Miss Ellen Scanlon, of Wash City.

Died: on Mar 15, in Warrenton, Va, after a short illness, Miss Janet Henderson, in her 73rd year. She was the eldest daughter of the late Alex'r Henderson, a resident of Dumfries, but for some years a highly respected resident of Warrenton.

Groceries, liquors, & shoes at auction: on Mar 27, at the Grocery Store of Mr S Brereton, corner of 7th & F sts, immediately opposite the Patent Ofc. –A Green, auctioneer

WED MAR 22, 1848
Senate: 1-Ptn from John Needles & others, citizens of Balt, in favor of the abolishment of the slave-trade in D C. 2-Ptn from Sarah Tyler, of Vt, widow of a Revolutionary ofcr, asking an increase of pension. 3-Ptn from John P Howard, offering to run a line of first class ocean steam ships between N Y & Marseilles for the same compensation & under the same restrictions as are contained in the contracts with the Southampton & Bremen & N Y & Liverpool lines. 4-Cmte of Claims: House bill for the relief of the heirs of Matthew Stewart: without amendment. Also, House bill for the relief of John Anderson: without amendment. Also, House bill for the relief of Wm Culver, without amendment, each bill accompanied by a report.

Wishing to close my business, I offer for sale the property on the corner of 11th & F sts west, being lot 1 in square 320, containing a 2 story frame store-house, with a 2 story brick dwlg adjoining, running back 75 feet to German Hall. Also, a 2 story brick, with basement & attic, finished complete, fronting 17 feet on F st. Inquire of the subscriber, on the premises. –A Carothers

The venerable Dr Strans, of N Y, died on Sat, after an illness of 2 weeks, caused by the absorption of virus while probing a mortified limb.

Passengers in the steamship **Cambria**, at N Y from Liverpool: Mr D Grimeke, Mrs Grimeke, Mr Strong, Mrs Strong, Mr R M Hoe, Mr Delius, 5 children, & servant; Augustus Delius, lady, & child; Mrs Wallack, S B Chittenden, lady, 2 children, & servant; Miss Chittenden, Robt Gillow, Mr Broadbent, Mons Cailleux, jr, Jas Turner, Mr Plate, Mr Nottbeck, Mr Colville, Mr Gray, Mr W Taylor, Mrs D W Coxe, Mr Marias, Mr McLean, Mr Dodge, Mrs C L Bartlett, Mr Ramsden, F Ramsden, J C Karouse, G Jackson, Mr P Bousefard, Lt Hallowell, Mr Shewerman, Mr Schult, Mr Grossman, G M Porter, Mr Klemm, Jas Hudson, Mr Coggill, L Gugniard, J Potsdamm, Mr Consilvi, J W Macomdry, H Casement, Mr Casement, W Smith, Mr Manifold, Mr Illins, & 5 in the steerage.

Mr John Cook, jr, of Winchendon, was arrested on Monday of last week, on a warrant from Justice Phillips, of Fitchburg, charging him with the murder of his wife, in 1834, by administering arsenic. The body was kept in a tomb & has continued in a remarkable state of preservation. The remains of the stomach & bowels were brought to Boston by Dr Alfred Hitchcock, of Ashby, & a chemical analysis was made by Prof Webster, at the Medical College, who obtained 4 or 5 grains of arsenic, as testified before the magistrate. The prisoner was committed to take his trial at the next term. –Boston Atlas

Mrd: on Feb 29, by Rev W P Saunders, Shepherd Laurie, M D, of Little Rock, Ark, son of the Rev Dr Laurie, of Wash City, to Miss Corinne J Fournier, of Demopolis, Alabama.

Mrd: on Mar 16, in Wash City, by Rev Mr Van Horseigh, Mr Alex'r More, of Belleville, Ill, to Miss Sarah Duncan, daughter of Wm Duncan, of Wash City.

House of Reps: 1-Ptn of Wm H Russell, late marshal of the district of Missouri, for an act of relief. 2-Memorial of Jas S Abeel, S Lansing, Edw Ingersoll & others, praying for adequate compensation to military storekeepers. 3-Memorial of Chas Findlay, praying that a draft drawn by the Shawnee Indians in favor of the Superintendent of Indian affairs at St Louis be paid. 4-Ptn & other papers of Geo S Chaflin, a sgt in the last war with Great Britain, showing hardship & consequent loss of health, & asking for compensation & relief. 5-Ptn of Valentine Miller, of Monroe Co, Va, praying for a pension. 6-Memorial of Maurice K Simons, of the commissariat dept, Mexico, but who was engaged in several battles & lost a leg in consequence of a severe wound, praying for a pension. 7-Ptn of Chas C Jell. 8-Memorial of John F McCoy & others, on the part of the old settler-party of Cherokee Indians, praying relief. 8-Ptn to have the memorial & papers of John Burke withdrawn from the files of the House. 9-Ptn of Job Chase & 421 others, for light-house or light-boat on Kill Pond bar near Monomoy, Capt Cod. 10-Memorial of Wm & Richd H Reedin for indemnity for property destroyed in the war of 1812. 11-Affidavit of Jas Sloan, of Black Rock, N Y, in support of his claim to prize money for his services in taking the ships **Caledonia** & **Detroit** in the war of 1812.

Orphans Court of Wash Co, D C. In the case of John F Ennis, adm de bonis non, with the will annexed, of Bernard Kelley, deceased: the administrator & Court have appointed Apr 11 next for final settlement of the estate. –Edw N Roach, Reg/o wills

Orphans Court of Wash Co, D C. In the case of Christopher Cammack, adm of Mary A Cooper, deceased: the administrator & Court have appointed Apr 11 next for final settlement of the estate. –Edw N Roach, Reg/o wills

THU MAR 23, 1848
By virtue of 5 writs of venditioni exponas, I will expose to sale, at public auction, on the premises, on Mar 24, 1848, for cash, the north half of lot 15 in square 878, with a frame dwlg-house thereon, in Wash City, late the property of Theodore B Acton. Taken in execution at the suits of Zadock Williams, Martin King, Dennis Callaghan, Christian Lederin, & John Pic. –H R Maryman, Constable

Lands in Hardy Co, Va, for sale, at Public sale, under a decree of the circuit Superior Court of Law & Chancery for Hardy Co, Va, pronounced on Sep 22, 1844, in the case of Norman Bruce, cmplnt, against the Potomac & Alleghany Coal & Iron Manufacturing Co, dfndnts: sale before the Court-house in Moorefield, in Hardy Co, Va. 400 acres on the east side of Stony river; 413 on Elk run; 400 s w side of Elk run; 400 acres near *Welton Glade*; 817 acres on *Difficult creek*; 684 acs known as *Slate Cabin Tract*; 2,005 acs near *Big Elk Lick*, of F & W Deakin's lands; 1,001 acs known as the *Buffalo Tract*, whereon Spencer Hendrickson now resides; 140 acres known as *Benj Ray Tract*; 1,740 acres: 200 excepted-being sold to Wm Shillingburg: on *Jonnycake creek*; 2,695 acres: 108 acres excepted-sold to Alex'r Smith, by deed Feb 3, 1817. Land conveyed by F & W Deakins to John Templeman, by said Templeman to Bruce, & by Bruce to the dfndnts in this decree. For more particulars refer to Wm Seymour, atty for plntf, or to Jos McNemar, my deputy, Moorefield, who are so authorized to give information.
–John G Harness, Sheriff of Hardy Co, Va

Valuable property for sale in Gtwn, D C: public auction on Apr 20, on Gay st, 2 lots south of R Dicks, & adjoining Dr J Riley's, fronting 75 feet on Gay st, with a 2 story dwlg house, a 3 story back bldg attached, & a brick smoke-house on one lot & a frame bldg on the other lot. –Edw S Wright, auctioneer

Gustavus B Alexander offers for sale about 30 acres of land, in Alexandria Co, 4 miles from Wash. The land is n w of the Columbian Factory, & adjoins the lands of Messrs Bronaugh, Fairfax, & others. Inquire of Messrs Swann & Swann, 5th st, near the City Hall. –G B Alexander

Appointments by the Pres, by & with the advice & consent of the Senate.
Bion Bradbury, Collector of the Customs for the district of Passamaquoddy, Maine, reappointed. Thos Stewart, Appraiser of Merchandise at Phil, vice Chas Francis Breuil, deceased.

Md Reformer, [Rockville,] reports the death of Mrs Sage, an aged & worthy lady, who, on returning home from a neighbor's house, on Mon week, fell into a stream & was found frozen to death the next day.

Senate: 1-Ptn from Cadwalader Evans, asking Gov't to purchase his patent for preventing explosions of steam boilers. 2-Ptn from Rebecca Robeson, widow of a Revolutionary ofcr, for a pension. 3-Ptn from D B Thuckley & others, for a modification of the patent laws. 4-Ptn from Nathan Cummings & other Citizens of Maine, asking relief. They state that under the treaty their lands had been declared in the province of New Brunswick, & they ask that Gov't will either pay them for their lands or exempt them from the colonial duties & remit the import duties. 5-Ptn from Wm Rall, asking a pension for services during the Revolutionary war. 6-Cmte on Patents: House bill for the relief of E G Smith: without amendment. 7-Cmte on Pensions: following House bills, without amendment: bill for the relief of Catharine Fulton, of Wash Co, Pa; of Jonathan Moore, of Massachusetts; of Robt Ellis; & of Mary Taylor-with a report.

Dr Sumner has been chosen Primate of England, to succeed the Archbishop of Canterbury, whose death has been already announced.

Monument to the Memory of Alex'r Barrow: made by Mr Maples, of Phil, to be placed over the grave of the lamented Barrow, late U S Senator from Louisiana: 12 feet high, being 4 feet broad at its base; inscription:
TO THE MEMORY OF
ALEXANDER BARROW.
He was born in the State of Tennessee, on the 27th day of March, 1801, & died in Baltimore on the 29th of December, 1846, being, at the time, a Senator in Congress from the State of Louisiana, of which he had been a citizen for twenty-five years.

Memphis, Tenn, Mar 9-during the noon adjournment Judge E W M King, presiding Judge, furiously assaulted, with a pistol & cane, C Irving, junior editor of the Enquirer, for an article published in the Enquirer of that morning, censuring Judge King's conduct & interference at the corporation & county election polls on Sat last. Judge King discharged three barrels of a revolving pistol, one of which lodged in the surface of Mr Irving's wrist & another striking the hand of Mr Dashiell, the hotel-keeper. Mr Irving is a small weakly man, & the Judge a stout six-footer & over. -Eagle

Movement of Troops. The transport ship **Christiana** sailed from N Y for Vera Cruz on Sat, carrying out a detachment of troops from **Fort Columbus**, under orders to join the army in Mexico. The detachment numbers 290 men. They were accompanied by the following ofcrs: Col A C Ramsay, 11th Infty, commanding; Capt C S Merchant, 3rd Artl, as passenger; 1st Lt P D Wallen, commanding Co I, 4th Infty; 1st Lt J J F Quimby, 3rd Artl, A C S, commanding Co D, 4th Infty; 1st Lt J W M Lane, mounted rifles, commanding Co I, 3rd Infty; 1st Lt J A Grove, 9th Infty; 2nd Lt G T Shackelford, 6th Infty; 2nd Lt J Bedell, 9th Infty; 2nd Lt W Schoonover, 11th Infty; & Acting Assist Surgeon, J Hewitt, U S Army.

FRI MAR 24, 1848
Mrd: on Mar 21, in Wash City, by Rev L J Gilliss, Mr John White to Miss Mary White, both of Montgomery Co, Md.

Wash Corp: 1-Ptn from John H Plant: referred to the Cmte of Claims. 2-Ptn from Wm C Riddall: referred to the Cmte of Claims. 3-Bill for the relief of Mrs M A Daly: passed. 4-Ptn from Jas Crutchett: referred to the Cmte of Claims. 5-Acts for the relief of Seth L Cole; of Albert Hart; & of Michl Keller: referred to the Cmte of Claims. 6-Ptn of Benedict Jarboe & others, for improvement of 4th st east: referred to the Cmte on Improvements. 7-Cmte of Claims: asking to be discharged from the further consideration of the ptn of Chas Middleton: agreed. 8-Cmte of Claims: bill for the relief of Moses Lazarus: indefinitely postponed.

House of Reps: 1-Ptn of Richd Pattison praying the passage of a special act allowing him a land warrant. 2-Ptn of Jos M Rhea, asking an increase of the pension he now receives, said pension to commence in 1837. 3-Ptn of Wm A Whitely, Andrew White, & 69 others, praying for a post route in Lousiana.

Died: on Mar 23, in Wash City, after a short illness of congestion of the lungs, Abraham, aged 10 months, youngest child of the Hon John Van Dyke, member of the House of Reps from N J.

Balt Conference of the Methodist Episcopal Church closed on Wed: list of appointments:
Wm Hamilton, Presiding Elder of Potomac District
Alexandria: J M Jones, J W Hoover, D Steele, supernumerary
Foundry & Asbury: J Lanahan, M A Turner, P Doll, sup
Wesley Chapel: Littleton F Morgan
McKendree Chapel: T M Reese
Ebenezer: Wm Prettyman, J M Hanson, sup
Ryland Chapel: Wm H Pitcher
Union Chapel: E F Busey
Gtwn: H Slicer & Wm H Wilson
Leesburg: Job Guest
Farifax: M G Hamilton & J W Kelly
Bladensburg: Thos McGee & E McCollum
Montgomery: Wm Hank & W H Chapman
Rockville: D E Thomas, C G Linthicum, Basil Barry, sup

Mr Rade, manufacturer & vender of Hemoeopathic medicines, residing in 4th st, Phil, was found yesterday, in his bedroom, stabbed & cut in fully 20 pieces, & in the agonies of death. Mrs Rade, wife of the unfortunate victim, was found in the same room with her husband, entirely dead, having been literally hacked & cut to pieces. No clue has yet been had to the perpetrators of this horrid crime.

Senate: 1-Ptn from John H Harris, late deputy collector of the port of Providence, R I, asking compensation for his services. 2-Ptn from Sarah Hubbard, asking compensation for property destroyed by the enemy during the late war with Great Britain. 3-Ptn from Sarah Beddinger, widow of a Revolutionary soldier, for a pension. 4-Cmte on Indian Affairs: asking to be discharged from the further consideration of the ptn of Jos Newell. 5-Bill introduced for the relief of Col Robt Wallace, aid-de-camp of Gen Wm Hull.

Jos Foster. Any person who will be kind enough to give information of the residence of this individual to the undersigned will be suitably rewarded. He is supposed to reside in Va, about 13 miles from Wash, probably in Fairfax, in the neighborhood of Prince Wm. He is a small man of dark complexion, with large whiskers, using large spurs when on horseback, & he is a farmer; or such was his appearance about 11 months ago, when last at our store. –T M & B Milburn, Aucts, 7th st, opposite Gales & Seaton's

SAT MAR 25, 1848
Wm Noell informs he is prepared to fill any orders in his line, of Venetian Blinds; wide Curtain paper; fire-board prints & paper screens; painted shades put up; & curled hair, moss, & shuck mattresses. Blind Depot, #1, south side, Pa ave, between 9th & 10th sts, Wash, D C.

Senate: 1-Ptn from Boston Starrit & other Cherokee Indians, asking the appointment of a board of com'rs for the investigation of Cherokee claims.

House of Reps: 1-Bills laid aside to be reported to the House-relief of: [All bills were passed.]

Zalpha White	Fred'k Durrive	Marcus Fulton	Saml Coney
Thos Badger	Elisha	Johnson	Wm P Brady
B O Taylor	Thomason	Jos Bryan	Wm S Holland
Medford Caffey	Jas P Sexton	Jonathan	John Morgan
G DeLirac	Wm Triplet	Fitzwater	Gideon Walker
Chas Waldron	Simon	Sarah Hildreth	heirs of Wm
Elijah H Willis	Rodriguesx	Wm Pool	Evans
Jas B Davenport		Aaron Tucker	

Dr A G Henry, of Ill
John B Rogers, of S C
legal reps of Jas Porterfield, deceased
heirs & widow of Francois Gramillon
Col Robt Wallace, aid-de-camp to Gen Wm Hull
legal reps of David Gardner, of Southboro, Mass
Archibald Bull & Lemuel S Finch
legal reps of Wm McKenzie, late a seaman on board the U S ship **Vincennes**
To confirm Eliz Burris, her heirs, or assigns in their tract of land
Joint resolution concerning the settlement of the accounts of Wm Speiden, purser in the U S Navy
Senate bill in addition to an act for the relief of Abel Gay & Walter Loomis, approved Jul 2, 1836.
2-Bill for the relief of Hervey Jones was amended by adding thereto the words, "during his natural life."-passed. 3-Bill to provide compensation to Saml Leech for services in the investigation of suspended sales in the Mineral Point district, Wisc: passed. 4-Bill providing payment of arrearages of pension to Anthony Walton Bayard: passed, & sent to the Senate for concurrence.

American claims in Europe: to persons having claims in Great Britain, Ireland, France, or Holland: a gentleman of much experience, who has resided in Balt nearly 40 years, intends embarking for Europe early in May next, & offers his services in the prosecution of any claims onpersons or estates. Apply to Neilson Poe, late Com'r of Insolvent Debtors, Law Bldgs, St Paul's st, Balt, Md.

Jesse E Dow, Notary Public & Genr'l Agent: ofc #3 Union Bldgs, Wash, D C.

An old citizen of N Y died a few days ago, having been for some time quite ill from pleurisy. Mr Elam Bliss, formerly of the house of Hastings, Etheredge, & Bliss, booksellers, at Boston, & afterwards of the firm of Bliss & White, for many years in N Y. His house was the publisher of many popular works.

Clothing & fancy articles at auction: on Tue next, at the clothing store of Mr Thos King, on Pa ave, between 4½ & 6th sts, the entire stock of ready-made clothing.
-R W Dyer, auct

Genteel furniture at auction: on Mar 29, at the residence of Rev Thos Seawell, on Gay st, Gtwn, his entire furniture. –Edw S Wright, auct, Gtwn

From the Boston Transcript: the U S ship **Supply** arrived at Port Mahon on Jan 6 from Gibraltar, & would sail about Feb 1 for the East. Cmder Lymch has been very seriously sick of the small-pox, but was recovering. His son & one of the sailors had also been attacked with the same disease & had recovered. The ship has been thoroughly cleansed & fumigated.

Died: on Mar 24, in his 68th year, Alex'r Tait, a native of Scotland, but a number of years a citizen of Wash City. His funeral is today, at 2 o'clock, from his late residence at G & 13th sts west.

Died: on Mar 22, at Coleman's Hotel, Henry Pirtle, aged 2 years & 2 months, youngest son of Rebecca & John Rowan, of Ky, [the lately appointed Charge d'Affaires to Naples.]

Died: on Mar 23, after a short illness, Drayden Milburn, 2nd daughter of Geo & Jane Lucinda Barber, aged 2 years, 2 months & 11 days. Her funeral is tomorrow at 2 o'clock from the residence of her father, on I st south, between 4th & 5th sts.

Two 2 story frame houses & lot at auction: by decree of the Circuit Court of Wash Co, D C, passed in a cause wherein Saml Redfern is cmplnt, & Barbara A Parker & others are dfndnts: sale on Mar 31, of part of lot 3 in square 56, with above improvements: fronts on G st, near 23rd. –John F Ennis, trustee -A Green, auctioneer

MON MAR 27, 1848
Fire in Watertown, N Y, Mar 21, in the factory bldg. Lemuel Wright & Levi Palmer were burnt to death.

Courage & Generosity handsomely rewarded. On Fri last a beautiful Silver Tankard was awarded. "Presented to Miss Sarah E Rogers, by Caleb Jones, Agent of the Va Woollen Co, as a mark of respect for & in compliment to her presence of mind, courage, & fortitude in saving the life of Jos Robinson, caught in a belt at the Factory, Mar 14, 1848." She saved his life by cutting the belt, immediately relieving him. His arm was broken, & he received other injuries, but is now doing very well. –Richmond Enquirer

New Orleans Bulletin of Mar 18 mentions the death of Maj Williams & Mr Lyons, the chief operator of the telegraph ofc in that city. They were visiting near **Fort Pike** on business, & took a boat to cross the lake. The boat capsized and they both drowned. The boatman saved himself by swimming.

Died: on Mar 15, at his seat, Tuckahoe, Va, Capt Thos Mann Randolph, in his 55th year. He was a man of highly cultivated intellect. When a young man he joined the U S army, at the commencement of the late war with great Britain, as a lt, & won the rank which he afterwards bore by service in the field. He was the youngest son of the late Col Thos Mann Randolph, of Tuckahoe, & half-brother to the former Govn'r of Va of the same name. –Richmond Whig

Appointments by the Pres: by & with the advice & consent of the Senate.
Consuls of the U S:
Jas McDowell, of Va, for Belfast, Ireland, vice Thos H Hyatt, declined.
T W Behn, of Ky, for Messina, Sicily, vice C Sherwood, deceased.
U S Attys: reappointed:
Jas A S Acklin, for the Northern district of Alabama.
Richd M Gaines, for the Southern district of Mississippi.
Henry W McCorry, for the Western district of Tenn.
Jas S Green, for the district of N J.
Henry R Jackson, for the district of Georgia.
Thos C Lyon, for the Eastern district of Tenn.
Robt L Chester, U S Marshal for the Western district of Tenn.
Land Ofcs: reappointed:
Wm N Wetterhurst, Receiver of public moneys at Wash, Miss.
Richd Whiting, Register of the land ofc at Tuscaloosa, Ala.
John S Howze, Register of the land ofc at Augusta, Miss.
Appointments in the Navy:
Henry W Ogden, to be a Capt in the Navy, from Feb 5, 1848.
Timothy G Benham, to be Cmder in the Navy, from Feb 5, 1848.
Geo H Preble, to be a Lt in the Navy, from Feb 5, 1848.
Thos B Huger, to be Lt in the Navy, from Feb 24, 1848.
Wm W Russell, to be a 1st Lt in the Marine Corps, from Nov 18, 1847.
J Hartley Strickland, to be a 2nd Lt in the Marine Corps, from Mar 22, 1848.
Henry Hurt & Danl B Martin, to be Chief Engineers in the Navy, from May 14, 1848.
Saml Britton Bennett, to be Navy Agent for the port of New Orleans, La.

Valuable property near the Navy Yard at public sale: on Apr 1, 2 brick house: one of them is on 8th st east, opposite the residence of Mr P Otterback, adjoining Mr Harrington's hotel. The other is on square 975, fronting K st, near 11th st east, in a good neighborhood. –A Green, auctioneer

House of Reps: 1-Bill for the relief of Capt Henry M Shreve: recommended that it do not pass: laid on the table. 2-Bill for the relief of David Myerle: passed: sent to the Senate for concurrence. 3-Ptn of G B Burr & others, praying for a post route in Lousiana. 4-Ptns & papers of Evander M Soper & others, of Wisc, heirs at law of Enos Soper, deceased, asking compensation in land for services & expenditures of said Enos Soper in raising a volunteer company as 1st Lt during the last war with Great Britain.

Excellent household & kitchen furniture at auction: on Mar 30, at the residence of Dr Blake, at the corner of C & 3rd sts. –R W Dyer, auct

On Sat last a man named Francis J Wood, in the employment of Capt Taylor, inventor of the Submarine apparatus, came to his death in this manner. He was engaged, with 2 other persons, to trying to raise a large stone from the bottom of the Potomac near Pomonkey, & after descending a 4th time, he was found to be perfectly dead. Physicians determined his death to be from blood in the head. By papers in his pocket, it was discovered he belonged to the Society of Odd Fellows, & his remains were taken charge of by that fraternity. His wife resides in Balt, & will be interred there today.

TUE MAR 28, 1848
Senate: 1-Ptn from Capt Reed & owners of the privateer **Gen Armstrong**, asking for indemnity from the Portuguese Gov't for the destuction of that vessel by the British at Fayal during the late war with Great Britain. 2-Ptn from Benj S Henning, in relation to a railroad communication connecting the waters of the Mississippi with the Pacific. 3-Ptn from Francis Hutinack: for a pension. 4-Ptn from John A Bryan, asking compensation for negotiating a treaty with the Wyandotte Indians in Ohio. 5-Additional papers in the case of Jonathan Tyner: presented. 6-Cmte on Private Land Claims: bill to be entitled an act for the relief of Jas G Carson. 7-Cmte on Patents: House bill for the relief of Calvin Emmons, with amendments: to be printed. 8-Cmte on Military Affairs: adverse report on the memorial of Joshua Shaw.

Laws of the U S passed at the First Session of the 13th Congress: Official publication. An Act granting frankling privilege to Louisa Catharine Adams, widow of the late John Quincy Adams: includes all letters & packets carried by post to & from Louisa Catharine Adams.

Valuable tavern property for sale: the subscriber [by authority from Capt John Brookes, the proprietor,] will sell the tavern in Upper Marlborough, lately occupied by Mr M E Clarke, a very large & commodious brick Tavern, large Stable & Carriage House, & all necessary outhouses. At the same time all the furniture belonging to the house.
–C C Magruder, Upper Marlborough, Md

Dr Valorus P Coolidge has just had his trial at Augusta, Me, on a charge of having murdered Edw Matthews, a young associate. The doctor is represented as a dashing young man, who had borrowed money of Matthews, & then destroyed him to get rid of the debt. The principal testimony against the prisoner was that of Thos Flint. Witness was a student with prisoner. [Coolidge had confided in Flint that he had killed the cursed Matthews.] Emily Williams, dght of the landlord in whose house Flint boarded, testified that the prisoner called for Flint; they met, & went off together. The jury found a verdict of guilty of murder in the 1st degree.

Information wanted of Francis Drummond, who, about 4 years ago, went to Mobile. A great favor will be conferred on his sister Eliz Drummond, in Wash, D C, by addressing her a note relative to him, as she has not heard from him since then.

Public sale on Apr 25th, of valuable personal property: by an order of the Orphans' Court of PG Co, Md: the undersigned admx of Notley Young, late of said county, deceased, will expose to sale at public auction, 2 farms of the deceased: *Poplar Ridge* & *Elverton Hall*; all the personal estate, consisting of a large number of negroes, horses, cattle, hogs, household & kitchen furniture, & farming untensils. –Martha Young, admx of Notley Young

Died: on Mar 24, in Gtwn, D C, Eliza A, daughter of Andrew M & Eliza Laub, in her 17th year.

WED MAR 29, 1848

Celebration of St Patrick's Day: commemoration of the Festival of the Apostle of Ireland was celebrated in Wash City on Mar 17, when a numerous party of Irishmen & friends of Ireland partook of an entertainment at the house of Fred'k Lakemeyer, [formerly Galabrun's.] Mr John Boyle, chrmn; at his right Geo W P Custis & Cmdor DeKay; on the left was seen Hon P W Tompkins, C J Ingersoll, & Gen Shields. Toasts by Mr Wm E Stubbs, Mr Peter Brady, Mr Jas Maguire, Mr J B McNamee, Thos W McCalla, Mr C B Closkey, Ambrose Lynch, John Foy, Owen Connolly, John Keenan, Anthony Best, C F McCarthy, Mr Porter, Mr Fitnam, Edw Stubbs, Thos Jordan, John Devlin, Andrew J Joyce, Wm P Faherty, John Connor, John W Keenan, Andrew Locks, & P McGarvey.

House of Reps: 1-Ptn of Eben Ritchie Dorr, praying compensation as acting Charge d'Affaires in Chili. 2-Ptn of John Emerson & 119 others, praying that Congress may pass a law emancipating Eliza Herbert & Caroline her dght; & to refund the money to the purchasers on a sale in favor of the U S. 3-Ptn of E J Chase, to inquire into revenue orders. 4-Ptn of David Jay & others, of Indiana, to withhold further supplies to carry on the Mexican war. 5-Ptn of C L Thompson, of Michigan, for relief on account of a mail contract. 6-Ptn of Joshua Russell, of Green Co, Pa, praying to be placed on invalid pension roll. 7-Memorial of Chas Lee Jones, of Wash City, asking redress for certain grievances connected with a btln of volunteers now in Mexico. 8-Ptn of Alfred F Randolph, of Genoa, DeKalb Co, Ill. 9-Ptn of Jos Hobbs, of Buscaw, for an extension of the benefits of the bounty land law. 10-Ptn of C S Thompson, of Michigan, for relief on account of a mail contract. 11-Cmte of Claims: bills for the relief of Dr Adolphus

Wislizeners; of Chas Ahrenfeldt & John F H Vogt; of Lawrence Daley; of David Shepherd; of Isaac Shepherd; & of A C Bryan, & others: committed. Same cmte: adverse reports on the ptns of Sylvester Comora, R P Whitney, Richd M Adams, & Wm Fitzpatrick: laid on the table. Same cmte: adverse reports on the ptns of Lewis D Offield & Sarah A Wirt, widow of John T Wirt: laid on the table. Same cmte: bills for the relief of Chas R Allen, of Richdmond, Va; & of Almedus Scott: committed. Same cmte: adverse reports on the ptns of Manuel Hoover, Isaac King, of Missouri, in behalf of J E Ball & G J Wasson, heirs of Wm Hudson & Wm D Gibson: laid on the table. Same cmte: bills for the relief of the widow & children of Col Wm R McKee; of Capt Dan Drake Henrie; of Maj John P Gaines; & of Sally Knowlton, widow of Elijah Bragdon, deceased: committed. 12-Cmte on Commerce: bills to refund to Chas A Kellet tonnage duties & light money paid on the Chinese junk **Keying** & to provide a customhouse at Wiscasset: committed.

Senate: 1-Ptn from Elijah McDougall, asking to be allowed a pension. 2-Ptn from Mehitable Gobbs, widow of a Revolutionary soldier, for a pension. 3-Cmte on Military Affairs: bill for the relief of Danl Wilkinson, with a report. 4-Cmte of Claims: recommended for passage: relief of Reuben Perry & Thos P Liggon; of Stalker & Hill; & of Bennet M Dell.

Boots, Shoes, & Palm leaf hats: W Noyes, Louisiana ave, near 7th st. [Ad]

Dr V P Coolidge was on Fri sentenced by Judge Whitman, at Augusta, Maine, for the murder of Edw Matthews, as follows: "That you be hanged by the neck until you be dead; & for this purpose you be conveyed to the State Prison, situated in Thomaston, in Lincoln Co; &, until this sentence of death shall be inflicted upon you, that you there be put to hard labor in solitary confinement." There is no foundation for the rumor of his suicide.

Mrd: on Mar 28, Mr Geo R Bruce, of Allegany Co, Md, to Miss Virginia L Sryock, of Wash City.

Died: Mar 28, in Wash City, Patrick Heffernan, born in the city of Cork, Ireland, & for the last 31 years a resident of Wash City, in his 54th year. His funeral is Thu, at 2 o'clock, from his late residence on N J ave.

For sale, those valuable Stone Quarries on the Chesapeake & Ohio Canal, situated about 3 miles above Gtwn, at present worked by Messrs O'Neale & Isherwood. Possession on Jun 21. –Wm H Murdock, Gtwn

$50 reward for runaway negro man Thos Brown, aged about 55 or 60 years. At the same time his wife Susan, eloped with him, & she is about 30 or 40 years of age. The said negroes I purchased of Dr Alex'r H Tolson, of PG Co, Md. He, by marriage, brought them from Prince Wm Co, Va, near Haymarket; they were the property of Miss Talliaferro. –Zachariah Berry, Blue Plains, opposite Alexandria, Va.

Groceries, liquors, boots & shoes, at auction: on Apr 4, at the grocery store of Mr Knot, at the corner of 15th & I sts. –A Green, auctioneer

Fine young mare at auction: on Apr 1, in front of the Centre Market House, which came astray to my property, & which has been duly advertised & appraised. –Mary Riley -A Green, auctioneer

THU MAR 30, 1848

House of Reps: 1-Resolved: that Jas Monroe, who contests the seat of David J Jackson, have leave to be heard in person at the bar of this House.

Boarding: a house on Capitol Hill, in Green's Row, formerly occupied by Mrs Whitwell. -Clements

City Affairs-Wash: 1-Ptn from C W Blackwell: referred to the Cmte of Claims. 2-Ptn from John O'Neale: referred to the Cmte on Police. 3-Ptn of R Farnham & others: referred to the Cmte on Improvements. 4-Ptn from Jeffrey Sampson: referred to the Cmte of Claims. 5-Ptn from John E Ager & brother: referred to the Cmte on Police. 6-Act for the relief of John H Plant; & for relief of Noel Penot: passed. 7-Bill for the relief of A G Herold: passed. 8-Bill for the relief of Albert Hart: passed. 8-Ptn of B L Jackson, praying payment of an assigned claim for paving on 7th st: referred to the Cmte of Claims. 9-Bill for the relief of M A Daly: referred to the Cmte on Improvements. 10-Bill for the relief of John Miller: referred to the Cmte of Claims. 11-Act to provide for the payment of Owen Summers' bill for mending market-house hose: referred to the Cmte on Police. 12-Cmte of Claims: asking to be discharged from the further consideration of the ptn of Anthony Holmead: agreed to.

Senate: 1-Ptn from Rebecca Heald, asking compensation for property destroyed during the war with Great Britain. 2-Cmte on Military Affairs: House bill for the relief of Col Robt Wallace, without amendment.

Died: on Mar 29, Mrs Catherine Sengstack, consort of Chas P Sengstack, in her 50th year. Assemble at the Foundry Church on Fri, at 10 o'clock, from whence the funeral will proceed.

Trustee's sale: by virtue of 2 deed of trust, executed by the late Chas King, deceased, to the late Clement Cox, deceased, on bearing the date of Jun 15, 1833, recorded in Liber B S 6, folios 90 thru 94, of the land records of Montg Co, Md, & the other dated Dec 12, 1842, recorded in Liber B S 11, folios 435 thru 438, of the land records, & a decree of the Circuit Court of Wash Co, D C, Court of Chancery, made in the cause of John Kurtz et al vs Geo King et al: sale on Apr 22, of a valuable tract of land in Montg Co, containing about 300 acs, embracing parts of **Friendship & Pritchett's Purchase**, being the entire farm in the occupancy & cultivation of the said Chas King at the time of his death. It has on it several tenements for residences, with other necessary bldgs. –Walter S Cox, trustee -Edw S Wright, auctioneer, Gtwn

Furnished rooms: 2 parlors & 2 bed chambers over J McColgan's grocery store, between 12th & 13th sts.

Old Capitol, Capitol Hill: H V Hill respectfully informs members of Congress & others, with or without families, that he has several large rooms unoccupied. Location on the n e corner of the Capitol square.

FRI MAR 31, 1848

John Jacob Astor, of N Y, so widely known for his great wealth, died at his residence in that city on Wed. His age is supposed to have been about 85 years.

Senate: 1-Ptn from Hall J Kelly asking a grant of land in Oregon for services in exploring & developing the resources of that country. 2-Cmte on Private Land Claims: bill for the relief of Henry Fredieu & other citizens of Louisiana. 3-Cmte on Commerce: House bill for the relief of Elijah H Willis, without amendment. 4-Cmte on the Judiciary: House bill for the legal reps of Wm McKenzie, late a seaman on board the U S ship **Vincennes**.

Mrd: on Tue, by Rev John C Smith, Mr Geo Jacob Foltz to Miss Margaret Hoffman, all of Wash City.

Died: on Mar 25, at Boston, Mass, after a brief illness, Col Geo Bomford, Col & Cmder of the Corps of Ordinance of the U S, a gentleman well known & highly esteemed in the walks of private life, & who had for more than 40 years spent in his country's service, faithfully discharged his duty. His remains have reached Wash City, & the funeral will take place this afternoon at 4 o'clock, from his late residence, near St John's Church.

Died: on Feb 23, of pulmonary disease, at the residence of her son, the Rev A A Lipscomb, in Montgomery, Ala, Mrs Phebe Lipscomb, wife of W C Lipscomb, sen, of Wash City. A change of climate it was thought would benefit her health, but alas! death had set his seal upon her. She died, as she had lived, trusting in God.

Died: on Mar 26, Lewis H France, in his 46th year.

Died: Mar 20, at Seaford, Delaware, in his 25th year, Dr Edw W Taylor, son of Geo Taylor, of Wash Co, D C.

Embezzlement, forgery, & fraud. Marvin McNulty, the confidential clerk of Messrs Vyse & Sons, silk merchants of N Y C, has absconded with from $75,000 to $100,000. It turns out he sailed on Sat for Matanzas, under an assumed name. The fugitive is a widower, & left 4 children behind him.

The house & garden at Spring Hill is offered for rent, either by the year or for the summer. It is within a half hour's ride of the Pres' House, on the heights n w of Gtwn. Inquire of Saml McKenney, Gtwn.

SAT APR 1, 1848
Pres sent the following diplomatic nominations to the Senate on Wed last: Dr J C Martin, now Sec of Leg in Paris, to be Charge d'Affaires to Rome. John Appleton, of Maine, now Chief Clerk in the State Dept, to be Charge d'Affaires to Guatemala. Elisha Hise, of Ky, to be Charge d'Affaires to Bolivia. Vanbrugh Livingston, now appraiser in the N Y Custom House, to be Charge d'Affaires to Ecuador.

House of Reps: 1-Cmte on Revolutionary Claims: adverse report on the ptn of the heirs of Robt Laughlin: laid on the table. 2-Cmte on the Judiciary: adverse report on the ptn of Maj G Tochman: laid on the table. 3-Cmte on Naval Affairs: adverse reports on the ptns of Nathl & Catharine Lawrence & Saml P Todd: laid on the table. 4-Cmte on Revolutionary Pensions: adverse report on the ptns of Anna Leech, of Maine; Martha Winans, widow of Abraham Winans, Jane Sulcer, Wm Sulcer, Sarah Sampson, widow of Peleg Sampson; Sarah Teas, widow of Wm Teas; John Victor, administrator of Sarah Victor; John Caldwell: laid on the table. Same cmte: bill for the relief of Mary McRea, widow of Lt Col Wm McRea, late of the U S army, deceased, recommended it do not pass. Same cmte: bill for the relief of Wm Parker & Wm Via: committed. Same cmte: adverse reports on the ptns of Rebecca Boyd, F Decatur Twiggs, Noah Clark, & Martin Dewey: laid on the table. Same cmte: adverse reports on the ptns of Henry Shafer & Sarah Knight: laid on the table. 5-Cmte on Invalid Pensions: bill for the relief of Elia A Mellon, or Benj Reisnyder, & Francis M Holton: committed. Same cmte: adverse reports on the ptns of Isaac Deaver & the heirs of Wilford Knott: laid on the table. Same cmte: adverse reports on the ptns of Theo Davis, Wm A Smith, Valentine Spaus, John Gilbert, Wm Gracy, John Steuart, & Ann H Allen, widow of Saml Allen: laid on the table. Same cmte: bills for the relief of Israel Bayles, of Arthur Wilson, of Benj G Perkins, of Beriah Wright, of John Savage, of Wm Paddy, & of Levi Colmus: committed. 6-Cmte on Patents: report on the ptn of Thos Gregg: laid on the table. 7-Resolved: that the Clerk of this House pay, on the audit of the Cmte of Accounts, the account of T Bailey Myers & F F Marbury, employed by the Solicitor of the Treas, under a resolution of the House of Jan 20, 1846, to take sworn testimony in the claim of Mathews, Wood, & Hall. 8-Cmte on Indian Affairs: adverse reports on the ptn of Jas McKibben & Isaac C Elston: laid on the table. 9-Cmte of Claims: bill for the relief of Manuel X Harmony, of A Baudenin, & A D Robert: committed. 10-Ptn of Eli Peterson, of Montg Co, Va, praying for bounty land, now on the files of the House: referred to the Cmte on Private Land Claims. 11-Ptn of Wm Wallace, of Lee Co, Ill, praying for a pension. 12-Concurrent resolution of the Legislature of N J urging provision to be made by Congress to refund to Capt Wm Napton & Lt Alex F Arnold, ofcrs commissioned by the Govn'r, the sum of $1,682.51, expended by them in raising, clothing, subsisting, & other necessary expenses of a company in the N J btln for the war with Mexico. 13-Memorial of Chas Fletcher, of Lancaster, concerning the Washington Monument. 14-Ptn of John Ferrah & many others, concerning the public lands. 15-Ptn from N H Skidmore & other citizens of Missouri, praying for certain post routes.

Committed to jail of Carroll Co, Md, on Mar 17, as a runaway, a yellow man, who calls himself John Jones: it is supposed he is not sane; says he lived in Balt with Mr Watson. The owner is to come forward, identify, & take him away. –Lewis Trumbo, Sheriff

Chas Co Court, sitting as a Court of Equity, 1848. Robt S Reeder, adm of John Fairfax & Ann L Fairfax, vs Buckner Fairfax & others. The object of this suit is to procure the payment to Ann L Fairfax, widow of John Fairfax, deceased, late of Preston Co, Va, of the purchased money of a tract of land sold by said John Fairfax, deceased, in his lifetime, to one Thos Perry, of Chas Co, Md. The bill & exhibits state that, in 1839, John Fairfax, of Preston Co, Va, sold to Thos Perry, of Chas Co, Md, a tract of land called *Franklin's Progress*; that, before the purchase money was paid, both Fairfax & Perry died, & that letters of administration were granted to Robt S Reeder, one of the cmplnts, by the Orphans' Court of Chas Co on the estate of said Fairfax, in Chas Co; that Reeder, as adm, recovered the said purchase money, & that Ann L Fairfax, widow of John Fairfax & one of the cmplnts, claims the purchase money as belonging to her on the ground that the land was hers, & demands a decree that it be paid to her. The bill further states that John Fairfax left the following heirs, all non-residents of Md, to wit: Buckner Fairfax, Wm Fairfax, Franklin B Fairfax, Eliz L Fairfax, Geo W Fairfax, & John A Martin, Alex'r E Martin, & Sophia Martin, children of Mary Martin, who was the dght of said John Fairfax. Absent dfndnts to appear in this Court on or before the 3rd Monday in Jul next.
–Peter W Crain Test: W Mitchell, clerk

The Jefferson Academy will resume on Apr 3: residence & Academy-6th & H sts.
–Rezin Beck

The locomotive Stephen Whitney, which was sunk in the Passaic river last week at the time of the railroad accident, has been recovered & placed on board of a vessel, on its way to Jersey City. The damage should not exceed $500. Abraham Quackenbush, the engineer, is able to be about again.

Mexico, Mar 9, 1848. This is the dullest place imaginable, & will continue during the armistice. Several ofcrs, anticipating no further active service, have resigned & returned home with the train which left on Mar 6 in charge of Col Black, of the Pa volunteers. Below you have a list of these ofcrs:

Sick Leave
Maj W Turnbull, Topographical Engineer
Maj E Kirby, Paymaster
Capt W H T Walker, 6th Infty, wounded
Assist Surg De Leon, to accompany Capt Walker to New Orleans

1st Lt D C Buell, Adj 3rd Infty, wounded
Lt Col F S Belton, 3rd Artl.

Resigned:
Capt J O H Denny, 1st Pa vol
2nd Lt J H Griswold, Mass vol
2nd Lt Jonathan Lee, 4th Regt Ill vol
2nd Lt Wm O'Sullivan, 2nd regt Ohio vol
2nd Lt J B Wadlington, 4th Regt Ky vol
2nd Lt G W Palmer, Ill mounted vol

1st Lt J J Martin, 12th Infty
2nd Lt J P Miller, 12th Infty
2nd Lt Lloyd Magruder, 12th Infty
Capt J M Crooks, 4th Regt Indiana vol
1st Lt H P Johnson, 3rd Regt Ky vol

Leave for Health:
Lt W H Gray, 1st Pa vol
2nd Lt W D Smith, 2nd Regt dragoons
2nd Lt W S Crittenden, 1st Regt infty
1st Lt A N Stoddard, 9th Infty
Capt W R Huntoon, Mass vol
2nd Lt J B Wing, Mass vol
2nd Lt J W Hague, 1st Regt Pa vol
2nd Lt J Young, 3rd Regt Tenn vol
Capt A W Bartlett, 4th Regt Ky vol
Assist Surg H H Steiner, Med Dept, resigned
Capt J S Simonson, Regt mounted riflemen
1st Lt H S Shields, 3rd Artl
Capt E B Alexander, 3rd Infty
Lt Col J Plympton, 7th Infty
Capt R H Ross, 7th Infty
Lt Col P O Hebert, 14th Infty, resigned
Brig Gen Lane
2nd Lt Wm M Faris, 3rd Ky vol, resigned
Capt J R Pritchard, 3rd Regt Ky vol, leave for health
1st Lt T Claiborne, Regt mounted riflemen, leave for health
Capt L M Corey, 3rd Regt Ky vol, leave for health
2nd Lt H H Richardson 4th Regt Tenn vol, resigned
Assist Surg De Leon, to accompany Capt Walker to New Orleans
Capt Geo E Pugh, 3rd Regt Ohio vol, resigned
Lt A Haye, 8th Infty, resigned
Capt g H Terrett, Marine corps, leave for health
1st Lt D H Hill, 4th Artl
Capt W J Clark, 12th Infty, leave for health
1st Lt R B Wynne, 4th Infty
Capt J H Barry, Mass Infty, leave for health
Brevet Maj G Wright, 8th Infty, leave for health
2nd Lt Wm Murray, 4th Regt Tenn vol, resigned
1st Lt G A Maney, 3rd Dragoons, leave for health
Lt J C Rich, Marine corps, leave for health

Capt Kelly's company of Florida volunteers, at Puebla, ordered to New Orleans to be discharged. Their time expired Apr 8. Among them you will see the name of Gen Lane, who found, on his arrival from his last expedition, letters informing him that the great flood of Ohio had made sad havoc with his plantation in Indiana, sweeping off all his stock.

Died: on Fri, in her 64th year, Mrs Sarah Thompson, wife of Gen Jas Thompson, & daughter of the late Col Burrows, of the U S Marine Corps. Her funeral will take place from the residence of Gen Thompson, near Gtwn, tomorrow, at 4:30 o'clock p m.

MON APR 3, 1848
Appointments by the Pres, by & with the advice & consent of the Senate:
Dr J C Martin, now Sec of Leg in Paris, to be Charge d'Affaires to Papal States.
John Appleton, of Maine, now Chief Clerk in the State Dept, to be Charge d'Affaires to Bolivia.
Elisha Hise, of Ky, to be Charge d'Affaires to Guatemala.
Richd K Watts & J Florentius Cox to be Justices of the Peace in Wash Co, D C.

Executors of the will of John Jacob Astor: Wm B Astor, Jas G King, Washington Irving, Jas Gallatin, J J Astor, jr, & Danl Lord. –Courier & Inquirer

Killed by the late steam boiler explosion at the Home Print Works, in R I, are: Owen Fearney, John McCuskey, Thos Thornton, Wm M Crawford, Susan Baker, Thos Thornton, & 3 of his children. The children were from 6 to 10 years of age. They were not at work in the mill, but were there with their father. Wounded: Geo D Cole, badly; Geo A Carpenter, slightly; Stephen Hunt, engineer, slightly; Saml Cutting, badly; Peter Berkley, slightly. Others, whose names have not been ascertained, may have perished.

To let: 3 story brick house at the corner of G & 22nd sts, recently occupied by Lt Maury, Superintendent of the Observatory. Apply to Chas E Eckel or M Adler.

Col Nicholas Van Rensselaer, a venerable soldier of the Revolution, expired in Albany, on Wed, in his 94th year. He was with Montgomery at the storming of Quebec, was at Ticonderoga, **Fort Miller**, **Fort Ann**, & at Bemis Heights, [in 2 engagements in the latter,] & was deputed to convey the intelligence of the surrender of Burgoyne to Albany.

Trustee's sale of improved real estate: by power of a deed of trust in me invested: public auction, on Apr 22: half of lot 3 in square 219, with a well built 4 story brick house thereon: on H st, one square north of St Matthews' Church: rents for $400 per annum. Also, the western half of lot 4 in square 286, with a well built 2 story frame dwlg, now occupied by Mr B Curran, at a yearly rent of $175. –P M Pearson, trustee

$50 reward for runaway negro man named Josiah. He ranaway from the farm of Jas Whiting, near Hopewell, Fauquier Co, Va, where he has been hired. He is about 20 years of age. –Dr Alex Chapman

City Ordinances-Wash: 1-Act for the relief of A G Herold: remit the fine imposed on him relative to the keeping of dogs: provided he pay the costs of prosecution. 2-Act for the relief of Albert Hart: remit the fine imposed on him relative to the keeping of dogs: provided he pay the costs of prosecution.

Senate: 1-Ptn from Nancy Haggard, asking the interest on the half-pay of her father. 2-Ptn from Peter F Dumas, in behalf of the heirs of the Marquis de Fougeres, asking the passage of a law to allow an appeal from the decision of the U S District Court of Florida to the Supreme Court of the U S. 3-Cmte of Claims: bill for the relief of J Throckmorton & the bill for the relief of Bent St Vrain & Co: recommending their passage.

Circuit Court of Wash Co, D C-in Chancery. Mar Term, 1848. Thos Blagden et al, cmplnts, vs Wm B Jackson, adm et al, dfndnts. Saml S Williams, Trustee, reported the sale to Wm B Jackson of lot 21 in square 977, in Wash City, for $940, & the terms of the sale have been complied with by the purchaser. -W Brent, clk

Circuit Court of Wash Co, D C-in Chancery. Scholfield & others vs Scholfield & others. The trustee reports the sale of lot 7 in square 576, with the appurtenances, to Selma Seibert, for $341.48; & also the sale of square 863, with appurtenances, to Geo W Dunlop, for $500. –Wm Brent, clk

In Chancery: Ephraim Wheeler & others vs Stanislaus Murray, exc of Martin Murray, deceased. Claims duly proved to be left with me or with S S Williams.
–W Redin, auditor

Died: on Mar 29, at Quincy, Mass, Mr John Greenleaf, in his 85th year.

In Chancery: Thos Blagden & others vs Wm B Jackson, adm of John Little & others. The estate of John Little will be audited on Apr 11. –W Redin, auditor

TUE APR 4, 1848
Ladies Furnishing Store, Pa ave, between 4½ & 6th sts. –Mary Alice Murray, agent

St John's Institute, *Mount Alban*, Gtwn Heights, D C. The Bishop of the Diocese, Visiter. The Rev Anthony Ten Broeck, A M, Rector: applications for information or admission of pupils, may be made to the Rector, Post Ofc address: St John's Institute, near Gtwn, D C.

The Laurel Milk Depot is removed to the basement on D st, near 10th, opposite Mr Foy's hotel. Pure milk is received morning & evening from the dairy of Col Capron at Laurel.
–P Bogert

Denistry: Wm Malster, Surgical, Operative, & Mechanical Dentist, [late assistant in the ofc of D L Parmele,] offers his services to the public. Ofc at Mrs Anderson's, Pa ave, between 11th & 12th sts.

Baltimore Female Academy, 117 East Balt st, Addison B Atkins, Principal: summer term will commence on May 1. The number of pupils is limited to 62. The principal would refer to the following gentlemen, some of whom have daughters in the Institution:

Rt Rev Alonzo Potter, D D, L L D, Robt A Dobbin, Balt
Bishop of Pa Andrew Coyle, Wash, D C
Rev H V D Johns, D D, Balt N D Coleman, Vicksburg, Miss
Rev L W Green, D D, Balt

Died: yesterday, at his late residence near the naval powder magazine, in Wash City, in his 80th year, Col Wm Hebb, a native of Md, of which State he was long a distinguished citizen, but more recently a resident of Wash City. His funeral is this afternoon at 4 o'clock.

Died: on Mar 28, at St Joseph's Valley, Emmetsburg, Sister Mary De Chantal, [Mrs Sarah Miles,] in the 39th year of her age, formerly of Wash City.

The copartnership under the name of Williams & Rand, is this day dissolved by mutual consent, the said Rand withdrawing from said firm, & assigning his interest to John Williams. –Jas B Rand, John Williams

WED APR 5, 1848
Senate: 1-Ptn from Mary Coleman, asking a pension on account of the services of her husband during the Revolution. 2-Ptn from Agnes Freeland, asking for a pension as widow of a Revolutionary soldier. 3-Bill granting a pension to Wm Pittman: introduced. 4-Cmte on Military Affairs: House bill for the relief of Col Robt Wallace, aid-de-camp of Gen Wm Hull, without amendment. 5-Cmte of Claims: House bill for the relief of Archibald Bull & Leonard S Finch, without amendment, recommending its passage. 6-Cmte on the Revolution: asking to be discharged from the further consideration of the memorial of Francis Hatinack, a soldier of the Revolution, &, that it be referred to the Cmte on Pensions. 7-Cmte on Accounts: unfavorable report on the resolution to allow all the messengers of the Senate the same compensation paid to R P Anderson & J L Club: agreed to. 8-Ptn of Richd Ames, a soldier in the war of 1812, for pay & bounty land. 9-Ptn & other papers of Amos Knapp, a soldier in the last war with Great Britian, for relief. 10-Obituary received from the House of Reps announcing the death of the Hon Jas Augustus Black, of the State of S C. He was seized on Mar 16 with a violent congestive chill, which terminated in an obstinate & incurable pneumonia, of which he died at his lodgings, in Wash City, last night. He was born of respectable parents in Abbeville district, S C, & at the time of his death was in his 57th year. He entered the army in 1812, at age 18, with the commission of lt, & was promoted to captain before the close of the war.

The Funeral of the Hon Jas A Black, will be on Apr 5, at 11:30 a m: in the hall of the House of Reps. Pallbearers:

Mr Lumpkin, of Ga	Mr Hunt, of N Y	Mr Rockwell, of Mass
Mr McClermand, of Ill	Mr Cranston, of R I	Mr Harmanson, of La
Mr Ligon, of Md	Mr Cocke, of Tenn	

Mr Jos L Ritchie, proprietor of an extensive vinegar establishment at Phil, was awakened early on Mon by the sound of groans on the premises. He found a negro in one of the vats, & in assisting him out, being stifled by the noxious gas rising from the fluid, fell in himself, & they both perished.

Leroy, N Y, Mar 28-two children of Mr L S Bacon were burnt to death by the accidental explosion of a can containing camphine or spirit gas. Grace age 6 years died that evening, & Lathrop age 3 years, died the next day. Jennett Shaw, the servant girl, aged about 13, was badly burnt, & her death is hourly expected.

The U S steamship **Edith**, from Vera Cruz on Mar 20, brought over a large number of passengers, among whom we notice the following: Gen Lane, Lt Col Plympton, U S A; Lt Col Belton, Maj Wright, U S A; Capts Ross & Pope, U S A; Capt Hunter, of the Mass volunteers; Capts Pugh, Doland, Clark, Pearson, Frekle, Claborn, Martin, Sibley, Nyne, Isacks, Young, Hughes, Maney, Tilghman, Hays, M Gander, Lee, Davis, & Gray; Drs Polk & Foot; Col Jackson, Maj Hatten, Messrs Bond, Reynolds, Stone, & Whittier, & 150 dischargd soldiers & teamsters.

Mrd: on Mar 28, in Shepherdstown, Va, by Rev Jos M Atkinson, Wm Moulder, formerly of Wash, to Miss Virginia Buckles, youngest daughter of the late Danl Buckles, of the former place.

Died: at Tunis, Barbary, Mrs Chas Ferriere, the youngest daughter of Dr S D Heap, Consul of the U S near his highness the Bey of Tunis. The European consuls causing their flags to be displaced at half mast, & all attending, with their employes, the funeral procession, was joined by several of the Bey's ministers, all the foreign ofcrs in his employ, many Greeks with their clergy, Jews, & Moors, & a numerous concourse of sympathizing friends. [No death date given-current news item.]

Mrd: on Mar 30, in New Bedford, Mass, by Rev Mr Wildes, Lt Chas Hunter, U S Navy, to Mary Stockton, daughter of Wm R Rotch.

Died: on Apr 1, at Balt, in her 23rd year, Mrs Maria Amanda, wife of Mr Walter M Clarke, & daughter of Jos Simms.

THU APR 6, 1848
John Jacob Astor's will: executed Jul 4, 1836; sundry codicils were made, 8 or more; ample provision for all the relations of Mr Astor & their children---his son, Wm B Astor, being the great residuary legatee. The only important bequest for the public benefit is one of $400,000 by the codicil of Aug 20, 1839, for erecting suitable bldgs & establishing a library in N Y for the free general use. He appropriated a plot of ground on the southerly side of Astor place, 65 feet front by 125 feet deep, for the bldg. There is a bequest to the poor of Waldorf, [his native town in Germany,] by establishing an institution for the sick or disabled, or for the improvement of the young, of $50,000. Bequests to: the German Society-$20,000; Institution for the Blind-$5,000; Half Orphan Asylum $5,000; Lying in Asylum-$2,000. The personal estate of Mr Astor is worth from 7 to 9 millions of dollars, & his real estate perhaps as much more. [Apr 10th newspaper: he leaves an annuity of $200 for life to Fitz Greene Hallack, who has been for some 25 years Mr Astor's chief & confidential clerk. Mr Astor's property value is about 20 millions of dollars; nearly three-quarters of it probably falls to his son, Wm B Astor, who is already worth several millions.]

Laws of the U S passed at the 1st Session of the 30th Congress. An act for the relief of the heirs of John Paul Jones: Sec of the Treasury is instructed to pay to the legal reps of the said John Paul Jones, & the ofcrs, seamen, & marine of the squadron under his command, being citizens of the U S, or their reps, their respective proportions of the value, as estimated by Benj Franklin, of 3 prizes captured by the squadron under the command of the said Jones, & delivered up to Great Britian by Denmark, in 1779; to be apportioned on the basis of the distribution of a settlement made with the captors, for prizes captured by the said squadron, & received from the court of France, & confirmed by Congress in 1787; deducting, however, from the share of Capt Peter Landais, the sum received by him or his legal reps under an Act of Congress, approved Mar 28, 1806: Provided, that in ascertaining the amount due the heirs of said John Paul Jones, if any, no interest shall be allowed on such claim. Approved, Mar 21, 1848.

Mrd: on Tue last, by Rev Mr Lanahan, Mr Jas H Perry & Miss Sarah Eliz Stairs.

Geo Slothower & Thos Camper, Agents, have this day bought out Geo W Adams entire stock of dry goods in Wash City.

The Hon Horace Mann was elected a Rep to Congress on Mon last, from the 8th district of Mass, to supply the vacancy caused by the death of Ex-Pres Adams.

Boarding School for Boys, located in the beautiful & healthy borough of York, Pa. Address the principal & proprietor at York, Pa. –R T Haughey [A Boarding School for Young Ladies has opened, having no connexion with the male dept.]

Meridian Hill for sale, or the Mansion House, with furniture, to let, with garden & grounds, for the summer or year. Apply at the north side of F st, next to 12th st. –J Florentius Cox

FRI APR 7, 1848
Senate: 1-Ptn from Eliza Ann & Mary Brewer, reps of a deceased Revolutionary soldier, asking to be allowed bounty land. 2-Ptn from Henry La Reintree, asking the interposition & influence of the Senate with the Pres of the U S to procure the appointment of purser in the navy. [This gentleman is appears is secretary to the Pacific squadron & is on board the U S ship **Independence**; he bases his request on long & faithful service, of all which the evidence is appended. The memorialist says in his letter that it is a new mode of making an appointment, but it is an upright course. I rely on the integrity of my motives & the justness of my cause.] 3-Cmte on Pensions: House bills, without amendment: relief of the heirs of Wm Evans; of Esther Russell; of Jonathan Fitzwater; & of Zilpha White. 4-Cmte on the Post Ofc & Post Roads: bill for the relief of John Lorimer Graham, late pastmaster of N Y C. 5-Cmte on Revolutionary Claims: adverse report on the ptn of the reps of Wm Russworm. 6-Cmte on Public Lands: bill for the relief of Wm Wynn. 7-Cmte of Claims: adverse report on the memorial of the administrator of Francis R Sanchez.

The Hon Richd Bache, a Senator in the Texan Legislature from Galveston Co, died at Austin on Mar 17. He was struck with palsy on Mar 7, while going to the Senate chamber; during the 10 days that elapsed before his death he is said to have been insensible, & perfectly unconscious. His funeral was Mar 18th.

The body of the late Dr A F Suter, U S A, has been brought from the city of Mexico & interred at Jefferson barracks, Missouri. This act of friendship was by Maj H V Sumner, of the U S Army, who, upon leaving Mexico, brought with him the remains of his friend, they they might have sepulture in his native land.

Lynchburg Virginian: Capt John Warwick, of Amherst Co, who died a few days since, manumitted by his will all his servants, numbering between 70 & 80. He has made ample provision for their removal, outfit, & settlement in one of the Western States.

Albany Journal: we announce the death of Gen Chas M Reed, an estimable citizen of Erie, Pa, who was most extensively & honorably connected with the commercial business of Buffalo & the Western Lakes.

The Baron d'Hautville, the father of the gentleman who married Miss Sears, of Boston, whose lawsuits respecting the custody of her child caused so much newspaper comment a few year since, recently died at his residence, *Vevay*, in Switzerland, at the age of 92. By his death Miss Sears would have been a Baroness-a very empty honor, which she appears willing to renounce for the sake of living in the U S with her child & parents.

Mrd: on Apr 5, in Wash City, at the Church of the Ascension, by Rev Mr Gilliss, Dr Danl Conrad, of Winchester, Va, to Sarah Jane, only daughter of the late Alfred H Powell.

House of Reps: 1-Ptn of A Z Donnet, praying compensation as Charge d'Affaires at the Court of Portugal from Apr 19 to Dec 28, 1844. 2-Ptn of Isaiah Williams, for a pension. 3-Ptn of Capt Silas Chatfield, for arrears of pension. 4-Ptn of John Warren & other citizens of Daviess Co, Mo, praying a grant of land to the Hannibal & St Jos Railroad.

Organization of the Army in Mexico: orders of the army in Mexico, recently issued. Headquarters Army of Mexico, Mar 1, 1848. Orders #16. Regular Troops-old & new regts:
I. Brevet Maj Gen Worth's Division:
Brevet Capt Geo Deas, Assist Adj Gen
Light Co A, 2nd Artl, the 2nd & 3rd Artl, 4th, 5th, & 6th Infty.
II. Brevet Brig Gen Smith's Division:
Brevet Capt J Hooker, Assist Adj Gen
Light Co K, 1st Artl, mounted rifle regt, 4th Artl, 1st, 2nd, 3rd, & 7th Infty, & Marine Corps.
III. Brig Gen Cadwalader's Division:
Brevet Capt P N Page, Assist Adj Gen
Field battery under the command of Capt Steptoe, 3rd Artl, 9th, 11th, 12th, 13th, 14th, & 15th Infty, & Voltigeurs.
<u>Volunteer Troops:</u>
I-Maj Gen Patterson's Division.
Brevet Capt W W Mackall, Assist Adj Gen
Btln Ga horse, 3 companies Ill horse, Mass, 1st & 2nd Pa, N Y, Dist of Columbia & Md, S C, 2nd & 4th Ohio, 2nd Ill regts of foot, N J & Ga btln of foot, & one company of Fla foot.
II-Brig Gen Marshall's Division.
Brevet Capt E R S Canby, Assist Adj Gen
1-Seven companies of La horse, btln Texas horse, Lawler's company of horse, 3rd & 4th Ky, 4th & 5th Indiana, 3rd, 4th, & 5th Tenn, La Regts of foot, Miss & La btlns of foot.
2-The field batteries under the command of Lts W H French, 1st Artl, & M Lovell, 4th Artl, are assigned to the 1st & 2nd divisions of volunteers, respectively.
3-Cmders of divisions will organize the troops under them into brigades; the regulars into 2 & the volunteers into 3 brigades.
4-The 14th Infty & Voltigeurs, under the senior ofcr, will proceed to Toluco, & there relieve the 6th & 8th Infty, which latter regts will then proceed to the city of Mexico.

5-Col Bonham, with the 12th Infty, will proceed to Cuernavaca & relieve the 1st Infty, which regt will then proceed to the city of Mexico. Col Bonham is assigned to the command of the dept of Cuernavaca, & will relieve Col Clarke, 6th Infty, who, on being relieved, will join his regt.
6-The chiefs of the several depts. will avail themselves of the change of troops to send supplies, should any be required, to Toluca & Cuernavaca, as well as to receive stores from those posts.
By order of Maj Gen Butler: L Thomas, A A G
Gen Orders #9. Mexico, Mar 2, 1848. Extract: Maj P H Galt, 2nd Artl, will relieve Lt Col F S Belton, 3rd Artl, in the duties of Lt Govn'r of the city of Mexico. By order of Maj Gen Butler: L Thomas, A A G

The New Bedford Mercury: the whale ship **Abraham H Howland**, arrived at this port on Sunday from the Sandwich Islands, having on board the following missionaries as passengers: Rev R C Forbes, lady, & 4 children; Mrs & Miss Dibble, & 3 children, & Master Emerson, all of the American Board of Missions.

Died: on Apr 6, of consumption, in his 34th year, Evan Evans, a native of Wales, but for the last 16 years a resident of Wash City. His funeral is this afternoon at 3 o'clock, from his late residence on B st, near 10th st, opposite the Smithsonian Institute.

Wash Corp: 1-Ptn from Julia Keep: referred to the Cmte on Improvements. 2-Cmte of Claims: bill for the relief of Wm C Riddall: laid on the table. 3-Cmte of Claims: bill for the relief of John J Joyce: laid on the table. 4-Cmte of Claims: bill for the relief of Thos Downey: passed. 5-Cmte of Claims: asking to be discharged from the further consideration of the ptn of Jas Towle. Same cmte: asking to be discharged from the further consideration of the ptn of Jas A Bower. Same cmte: bill for the relief of J C Peetch, reported the same without amendment. Same cmte: ptn of Washington Rawlings for his relief: passed.

SAT APR 8, 1848
Jno W Bronaugh & Henry B Blagrove, having associated themselves in the Lottery business, under the firm of Bronaugh & Co, at the old-established U S Prize Ofc, #141, one door east of Bradshaw's U S Hotel. Lottery is drawn under the management of D Paine & Co. –Bronaugh & Co, Balt

Florida Sentinel, Mar 28. Thos H Hagner died last Sunday of a disease of the liver, indications of the existence of which first became manifest during the last session of the Genr'l Assembly of this State, of which he was a prominent & influential member. His death is a great public loss. He was a native of Md, a son of the present 3rd Auditor of the U S Treasury. He had been a resident of Florida 8 or 9 years, & was a successful practitioner at the bar in Middle Fla. He has left a widow & 2 infant children to mourn his loss.

Died: on Apr 6, at ***Chilolmwood***, the residence of John B Wiltberger, near Rock Creek Church, Benj Burche Wright, in his 25th year. His funeral is from his late residence today at 3 o'clock.

Died: on Apr 7, of consumption, in his 36th year, Geo Hensley, a native of Gloucestershire, England, but for the last 15 years a resident of Wash City. His funeral is on Sun at 5 o'clock, from his late residence on the south side of Pa ave, between 11th & 12th sts.

MON APR 10, 1848
Trustee's sale of improved real estate: by the power of trust in me vested, I shall sell at public auction, a part of lot G in subdivisionof lot 2, in square 570, generally known as ***Pollard's Row***, fronting on D st north. Improvements: 2 story brick dwlg, with basement.
–Geo W Donn, trustee -A Green, auctioneer

J Mortimer Kilgour, Atty at Law, Rockville, Montgomery Co, Md. [Ad]

In Chancery, Apr 3, 1848. Ann S Hill & others, vs Martha Young, admx of Notley Young & others. Object of this bill is to procure a decree for a sale of mortgaged premises & real estate in PG Co, Md, of which Notley Young, late of said county, died seized & possessed, & a greater portion of which was, on Jan 18, 1838, mortgaged by him to Ann S Hill. On or about Jan 18, 1838, Young conveyed certain real estate & land unto Ann S Hill, by way of mortgage, to secure the payment of $1,270.62, which was then due & owing to the said Ann S Hill as guardian of her 2 children, Eleanor Ann Hill & John Hill, the half of said sum to be paid on Sep 1, 1840, & the balance on Oct 1, 1842, with the interest on the whole sum to be paid annually. The bill further states that Notley Young departed this life without having paid to the said Ann S Hill the money & interest, except to Jan 18, 1844, without a widow, & leaving 5 children his heirs-at-law & personal reps, to wit: Martha Young, to whom the bill states letters of administration upon the personal estate of Notley Young have been granted; Benj F Young, of PG Co; Eleise Young, intermarried with Geo H Smith, of St Mary's Co; & Clement Young & Julia F Young, who are minors; & that the 2 last reside out of the State of Md. The bill also alleges that the said Notley Young died indebted to Geo Parker & Thos Parker, trading under the name of Geo & Thos Parker, as the payees & endorsers of certain notes & on open accounts, in the sum of $1,824.72, & interest thereon, as will appear from the exhibits filed with the bill; that the deceased left a personal property which is insufficient to pay his debts, & prays a decree for the sale of the said lands to pay first the mortage debt of the said Ann S Hill, & to aid the personalty to pay the debts of the cmplnts Geo & Thos Parker, & such other creditors of the said Notley Young as shall become parties to the said bill; & that the said Martha Young resides out of the State of Md. Dfndnts to appear in this court on or before Sep 20 next. –Louis Gassaway, Reg Court Chancery

$4 reward for a black Mare that strayed or was stolen on Sun last, from Isaiah King, living at 3rd & K sts.

Papers wanted relating to a foreign claim in favor of Wm P Robinson-supposed to have been left in the hands of some person at Washington by A W Paine, who left Washington about 2 years since fo Boston, & has since died. –Chas Monroe, Patent Ofc Dept

Boarding on Capitol Hill: at J Owner's, #2, *Dowson's Row*.

By order of distrain for house rent due & in arrears to Saml Wroe by Wm C Smith, I will expose at public sale, on Apr 15, the goods & chattels of Wm C Smith. Terms cash. –Horatio R Maryman, Bailiff

$50 reward to the person who will furnish me with such information as may lead to the conviction of the person or persons who maliciously entered my ice-house, on *Analostan Island*, opposite Gtwn, by tearing down a portion of the partition, uncovering the ice, & subjecting it to much waste. –John Pettibone

Lost: chain with a pencil with the name of Miss C S Whitney marked in full. Leave it with Mr Chas W Stewart at the Capitol, for a suitable reward.

For rent: residence, adjoining that of the subscriber, on H st, between 6th & 7th sts; house is nearly new. Possession immediately. Apply on the premises or at the Bank of Wash to Hugh B Sweeny.

New Spring Millinery: Mrs H Tucker, 8th st, & Pa ave.

Senate: 1-Ptn from David Penrod, asking to be allowed to change the entry of a tract of land. Also, from Jesse Toler, to the same effect. 2-Ptn from Christopher Cunningham, asking a pension for wounds received at the battle of Buena Vista. 3-Cmte on Revolutionary Claims: adverse report in the cases of Robt Piatt, legal rep of Danl Piatt, & of Nancy Haggard; which were ordered to be printed. Same cmte: bill for the relief of Fred'k Vincent, adm of the estate of Jas Le Casse. 4-Cmte of Claims: bill for the relief of Chas Waldron, without amendment, with a report recommending its passage. Same cmte: asking to be discharged from the further consideration of the ptn of Sarah Hubbard.

House of Reps: 1-To be reported without amendment: relief of-Peter Engels, sen; of Eliz Converse, widow of Joshiah Converse; of Capt John Percival, capt in the U S Navy; of H Carrington, exc of Paulina Le Grand, deceased; of Richd Reynolds; of Wm Harding; of John S Conger; of H M Barney; of Sarah D Coldwell, wife of Jas H Brigham; of Edna Hickman, wife of Alex'r D Peck; of Wm M Blackford, late Charge d'Affaires to the republic of New Granada; of Francis Hutinack; of Eliza S Roberts; of Seth Morton; of Jos Johnson; & of Christopher H Pix, of Texas. Also, a pension to John Morrison. 2-Joint resolution for the relief of J Melville Gillis & other: laid on the table. 3-Bills for the relief of Chas Reeder, Walter R Johnson, & legal reps of Thos P Jones, deceased: with amendment-reasonable compensation should be allowed not exceeding $100 per month: agreed to.

The case of Lee & others vs Chichester, which has excited no little interest, removed from Fairfax to Loudoun, & from Loudoun to Alexandria, Va, & has been in Chancery for the last 18 years, was tried before a jury at a special term of the Superior Court of this county. The case was decided on Wed last, by a verdict of the jury in favor of the plntfs. –Alexandria Gaz

The Phil Bulletin announces the death of Jas P Wilson, Cmder in the Navy, which took place at Alvarado, from apoplexy. He was a native of Balt, & entered the service in 1817, & was appointed Cmder in 1842.

Splendid carriage exhibited on Pa ave may be seen at Walker & Kimmell's stables. Will be sold for less than half the price it cost to build it. –Isaac Walton

Mrd: on Apr 6, by Rev F S Evans, Mr Robt Nash to Miss Eliz T Sloan.

Mrd: on Apr 6, by Rev Jas B Donelan, Mr Jas E F Dunawin, of Wash City, to Miss Ellen A Regan, of Fred'k, Md.

The North American [Mexican:] Jas Manly, 1st Sgt of Co F, [Capt Porter's] mounted rifle regt, died on Mon from the effects of poison, by whom administered is not known. Sgt Manly was one of the bravest & best soldiers in the army. At Cerro Gordo he received honorable mention for his gallantry, & also at Contreras. At Chapultepec he was the first man of Twiggs' division to reach the heights beside his captain, & his hand raised the stars & stripes first on the national palace on Sep 14. He was a good soldier & an honest exemplary man. His residence was Phil, his recruiting post Norfolk.

Chas Bain was so shockingly burnt by the falling in of a lime-kiln in Jefferson Co, Va, on Mar 24, that he died an hour later.

TUE APR 11, 1848
Senate: 1-Ptn from Cyrus H McCormick, asking an extension of his patent for a reaping machine. 2-Presented: papers relating to the claim of J S Bowen. Also, documents relating to the claim of Manuel X Harmony. Also, papers relating to funds withheld from the Seneca Indians by a late com'r. 3-Ptn of Jos K Boyd, of Wash, the only survivor, with the exception of Com Morris, of the party engaged in the destruction of the frig **Philadelphia** at Tripoli in 1804, asking such compensation as may be deemed just. 4-Cmte on Private Land Claims: House bill for the relief of Eliz Buriss, with an amendment. Also, same cmte, House bill for the relief of Anthony Bessee. 5-Cmte on Public Lands: bill for the relief of Jesse Toles; & a bill for the relief of David Penrod.

Orphans Court of Wash Co, D C. Letters testamentary on the personal estate of Ann Coomb, late of said county, deceased. –Mary Ann Graham, excx

Died: yesterday, at his residence, near the Observatory, Mr Azariah Fuller, in his 58th year. His funeral is this afternoon at 4 o'clock.

Died: on Apr 3, at the residence of Mr Henry Sewell, Fairfax Co, Va, Thos Lee Orr. Obliged by ill health to leave Washington & abandon his profession, Mr Orr has sought retirement in the country, & resided in Fairfax for many years. He was a man of hightly polished & cultivated mind & of most benevolent disposition. He died without a blot or stain upon his memory, in full confidence of a happy eternity.

Headquarters Army of Occupation, Monterey, Mexico, Feb 27, 1848. A band of American robbers, composed principally of deserters, [chiefly from the Texas btln & Capt Meare's company of volunteer cavalry,] dishonorably discharged soldiers, & followers of the Army, have been ravaging the country from Pritas to the Presidio de Rio Grande, ravishing the women, & committing every species of atrocity on the defenseless inhabitants. A similar party has recently robbed an entire village, under the pretence of being a detachment of the American army sent to levy a contribution on the place. These acts call upon everyone to make exertions to apprehend the villains. The Ofcrs commanding at Monclova, Presidio, Laredo, Mier, & Ceralvo, will endeavor to effect this object. All soldiers dishonorably discharged the service will be held in confinement till they can be sent under guard to the Brasos, & no person will be permitted to follow the army who does not belong to it. By command of Brig Gen Wool: Irvin McDowell, AAG

WED APR 12, 1848
Senate: 1-Cmte on Private Land Claims: House bills, without amendment, for relief of Edna Hickman, wife of Alex'r D Peck; & for relief of Sarah C Caldwell, wife of Jas H Brigham. 2-Cmte of Claims: bill for relief of Henry Williams & others, owners of the schnr **Ticonic**. Same cmte: joint resolution for relief of the heirs of Caleb Swann.
3-Cmte on Indian Affairs: bill for relief of P Chouteau, jr & Co. 4-Amendments of the House to the bill for relief of the legal reps of Geo Fisher were concurred in.
5-Cmte of Claims: unfavorable report on the ptn of Jas Edwards. Same cmte: House bill for relief of Wm Ralston, without amendment, & recommending that it do not pass.
6-Cmte on Foreign Relations: House bill for relief of Wm M Blackford, late Charge d'Affaires at New Granada, without amendment. Same cmte: joint resolution for relief of Mrs Ann Chase.

House of Reps: 1-Memorial of W R Ashard for relief. 2-Ptn of the legal reps of Capt Wm Armstrong. 3-Ptn of J B Hyde, praying for an alteration in the laws of the U S, in relation to the granting of patents to foreigners.

Cassuis M Clay has recovered $2,500 damages from Jas B Clay & T H Waters, two of the persons who were prominent in forcibly transporting his abolition newspaper ofc from Ky to Ohio.

Col Jason Rogers, of Louisville, died in that city on Apr 3. He was for many years an ofcr in the regular army of the U S. He was Lt Col of the Louisville Legion in Mexico, & was appointed Military & Civil Govn'r of the city of Mexico. In the same city, on Apr 2, died Lt Stephen Johnston, U S Navy.

Died: at the residence of W Kirkwood, PG Co, Md, of whooping cough, Wm Henry, infant son of Rosa S & Jos B Pleasants, aged 7 months & 13 days.

Members of the New Jerusalem Lodge #9 to meet at the Masonic Hall, 10th & E sts, on Apr 13, A L 5848. By order, Urias Hurst, sec.

The Legislature of Va has voted Swords to the following ofcrs for services in the campaigns against Mexico:

Col Jas Bankhead	Capt Larkin Smith	Capt Geo D Ramsey
Lt Col Jos E Johnston	Capt Francis Taylor	Capt Chilton
Lt Col Graham	Capt Lewis S Craig	Capt Jas Monroe
Lt Col M M Payne	Capt Edw J Steptoe	Capt J W Smith
Maj Gwynn	Capt Francis Nelson	Capt Galt
Maj Chevallie	Page	Capt Edwards
Capt John B Magruder	Capt Geo G Waggoner	Capt A C Cummings
Capt John Washington	Capt Lawrence P	Capt Turner
Capt Robt E Lee	Graham	

Capt J W Anderson, [fell at the battle of Churubusco,] Wm Bertrand Alburtis, of Berkeley Co, only son of Capt Wm Alburtis, who was killed at Vera Cruz

Lts:

Geo W Lay	___ Armistead	J W Martin
Jos E Selden	Wm H Tyler	J W Leigh
Geo H Thomas	S Anderson	John M Blakely
Brevet R S Garnett	Hamilton Shields	Thos Easley
Dabney H Maury	Edw Johnston	D S Lee
Lewis Neill	Geo Pickett	Theodore Laidley
Wm B Blair	R W Johnson	R S Ewell
J S Reno	E H Fitzgerald	Geo Minor
T J Jackson	___ Fry	
Wm Patterson	___ Terrett	

Dead:

Capt S Thornton	Lt Weley P Hale	Lt J P Johnstone
Capt Stephens T Mason	Lt Shackleford	Lt Irwin
Capt Oscar E Caldwell	Lt Sidney Smith	Lt Geo T Mason
Capt Hooe	Lt Ewell, [of the Rifles]	

To Sgt Undergraff, a silver medal.

Rev Enos Dudley has been arrested in Grafton, N H, on a charge of the murder of his wife, who was tipped over with her husband in a sleigh, 2 or 3 weeks ago, & buried without much ceremony.

Mr Wm Walter, a respectable citizen of West Balt, aged about 50 years, while walking to church on Sunday morning, fell at Fayette & Poppleton sts, & expired in a few minutes.

The remains of Lt Alex'r Perry Rodgers, of the 4th Infty, son of the late Cmdor John Rodgers, of the Navy, arrived yesterday from Norfolk, & were transferred, under a guard of honor, to the depot on Pratt st. He was in his 21st year & had just graduated at West Point when he was ordered to join Gen Scott's column in Mexico. He was engaged at the siege of Vera Cruz, & in the battles of Cerro Gordo, Contreras, Milino del Rey, Churubusco, & Chapultepec. He was killed by a ball through the forehead, when within 10 feet of the batteries. His remains were brought from Mexico by the U S ship **Germantown**, & they are under the charge of his brother, Lt C R P Rodgers, of the Navy, to their final destination in the family vault at New London. The friends of the deceased beg leave to make their public acknowledgments to Mr Jacob I Cohen, Vice Pres of the Phil Railroad Co at this point, & to Mr Robt A Taylor, & Mr Falls, of the Balt Steampacket Co, for their courtesy & liberality in affording free transportation to the remains of a gallant ofcr. Their warm thanks are also tendered to Messrs John Stewart & Son, who with great public spirit volunteered a hearse & their personal services on this occasion.

Obit-died: on Apr 2, Miss Ann Catherine Fitzhugh, the last of the lovely dghts of Saml & Ellen Fitzhugh, in her 22nd year.

For rent: comfortable 2 story brick dwlg on 7th st, near I st, & adjoining the residence of A Rothwell. Apply to R W Dyer, auctioneer, or to the subscriber. –John F Boone

Valuable property for sale: 3 story brick bldg, adjoining the residence of Judge Cranch, on Capitol Hill. –Henry May, Wm Brent

By virtue of a writ of fieri facias, I shall sell for cash, a large gray mare, opposite the Centre Market, the property of John Mulliken & W B Magruder, seized & taken to satisfy a judgment in favor of Geo Crandell. Sale on Apr 15. –John Magar, Constable

TUE APR 13, 1848
Senate: 1-Memorial in relation to the claim of Wm Parkeson, a soldier in the war of 1812, for a pension. 2-Ptn from J F Callan, & other citizens of D C, asking the enactment of a law to incorporate the Wash Gas light Co. 3-Ptn from Isaac W Taylor & other legal reps of Jacques Clamorgan, in relation to claim on lands. 4-Cmte on Foreign Relations: House bill directing the mode for settling the claims of Chas G Ridgely, with an amendment. 5-Cmte on Public Lands: asking to be discharged from the further consideration of the memorial of David B Sears. 6-Cmte on Revolutionary Claims: unfavorable report on the claims of the excs of Nathan Lamme. 7-Cmte on Pensions: bill for the relief of Christopher Cunningham. 8-Bill for the relief of Eliz Converse, widow of Josiah Converse: be referred to the Cmte on Revolutionary Claims. 9-Cmte on Pensions: relief of Thos Badger; granting a pension to John Morrison; relief of Wm P Brady; relief of Saml Cony: without amendment. 10-Cmte on Private Land Claims: bill for the relief of the legal reps of the Marquis de Fougieres, & asked its immediate consideration. Bill was read a 3rd time, by unanimous consent, & passed. 11-Bill for the relief of Capt Foxall A Parker, of the U S Navy: passed.

Information wanted of Benj Hair, formerly of Cobcroft Hall, near Ferrybridge, Yorkshire, Old England. He left England about 50 years ago & came to this country, &, if living, would be about 72 years of age. Information will be thankfully received by his niece, Eliz Schofield, [only daughter of his sister the late Lucy Hall,] now resideing at 299 South Front st, Phil. The above Lucy Hall lived in London Road, Manchester.

Wash Corp: 1-Ptn of H G O'Neale: referred to the Cmte of Claims. 2-Relief of David Rich: passed. 3-Cmte of Claims: asking to be discharged from the further consideration of the ptn of Richd Eaton & wife. Same cmte: asking to be discharged from the further consideration of the ptn of John Fleming. 4-Cmte of Claims: act for the relief of Michl McDermott-[passed]; relief of Wm Jasper: both read. 5-Ptn of John Y Bryant & H O'Neal, remonstrating against the assessment of certain property belonging to them: referred to the Cmte of Ways & Means. 6-Bill granting permission to John E Ager & Brother to erect a frame bldg on lot 2 in square 343, was referred to the Cmte on Police. 7-Bill for the relief of Tos Downey: referred to the Cmte of Claims. 8-Bill for the relief of J C Pertch: rejected. 9-Bill for the relief of Chas Steward, jr: passed.

Gen Lafayette is buried in a private cemetery in the Rue Picpus, at the eastern extremity of Paris.

For the seat of the war: the U S steamship **New Orleans** left New Orleans on Apr 2 for Vera Cruz with Gov't store. The following passengers were on her: Gen Kearny, Hon Mr Sevier & suite, Jas D Mix, Com'r G F Pierson, U S N; Col Fiesco, Capt Hunter, 2nd Ill Regt; Capt D C Berry, Mass Regt; Lt Gilmer, Engineer corps; Capt Badger, Lt Wood, Lt G Patton, Capt H H Niles, 2nd Ohio volunteers; Lt A Jackson, Capt Blanding, Capt Osmur, one detachment of dragoons from Jefferson barracks, [Missouri] & one detachment of mounted men from Tenn, & one detachment of infty recruits.

A duel was fought on Mar 18 at Mier, between 2 ofcrs of the 3rd Dragoons: Lt Jos H Maddox & Lt Acting Adj Edw McPherson. On the fourth fire Lt McPherson was shot through the heart & died immediately. The cause of the quarrel was not known.

Died: on Apr 11, in Wash City, John Davis, a clerk in the ofc of the Com'r of Public Lands, aged 79. His funeral is this day, at 12 o'clock, from his residence near the Lower Bridge.

Died: Seneca M Conway, an esteemed & gifted member of the bar of Wisconsin Territory. Announcement was made on Mar 9 at the Court-house of Mineral Point. Although he had not been long among us, yet he became extensively known by his talents. –Wisconsin paper [No date.]

FRI APR 14, 1848
J F Kahl, manufacturer & importer of Pianos, Pa ave, between 10th & 11th sts.

Beautiful Boots: comfort, elegance, & durability combined.
–Henry Janney, 8th st, near the Gen P O.

Senate: 1-Documents in support of the claim of W Lee. 2-Cmte on Pensions: adverse report on the ptn of Elijah McDougall: to be printed. 3-Cmte on the Post Ofc & Post Roads: relief of H M Barney, without amendment. 4-Cmte on Pensions: bill for the relief of Gustavus Dorr. 5-Cmte on Naval Affairs: act for the relief of D Myerlee; of Stephen Champlin; of Jos Bryan; of G F de La Roche & W P Sanger; of Jas H Conley; of Jas Glynn; of Nancy Tompkins, of Eliz Mays; of Anne W Angus; of John Percival, a capt in the U S Navy; of Edw Quinn; & the joint resolution concerning the settlement of the accounts of Wm Speiden, purser in the U S Navy. 6-Resolved: the Secretary pay to John Skirving for his services in ventilating the Senate chamber during this session an allowance not exceeding the pay of a messenger, together with one dollar a day for an assistant laborer.

House of Reps: 1-Cmte on Revolutionary Claims: to inquire into allowing to the heirs of Capt John D Treville, a capt in the 4th Regt of Artl of the S C line, commutation pay, on account of his military services in the Revolution. 2-Ptn of C C Hopkins & Jas A Stuart, postmasters, & others, of Wayne, Marion, & Hamiton Counties, praying for a post route from Hickory Hill, in Marion Co, to McCleansboro, in Hamilton Co. 3-Ptn of W Baker, for compensation for wheels & looms furnished the Choctaws. 4-Ptn of Silas Reed, a citizen of Mo, preferring numerous charges of official misconduct against F R Conway, surveyor genr'l for the States of Illinois & Missouri. 5-Ptn of John Davenport, for arrears of pension, be taken from the files of the Clerk's ofc. 6-Ptn of Jas Rankin & others, citizens of township 38, of range 22, Hickory Co, Mo, praying to be permitted to select section 29, of same township, in lieu of the 16th section.

Com'rs sale of that portion of Geo Semmes' real estate remaining unsold, on Apr 28, nearly opposite Alexandria, containing a dwlg-house & outbldgs. The property is well known as the **Head of Frazier**. The sale is under a decree of the Circuit Court of D C. –Zach Walker, David Barry, Jas C Barry, Benj T Smith, Thos Jenkins, Com'rs

Appointments by the Pres: J W Lugenbeel, of Md, to be Commercial Agent of the U S at Monrovia, in Liberia. Vanbrugh Livingston, of N Y, to be Charge d'Affaires of the U S to the Republic of Ecuador. Jos W Fabens, of Mass, to be Consul of the U S for the port of Cayenne, in French Guiana.

Appointments of Postmasters by the Postmaster Genr'l:
Wm L Berry, Beavertown, Chas Co, Md, vice John Montgomery, deceased
Richd Owings, Friendship, Anne Arundel Co, Md, vice Wm H Ward, resigned
Constantia F Black, Charlestown, Cecil Co, Md, vice Wm C Black, deceased
Danl Witmer, Beaver Creek, Wash Co, Md, vice Larkin C Cook, resigned.
New Post Ofc: at Keedysville, Wash Co, Md, & Edw Reiley appointed Postmaster.

The Catholic Bishop the Rt Rev Wm Quartier died lately at Chicago.

Hon Levi Lincoln, of Worcester, Mass, has been elected the first Mayor of that "city" under its new charter.

Mrd: Apr 12, by Rev F S Evans, Mr Jas H Robertson, of Alexandria, to Miss Ann E Garrett, of Wash City.

Valuable Wash City property for sale: on Apr 15, his excellent 2 story brick house & lot, at the corner of E & 20th sts. –S D Finckel, G & 20th sts -A Green, auctioneer

SAT APR 15, 1848

Genteel furniture at auction: on Apr 18, at the residence of Mr Appleton, on the corner of Washington & Dunbarton sts. –Edw S Wright, auctioneer

For sale: 2 story frame dwlg-house, in a rapidly improving part of the city. –S Merwin Tucker, at Tucker & Daniel's, 3 doors east of Brown's Hotel.

For rent: in Gtwn, a 2 story brick house, on Fred'k & Second sts, with all necessary outbldgs: rent will be $200 a year, payable quarterly. –Wm G Ridgely

In Chancery: Benj L Jackson & Wm B Jackson, vs Catharine Ledden & Jas S Harvey, adms of Benj Ledden & others. On Apr 22, at the City Hall, the account of the trustee, & the interest of the widow will be audited. –W Redin

Senate: 1-Ptn from Saml Simonton, asking the payment of a certain sum of money due a deceased relative, under the treaty of 1837 with the Saginaw Indians. 2-Ptn from Wm J Bend, asking the return of duties paid by him on merchandise destroyed by fire. 3-Ptn from John Irons, asking indemnity for money to which his relative was entitled while an ofcr of the army. 4-Ptn of Catharine Crosby, legal rep of T D Anderson, late Consul of the U S at Tripoli, asking to be allowed credit for certain expenditures made by him in his official capacity. 5-Cmte on Indian Affairs: joint resolution for the relief of John A Bryan. 6-Bills passed: Relief of:

Jesse Turner	Nathl Kuydendall	Jonathan Lewis
Creed Taylor	Thos Brownell	Oliver C Harris
J F Caldwell	Thompson Hutchinson	Reynolds May

Abigail Garland, widow of Jacob Garland, deceased
Thos Douglas, late U S atty for east Florida
Saml W Belt, a native of the Cherokee nation
Eliz Pistole, widow of Chas Pistole, deceased
Eliz Jones & the other children, if any, of John Carr
Jeanette C Huntington, widow of & excx of Wm D Cheever, deceased.
7-Settlement of the claim of Henry Washington, late a deputy surveyor of the public lands in Florida.
8-Bill authorizing the purchase of the papers of Alex'r Hamilton. 9-Bill for the relief of the legal reps of Capt Jesse D Elliott was indefinitely postponed. 10-Sec of the Treas to make arrangement with Mangel M Quackenboss & his co-obligors, if any of them, for claims on bonds given by them as sureties to the U S.

House of Reps:: 1-Ptn of Cary H Fry, late major of the 2nd Regt of Ky volunteers, for losses sustained in the present war with Mexico. 2-Ptn & documents of Eliz Kinney, of Pa.

Circuit Court of Wash Co, D C-in Chancery. Nicholas Febrey vs Jas Thrift, trustee, & John Sessford. The bill charges that Sessford is indebted to the cmplnt in a certain sum of money, to wit: $700, with interest from Jan 1, 1846, subject to 2 payments amounting to $130, long since due & in arrears, which is secured by a deed of trust executed by said Sessford to said Thrift as trustee for a certain lot or parcel of ground in Wash City, with the appurtenances; that Thrift has removed out of the U S, & cannot execute the trust of said deed; the objects of the bill are the substitution of another trustee & general relief. It appears that Jas Thrift resides & is out of D C, & is in parts beyond the seas. It is ordered that Jas Thrift do, on or before the third Monday of Oct next, appear in Court. By order of the Court, Wm Brent, clerk

House for sale: new 2 story frame house on 8th st, between I & N Y ave. Apply to Simeon Matlock, 2 doors above Patterson's drug store, on 9th st.

Died: on Mar 31, at the residence of her father, in Montg Co, Md, Ellen R, only daughter of Thos J & Catherine W Bowie, in her 11th year.

Died: on Mar 16, at her residence in Decatur, Ill, Mrs Eliza Duley, widow of the late Benedict H Duley, of Montg Co, Md, in her 49th year.

A mother & 3 children, by the name of Stier, were burnt to death on Tue at Bloomfield, N Y.

MON APR 17, 1848

From Mexico: Gen Valencia died at Mexico on Mar 25, from an attack of apoplexy. This is the ofcr who was in command of the Mexican troops at Contreras, & upon whom Santa Anna throws the responsibility of all his reverses in defence of the city of Mexico.

Pottsville, Apr 12: Two of the locomotives of the Reading railroad Co ran together at the crossing of the Minehill & Reading railroad, & killed Martin Kowen, jr, age 18 years, an employee of the Reading Co.

Thos Sinclair, a son of Mr Geo Sinclair, of Wash City, age 5 years, was drowned yesterday in the creek near the Long-bridge Fishlanding. How he got into the water has not been ascertained. His body was found.
+
Died: yesterday, in his 6th year, Thos Sinclair, son of Mr Geo Sinclair, of Wash City. His funeral is from his father's residence on 7th st, this afternoon, at half-past 3 o'clock.

John Rowan, U S Consul to Naples, sailed from N Y with his lady & 4 children in the packet ship **West Point**, for Liverpool.

New Orleans Picayune of Apr 5. Jas Erwin committed suicide on Mon in his chamber at the St Chas Hotel, by shooting himself through the head. He was about 20 years of age, son of Mr Jas Erwin, long a resident of this city, & grandson of Henry Clay, & on either side of his family connected with names of great merit. [Apr 18th newspaper: a private letter states that Mr Erwin did not commit suicide, but accidentally shot himself while in the act of putting a loaded pistol under his pillow on going to bed at night.]

Last Sat, says the Worcester Journal, Rev Erastus Hopkins, of Northampton, lost a fine little boy, about 3 years old. Previous to putting him to bed, the girl having charge of the nursery put boiling water in the bathing tub, & left the room without qualifying the temperature. The little naked boy, supposing the water ready for his use, jumped into the tub, & was immersed in scalding water. He died on Sunday.

A boy, 7 years of age, son of Mr Adam Book, living in St John st, died yesterday from the effects of whiskey which he drank the afternoon previous. Two younger children sipped some, but are well. –Phil Ledger

House of Reps: 1-Ptn of Chiefs of different tribes of the N Y Indians, praying for relief to the survivors of the N Y Indians, who emigrated west of the Mississippi, & for the reps & relatives of those who have died. 2-Memorial of Thos W Chinn, M Courtney, & others, securities of Thos Gibbs Morgan, late collector of the revenue for the port of New Orleans, praying for relief. 3-Claim of W H Brockwa, adm on the estate of John & Susan Johnson, late of the village of Mackinac, deceased. 4-Ptn of John Plunkett, of Fayetteville, N C, asking an indemnity for injuries sustained from an explosion in the laboratory of the North Carolina arsenal.

TUE APR 18, 1848
Senate: 1-Ptn from Dennis Harris, merchant of N Y, asking for a return of duties on sugar destroyed by fire in N Y C while yet subject to exportation. 2-Ptn of John Campbell & Co of Pensacola, asking payment for subsistence furnished troops in the service of the U S in 1847. 3-Memorials from numerous citizens of the U S for the purchase of *Mount Vernon*. 4-Ptn from the heirs of Col Truman Cross, asking to be allowed compensation for extra official services rendered by deceased. 5-Cmte on Patents: bill authorizing the renewal of the patent for the benefit of the widow & heirs-at-law of Timothy P Anderson, deceased. 6-Cmte on Public Lands: House bill for the relief of Thos Scott, without amendment. 7-Cmte on Public Lands: asking to be discharged from the further consideration of the ptn of Isaac W Taylor & other reps of Jacques Clamorgan, & that it be referred to the Cmte on the Judiciary.

To the great satisfaction of his family & connexions in Wash City, & his friends generally, we are glad to announce the return home from service with the army in Mexico, in apparently excellent health, of Maj Wm Turnbull, of the corps of Topographical Engineers.

Late from Calif: Passed Midshipman T McLanahan was killed on Feb 11.

For rent: brick house on L st, between 15th & 16th sts west; & a house on 12th st, near *Franklin Row*, large lot, & a pump of good water in the yard. Inquire of Alex Borland.

The subscriber has several hundred acres of land in Wash Co which he will dispose of upon reasonable terms. It lies between the Washington & Rockville Turnpike Road & Rock Creek, on both sides of the Piney Branch Road. Apply to the subscriber, near the land, or to Thos Carbery, in Wash. –Abner C Peirce

Sat, as Mr J P Bigelow, of Abington, brother-in-law of the younger Mr Chamberlain, whose property was destroyed at Neponset, attempted to get into the cars to return home, he having been assisting at the fire the previous day, he fell, & the wheels passed over his leg, severing it at the ankle, & he was obliged to submit to amputation afterwards.

Mrd: on Apr 16, by Rev Levi R Reese, Isaac P Baldwin, of N Y, to Miss Harriet Sexsmith, of Wash City.

The subscriber has been appointed by Dr Henry Brooke & Mr John L Waring trustees of John Waring, late merchant in Wash, D C, as their agent. –John B Brooke, jr

The Shelby News of Apr 5, contains a long interesting letter from Lt Whitaker, of the Shelby volunteers, 3rd Ky Infty, dated Mexico, Feb 26, 1848, from which it appears that the following deaths have occurred in Capt Todd's company up to the date above: Jas Ashby, Jas B Telley, John C Drake, Wm Boothe, A C Sill, N M Pifer, Moses R Garnett, Warfield Bright, Cyrenus W Doss, John J Williamson, John W Berry, Ezekiel Brown, & Dr Joel D Sublett. From this letter we learn that of the regt over 100 have died, 30 or 40 discharged, & 108 on the sick list. -Commonwealth

WED APR 19, 1848

N Y Correspondent: N Y, Apr 15, 1848. I saw yesterday the original patent given in this country for the first cast iron plough. The document, which is on strong parchment & well preserved, bears date Jun 26, 1797, & is signed by John Adams, Pres of the U S, Timothy Pickering Sec of State, & certified by Chas Lee, Atty Gen. It was given to Chas Newbold, of Burlington Co, N J, for an improved plough, which consisted of solid cast iron, except the handles & beam.

Senate: 1-Ptn from Geo F Raub, asking Gov't to purchase the patent right of Raub's safety valve for steam engines. 2-Ptn from Jas Lowry Donaldson, an ofcr of the U S army, asking indemnity for losses sustained in consequence of having been robbed of public money. 3-Cmte on Naval Affairs: House bill for the relief of J Mellville Gilliss & others, with an amendment. 4-Cmte of Claims: bill for the relief of John McIntosh; also, a bill for the relief of A H Cole. 5-Cmte on Public Lands: bill to provide for the final settlement of the accounts of Thos C Shelden, late receiver of public moneys at Kalamazoo, Mich. Same cmte: bill to provide for the settlement of the accounts of Abraham Edwards. 6-Cmte on Military Affairs: bill for the relief of Midshipman Robt C Rogers.

For sale; country residence, called *Joseph Park*, on the Brookville & Gtwn rd, bordering on Rock Creek, Montg Co, Md. Improvements include a small frame house. Apply to R Jones, of *Cleandrinking*, or J C Jones, of *Norwood*, near Gtwn.

I will offer at public sale, on Apr 22, on the premises, 100 acres of land. This farm lies on the turnpike leading from Gtwn to Rockville. Apply to John C Jones, Norwood.

Orphans Court of Wash Co, D C. Letters testamentary on the personal estate of Evan Evans, late of said county, deceased. –W B Magruder, exc

New Hardware & Variety Store: on Pa ave, opposite Brown's Hotel. –T G Russell & Co

House of Reps:: 1-Cmte of Claims: adverse reports on the ptns of Wiltshire Minor, David Cook, Richd S Schaffelin, J P McElrath, Jos Ingle, the legal reps of Wm H Freeman, & Ebenezer Hazard: laid on the table. Same cmte: bills for the relief of John H Baker, & relief of the legal reps of Oliver Lee: committed. Same cmte: adverse reports on the ptns of Jas H Chezun; Geo W Biscoe; Lewis F Beeler & others; Caleb Bell; adm of Matthew Bell; & Danl G Garnsey: laid on the table. Same cmte: bill for the relief of Joshua Barney, U S agent; relief of Eleanora B Watkins, widow of Gassaway Watkins; & relief of Saml A Grier: committed. 2-Cmte on Public Lands: bill for the relief of Shadrach Gillet & others, moved that the cmte be discharged from the same: agreed to. 3-Cmte for D C: bill for the relief of John Dixon: committed. 4-Cmte on the Judiciary: adverse report on the ptn of Josiah McCaskey: laid on the table. 5-Ptn of Wm Gott for a pension.

Mrd: on Apr 13, by Rev Chas A Davis, Mr Geo Chism to Miss Eliz Mohldr, all of Wash City.

Clarence, a son of of Hon David Wilmot, aged about 11 years, came to his death on Mon last [says the Bradford Reporter] by eating wild parsnip. He was attending the Misses' Robbs' school, at Athens, & with another lad, in the fields, ate the root, which caused his death, after much suffering, in about 2 hours. –Albany Atlas

THU APR 20, 1848
Senate: 1-Cmte of Claims: unfavorable report on the ptn of Richd P Dunn: adverse report on the ptn of J Harris, late deputy collector at Providence, R I.

$50 reward. I am authorized by her owner to offer a reward for recovery of servant woman, Evelina, who left her house on Sat: a dark-colored woman, about 40 years of age, short, & very fat. –John Dewdney

Died in Buffalo, on Apr 6, Ezekiel Lane, at the great age of 102 years. He was the first white resident of that city, & built the first house in 1784. He lived, says the Advertiser, to see that single hut multiplied to over 4,000 bldgs, & more than 40,000 people in a city of which himself & family were the first sole inhabitants. He was a soldier of the Revolution.

Chicago Journal: Rev Wm Quarter, Bishop of Chicago, died at that place on Apr 10, deeply lamented by those who knew him.

Wash Corp: 1-Ptn of A C Draper: referred to the Cmte of Claims. 2-Cmte of Claims: asking to be discharged from the further consideration of the ptn of H B Sawyer: agreed to. 3-Relief of Chas Steward, jr: referred to the Cmte of Claims. 4-Cmte of Claims: bill for the relief of Thos Downey: reported without amendment.

For rent: commodious dwlg-house on F near 21st st, formerly occupied by T Ritchie. Inquire at the Assist Quartermaster's Ofc, near the War Dept.

FRI APR 21, 1848
Six young men went out from Camden, Me, on Sun last in a boat, & capsized. John Tyler, Putnam T Simonton, Arelius Faly, & Geo Duncan, being burdened with overcoats, were drowned. Levi Turner & Geo Hodgman were rescued.

Dr John Fred'k Sickles, Surgeon on board the U S ship **North Carolina**, lying in the habor of N Y, suddenly expired on Tue last, from disease of the heart, while engaged in conversation with one of the Lts on board the ship. He had been in the U S service for 15 years, & with Lt Wilkes on the exploring expedition, during which time he became afflicted with the malady which has so suddenly terminated his life.

Hudson [N Y] Gaz of Tue. Deputy Sheriff John H Smith, of Livingston, was shot & critically wounded by 2 men who ambushed him as he drove past a patch of pine wood. He was to attend the sale of some property which he had levied upon, belonging to Geo L Finkle, on an execution in favor of Mr Wicks, for his oxen, which had been shot. No sale took place. Smith proceeded to Philip R Miller's house, a mile from Yager's tavern, when he was shot. [See Apr 22nd newspaper.]

Orphans Court of Wash Co, D C. Case of Jas Selden, adm of Jas M Selden, deceased: administrator & Court have appointed May 9 next for the settlement of the estate of Jas M Selden. --Ed N Roach, Reg/o wills

For rent: dwlg, recently occupied by Mon Pageot. Apply to W W Corcoran.

Wash City Canal: sealed proposals will be received for renting, for 1 year, commencing on May 1, 1848, all the wharves & sites on the canal, [including Market Space between 7th & 8th sts,] from 17th st wharf. -Jas A Tait, Com'r of Canal, Western Division

Some persons, regardless of the interest of their neighbors, have removed from my square 369 large quantities of sods & earth, thereby greatly injuring the property. This is to notify such that I expect them to fill the cavities they have made, & to warn all others against committing similar depredations at their peril. -Jas Caden

To let, 2 story brick dwlg, neatly furnished, at H & 20th sts. Apply to Wm Wilson, next door.

SAT APR 22, 1848
Virginia, to wit: At a quarterly Court, continued & held for Pittsylvania Co, Jun 22, 1847. Wm Dews & Nancy his wife, & the said Wm Dews, as adm de bonis non with the will annexed of Joshua Stone, deceased, plntfs, against the distributees of the said Joshua Stone, deceased, dfndnts. In a suit in Chancery for the distribution of the estate bequeathed to the testator's widow for life. The Court doth adjudge, order, & decree that Wm Dews, as adm d b n of Joshua Stone, deceased, with his will annexed, & com'r under the decree to sell the land bequeathed to Mary Stone, his widow, for life, do pay to the heirs of D C Harrison, deceased, the following sums of money, to wit: to Joshua Harrison, $45.08; to Wm Dearing & Polly his wife, $45.08; to Harrison Coleman & Nancy his wife, $45.08; to Stith Harrison, $45.08; to Doke & Koley his wife, $45.08; to Answorth Harrison, $45.08; to Clack Harrison, $45.08; & to the descendants of Polly Terry, deceased, the following sums, viz: to Joshua Terry, $90.16; to Nathl Terry, $90.16; to John H Buckley & wife, $90.16; to Creed McHaney & wife, $90.16. That he pay the descendants of Joshua Stone, jr, deceased, son of Joshua Stone, the elder, deceased, the following sums of money, viz: to Joshua Stone, $40.07 2-9; to Henry Paris & Prudence his wife, $40.07 2-9; to the descendants of Patsy Dews, wife of Ezekiel Dews, viz; Joshua, Sarah, Polly, & Ann Dews, $40.07 2-9; to Dianna Stone, widow of Joshua Stone, & her child Prudence, $40.07 2-9; to the children of Polly, wife of McCoil Graven, $40.07 2-9; to an unknown child of Wm W Dews & Eliz his wife, the said parents being dead, $40.07 2-9; to an unknown child of Memory Thompson & Judith his wife, $40.07 2-9; to the rep of Saml Stone, deceased, $40.07 2-9/ that the said Wm Dews retain the sum of $40.07 2-9, in right of his wife Nancy. That he pay to Saml Stone, son of the testator $360.65; that he pay to Clack Stone, $360.65; that he pay to the descendants of Wm H Stone, deceased, the following sums, viz: to Wm H Plunkett & Mary his wife, $47.73; to Cornelius Gilbert & Eliza his wife, $47.73; to Saml E Stone, $47.73; to John Gilbert & Dolly C his wife, $47.73; to Gunnery Wilbourn & Sarah his wife, $47.73; to Joshua R Stone, $47.73; to Thos Dews & Martha his wife, $47.73; to Susan, widow of Jesse Hubbard, deceased, $47.73; to Applewight, wife of John Stone, deceased, & their children, Martha, Laura, & Jas J Stone, $47.73; to Eliz, wife of Wm Stone, deceased, which said Eliz has since married, & their 3 children, Susan Ann, Mary L, & Eliz M Stone, $47.73. That he pay to the descendants of Coleman Stone, deceased, $360.65. The aforesaid amounts being all the estate of the testator Joshua Stone, deceased, which at the time of making up the said amount had come to the hands of the said Wm Dews, adm of Joshua Stone, & as com'r in this cause. It appearing to the Court that the names & residences of many of the parties in this suit are unknown. An extract-Test: Wm H Tunstall, clerk Note: Since the rendition of the foregoing decree, the amount payable to the children of Polly, wife of McCoil Graven, has been decreed to be paid to a transferee of said Graven.

Much excitement at Vera Cruz on Mar 30th, it being discovered that 2nd Lt John Smith, of Capt White's company of mounted men, had deserted, taking with him 7 men of his company. They fell into the hands of Zenobis, or Cenobio, the guerilla chief. He would not accept the men & kept them prisoners. He sent word to Govn'r Wilson, who dispatched Capt Kerr & his command to escort the worthies into Vera Cruz, & they arrived on Apr 2. It is hoped that Govn'r Wilson will not let him off with impunity.

$1,000 reward has been offered by Govn'r Young, of N Y, for the arrest of John Mosher, of Columbia Co, who has been indicted for burglary, arson, & conspiracy, & John Miller & Coonrod C Wheeler, of Taghkanic, charged with the murderous assault on Sheriff John H Smith. [See Apr 21st newspaper.]

Alex'r Addis, about 17 years old, a son of Jos Addis, engineer of the steam saw mills at Forestville, Queen Anne Co, Md, was caught in a belt of the machinery & instantly killed on Apr 14.

Chancery sale of valuable & extensive iron works, & of a large body of mineral, wood, & farming lands, in Wash Co, Md: by decree of the High Court of Chancery. Sale on May 24, *The Antietam Iron Works*, with all bldgs & improvements. Comprises upwards of 13,000 acres. A plat of the property can be seen at the ofc of J S Nicholas, one of the trustees, in Court-house land. Reference may be had to Thos H O'Neal, Surveyor, Fred'k, Md. –J Meredith, J S Nicholas, Trustees

$50 reward for runaway negro Daniel, about 25 years old. –Saml L Brooke, living near Upper Marlborough, PG Co, Md.

Danl Drayton, Chester English, & Edw Sayres-capt of the vessel, were yesterday finally committed to answer at the June term of the Criminal Court to the charge of having "stolen, taken, & carried away," 76 slaves, residents in this county, on Apr 15, 1848. Bail demanded by the magistrates is $1,000 for each slave. As yet no bail has been offered for either of these men. [Apr 24th newspaper: slave abductors were finally committed. The Criminal Court meets in June. Nearly all of the runaway slaves have been sold to dealers in that line -News]

MON APR 24, 1848
Mrs Jane C Washington, of *Mount Vernon*, has authorized a contradiction of the current report that Mr Stephens has purchased the Library of Gen Washington, or 3,000 volumes of it, for $5,000. She says that there is not the slightest foundation for it. The family has never entertained the thought of selling that property, & five times the sum named could not purchase it.

A young man named Gibbs, of Somerset, Mass, about 27 years of age, having been jilted by his sweetheart, in Dighton, committed suicide by throwing himself into Taunton river.

David Baldwin, of Preston, Senator elect in the Legislature of the State of Conn, died last Mon, aged 49. Col Baldwin is highly eulogized in the Conn papers, & his loss is deeply deplored.

Fire on Fri in the Catholic Church in the city of Richmond, when a candle accidentally fell against the drapery surrounding the repository. The fire was confined to a small area, but Rev Timothy O'Brien, had his hands & face severely burnt. A son of Mr Henry Miller, one of the attendants, was also badly burnt.

Mrd: on Apr 20, by Rev Littleton F Morgan, Mr Wm Butler, formerly of Balt, to Miss Ann Eliz Mattingly, of Wash City.

Mrd: on Apr 18, at Carlisle, Pa, by Rev Mr Nadal, Hon T Pilsbury, Rep in Congress from Texas, to Rebecca S, 2nd daughter of Col J Carpenter, of Penobscot Co, Maine.

Died: on Apr 22, in Wash City, Col Jas Long, a native of Berkeley Co, Va, & for upwards of 20 years a resident of Wash City.

Died: on Sat, Thos Bingey, aged 58 years, an amiable, honest, & sober man, & for more than 30 years a faithful watchman at the Navy Dept.

Died: on Apr 22, Mary Emma, infant daughter of Francis & Caroline M Lombardi, aged 11 months.

Missing Vessels: the British brig **Charles Grey**, of Bermuda, which cleared at Balt on Oct 15 last for Barbadoes, has not since been heard from. The brig **Evelina Sandel**, of & from Balt, cleared this Oct, for Demerara, has likewise never been heard from.

At the fire of last Tue 3 children of Mr Weedon who slept in the 4th story of the burning house, narrowly escaped. They were saved by the praiseworthy & prompt exertions of a warm-hearted Irishman named Kelleher, who bore off the children to safety, at the peril of his own life.

Appointments by the Pres: Montgomery D Parker, of Mass, to be Consul of the U S for the Cape de Verd Islands, vice Ferdinand Gardner, deceased. Geo F Thompson, to be Appraiser of merchandise for the port of N Y, N Y, vice Vanburgh Livingston, appointed Charge d'Affaires to Ecuador. John Bryan, jr, to be Appraiser of merchandise for the port of Charleston, S C, vice John Bryan, sen, resigned.

TUE APR 25, 1848
Senate: 1-Cmte on the Post Ofc & Post Roads: bill for the relief of Wm Greer. 2-Memorial of Sarah Ann Hart: referred to the Cmte on Naval Affairs. 3-Ptn of Arnold Naudain: referred to the Cmte of Claims. 4-Cmte of Contingent Expenses: adverse report on the ptn of Jas Moore. 5-Cmte of Claims: bill for the relief of Jas Lawton ordered back to the Cmte of Claims. 6-Bill for the relief of Gamaliel Taylor, late marshal of the U S for the district of Indiana. 7-Bill for the relief of Lomer Graham was considered in the Cmte of the Whole & passed.

Railroad Journal, Ironmaster's & Mining Gaz: now in its 17th publication; at the Bookstore of Frank Taylor, or the the publisher in Phil, for current year, or from commencement, 1832. –D K Minor, Phil

House of Reps: 1-Ptn of John Downey, of N Y, for a pension. 2-Ptn of Dickenson Lumpkins, of Campbell Co, Tenn, a Revolutionary soldier, praying for a pension for services rendered in the war of the Revolution.

Lewisburg [Va] Chronicle of Apr 13 states that about the Apr 1, Eastep shot & killed a man named Harris. He shot him through the back & he died immediately. A party left Nicholas Court House, on Sat, to arrest him. The controversy was over a piece of land.

Died: on Mar 31, at the residence of Mrs Hawley, [her sister,] at Albany, after a long & painful illness, Mrs Anna Maria Tyler, wife of Mr Benj O Tyler, formerly of Wash City, in her 54th year. One son, aged 18 years, is the only child remaining to console her surviving partner, himself suffering & disabled for the last year & a half, & still, by the effects of an accidental fall from a ladder.

Died: on Apr 23, in Boston, Mrs Mary Anne Philips, wife of Geo Wm Phillips, of that city, & daughter of the late Mr Geo Bladen, of this place.

Died: on Apr 12, at Peakland, Bedford Co, Va, Laura Virginia, infant daughter of the Hon W L & Eliz Goggin, aged about 1 year & 3 months.

Died: on Mar 31, at the residence of her father, in Montg Co, Md, Ellen R, only daughter of Thos J & Catherine W Bowie, aged 11 years, after a painful illness.

Died: on Apr 23, in Wash City, Edward, infant son of Thos S & Caroline B Devaughan, aged 17 months.

Mrd: on Apr 23, at St John's Church, Wm B Avery, of Conn, to Miss Margaret Smith, daughter of the late Henry Smith, of Wash City.

Celebration of the French Revolution: owing to the unfavorable condition of Pa ave, which was literally a cloud of dust all the morning & when the procession passed along, there was not so full a turnout. In front of the line was the Chief Marshal, S R Hobbie, & his side, Jos H Bradley & John P Heiss, on horseback. The Marine Band following playing the Marseilles Hymn; then the Wash Light Infty; Ofcrs of the Day & City Authorities; Orator & Chaplain; Exec Cmte; Mayor, Aldermen, & Common Council; the Clergy; College of Gtwn, Pres, Ofcrs, & Students; Columbus College, Pres, Ofcrs, & Students; German citizens; then a Car & Printing Press, the car being ornamentd with the tri-colored flag & with the U S flag, & drawn by 4 horses, led by grooms; strangers & visiters; & citizens of Wash. Prayer by Rev Chas A Davis. Richd S Coxe, was Orator of the Day.

Valuable improved property for sale: by excs of the late Alex'r McDonald: 2 adjoining brick houses, & the lot, on the n w corner of square 223, fronting on N Y ave & 15th st west. –Michl Nourse, Alex'r McIntyre

WED APR 26, 1848
Santa Anna took his departure from Mexico, after a long farewell address to his fellow-citizens.

Deaths in Maine: on Apr 17, the Hon Asa Clapp, aged 86 years. Also, at Wiscasset, Maine, on the same day, Capt Nathan Clark, aged 80 years. These 2 gentlemen were the respected parents of Messrs A W H Clapp & Franklin Clark, 2 Reps from Maine, who occupy seats side by side in the present Congress.

Knoxville [Tenn] Tribune of Apr 11: On Sat last, Capt Henry B Newman, an esteemed citizen of Knoxville, was shot down in the ofc of the county court clerk, in the courthouse, by Thos D Murray, & lived but 15 minutes afterwards. The instrument of death was a large holster-pistol, heavily loaded. There were 41 buckshot deeply imbedded in the breast of the victim. Murray was taken into custody.

City Ordinances-Wash. 1-An act for the relief of sundry persons therein named: to Valentine Harbaugh, $30.25; to Wallace Elliot, $16.75; & to T P Morgan, $85.22.

Senate: 1-Ptn from Frink & Hadduck & L P Sanger, asking payment of a balance due under a contract for carrying the U S mail. 2-Cmte on Revolutionary Claims: adverse report on the House bill for the relief of the heirs of Rignald, alias Nick Hillary. 3-Cmte on Indian Affairs: bill for the relief of Wm Lee.

House of Reps: 1-Ptn of L P Sanger, praying compensation for carrying the mails from Feb 13, 1847, until Jun, 1847, over routes abandoned by O Hinton & Co. 2-Ptn of Thos Harrison & many others, for a mail route from Mount Carroll, Ill, to Pleasant Valley & Howardsville, Ill. 3-Ptn of Henry Little & Jacob Felch, of Newbury, Mass, for indemnity for damages sustained by the erection of a breakwater connecting with Woodbridge's island, in Merrimac river. 4-Memorial of Benedict J Heard, that his claim for the destruction of his houses may be paid. 5-Ptn of David Jones for a pension. 6-Ptn of W H Y Haskett & 27 other citizens of Portsmouth, N H, praying that Congress will purchase **Mount Vernon**, agreeably to a proposition of John A Washington to the Hon Geo M Dallas. 7-Ptn of Saml Davis for bounty on schnr **Daniel**. 8-Ptn of Ephraim Spoor, praying for a pension. 8-Ptn of Wm Linville & 25 others, ofcrs & soldiers in the last war with Great Britain, asking an extension of the pension laws. 9-Ptn of Wm Tee, of Portsmouth, Va, for a pension. 10-Ptn of 2nd Lt John S Devlin, for compensation for acting as assist quartermaster in the marine corps. 11-Ptn of Geo Pitt Stevenson, for an allowance for service as judge advocate on the coast of Brazil. 12-Ptn of Charlotte S Newcomb for arrears of pension due her grandfather, Thos Lincoln, deceased. 13-Ptn of Robt Perry, for a pension for services rendered & injuries received during the Indian war.

Died: on Apr 24, John N Pumroy, of Wash City, in his 41st year. His funeral is this morning, at 10 o'clock, from his late residence on 11th st, a few doors above G st.

Brandywine Chalybeate Springs, in Delaware, for sale: a fashionable resort for many years; consists of a 3 story stone bldg, used as a Hotel; bath house; billard room & ten-pin alley; besides 3 ornamented cottages; about 60 acres of land.
–Matthew Newkirk, 80 Walnut st, Phil, Pa.

A Naval Court Martial has been sitting at Annapolis during the past week, composed of the following ofcrs: Cmdor Morris, Cmdor Morgan, Cmdor McCauley; Cmder Eitchie, Cmder Buchanan, Cmder Faragut, & Com Barron. It is for the trial of some midshipmen.

THU APR 27, 1848

Wm A Richardson, Merchant Tailor, west side of 8th st, near Pa ave, is about to close his business on account of continued ill-health. Those indebted to him should call & settle their accounts.

House & lot for sale or rent on C st, between 2nd & 3rd sts. Inquire of W C Choate, La ave & 6th st.

$50 reward for runaway negro man Allen Hawkins, slave for life, aged about 24 or 25. –Jno A Pye

Wash Corp: 1-Cmte of Claims: act for the relief of Michl McDermott; act for the relief of Chas Stewart, jr: both passed. 2-Cmte of Claims: asking to be discharged from the further consideration of the ptn of Caleb Dulany. Same cmte was referred the ptn of Thos Kingsbury, made a similar report. Same cmte: bill for the relief of John Miller, without amendment.

Senate: 1-Ptn from Maj Wm Bayly, asking to be discharged from liability for certain public property which has been applied to the service of the public. 2-Cmte on the Library to purchase the full length original portrait of Gen Zachary Taylor, painted by Wm G Brown, of Richmond, if the same can be obtained at a price deemed by the cmte to be reasonable.

House of Reps: 1-Cmte of Claims: bill for the relief of Jose Argote Villalobos, Marie Rose, Francois Felix, Marquis de Fongeres, their heirs or legal reps, reported the same without amendment: committed. 2-Cmte on Naval Affairs: bill for the relief of the legal owners of the ship **James Mitchell**; bill for the relief of Capt Lewis Warrington & others: committed. 3-Same cmte: bill for the relief of Edmund L DuBarry, & a bill for the relief of Edw Myers: committed. Same cmte: bill for the relief of Lot Davis; relief of Wm Gove; & a bill for the relief of Benj Cressey. 4-Cmte on Foreign Affairs: bill for the relief of Joshua Dodge; relief of Peter Parker & Jacob L Martin: both committed. 5-Cmte on Revolutionary Pensions: adverse reports on the ptns of M A Richard, Drusilla Bukey, A P Campbell, A Garlick, J Gere, L Van Dyke, & C Kellar: laid on the table. Also, a bill for the relief of Sarah White, & a bill for the relief of Eliz Williamson: committed. 6-Cmte on Revolutionary Pensions: adverse reports on the ptns of A M Dade, widow of the late Maj F L Dade, & Wm Pelfrey: laid on the table. Same cmte: adverse reports on the ptns of Henry Freeman, Hannah Weston, Catharine Riddle, Esther Bartlett, Lydia Shurtliff, Nancy King, & Henry Johnson: laid on the table. Same cmte: bill for the relief of Polly Aldrich: committed. Same cmte: bill granting pensions to the surviving petty ofcrs, seamen, & marines, who, under the command of Capt Stephen Decatur, jr, captured & destroyed the frig **Philadelphia** in the harbor of Tripoli on Feb 10, 1804: read twice. [Besides Decatur there were 3 other Lts, Lawrence, Bainbridge, & Power.

Decatur was dead & his lady put on the roll of pensioners in which capacity she had drawn some $10,000 out of the Treasury. Lawrence was dead, & his widow was pensioned. Bainbridge was dead, & his surviving child was enjoying a pension. Power, too, was deceased, & his child was provided for in like manner. So there were no surviving Lts to be provided for by this bill. Of midshipmen there had been 7. Of these all were dead but one, & either their widows or children were on the pension list. The sole survivor was now in employment by the Navy Dept.] The bill was ordered to be printed. 7-Cmte of Claims: bill for the relief of the widow of Lt Richd E Cochran: committed. Same cmte: bill for the relief of John B Smith & Simeon Darden: committed. Same cmte: adverse report on the ptn of A Fenton: laid on the table. 8-Cmte on Commerce: bill to refund a penalty remitted by the Sec of Treas to John Hurdorp: committed. Same cmte: bill for the relief of Thos H Leggett: committed. 9-Cmte on Public Lands: bill for the relief of the widow & children of Capt Robt Grey, the discoverer of the Columbia river: committed. 10-Cmte on Revolutionary Claims: discharged from the ptns of the heirs of Jos Frederick, deceased, & of the heirs of Jacob Nutter: laid on the table. Same cmte: bill for the relief of the legal reps of Thos Jett, deceased: committed. Same cmte: adverse reports on the ptns of the legal reps of Wm Shippen, deceased, & of the heirs of Wm Campbell, deceased: laid on the table. 11-Cmte of Claims: bill for the relief of H M Salomon, legal rep of Haym Salomon: committed. 12-Cmte on Private Land Claims: adverse report on the ptn of Mary Toorea & Frederic Grove, heirs of Wm McGhee, deceased: laid on the table. 13-Cmte on Indian Affairs: bill for the relief of Israel Johnson: committed. Same cmte: House bill for the relief of Abraham Hogeboom, deceased: committed. Same cmte: adverse report upon the ptn of Geo McGuire: laid on the table.

Dissolution of the partnership under the name of Boteler & McGregor, by mutual consent. —C W Boteler, N M McGregor [N M McGregor continues the house-furnishing business at the old stand.]

Died: on Apr 26, Mr Richd Tonge, in his 67th year. His funeral is tomorrow at 3 o'clock, from his late residence, on 7th st, next to Odd Fellows' Hall.

Died: on Sat last, at his residence in Buckingham Co, Va, after an illness of some weeks, Thos M Bondurant. Col Bondurant represented his county for several sessions in the House of Delegates of Va.

Died: on Apr 1, at West Hill, Wandsworth, England, of consumption, Frances Allan Aspinwall, aged 26, daughter of Col Aspinwall, U S Consul in London.

Died: on Feb 14, at the residence of her son-in-law, Rev Ferdinand Jacobs, near Milledgeville, Ga, of pneumonia, Mrs Abigail O Ripley, relict of the late Hon Jas Wheelock Ripley, of Maine.

Died: on Apr 23, at his residence, in Chas Co, Md, Gerrard Briscoe, after a very short illness, aged about 38 years, leaving a wife & 4 children to deplore his early death.

Capt Wm C De Hart, of the 2nd Regt U S Artl, died at Elizabethtown, N J, on Fri last, after lingering for months from disease contracted while in the active discharge of arduous service in his regt in Mexico. He was a graduate of West Point, & joined his regt just prior to the masterly demonstration upon Vera Cruz. He led his regt gallantly into action at the triumphant battle of Cerro Gordo, & was installed in the post of Lt Govn'r of the city of Puebla, memorable for its brilliant defence under the chief command of Col Childs against the obstinate assaults of a vastly superior Mexican force. It was during this siege that Capt De Hart's health finally gave way. He had lingered since his return, now some months, upon a bed of sickness.

Mrd: on Apr 13, in Chas Co, Md, by Rev Mr Moore, Tho Milstead to Miss Verlinda Ann, eldest daughter of Edw Welch.

Wm Gibbons, Sheriff of Allachia Co, Florida, was recently shot dead by a man named Black.

Wm R Jones, father of the Hon John W Jones, of Ga, died at his residence in Nicholas Co, Ky, in his 73rd year, on Apr 17

FRI APR 28, 1848
House of Reps: 1-Ptn of Jos Chaffee, praying Congress to adjust & pay his claim against the Wyandott Indians, in accordance with the treaty with that people in 1842. 2-Ptn of Wm Pitman, of Pa, a soldier of the late war, praying for relief. 3-Ptn of David McNair, for a pension for services in last war with Great Britain. 4-An application for the renewal of the patent of Jas Harley, for casting chilled rolls.

City Ordinances: 1-Act for the relief of Mrs M A Daly: to pay to her one-half the amount expended by her late husband in sinking a well & fixing a pump on the street at L & 14th st, the same being now used as a Corp pump. 2-Act for the relief of Chas Steward, jr: to pay him the sum of $17.93, being a balance due him for improving 4½ st. 3-Act for the relief of Washington Rawlings: fine imposed for an alleged violation of a law relative to retailing firewood: remitted: provided he pay the cost of prosecution. 4-Act for the relief of Michl McDermott: fine imposed for an alleged violation of a law relative to the erection of wooden bldgs; remitted; provided he pay the cost of prosecution.

Senate: 1-Ptn from David Baker, for a renewal of his patent for an improvement in a saw mill for cutting ship timber. 2-Ptn from Capt Richd Merrick, asking relief for the loss of his vouchers after they had been filed with the proper accounting ofcr of the Gov't. 3-Ptn from the heirs of John Riggs, asking for 7 years half pay due said Riggs.
4-Ptn from citizens of Winnebago Co, Ill, asking that a law may be passed to emancipate Eliza Herbert & Caroline, her dght, who were sold to satisfy a judgment in favor of the U S, & refunding the money to the person purchasing them.

Richd J Turner, whose trial, for conspiracy to defraud the Mechanics' Bank of Balt of a large sum of money, was removed to Annapolis, has been tried & convicted. His sentence is confinement in Anne Arundel Co jail for 7 years & a fine of $500.

Robt Love, of Balt, some days since, tramped upon a nail, which pierced his foot, going almost through it. The wound healed up, but on Sat he was attacked with tetanus, & died on Monday. He was a young man, a carpenter, & leaves a wife & child.

Passengers in the steamship **Acadia**, from Liverpool for Boston: Mr & Mrs Bridel, Mr & Mrs Foy, Mr Herbrailt, Capt Prichard, Messrs French, McTavish, Martineau, Escandon & friend, C Campbell, Wutherland, Rev Dr Dixon, Mr Noad, John Sterling, Mr Russell, S Brown, J T Knight, T Teter, John Aiken, Messrs L Charnon, J L Barclay, C D Roy, W T McKinstry, Mr Sutzens, Peard, J B Brugere, Weston Hay, A Leveagne, Gravel, Jas Lodge, Lewis Lay, P L Bogart, Mr Thompson, Gilbert Heron, Alex'r Ewing, & Lunsden Clementon.

Household & kitchen furniture at auction: on May 2, at the residence of Mrs Reed, on C st, between 4½ & 6th sts. -A Green, auctioneer

Died: on Apr 23, at Lebanon, West River, Md, Ann Thomas, in her 70th year.

Mrd: on Apr 27, by Rev J W R Handy, Prof J S Hubbard, U S Navy, to Sarah E L, daughter of the late Jas H Handy, of Wash City.

Mrd: on Apr 18, by Rev W Prettyman, Mr Chas A Vermillion to Miss Eliz Stewart, both of Wash City.

An impression has existed in this community, that I was instrumental in detecting & preventing the recent escape of slaves from this District. I deem it due to myself to state that I had no knowledge whatever of the contemplated escape of the slaves, & was not in any manner concerned in their capture. My good character I hope, will not not suffer from such base slander. –Judson Digges, Hack 100

SAT APR 29, 1848
C Gill, of Wash Co, D C, brought before me, as strays, a buffalo cow with a calf about one week old. -J L Smith, Justice of the Peace [Owner to prove property, pay charges, & taken them away. C Gill, near the Long Bridge.]

Senate: Ptn from Saml C Williams, & other citizens of Fred'k & Shenandoah Counties, Va, asking mail facilities. 2-Cmte of Claims: bill for the relief of Jacob Godeon, with an amendment. Same cmte: bill for the relief of Gad Humphreys, with a report; & relief of Eugene Van Ness & John M Brush, excs of Nehemiah Brush, with a report. 3-Cmte on the Library: asking to be discharged from the further consideration of the ptn of Thos F Gordon: referred to the Cmte of Claims.

House of Reps: 1-Bills reported-relief of:
Joel Thacker	Isaac Shepard	Wm Via
John Knight	David Shepard	Eliza A Mellon
Thos Flanegan	A C Bryan & others	Benj Reifsnyder
Jonathan Slyter	Almedus Scott	Francis M Holton

Israel Bayless Beriah Wright Wm Paddy
Arthur Wilson John Savage John H Baker
Benj G Perkins Levi Colmus Saml A Grier
Widow of Lt Richd E Cochran Eleanora B Watkins, widow of
Baudonin & A D Roberts Gassaway Watkins
Chas Allen, of Richmond, Va Parmelia Slavin, late the wife of John
Chas Ahrenfeldt & John F H Vogt Blue, deceased
Widow of Elijah Bragdon, deceased
John Black, late U S Consul at the city of Mexico
2-Cmte on Revolutionary Pensions: adverse reports on the ptns of John Jones & Christopher Moore: laid on the table. 3-Cmte on Invalid Pensions: bill for the relief of Christopher Cunningham, without amendment. Same cmte: bills for the relief of Robt Whittell & John Wilson: committed. Same cmte: adverse reports on the ptns of Fred'k Taylor, Matthew Machlin, Jos J Watson, Lemuel Parker, Jos Kelley, Jos Brown, Thos Thompson & Wm Roberts: laid on the table. 4-Cmte on Invalid Pensions: discharged from the ptns of Nehemiah Holladay, Jas Chester, & Henry Neely: laid on the table. Same cmte: bill for the relief of Wm H Wilson; of Amos Bull, & of Amos Armstrong: committed. 5-Cmte on Invalid Pensions: adverse reports on the ptns of Jonas Dutton & Geo Cassady: laid on the table. Same cmte: adverse reports on the ptns of Linchfield Sharpe, John Holland, Fred'k Perrigo, Cornelius Hughes, Jeremiah Harpham, Maria Hogue, Nathl Lansdown, Jas M Lewis, & Jas Coe: laid on the table. Same cmte: bills for the relief of Edw Taylor, of Warren Raymond; of Hubert H Booley; of Wm Miller; of Maurice R Simmons; of Eliphus C Brown, & of Henry N Halstead: committed. Same cmte: bills for the relief of Robt Ramsey; of John Farnham; of Andrew Flanagin; of Wm Gott, & of Catharine Hoffman: committed. 6-Cmte on Revolutionary Pensions: discharged from the ptn of Miles Devine: laid on the table. 7-Cmte on Patents: bill for the relief of John Goulding: committed.

The lifeless body of Miss Morrisette has been found in the Alabama River. The cause which led to her suicide was mortification from an outrage against her father by a mob in Mobile, who had taken umbrage at a vote given by Mr Morrisette in the State Senate, of which he was a member.

Petersburg Republican: on Apr 15, Grief Nunnally was shot by his own dght, Mrs Moody, in the public road, in Dinwiddie, & survived only 3 days. Mrs Moody is in custody. Mr Nunnally was an industrious man, but at times intemperate, when he was cruel in his family & turbulent in his neighborhood.

Died: on Apr 28, of croup, in her 4th year, Emma, youngest daughter of B F & Eliz Middleton. Her funeral is tomorrow at 4 o'clock, from the residence of her father.

For rent: the house & grounds belonging to Col Jas Kearney, on the corner of 14th & F sts. Inquire of J B H Smith, at his ofc on F st.

House & lot at aution, under a deed of trust. Brick house & lot at 9th & D st, under rent to Mr Geo Stettinius. –C Bestor, Trustee -A Green, auctioneer

Dry Goods at auction: on May 5, at the Dry Goods store of Mr S T Drury, on Pa ave, near the West Market House. -A Green, auctioneer

Orphans Court of Wash Co, D C. Letters of administration on the personal estate of Geo Bomford, late of said county, deceased. –J B H Smith, adm

MON MAY 1, 1848
Ladies with letters in the Wash Post Ofc, May 1, 1848:

Allen, Ellen
Aguiel, Miss Louisa
Anderson, Miss M R
Berry, Miss Chris'a
Boswell, Miss Eliz
Bright, Mrs Eliz B
Butler, Miss Hellen
Boyden, Mrs J C
Boyle, Miss Mary
Burrows, Mrs
Blane, Miss M L
Birch, Miss Verlin'a
Cook, Mrs Mary
Coston, Mary E
Clarke, Miss M C
Campbell, Mrs
Cook, Miss M A
Coxeaden, Miss A
Costney, Miss A
Craken, Miss C V
Cliver, Miss Georg
Chaules, Miss
Clifford, Miss Jane
Cogswell, Miss L
Davis, Miss Cath'e
Duncan, Mrs D-2
Dunnington, Miss Anna E
Dodson, Miss M A
Day, Mrs Mary E
Donally, Miss W A
Eld, Mrs Eliz
Edwards, Mrs M A
Fries, Mrs Ellen
Ford, Miss H
Foote, Miss Jane E

Ficket, Mrs Jane
Gladen, Miss J E
Gardiner, Miss M A
Goins, Sarah
Grason, Mrs Sarah
Hebron, Miss Ame
Hall, Mrs Ann E
Hepburn, Miss L
Howard, Mrs M
Hewitt, Miss M B
Henderson, Nancy
Humphreys, Mrs S
Howe, Mrs A A
Johnson, Mrs Henry
Jamaison, Mrs
Jones, Mrs Mary
King, Miss Cealey
Kuntz, Sarah
Lane, Mrs A E
Lillett, Mrs Eliz
Lucas, Miss E A
Lee, Miss Matilda-3
Lewis, Miss Susan
Moreau, Mrs A M
Miller, Eliza H
Magruder, Mrs H
Merry, Miss L B
Moore, Miss Mary
McKonkey, Eliza
Porter, Mrs Eliz
Pyles, Mrs Sarah A
Peyton, Mrs S A
Queen, Miss M E-2
Raub, Miss Eliz
Ragan, Mrs Elias
Read, Miss H Fanning-2

Ransom, Miss Lucia
Robinson, Miss M
Ratcliff, Mrs S Ann
Stewart, Mrs Emily
Smith, Mrs Jane
Sturms, Mrs S W-2
Suter, Miss A M
Smith, Miss Mary
Smallwood, Patsy
Selden, Miss Sophia
Tait, Miss Anna
Thompson, Miss E
Turner, Mrs Jas C
Thornton, Mrs Jas D
Tozer, Mrs Julia A
Thompson, Mrs
Travers, Mrs M
Talbott, Miss Mary
Whitaker, Miss A
Wineberger, Miss
Williams, Mrs C
Williams, Mrs F A
White, Miss Fr-2
Wilkins, Mrs G M
Walker, Miss H B-3
Walker, Mrs Jane
Walters, Miss L-2
Weaver, Mrs Lydia
Williams, Lucy
Wilson, Mrs Maryy
Williams, Martha A
Wise, Miss Madal'e
Wilkinson, Mrs S

Van Dieman paper of Dec 8: an account of the accidental death of Lady Mary Fitz Roy, wife of the Govn'r, & Lt C C Masters. They were about to visit Sydney, when the horses ran away, dashed the carriage to pieces, & killed them both instantly. Lady Mary was daughter to the late & sister to the present Duke of Richmond.

From the Union of yesterday. Mr Chester Ashley, one of the U S Senators from Arkansas, was walking about in perfect health on Mon, & was attacked on Tue, & is now no more.

Appointments by the Pres: 1-C S Whitner, Register of the land ofc at Falls of St Croix, Wisc-new ofc. 2-Saml Leech, receiver of public moneys at Falls of St Croix, Wisc -new ofc.

The Snow Hill Shield announces the death, at his residence in Onancock, Accomac Co, Va, on Apr 11, after a protracted & most painful illness, of the Rev Wm Lee, in his 81st year. He was a member of the Methodist church for more than 60 years, & a preacher for half a century.

Trustee's sale: by decree of the Circuit Court of D C, sitting in Chancery. Public auction on May 23: the undivided moiety or half part of the centre one of the three 3 story brick houses on Pa ave, which were built by John Cruikshank & Geo Thompson, on part of lot 5 in square 461, & of that part of the ground on which the said house stands. The house & lot lie west of & adjoining to the large new storehouse & dwlg recently built on the said lot by Messrs B L Jackson & Brother, & runs back to & fronts on Canal st. –John Marbury, trustee [The subscriber, being the owner of the undivided half of the above, will offer his interest & estate therein, at public sale. –W Morton]

Trustee's sale: by deed of trust from Jos Libbey, Chas King, & the Farmers & Mechanics' Bank of Gtwn to Clement Cox, dated Feb 15, 1836, recorded in Liber W B 59, folios 174-in the land records of Wash Co, D C, & a deed from Chas King to Clement Cox, dated Sep 18, 1838, recorded in Liber W B 70, folio 474, of the land records, & of a subsequent decree of the Circuit Court of D C, sitting as a Court of Chancery, made in the cause of John Kurtz et al, vs Geo King et al: I will offer at auction, on May 24, on the premises, all the following property situated in Gtwn, D C, viz: 1-Wharf property beginning at the s e corner of Water & Congress sts. 2-All that part of lot 63 in old Gtwn: a boundary being a lot conveyed by Wm H Dorsey to Walter Smith. 3-All that part of lots 21 & 22 of the water lots on the south side of Water st: a boundary is the lot formerly Jas Kennedy's; another boundary is Walter Smoot's line. –Walter S Cox, trustee -Edw S Wright, auctioneer

On Mon, Miss Bridget Morgan, daughter of Mr Morris Morgan, of Lowell, was struck by a horse & buggy, which came at full speed up Merrimack st, & dragged her for a considerable distance, her head striking the pavement. She lived but a few minutes when taken up.

Mr F Minor intends opening a school on May 26, in the First Ward, for the instruction of youths.

Affair on Thu at Lewistown, Ill: Norman Berris was shot by N Northup on the afternoon of the wedding of the former. Northup, by way of a joke, dressed himself in female garb, got a gun which he supposed not loaded, met Berris, &, intending simply to frighten him, shot him dead.

Died: on Apr 30, at Congress Hall, after a short illness, Capt John H Martin, of Michigan, in his 65th year. His funeral is tomorrow at 4 o'clock, from the above named place.

Household & kitchen furniture at auction: on May 4, at the late residence of J N Pumroy, deceased, on 11th st, between G & H sts north. –H S Pumroy, admx -A Green, auct

TUE MAY 2, 1848
Magnificent country seat for sale: **Fountain Park**, at the Falls of the Schuylkill, 4 miles from Phil, on the Ridge Turnpike: contains about 20 acres: improvements are a large hewn-stone dwlg house, with stone wings, bath houses, stables, barn, smoke house, & stables. The flower garden alone occupies an acre. -Andrew McMakin, Phil

House of Reps: 1-Obit of Chester Ashley, late a Senator of the State of Arkansas, who died on Apr 29, in Wash City, after a short but painfully afflicting illness. He was born in Westfield, Mass, &, when less than a year old, was taken with his father & family, who removed to Hudson, N Y. He was educated to the legal profession, &, at age 27, emigrated to Ill. He married in Missouri, & in 1819 removed to & settled in the then Territory of Arkansas. He was elected to the Senate in the fall of 1844; re-elected in 1846. His funeral is today at 11 o'clock, from the Capitol.

Died: on Apr 30, at the residence of her brother, on 9th above I st, in her 55th year, Miss Isabella Price Hood, daughter of the late John Hood, of Phil. The body will be removed to Phil for interment.

WED MAY 3, 1848
At Boston, on Thu, a Frenchman named Dutee, instigated by jealousy, shot Miss Oakes, to whom he was engaged to be married, in the neck & temple. He then shot himself. Neither were expected to survive.

Mr David Estes, or Esters, the watchman shot by a burglar at Boston, died on Thu. A reward of $1,000 has been offered by the Govn'r for the detection & conviction of either of the burglars.

The Boston papers inform us of the realization of the painful anticipations of her friends, in the death, on Fri last, of Mrs Julia Webster Appleton, only daughter of the Hon Danl Webster.

Wash Corp: 1-Ptn from Wm C Bamberger & others, in relation to enclosures in the 7th Ward: referred to the Cmte on Improvements. 2-Ptn from Jas A Wise & others: referred to the Cmte on Improvements. 3-Cmte of Claims: bill for the relief of Seth L Cole: passed. 4-Cmte of Common Council: bill for the relief of John Simmons: referred to the Cmte on Improvements. 5-Cmte of Claims: asking to be discharged from the further consideration of the ptn of Thos Kingsbury. Bill for the relief of John Miller: passed. 6-Cmte of Claims: asking to be discharged from the further consideration of the ptns of Richd Patton & wife, John Fleming, & of Moses Lee: agreed to. 7-Bill for the relief of Thos Downey: passed. 8-Cmte of Claims: asking to be discharged from the further consideration of the ptn of Jas Towles: agreed to. Same cmte: asking to be discharged from the further consideration of the ptn of Jas A Bowen: agreed to. Bill for the relief of John Burch: passed. 9-Ptn of Wm B Wilson, praying payment of a claim for work done in the 5th Ward: referred to the Cmte on Improvements. 10-Ptn of Wm Mullen, praying remission of a fine: referred to the Cmte of Claims.

Mrs Flournoy, wife of Thso S Flournoy, the Rep in Congress from the Halifax district, died on Apr 21, [as we learn from the last Danville Register,] Mrs Flournoy was called suddenly to the assistance of a little negro who was choked, &, although she was in her usual health, her feelings were so overcome by the scene that she was seized with spasms, & died 2 hours afterwards. She leaves a devoted husband & 5 small children. -Richmond Whig

Died: on May 1, in her 23rd year, Imana, wife of Mr Wm H Minnix, of the Genr'l Land Ofc. Her funeral is tomorrow at 4 o'clock, from her late residence, F & 22nd sts.

Passengers in the steamship **America** at N Y from Liverpool: Mrs Woodward, Mrs E Johns, Miss Robertson, Mr Gardner & lady, Mr Johnson & lady, Mr Lewis & lady, Mr Wright & lady, Mr Schenley, lady, nurse, 3 children, & man servant; Chas Sharples, lady, nurse, & infant; Lt Pipon, Rev Alex'r King, Dr Ogilby, Messrs Cavallier, Geo Taylor, John Edwards, Robt Muir, Truianame, Thibanden, A Easton, W H Jones, Alden Schlacher, Thos Kerr, Henry Reeves, Walter H Walsh, Columb, Jesse Joseph, Ferguson, R F Maitland, Mitchell, W C Rudman, jr, Jas Johnson, Henry Jevons, Klingenden, Alex Prouan, Collis, Culonne, Doughlass, Munroe, [bearer of dispatches,] Thos Crigan, Jolys, Edw Ryan, Ross, Langloid, Jas Kerr, Anderson, Chas Ready, Francis Mulling, Frazer, Lynch, Andrew Patterson.

Circuit Court of Wash Co, D C-in Chancery. Amos Binney, adm, vs, the heirs of Jas Thomas, deceased, & others. By a decree passed in the above cause, will be sold at public auction, on May 17, lots 9 thru 11 in square 490, in Wash City, at the junction of C & 6th sts, having 102 feet 8 inches on C st, with improvements. –David A Hall, Trustee

Circuit Court of Wash Co, D C: in the case of John W Maury & others vs Thos A Scott, the jury yesterday returned a verdict for the plntf, awarding damages $4,950, with interest on $2,350 from Jan 13, 1845, & on $2,600 from Jan 24, 1845.

THU MAY 4, 1848
Noah Webster, descended on the father's side from one of the early Govenors of Conn, on the mother's from Bradford the 2nd Govenor of the Plymouth colony, was born in Hartford, Oct 16, 1758, & died in New Haven, on May 28, 1843. His father was a respectable farmer, apparently neither poor nor rich, whose utmost civil & military dignites seem to have been a Justiceship of the Peace & a Revolutionary captaincy of what was called the alarm list of his native town, a corps formed for emergencies. He appears to have given, [one of 4 sons & 6 children,] no patrimony but an honoest & pious mind. He united himself with a lady of Boston, the daughter of Mr Wm Greenleaf. She survived him 4 years, dying in 1847, at age 82 years.

Orphans Court of Wash Co, D C. Letters of administration on the personal estate of Jas Long, late of said county, deceased. –Richd Wallach, adm

Wanted, a Servant to do the housework of a small family. Liberal wages. Apply on 7th st, opposite the ofc of the Nat'l Intell, to Jas W Berry, Commission Merchant.

Senate: 1-Ptns referred: from the heirs of Robt Libby, asking arrears of pension; from Jos Masterson, a wounded soldier, asking for a pension; from John S Luce, asking to be allowed remuneration for certain losses incurred. 2-Cmte on Pensions-House bills without amendment: relief of Harvey Jones; of Richd Reynolds; of Seth Morton; of H Carrington, exc of Paulina Le Grand, deceased; & of Jos Johnson. 3-Cmte on the Judiciary: House bill for relief of Chas Reeder, Walter R Johnson, & the legal reps of Thos P Jones.

Appointments by the Pres:
1-Alex'r G Gordon, promoted to rank of Cmder in the Navy, from Mar 14, 1848, vice Jas P Wilson, deceased.
2-Robt B Riell, promoted to rank of Lt in the Navy, from Mar 14, 1848, vice Lt A G Gordon, promoted.
3-Mathew C Perry, promoted to rank of Lt in the Navy, from Apr 3, 1848, vice Lt Stephen Johnston, deceased.
4-Jos Beale promoted to rank of Surgeon in the Navy, from Apr 19, 1848, vice Fred'k Sickles, deceased.
5-Albert Pearson, of Pa, appointed an Assist Surgeon in the Navy, from Apr 26, 1848, vice Saml H Stout, who declined to accept his appointment.
6-John Ward, of Va, appointed an Assist Surgeon in the Navy, from Apr 28, 1848, vice Passed Assist Surgeon Jos Beale, promoted.

Died: on Apr 26, at *White Marsh*, PG Co, Md, the residence of his father, Mr Richd N Summers, aged 24 years, after a protracted & painful illness of several months, which he bore with great calmness.

FRI MAY 5, 1848
Dedication of the new Methodist Episcopal Church in Wash City, in the First Ward, is to take place on Sun next, & Rev Mr Sargent to deliver the dedication sermon.

City Ordinances-Wash: 1-An act for the relief of John Burch: fine imposed for an alleged violation relative to forestalling the market, be remitted: provided he pay the costs of prosecution. 2-Act for the relief of Thos Downey: $5 to be paid to him, the said amount imposed on him for harboring a dog. 3-Act for the relief of W C Reddall: fine imposed on him for harboring a dog: remitted: provided he pay the costs of prosecution. 4-Act for the relief of John Miller: fine imposed on him for harboring a dog: remitted: provided he pay the costs of prosecution. 5-Act for the relief of Seth L Cole: fine imposed on him for harboring a dog: remitted: provided he pay the costs of prosecution.

House of Reps: Acts Referred: 1-Act for the relief of John Lorimer Graham, late postmaster in N Y C. 2-Act to provide for the settlement of the claim of Henry Washington, late a deputy surveyor of the public lands in Florida. 3-Act for the relief of Reynolds May. 4-Relief of-Jonathan Lewis; Jeannette C Huntington, widow of & sole excx of Wm D Cheever, deceased; of Creed Taylor; of Eliz Pistole, widow of Chas Pistole, deceased; of Jesse Turner; of Jos F Caldwell; of Nathl Kuykendall; of Thos Brownell; of Eliz Jones & the children of John Carr; of Thompson Hutchinson; of Thos Douglas, late U S Atty for East Fla; of Saml W Bell, a native of the Cherokee nation; of Olver C Harris. Also, act to compromise with Mangle M Quackenboss & his co-obligors for claims on bonds given by them as sureties to the U S. 4-Ptn of Saml Graves, praying for a pension for injuries sustained while acting as a pilot on Lake Champlain during the late war with Great Britian. 5-Memorial of Clarissa Sumner & Lucy Due, heirs of Col John Sumner, of the Connecticut continental line of the Revolution, praying pay for 2 final settlement certificates, which were funded in 1790, still due & unpaid. 6-Ptn of Thos R Clarke, of Detroit, for a land patent. 7-Ptn of Archibald McAllister for a renewal of letter patent. 8-Ptn of Henry Childs, praying for a pension on account of a disability received while in the service of the U S. 9-Cmte on Naval Affairs: asking to be discharged from the further consideration of the ptn of Cevans, of Pittsburg, Pa: laid on the table. Same cmte: bill for the relief of S B Elliot, of the U S Navy: committed. 11-Cmte of Accounts: asking to be discharged from the further consideration of the resolution of the House in relation to the funeral expenses of John M Holey: laid on the table. 12-Cmte on Pensions: bill granting a pension to Eliz Munroe. 13-Cmte of Claims: bill for the relief of John P B Gratiot, & the legal reps of Henry Gratiot: committed. Same cmte: adverse reports on the ptns of David Little & of Alex'r H Mechlin: laid on the table. 14-Cmte for D C: bill for the relief of J W Nye, assignee of P Bargy & H Stewart: committed.

By order of distress & to me directed, I shall expose at public sale for cash, on May 12, at the Monterey House, on Pa ave, Wash City, the goods & chattels of Jas S Hall. Seized & taken for house rent due in arrears by Jas S Hall to Ann Lowry. –R R Burr, bailiff -A Green, auctioneer -Chas H Wallach, trustee

Senator Downs arrived at New Orleans on Apr 25 from Washington. He had been summoned home by the death of an only child, & the dangerous illness of his wife.

Mr E L Andrews, one of the most active merchants of Mobile, the head of the firm of E L Andrews & Co, committed suicide at that place on Sat week by throwing himself into the river. His friends cannot account for this act. He left a letter to his wife. His brother in New Orleans, Mr Z Andrews, of the firm of Andrews & Brother, suddenly left his ofc on the same day as his brother's death, & has not since been seen or heard of. It is feared that he too has committed suicide. Anticipated bankruptcy may have caused these events.

The remains of Maj Edw Webster, of the Mass Volunteers, who died in Mexico, arrived at Boston on Mon from Vera Cruz. The remains of the son arrived just as the father was performing the last sad offices to the corpse of a beloved daughter, whose decease was announced a few days ago.

The store I now occupy, on the corner of Pa ave & 10th st, will be for rent in a few days. –Wm Q Force

Mrd: on Tue last, by Rev Mr Cushman, Mr Wm H Ward to Miss Sarah Otterback, both of Wash City.

Mrd: on May 2, by Rev Mr Foley, Mr John Waters to Mrs Catherine S Davis, all of Wash City.

Died: at his residence on M st north, Mr Zachariah Dove, in his 89th year, formerly from Va, but for the last 33 years a resident of Wash City, leaving a large family of relatives & friends to mourn him. [No death date given-current item.

SAT MAY 6, 1848
Administrator's notice. Letters of adm on the estate of Miss Sally Crook, late of this county. Having settled up the estate, I am prepared to distribute to her heirs. She is a native of England, I believe from near London. She lived near 20 years in the family ot the late Clack Robinson, of this country. –Henry G Goodloe, Warrenton, Adm, Warren Co, N C.

Senate: 1-Cmte on Naval Affairs: bill for the relief of Cmder Jas M Macintosh. Same cmte: asking to be discharged from the further consideration of the ptns of John H Williams; Passed Midshipmen John L Worden; Susan T E Williamson, widow of Chas L Williamson; Henry La Reintree, & of Saml Raub. 2-Cmte of Claims: bill for the relief of John Morgan, with an amendment; relief of G De Lirac; & relief of Wm T Holland.

House of Reps: 1-Ptn & papers of Thos C Green: referred to the Cmte of Private Land Claims. 2-Letter from W W Brent, of Wash, that he has just received from Robt Walsh, the U S Consul at Paris, a portrait of Maj Gen Baron de Kalb, to be presented to Congress as an offering from the surviving family of De Kalb, which awaited the decision of Congress as to its reception & disposition: referred to the Cmte on the Library.

Orphans Court of Wash Co, D C. In the case of Wm Bird, adm of Simon Fraiser, deceased, the Court & adm have appointed May 26 for settlement of the estate, with the assets in hand. –Edw N Roach, Reg/o wills

Valuable property for sale: part of lot 3 in square 166: running with the line of Pa ave, 43 feet 5 inches; thence with the western line of that part of lot 3 granted to Tench Ringgold to Francis Lear & Benj L Lear, by deed dated Aug 19, 1823: with brick tenement thereon: between 17th & 18th sts west. Apply to Mechlin & Winder, Gen Agents, ofc 17th st west, opposite the War Dept.

Delinquent lands in Alleghany Co, that Wm Ridgely, of Eli, Collector of the State & County Taxes for the year 1847, in said county: advertisement embracing the statement returned by him, & give notice that unless the taxes be paid to the said Collector, or his agents, Chas Farquharson & Son, in Balt city, on or before Jun 1 next, the land will be sold at public auction for the payment of the same. –Geo W Devecmon, Clerk to Com'rs of Alleghany Co, Md.

District #1:
Battle, Robt H & John W Ott & John T Ritchie & others: 6 lots: 300 acres: $1.10
Cook, Wm: *Stony Ridge* 383 acres, *Deer Park*, 2,000 acres $1.45
Conner, Marmaduke W: lot 1733: $1.45
Donaldson, Thos: 14 lots: 700 acres: $2.54
Davis, John, of Balt: 3 lots: 150 acres: $1.65
Donaldson, Saml I: 3 lots: 150 acres: $2.17
Donaldson, Saml & John: 4 lots: 200 acres: $2.90
Ellicott, Thos & Meredith: 18 lots: 900 acres: $6.50
Galloway, Thos: part of *Rights of Man*: 198 acres, $4.10
Johnson, Wm & John: *Polly & Addition to Polly*, 513 acres; *Mount Airy*, 108 acres: $8.19
Johnson, Reverdy: *Eden's Paradise Regained*: 1,000 acres: $10.80
Jones, Richd J: 3 lots: 150 acres: $1.65
Kenney, Anthony: 6 lots: 1,300 acres: $2.17
Leakin, Shepherd C: lot 1309: 50 acres: .37
Markell, Jacob: 3 lots, 50 acres each: $1.65
McCutchen, Geo: 14 lots: 700 acres: $5.06
Mullen, Peter: 4 lots: 200 acres: $1.45
Neth, Lewis, jr: part of *Eden's Paradise Regained*, 1, 500 acres; & lots-100 acres: $15.58
Ritchie, Joshua & Mary R Ritchie & John W Ott: 300 acres: $1.10
Sinclair, Alex'r: *Alexander the Great*: 176 acres: $9.15
Smith, Clement: *Green Meadows & Deep Creek*: 1,408 acres: $5.07
Singleton, John: One-third of *Goodly lands*: 201 acres: $1.47
Swartzwelder, Saml A: *Republican Bonam*, 200 acres; lot 45, 50 acres: $2.54
Turner, Thos: 200 acres: $1.45
Vanmeter, Jacob: *Roby's Adventure*: 169 acres: $2.46
Vanbibber, Andrew A & Hester: *Friendship*, 50 acres; lots 135 & 138, 100 acres: $1.65
Vandiver, Wm-heirs: *William's Discovery*: 400 acres: $2.17

District #1-cont'd:
Webb, Henry W: lot 1546, 50 acres: .37
District #2:
Brice, John: *Huron* 200 acres; *Groove* 200 acres; *Ington* 200 acres; *Ipso* 200 acres; *Bumpton* 200 acres; *Aristotle* 200 acres; & *Drummond tract* 200 acres: 1,400 acres: $7.57
Clayton, Philip: lot 1235: 50 acres: .73
Enlow, Josephus: [no name given] 50 acres: .72
McCurdy, Alex'r: lots: 675 acres; *Buck Shooting*: 200 acres: $15.40
Meley, Wm-heirs: 4 lots: 200 acres: $2.17
Magruder, Wm: lot 3025: 50 acres: .54
Pearce, Eliz: lot 3035: 50 acres: $1.10
Rizer, Geo, Jr: *Norwood Farm*: 100 acres: $1.45
Vanbibber, Andrew, A, & Hester: lots 3455, 3456, 3458: 150 acres: $2.17
District #3:
Armstead, John B: part *Internal Improvements*: 1,616 acres: $8.05
Armistead, Walter K: one-half *Internal Improvements*: 3,916 acres: $13.82
Adams, Levon H: 8 lots containing 400 acres: $2.17
Carr, Jos G: 4 lots containing 600 acres: $1.45
Clements, Bennett: *Lorrain*: 200 acres: $4.32
Parker, Jas: 4 lots containing 200 acres: $1.45
Beddinger, Geo, sen: *Sanca Panca*: 159 acres: 3.44
Hawkins, Henry: 4 lots: 400 acres: $2.89
Hannwalk, Peter: lots 2136 & 2137: 100 acres: $1.45
Jewell, Wm: *Jewelry* 702 acres; *Test* 209 acres: $3.30
Kennedy, Thos-heirs: 11 lots, 50 acres each: $3.97
Kelly, Wm: lots 1348 & 3132, 50 acres each: $1.45
Mason, Thos-heirs: 4 lots, 50 acres each: $2.17
Marberry, Jos-heirs: 4 lots, 50 acres each: $2.17
Most, John: lots 3473 & 3474: 100 acres: .73
Nourse, Mary: 10 lots, 50 acres each: $10.98
Rease, Thos: lots-200 acres: $1.45
Raymond, Danl: part *Bear Camp*: 500 acres: $3.61
Slabaugh, Jacob: *Price's Desire*: 45½ acres: $1.56
Swartzwelder, Sam A-heirs: 4 lots, 50 acres each: $2.89
Tomlinson, Jesse: *Mud Spring*, 50 acres; *Mount Clear*, 119 acres: $1.45
Templeman, Geo: half of lands charged to Wm Grindage-*Cut & Come Again*, & *Apart*: 7,000 acres: $31.11
Thomas, John: lots 2917 & 2919: 250 acres: $1.45
Vanbibber, Andrew A: 4 lots, 50 acres each: $7.55
Wood, Gerr'd-heirs: 4 lots, 50 acres each: $1.45
Willett, Chas S: 2 lots, 50 acres each: $1.45
District #4:
Brant, John, sen: *Brant's mill*: 438 acres: $9.48
Beatty, Thos-heirs: *Flowery Mead*: 528 acres: $3.79
Burke, Garrett: 4 lots, 50 acres each: $1.45

Broadwaters, Jefferson: ***President Jefferson***: 250 acres: $2.72
Baker, Richd: ***Forge Seat & Mill Seat***: 16 acres: $2.17
Fowler, Benj: ***Fowler's lot***: 1, 298 acres: $7.03
Green, Duff: ***Burnt Mill seat***, 100 acres; ***Limestone***, 50 acres; 6 lots, 50 acres each; ***Leatherwood Bottom***, 29 acres; ***Boot Yard***, 1 acre; ***Shepherd's Park***, 21 acres; ***Pretty Prospect***, 430 acres; ***Poland Sugar Camp***, 86 acres; half of ***Ray's Discovery***, 124 acres; part lot 313, 7 acres; ***Coal in Storer***, 15 acres; ***Pig Iron***, 66 acres; ***Factories tract***, 1,016 acres: $81.27
Howard, John E, jr: ninth of ***Beatty's Plains***: 900 acres: $19.45
Junkins, Benj: ***Reverton tract***: 66½ acres: ,51
Union Co: ***Coal & iron banks***, 5, 631 acres; ***Gen Duff Green's Iron & Ore lands***, 5,128 acres; ***Hoye's Coal, Iron, & Lime Discovery***, 2,752 acres; the ***Rose Buds***, 28 acres; part ***Flowery Meads***, 414 acres; ***Coromandel***, 151 acres; ***Hoye's Fortune***, 47 acres; ***Dan's Mountain***, 139 acres; ***Jubax & Syphax***, 50 acres; ***Hamborough***, 116 acres; ***Stripe***, 5 acres; ***Millstone Point***, 363 acres; ***A Rustie's Hat***, 50 acres; lot 20, 50 acres; ***What You Will***, 10 acres: $215.07

District #5:
Brogan, Thos: house & lot near Arnold's: $1.78
Bruce, Andrew: ***Coincidence***: 135 acres: $1.95
Copperwalt, Jos & Thos Dunlap, & Herman Cope: ***Soldier's lot***, 50 acres; a tract [no name] 2,933 acres: $22.93
Guyer, John: 9 lots, 50 acres each: $3.26
Green, Duff: 5 lots, 50 acres each: $18.00
Griffin, Francis: lot 3380, called ***Hope tract***, 50 acres; lots 3381 & 3382, 95 acres; part ***William's Good Luck***, 50 acres: $11.28
Harden, Savel: ***Bear Wallow*** & part ***Chestnut flat***: 29 acres: .87
Howell, Lewis: ***Kingman's Discovery***: 39 acres: $5.14
Logsdon, John: part resurvey on ***Stony Lick***, 1,591 acres; & lots 3567 & 3568, 100 acres: $14.48
Nelson, John: 2 lots & part of a tract of land: 150 acres: $1.10
Thompson, David H & Hamilton Golman: lots 16 & 38 of ***Logsdon's estate***: $2.17
Vaughan, Benj G: ***Traveller's Rest***, 125 acres; ***Sapp's Neglect***, 7½ acres; ***Addition***, 16 acres; ***Mount Hope Resurveyed***, 102 acres; ***Addition***, 155 acres; ***Liberty***, 201 acres; ***Subtraction*** 68 acres: $5.95

District #6:
Beatty, Jas: ***The Request*** 156 acres; ***Lost Glove***, 56½ acres: $4.63
Devore, Saml: ***Black Range***: 67½ acres: $3.89
Hunter, Talliferro: part of ***Hoffman's Delight***, 46 acres; ***Crooked Billet***, 62 acres: $3.14
Krebs & Falls: ***Lock Valley***, 74 acres; ***Mount Pleasant***, 50½ acres; ***Mud Lick Mine***, 29 acres; half of ***Godman's Level***, 23 acres; lot 3369, 25 acres; lots 3 & 4 in Cresaptown: $7.
McCrackin, Jas P: house & lot in Cresaptown: $1.45
Maxey, Virgil & others: ***Quarts***, 126 acres; ***Rabbit's Walk***, 116 acres; ***Trio***, 100 acres: $7.41
Purgentt, Henry-heirs: house & lot in Cresaptown: $1.45
Potts, Wm: ***Friendship tract***: 15½ acres: $1.45
Schley, Wm: lots 3, 4, & 5, ***Slicer's Lands***: 43 acres: $4.76

District #6-cont'd:
Tobin, John-heirs: part of *Reuben's Desire*, 155 acres; lot 3412, 10 acres: $3.51
Cumberland Town:
Buchanan, Judge John-heirs: *Old Men's Follies never cease*: 978 acres: $7.06
English, Wm & Louisa Violett-heirs: lot 1 on Mill st: $2.17
Gray, Valentine: part *Walnut Bottom*: $1.65
Miller, Michl: part *Walnut Bottom*: $1.45
Ramsey, Jane C: *Commercial Mart*: $1.31
Violett, Robt G: lots 2 & 3 on Mill st: $5.06
District #7:
Hesselin, John-heirs: lots 3 *Skipton*, part of *Seven Springs*: 46 acres: $1.74
Hettick, Chas F: *Miller's Chance*, 20½ acres; *Wilson's Risk*, 57½ acres: $1.41
Jacobs, Robt-heirs: *Cow Pasture*: 110 acres: $1.59
Luddington, Zalmon: *Patteron's Creek Warehouse*: .97
District #8:
Bargy, Peter: *Sparking Camp*: 113 acres: $1.23
Cairmell, Ann: *Land off*: 122 acres: $1.78
Carroll, Wm: Half of the following tracts: *Jacob's Ladder*, 300 acres; *Resurvey on Three Springs*, 108 acres; *White Oak Plains*, 103 acres; *Canal & Railroad*, 1006 acres; *Water lot*, 34 acres; *Webster tract*, 106 acres; *Take All*, 327 acres; *Villiers*, 216 acres; *Cat Point*, 33 acres; *Pleasant Vale*, 99 acres; *Timber Land*, 117 acres; *Rocky Point*, 73 acres; *Look Up*, 53 acres; *Jos' Dreqam*, 196 acres; *Cornwall*, 117 acres; *Prospect Hill*, 64 acres; *Last Shift*, 100 acres; *Town Hill*, 41 acres; *Land of the Living*, 47 acres; *Jenkins' Deer Park Resurveyed*, 30 acres; *Quincy*, 65 acres; *Steam Mill*, 68 acres; *Keenan's Fancy*, 73 acres; *Depot*, 1 acre; *Lick*, 4 acres; *Town Ridge*, 68 acres: $58.38
Dickerson, Israel: *Fifth survey*, 20 acres; *Mount Pleasant*, 68 acres; *Lambelle*, 6½ acres; *Clapper's Hollow*, 26½ acres: $3.62
Fouty, Jacob: *Larewson*, 26 acres: *Half Moon*, 64 acres; *Sagar Camp*, 22 acres; *Groper lot*: $7.46
Galloway, Benj-heirs: part of *Hope*: 2,031 acres: $21.94
Goodrich, Saml: *Dry Hill*, 22 acres; *Fox Chase*, 29 acres; *What you Please*, 73 acres: $1.45
Goodhue, Jonathan, Pelatiah, Perit & Francis Durand: half of *Railroad & canal*, 5,003 acres; *Villiers*, 108 acres; *Webster*, 53 acres; *Water lot*, 17 acres; *Take All*, 163 acres; *Last Shift*, 50 acres; *Jos' Dream*, 98 acres; *Timber Land*, 58 acres; *Rock Point*, 37 acres; *Look Up*, 27 acres; *Cat Point*, 17 acres; *Deer Park Resurveyed*, 15 acres; *White Oak Plains*, 52 acres; *Prospect Hill*, 32 acres; *Cornwall*, 39 acres; *Land of the Living*, 24 acres; *Town Hill Prospect*, 21 acres; *Jacob's Ladder*, 150 acres; *Resurvey on Three Springs*, 54 acres; *Pleasant Vale*, 50 acres: $36.51
Mann, Ann, Chas, & Harriet: *Tracts United*: 797 acres: $17.22
Vansant, Chas-heirs: *Beef & Chickens*, 25 acres; *Mount ry*, 25 acres; *King's Sorrowr*, 8 acres; $1.28
Warfield, Chas-heirs: part of *Far-enough*: 130 acres: $6.58
District #10:
Armstead, John B: *Sportsman's Field*: 280 acres: $2.02
Bosely, Jas: 16 lots, 50 acres each: $2.89

Buamyer, Fred'k: house & lot in Hoyesburg: $1.45
Chapman, Henry H: part of *William & Mary*: 225 acres: $1.68
Davidson, Mgt: part of *William & Mary*: 225 acres: $1.92
Davidson, Eleanor: part of *William & Mary*: 175 acres: $1.92
Hone, Chas: 6 lots: 300 acres: $2.17
Harris, Thos, jr: part of *William & Mary*: 1,375 acres: $9.92
King, John: 27 lots, 50 acres each; part *Cherry Hill* 97 acres: $11.14
Koontz, Jacob: 15 lots: 750 acres: $2.72
Lawrence, Benj H & Elias D, & Mary Riddle: part of *Transylvania*: 400 acres: $1.45
McCubbin, Richd: 8 lots: 400 acres: $2.17
McLaughlin, Marietta: 16 lots: 800 acres: $4.32
McCobb, John & Wm H Miller: *Brotherly Love*, 150 acres; 9 lots, 50 acres each; *Hard Bargain Resurveyed*, 109 acres; *New Addition*, 202 acres; *Prospect*, 85 acres; *Taylor's Addition*, 44 acres; *Last Shift*, 100 acres; Part of *New Addition*, 195 acres; *Half Small Meadows*, 2, 512 acres; *Carrollville*, 26 acres: $20.93
Lawrence, Leven, guard of Mary, Benj, & Elias D Lawrence: *Elk Garden*, 5,421 acres; *Yohegany Bottom*, 50 acres; *Choice*, 100 acres; lots 34, 26, 24, 28: 200 acres; lots 193 & *Beckwith's Disappointment*, 80 acres: $22.61
Nelson, Robt & Richd H Beattie: 3 lots: 150 acres: $1.64
Nordeck, Mgt M: lot 316: 50 acres: .73
Paca, John P: *Buck's Bones*: 500 acres: $2.68
Parsons, David & Isaac Kuykendall: *Piney Bottom*, 270 acres; 3 lots, 50 acres each: $3.00
Richie, John: *Constitution Vale*, 301 acres; Addition to *Hunting ground*, 533 acres; *Rich Glades*, 306 acres; **Elk Lick**, 211 acres; 4 lots, 200 acres: $8.40
Saunders, Adam: house & lot in Hoyesburg: $1.45
Schlutter, Henry: house & lot in Hoyesburg: $1.45
Templeman, Geo & Jas W McCulloh: half the following tracts: *Cinque Foil*, 147 acres; *Delacalia*, 109 acres; *Mechlenburg*, 430 acres; *Crotia*, 225 acres; *Bridgeport*, 25 acres; *Sweet Pink*, 101 acres; *Rhinoceros*, 322 acres; *Troad*, 1,566 acres; *Siege of Acre*, 916 acres; *Thessalia*, 16 acres; *Fairfax tract*, 529 acres; *Alhambra*, 127 acres: $17.74
Walters, Henry: house & lot in Hoyesburg: $1.45
Waring, Marucs S: lots 358 & 1013: 100 acres: $1.45
Wood, John & David: part of *Western Connexion*, 1,108 acres; Part *Roanoke tract*, 200 acres; the *Request*, 156 acres; *Lost Glove*, 56 acres; House & lot in Hoyesburg, 50 acres: $1.45

House of Reps: 1-Bills passed: Relief of John B Smith & Simeon Darden; of Thos H Leggett; of Lot Davis; of Christopher Cunningham; of Wm H Wilson; & of Amos Bull.

Died: on May 5, of a disease of the lungs, after a short & painful illness of only 3 days, Mrs Ellen J Burche, son of Mr John Covington Burche, of Wash City, & daughter of the late Jos Kambrick, of Balt. Her funeral is on May 8, at 12 o'clock, from the residence of the late Capt S Burche. [Balt & Phil papers please copy.]

Died: yesterday, in her 70th year, Mrs Maria A Baker, relict of the late Philip Baker, of Md. Her funeral will take place today at 5 o'clock, from the residence of her son-in-law, John P Ingle, Capitol Hill.

Mrd: on May 4, by Rev Mr Cushman, Mr Southey S Parker to Miss Mary Ann Waters, both of Wash City.

The Osage Chief Black Dog is dead. He died, says our informant, on Apr 24, at his village. He has been lingering for 2 or 3 years under a tormenting disease & was literally a self-made hero. As a warrior he had no equal among his people. In stature he was about 7 feet, weighing some 275 pounds. –Cherokee Advocate of Apr 10.

By writ of venditioni exponas, I have seized the right, title, & interest, of John Hollohon & Jas Hollohon, in lot G, in square 731, with improvements-a 2 story brick house-to pay & satisfy a judgment in favor of Enoch Ridgway for the use of Thos N Brashears: sale of same on Jun 6. –H R Maryman, Constable

MON MAY 8, 1848
John F Watson has resigned as Cashier of the Germantown Bank, after an uninterrupted service of nearly 35 years. He is especially esteemed in this quarter for his valuable "Annals of Phil."

Register's Ofc, Wash, Apr 28, 1848: persons who have taken out licenses under the laws of the Corp during the months of Dec, Jan, & Feb last

Albert, Lee: sleight of hand-4	Brown & Nichols: theatrical
Anderson, Eliza: hardware	Burns, Geo: hats, boots & shoes
Addison & Cochran: retail	Boteler & McGregor: dry goods
Atkins, Davy: huckster	Brodbeck & Riggles: shop-transfer
Aigler, Jacob: dog	Brener, F & Son: dry goods
Aileir & Thyson: dog	Bartlett, J C: grocery
Atkins, David: dog	Boulanger, Jo: shop
Adams, Wash: dog	Brown & Nichols: theatrical-6
Abbott, Jos: dog	Buckley, F K; pedlar
Adams, Jemina: dog	Brown, Reuben: huckster
Atkins, David: dog	Bradley, J T: huckster
Andrew, Jas F: dog	Brown, C W: huckster
Adams, Nace: hack	Bayliss & Skidmore: huckster
Adams, S J: hack	Berryman, L H: huckster
Brodback, G: dry goods	Bicksler, Jno: huckster
Bayly, B S: retail	Birch & Moses: huckster
Brereton, John: retail	Brown, H Y: huckster
Baker, Thos: tavern	Bede, Geo: huckster-transfer
Brown, R W: retail	Borland, Alex'r; slave
Brown, John: porter	Burke, Jos: concert-2
Burch, Fielder: tenpins	Boarman, Chas: confectionary
Bushman, J H: retail	Benson & Ludwig: huckster

Beasley, Jos: hack
Buckley, J S: dogs
Briel, Conrad: dog
Brown, Anthony: dog
Brown, Wm: dog
Black, Moses: dog
Bryan, Jos: dog
Blake, J B: dog
Birch, Thos: slut
Bronaugh, A W: dog
Butler, Jos: dog
Bickler, Gotleig: dog
Boyle, John: dog
Bache, A D: dog
Brady, Peter: dog
Boyle, J P: dog
Brown, Chas: dog
Brashear, W B: dog
Brooke, F J: dog
Brereton, Jno: dog
Blagden, Thos: dog
Bradley, Chas: dog
Browning, P W: dog
Burr, H A: dog
Bowling, Jos: dog
Barcroft, Maria: dog
Barber, Geo: dog
Brown, Eliz: dog
Brown, Simon: dog
Byrne, Thos: dog
Butler, Abram: dog
Bignam, Gip: dog
Brown, Archy: dog
Bates, Fred: dog
Brent, Wm: dog
Brown, Basil: dog
Bohlayer, John, jr: dog
Benter, Wm: dog
Burr, Thos A: dog
Beall, M: dog
Beale, Robt: dog
Bache, E C: dog
Beady, Mgt: dog
Bell, Lloyd: dog
Birch, Fred: dog
Brown, Thos: dog

Bosse, Martin: dog
Burgess, Jas: dog
Balley, A F: dog
Brown, Jas: dog
Boyd, J K: dog
Bohlayer, J, jr: dog
Brenner, Hy: dog
Birch, G A: dog
Barnhill, J L: dog
Bayly, F: dog
Bohrer, Benj: dog
Butler, John: dog
Beady, Jo: hack-2
Boteler, Phil: hack
Begnam, Wm: hack
Bush, Jas: hack
Cole & Israel: retail
Cammack, Chr: dry goods
Callan, J F: medicine
Cook Mathew: grocery
Cannon, Danl: retail
Crutzfeldt, W: shop
Clarke, R B: retail
Clarke, E B: hats, boots, shoes
Costigan, John: retail
Costigan, John: hats, boots, shoes
Crawford, D: slave
Carlin, J E F: retail
Copp, Moses: shop
Copp, Moses: tenpins
Clarke, J B: dry goods
Collier, R M & Co: model artists-3
Cruitt, Richd: huckster
Cross, Harrison: huckster
Carroll, Jno: huckster
Cook, Abm: dog
Collins, Thos: dog-2
Cripps, Wm L: dog
Cohen, Robt: dog
Cathcart, J L: dog
Coyle, Fitzhugh: dog
Cookendorfer, Thos: dog
Calvert, Betsey: dog
Collard, G W: dog
Carter, J H: dog
Clements, A H: dog

Clitz, Fm: dog
Cornish, Harriet: dog
Costello, Jno: dog
Campbell, Amelia: dog
Colt, C A: dog
Chubb, J M: dog
Cook, J F: dog
Comas, R M: dog
Crutzfeldt, W: dog
Crutzfeldt, W: slut
Cook, Jno F: dog
Clarke, W H: dog
Casparis, J: dog
Clarke, M M: dog
Crutchett, J: dog
Cash, Leon: dog
Catalano, A: dog
Caldwell, J P: dog
Clarke, Wm: dog
Crowther, Thos: slut
Cross, Wash: dog
Cole, S L: dog
Cheseltine, Elex: dog
Caden, Jas: dog
Clarke, Cornelius: hack
Coumbe, J T: hack
Costin, W P C: hack
Collier, Peyton: hack
Donovan, John: tavern
Douglas, John: shop
Dyer, R W: auction
Drury, Tarrence: retail
Doyle, E: dry goods
Dyson, Chas: huckster
Dumbleton J M: concert
Dyson, Chas: huckster
Dumbleton, J A: concert
Dodson, Wm: retail
Delany, A H: huckster
Delany, Caleb: huckster
Dowell, John: huckster
Davis & Ellis: huckster
Deneale, J W: huckster
Dyer, Giles: slave
Dorsey, Rebecca: slave
Desmond, Danl: retail

Donovan, Danl: stage
Demar, Elias: dog
Dyvenau, G E: slut
Dyson, Chas: dog
Donovan, Wm: dog
Dement, Richd: dog
Duvall, Wash: dog
Dunwell, Saml: dog
Dunnington, C W: dog
Dent, Bruce: dog
Davis, J of A: dog
Downer, Joel: dog
De Saules, P A: dog
Dooley, Mich: dog
Dove, Wm: dog
Donoghue, P & T: dog
Dermott, Ann: dog
Dyer, Giles: dog
Downs, Solomon: dog
Delany, Caleb: dog
Deneale, Kin: hack
Dalton, Wm: hack
Dent, Bruce: hack
Dumphy, Thos: hack
Eversfield, E: slave-3
Ehrmanbrent, Jno: shop
Eaton, Richd: huckster
Elias, Thos: dog
Elliot, Wm P: dog
Earle, Robt: dog
Edwards, Geo: dog
Eaton, J H: dog
Ennis, Philip: dog
Eichorn, Geo: dog
Emmert, H Y: dog
Edelin, Nancy: dog
Entwistle, T B: dog
Edgerton, Jos: dog
Ellis, Jas G: dog
Fuller, F W: medicine
Fischer, Wm: hardware
Fitzgerald, J: tavern
Fowler, Chas S: dry goods
Foy, John: tavern-2
Farnham, R: hardware
Fraiser, G W: huckster

Flenner, Wm: boots & shoes
Fowler, J E: hats, boots & shoes
Frunk, Michl: grocery
Frasier, G W: huckster
Fitnam, Thos: retail
Fraunck, Jacob: huckster
Fowler, w R: huckster
Favier, A: tavern
Fuller, Cornelius: shop
Ford, Jas: shop
Follansbee, Ja: dog
Fitnam, Thos: dog
Farrar, J W: dog
Fearson, J C: dog
Fries, John: dog
Forrest, Step: dog
Finkman, Conrad: dog
Ford, Wash: dog
Ford, J N: dog
Fraler, Chas: dog
Fitzgerald, J: dog
Franklin, S P: dog
Fitton, W H; dog
Fister, John: dog
Flemming, Pat: [blank]
Gibbs, J H: hardware
Gibbs, J H: dry goods
Gardner, C T & Co: medicine
Gadsby, Wm: tavern
Galt, M W & Bro: hardware
Gough, Stephen: slave
Green, Ammon: retail
Garret, Milton: huckster-3
Goldin, R R: huckster
Gorden, D S: huckster
Gooding, Peter: huckster
Green, Ammon: auction
Gunnell, J S: dog
Goodrich, J C: dog
Groupe, Wm: dog
Green, Mantroy: dog
Guists, M A: dog
Goodhall, Thos: dog
Gardner, J B: dog
Gunton, Thos: dog
Gibson, Saml: dog

Gadsby, Wm: dog
Goldsborough, W: dog
Griffith, Wm A: dog
Gillott, Jos: dog
Guyer, Burr: dog-2
Greeves, Jno: dog
Goddard, Thos: dog
Grimes, M H: dog
Gess, J G: dog
Griffith, W T: dog
Gladman, A: dog
Grayson, Wm: dog
Graham, Susan: dog
Green, John: dog
Golding, J A: dog
Golding, F: hack
Grimes, C W: hack
Gibson, John: hack
Harbaugh, L: retail
Holland, J E: retail
Hughes, Wm: retail
Hepburn, D: retail
Hodge, Mary: retail
Hillyard, C: retail
Hardy, W C: huckster
Hall, Edw: retail
Heydon, C W: hardware
Howell, W P; retail
Hall, John: grocery
Henck, Eliz: huckster
Harkness, J C: grocery
Hall & Scott: tavern
Hawkins, Philip: huckster
Hawkins, Edw: huckster
Haines, Wash: huckster
Harris, M: huckster
Hensley, Geo: huckster
Holmedan, Anthony: retail
Howell, John: huckster
Hough, Wm: huckster
Hagerty, Danl hack
Hammersley, E: dog
Hunter, Wm: dog
Hess, Jacob: dog
Henley, Jane: dog
Hobbie, S R: dog

Hagner, J E: dog
Hicks, Chas: dog
Howle, P G: dog
Hall, Edw: dog
Harvey, J S: dog
Hairmiller: dog-2
Hess, Paul: dog
Howard, John: dog
Huddleston, John: dog
Hall, Jas C: slut
Hawkins, M: dog
Hill, Richd S: dog
Hill, Richd S: dog
Horning, G D: dog
Hickman, J: dog
Handy, Saml W: dog
Hickman, Anthony: dog
Hurtscamp, H: dog
Harris, A: dog
Hanly, J G: dog
Howe, Ignatius: dog
Hager: dog
Haislip, T H: dog
Hollidge, J: dog
Hitz, John: dog
Hampton, Emily: dog
Harbaugh, Val: dog
Hart, Albert: dog
Henson, G D: dog
Herald, A G: dog-2
Huffman, Geo: dog
Hamilton, W H: dog
Henly, Eliza: dog
Hickerson, Wm: hack
Holbrook, Jno M: hack
Henley, John: hack
Homer, Wm: hack
Jones, J H: confectionary
Jones, Ann: retain
Jenkins, Chas: theatrical
Jones, Alfred: huckster
Jenkins, David: huckster
Johnson, W C: huckster
Johnson, Thos J: huckster
Johnson, Wm: dog
Jackson, B L & Bro: dog

Johnson, Richmond: dog
Ingle, John P: dog
Jones, Alfred: dog
Jones, Raphael: dog
Jordine, Harriet: dog-2
Jennings, Polly: dog
Johnson, Lewis: dog
Johnson, John: dog
Jenkins, David: dog
Jenkins, A D: dog
Jackson, Susan: dog
Jamieson, J W: dog
Jost, Benedict: dog
Jasper, Wm: hack
Jenkins, A D: hack
Johnson, David: hack
King, Pat C: tavern
Krafft, Geo: confectionary
Krafft, J M: confectionary
Kilmiste, M: theatrical-2
Kennan, Chas: huckster
Kinney, Jeremiah: retail
Keller, Michl: grocery
Kanaley, Jas: retail-transfer
King, J H & Co: dry goods
Kirby, Saml: dog-2
Kleindenst, J P: dog
Kepler, Henry: dog
Kingman, Eliah: dog
Kuhn, Henry: dog
Krafft, J M: dog
Keys, Gillis: dog
Keyworth, Geo: dog
King, Martin: dog
Kelcher, Jas: hack
Kinsley, Hy: hack
Long, Jas: tavern
Laurel Milk Co: huckster
Lazarus, M & Co: dry goods
Leddy, Owen: huckster
Lucas, Bennet: retail
Lord, F B, jr: retail
Lavender, Jas: huckster
Lowe, Melchi: huckster
Lefler, John: huckster
Lane, J: huckster

Lathan, R W & Co: exchanges
Lover, Saml: concert-3
Leddy, Hugh: huckster-transfer
Longden, M: retail-transfer
Leddy, Owen: dog
Lewis, John: dog
Larned, Jas: dog
Landrick, Isaac: dog
Landrick, Fanny: dog
Leach, Wm: dog
Laub, J Y: dog
Lewis, Saml: dog
Lawson, Thos: dog
Lord, Wm: dog
Lowry, Wm H; dog
Law, J G: dog
Liomin, Eugene: dog
Lepreux, Lewis: dog
Lasky, R H: dog
Lavender, Jas: dog
Lancaster, Cath: dog
Lauxman, Mart: dog
Lambell, H K: dog
Lusby, John: dog
Lee, Josias: dog
Lemon, Chas: dog
Looby, Terrence: hack
Murray & Semmes: retail
Moran, Pat: tavern
Masi, F & Co: hardware
Martin, Wm: retail
Maher, Jas: tavern
Morrison, W M; auction
Maxwell & Sears: dry goods
Masi, Seraphim: hardware
Middleton, Chas: slave-2
Mills, R T: retail
Magee, Owen, retail
McKnight, J M: dry goods
Milburn, T M & B: auction
Meashun, Richd: huckster
Morell & Miller: confectionary
Mullikin, J W: huckster
McQuay, Benj: huckster
Munkins, G W: huckster
Moore, W H: huckster

Murray, W A: huckster
Mortimer, J T: huckster
Murray, Sarah: slave
Milburn, R M & B: retail
Mecklin, J P: dog
Magruder, R: dog
Muse, Lindsay: dog
Mankin, Jas: dog
Miller, J S: dog
Marks, S A: dog
McNorton, Geo: dog
Mullin, Basil: dog
McGinnis, J, jr: dog
Meehan, C H W: dog
McClery, Jas: dog
Mason, Is: dog
McIntire, Alex: dog
Martin, J W: dog
McWilliams, A: dog
Maury, J W: dog
Maury, C B: dog
Maury, J & C: dog
Mohler, Fred: dog
Murphy, John: dog
Miller, Chas: dog
Miller, Jo: dog
Mattingly, Geo: dog
Mohler, J: dog
Matthew, Sam: dog
Masi, Seraphim: dog
McDermott, Michl: dog
Marks, Jacob, sen: dog
Miller, John: dog
Morris, Wm: dog
MeKelden, John C: dog
Murray, Wm: dog
Mullen, W S: hack
Mercer, Jas: hack
Mason, H [Geot'n]: hack
Nailor, Dickinson: retail
Noland, Caroline: slaves
Nailor, Thompson: stage-4
Nourse, John: dog
Nichols, J W: dog
Norbeck, Geo: dog
Nokes, Jas: dog-2

Noble, Martha: dog-2
Noerr, And: dog
Nugent, E: dog
Newton, Benj: dog
Nepp, Dan: dog
Netle, Kitty: dog
Oyster, J H: hackster
Ogle, Chas: hackster
Orr, S L: dog
Ober & Ryon: dog
Owner, Jas: dog
Otterbach, Phil: dog-2
Owens, John: dog
O'Neale, H G: dog
O'Neale, J H: dog
Phillips, Geo W: dry goods
Peters, J R: Chinese Museum
Parker, Selby: dry goods
Plant, J K: retail
Pierce, G C: huckster
Paxton, John: huckster
Payne, C H: huckster
Pursell, Thos: dog
Parris, A K: dog
Picken, Thos: dog
Pleasanton, Step: dog
Parker, G & T: dog
Peck, Jos: dog
Powell, Thos S: dog
Pettit, Chas: dog
Pulizzi, V: dog
Poston, F B: dog
Prather, Alfred: dog
Pumphrey, L: dog –2
Preston, O J: dog
Plumsill, Thos B: dog
Perkins, Saml: dog
Perkins, Richd: dog
Page, Y P: dog
Powell, Abraham: hack
Page, Geo: hack-2
Pywell, R R: hack
Powell, Alex: hack
Queen, E F & Bro: retail
Quigley, Wm: shop
Richards, Wm: grocery

Radcliff, J T: grocery
Robey, Jane: retail
Redstrike, W J: retail
Ruff, J A: boots & shoes
Robertson, D: grocery
Reilly, F B: slave
Richardson, C F: huckster
Rabbit & Springman: huckster
Ricketts, A: huckster
Row, Geo: dog
Rhodes, Jas: dog
Roberts, J M: dog
Roach, Abm: dog
Redfern, Saml: dog
Robinson, T J: dog
Ritter, H G: dog
Randolph, H K: dog
Ross, Augustus: dog
Ried, B W: dog
Richardson, Luke: dog
Riordan, Jas: dog
Roane, J J: dog
Rochat, Henry: dog
Rawlings, Dav: dog
Ross, J W: dog
Rives, John C: dog
Robertson, H B: dog
Ramsay, Douglass: dog
Ross, Dan: hack
Sheckell, B O: tavern
Smallwood, E W: retail
Smallwood, E W: hats, boots, & shoes
Sweeting, Ellen: tavern
Simms & Son: retail
Stutz, Fred'k: tavern
Samuels, Wm: shop
Simpson, Presley: grocery
Stewart, Wm M: lottery
Sweeny, Mary: retail
Scott, R M: slave
Simms, J M: shop
Stepper, And: huckster
Stoops, Jas: retail
Stoops, Jas: huckster
Sherwood, Saml: huckster
Shreve, C H: huckster

Shreve, John: huckster
Shreve, Saml: huckster
Sullivan, Pat: huckster
Spignal, W B: huckster
Soper, Wm: huckster
Sedgwick, R H: huckster
Shaw, John: huckster
Steyermarkschen: concert-2
Sothoron, W B: retail-transfer
Saner, Lewis: retail
Stewart, L C: dog
Syfferly, G H: dog
Simms, Ann: dog
Slight, Jas: dog
Scaggs, Susan: dog
Shorter, Basil: dog
Sweeny, H B: dog
Smith, w C: dog
Saunders, H: dog
Sioussa, Jno: dog
Schweitzer, A: dog
Stubbs, Edw: dog
Stallings, Jno S: dog
Sewell, Richd: dog
Sioussa, Fred: dog
Shirley, John: dog
Stewart, Geo: dog
Scott, Stephen: dog
Springman, J M: dog
Sheppard, P: dog
Speiser, Fred: dog
Shiner, Mich: dog
Shaw, Alex: dog
Smith, J C: dog
Shedd, W P: dog
Scott, S E: dog
Steiger, W T: dog
Spignull, W B: dog
Sweeting, Mrs: dog
Storm, Leon: dog
Simms, Basil: dog
Smith, Thos: dog
Seitz Geo: dog
Sprigg, T B: dog
Smoot, Jno H: dog
Smallwood, John: dog

Shelton, Sarah: dog
Shannon, John: hack
Smith, Thos: hack-5
Thomas, Jos: shop
Thompson, C F: slave
Thompson, E L: slave
Tyson, Saml E: medicine
Taylor, J H: wood
Topham, Geo: tenpins
Tenant, John: huckster
Triplett, Thos: huckster
Thomas, Wm: tavern
Tastet, N: dog
Tonge, J T: dog
Todschinder, J A F: dog
Tschiffely, F A: dog
Taylor, Hudson: dog
Tanner, Lethe: dog
Tinney, Pompey: dog
Tophan, Geo: dog
Thomas, Chas: dog
Taylor, R A: dog
Tarlton, L A: dog
Talbot, Adelaide: dog
Tastett, J M: dog
Thomas, J G: dog
Tench, Stan: dog
Tucker, John F: dog
Tucker, Jas: dog
Trott, Thos P: dog
Thompson, Geo W: dog
Travers, Elias: dog
Tilghman, H H: dog
Turner, Hy: hack
Venable, Pat: shop
Van Zandt, N B: dog
Vanderlick, Jno: dog
West, John: tavern
Wilson, Patrick: retail
Williams, Barbara: slave
Wilson, Pat: huckster
Wannall, C P: retail
Willard, E & H: tavern
Wheatley, Geo: retail
Whittlesey, O: hardware
Webb, S B: lumber

Westerfield, Jas: retail
Williams, H: huckster
Wallace, Jas: huckster
Wollard, H: huckster
Whaley, Martha: dog
Wheat, Mary: dog
Warrington, L: dog
Willett, V: dog
Whitwell, J C: dog
Weichman, J C: dog
Watson, J W: dog
Wallach, Richd: dog
Weber, Christian: dog
Werner, J H T: dog
Wilcox, A F: dig
Weyrick, Jos: dog
Woodey, C F: dog
Williams, Zad: dog
Winster, J N: dog
Wallis, Wm: dog
Watts, Wm: dog
Wheeler, E: dog
Wirt, Jno L: dog
Winchester, R: dog
Wilson, J D: dog
Walker, Wm: dog
Wheat, Wm: dog
Warner, Hy: dog
Weaver, Sandy: dog
Willis, Wm: dog
West, John: dog
Wormly, Jas: hack
Welsh, Thos: hack
Walker & Kimmel: hack
Young, A H: retail
Yatemen, J H: huckster
Young, A H: huckster
Young, A H; dog
Young, J W: dog

Persons fined during the months of Dec, Jan, & Feb last, for failing to procure their licenses.

Brown, O B: dog
Bogan, B L: dog
Beall, Eliz A: dog
Benter, Wm: non-resident slave
Brenner, P & Son: dry goods
Carothers, A: groceries
Cole, Seth: dog
Clarke, Jas B, agent: retail
Carroll, Jas T: cart
Cash. Leonard: dog
Copp, Moses: bowling alley-2
Casparis, Jas: liquors
Dowell, Rebecca: dog
Dessnell, Dennis: peddling
Fuller & Co: wagon
Farrar, John M: bowling alley
Flenner, Wm: boots & shoes
Gardner: dog
Goddard, Thos: dog
Howell: retailing
Hollidge: dog
Jasper, Wm: hack
Killion, John: dog
Kirdwood, Jonathan: dog
Keyworth, Robt: dog
Lahmin: dog
Lazarus, Moses: retailing
Lambright, Geo: dog
Miller, John: dog
Mason, John: dog
Middleton, L J: liquors
McKnight, J: retailing
Metclear, Wm: cart
Mustin, Thos: dog
Mullen, John: hack
Nugent, Eli: dog
O'Neale, H G: dog
Pestch, T C: liquors
Plant, J H: liquors
Prosser, John: liquors
Parker, Geo & Thos: exchanging
Pearson, P M: lumber
Peall, Resin: dog
Purdy, John: lumber
Quigley, Wm: retail
Ramsay, Wm: dog

Ready, Jno: liquors
Skinner, John: dog
Sanford, Louisa: dog
Sears, Maxwell: retail
Smith, Henry: peddling
Smith: wagon
Sweeny, Edw: dog
Thompson, E C B: dog
Traverse, N: dog

Tyson, Saml E: medicine
Tarin, Madam, & Co: dry goods
Valentine, Dr: theatrical
Weeden, Susan: slut
Weeden, Susan: dog
Wilson, J L: huckstering
Welsh, Thos: hack
-C H Wiltberger, Register

At the editorial head of the Knoxville [Tenn] Standard, of Apr 11, new way of telling a man's death: Died, on Sat last, within 20 minutes after the reception of the contents of a pistol fired by Thos D Hurray, Capt Henry B Newman, citizen of this place, & in the full vigor of health.

The Rockingham [Va] Register announces the death of Dr Peachy Harrison, a distinguished citizen & native of that county. He died on Tue last, in his 72nd year. He has represented Rochingham in the Legislature of Va, & was a member of the Convention that met in 1829 to revise the State constitution.

Died: on May 2, at Phil, at an advanced age, Richd Peters, formerly a leading member of the Phil bar, & for many years official Reporter to the Supreme Court of the U S.

Died: yesterday, after a short illness, at *Haddock's Hills*, Wash Co, Edward, youngest child of Robt W & Mary Eliza Dyer, aged 13 months & 21 days. His funeral is on Tue at 10 o'clock.

In Mobile, on Apr 26, an old man named Elisha Palmer was shot dead near Mr Wragg's residence, on the Gov't street road. He was going home from his daily labor. The person who fired the gun was concealed in the woods.

Commissioners' sale: by decree of the Circuit Court of Wash Co, D C, in the matter of the heirs of Fred'k Reitz, late of said county, deceased: public sale on May 29, of the property in square 254, belonging to the estate of Reitz: one 3 story brick dwlg-house fronting on E st, & also one 2 story brick dwlg-house on the same st, adjoining the former; both houses being immediately west of the residence of John C Rives, near the Treas Dept. –Lewis Johnson, Chas H James, N Callan, E Simms, Com'rs

For rent: a large 3 story brick house, with back bldgs, on the north side of F st, between 6th & 7th sts, near the Patent Ofc, built by & known as the residence of the late Thos P Jones. Persons intending to take boarders need not apply. Persons calling may see the house.

House of Reps:: 1-Memorial of John Poe.

TUE MAY 9, 1848
Orphans Court of Wash Co, D C. Letters of administration on the personal estate of Geo Fisher, late of Florida, deceased. –Susan E Gordon, admx -D Gordon, adm

For rent-2 story brick house on B st near 3rd, in rear of Pa ave & near railroad depot. Apply at Dr Schwartze's Drug Store.

Belle Plain for sale: my little farm in Fairfax Co, adjoining the land attached to the Episcopal High School, half a mile n w of the Theological Seminary of Va: with a 2 story brick dwlg, barn, stable, cow-house, & all necessary bldgs. –Isaac George

From 550 to 600 acres of land for sale: at public auction, on Jun 2, 1848, at the courthouse of Fauquier Co, Va, the land of which John T Mason died seized & possessed, & which descended to his heirs, of whom one of them now owns an undivided moiety. It is Fauquier Co, & adjoins the lands of John Porter, Wm W Wallace, J Horner, Walter Smith, Robt Tompkins, & Mrs Chichester. –John T Mason -Inman Horner, Atty

The funeral of the late Maj Edw Webster took place at Boston on Thu. His remains were attended to the grave by a large concourse of his friends & fellow citizens in military & civic procession.

Orphans' Court for Balt Co: upon the application of Jos Anthony & others, claiming to be distributees & reps of John alias John P Anthony, & John Anthony, the younger, late of Balt City, intestate deceased, the latter of whom resided in one of the Southern States in 1826. It is May 4, 1848, orderd by the said court that Sep 1 next be, & is appointed for all persons entitled as distributees or next of kin of said deceased to appear, in person or by atty, in this Court. –Chas Howard, John Burnes Test: D M Perine, Reg/o wills- Balt Co, Md.

Dr Wm L Fraser offers his professional services: ofc on 9th st, near Mckendree Chapel.

The steam propeller **Sarah Sands** left N Y on Fri for Liverpool, taking out the following passengers: Mr Frank Perkins, Dr Chas Craitzer, Boston; Mad'lle Blangy, Mr Robert, of N Y; Mr & Mrs Ephraim, C S Ducouren, of Balt; J G Woener, Augustus Koeger, St Louis; H T W Geddersen, Lancaster; H D Andrews, N Y; Mr Welch, lady & child, Miss Matthews, Honduras; Mr G Mass & lady, France; Mr Higgins, lady, & 2 children, Mrs Town, Miss Hassitt, Mrs Turner, Mr Stevens, Mr Gibson, Robt Ellington, England.

Died: on May 2, at the Union Hotel, Gtwn, D C, Mrs Margaret R Wilson, consort of Peter F Wilson, in her 19th year, a native of Martinsburg, Va. [Steubenville & Iowa papers please copy.]

Died: on Apr 28, at his residence on Wye river, Queen Anne's Co, Md, Wm H De Courcy.

Died: yesterday, Mary Eliz, youngest daughter of John W & Isabel Maury, aged 1 year & 2 days. Her funeral will take place from the residence of her father, on C st, today at 4 o'clock.

WED MAY 10, 1848
A 17 year old lad named Macafee, who had been at work on the railroad, leaped from the freight train at Manchester, N H, fell between the cars & was killed.

House of Reps: 1-Ptn from the reps of Wm Armstrong, asking compensation for his services as U S Indian agent. 2-Cmte on Naval Affairs: bill for the relief of Michl Hanson. 3-Cmte on Military Affairs: bill for the relief of the legal reps of Thos J V Owen, deceased. 4-Cmte on Pensions: asking to be discharged from the further consideration of the House bill for the relief of Francis M Holton: referred to the Cmte on Naval Affairs. 5-Ptn of Sally Hart for a pension. 6-Ptn of Philip Tabers for arrears of pension. 7-Ptn of Mrs Harriet Gay, of Monroe Co, N Y, praying further relief for her aged father, Elkana Stevens, of Chelsea, Vt, who was a soldier of the Revolution, & is now destitute & infirm. 8-Ptn of Rezin Tevis for an increase of pension. 9-Memorial of Mary E Carney, praying for a pension: referred to the Cmte on Revolutionary Pensions.

Passengers in packet-ship **Mediator**, at N Y from London: Madame Fallofield, Paris; Thos B Kay, Boston; Mrs S Bradley, Utica; Mr S Unwin, London; Mrs Ann Hill, N Y; Miss Sarah Ann Hill, N Y; John Perry, Montreal, Miss Louisa Hall Chatteras, Kent; Miss Harriet Betbel, Essex; Capt Thos Boland & lady, Boston; Mr Lewis Bossot, Switzerland; H Wilmott, Somersetshire; Mr A Lyon, Bedford; W Henman, Bedford; Edw Partridge & lady, Boston; W R Lucas & lady, London; Miss Pratt, Wash; Miss A Bloomfield, Arthur Bloomfield, Windsor; Cyrus Lucas, London; Wm Blakely, Greenwich; Wm Pierce, Kent; H Parton, Bristol; J Thompson, Scotland; Wm Perry, jr, Montreal; Capt Eytinge, N Y; & 170 in steerage. In the ship **Iowa** at N Y from Havre: J Phillips, Phil; J Marcole, France; A Pracole, France; E Eckeher, N Y; L Butler, France; A Sevoige, Switzerland; W Stanburcher, lady, 2 children, & servant, Germany.

Senate: 1-Ptn from Nancy Jillson, asking an increase of her pension. 2-Cmte on Foreign Relations: bill for the relief of the personal reps of Wm A Slacum, deceased. 3-Bill for the relief of John W Simonton.

Mrd: on May 4, by Rev Mr Butler, Thos D Larner to Caroline, daughter of Mr Geo Hill, all of Wash City.

Mrd: on May 8, by Rev Mr Vanhorseigh, Mr Jas W Johnson to Miss Catherine Sophia Greenwell, both of Wash City.

Mrs: May 9, by Rev Jas B Donelan, J C Moran, of Balt, to Susan W, eldest daughter of John T Caro, of Wash City.

Boots & Shoes: J A Ruff has removed his store on Pa ave, opposite the Theatre.

Store & house for rent: occupied by Messrs B L Jackson & Brother for the last 10 years as a Wholesale Grocery, is offered for rent; also, the dwlg house above. Inquire of B H Cheever.

THU MAY 11, 1848
Senate: 1-Bill for the relief of Nehemiah Brush, with a report. 2-Cmte on Pensions: bill granting a pension to Wm Pittman, with a report. 3-Cmte on Pensions: House bills without amendment: relief of Joel Thatcher; of John Knight; of Benj Reefanyder; of Wm Paddy; of Israel Bayless; of Arthur Wilson; of Benj G Perkins; of Beriah Wright; & of John Savage.

Wash Corp: 1-Ptn from Chas Shorter for remission of a fine: referred to the Cmte of Claims. 2-Ptn from Philip Otterback & others, respecting the fences before private residences in the 7th Ward: referred to the Cmte on Improvements. 3-Cmte of Claims: bill for the relief of W C Johnson: passed. 4-Bill for the relief of Louisa Collins; of Andrew D Jenkins; & of Wm Jasper: all referred to the Cmte of Claims. 5-Ptn of Thos Fevan & others, praying that iron pipes may be substituted for the wooden ones now in use for conveying water on 13th st, between G & H sts: referred to the Cmte on Improvements. 6-Ptn of Owen McGee, for remission of a fine: referred to the Cmte of Claims. 7-Ptn of Caleb Dulany, was recommitted. 8-Cmte on Unfinished Business: asking to be discharged from the further consideration of the ptns of: Alfred Prather, John N Moulder, C S Fowler, Stephen J Ober, H Skidmore, Thos Hurdle, Ann Stewart, John Cotter, Enoch Ward, & Thos Welsh: agreed to.

Circuit Court of Wash Co, D C-in Chancery. Henry Ould, adm of Eliz Peirce, against Abner C Peirce, Joshua Peirce, Saml Simington & Ann his wife, Hayes Speakman & Hannah his wife, Abilgail Shoemaker, Peirce Shoemaker, & Abner Shoemaker. The bill states that Isaac Peirce bequeathed to the cmplnts intestate a legacy of $3,000, & subject to the payment of the same, devised all his estates to the dfndnt, Abner C Pierce: that he bequeathed to the other dfndnts legacies to be paid by his said residuary devisee; that some of said legacies have been paid, & others remain unpaid, the time for payment having expired; that the bill is filed by the cmplnt on behalf of himself & all the other legatees who shall come in upon the usual terms; & the object of the bill is to obtain payment of said legacies, & a sale of the real & personal estates of said Isaac Pierce, if the same should not be paid by his said residuary devisee; & it appearing to the Court that Saml Simington & Ann his wife, reside out of the jurisdiction of this Court: ordered that said dfndnts are to appear in this Court on or before the 1st Mon of Oct next.
–W Brent, clerk

Exec's sale of good 2 story frame house & lot at auction: by powers vested in me by the last will & testament of Richd M Warring, deceased: sale on May 10, of lot 26 in subdivision of square 435, with the improvements, situated on the island, on 7th st west, between E & D sts south. –Chas S Wallach, exc -A Green, auctioneer

Household & kitchen furniture at auction: May 15, at the late residence of Mrs Rebecca Burche, deceased, on East Capitol st: first 3 story brick house east of the Capitol: order of Orphans' Court. -A Green, auctioneer

Circuit Court of Wash Co, D C-in Chancery. Wm Stabler & Benj Hallowell, vs, Richd Thompson, Lydia Thompson, Wm D Prout, Sarah S Prout, Danl F Prout, Martha H Prout, Mary C Prout, Francis R Prout, & Julia Prout. The bill states the dfndnt, Richd Thompson, is indebted to cmplnt, Wm Stabler, for $3,000, with interest from Oct 14, 1837; to the cmplnt, Wm Stabler, adm of Edw Stables, deceased, for $1,000, with interest as aforesaid; & to cmplnt Benj Hallowell, for $1,000, with interest as aforesaid; the payment of which debts is secured by a deed of trust executed by the dfndnts, Richd Thompson & Lydia Thompson, to Wm Prout, since deceased, as trustee, conveying lots 2, 6, & 8, in square 518, Wash City; that Wm Prout died without having executed the trusts of said deed, leaving children & heirs at law, namely, the dfndnts, Wm D Prout, Sarah S Prout, Danl F Prout, Martha H Prout, Mary C Prout, Francis R Prout, & Julia Prout. Bill prays for substitution of another trustee & general relief. Wm D Prout resides & is out of D C: ordered he appear on or before the 3rd Mon in Oct next, in this Court. –Wm Brent, clerk

FRI MAY 12, 1848
Tragic affair near Natchez a few days ago is mentioned in the New Orleans Delta: Mr Chas Jones, originally from Red river, & has practiced law in Louisiana, was shot at his residence on Black river, by a highly respectable lady, said to be a relative of his. At last accounts Jones was not quite dead.

Senate: 1-Cmte on Indian Affairs: asking to be discharged from the further consideration of the memorial of Patrick Marraulette. Same cmte: adverse report on the ptn of Jas Wilkins.

The body of Mr Nathl Hardy, long known as a hardware merchant, of Louisville, Ky, was found in the river a few days ago. Verdict of the coroner: found drowned.

The Delaware Gaz reports the death, by suicide, on May 4, of Warren Jefferson, a member of the last State Senate. He shot himself through the heart with a horse pistol, in the rear of his own house, in Sussex Co. The committal of the awful deed is attributed to family afflictions, causing partial insanity, which is said to be hereditary in his family. His son committed suicide some years ago. He was about 70 years of age, in easy circumstances, & enjoying a high reputation.

The Massachusetts Regt: the Boston Post published an official list of the deaths in this regt since its arrival in Mexico, dated San Angel, Mar 20, 1848: deceased:-Maj Webster, Capt J A Felt, Lt E S Green, & 2nd Lt G F Gardner. 71 privates are deceased, 2 of whom were killed by Mexican. 7 ofcrs have resigned, & their resignations have been accepted, viz: Capts Ashley, Whiting, & Nichols; Lts Griswold, Roby, Myers, & Thompson. Capt Geo Walsh, Lts J P Caldwell & Amos Wood have been dismissed from the service by sentence of general court martial.

Explosion on Sat last a mile below West Point, killed Mr Stephen Garrison; some 7 or 8 others were seriously injured. A shanty containing powder was fired by an incendiary, & the bldg blown to atoms.

Horace Stockman & Wm Stockman, residing near Pontiac, were drowned in Lake Huron, on Apr 23. They were in the employ of Mr Henry Butts as fishermen, when the yawl capsized.

Balt City Court: Wm S Birch, convicted of conspiring with Richd J Turner to defraud the Mechanics' Bank, has been sentenced to 4 years' imprisonment in the county jail, & fined $500.

House of Reps: 1-Ptn of Susannah Kimball, of Ipswich, for pension for Revolutionary service of her her late husband. 2-Ptn of the heirs of Jonathan Faire for arrears of pensions. 3-Applications of Mrs Dorothy Mead, Mrs Barbara Baughman, & Mrs Abigail Williams for arrearages of pay & pensions.

The Watch Tower, printed in Jalapa, Mexico, has the following: We hear from Perote of the death, in that place, of Lt Gough, of Col Black's Pa Regt. He was on duty in Perote as assist quartermaster, & had a slight difficulty with Capt Foster, of the Georgia btln. About 4 days since, Capt Foster attacked Lt Gough, & stabbed him in 4 places. He died a few hours later. Capt Foster has been removed to Puebla for trial.

Suitable reward for runaway servant boy Charles, age 13 years, dark copper color; stutters very badly. His mother lives in the 1st Ward, by the name of Vigle. –Alex'r Lee

Mr Dewitt Clinton Winchell, of Ulster Co, N Y, brought a suit against Miss Eliz Bogart, for a breach of the marriage promise. They kept company with each other for over 5 years & declared their intention to marry. A man named Chamber cut Winchell out of his intended wife. The jury awarded Winchell $25.00

Contributions for the Nat'l Washington Monument received since May 2:
John G Mosley, Richmond dist, Va: $120.
Wm D Acken, Florida: $270.
Thos F Martin, Botetort district, Va: $50.
Saml Whitcomb, jr, Windsor district, Vt: $150.
Francis E Luckett, Berkeley district, Va: $118.

Pres Polk restored Midshipman Pollock, who was sentenced to the State Prison for shooting an editor in Buffalo, N Y, to his rank in the Navy. He had been previously pardoned from prison by Gov Young.

Mrd: on May 9, by Rev Jas B Donelan, Lemuel S Clark, of Wash City, to Frances Olivia, daughter of the late Thos Burch, of PG Co, Md.

Mrd: on May 9, at Normanstone, near Gtwn, by Rev R T Berry, John H Higgins, of Rockville, Md, to S Dora, daughter of Robt Barnard, of the former place.

Mrd: on May 9, at St John's Church, by Rev Smith Pyne, Capt E D Townsend, U S Army, to Ann Overing, daughter of the late Col Wainwright.

Mrd: Mar 14, at Woodland Cottage, Taycheidah, Wisconsin, by Rev Fabius Bernard, Mr Albert Brewster, of Fond-du-lac, Wisconsin, to Miss Harriet Daingerfield Preuss, of Wash City, daughter of the late A W Preuss.

Died: on May 7, in Gtwn, at the residence of her sisters, the Misses Bootes, of pulmonary consumption, Mrs Matilda Edmonson, relict of Thos Edmonson, & daughter of the late Saml Bootes.

Died: on May 5, in Montg Co, Md, Priscilla, in her 63rd year, consort of Saml Shreve, of Montg Co.

Died: on Mar 14 last, in Mexico, Capt J Oswald Dunn, formerly of Wash City.

Died: on Apr 17 last, at Louisville, Ky, Miss Susan Hughes, formerly of Wash City. [Phil papers please copy.]

Died: on May 9, at his residence, in Fredericksburg, Va, at age 74, Wm J Roberts. He had been the cashier of the Branch Bank of Va at Fredericksburg ever since its establishment. His private life illustrated the highest virtues of a man & a Christian.

Died: on Apr 20, at New Orleans, on his return from Verz Cruz, where he had been for the recovery of his health, Mr David Sleator, of Debuque, Iowa.

SAT MAY 13, 1848
Senate: 1-Ptn from David Hunt & Aylett Buckner, asking to be confirmed in the entry of certain public lands.

House of Reps: 1-Cmte of the Whole: bill for settling the claim of the legal reps of Richd W Meade, deceased.

David S Jones, for 50 years a member of the N Y Bar, & recently a Judge of Queen's Co, died in N Y C on Wed. He was a brother of the venerable Saml Jones, late Chancellor of the State.

Col Wm Chambers died on May 2 at the residence of his nephews in the city of St Louis. He had been ill for a few days only. He was 91 years old, a remarkable man in many respects. He leaves a vast estate, both in St Louis & Ky, & only one child, the wife of Robt Tyler, of Louisville. –St Louis Union

Matthew Reed, late Pres of the Tradesmen's Bank of N Y, & formerly one of the Aldermen of the 6th Ward, accidentally lost his life on Wed while assisting in the removal of a bale of leather from one of the upper lofts of a store. He fell through the hatchway to the floor below, breaking his neck.

Died: on Apr 29, at Wordsfield, Ohio, in her 25th year, Mrs Phebe Smith, wife of Isaac Smith, & daughter of the Hon Jos Morris.

Died: on Apr 26, near Martinsburg, Gerard B Wager, formerly of Harper's Ferry, in the 43rd year of his age, leaving a young & interesting family.

In Chancery: Robt W Dyer, against Sarah G Stewart, Chas A Stewart, & Wm H Stewart. The creditors of the late Wm H Stewart are notified to file at my ofc their claims, duly proved, on or before Sep 1 next. -W Redin, auditor

MON MAY 15, 1848
Some miscreant attempted on Sat to set fire to the dwlg of the venerable relict of Ex-Pres Madison, near St John's Church, but the alarm quickly given, prevented serious injury.

One cent reward for John F Sewall, an indented apprentice to the coach wood-work business. –Michl McDermott, living on Pa ave, near 3rd st.

Letter from a gentleman in Montgomery from which we learn that the north end of the county was visited by a destructive storm on May 6, by which the dwlgs of Mr Kemper & Mrs Mitchell were prostrated, & the family of the latter buried beneath her dwlg. Mrs Mitchell & Mrs Anderson were both killed instantly. Jas Mitchell, Mr Calahan, Miss Treadway, & Mrs S Mitchell, & her little son, were severely injured: the latter, it is feared, mortally. –Frankfort [Ky] Commonwealth

Appointments by the Pres: 1-John N A Griswold, of N Y, Consul for the port of Shanghai, in China, vice Caleb Lyon, resigned. 2-Horatio I Sprague, Consul for the port of Gibraltar, vice Horatio Sprague, deceased.

U S ship **Ohio**, Harbor of Callao, Mar 13, 1848. The storeship **Erie**, Lt Commanding Jas M Watson, sailed on Mar 4, homeward bound, having in charge the remains of Cmdor A J Dallas, who died here on Jun 4, 1844. The day previous there was a solemn funeral procession of boats to escort the remains from the shore to the Erie. The ship **Ohio**, Capt W V Taylor, detained here awaiting the arrival of the storeship **Matilda**, will sail for the coast of Mexico by the close of this week. The ship **Preble**, Cmder Jas Glynn recently transferred to her, sailed Mar 4 for Monterey, ofcrs & crew all well. Among the ofcrs, passengers on board the **Ohio**, are: Cmdor Thos Ap Catesby Jones, Cmder-in-Chief, & suite; Cmder C K Stribling, Capt of the Fleet; Lt Jas McCormick, Flag Lt; Bailey Washington, Surgeon of the Fleet; Wm M Steuart, Cmdor's Sec; Passed Midshipman M P Jones, & Midshipman E O Carnes, Cmdor's Aids.

Senate: Ptn from J Anthony King & Cuyler W Young, asked to be allowed to organize a military force to aid the people of Yucatan.

Mrs Sweeny was killed 2 or 3 days ago, at Little Falls, N Y, by a stone thrown out by a sand blast. Two stones, about 30 pounds each, were dashed into her house, one of which struck her just above the breast as she sat in her chair with her infant 10 days old. She was killed instantly.

Mrd: on May 10, at Sharon, Fairfax Co, Va, by Rev L H Christian, Wm Beall, M D, formerly of PG Co, Md, to Mary Eliz Lee Jones, daughter of Cmdor Thos Ap Catesby Jones, U S Navy.

Mrd: on May 10, according to Friends' ceremony, at Sandy Spring, Montg Co, Md, Warwick P Miller, of Alexandria, Va, to Mary M, only daughter of Caleb Stables, of that county.

Died: on May 13, at his residence, Palermo, near Alexandria, the Hon Wm Brent, jr, of Richland, Va, late Charge d'Affaires of the U S at Buenos Ayres. His funeral will take place at Christ's Church, Alexandria, on May 15, at 4 o'clock.

Died: on May 13, in Wash City, in her 13th year, Columbia Washington, 2nd daughter of Dr A J & Eliz A K Schwartze. Her funeral is this morning at 10 o'clock, from the residence of her father, Pa ave, near 3rd st.

Died: on Apr 29, Jas L Woodville, Pres of the Bank of Va, at Buchanan, aged about 56 years.

TUE MAY 16, 1848
For sale: new frame house, containing 10 rooms, with a good cellar & fine lot, on Mass ave, between 11th & 12th sts, north side. Apply to W H Clampett, on the premises, or his carpenter's shop, N Y ave & 14th st.

Senate: 1-Cmte on Patents: bill for the relief of Obed Hussey. Same cmte: bill for the relief of Bancroft Woodcock. 2-Bill for the relief of Wm B Grady: passed.

Household furniture, piano forte, silver, & carriages at auction, by order of the Orphans Court of Wash Co, D C. Sale on May 31, at the residence of the late Col Geo Bomford, on I st, between 16th & 17th sts, near St John's Church. -R W Dyer, auct

Mrd: on Sun last, by Rev Mr Vanhorsigh, Wm Quigley to Miss Mary Eliza McNamee, both of Wash City.

Died: on May 14, in Wash City, Mrs Eliza R, relict of the late Cmdor Thos Holdup Stevens, U S Navy. His funeral is from Lakemeyer's [late Hand's & Galabrun's] Hotel, today, at 12 o'clock.

Recent deaths at Vera Cruz: from the Free American-report of deaths at the Genr'l Hospital at Vera Cruz for the half month ending on Apr 15. Regulars: John Henderson, Richd T Avery, Meale McPeake, Jas P Allen, Wm McShane, Jeremiah Williams, Jacob Oake, Lt Gray, 13th Infty; Nelson C Slater, Wm Ryder, Geo Sidlinger, Joshua D Holt, Jos Morris, John W Steward, Casper Bates, Wm Bryant, Geo Sailling, John Setter, F Schlem. Volunteers: Henry Clark, Jos Differt, David High, Wm Thatcher, John C Ward.

Died: on Sun last, in Wash City, of brain fever, Milton M Bernard, in his 16th year. His funeral is this morning, at 10 o'clock, from his late residence, 13½ st, between C & D sts.

Circuit Court of D C: John L Wilson, insolvent debtor, has applied to be discharged from imprisonment. -Wm Brent, clk

WED MAY 17, 1848
Senate: Ptn from Elijah Pratt, asking compensation for the use of certain valves by the Gov't, in violation of his patent right, & for the purpose of his invention by the Gov't for the use of the Pountonier service.

Wash Corp: 1-Mayor's nomination as Assessors for the present year, Geo W Harkness, John Sessford, Geo Collard: laid on the table. 2-Ptns from John Davidson, from Jas Hollidge, & from John Fletcher: referred to the Cmte of Claims. 3-Bill for the relief of Michl Shanks: concurred in. 4-Ptns from Jonathan Kirkwood & from Caleb Buckingham: referred to the Cmte of Claims.

Decree of the Circuit Court of Wash Co, D C, in Chancery: in a case wherein Chas Thomas et al are petitioners for sale of real estate, all that piece of ground of which the late Ann Thomas died, seized & possessed, being part of lot 1 in square 317, with 2 story frame house thereon. –S S Williams, trustee -A Green, auctioneer

House of Reps: 1-Ptn of Calvin Blythe, exc of the last will & testament of Cmdor Jesse D Elliott, deceased, asking to be remunerated for certain expenses incurred while cmder of the naval force in the Mediterranean from 1835 to 1839. 2-Ptn of Thos B Grose & 200 others, asking the construction of a light-house on Indian Island, near Goose river village, in Camden, Maine. 3-Memorial of Lawrence Y Morton & others of the pay dept of the U S army at New Orleans, for an increase of pay.

The Hon Wm A Newell, the Rep in Congress from the 2nd district of N J, has just been presented with a gold ring from Mrs Adams for his unremitting attention to her lamented husband from the first of his illness. The ring has a table of cornelian opening by a hinge, & disclosing the hair of the deceased, with the inscription, "J Q Adams, Feb 23d, 1848." This note accompanied the gift: "As a very small appreciation of Dr Newell's kind services & attention to her husband, Mrs Adams begs his acceptance of the accompanying hair ring. "Washington, April 27, 1848."

Mrd: on Tue, by Rev John C Smith, Mr Edmund Carr to Miss Ann Eliza Waters, of Va.

A young man named Dillingham, about 21, belonging to Camden, Maine, committed suicide there by taking arsenic on Tue last. Some ascribe it to domestic affliction. –Belfast Republican of Fri.

John Peirce, age 25, at Avon Springs, because of his health, was found hanging to a tree in the north part of Genesco, near the house of Mr E C Goodrich. Peirce was a nativeof Salem, N Y, & resided in Sandgate, Vt, with his father-in-law. –Rochester American-Fri

Trustees Sale: by decree of the Circuit Court of Wash Co, D C-in Chancery: in a cause in which Fred'k L Keller-cmplnt & Henrietta C Keller & Chas Keller-dfndnts: public auction on May 24, on the corner of 11th st & Md ave, Wash City, lots 18 through 23 in square 327. –A H Lawrence, trustee -R W Dyer, auct

The remains of the late Senator Ashley were conveyed from our city on Mon under charge of Mr Isaac Holland, Assist Doorkeeper of the Senate, on their way to the family residence of the deceased in Arkansas.

Arrivals from Mexico: ofcrs came passengers on the last vessel from Vera Cruz: Maj Gen Pillow & staff, Gen Towson, Gen Cushing & staff, Cols Childs, Belknap, Randal, Duncan, Withers, Walton, Maj Crutchfield, Capts Huger, Swasey, Toulmin, Brown, Sibley, Asquith, Lts Wayne, W B Gray, A J McCallan, G W May, McElroy, S C Ridgely, Auger, Ripley, Twing, Steener, Hull, 2 companies Texan Rangers, & 5 sick & discharged soldiers & teamsters.

List of the ofcrs of the U S ship **Albany**, at sea, Apr 15, 1848: John Kelly, Capt; A Gibson, Z Holland, & B S Gantt, Lts; John Wilkes, jr, Acting Master; G F Cutter, Purser; R T Barry, Surgeon; W Sherman, Assist Surgeon; J W Curts, 1st Lt Marines; Geo H Hare, G U Morris & J C Eggleston, Midshipmen; John Bates, Boatswain; Wm Arnold, Gunner; Jacob Stevens, sailmaker; R Sheffield, Carpenter; G W Ingolls, capt's Clerk. Bound to Laguyra, South America.

Richmond Whig of yesterday announces the death of Richd H Toler. Our paper goes forth clad in the sable garb of mourning for one who has, for more than 2 years, directed its course with consummate address, & inspired its columns with an interest only inferior to the skill with which its general aim has been preserved. He expired yesterday at his lodgings at the Powhatan House, in his 49th year.

The Bldg Cmte of the Nat'l <u>Washington Monument</u> are happy to announce that the excavation for the foundation of the Monument has been completed, & the masonry will be very soon commenced. The corner-stone, a white mable block of 6 to 8 tons, will be at the railroad depot in a few days, when it is intended to place it upon a large stone-wagon, & is expected to be conveyed to the site of the Monument by our fellow citizens, under the direction & management of Mr Philip Ennis, of which due notice will be given to the public. This stone is a present, & has come free from the quarry to the depot, the cmte wish it to go free to its resting-place. –Thos Carbery, Geo Watterston, Wm A Bradley, Blgs Cmte

House of Reps: 1-Cmte of Claims: bill for the relief of Archibald Beard & 21 others, mounted Tennessee volunteers: committed. Same cmte: bills for the relief of Wm J Turner & the relief of Wm P Yonge: committed. Same cmte: adverse report on the ptn of Thos Chaney: laid on the table. 2-Cmte on Commerce: bill for the relief of Philip J Fontane: committed. 3-Cmte on Public Lands: adverse reports on the ptns of Evander M Soper & others; & of Alfred R Randolph: both laid on the table.

Died: on May 15, in her 35th year, after a short but severe illness, Mrs Eliza F Haw, wife of Dr Henry Haw, & daughter of the late Mr Jesse Brown. Her funeral is this day at 11 o'clock, from her late residence near Wash City.

Good 2 story frame house & lot at auction: by decree of the Circuit Court of Wash Co, D C, wherein Saml Redfren, cmplnt, & Barbara A Parker & others, dfndnts. Sale on May 19, of half or part of lot 3 in square 56, with improvement. The property fronts on G st north, near the corner of 23rd st west. –John F Ennis, Trustee -A Green, auctioneer

THU MAY 18, 1848
Brevet promotions by the President, by & with the advice & consent of the Senate. List of ofcrs for brevet promotions for gallant & meritorious conduct in the battles of Palo Alto & Resaca de la Palma, in Texas, on May 8 & 9, 1846, to date from May 9, 1846.
Brevet Maj Geo A McCall, since Major of the 3rd Infty, to be Lt Col.
Capt Wm W S Bliss, Assist Adj Gen, to be Major.
2nd Lt Delos B Sackett, 1st Dragoons, to be 1st Lt.
2nd Lt Thos J Brereton, ordnance dept, to be 1st Lt.
Brig Gen David E Twiggs, to be Maj Gen, "for gallant & meritous service in the several conflicts at Monterey, Mexico, on the 21st, 22nd, & 23rd of Sep, 1846," to date from Sep 23, 1846.
List of ofcrs for brevet promotion for gallant & meritorious conduct in the several conflicts at Monterey, Mexico, on the 21st, 22nd, & 23rd of Sep, 1846, to date from Sep 23, 1846.
Capt Geo D Ramsay, ordnance dept, to be Major.
Capt Henry Bainbridge, 3rd Infty, since Major of the 7th Infty, to be Major.
Capt Wm S Henry, 3rd Infty, to be Major.
1st Lt Wm W Mackall, 1st Artl, to be Capt.
1st Lt Don Carlos Buell, 3rd Infty, to be Capt.
1st Lt Wm T H Brooks, 3rd Infty, to be Capt.
2nd Lt Chas L Kilburn, 3rd Artl, since 1st Lt, to be 1st Lt.
2nd Lt John L Reynolds, 3rd Artl, since 1st Lt, to be 1st Lt.
2nd Lt Saml G French, 3rd Artl, since 1st Lt, to be 1st Lt.
2nd Lt Schuyler Hamilton, 1st Infty, to be 1st Lt.
Ofcrs for brevet promition for gallant & meritorious conduct in the battles of Buena Vista, Mexico, on Feb 22 & 23, 1847, to date from Feb 23, 1847.
Brig Gen John E Wool, to be Maj Gen.
Col Sylvester Churchill, inspector gen, to be Brig Gen.
Brevet Lt Col John Monroe, Maj 2nd Artl, to be Col.
Brevet Lt Col Jos K F Mansfield, Capt Corps of Engineers, to be Col.

Maj John M Washington, 3rd Artl, to be Lt Col.
Maj Roger S Dix, paymaster, to be Lt Col.
Brevet Maj Wm W S Bliss, Assist Adj Gen, to be Lt Col.
Brevet Maj Braxton Bragg, Capt 3rd Artl, to be Lt Col.
Capt Thos B Linnard, Topographical Engineers, to be Maj.
Capt Amos B Eaton, Commissary of Subsistance, to be Maj.
Capt Ebenezer S Sibley, Assist Quartermaster, to be Maj.
Capt Wm W Chapman, Assist Quartermaster, to be Maj.
Capt Thos W Sherman, 3rd Artl, to be Maj.
Brevet Capt Wm H Shover, 3rd Artl, since Capt, to be Maj.
Brevet Capt Jas L Donaldson, since Assist Quartermaster, to be Maj.
Brevet Capt Geo H Thomas, 1st Lt 3rd Artl, to be Maj.
Brevet Capt Robt S Garnett, 1st Lt 4th Artl, to be Maj.
Capt John P J O'Brien, Assist Quartermaster, to be Maj.
1st Lt Henry W Benham, Corps of Engineers, to be Capt.
1st Lt Thos L Brent, 4th Artl, since Capt & Assist Quartermaster, to be Capt.
1st Lt Lorenzo Sitgreaves, Topographical Engineers, to be Capt.
1st Lt Irvin McDowell, 1st Artl, since Assist Adj Gen, to be Capt.
Brevet 1st Lt John Pope, 2nd Lt Topographical Engineers, to be Capt.
1st Lt John F Reynolds, 3rd Artl, to be Capt.
1st Lt Chas L Kilburn, 3rd Artl, to be Capt.
Brevet 1st Lt Saml G French, 3rd Artl, since 1st Lt & Assist Quartermaster, to be Capt.
2nd Lt Chas P Kingsley, ordnance dept, since 1st Lt, to be 1st Lt.
2nd Lt Henry M Whiting, 4th Artl, since 1st Lt, to be 1st Lt.
2nd Lt Darius N Couch, 4th Artl, since 1st Lt, to be 1st Lt.
Brevet 2nd Lt Francis T Bryan, Topographical Engineers, to be 1st Lts.

Senate: 1-Cmte on Pensions: House bill for the relief of Wm Via: without amendment. 2-Cmte on Pensions: adverse report on the ptn of Hugh W Wormley. 2-Bill for the relief of Robt Purkis: taken up. Mr Green explained the grounds on which the bill rested, & gave a history of the gallantry of Mr Purkis in recapturing a vessel taken by the British in the war of 1812, & delivering to the authorities of Newport 4 British prisoners. The bill was amended to insert $700 in the place of $400: passed. 3-Bill for the relief of Clement, Bryant & Co: recommitted to the Cmte of Claims.

Wash Corp: 1-Ptn of Caleb Buckingham, praying to be reimbursed the expense of laying certain pipes in the 2nd Ward over & above the contract price: referred to the Cmte on Improvements. 2-Ptn of John T Clements & others, for a paved footway on south front of square 516: referred to Cmte on Improvements. 3-Cmte on Police: bill for relief of David Rich, & ptn of Dennis Orme: read twice. 4-Cmte of Claims: asking to be discharged from further consideration of the ptns of A Queen, of Jas H Shreve, & Harrison Taylor. 5-Ptn of Chas Finkmann, for remission of a fine: referred to cmte of Claims. 6-Bill for the relief of Wm C Johnson: referred to the Cmte of Claims. 6-Bill for the relief of John H Plant: passed. 7-Bill to provide for the payment of Owen Summers' bill for mending Centre Market hose: indefinitely postponed. 8-Bill for the relief of Wm B Wilson: passed. 9-Cmte of Claims: Act for the relief of B L Jackson & Brother: read twice.

House of Reps: 1-Cmte on the Judiciary: bill for the relief of Levi H Corson & for other purposes: committed. Adverse report on the ptn of Wm Fuller: laid on the table. Same cmte: Senate bill for the relief of Reynolds May, reported to the House without amendment. 2-Cmte on Revolutionary Claims: that D F Manice have leave to withdraw from the files of the Clerk the papers presented by him, & that the Com'r of Pensions transmit to the Clerk the ptn & papers in the case of Charity Freeman. 3-Cmte on Revolutionary Claims: bill for the relief of the heirs of Lt Bartlett Hinds, & for the relief of the heirs of Nehemiah Stokely: committed. Same cmte: adverse report on the ptn of Abram Brinker: laid on the table. 4-Cmte on Indian Affairs: adverse reports on the joint resolutions of the Legislature of Indians in relation to the Miami Indians, on the ptns of the Catawha tribe of Indians, & of Jos Keener & others in behalf of the same: committed. Same cmte: bill for the relief of E B Cogswell, & a bill for the relief of Jesse Sutton: committed. Mr Thompson, of Mississippi, presented the ptn of B Marshall, Tuchahatchee, G W Stidham, & Geo Scott, delegates of the Creek nation, for the passage of a law for the adjustment of their unsettled business: referred to the Cmte on Indian Affairs. 5-Cmte on Military Affairs: discharged from the further consideration of the ptn of John Campbell & Co, of Pensacola, for payment for subsistence furnished troops in the U S service; & of the ptn of Geo W Crawford for payment of his account for supplies furnished: laid on the table. Same cmte: adverse reports on the ptns of John F Staser & Geo F Blake, administrator: laid on the table.

For sale: on north 10th st, one door from Pa ave, in proximity to Mr King's Lace Store: Patent Shoulder Braces, for both sexes, recommended by the Medical Faculty. Wanted-a neat seamstress; none other need apply. –Madame Clermon

Great variety of tea & fancy cakes; loaf bread of superior quality. –Thos Havenner & Son, C st, before 4½ & 6th sts.

Died: on May 13, at Fruit Hill, his residence in Jefferson Co, Va, Archibald Robinson, in his 50th year.

Whole family butchered. The Eastern Times contains the shocking tragedy, which was enacted on May 11, in Edgecomb, about 5 miles from Wiscasset village, Maine. Mr Pinkham, aged about 45, a ship-carpenter by trade, with a sharp axe, completely decapitated his wife & 4 children, the oldest child about 12 years of age. The house stands some distance from other dwlgs, & the awful deed was discovered on Fri by the mother of Mr Pinkham. Mr & Mrs Pinkham had jointly written a note that they had become tired of living.

Chas W Schuermann, [formerly a pupil of Spohr,] gives instructions on the piano, violin, flute guitar, & in vocal music. Residence at Mr McLeod's cottage, corner of 9th & H sts.

Two daughters of Mr Davis, who is employed at the Reading Furnace, were instantly killed on Mon last by the first line of passenger cars. They were gathering coal near a curvature, & were crushed. –Pottsville [Pa] Miners' Journal of the 13th.

FRI MAY 19, 1848
Appointments by the Pres: Geo W Phillips, Henry Haw, & Richd Jones, to be Inspectors of the Penitentiary in the Dist of Col, for the ensuing year.

Senate: 1-Ptn from Sarah A Mackay, asking for a renewal of pension. 2-Ptn from Johnson Rice & R McKee, asking a grant of land for a number of families ready to settle in Oregon. 3-Cmte on Naval Affairs: bill for the relief of the legal reps & sureties of Benj F Hart, late purser in the U S Navy. Same cmte: asking to be discharged from the further consideration of the ptns of: John Crosby; & of Henry W Paine. 4-Cmte on the Post Ofc & Post Roads: bill for the relief of L P Sauger, accompanied with a report.

Gen Wm B Carter died in Carter Co, Tenn, on Apr 17, aged 56 years. During his life he filled the ofc of State Rep & Senator, Pres of the Constitutional Convention, & served 2 terms as member of Congress from his native State. His personal character was unusually amiable, & endeared him to a large circle of friends.

House of Reps: 1-Leave was granted the administrator of John Johnson, deceased, to withdraw papers pertaining to the claim of said Johnson. 2-Leave was granted for the withdrawal of the papers in the case of J M Bates; also the ptn of Danl G Garney. 3-Cmte on Naval Affairs: bills for the relief of the forward ofcrs of the late Exploring Expedition & for the relief of Thos Brownell: committed. 4-Cmte on Revolutionary Pensions: adverse reports on the ptns of Olive King, Eunice Clark, Caty Burnham, & Eliz K Brunot: laid on the table. Same cmte: bill for the relief of Mary Pike: committed. 5-Cmte on Invalid Pensions: bill for the relief of Sarah Wood; of Henry Miller; & granting a pension to Gideon A Perry: committed. Same cmte: bill for the relief of Fielding G Brown; & relief of Jos Taylor: committed. Same cmte: adverse reports on the ptns of Benj Holland, Abner Long, & Chas Taylor: laid on the table. Same cmte: adverse reports on the ptns of Ephraim Spoor & Robt Milligan: laid on the table. Same cmte: bills for the relief of Mary W Thompson & John Haup: committed. Bill for the relief of Wm Tee: sent to the Senate for concurrence. 6-Ptn of W Woodward praying for a remission of a fine imposed on him. 7-Ptn for the relief of John Phagan.

Newbern, N C, May 9. Correspondent, Elijah S Bell, of Carteret Co, tells of the tragedy which took place in his neighborhood, Hadnote, on Apr 23. Mr Wilson Chance discovered a bee tree, & took his son Henry, about 10, & 3 half brothers, Stanly, Isaiah, & Jas Mabley, to cut it down. The boys ate the honey & all became sick, Jas dying in half an hour. Persons should be careful eating honey from bee trees.
-Newbernian

Mount Ida for rent: now occupied by John Selden, about 10 miles from Alexandria, Va: with a comfortable brick dwlg about 50 feet front, with stable, carriage house, & other out-bldgs. From 30 to 50 acs fronting east & south, with a good dwlg, & stable, thereon, adapted for a Florist & Gardner. Apply to John Lloyd, of Alexandria, or address the subscriber John J Lloyd, Balt, Md.

Mrd: on May 16, at Congress Hall, by Rev Mr Butler, Wm H Gaskins to Sue, youngest daughter of Robt Roach, all of Balt.

SAT MAY 20, 1848

Senate: 1-Ptn from Ed A Buttolpk asking the purchase of the papers found in possession of Maj Andre at the time of his capture during the Revolutionary war. [Mr Buttolpk states that he has in his keeping the original papers found in the boot & upon the person of the unfortunate Maj Andre at the time of his capture, & believing them to be important for preservation among the archives of the nation, asks Congress to purchase them.] 2-Bills in the Cmte of the Whole-passed: relief of Purser Benj J Cohoone; relief of Messrs Cook, Anthony, Mahon, & others; relief of Wm H Prentiss; relief of Anna J Hassler; relief of Welcome Parmeter; relief of David Currier; & relief of Mary Brown, widow of Jacob Brown.

For sale by public auction on Jun 6: the excellent built 3 story brick house, on Capitol Hill, adjoining the residence of the Hon Judge Cranch. -R W Dyer, auct

Judge Jas M Marshall, son of Col Thos Marshall, cmder of the 3rd Va Regt in the war of Independences, & eldest surviving brother of Chief Justice Marshall, died at his residence in Fauquier Co, Va, on Apr 26, aged 85 years.

One by one the bearers of the old Knickerbocker names among us go down to the grave. Henry Brevoort, departed on Wed, in his 64th year, following, at no long interval, the aged father whose estate became in his hands a princely inheritance, & the wife who shared & adorned his opulence. His noble mansion on the 5th ave, N Y, was among the earliest erected of the costly structures which adorn that 'street of palaces."

Mrd: on May 19, by Rev C M Butler, Wm B Davis to Miss Evelina O Taliaferro, both of Va.

Mrd: on Thu, by Rev John C Smith, Mr Chas F E Richardson to Miss Charlotte A, daughter of Mr Benj Williamson, all of Wash City.

Mrd: on May 16, by Rev Mr Coskery & Rev Mr Pyne, Geo Guest to Nora, eldest daughter of Col Bankhead, U S Army.

Mrd: on May 16, in N Y C, by Rev Dr Taylor, of Grace Church, Francis R Rives, eldest son of the Hon Wm C Rives, of Va, to Matilda A Barclay, only daughter of Geo Barclay, of that city.

MON MAY 22, 1848

The trial of Dr Geer, the companion of Du Charm, the bigamist, came on at the County Court last week at Rome. The jury returned with a verdict of guilty of bigamy as principal in the 2nd degree. He was sentenced to 3 years' imprisonment at Auburn.
–Utica Daily Herald

At the head of one of the graves in the burial ground at "Old St Mary's," [Md] there stands a cedar slab, which, as the inscription upon it indicates, was placed there in 1717. Notwithstanding it has been exposed to the weather for so long a period, it is still perfectly sound, &, if unmolested by desecrating hands, it will doubtless be standing when every man, woman, & child that now moves upon the earth shall have gone down to "darkness & the worm."

Lt Jenks, of the 7th Infty, died at Tampico on May 6 of yellow fever.

The dwlg of Francis Scott Key, in Anne Arundel Co, about a mile from the Relay House, [recently the property of Richd B Dorsey] was destroyed by fire on Thu, & with it nearly all the furniture & other contents of the bldg. The progress of the flames were so rapid that the family, hastily aroused from their sleep, barely escaped with life & a scanty supply of night clothing.

A connexion has been made between the man called Harrison arrested at Matamoras, Mexico, on suspicion of being concerned in the robbery of the Chester Co Bank, Pa, &, of Mr Hitchcock, a cattle drover living in Pa, who mysteriously disappeared from Phil, whither he had gone to sell cattle. Harrison confessed that he is no other than the missing Mr Hitchcock.

House of Reps: 1-Ptn of Ezra Finney & others, for a breakwater near the n e point of the Island of Nantucket, Mass. 2-Ptn of Mason C Darling & 49 other citizens of Wisconsin, praying for the purchase of **Mount Vernon** by the Gov't. 3-Senate bills referred to appropriate cmtes: relief of Purser Benj G Cahoone; relief of Cook, Anthony, Mahon, & others; relief of Wm H Prentiss; relief of Anna J Hassler; relief of Wm Parmenter; & of David Currier.

Rev Ashbel Green, D D, died at his residence in Phil on Fri last, at the ripe age of 86 years. He was the only surviving member of the assembly which met to form the constitution of the Presbyterian church in this country, & was the oldest minister in the connexion, it having been 61 years since he was ordained. In early life he was a soldier of the Revolution, was a Chaplain to Congress when it sat in Phil, & for a considerable time President at Princeton College.

I forewarn all persons from crediting any person on my account from this date, without an order signed by myself, as I will pay no debts except where the orders can be shown. –N Travers

Dr Henery D Magill, long a physician in Leesburg, Va, came to a sudden death on May 15, by being thrown from his horse & dragged in consequence of his feet hanging in the stirrup.

Household & kitchen furniture at auction: on May 6, at the residence of Mr Preston, on D st, between 12th & 13th sts. -R W Dyer, auct

TUE MAY 23, 1848
Mrd: on May 21, by Rev L F Morgan, Jos Anthony to Mrs Eliz Thompson, both of Wash City.

Died: on Apr 14, at her residence, near Lancaster, Ky, Mrs Martha McKee, widow of Saml McKee, once a distinguished member of Congress, & mother of Col Wm Robertson McKee, who gloriously fell in the battle of Buena Vista.

Col Elisha Jenkins, an aged an estimable citizen of State of N Y, died in N Y C in May, aged 78 years, 7 months & 18 days. Col Jenkins was a native of Nantucket, but moved in early life with his father to the city of Hudson. During the war with England, 1812-1815, he was Quartermaster Gen upon our northern frontier. He was Sec of State & Mayor of Albany; & the oldest regent of the Univ of N Y. -Albany Journal

City Ordinances-Wash: the following have been appointed Assessors-14:
Wm Wilson
David Hines
Geo H Plant
Wm W Curran
Jas C McGuire
Jonathan T Walker
Jas M Towers
Michl P Mohun
Jeremiah Hepburn
Robt M Coombs
Chas Newton
Jas S Magee
Thos Allen
John Thompson Van Reswick

Household & kitchen furniture at auction: on May 29, at the residence of the late Capt Hetzel, on F st, between 20th & 21st sts: excellent furniture. -R W Dyer, auct

WED MAY 24, 1848
Ka-ge-ga-gah-bowh, or Geo Copway, a converted Indian Chief of the Chippewa Nation, will, in complete costume of an Indian Chief, deliver a lecture on the early history of the Indians, in the Temperance Hall, E st, this Wed, at 3 o'clock. Admittance: 12½ cents, to be paid at the door.

For sale: most desirable residence in Wash, on L st, adjoining the property of Maj Heiss, suitable for a small family. Inquire at Butt's Drug Store, Pa ave & 12th st.

Saddles, Harness, whips, & furniture at auction: on May 27, at the store lately occupied by D S Waters, on 7th st. -A Green, auctioneer

Genr'l Scott arrived on Sun at his home, in the sequestered village of Elizabethtown, N J, which for many years has been his residence when not absent on duty. The brig **St Petersburg**, in which he was a passenger, arrived on Sat at Quarantine. He took a boat early on Sun for Elizabethtown. His suite, consisting of Capt Scott, Capt Williams, & Lt Schuyler Hamilton, Aides-de-Camp, & Dr Tripler, Surgeon of the U S A, went on to N Y. The General is in excellent health.

House for sale: 3 story brick dwlg-house on Indiana ave, at present occupied by the Hon Jas Dixon. Inquire at my residence on D st near 3rd. –A Baldwin

Died, at Wexford, Canada West, Mr Danl Aiken, aged 120 years. He had, during his life, contracted 7 marriages, & had 270 grandchildren & great grandchildren.

The house in which Gen Henry Dearborn lived in Gardiner, Maine, & which Louis Philippe & Talleyrand abode some time in on a visit during the French revolution under Napoleon, was burnt on Monday of last week. It was one of the oldest bldgs in Gardiner, having been built in 1785.

The trial at Rochester of Dr John A Salisbury for counterfeiting resulted in a verdict of guilty. Previous to this crime he bore an unblemished character, & was much respected by the citizens among whom he lived.

U S District Court on Sat: John Wyle, master of the ship **Wenham**, & Edw Bill, master of the ship **Eliza Caroline**, were arrested on a charge of violating the law of Congress regulating the number of passengers, by bringing more than the number allowed by the law. They were held to bail in the sum of $2,000 each.

Died: on May 20, at *Oak Hill*, near Gtwn, Capt John McCobb, aged 70 years.

THU MAY 25, 1848
Indian war in Oregon: Louisville, May 21, 1848. News from Oregon by the arrival of Maj Meek from the West. Four battles took place in Jan: 500 Whites fought a body of 2,000 Indians. On Nov 29 a most horrid massacre was committed by the Cayuse Indians, at the Presbyterian Mission, at the Wallah Wallah Valley. Dr White, his man & wife, with 18 others, were killed, & 60 or 70 taken prisoners. The houses were burnt to the ground. The unfortunate prisoners were subsequently ransomed, throught the agency of Peter Sken Ogden, chief factor of the Hudson Bay Co.

Houses & lots at auction: deed of trust from Wm Bush to me, dated Nov 30, 1847, recorded in Liber W B 138, folios 218 thru 221, of the land records of Wash Co, D C: sale on May 31, of lot 2 & east half of 3, in square 734, with 2 frame houses, with stables: property fronts on N C ave, between 1st & 2nd sts. Terms cash. -A Green, auctioneer

Mrd: on May 23, by Rev Henry Slicer, Mr John Sioussa, jr, of Wash City, to Miss Mary Cammack, of Gtwn, D C.

Died: on May 19, at the residence of her father, near Wash City, Mary Plummer Seaver, aged 14 years.

Capt Saml Upham, father of Senator Upham, died at the residence of his son, Saml, in Randolph, Vt, on May 12, aged 85 years. He was a Revolutionary hero, & one of the earliest settlers of Montplier.

Mr McCarty O'Reidy, Member of the Young Ireland Confederation, will deliver a lecture on May 26, in the hall of the Wash Benevolent Society, G st, between 6th & 7th sts.

Virginia Camp at A-rispa's Mills, near Saltillo, Mexico, Apr 23, 1848. I regret to inform that Capt Deas, 4th Artl, who, with his fine battery, has been stationed at Buena Vista almost every since the battle there, has been lately tried by a court martial convened at Saltillo, was found guilty, & sentenced to be dismissed the service; which sentence was approved by Gen Wool, at Monterey. He is now on his way home to await the issue of a application to the executive in his behalf by many influential personal friends on this line & elsewhere. The American public will well recollect him as the Lt Deas who swam the Rio Grande at **Fort Brown**, just before the time of its bombardment, to procure an interview with a Mexican maiden on the opposite bank who had struck his fancy, & who, by way of a continuation of his adventure, was taken prisoner by the Mexicans, & remained so for some time before Gen Taylor would consent to exchange for him. At the battle of Monterey Lt Deas did noble service, & was later was promoted to a captaincy, & put in command of what became known as "Washington's battery," at the battle of Buena Vista.

+

The 13th company held an election a few days since to fill the ofc of 2nd Lt, made vacant by the resignation of Van Dyke Neale, gone to the States. 2nd Lt Thos Moore was chosen. He is from Fairfax Co, Va, & is brother of the lamented Lt Moore, of the 1st Mississippians, who fell at Buena Vista before one of the most desperated charges which the Mexican lancers made during that memorable conflict. He had been wounded by a ball in the hip but refused to be carried from the field; & when, just before the charge mentioned, the regt was ordered to fall back & reform on a more suitable position, Lt Moore lingered in the rear from loss of blood & exhaustion, & was borne down by the cavalry which came pressing on, & dispatched by no less than 21 distinct thrusts of the lance. His remains were conveyed home by the order of the authorities of his adopted State. He was a son of A Moore, of Fairfax Co, Va, as is also the present Lt Moore, of the 13th. -X

FRI MAY 26, 1848
The father of Mrs J Q Adams, written for Neale's Sat Gaz. Mr Johnson was the 5th son of a highly respectable family of Calvert Co, Md, who came to America in the reign of Queen Anne of England. His mother was a Miss Baker, also of England, the daughter of the cmder of an English vessel, & possessed of some landed property in Md, where the family was originally established in a handsome mansion on the banks of the Patuxent, [burnt down by the English in the war of 1812, but at that time not in their possession.] Mr Johnson was one of 11 children, 5 of whom served in the Revolutionary war, & one of whom was Thos Johnson, the 1st Govn'r of Md, Judge of the Supreme Court, Com'r for the Public Bldgs & Dist of Columbia on the first plan of Wash City, & the personal friend of Gen Washington. Mr J Johnson, previously to the Revolutionary war, had been established in London, Eng, as a merchant. When the war was declared, he, being a staunch republican, could no longer remain in England with safety, & removed his family to Nantz, France, & was presented by Dr Franklin to the King & Queen in the capacity of commercial agent, being appointed by the Congress of the old confederation in 1778 or

1779. He remained at Nantz until 1783, after the peace, as consul & agent for the ports of Nantz, Brest, & Morfaix. In 1783 he was transferred to London as Consul Gen, but with a salary inadequate to support his family. When the constitution went into operation, Gen Washington, the Pres of the U S, renominated Mr Johnson to the same ofc, Congress having substituted fees of ofc instead of the salary which had been annexed to an ofc of drudgery & expense at that station, quite insufficient for support & ruinous to his health & fortune. The fees of ofc were small, & not well paid. In 1796 he offered his resignation of the ofc, but it was not accepted. In Oct, 1797, he returned to his native country, without the means to subsist a wife & 7 children, 6 of them dghts, with one son, who was, after Mr Johnson's death, appointed postmaster at New Orleans, where he served faithfully for many years. Mr Johnson was nominated to the senate by Pres John Adams. In very feeble health, he accompanied his dght, [Mrs J Q Adams, who had just arrived in America for the first time,] to pass 2 short months with him, after an absence of 4 years, to introduce her to his relatives in Fredericktown, Md, where he was seized with a dangerous illness, of which he died, after great suffering, at the house of Baker Johnson, his brother, from whom he received every kindness, as well as from all his brothers & connexions. He expired on Apr 2, 1802, a few days after his ofc had ceased, leaving a widow & family in the most destitute circumstances. His vouchers were destroyed by fire in the Dept, & his accounts were never settled.

House of Reps: 1-Ptn of Stephen Howard, praying for arrears of pay & bounty land as a soldier in the War of 1812.

Messrs G & T Parker has commenced the erection of an extensive brick bldg on the corner of 6th & La ave. Mr Towers is to occupy the upper part of his bldg as a printing ofc. Messrs Jackson & Brother have lately erected an excellent brick bldg, 4 stories high, on the south side of Pa ave.

Wash Corp: 1-Ptn of Lewis H Sneider: referred to the Cmte on Improvements. 2-Ptn of Owen Connolly: referred to the Cmte of Claims. 3-Ptn from Jas Crutchett: referred to the Cmte of Claims. 4-Ptn of Wm Dowling & Jas E W Thompson: referred to the Cmte of Claims. 5-Ptn of Peter Conlan & others, for a footway from 4th st west to North Capitol st: referred to the Cmte on Improvements. 6-Ptn of E D & H A Willard, praying remission of a fine: referred to the Cmte of Claims. 7-Act for the relief of Emily G Jones, excx of the late Thos P Jones: read twice.

U S Patent Ofc: inventions patented by this ofc in 1847:
Improvements in portable steam-pumps, invented by Wm Boardman, jr.
Improvements in printing oilcloth carpeting, invented by Jas Albro, jr.
Improvements in casting ordnance, invented by Thos J Rodman.
Improvements in cars for transportation of coal, invented by Ross Winans.
Improvements in lead pipe machinery, invented by Saml G Cornell.
Improvements in cotton presses, invented by Philos B Tyler.
Improvements in machinery for twisting & rolling iron, invented by G Wetheret, patented to H Ames.
Improvements in sofa-tables, invented by C Brigg.

Improvements in gearing for connecting feed pressure rollers, invented by Wm E Cornell & C W Brown.
Improvements in stocking looms, invented by John Vickenstaff.
Improvements in preparing raw hides, invented by H Halverson, assigner of T Earle.
Improvements in preparing India rubber, invented by Jas Thomas.
Improvements in ventilating the timbers of vessels, invented by E Knight.
Improvements in bleaching rosin, invented by J W Harman, patented to H B Dunbar.
Improvements in horse-rakes, invented by John M Stafford.
Improvements in self-adjusting pendulums, invented by John S Grigg.
Improvements in mariners' compasses, invented by Hall Colby.
Improvements in ditching machines, invented by E W Thomas.
Improvements in connecting side-presses with steam chests, invented by H R Dunbar.
Improvements in India rubber fabrics, invented by C J Gilbert & G Gay.
Improvements in machinery for the manufacture of wire-rope, invented by E S Townsend. –Edmund Burke

A private letter received in this city this morning, makes it highly probable that Mr C Austin Coolidge, of Boston, son of the late Chas D Coolidge, & Commissary of the Mass Regt, was on board the transport **Dolphin**, which sailed from Brasos on Dec 4 last for Vera Cruz, & has not since been heard from. The **Dolphin** is supposed to have foundered at sea. –Boston Raveller

Mrd: on May 25, in Balt, by Rev Mr Grapnell, David J Bishop, of Wash, to Miss Susan Crook, of Balt.

Mr J S Stores, who resides near Onion river, in Burlington, Vt, had 2 dghts, one 11 & the other 13 years, drowned on Fri.

SAT MAY 27, 1848
House of Reps: 1-Leave was given for the withdrawal of the papers in the case of Saml F Reed, of Tenn. 2-Cmte of the Whole reported the following bills: relief of Sarah Wood, widow of Maj Jas Wood; Levi Corson, & for other purposes; Mary W Thompson, widow of Lt Col Alex'r R Thompson; Archibald Beard, & 21 other mounted Tenn volunteers; John P B Gratiot & the legal reps of Henry Gratiot; &

Maurice R Simons	Philip J Fontane
Eliphas C Brown	Elisha F Richards
Henry N Halstead	Gideon A Perry
Robt Ramsey	Fielding G Brown
John Farnham	Jos Taylor
Andrew Flanagin	John Haup
Wm Got	Mary Pike, widow of
Catharine Hoffman	Ezra Pike
Mrs Mary B Renner	

3-Senate bills, severally without amendment: relief of: Reynolds May; Thos Brownell; Edw Bolon; & Saml W Bell, a native of the Cherokee nation. 4-Cmte reported the following bills, with an amendment to each: relief of: legal reps of Lt Francis Ware; of

Hugh Riddle; of Jos Perry, a Choctaw Indian, or his assignees; & of Jos Gerard. 5-Bill to authorize the settlement of the account of Jos Nourse, deceased. 6-House bill to pay Jas Crutchett $2,000 for lighting the Capitol & Capitol grounds, & also a Senate bill of the same title, were reported to the House, with the recommendation that they be laid on the table.

To the Editors: Capt Deas' object in crossing the Rio Grande was solely to obtain information relative to the whereabouts of Col Cross, who had been captured, & who, as subsequently proven, was murdered by the Mexicans. The above fact was well known to the whole army & will be attested by them. [The author of the above is, of course, known to us. –Editors]

Strayed or stolen: a black horse, 6 years old. Suitable reward. -F A Tucker, 1½ miles west of Bladensburg.

Household furniture at auction: on May 30, in front of the Centre Market, the remainder of the furniture of J S Hall, seized & taken for house rent due in arrears to Ann Lowry. –R R Burr, Bailiff -A Green, auct

$5 reward for the 3 cows which left the grounds of Columbian College on Mon last under suspicious circumstances. If they strayed they are no doubt together. –Jas B Clarke

Shocco Springs, Warren Co, N C: pleasant summer retreat. –Saml Calvert, Proprietor

MON MAY 29, 1848
The steamboat **Halifax**, a small boat running from Waterville to Hallowell, on the Kennebec, with passengers for the larger boats plying between Hallowell & Boston, burst her boilers on Tue. The Capt, Chas Paine, was torn to pieces. Anael Brackett, & another, named Williams, were killed.

Fire at Balt yesterday broke out in the cotton factory of John Knox, at Poppleton & Fremont sts, & consumed surrounding tenements, including the logwood factory of Robt J Baker.

Wash Corp: 1-Cmte of Claims: asking to be discharged from the further consideration of the ptn of Maria A Queen. 2-Bill for the relief of David Rich & Dennis Orme: passed. [Free persons of color, who had been fined. Rich was the property of the late Judge Upshur, by whose will he was set free, & for long & faithful service of 24 years. Va was his former home. Orme was brought to this city when a boy 10 years old from PG Co, Md, & raised here, & about 10 years since sold to Mr McKenny, of Gtwn, where he was carried. By an arrangement with his master, he was permitted to return to the city, & was set free.] 3-Bill for the relief of Wm Campbell: passed. 4-Act for the relief of Emily G Jones, excx of the late Thos P Jones: passed. 5-Bill for the relief of Thos Jacobs & the bill for the relief of John J Joyce: both passed.

Fatal accident at the iron rolling mill in this village, on Wed last, when Francis Rhind was struck by a piece of hoop iron in a redhot state. He expired in about 6 hours.
–Ulster Telegraph

House of Reps: 1-Bills for the relief of Wm Fuller & Orlando Saltmarsh & for the relief of H D Johnson: laid aside to be reported. 2-Bill for the relief of Wm B Slaughter, late Sec of the Territory of Wisconsin, was amended by adding a proviso, providing that the said balance shall not exceed $1,731.51. 3-Bill for the relief of the legal reps of Joshua Kennedy, deceased: taken up. 4-Ptn of Pope & Morgan, & other owners of ship **Chandler Price**, asking compensation for expenses incurred in ransoming the crew of the whale-ship **Columbia**, of New London, from the inhabitants of the Kings Mill Islands, Pacific Ocean.

On Sat, Wm Patterson Colmary, a young gentleman of this city, was killed by lightning. He took shelter under trees, being overtaken by a storm, & rider & horse were instantly killed. –Wilmington [Del] Journal

Mrd: on May 24, by Rev Mr Lanahan, Mr Wm E Spalding to Miss Maria P Robinson, both of Wash City.

Mrd: on Thu, by Rev John C Smith, Mr John Cumberland to Mrs Susan Johnson, all of Wash City.

Mrd: on May 25, by Rev John P Donelan, of St Vincent de Paul's Church, Balt, Md, Jas W Sheahan to Miss Lizzie, daughter of Saml Drury, all of Wash City.

Died: on May 23, in Gtwn, D C, Mary Kurtz, aged 72 years.

Died: in her 23rd year, of consumption, Diana, wife of Wm H Minnix, the youngest daughter of the late Thos Sandiford, of Wash City. Long & well has she been known in our community. Her early departure has left a large circle of mourning friends & a bereaved husband. [No death date given-recent item.]

TUE MAY 30, 1848
Circuit Court of Wash Co, D C-in Chancery. Jacob Snider, jr, vs Wm Vaughan, John Merrick & Rebecca his wife, Chas Vaughan, & Petty Vaughan, heirs at law of John Vaughan, deceased. The bill states that John Vaughan, late of Phil, died in Dec, 1841, having just made his will, by which he bequeathed all his property, subject to the payment of debts & legacies, to the cmplnt, & that he appointed him his exc; that the will was executed in the presence of 2 witnesses only, & was inoperative to pass real estate in D C; that the cmplnt qualified as excecutor, & has paid all the debts of the estate, except that due to himself, amounting to about $4,116; that the personal estate is exhausted; that certain real estate remains, consisting of lots in squares 583, 584, 587, & 643, in Wash City, which the said cmplnt prays may be decreed to be sold for the payment of the debt of said Vaughan due to him. The dfndnts do not reside within D C or the jurisdiction of this Court. –W Cranch –Wm Brent, clerk –D A Hall, Solicitor for cmplnt.

Senate: 1-Ptn from Jedediah Gray, asking a pension for injuries received while in the service of the ordnance dept. 2-Ptn from Saml F Read, asking compensation for a horse taken for the U S service during the Florida war. 3-Ptn from Lawrence M Morton & others, clerks in the pay dept of the army at New Orleans, asking an increase of compensation. 4-Ptn from Candace Munn, asking to be allowed a pension. 5-Cmte on Naval Affairs: asking to be discharged from the further consideration of the memorial of Wm Norris, & that it be referred to the Cmte on Finance. Same cmte: asking to be discharged from the further consideration of the memorials of Sarah Hebbard & Sarah Ann Hart. Same cmte: adverse report in the case of Abel Gregg. Same cmte: asking to be discharged from the further consideration of the memorials of John Erickson & of Ann Kelly, accompanied by a report in each case. 6-Cmte of Claims: asking to be discharged from the further consideration of the memorial of Amos Holton, on the ground of insufficient evidence. 7-Cmte on Naval Affairs: House bill for the relief of Francis M Holton, without amendment, & recommending its passage.

On Thu, as a wedding party was leaving the Catholic Church, in Northampton st, Boston, a dispute arose between the bridegroom & Michl Brady. The cry of Police was raised, & Brady, becoming frightened, ran down the street & accidentally fell into a creek & drowned. When taken out, life was extinct.

Abram Williams, of Bracken Co, Ky, died on May 1. He was born on the Eastern Shore of Md on Jan 13, 1742: served in the Revolutionary war, & received a pension. He has been a resident of Ky for upwards of 50 years, & enjoyed tolerably good health up to his death. He was in his 106th year when he died.

The Oregon Massacre: Dr Whitman, his lady, & others, have fallen victims to the fury of remorseless savages, who appear to have committed this crime, under the horrible suspicion that, in consequence of the number of deaths from dysentery & measles in their tribe, that Dr Whitman was silently administering poisonous drugs to destroy them. List of persons killed on this occasion: Dr Whitman, Mrs Whitman, Mr Rogers, Mr Hoffman, Mr Sanders, [schoolmaster,] Mr Marsh, John Sager & Francis Sager, [youths,] Mr Kimball, Mr Gellen, Mr Bewley, Mr Young, jr, Mr Sales, Mr Hall, [supposed to have been killed at John Day's river.] Mr Ogden, of the Hudson Bay Co, immediately succeeded in gathering a council of the chiefs. The chiefs agreed to give up their prisoners within 6 days on the promise of a ransom being paid for them. Speeches were also made in the intermediate time to the Nez Perces, & they agreed to deliver up Mr Spalding & his family.

Capt Thos Postley, of the 10th Infty, was killed at Camargo on May 7, by a soldier of Co K, names Francis Darlington. The man in the early part of the day had been in Capt Postley's camp, & was ordered away by the Capt. He went & procured a pistol & waylaid & shot Capt Postley in the vicinity of his quarters, the ball striking him in the groin. Capt Postley lingered in great agony until the next day, when he died surrounded by his friends.

Died: on May 28, in Wash City, Mrs Jane Ennis, wife of Mr Philip Ennis, in his 48th year. Her funeral will leave the residence of her husband on May 30, at 9 o'clock, & will proceed to St Patrick's Church, where the burial service will be performed. The friends of the family are invited.

WED MAY 31, 1848
Mr J B Bechtel, a gentleman of great amability of character, committed suicide at Balt last Mon, by putting the muzzle of a pistol in his mouth & discharging the contents into his brain. He was bookkeeper in the banking-house of Mr Josiah Lee, the duties of which he discharged with great fidelity. An addiction to intoxicating drink was no doubt the inciting cause of this rash act. -American

Mrd: on May 25, by Rev Mr Lockwood, Nathl Chapman Hunter to Miss Amelia, daughter of the late Capt Geo H Terrett, of Fairfax Co, Va.

Died: yesterday, suddenly, Mrs Susan Griffin, wife of Thos B Griffin, in her 54th year. Her funeral is this afternoon, at 3: 30 o'clock, from her late residence, on the corner of 12th & K sts, opposite Franklin Row.

Com'rs for the election for the Wash Corp, D C: [Alderman, surveyor, assessor, register, & collector.]

Jas L Cathcart	Wm J Wheatly
W N Waters	Chas Munroe
Wm H Perkins	Geo W Thompson
Willard Drake	Noble Young
Elex Simms	Wm M Ellis
John Ferguson	Jas Crandell
John Boyle	J S Harvey
Geo Crandell	Wm Bird
V Harbaugh	Craven Ashford

House of Reps: 1-Cmte of Ways & Means: adverse report on the ptn of Henry Simpson, surviving adm of Geo Simpson, deceased: laid on the table. 2-Cmte of Claims: bill for the payment of a sum of money to Robt Purkis, reported the same without amendment: committed. Bill for the relief of the legal reps of Darius Garrison: committed. Adverse reports on the ptns of J B Cooper & Cary H Fry: laid on the table. Same cmte: bill for the relief of Staunton W Gaar: committed. Adverse report on the ptn of Jas Sloan: laid on the table. 3-Cmte of Claims: discharged from the ptns of Augustus Steele & Peyton A Key: laid on the table. Same cmte: bill for the relief of Mr Snavely, of Indiana: committed. 4-Cmte on Commerce: bill for the relief of Henry Little & Jacob Felch: committed. 5-Cmte on Public lands: adverse reports on the ptns of Thos G Holmes & of the citizens of the State of Maine, praying an appropriation of the public lands for the extinction of slavery in the U S: laid on the table. 6-Ptn of Andrew McKim, praying to be placed on the pension list. 7-Ptn of Chas McClain, of Missouri, praying the confirmation of a tract of land to him. 8-Ptn of Timothy Carman for a register for the schnr **James**, of N Y. 8-Ptn of Dennis Harris for return of duties on sugars destroyed by fire in N Y C.

Republican Genealogy: Col Wm Preston, senior, commenced serving his country at age 18 as secretary to the Log-house treaty, [before Braddock's defeat,] of which his uncle Col Jas Patton, was a Com'r; in the Revolution he commanded a regt of militia, was slightly wounded in the battle of Guilford, N C, & died soon after the peace. His sons were too young to be engaged in the first war. His 2nd son, Gen Francis Preston, was in the service at Norfolk during the late war with England; his 3rd son, Maj Wm Preston, was in the regular service during our war with the northwest Indians, & attached to Gen Wayne's command during his campaigns; his 4th son, Col Jas P Preston, was in the regular service to the close of the war of 1812, recruited & marched his regt to Canada, & was most dangerously wounded at the battle of Chrystler's field, in Canada. Lt Col Wm Preston, of Ky, lately appointed to one of the new regts; Capt John Preston, of Arkansas, who fought at the battle of Buena Vista; Capt Jas Preston, of the 1st Regt of Va volunteers; Lt Jas Preston, of Capt Cumming's company now in service, are his grandsons. Capt Edw Carrington, of the 1st U S Artl, who so gallantly fell at the battle of Contreras, & Sgt John Preston Bawyer are his [the first Col Preston's] great grandsons. Col Wm C Preston, of S C, & Wm Ballard Preston, members of Congress, are also his grandsons. All patriots, all Whigs! '78
+

We may add to the above list the name of Isaac, the son of Gen Frank Preston, who served in the war of 1812 as a captain in the regular army. Studying law afterwards he established himself at New Orleans, where he has risen to much eminence. Senator Wm Campbell Preston, of S C, now Pres of the State College, volunteered as a private in a troop of cavalry raised in the town of Abingdon on the news of the taking of Washington. It marched within a few days; but, of course, did not arrive until after the re-embarkation of the enemy. But his branch of the family drew patriot blood from other sources. His mother was the only daughter of Wm Campbell, the victor of that singular battle of King's Mountain, & of Eliz, the youngest sister of Patrick Henry, who, by his bold & successful resisitance of the Stamp Act, may be fairly considered the originator of the Revolution of 1776; in which, besides, he bore the most leading part of all who brought up the South to stand by Massachusetts against Lord North's taxes. A word more of the bright, & brave young West Pointer who fell at Contreras, pushing on so gallantly & gaily over most difficult ground, against an overwhelming fire, his two advanced guns of Magruder's battery. Like his father's cousin, Wm Campbell Preston, he united with his immediate family names the blood of the Henrys, & was connected with the Madisons, Christians, & other Revolutionary families. His grandfather was Judge Peter Johnston, who, running away from college at 16, enlisted as a trooper in Lee's Legion, distinguished himself in his first battles under that cmder's eye, was at once promoted to an ensigncy, & fought on alongside of Manning & Rudolph through Guilford, Eutaw, & many battles of the campaigns of Greene, leading the forlorn hope at the storming of **Fort Watson**, &, as may be seen in Garden's "Anecdotes of the Revolution." Chas Clement, the 3rd of his sons, served at Norfolk in the war of 1812; came afterwards to the bar, married Eliza Madison, the eldest daughter of Gen John Preston, rose to much eminence in his profession; was elected to Congress in 1831, but by a sad casualty & an untimely fate lost his life in the Potomac, at Alexandria, in Jul, 1832. He was already a widower & left 2 orphans, a son, Preston, & a daughter. The youth perished like his father in the public service.

Trustee's sale of valuable bldg lots at auction by order of the Orphans Court of Wash Co, D C. Sale on Jun 15, of the following property belonging to the estate of Jas Douglas, deceased, viz: lots 3 thru 6 in square 529, at the corner of 4th st north & G st west. Also, lot 11 in square 493, situated on the island, on C st, between 4½ & 6th sts west.
–Wm G Gorsuch, adm -A Green, auctioneer

Died: on May 28, at Urbana, Fred'k Co, Md, Mr Jos McClain, in his 32nd year. The deceased was formerly a resident of Gtwn, D C.

Deaths by Intemperance. 1-On Thu Simon Dunn, of Bath township, in this county, committed suicide by hanging himself on his porch a few hours before daylight. He has filled the ofc of County Com'r, served 2 terms in the lower branch of the Legislature- 1833 & 1834-& 14 years as Associate Judge of the Court of Common Pleas. He was about 70 years of age, & in good circumstances, & highly respected. He leaves a large circle of relatives & friends. 2-About 2 weeks since Wm Chambers, of the same township, was returning from Dayton, when about 2 miles from the city was thrown from his horse, alighting on his head & shoulders, &, as was supposed, considerably hurt. On Sunday morning his body was found in Mad river; appears to be entertained that he committed suicide; he was under the influence of intoxicating liquor. He was a man in comfortable circumstance, & highly respected in his neighborhood. –Xenia Torch Light

Orphans Court of Wash Co, D C. Letters of administration on the personal estate of Wm Bergman, late of the U S Army, deceased. -Peter Bergman, Priscilla Bergman, adms

The trial of John Houck for the murder of Isaac D Adkins, terminated at **Fort Wayne**, Indiana, on May 16. Houck was found guilty & sentenced to be imprisoned at hard labor for life. Houck boarded with Adkins; a criminal attachment existed between him & Adkins' wife; he procured arsenic, which his guilty partner administered to her husband, & he sickened & died. Mrs Adkins, after being arrested, was discharged. She left the country, & has escaped for the present the punishment due her atrocious crime.

$5 reward for the return of a strayed white mare, about 10 years old. When last seen she was about 12 miles on the 7th st Turnpike on Monday, about dusk. –Chas Tinney

Senate: 1-Cmte on Naval Affairs asking to be discharged from the further consideration of the memorials of the surviving ofcrs & crew of the U S brig **Somers**; from that of Ebenezer Whitten; & from that of Wm Davis: which was concurred in.

Wash City Improvements. We observe that 2 new brick dwlgs are now being erected on the south side of E st, fronting the Medical College. They are being erected for Mr Wm Orme. Two other brick bldgs are being erected near the Centre Market-house, & on the west side of it, for Mr Briscoe. The road all the way from the Capitol to Congress Burial Ground is now in excellent condition.

THU JUN 1, 1848
Fashionable Ready-made Clothing of every style, can be found at the N Y Mammoth Clothing Store: -J Galligan & Son, Pa ave, next door to D Clagett & Co.

Orphans Court of Wash Co, D C. Letters of administration on the personal estate of Thaddeus Kosciusko, late of Poland, deceased. –Lewis Johnson, adm de bonis non, will annexed

Simon Gormley, insolvent debtor, has applied to be discharged from imprisonment. –Wm Brent, clerk

House of Reps: 1-Cmte on the Post Ofc & Post Roads: Senate bill for the relief of John Lorimer Graham, late postmaster of N Y C, reported the same back to the House without amendment: committed. 2-Cmte on D C: discharged from the ptn of Chas Fletcher: laid on the table.

The graining mill attached to the powder works of Mr Jas Beatty, on the Balt & Susquehanna Railroad, exploded on Tue. Two of the workmen, John Lyons & Wm Eaton, were killed.

Distribution of Prize-money to the ofcrs & crew of the ship **Bon Hommer Richard**, & frig **Alliance**. Treas Dept, First Auditor's Ofc, May 11, 1848. Act of Congress entitled "An act for the relief of the heirs of John Paul Jones," approved Mar 21, 1848, provides for the payment to the legal reps of the said John Paul Jones, & the ofcrs, seamen, & marine of the squadron under his command, being citizens of the U S, or their reps, their respective proportions of the value, as estimated by Benj Franklin, of the 3 prizes captured by the squadron under the command of the said Jones, & delivered up to Great Britain by Denmark in 1779. –Wm Collins, First Auditor. Distribution among the ofcrs & crew of the Bon Homme Richard is:
To lts, capt of marines, & master, each: $2,275.61
To lts of marines, surgeon, chaplain, purser, boatswain, gunner, carpenter, master's mates, & sec of the fleet, each: $949.17
To midshipmen, capt's clerk, surgeon's mates, boatswain's mates, carpenter's mates, gunner's mates, steward, sailmaker, cooper, armorer, cook, cockswain, sgt of marines, each: $262.57
To seamen, ordinary seamen, boys, each: $130.26
Among the ofcrs & crew of the frig **Alliance**:
To lts, capt of marines, & master, each: $2,237.22
To lts of marines, surgeon, chaplain, purser, boatswain, gunner, carpenter, master's mates, & sec of the fleet, each: $847.43
To midshipmen, capt's clerk, surgeon's mates, boatswains's mates, carpenter's mates, gunner's mates, steward, sailmaker, cooper, armorer, cook, cockswain, sgt of marines, each: $385.73
To seamen, ordinary seamen, boys, each: $188.66.

Gentlemen invited to attend the examination of the cadets of the Military Academy, to commence on Jun 5:

Hon Wm Prescott, of Maine
Hon Dutee J Pearce, of R I
Maj Gen J McDaniels, of Vt
Col Robt Hamilton, of N J
Dr H F Askew, of Delaware
Col Geo W Wilson, of Va
Col Jas Gadsden, of S C
Patterson C Lander, of Ky
Dr J G M Ramsay, of Tenn
Prof W C Larabee, of Indiana
Isaac N Morris, of Ill
Gen Jas Yell, of Ark
Col Alex'r H Redfield, of Mich
Col A W Doniphan, of Missouri
Dr Ashbell Smith, of Texas

Died: on May 24, at Greenville, S C, Emmala E Thompson, wife of the Hon Waddy Thompson, for many years a member of Congress from S C, & subsequently Minister to Mexico. She was the daughter of Gen Wm Butler, a distinguished partisan ofcr during our Revolutionary war, & afterwards a Member of Congress from S C, & sister of Senator Butler & the late Col Pierce Butler, who so gallantly fell at the head of his regt in Mexico. As a wife, mother, sister, & friend, she was earnest, affectionate & true.

Mrd: at St John's Church, by Rev Mr Shiras, the Rev Edmond T Perkins, of Parkersburg, Va, to Mary E, daughter of Thos B Addison, of Gtwn. [No date-current item.]

Mrd: on May 30, at Bloomingdale, near Washington, by Rev N P Tillinghast, Lt Wm Read, U S Army, to Miss Mary Eliza, daughter of the late Geo Beale, U S Navy.

Great sale of lands, town lots, & water power, on the Illinois & Michigan Canal: under authority granted by the State of Ill: about 230,000 acres of land. Wm H Swift, David Leavitt, Chas Oakley, Trustees Ill & Mich Canal. Ofc of the Board of Trustees of the Ill & Mich Canal, Jun 1, 1848.

FRI JUN 2, 1848
Among the passengers by the ship **Hibernia**, which arrived at N Y on Sat last, we notice the name of Mrs Fanny Kemble Butler.

Five persons were drowned on Sun last, while returning home from church, at Trenton, on a truck upon the railroad. While crossing over the inlet from the canal into the Millham basin, the car was accidentally titled & those upon it slid into the water. One escaped, John Raywood. The others, Mrs Raywood, his wife, her son Thos, Michl Fogarty & his wife Julia, with their child Julia, about 3 months old, perished. The men were employed upon the railroad.

City Ordinances-Wash: 1-Act for the relief of John H Plant: Fee imposed for an alleged violation relative to grocer's license, is remitted, provided he pay the costs of prosecution. 2-Act for the relief of Michl Shanks: to be paid the amount & interest of 5 certificates of paving stock issued to Philip Mohun on Jan 24, 1838. 3-Act for the relief of Wm B Wilson: to pay to him the sum of $79.07, being the balance due him for gravelling 2nd st, in pursuance of the act approved Oct 13, 1845.

The delegation of Chickasaw Indians, consisting of their principal chief, McLawghlin, & Messrs Pitman Colbert, Isaac Albertson, Jas Gamble, Edmund Picken, Davis James, Capt McGilvay, & Capt Shepawney, arrived in this city on Mon last, & yesterday called on the Com'r of Indian Affairs, who, together with the Acting Sec of War, accompanied them on a visit to the President of the U S. Col Pitchlynn, of the Choctaw Nation, accompanied the delegation, at their request, & acted as interpreter between the Pres & the Chickasaws.

Fr P J De Smet, the philanthropic Jesuit missionary to the Snake, Flat Head, & Black Foot Indians beyond the Rocky Mountains, is on a visit to Albany, N Y. This good man, who some 10 years ago went alone thousands of miles beyond the frontier of civilization, has since supplied the wildest & most savage tribes of Indians with seeds, farming implements, cows, oxen, & sheep. Turned them to peaceful habits.

In the U S Circuit Court, sitting at Newcastle, Dela, last week, the 2 most important cases that came up were those of Thos Garrett, of Wilmington, Dela, & John Hunn, of Cantwell's Bridge, for aiding & abetting in the escape of 5 or 6 slaves, who belonged to persons residing in Queen Anne's Co, Md. Hunn was fined $500 in each case-the whole amounting to $2,500. Mr Garrett was fined $3,500. An action for the recovery of the value of the negroes was to be brought against the latter.

In Chancery, May 29, 1848. Benj Young & others, vs Geo H Smith & Eloise his wife, & others. Object of this bill is to enforce the execution of the trusts created by a certain deed of conveyance from the cmplnt, Benj Young, sen, to Notley Young, lately deceased. On Jan 23, 1828, certain real & personal property in PG Co, Md, & in D C, were conveyed to the said Notley Young, deceased, in his lifetime, in trust to pay the debts of the grantor, to provide for the support of the grantor & his family, & to apply the residue as the grantor by last will should appoint. It states that the trustee accepted said trust, sold from time to time parcels of said trust estates, & applied the proceeds to his own use. The bill states some particulars of said sales, & calls for a full account thereof. It charges that the said trustee suffered the bldgs & improvements on parts of the real estate to go to waste & decay, & that by his default many of the lots in D C were sold for public dues & taxes at gross undervalues. It insists that the cmplnts are entitled to charge the said trustee with the full values of the lots as if they had been properly repaired & judiciously sold. They charge likewise sundry other violations of duty on the part of said trustee; that the debts of the grantor were of small amount; that he & his children have not been supported from said fund, as they ought to have been; on the contrary, the funds have been converted by the trustee in his private & gainful speculations; that Notley Young is dead, & the dfndnts are his administratrix & children, who are entitled to his real estates as his heirs at law, or as devisees under a certain instrument of writing which some of said children claim to be his last will & testament. The bill is filed by the grantor & his children. It states likewise that the dfndnts, Martha Young, Clement Young, & Julia Fidelia Young, reside out of the State of Md. All to appear in this Court on or before Nov 6 next. –Louis Gassaway, Reg Cur Can

Hunter Hill, who was convicted in Nansemond Co, Va, in Oct, 1845, of the murder of Robt R Smith, has been pardoned by the Govn'r of Va, & is now at liberty.

The steamer **Benjamin Rush** was totally destroyed by fire last night. No lives were lost.

Died: on Jun 1, Cornelius Riley, late of Castle Sanderson, near Belturbit, county Cavan, Ire, in his 27th year. His funeral is this afternoon at 4 o'clock, from the residence of P McGarvey, near the Railroad Depot.

Lord Armstrong, better known as Alex'r Baring, died on May 12, in his 75th year. In early life he passed much time in the U S, where he married the daughter of Gen Bingham. His visit to Washington in 1842 as English Ambassador was for the settling of the Maine boundary question. His chief wealth was derived from the successful French loan in 1815. He is succeeded by Wm Bingham Barring, in the title & estate. His 2nd son, Francis, continues at the head of the mercantile firm; Mr Mildmay, Lord Ashburton's son-in-law, having retired about 2 months ago, Mr Joshua Bayes & Chas Baring Young are now the other remaining partners. The death of Lord Ashburton was followed close upon the decease of his brother, Sir Thos Baring & Mr Henry Baring, both of whom died within a month. –Cor N Y Cour

House of Reps: 1-Ptn of Chas Hibbs, a messenger in the Pension Ofc, praying an increase of salary. 2-Ptn of Capt Alex'r McEwen was referred to the Cmte on Invalid Pensions.

SAT JUN 3, 1848
House of Reps: 1-Bills taken up-relief of: Peter Shaffer; of John Ozias; of the legal reps of Robt Fulton, deceased; relief of Anna Giffin of Wyoming Co, N Y; of Wm Butler; of Wm DeBuys, late postmaster at New Orleans; of Artemas Conant; of Ruth Hollenbeck; of Jesse Washington Jackson; of Jas Fugate; of Saml Gray; of L B Canfield; of John Hibbert; of Danl H Warren; of Nathl Shiflett; of Skelton Felton; of Edmund Berd & John M Keene; of Richd Bloss & others; of Jones & Boker; of Chas L Dell. 2-Joint resolution of the Senate in favor of David Shaw & Solomon T Corser, & the House bill for the relief of Lewis Hastings. 3-Bills acted on & ordered to be reported to the House: bills authorizing the Sec of War to issue a duplicate of land warrant 1,469, which originally issued in favor of Adam Hart, Feb 3, 1829, & for the relief of Thos B Graham, & Senate bill for the relief of Fernando Fellany. 4-Bill for the relief of John P Converse: recommitted to the Cmte of Claims. 5-Bills for the relief of Jos Wilson, & relief of W B Slaughter, late Sec of the Territory of Wisconsin: passed. 6-Bill for the relief of Wm Fuller & Orlando Saltmarsh, & relief of H D Johnson: sent to the Senate for concurrence. 7-The bills for the relief of Peter Shaffer & relief of Wm DeBuys, late postmaster at New Orleans: laid over for further discussion.

Late news from the South is a report of the death of Cmder Harris & Cmder Pinckney, of the U S Navy, who are stated to have drowned on the 15th ult, on the bar off Tuapan, by the swamping of a boat.

Died: yesterday, Miss Jane Ashwood, a native of England, but for many years a resident of Wash City. Her funeral is today, at 2 o'clock, from the residence of Mr Little, on D between 9th & 10th sts.

Ladies with letters in the Wash Post Ofc, Jun 1, 1848:

Arthur, Mrs Mary H
Allison, Miss Rebecca
Burton, Mrs Cath-2
Brooke, Miss Emily
Bogue, Mrs Eliz
Brown, Mrs Mary J
Bryant, Mrs Mary
Bell, Miss Matilda
Ball, Mrs Mary C
Beams, Miss Susan
Bennett, Miss Clara S
Byar, Miss Henrietta
Boarman, Mrs Jen'te
Brooke, Miss Jane E
Briasmade, Mrs M M
Carroll, Miss Ann
Clarke, Mrs Har E
Clarke, Miss Mar E
Custis, Miss Mary
Cross, Mrs Rachael
Colston, Teresa
Campbell, Mrs Mary
Day, Mrs Agnes
Dunn, Mrs Louisa
Dulany, Mary
Drury, Miss Adelaide
Douglass, Mrs Lucy A
Douglass, Mrs M D M
Esher, Mrs Ann M
Ewell, Miss Reb L
Finch, Mrs Mary E
Fletcher, Miss M E
Fairfield, Mrs M A
Fisher, Miss Sarah
Goldsberry, Miss J
Gahan, Mrs Marg
Gates, Mrs Mary
Gould, Mrs Sarah A
Hellemes, Mrs Cath
Hurburt, Mrs Eliz
Hinton, Miss Mary
Hill, Miss Sophia
Henson, Mrs Susan
Herbert, Mrs Har A
Jackson, Mrs Lucin
Jackson, Miss M A
Jennings, Mrs Mah
Jamaison, Mrs M E
Jones, Miss Mary
Johnson, Miss Marg
Jones, Miss Susan'h
Kirk, Miss Mary
Lancaster, Miss Chr
Lyons, Mrs Jos
Lewis, Mrs Jane E
Lewis, Mrs Lucy
Loomis, Mrs S C
Loomis, Miss Martha
Landen, Miss Rach'l
Morris, Eliza A
Mathews, Miss H
Mills, Mrs Mary E
Morse, Mary
Mills, Mrs Mary
Mitchell, Miss R
Marks, Miss Nancy J
McClelland, Mrs M
McKnight, Miss
McCormick, Mrs E T
Newton, Miss Ann
Naughton, Mrs Brid
Newton, Martha
Newman, Miss Rach
Noble, Miss Patsy J
Osburn, Mrs Lucy A
Peddicord, Mrs Cath
Phelps, Mrs M C
Page, Miss Eliz G
Quesenbury, Mary
Roche, Miss Joanah
Rogers, Miss Lucy
Russell, Mrs Sarah A
Robinson, Mrs Susan
Robinson, Eliz
Rollins, Mrs Mary A
Smoot, Mrs Henley
Sith, Mrs Margaret
Sutton, Mrs
Spencer, Mrs
Solomon, Mariah
Suter, Miss Anna M
Thaw, Mrs Eliz
Taylor, Mrs Maria
Tazco, Miss Mary J
Thompson, Miss J E
Taylor, Mrs Marg E
Waller, Mrs Eliz-2
White, Mrs J C
Williams, Miss Jos
Ward, Mary
White, Mrs Eliz
Woodward, Caroline
Winebury, Mrs Eliz
Whiting, Mrs Ann B
Wheatley, Miss Mar
Wise, Miss My [c'd]
Williams, Mrs Mary

MON JUN 5, 1848

Rt Rev Dr Kyle, Bishop of Cork, Ireland, died in Dublin on May 18, in his 78th year.

Wm K Gordon appointed Cashier of the Branch Bank of Va in Fredericksburg, vice Wm I Roberts, deceased.

House of Reps: 1-Ptn of Nancy Hough, in her own right & on behalf of Andrew Finley, Polly Finley, now the wife of Walter Bell, & the widow & children of John Finley, deceased, heirs of Saml Finley, deceased, who was a Lt in the Revolutionary war, praying the commutation pay.

Orphans Court of Wash Co, D C. Letters of administration with the will annexed on the personal estate of Ann Gamlin, late of said county, deceased. –Enoch Brunett, adm will annexed

Cmders Pinkney & Harris, of the U S Navy, were in 2 boats belonging to the steamers **Iris** & **Vixen**, & were attempting to cross the bar of Tuspan, on the coast of Mexico. A rain the night before had caused a strong current in the river, making the undertow very great, to which the accident is partially attributed. Cmder Harris' boat had passed over in safety, but Cmder Pinkney's boat having become unmanageable, the former was put about to render assistance, when both boats were swamped, & both their principal ofcrs were drowned. A French resident at Tuspan & 2 seamen were also drowned. Three other ofcrs, Lt Ward, of the ship **Cumberland**; Lt Doughty, commanding ofcr of the marines in the squadron; Dr Bell, of the **Vixen**, & 9 seamen, were saved by the boats of the U S schnr **Mahonese**, in charge of Acting Master Dyer & Passed Midshipman N C West.

To the Voters in Washington:
W H Winter is a candidate for a seat in the Common Council in the 4th Ward.
W Wilson has declined his name being entered as Assessor of the 1st Ward.
Wm P Elliot declines being a candidate as Surveyor of Wash City, an ofc he filled for many years.
Butler Baker declines being a candidate for Assessor.
Josiah Ray offers himself a candidate for Assessor.
Jas Clephane withdraws his name as a candidate for the Board of Aldermen.
Rd Dement & Wm W Birth announce they are not candidates for the Board of Common Council.
J W Deeble states he has not determined to retire from the contest for Register.
Ignatius Mudd presents himself as a candidate for the ofc of Collector.
P M Pearson announces himself for the ofc of Collector of Taxes.
Wm J McCormick has consented to be a candidate for the ofc of Register of the city.
C H Wiltberger is a candidate for the ofc of Register of the City, so long held by him, & now made elective by the new Charter.
Thos C Magruder is a candidate for the ofc of Collector of Taxes.
A Rothwell is a candidate for the ofc of City Collector, now held by him.
Thos C Magruder will be supported for Collector of Taxes by many voters of all wards.
Geo W Philips offers himself as a candidate for the ofc of Collector of Taxes.
Wm W Birth does not desire to be a candidate for the ofc of Surveyor.
Jno M Moore will not be a candidate for a municipal ofc at the coming charter election.
Dr F Howard declines being a candidate for the council.

Fielder R Dorsett will be supported for the ofc of Assessor in the 1st Ward.
Announce Thos F Harkness as a candidate for Assessor.
Saml Drury is recommended as a suitable person to fill the ofc of Assessor.
Mr Alex'r Borland is recommended as a competent person for Assessor & will serve if elected.
Mr R Farnham declines being a candidate of the ofc of Assessor.
Jas F Haliday is a candidate for re-election in the 2nd Ward.
John M Moore is recommended for the ofc of Register of the city.
Wm J McCormick is recommended for ofc of Register.
Announce Geo W Stewart for the ofc of Assessor of the 2nd Ward.
Mr Jas Carbery states he is not a candidate for the Board of Aldermen for the 5th Ward.
Mr John McCauley is presented to the voters of the 5th Ward for the Board of Common Council.
Geo Collins will be supported for the ofc of Assessor in the 6th Ward.
Election in Wash City on Jun 5 for the following ofcs:

For Mayor: Wm W Seaton; Peter Force

For Alderman:
J D Barclay	Walter Lenox	Saml Byington
Alex H Michlin	Geo S Gideon	Wm Ashdown
Wm Orme	B B French	
John T Towers	Thos Thornly	

For Common Council:
Wm Easby	Silas Hill	Geo M Dove
Wm T Dove	Jos Bryan	W W Birth
Saml F Douglass	Jos Borrows	J Cull
Saml E Douglass	Jas A Wise	G H Fulmer
J B H Smith	Jos Borrows	John R Queen
T B J Frye	Wm H Rinter	Jonas B Ellis
Saml Stott	Richd Wallach	Michl Carroll
Dr T B J Frye	H B Sweeny	Chas Venable
Geo J Abbot	Saml Bacon	Joel W Jones
Jas L Cathcart	Francis Y Naylor	John T Cassell
Lewis Johnson	John McCauley	Dearborn B Johnson
Jesse E Dow	Chas W Stewart	W Lloyd
Nicholas Callan	John Johnson	J W Jones
Jas F Haliday	C E Tims	Craven Ashford
Jas Clephane	Enoch W Smallwood	
Dr F Howard	John M Brodhead	

For Register:
C H Wiltberger	Jas W Deeble	
John M Moore	W J McCormick	

For Collector:
I Mudd	Thos C Magruder	Walter Warder
John Hands	John A Blake	Peter M Pearson
Andrew Rothwell	Thos L Magruder	

For Surveyor: R Coyle; Randolph Coyle

For Assessor:
Wm Wilson	Benj F Middleton	Jeremiah Hepburn
Thos F Harkness	Geo S Noyes	Danl Kealey
Saml Drury	Washington Lewis	J W Shiles
D Hines	J Thompson Van Reswick	Wm Bird
Geo H Plant		
John Sessford, sen	Jos W Beck	

TUE JUN 6, 1848
Senate: 1-Ptn from R W Richardson, asking confirmation of a tract of land. Shall we, the Congress & people of the U S, become accessory to an injustice towards the heirs of the gallant Kosciusko, whose valiant conduct on the battlefields of the American Revolution, as those of his native land, render even his descendants conspicuous objects of hatred to the Russian Autocrat?

Handsome household furniture, piano forte, carriage, & horse at auction: on Jun 7, at the residence of his Excellency Col Beaulieu, Belgian Minister, residence on Pa ave, between 24th & 25th sts. -R W Dyer, auct

House of Reps: 1-Ptn of Maj Tochman is before the House, the case is of high-handed tyranny in the Minister of the Autocrat of Russia. The Emperor of Russia, holding Maj Tochman in unbounded hatred for his noble efforts in behalf of his native land in her struggle of 1830, has thought proper to persecute him through his minister, Mr Bodisco, on an occasion presented for the adjustment of the claims of the heirs of Kosciusko, & all the force & power of his position is bought to bear upon his destined victim. So far he has succeeded. He is by birth a fellow-countryman of Thaddeus Kosciusko, & represents the rights of his heirs for certain properties in this country. We are now appealed to by the victim of Russian tyranny to vindicate his rights as an American citizen. Maj Tochman is only one party aggrieved; but, through him, the heirs of Thaddeus Kosciusko. Referred to the Cmte on the Judiciary

Two steamboat disasters. 1-On May 27, the steamboat **H Kenney**, Capt Miller, exploded on the Tombigbee river, Ala: 30 persons were killed or missing; 12 badly maimed, & 2 shockingly scalded. The boat sunk a few minuted after the explosion. 2-The steamer **Clarksville** was burnt, near Ozark's Island, on May 27: the captain & crew, 8 or 10 in number, & 30 deck passengers were lost. The cabin passengers were saved.

Railroad accident last Sat on the way to Fred'k: Richd Wood, of Phil, had one of his legs so severely injured, it will probably be amputated.

Sale of valuable lands in the Lake region of Indiana: pursuant to a deed of trust from John B Steenbergen to the subscribers. David G Rose, of Laporte Co, will show any of the lands to persons desiring to see them. –Robt Y Conrad, Jas Marshall, jr, Rhesa Allen

Twenty-five years have elapsed since the mortal remains of the lamented Wm Lowndes were consigned to the bosom of the ocean. In the Encyclopedia Americana, recently published, we find a brief notice of him. Something more than this is due to the memory of one of the purest statesman which the country has produced. We trust that some gifted son of the Palmetto State will rescue his name & fame from oblivion. –A Native of Pa.

Trustee's sale of valuable lots near the War Dept: deed of trust to me, dated Oct 6, 1847, recorded May 3, 1848, in the land records of Wash Co, D C: sale on Jun 15, of all that piece or parcel of land in said city, being part of lot 3 in square 166, bounded with the western line of that part of said lot 3, which was conveyed by Tench Ringgold to Benj Lincoln Lear & Francis L Lear, in 1824, duly recorded, to an alley; in a direct line to the same property sold under a decree of the Circuit Court of Wash Co, D C, sitting as a Court of Chancery, by John J Stull, trustee, & by him conveyed by deed, dated Mar 25, 1835, recorded in Liber W B 55, folio 165, with a small tenement thereon. This property is on the north side of Pa ave, a few doors west of 17th st west. –Thos J Semmes, trustee –R W Dyer, auct

Shoes: ladies Gaiters, Kid slippers, Morocco slippers. –A Hoover, opposite Seven Blgs, Pa ave.

Balt, Jun 6. State of Md vs John Cochrane, Jas Cochrane, & Wm H Hunt: on an indictment for a conspiracy to falsely charge G Warner with the crime of perjury, John Cochrane alone being on trial. The jury returned with a verdict of guilty.

For rent: large brick dwlg on 10th st, south of Pa ave. Inquire of Mr Robt W Dyer, Wash, or address Jno F M Lowe, Alexandria, Va.

WED JUN 7, 1848

Immigrants robbed on Jun 2 on the steamboat **Admiral**-Mrs Rugglesworth of $110 in gold, Mrs Little of 7 sovereigns, & Wm Burgess of 8 sovereigns, & one Queen Anne shilling. They were on their way West & are now destitute. Mr Nelligan, the immigrant agent, has taken hold of the matter. –Albany Evening Jrnl

Pottsville Emporium: Mr Edw Kearns, a highly respectable citizen of Schuylkill Co, Pa, was recently robbed of $1,027, while on board a canal boat commanded by Capt Elliott, on the Pa canal. He carried the money in 2 separate packages in his coat pocket.

John C Lyon, a son of Mr Wm Lyon, of St Mary's Co, Md, was drowned on Sun last in a mill-pond near the village of Charlotte Hall. He had entered the pond with a parcel of boys for the purpose of bathing, & while swimming in the deepest part of it was taken with a cramp, as is supposed, & disappeared. He was about 19 or 20 years of age. –St Mary's Republican

Fire at N Y on Sat seriously & probably fatally, injured a brother & sister named Edw & Margaret Wisely. Some persons were engaged in making fireworks & some exploded, setting fire to the premises.

At Louisville, Ark, about middle May, Judge Hightower was shot by a young man named Garland, against whose father the Judge was engaged in a suit as counsel. The result was fatal. In another homicide, Rowland Robinson was shot dead by Elijah Adams, at a ball in Point Coupee, La, on May 9. Cause was an old family quarrel.

Wash Corp: 1-Cmte of Claims: act for the relief of Richd Harrison: passed. Same cmte: act for the relief of Caleb Dulany: passed. 3-Cmte of Claims: bills for the relief of Wm Dowling; relief of John Fletcher; & relief of J Fletcher: passed.

City Ordinances-Wash: 1-Act for the relief of Andrew D Jenkins: to be paid the sum of $10, being the amount of a certain judgment paid by Jenkins. 2-Act for the relief of Wm C Johnson: to refund to him the $10 paid by him for a vegetable stand in the Northern Market in Wash City. 3-Act for the relief of Anne Wheeler: remit the fine imposed on her for an alleged violation relative to the keeping of dogs: provided she pay the costs of prosecution. 4-Act for the relief of John J Joyce: fine imposed for alleged violation of selling liquor less than a pint without a license is remitted: provided Joyce pay the costs of prosecution.

Wash City Election Returns:
1st Ward:
Mayor: Wm W Seaton 218; John Boyle 68; Peter Force 62.
Alderman: Saml Drury 147; Alex H Mechlin 108; J D Barclay 65.
Common Council: Saml E Douglass 217; Wm T Dove 189; Saml Stott 112; J B H Smith 104; Wm Easby 99; J L Catchcart 90; T B J Fry 87; G J Abbott 47.
Register: C H Wiltberger 181; Jas W Sheahan 95; Wm J McCormick 29; J W Deeble 24; P M Pearson; 3; scattering 2.
Collector: Andrew Rothwell 106; John Hands 196; scattering 38.
Assessor: Thos F Harkness 234; David Hines 45; F Dorset 20; Wm Wilson 15; A Borland 12; S Drury 3.
Surveyor: Randolph Coyle 335.
2nd Ward:
Mayor: Wm W Seaton 191; John Boyle 177; Peter Force 89.
Aldermen: Wm Orme 230; Jas Clephane 123; Andrew Hancock 68.
Common Council: Jesse E Dow 317; Lewis Johnson 302; Nicholas Callan 280; Jas F Haliday 270.
Register: Jas W Sheahan 186; Wm J McCormick 151; C H Wiltberger 65; Jas W Deeble 44.
Collector: John Hands 282; A Rothwell 71; John A Blake 45; Walter Warder 13; T C Magruder 13; G W Phillips 11; B K Morsell 7; P M Pearson 7; Ignatius Mudd 2.
Surveyor: Randolph Coyle 408.
Assessor: Geo H Plant 371; John Sessford 67.
3rd Ward:
Mayor: Wm W Seaton 265; John Boyle 122; Peter Force 83; G Baily, jr 2.
Alderman: John T Towers 494; scattering 7.
Common Council: S H Hill 368; Jos Borrows 305; Jos Bryan 304; Jas A Wyse 71; O J Prather 8; John Y Bryant 6; scattering 9.

Register: C H Wiltberger 154; J W Deeble 119; J W Sheahan 93; Wm J McCormick 92; scattering 6.
Collector: A Rothwell 208; John Hands 97; Thos C Magruder 53; J A Blake 29; Geo W Phillips 22; B K Morsell 13; I Mudd 12; W Warder 9; scattering 1.
Surveyor: R Coyle 413; scattering 5.
Assessor: John C Harkness 390; J Downing 12; scattering 4.
4th Ward:
Mayor: Wm W Seaton 403; John Boyle 150; Peter Force 63; G Baily, jr 1.
Alderman: Walter Lenox 436; Geo S Gideon 143; scattering 2.
Common Council: Hugh B Sweeny 465; R Wallach 453; W H Winter 318; Sam Bacon 273; scattering 4.
Register: C H Wiltberger 230; Wm J McCormick 143; Jas W Sheahan 139; Jas W Deeble 79; scattering 4.
Collector: A Rothwell 312; T C Magruder 92; J T Hands 63; G W Phillips 48; B K Morsell 25; Ignatius Mudd 16; P N Pearson 14; J A Blake 8; W Warder 7; scattering 10.
Surveyor: R Coyle 554; scattering 10.
Assessor: Washington Lewis 221; Benj F Middleton 207; Geo S Noyes 142; scattering 3.
5th Ward:
Mayor: Wm W Seaton 163; John Boyle 78; Peter Force 54.
Alderman: B B French 171; Wm Dickson 99.
Common Council: Geo M Dove 171; F Y Naylor 142; John Johnson 95; J M Brodhead 94; C E Tims 79; E W Smallwood 62; John McCauley 63; Wm J Wheatley 50.
Register: Wm J McCormick 178; C H Wiltberger 56; J W Sheahan 48; J W Deeble 5.
Collector: A Rothwell 130; J T Hands 49; Peter N Pearson 45; G W Phillips 19; T C Magruder 15; J A Blake 8; I Mudd 8; B K Morsell 4.
Surveyor: R Coyle 258; scattering 4.
Assessor: J Hepburn 120; J T Van Reswick 90; J W Beck 36; J P Ingle 33; scattering 3.
6th Ward:
Mayor: Wm W Seaton 176; John Boyle 147; Peter Force 10.
Alderman: Thos Thornley 326.
Common Council: J R Queen 227; Jas Cull 184; G H Fulmer 164; Jonas B Ellis 137; Michl Carroll 86; Chas Venable 21.
Register: Wm J McCormick 151; J W Sheahan 94; C H Wiltberger 64; J W Deeble 3; C Dubb 2.
Collector: P M Pearson 127; A Rothwell 83; J T Hands 58; T C Magruder 28; G W Phillips 11; I Mudd 4; scattering 7.
Surveyor: R Coyle 317.
Assessor: D E Keally 258; Geo Collard 68; Jas Crandell 1.
7th Ward:
Mayor: Wm W Seaton 212; John Boyle 71; Peter Force 63;
Alderman: Saml Byington 193; Wm Ashdown 138.
Common Council: Joel W Jones 231; John T Cassell 247; Wm Lloyd 195; D B Johnson 148; C Ashford 89; John L Smith 5; Jos Cross 1.
Register: Wm J McCormick 164; J W Sheahan 59; P M Pearson 4; C H Wiltberger 57; J W Deeble 29; scattering 5.

Collector: T C Magruder 69; J T Hands 61; Adw Rothwell 59; I Mudd 43; P M Pearson 47; W Warder 24; G W Phillips 17; scattering 5.

Surveyor: R Coyle 198; W J Elliot 30.

Assessor: Wm Bird 122; Jas S Magee 86; Peter Hepburn 19; J W Shiles 49; Jackson Pumphrey 44; scattering 3.

Recapitulation: total votes for the 7 Wards:
Mayor: W W Seaton 1,628; Peter Force 424; John Boyle 813
For Register: W J McCormick 968; C H Wiltberger 807; J W Sheahan 714; J W Deeble 302
For Collector:
Andrew Rothwell 969
John Hands 806
P M Pearson 240
Th C Magruder 270
Geo W Phillips 111
For Surveyor: Randolph Coyle 2,483

John A Blake 94
Ignatius Mudd 85
Genj K Morsell 52
Walter Warder 63

Died: on Jun 4, in Wash City, Ann Maria S, consort of Wm Tell Steiger, of the Gen Land ofc, & daughter of the late Andrew Shriver, of Carroll Co, Md, at the age of about 44 years. Her remains were yesterday interred in the Congressional Burying Ground, attended by a large number of mourning relatives & friends. Her malady was of such a nature as to render medical treatment of no avail. Her disease manifested itself several months before her death. Although confined during that period, she experienced but little acute pain, & died calmly, in the full possession of her mental faculties. Her duties as head of a family she performed in the most affectionate & tender manner.

Died: on May 24, at Savannah, Ga, Capt Geo L Welcker, of the U S Corps of Engineers.

Died: on May 31, at Savannah, Ga, Capt John Mackay, of the U S Topographical Engineers. He was a graduate of West Point in 1826; his last duty was the survey of Matagorda Bay. He has found an early tomb at the homes of his childhood, & his native city has never seen one of her younger sons pass from the cradle to the grave more honored, more esteemed, more deeply regretted.

Died: on Jun 5, Morton Burr, son of E B & Adelaide St M Stelle, aged one year & 9 months.

Died: in March, at Dayton, Ohio, Rufus Given, youngest child of W J & Anna Delano, aged 1 year & 3 months.

Lost, on last Sat, a blue morocco pocketbook. Suitable reward will be paid to any person who will return the same to me at the Smithsonian Institute Bldgs. –Gilbert Cameron

Household & kitchen furniture at auction: on Jan 7, at the residence of Mr Henry Ould, 4 miles from the city on 7th st or Rockville turnpike road, adjoining the farm of Richd Butt. –A Green, auctioneer

THU JUN 8, 1848
Mrs John Quincy Adams & family arrived at Balt, on Mon, & left the next morning in the cars for the family mansion in Quincy.

The corner-stone of the <u>Washington Monument</u> being yesterday afternoon raised without accident from the 14 st bridge, was safely transported to the site of the Nat'l Monument. The Marine Bank attended & played excellent music.

An accident occurred last week in Wash Co, Pa, by which David Patterson, David & Danl Sutherland [the last 2 being brothers,] drowned in a milldam in West Finely township. Danl sunk in a hole & the other two attempted to rescue him, but they too were lost.

By the death of Mr Winter, of the Savannah [Geo] Republican, J L Locke, the surviving partner, is left sole proprietor & editor of that journal.

Matthew Gregory died at Albany on Jun 4, in the 91st year of his age. He was one of the men of the 'better days of the republic." He entered the army, in Conn, as a non-commissioned ofcr, & served during the whole of the war. He participated in all the sufferings of the army at Valley Forge. Before the close of the war he received a lt's commission, & was in Hamilton's brig at the capture of Cornwallis. He was one of the last, if not the very last surviving member of the Society of Cincinnati. –Albany Journal

New Grocery, Feed Store. The subscriber has opened at the stand, formerly occupied by Mr Cartwright, & recently by Mr Iardella, on N J ave, one square south of the Capitol.
–Jos Ingle

FRI JUN 9, 1848
Senate: 1-Ptn from Maria Caldwell Robertson, asking the payment of certain loan certificates. 2-Cmte of Pensions: pension to Ruth Hallenbach. Same cmte: the following House bills without amendment: act for the relief of:

Hannah Yarrington	Henry N Halsted	Mary Pike
Eliza A Mellon	John Farnham	Gideon A Perry
Wm H Wilson	Andrew Flanegan	Jos Taylor
Amos Bull	Wm Gott	Henry W Thompson
Maurice R Simmons	Catharine Hoffman	John Haup

Anna Griffin, of Wyoming Co, N Y
2-To be referred to the Cmte on Naval Affairs: relief of Robt Ramsay; relief of Wm Butler. 3-Sec of Navy report on the papers filed by Mary Cassin in her application for a pension. 4-Cmte on Public Lands: bills for the relief of Charity Herrington; relief of Wm L Wigent. 5-Cmte on the Library: bill authorizing the purchase of the papers & manuscripts of the late Thos Jefferson, with a report; which was ordered to be printed.

Salt Water Bathing at *Piney Point*, Md-the Potomac Pavilion. –A W Kirkwood, F L Keller, Proprietors

The expedition under Lt W F Lynch, of the U S Navy, authorized by Gov't to explore the Dead Sea, had reached its destination on Apr 23, & was afloat on that sea, with boats launched, the weather mild, & all the party safe & well. We believe Lt Lynch is the first to visit it under the authority of a foreign Gov't.

Headquarters Army of Mexico, Mexico, May 17, 1848. Orders #95.
I-Before a Military Commission convened at the Nat'l Palace, city of Mexico, by virtue of Orders 53, of Apr 9, 1848, & of which Col M V Thompson, 3rd Regt Ky Volunteers, is Pres, were tried:
First Lt Isaac Hare, 2nd Regt Pa Volunteers. Charge 1: Murder. Specification: In this, that the said Lt Hare did on Apr 5, 1848, in Mexico, commit murder upon Manuel Zorriza, a citizen of Mexico, by shooting him in the head. Charge 2: Burglary. Specifications: In this, that Lt Hare did on Apr 5, 1848, forcibly, & with a felonious intent, break into & enter a house in the city of Mexico, #5 de la Palma st. To all which the accused pleaded "Not Guilty." Sentence: The Commission found the accused guilty as charged, & sentenced him to be hanged by the neck until he is dead, dead, dead; 2/3rd of the members of the Court concurring therein.
Here follow similar charges & sentences against Lt B F Dutton, 2nd Regt Pa Volunteers; Lt B P Tilden, 2nd Regt Infty; John Laverty; Sgt B F Wragg; Sgt Stewart; & Pvt John Wall.]
II-The Major Gen Commanding approves the proceeding, findings, & sentences of the Military Commission in the foregoing cases. Lts Isaac Hare & B F Dutton, 2nd Regt Pa Volunteers, & B P Tilden, 2nd Regt Infty, & John Laverty, will be executed on May 25, between the hours of 8 & 11 a m, under the direction of the Military & Civil Govn'r of the city of Mexico. Upon the recommendation of the Court, the sentences in the cases of Sgts B F Wragg & Stewart & Pvt John Wall, of the 7th Infty, are respectively remitted. They will be kept in close confinement until the close of the war, when they will each be dishonorably discharged from the service. No further proceeding will be taken against the prisoners Jesse Armstrong & J A Hollister, who appeared as witnesses for the prosecution. They will be kept in close confinement until the close of the war, & then set at liberty. III-The Military Commission is hereby dissolved. By order of Maj Gen Butler. –L Thomas, Assist Adj Gen
[Jun 13th newspaper: City of Mexico, May 25, 1848. The ofcrs & others who had been sentenced to be hanged on today have been respited by Gen Butler, by a special order: "The sentence of death which has been passed upon persons by courts of the American army, whether Americans or Mexicans, is hereby suspended until further orders."]

Died: in Oct last, at Knoxville, Ill, Edmund Law, aged about 30 years, 2nd son of the late John Law, of Wash City.

SAT JUN 10, 1848
Lumber, Lime, & Coal: John Purdy, 1st st, near Pa ave.

House of Reps: 1-Ptn of Jos D Ward, praying an additional pension, he having faithfully served as a non-commissioned ofcr up to & during the battle of Buena Vista, in which engagement he was literally shot to pieces, & thereby rendered perfectly helpless. 2-Ptn of D Nash, coroner of Norfolk Co, Va, & cmte of the estate of Thos Bressie, deceased, praying for half-pay for Revolutionary services of the said Bressie.

Orphans Court of Wash Co, D C. In the case of Huch C Smith, adm of Henry S Fox, deceased, the adm aforesaid, with the approbation of the Orphans' Court, appointed *Jun 9 next for the settlement & distribution of the estate of said deceased, at the ofc of Jas M Carlisle, of the assets in his hands as administrator, so far as the same has been collected & turned into money. –Ed N Roach, Reg/o wills [*Jun 9 as copied.]

Valuable oil paintings, books, fine engravings, mathematical instruments, & telescopes at auction on Jun 13, at the residence of the late Col Geo Bomford. His collection of Oil Paintings, amongst which are a fine piece by Gainsborough, & one by Woeverman.
-R W Dyer, auct

MON JUN 12, 1848
The Military Heroes of the Revolution, with a narrative of the war of Independence, by C J Peterson: just issued from the press of Mr W A Leary, of Phil, highly deserving of public patronage. Mr Chas Snow is agent for making sale of copies of the work in this city.

Miss Maria Mitchell, of Nantucket, discoverer of the comet which bears her name, was unanimously elected an honorary member of the American Academy of Science at their last general meeting. She is the first female member of that association. [Dec 7th newspaper: Miss Mitchell is not the daughter of Prof Mitchell, of Cincinnati, as stated in the London Atheneum. She is the daughter of Prof Wm Mitchell, of Nantucket. This is the first honor of the kind ever bestowed upon an American; & we believe that Miss Mitchell is the only lady of any country to receive this high compliment.]

Caution. All persons are forewarned against receiving a note drawn by me about 2 years ago in favor of Michl Smith, for $20, as I am determined not to pay the same.
–P A Byrne

By 2 writs of venditioni exponas, I will expose to sale at public auction on Capitol Hill, lot G in square 731, with brick house thereon, on Jul 13, for cash, late the property of John Hollohan & Jas Hollohan, seized & taken in execution at the suits of Enoch Ridgway, use of Thos N Brashears & Jos S Clarke, surviving partner of the late firm of Clarke & Orme. –Horatio R Maryman, constable

House of Reps: 1-Ptn of Jonathan Church & others, praying Congress to authorize the sale of certain lands in Monroe Co, Ill, known as the **Renault grant**. 2-Memorial of Capt P Lamothe, praying compensation for mail service performed by him in carrying the mail from Alton, Ill, to St Louis, Missouri.

Notice: Stores to be closed. In order that the Clerks employed in the dry goods stores may have some time for recreation, all the dry goods stores in Wash City will, from this day until Sep 1, be closed *precisely* at sunset.

Army Order: War Dept: Adj Gen's Ofc, Wash, Jun 8, 1848. Orders #25. 1-At the termination of the war with Mexico, measures will be taken to transport the Volunteers as near to their homes as circumstances will permit. The Mass Regt will be sent to Boston; the N Y & N J Regts to **Fort Hamilton**, N Y harbor; the Pa Regts, one to Phil & one to Pittsburg; the Md & D C Regt to **Fort McHenry**; the Va & N C Regts to **Fort Monroe**; & the S C Regt to **Fort Moultrie**, where they will be paid & regularly mustered out of the service. 2-Col Crane, commanding the 5th & 6th military depts., will designate & give the orders to the mustering ofcrs at Boston, **Fort Hamilton**, Phil, & Pittsburg. Col Walbach & Capt Van Ness, commanding respectively at **Fort Monroe** & **Fort Moultrie**, with like service, & Lt Col Belton with like service at **Fort McHenry**. 3-The Mich Regt will be paid & mustered out at Detroit, & Capt Gage's company at **Fort Mackimac**, under direction of Bvt Brig Gen Brady. 4-The Volunteers from Ga & Ala, & Livingston's company from Fla, will be sent to Mobile. Those from the Western States, including La & Miss, will be sent to the places where they were mustered into service, or to points accessible to steamers, as Bvt Brig Gen Brooke, commanding at New Orleans, may direct. He is authorized to call on Lt Col Erving, at Cincinnati, for aid as the service in the States bordering on the Ohio may tender necessary. 5-The Volunteers in New Mexico, under Brig Gen Price, will be marched, the Missouri troops to Independence, the Ill troops to Alton, & mustered out under Lt Col Wharton. 6-The companies from Wisc & Iowa will be mustered out under Bvt Col Garland at **Fort Crawford** & **Fort Atkinson**, respectively. The Florida company at Tampa Bay under Bvt Maj Wade. 7-Bvt Brig Gen Churchill, Inspector Gen will repair without delay to New Orleans, & report to Gen Brooke for mustering service. [We learn that Bvt Lt Col Washington, of the Artl, will command the troops detached from Gen Wool's command, & that, on his arrival at Santa Fe, he will act of Govn'r of the Territory of New Mexico. The Sec of War could not perhaps have chosen a better ofcr, or of sounder judgment & discretion, than the distinguished Capt [now Bvt Lt Col] Washington. -Editors]

Mrd: on Jun 7, in Alexandria, Va, by Rev Mr Jones, Mr John T Laskey, of Wash, to Miss Mary Walker, of the former place.

Died: on Jun 10, after a very short illness, Eliz Chew Hill, daughter of Wm B Hill & of Catharine B Hill, of PG Co, Md, aged about 6 months.

Died: Thu last, in Gtwn, Joseph, son of Robt M & Ann H Lauck, aged 21 months & 25 days.

Orphans Court of Wash Co, D C. Letters of administration on the personal estate of Dumson Addison, late of the U S Navy, deceased. –Chas De Selding, adm

TUE JUN 13, 1848

Private sale of the east half of the west part of lot 3 in square 575, fronting 19 feet on Pa ave. Apply one door east of the Railroad Hotel to F F Stuck.

Senate: 1-Ptn from D G Ingraham, asking payment of a balance due for the manuscript papers of his father, Jos Ingraham, furnished to the Dept of State. 2-Ptn from Geo C De Kay, asking reimbursement of moneys expended by him while engaged in transporting provisions to Ireland in the U S frig **Macedonian**. 3-Ptn from the ofcrs of the regt of volunteers from D C & Md, denying certain allegations contained in the memorial of Chas Lee Jones to Congress, & soliciting an investigation of the same. 4-Ptn from Jas Ferrell, asking an increase of pension. 5-Ptn from Isaac Davenport, asking for a pension. 6-Ptn from Nathan Worthen, in relation to a pension. 7-Ptn from Geo Colee P Martin, of Picolata, Fla, for increase of compensation. 8-Cmte of Pensions: bill granting a pension to John Le Roy.

House of Reps: 1-New member, to wit, Mr Danl Wallack, a rep from the State of S C, elected to supply the vacancy occasioned by the death of the Hon Jas Black, appeared this day & was sworn in. 2-Ptn of Capt David Van Ness for compensation for Revolutionary services. 3-Ptn of Benj Watson for a pension.

Medical Staff of the Army: candidates approved for the appointment of Assist Surgeon in the Medical Dept of the [old] regular army, who were examined in N Y C on Jun 1:

John Byrne, of Missouri   Wm F Edgan, of Missouri
Lafayette Guild, of Ala   Thos H Williams, of Md

Assist Surgeon J W Russell was examined & found qualified for promotion.

On May 15, the residence of Eugene Oubre, near the village post ofc in the parish of Point Coupee, was lighted up with splendor for a magnificent entertainment proffered to his friends by the owner of the mansion. The occasion had been anticipated with hopes of delight. In the room adjoining the dancing, 2 gentlemen, Elijah Adams & Rowland Robertson were conversing, when Robertson was seen striking Adams. Adams shot Robertson with a revolver. Confusion, consternation, & shrieks, swallowed up all the happiness of the scene. The two had been brothers-in-law. Adams was a widower, having been the husband of Robertson's deceased sister. The unfortunate Robertson had scarcely realized the passing away of the honey-moon, & his young & unsuspecting bride was mingling happily in the life of the ball-room, when the report of death in the room adjacent staggered the senses of all. Robertson expired on the succeeding evening. Adams surrendered himself in open court on Sat. He was held to bail in the sum of $5,000.

Mrd: on Jun 11, by Rev Wm H Pitcher, Mr Geo L N Hall to Miss Ann Maria Beck, all of Wash City.

Mrd: on Jun 11, by Rev Mr Foley, Mr Nathan H Topping to Miss Mary E Culverwell, eldest daughter of Richd Culverwell, all of Wash City.

Mrd: on May 30, by Rt Rev Bishop Cobbs, in St Paul's Church, Greensborough, Ala, Rev J Somerville Marbury, rector of the church, to Miss Fanny M Sawyer.

Circuit Court of Wash Co, D C. Murray Barker vs David Riley. This is a creditor's bill of cmplnt, in which the cmplnt charges that Catharine Campbell died intestate, leaving sundry debts; that her personal estate is insufficient to pay her debts; that she was seized at the time of her death of lot 8, in square 16, of Wash City, which has descended to her heir-at-law, David Riley, dfndnt, subject to the charge of the payment of her debts; & that the cmplnt is the administrator of her personal estate, & one of her creditors; & the objects of this bill are a sale of the said real estate in aid of the personalty for the payment of her debts & for general relief; &, for as much as it appears that the dfndnt resides out of D C, it is ordered he appear in Court here on or before the 3rd Mon in Oct next.
–W Cranch -W Brent, clerk

Died: on Jun 2, at **Millwood**, the residence of her father, Harriet Fludd Hampton, eldest daughter of Col Wade Hampton, of S C, in her 25th year.

Died: on Jun 11, after a short but painful illness, Mr Richd Rice, in her 52nd year, for the last 30 years a resident of Wash City.

Died: on Mon, after an illness of 2 weeks, Miss Hannah L Barrett, in her 10th year. Her funeral is today at 4 o'clock, from the residence of Mr John Thos Caro, on H between 6th & 7th sts. The corpse will be borne to McKendree Chapel, where the usual funeral obsequies will be observed.

WED JUN 14, 1848
Senate: 1-Ptn from Geo C Hutter, asking arrears of pay as an ofcr of the U S Army. 2-Ptn from Jas C Chapman, asking to have paid over to him one-fourth part of the proceeds of the cargo of the brig **Diana**, condemned for a violation of the non-intercourse laws. 3-Cmte of Claims: asking to be discharged from the further consideration of the ptn of Thos F Gordon. Same cmte: House bill for the relief of Wm Ralston, without amendment.

City Ordinances-Wash. 1-Act for the relief of Dennis Orme & David Rich, free persons of color: that the fines of $20 & costs, each, imposed on them, for non-compliance with the laws of the Corp, be remitted, provided they pay the costs of prosecution & the remaining $5 of the fine within 30 days after the passage of this act, which $5, in each case, shall go to the credit of the police ofcr who made the arrest. 2-Act for the relief of John Fletcher: to remit fine imposed for violation of the law relative to cart license: provided he pay the costs of prosecution. 3-Act for the relief of Wm Dowling: to remit fine imposed for an alleged violation relative to the keeping or harboring of dogs: provided he pay the costs of prosecution. 4-Act for the relief of J Kirkwood: to remit fine imposed for an alleged violation relative to keeping or harboring of dogs: provided he pay the costs of prosecution. 5-Act for the relief of Caleb Buckingham: to pay to him the sum of $30.07, for laying iron pipes in 13th st west, between Springhead & N Y ave, on Sep 22, 1847.

Judge Monroe, of Ky, elected to the chair of the Law Professorship of the Lousiana Univ, made vacant by the death of the Hon Richd Henry Wilde.

Paris, May 26, 1848. The proposed decree for the banishment of Louis Philippe & his family was brought forward today in the Assembly: in favor-632; against it 63; majority for banishment-569.

House of Reps: 1-Ptn of Lucien Clavadetscher for the removal of Capt Wm Ramsay from the naval service for fraudulent conduct, & using his official position for the purpose of perpetrating deception & of cheating private citizens. 2-Memorial of the reps of Col John Crowell, late Indian agent, for compensation for his services.

Boston Post: Mrs Olive Bliss, mother of Col Bliss, the brave soldier & accomplished scholar, died at Lebanan, N H, on Jun 2. Col Bliss was her only child, & on him all her hopes & anticipation seemed to center. She lived to see her son honored & respected. Col Bliss visited his mother last winter, after an absence of nearly 7 years.

Information has reached St Louis, from the Indian country, that Keokuk, the head chief of the Sac & Fox tribe of Indians, has been poisoned by one of his band. His death followed soon after. The murderer has been arrested & confessed the crime.

Balt, Jun 13. Saml McCabe, a worthy young man, was killed a short time ago on the Balt & Susquehanna railroad, by being crushed between the cars. The brother of the deceased was killed in a similar way some weeks ago.

Mrd: on Jun 6, by Rev O B Brown, Mr Robt Merchant, of Portsmouth, England, to Miss Isabel Fryer, of Wash City.

Death of a Sister of Charity. Sister Victorine Kenny died in the Charity Hospital, at New Orleans, on May 31; she was aged 26 years, & was a native of Ireland. She ministered to the wants of the unfortunate in the hospital since 1843, & was universally beloved by all who knew her.

$2 reward for return of a small bluish-white Cow. I had exchanged some dry cows for her with Mr Bouldings, of P G Co, & she may have returned to Md. –Louis Vivans, home on Boundary st, at the head of 20th & 21st sts, immediately east of Kalorama.

Orphans Court of Wash Co, D C. Letters of administration de bonis non, with the will annexed, on the personal estate of Benj L Lear, late of said county, deceased.
–J B H Smith, adm D B N W A

THU JUN 15, 1848
Public sale of valuable property: the tract of land in Nelson Co known as **Bellevue Estate**: public auction on Jul 20th: contains 1,088 acres. At the same time & place, will be sold all the stock. The negroes, amounting to 40, may be obtained also, if the purchaser wants them. –L C Rives

Senate: 1-Ptn from Danl G Garnsey, an ofcr in the late war with Great Britian, asking compensation for military service. 2-Cmte on Finance: asking to be discharged from the further consideration of the memorial of John Golden in relation to his discoveries in finances. 3-Cmte on Commerce: House bills without amendment: relief of Philip J Fontain; & relief of the owners of the Spanish brig **Restaurador**. 4-Cmte on Naval Affairs: bill for the relief of Robt Ramsay, without amendment. 5-Cmte on Pensions: without amendments: house bills for the relief of Artemas Conant; of Jesse Washington Jackson; of Nathl Sheflett; of Hugh Riddle. Same cmte: asking to be discharged from the further consideration of the House bill for the relief of Wm Tee, of Portsmouth, Va, & that it be referred to the Cmte on Naval Affairs. Same cmte: adverse reports on the House bills for the relief of Sarah Wood & the relief of Danl E Warren. 6-Cmte on Naval Affairs: adverse report on the bill for the relief of Jno R Bryan.

House of Reps: 1-Cmte of Claims: reported bills for the relief of Ira T Horton & Augustus Ford; & of Jas Morehead: committed. Same cmte: bill for the relief of Jas Y Smith: committed. Same cmte: adverse reports on the ptns of Wm H Russell & W H Brockway, administrator of John Johnson, deceased: laid on the table. 2-Cmte on the Judiciary: was referred the Senate bill for the relief of Thos Douglass, late U S Atty for East Florida, reported the same back to the House without amendment: committed. 3-Cmte on Revolutionary Claims: adverse reports on the ptns of Moses Matthews & Noah Smith: laid on the table. Same cmte: bills for the relief of the heirs & legal reps of Presley Thornton; for the relief of the heirs of Larkin Smith; to provide for the payment of 7 years' half pay to Sarah Ann Dye, who was the widow of Lt Jonathan Dye an ofcr of the U S Army, & who was killed at Brandywine; & for the relief of the legal reps of John Mandeville: all committed. 4-Cmte on Indian Affairs: relief of Jonathan Lewis: committed. Same cmte: bill for the relief of Robt S Mitchell: committed. 5-Cmte on Military Affairs: bill for the relief of Josiah P Pilcher: committed. 6-Cmte on Naval Affairs: bill for the relief of Purser Benj G Cahoone, & for the relief of the widows & orphans of the ofcrs, seamen, & marines of the brig of war **Somers**, reported the same without amendment: committed.

Circuit Superior Court of Law & Chancery held for Bath Co, May 1, 1848. The Commonwealth of Va, who sues for the benfit of the Literary Fund, plntf, against Wm Wilson, adm of Adam Bowyer, deceased, Wm McClung, & Thos Graham, dfndnts. The plntf's bill alleges that Adam Bowyer, late of this county, departed this life intestate as to his goods & chattels, & that, after the payment of funeral charges, debts, & just expenses, there is no person entitled to take the residuum under the laws of this commonwealth directing the distribution of intestate's estates, & that such residuum has vested in the commonwealth for the benefit of the Literary Fund; & prays that the dfndnt, Wm Wilson, the admistrator of Adam Bowyer, deceased, be decreed to pay to the plntf, for the benefit of the Literary Fund, the said residuum of the personal estate of the Adam Bowyer, deceased. It is stated in the answer of the said Wm Wilson that his said intestate removed to this county from Pa many years since, but that the nativity of the Adam Bowyer does not appear from the papers in this cause. It is ordered & required that all persons claiming an interest, as distributees in the personal estate of said Adam Bowyer, do appear here on the first day of the next term of this Court. –Chs L Francisco, Clerk

The Hon Abbott Lawrence is said to have given $50,000 to Harvard Univ for the use of the Scientific School which bears his name.

Matamoros Flag of May 24: Col Harrison W Goyne, who some months since shot Assist Surgeon John C Glen in that city, has been tried by a military commission convened in Matamoros, & acquitted-the finding of the court being justifiable homicide.

The Louisville papers announce the death of Alex'r Gordon, for many years a distinguished merchant of London, Liverpool, & New Orleans. He died on May 27,

Household & kitchen furniture, piano forte, books & music at auction: on Jun 22, at the residence of Mr Whittaker, on D st, between 9th & 10th sts, [*Parker's Row*.] -A Green, auctioneer

FRI JUN 16, 1848

The Surgeon Gen of the Army has selected a small island called *Greenwood*, about 3 miles east of Pascagoula, for a military hospital, on the Gulf. The island contains some 80 or 90 acres of land & is thickly covered with live oak. John K Collins has been appointed to superintend the erection of the proper bldgs..

Senate: 1-Ptn from W H Eaton, asking remuneration for a horse purchased from the U S which proved unsound. 2-Cmte of Claims: bill for the relief of John G Mackall, with a report: ordered to be printed. Same cmte: adverse report on the claim of Ann B Cox.

City News: the late fire in the First Ward destroyed the shoe store of Mr Drury, & a great deal of damage was done to the household articles of Mr Favier & other sufferers.

Louisville, Jun 7, 1848. Maj G D Ramsay, Ord Dept, U S Army. The undersigned, in behalf of the ofcrs & members of the Louisville Legion, welcome you on your arrival in the city, & offer you the hospitalitles of the Legion, & invite you to a dinner on Jun 8. John B Shepherd, Maj; Thos L Caldwell, Surgeon; J J Matthews, Assist Surgeon; Chas H Harper, Conrad Shroder, E B Howe, Chas W Bullen, B F Stewart, F Kern, John Fuller, Capts L Legion, late 1st Reg Ky Vol. Reply: steamboat **Price**, Ohio River, Jun 7, 1848. I had the honor to receive this morning, just as I was leaving Louisville, your kind invitation, & am compelled to forego so great a pleasure. –Geo D Ramsay, Brevet Maj Ordnance, U S A to Maj John B Shepherd & others.

Negro boy, family horse, wagon, cart, saddles, & bridles at auction: on Sat next, on the Centre Market space, a colored boy, 18 years of age, for a term of years.
–T M & B Milburn, auctioneers

A vein of salt water, sufficient to turn an overshot mill, burst through a rock on the farm of Milton Smiley, in Cumberland Co, Ky, on May 26. It produces a pint of salt to every 2 gallons.

Rev Dr Stony, of Brooklyn, has recently inherited, through his son by a former wife, by the death of an English gentleman named Morrison, an estate of $400,000. The Dr & his family sailed for England on Sat last in the ship **United States**. –Eve Post

Valuable brick house & lots at auction: on Jun 19: lots 11 & 12 in square 424, with a 2 story brick house: fronts the Poor House square, being the property formerly belonging to the late Thos T Belt, deceased; the lots front 159 feet on 7th st between M & N sts. –A Green, auctioneer

Died: yesterday, Columbus Choate, son of Warren C Choate & Susannah G Drew, aged 3 years & 7 months. His funeral is this day at 10 o'clock.

Farm for sale-93 acres, on the old Bladensburg road, & adjoins the farm of E Tucker: improvements consist of a good dwlg, & all necessary out-bldgs. Apply to Isaac Clarke, corner of H & 8th sts.

House of Reps: 1-Ptn for the relief of the heirs & legal reps of Jos Spencer, deceased, a captain in the Revolutionary army. 2-Ptn of the heirs & legal reps of Col Jos Crockett, deceased, praying relief. 3-Ptn of Chas Stuart. 4-Memorial of Luther Bradish & others, members of the Historical Society of N Y, urging upon Congress to purchase *Mount Vernon*.

Mrs Sprigg, *Green's Row*, fronting the Capitol, east, has several unoccupied rooms. Gentlemen with or without families can be accommodated with board. The location is the most healthful in the city.

SAT JUN 17, 1848
All persons indebted to the Gtwn Plough Factory will please call & settle their accounts, as I wish to close the business as soon as possible. Settle with me or Chas Myers, my only agent. –Jos Libbey, Gtwn

Washington National Monument-cmte of arrangements for the ceremony of laying the corner stone: Arch Henderson, Walter Lenox, Jos H Bradley, & M F Maury.

House for rent: the commodious house & grounds lately occupied by Col Geo Bomford. –J B H Smith, Atty at Law

From our European correspondent: London, May 30, 1848. The court & aristocracy have been thrown into mourning by the death of the Princess Sophia, aunt to the Queen, & 12th child of George III. The Princess was in her 71st year, & had long been in a state of ill health. Only 3 of the once numerous family of George III now survive, viz. the King of Hanover, the Duke of Cambridge, & the Duchess of Gloucester, formerly the Princess Mary.

Died: yesterday, Columbus A Birch, in his 21st year. His funeral is Sunday at 5 o'clock, from the residence of his father on 14th st, between F & G sts.

Senate: 1-*Letter from Mr Bagby, of Alabama, resigning his seat as Senator of that State. 2-Bill directing the Sec of the Navy to purchase from Dr Jas P Espy his patent right for the conical ventilator: passed. 3-Passed: bills for the relief of: Jas F Sothoron; of John Clark; of the heirs of Jean F Perry, Josiah Blakely, Nicholas Jarrot, & Robt Morrison; of David N Smith; & of Silas Waterman. 2-Bill to provide compensation to Wm Woodbridge & Henry Chipman for services in adjusting titles to land in Michigan, & for other purposes: passed. 3-Bills laid on the table: relief of Geo Newton; of Russell Goss; of John Caldwell; of John P Baldwin; of the heirs & legal reps of Wm Grayson. 4-Took up the House bill for the relief of Phineas Carpenter, administrator of John Cox, deceased, of Boston. [*The Hon Arthur P Bagby has been appointed by the Pres to be Envoy Extraordinary & Minister Plenipotentiary from the U S to the Court of Russia, to succeed Hon R J Ingersoll, recalled at his own request.]

Special Order #53. War Dept, Adj Gen Ofc: Wash, Jun 15, 1848. Ofcrs detailed for special service connected with the muster & discharge of the volunteer troops, will report by letter for instructions to the ofcrs charged with the superintendence of the same, viz:
1-Brevet Col T Childs, 1st Artl; Maj C A Wait, 8th Infty; Maj G Wright, 4th Infty; Capt H Day, 2nd Infty: to Col J B Crane, 1st Artl, N Y C.
2-Maj J L Gardner, 4th Artl, to Col J B Walbach, 4th Artl, **Fort Monroe**.
3-Capt E B Alexander, 3rd Infty, to Brevet Maj Gen Twiggs, Wash City.
4-Capt S M Plummer, 1st Infty, to Lt Col Ewing, 2nd Artl, Cincinnati, Ohio.
–R Jones, Adj Gen

Mrd: on May 15, in Wash City, by Rev C M Butler, D D, Francis M Whittle, Rector of Kanawha Parish, to Emily C, eldest daughter of W M C Fairfax.

Mrd: on Jun 10, at St Peter's Church, by Rev Mr Van Horsigh, Josse Pablo Roura, of Barcelona, to Lavinia G, youngest daughter of the late Guiseppe Franzoni, of Florence, Italy.

The following missionaries were to sail from Providence on Tue for Africa, in the brig **Smithfield**, Capt Duff, bound for Gaboon River: Rev J L Wilson & wife, Rev A Bushnell & wife, Rev J M Preston & wife, Rev W T Wheeler, Mrs Griswold; also, John Wesley, a native youth, who came to the U S 2 years since, & has learned the art of printing.

Appointments by the Pres: 1-Andrew G Miller, to be Judge of the District Court of the U S for the District of Wisconsin. 2-Thos W Sutherland, to the U S Atty for the District of Wisconsin. 3-John S Rockwell, to be U S Marshal for the District of Wisconsin. 4-Geo W Thompson, to be U S Atty for the Western District of Va, in the place of Geo H Lee, resigned.

MON JUN 19, 1848
Gen Pierre Van Cortland died on Tue at Peekskill, N Y, in his 86th year, after a life honorable to his fame & useful to his country.

Senate: 1-Act for the relief of Phineas Carpenter, adm of John Cox, deceased, of Boston: passed. 2-Passed: act for the relief of the legal heirs of John Snyder, deceased. 3-Act for the relief of the legal reps of Jas Brown, deceased: passed. 4-Bill for the relief of B W Slaughter, late Sec of the State for the Territory of Wisconsin: passed. 5-Bill for the relief of J W Nye, assignee of Peter Bargy & Hugh Stewart: passed.

House of Reps: 1-Bill for the relief of the legal reps of Joshua Kennedy, deceased, & progress on the bill for the relief of Lyon & Howard:passed. House adjourned.

The remains of the Hon Chester Ashley, late Senator from Arkansas, in charge of Mr Isaac Holland, Assist Dock-keeper of the U S Senate, reached Little Rock, Ark, on the vessel Cotton Plant, on May 27. After the religious ceremonies, the corpse was followed by the family & relatives & a large concourse of citizens to Mount Holly Cemetery, where it was deposited in the family burial ground.

Thos Fitzgerald has been appointed Govn'r of Michigan to supply the vacancy in the U S Senate caused by the resignation of Gen Cass.

Letter from City of Queretaro, May 25, 1848: to Hon Jas Buchanan, Sec of State. We have reached this city, & the treaty, as amended by the U S Senate, passed the Mexican Senate about the hour of our arrival by a vote of 33 to 5. It had previously passed the House of Deputies. –A H Sevier, Nathan Clifford

Gtwn, Jun 13, 1848. Meeting to organize a Taylor Club, Mr Henry King was called to the chair. Mr J T Bangs moved that a cmte be appointed by the Chair to name the Club. Cmte appointed: Messrs Wright, Nicholson, Craig, Donnellan, & Bronaugh. Club shall be styled Gtwn Taylor Club, No 1. Elected:
For Pres: W H Edes
For Vice Pres: Hugh Caperton, Henry King, Bladen Forrest, O M Linthicum, Ths Jewell, Ezekiel Hughes, D Wm Sothoron, Jer Orme, A H Dodge, Walter S Cox, Wm McK Osborn & John Wilson.
For Recording Sec: John W Bronaugh
Assist Recording Secs: Wm H Tenney, Richd Jackson, & Henry King.
For Corresponding Cmte: J T Bangs, W D Blunt, C A Upperman, P Donellan, & Wm T Lang.
For Treasurer: Danl S Gordon
For Executive Cmte: Robt Ould, John Crockwell, Peter Berry, Geo M Sothoron, & Saml Cropley.

Among the passengers from Europe in the ship **America** at Boston are John Ridgley & family, & Mrs Isaac McKim, of Balt.

The nomination of Gen Zachary Taylor & Millard Fillmore was received with every demonstration of joy & enthusiasm by our neighbors in the State of Indiana.

Isaiah A Blakelee was killed at New Haven, Conn, on Wed by falling from a new church bldg. He went upon the church from motives of pure curiosity.

Henry Bancroft, an estimable young man, was accidentally shot at Chagrin, Ohio, on Fri last. He lingered but 12 hours.

Casualties: 1-Mrs Stevenson, wife of Jas Stevenson, of Lockport, fell from her chair a corpse on Sat last. She was sewing at the moment. She had recently been ill, but was supposed to have fully recovered. 2-Mrs Hickley, of Milwaukie, was in company with her husband, on Jun 6, on her way to an insane asylum. While left alone a moment she jumped from the steamboat & was drowned. 3-Chas Olds, a hand on the canal boat **Verona**, fell into the lock at West Troy, on Jun 9, & was drowned. He was 21 years of age, & a temperate young man. –Albany Journal

Died: on Fri, in Wash City, after a long & painful illness, Mrs Barbara Hoover, aged 78 years. She was one of the first settlers of Wash City.

Appointments by the Pres: 1-Colin M Ingersoll, of Conn, to be Sec of the Legation of the U S to Russia, in the place of John R Clay, appointed Charge d'Affaires for the U S to Peru. 2-H T A Rainals, to be U S Consul for the port of Elsinore, vice E L Rainals, resigned. 3-John Taylor, register of the Land Ofc at Defiance, [removed from Upper Sandusky,] Ohio, vice R McKelly, resigned. 4-Wm L Henderson, receiver of public moneys at Defiance, [removed from Upper Sandusky,] Ohio, vice Purdy McElvaine, deceased. 5-Joel S Fisk, register of the Land Ofc at Green Bay, Wisconsin, vice John F Mead, removed.

TUE JUN 20, 1848
Trustee's sale of houses & lots at auction: on Jul 5, on the premises, by deed of trust recorded Apr 19, 1847, in liber W B 133, folios 235 thru 237, of the land records of Wash Co, D C: lots 5 & 6 in square 583, with 2 two-story frame houses: located on the corner of south F & 3rd st west. Terms at sale. –Henry Naylor, Trustee -A Green, auctioneer

Senate: 1-Ptn from Chas Colburn asking payment of the full term of his enlistment in the U S Navy. 2-Ptn from the inhabitants of Rosendale, Wisconsin, remonstrating against granting land to Mr Whitney for the construction of a road from Lake Michigan to the Pacific Ocean. 3-Ptn from Capt Paynes, of a company of Florida volunteers, for pay. 4-Cmte of Indian Affairs: House bill for the relief of Jos Perry, a Choctaw Indian, or his assigns, without amendment. 5-Cmte of Claims: adverse reports on the House bills for the relief of Thos B Graham; & of Jas Porterfield's legal reps. 6-Cmte on the Judiciary: Senate bill for the relief of Gamaliel Taylor, late Marshal of the State of Indiana, & his sureties, with an amendment. 7-Cmte of Claims: House bill for the relief of Alborne Allen, without amendment.

Rev John Healy, pastor of the Second Baptist Church of Balt, died Jun 19, at the advanced age of 85 years.

House of Reps: 1-Communication from Capt Wm Ramsay, U S Navy, stating that in the proceedings of the house on June 13, he found that a ptn had been presented which reflected on his character, in relation to which he submitted a long statement: referred to the Cmte on Naval Affairs.

Loudoun Land for sale: in pursuance of the last will & testament of Chas Gassaway, deceased, the undersigned will offer for sale, at public auction, on Aug 3 next, a very valuable Farm in Loudoun Co, containing by survey 358 acres, 2 roods, & 11 poles; with a large & comfortable stone dwlg & all necessary out-bldgs. Sale on the premises.
–C B Gassaway, F W Luckett, excx & exc of Chas Gassaway, deceased.

Improved property at auction on Mon next, in front of the premises: lot 3 in square B, fronting on Missouri ave, between 4½ & 6th sts, with a valuable bldg thereon, occupied by Mrs Williams as a boarding house. Also, I shall sell lot 3 in square 453, with improvements, which are 2 brick houses. -R W Dyer, auct

Household & kitchen furniture at auction: on Jun 23, by order of the Orphans Court of Wash Co, D C: at the late residence of Mrs Ann Camlin, deceased, on 5th st.
-A Green, auctioneer

Mrd: on Jun 1, in Fayetteville, N C, by Rev Mr Gilchrist, Lt Chas P Kingsbury, of the Ordnance Dept U S Army, to Mis Mary Isabella, youngest daughter of the late John McMillan, of Fayetteville.

Died: on Jun 16, of cholera infantum, John C Rives, only son of Josiah & Harriet Goodrich, aged 11 months.

Notice is hereby given to the next of kin of Henry W Colbey, late Passed Midshipman in the U S Navy, who died at Vera Cruz, in Mexico, in Nov, 1847, to apply for letters of administration before the Orphans Court of Wash Co, D C within 3 weeks from this publication, otherwise the administration will be granted to a creditor of said Colbey.

The packet sloop **Ceres**, Capt Hickman, will leave for the Phil port on Jun 22. For freight apply on board, or to E Pickrell & Co, Water st, Gtwn.

Subscriber is always ready to furnish Picnics, Excursions, Balls, Weddings, & all parties of pleasure, with pure & excellent Ice creams, pound, fruit & every other kind of cake.
–L A Tarlton, 10th st, between E & F

Clarence for sale: that beautiful place known as the estate of Robt Leckie, deceased, more lately the property of A Fuller, deceased: will be sold at public auction on Jul 1: located on 23rd st: about 4 acres, a fine residence, 3 frame houses, out-houses, & ice-house. Inquire of M E Clark on the premises. -E H Fuller

WED JUN 21, 1848
Senate: 1-Memorial from Emily Maria Pinkney, infant daughter of Cmder Pinkney, who was drowned at Tuspan on May 15 last. The memorial in in the handwriting of Miss Pinkney, & set forth that she is 9 years old, & that her father was drowned in the execution of his duty; & that, having lost her mother, she is thereby cut off from the support which the law allows only to widows, & she asks that Congress will pass a special act for her relief. 2-Memorial from Margaret Deveal & Littleton Bailey, asking the confirmation of their titles to tracts of land. 3-Cmte of Claims: House bill for the relief of B O Tayloe & John H Baker, without amendment. Same cmte: unfavorable report on the ptn of Arnold Naudain. Same cmte: House bill for the relief of Mary B Renner, with a recommendation that it do not pass. 4-Cmte on Military Affairs: asking to be discharged from the further consideration of the ptn of Albert Pine. Same cmte: House bill for the relief of Dr A G Henry, of Ill, without amendment. 5-Cmte of Claims: House bills, without amendment: relief of Almedeus Scott; & of Elijah Bragdon's widow. Same cmte: with amendments: House bills for the relief of Saml A Greer; & of Eleanor B Watkins, widow of Gassaway Watkins.

House of Reps: 1-Cmte on Naval Affairs: Senate bills for the relief of Cmdor Foxall A Parker & for relief of Anna J Hassler: committed. 2-Cmte on revolutionary Pensions: bill for relief of Eunice Crossman: committed. Same cmte: adverse report on the ptn of Geo Bock: laid on the table. Same cmte: bill for relief of Polly Damrow & Eliz Kinney: committed. Same cmte: adverse reports on the ptns of Lucy Clark, Abigail Higbee, & Anna Oldhan: laid on the table. 3-Cmte on Revolutionary Pensions: discharged from the futher consideration of the ptns of Frances P Gardner, Frances Fowler, Catharine Freeman, Mary Martin, of Tenn, Hannah Lord, Jas Oldham, of Md, Valentine Miller, Jos Phelps, Sarah Hammond, Levi Nichols, & Thos Pritchard: laid on the table. Same cmte: bill for relief of Mary G Leverett: committed. Same cmte: adverse reports on the ptns of John Cripps, J L Fair & others, heirs of Jonathan Fair, Francis Ingraham, & Jos Cogswell: laid on the table. Same cmte: adverse reports on the ptns of Henrietta Moore & other widows of Revolutionary soldiers, praying for a continuance of their pensions during life, of the heirs of Robt McNeill & Catharine O'Neale: laid on the table. Same cmte: adverse reports on the ptns of Ada Smith, David Troxell, Wolcott Burham, the widow of Geo Hubbard, & of Asa Day: laid on the table. Same cmte: adverse reports on the ptns of Mary Stanton, Rhoda Drury, Ann O Wright, Sally Hart, & Susan Oglesby: laid on the table. Same cmte: Senate bill for relief of Eliz Pistole, widow of Chas Pistole, deceased: committed. 4-Cmte on Invalid Pensions: adverse report on the ptn of Stephen A Cory: laid on the table. Same cmte: discharged from the further consideration of the ptns of Jas Somers, Saml T Winslow, John Gordon, Mary Ann Fitch, Chester Parish, & Hugh G Smith: laid on the table. Same cmte: bills for relief of David Currier; Francis Trebon; Edw Cole; & Wm Whitcher: committed. Same cmte: adverse reports on the ptns of Solomon Street, Martha Flood, & March Farrington: laid on the table. Same cmte: discharged from the further consideration of the ptns of Wm Linville & others, Thos L Richardson, John Davenport, & David Ladd: laid on the table. Same cmte: bills to increase the pension of Henry Click, for relief of David Towle, for the relief of Geo S Claflin, for the relief of Henry Chiles, for relief of Wm Pittman, for relief of Catharine Clark, for relief of Jos D Ward, & for relief of Isaac Downs: all committed. Same cmte:

bills for relief of Giles London, for relief of Gardner Hening, & for relief of David Murphy: committed. Same cmte: discharged from the further consideration of the ptn of Jonathan M Young, Hugh W Dobbin, A A Whitlock, & others, in behalf of Saml House: laid on the table. Same cmte: adverse report on ptn of Russell Jefferson: laid on the table.

West Point Academy: annual examination of the Cadets of the U S Military Academy at West Point was brought to a close last Thu. On Fri there was an artillery target exercise, under the charge of Lt Clark, of Pa, late of Duncan's command in Mexico, The distance of the target was 1,360 feet, & the target was shattered 3 times in 20 discharges, while shell, thrown from a mortar, & calculated to explode at a great & definite distance, did so with wonderful accuracy. Names of Board of Visiters:

Mr Ashbel Smith, of Texas, Pres
Prof W C Larrabee, of Indiana
Hon Wm Prescott, of N H
Col C W Wilson, of Va
Col A W Doniphan, Missouri
Gen J McDaniels, Vt

Maj Patterson Lander, Ky
Col A H Redfield, Michigan
Dr J G M Ramsey, Tenn
Dr H Askew, Delaware
Hon Dutee J Pearce, R I
Col Robt Hamilton, N J

Invited but did not attend:
Col Gadsden, of S C
Gen Jas Yell, of Arkansas

Isaac N Morris, of Ill

Members of the Graduating Class:

Wm P Trowbridge	Geo H Paige	Nathl H McLean
Jas C Duane	Wm G Gill	Geo C Barker
Robt S Williamson	John Buford, jr	Ferdinand Paine
Walter H Stevens	Truman K Walbridge	Chas H Ogle
Andrew J Donelson	Richd I Dodge	Wm N R Beall
Jas M Haynes	Thos F M McLean	Wm T Mechling
Jos C Clark, jr	Thos S Rhett	Chas W Greene
Rufus A Roys	Robt M Russell	Hugh B Ewing
Nathl Michler, jr	Wm A Slaughter	Geo W Howland
John C Tidball	Grier Tallmadge	N Geo Evans
Wm E Jones	Chas H Tyler	Thos D Johns
Edw B Bryan	John C Booth	Danl Huston, jr
Benj D Forsythe	Thos K Jackson	Jas W D Lyon
Jas Holmes	A Galbraith Miller	Geo H Steuart, jr

Father Mathew. The friends of temperance will regret to hear that Mr Mathew has suffered a paralytic attack, which will probably compel him to abandon altogether his anticipated visit to this country.

Deaths from Clams: Mr John Nowland, of Marblehead, last week, & the death in Lynn on Sun last, of a Scotchman employed in the print-words there, named Wm Austin, aged about 30, who ate a few raw clams upon the borders of Saugus river on Sunday, expired in convulsions shortly after. –Salem Reg-Thu

Thos J McKain has been elected President of the Mineral Bank of Cumberland, vice C M Thurston, resigned.

Family reunion: the descendants of Mr Jacob Bradbury, of Pittsfield, Ill, says the Free Press, to be number of 85, recently assembled by appointment at the house of Saml Bradbury, the 2nd son. After an impressive discourse by Rev B B Carpenter, they repaired to a richly furnished table, 110 feet long, where they passed the afternoon in social chat. They all reside within 6 miles of the father's house, are all of them upright, correct, & honest men, &, of course, they are all, men, women, & children, staunch Whigs & Taylor men.

The Huntsville papers announce the death of Col Jas W McClung, a member of the State Senate of Alabama & one of the Democratic Electors for the State.

Mrs Thurston made a balloon ascension at Hemlock Lake, Livingston Co, N Y, on Jun 6, & went a distance of 42 miles in one hour.

Sale by order of the Orphans Court of Wash Co, D C of Bonnets, Laces, Ribands, Scarfs, & Caps at auction: on Jun 24, at the store lately occupied by Miss Ashwood, deceased, on Pa ave, between 9th & 10th sts, the entire stock of the deceased. –John Sessford, adm –A Green, auctioneer

Criminal Court-Wash: summoned to serve on the Grand Jury, viz:

Peter Force, Foreman	Hamilton Luftborough	Joshua Peirce
John Boyle	Henry Haw	Isaac Clarke
John Kurtz	John Pickrell	Judson Mitchell
John C Rives	Zachariah Walker	Chas R Belt
John Mason, jr	Wm Gunton	Saml Bacon
Thos Brown	Evan Lyons	Geo Parker
John P Heise	Robt S Patterson	

Mrd: on Jun 15, by Rev Mr Austen, Dr B Franklin Bohrer, formerly of D C, to Mary A, only daughter of the late Wm Owings, of Balt Co.

Died: Jun 20, after a protracted illness, Mrs Mary Wannall, wife of Mr Chas P Wannall, of Wash City. Her funeral is from the residence of her husband, tomorrow, at 4 o'clock.

Dwlg house & lot at public auction, by deed of trust from Jos Thaw, deceased, & in execution of the power confided to the subscriber: sale of the dwlg-house & grounds on N Y ave, in Wash City, in which the said Jos Thaw resided at the time of his death, adjoining the 2nd Presbyterian Church: the ground is lot 2 in square 251; the dwlg is a very handsome & commodious 2 story brick house. –D English, trustee

The partnership existing in the name of Isherwood & O'Neale, has this day expired by limitation. Payment of accounts to be made to Timothy O'Neale.
–Robt Isherwood, Timothy O'Neale

THU JUN 22, 1848

Valuable household & kitchen furniture & plate for sale at public auction: by order of the Orphans Court of Wash Co, D C. The whole of the personal effects of the late Capt J T McLaughlin: on Jun 29, at the house lately occupied by the late Capt McLaughlin, at the corner of F st west & 21st st. The household furniture is very beautiful. Also, a pew in St John 's Church. –A Green, auctioneer

Senate: 1-Ptn from Capt L Warrington, in behalf of himself, ofcrs & crew of the U S sloop-of-war **Peacock**, asking the payment of certain prize money due them & improperly retained in the Treasury. 2-Cmte on Revolutionary Claims: bill for the relief of the legal reps of Col Geo Gibson, accompanied by a report. 3-Cmte on the Judiciary: adverse report on the memorial of John B Luce. Same cmte: bill for the relief of Jas Chapman, adm of Thos Chapman. 4-Cmte on Pensions: House bills without amendment, & recommending their passage: acts for the relief of Eliphas C Brown; of Jas Fugate; of John Hilbert; of Lewis Hastings; & of Saml Gray. 5-Bill for the relief of Wm A Slacum: passed.

For sale: a young family horse, of good action, very free & gentle, & perfectly broke; also, a one-horse Carriage & Harness, nearly new, will be sold a bargain if applied for soon. –D A Gardner, 14th st, between H & I sts, Washington.

Teacher wanted: the Trustees of Primary School #1, in Marlborough district, P G Co, Md, wish to employ a teacher. Letters may be addressed to either of the Trustees, post paid, Long Old Fields. –Allen P Bowie, Benj Berry, Correl Brooks, Trustees

Valuable farm for sale: by the Trustees of the estate of Wm C Walton, deceased: farm known as **Bethany**, 7 miles south of Charlestown, Jefferson Co, Va, joining the farms of H L Opie & Mrs Lewis, lying on the west bank of the Shenandoah river: good brick dwlg house & out-bldgs: 280 acres of cleared land, & 147 well-timbered. Application may be made to Mr Robt Jamieson, of Alexandria, Va, & to John T Hargrave, Shepherdstown, Jefferson Co, Va, Trustees.

Virginia House, Staunton, Va: our Hotel is the terminating point of stage lines coming from the four quarters of the compass. –Wm H Garber, M G Harman, proprietors

Mrd: on Jun 19, by Rev Mr Wilson, Jenkin Thomas to Ann E Barrett, all of Gtwn.

Mrd: on Jun 20, at **Mount Oak**, PG Co, Md, by Rev Mr Kepplar, Wm A Gunton to Mary R, daughter of John B Mullikin.

Died: on Jun 15, Miss Loretto Gallaher, in her 24th year.

Died: on Tue, Lydia Isadore Lord, eldest daughter of Wm & Eliz Lord, aged 6 years & 3 months. Her funeral is this afternoon, at 5 o'clock, from the residence of her father, corner of 5th & G sts.

Died: on Tue last, Mrs Sarah A Sessford, wife of Mr Jos Sessford, of Wash City. Her funeral is this afternoon at 3 o'clock, from the residence of her husband, on C, between 11th & 12th sts.

To The Public: I have this day withdrawn from all connexion with the Nat'l Whig newspaper. —W G Snethen, 8 Missouri ave

FRI JUN 23, 1848
Senate: 1-Memorial from Jas W Day, messenger to the Pres of the U S, asking extra compensation. 2-Cmte of Claims: act for the relief of Danl Robinson, without amendment. 2-Bills referred: relief of David N Smith; & granting a pension to John Clark. Also, a bill to provide compensation to Wm Woodbridge & Henry Chipman. Bill for the relief of the heirs of Jean F Perry, Josiah Bleakley, Nicholas Jarrot, & Robt Morrison. Bill for the relief of Jas F Sothoron; & of J E Nye, assignee of P Bargy & H Stewart.

Capt Edw Deas, a highly meritorious ofcr, who was recently, by court-martial, sentenced to be dismissed the army, has been ordered back to his regt, the President restoring him to his rank & position, by the advice & consent of the Senate. -Union

House of Reps: 1-Ptn of John Cassedy, praying compensation for services.

The ship **America**, arrived at New Orleans from Vera Cruz, brought a detachment of 452 sick soldiers from the general hospital at Jalapa, Capt F N Page, A A G, commanding; Surgeon P H Craig, U S A; Assist Surgeon J Simpson, U S A; Acting Assist Surgeons L C Kinney, J A McBrayar, F M Ringgold, & B F Mullen. Passengers: Brevet Maj R S Garnett, A D C; Capt J Banks Anthony, 12th Infty; Lt F Moon, 10th Infty; Lt J S Kingsland, Michigan volunteers; & Lt McCawley, Marine Corps.

The immense estate of M d'Aligre, who died last year in France, was still unsettled when the revolution of February broke out. This estate was inventoried at 53,000,000 francs, but it was incumbered with legacies & gifts to the sum of 15,000,000 francs.

Obit: Thos Snowden, who for nearly 20 years has been the Cashier of this establishment, died yesterday. He was formerly the proprietor of the Nat'l Advocate, & was universally & highly esteemed. In all the relations of life, as father, husband, brother, & friend, he was all that could be desired.

Mrd: on Wed, at the U S Hotel, in Wash City, by Rev John C Smith, Wm R Brown to Miss Mary M Moore.

Mrd: on Jun 21, by Rev Mr Evans, Mr Wm H Thomas, of Alexandria, Va, to Kate L, 2nd daughter of Levi Pumphrey, of Wash.

Mrd: on Jun 13, at Olney, Accomac Co, Va, by Rev Mr Jones, Dr Alex'r Y P Garnett, U S Navy, to Miss Mary E, daughter of Hon Henry A Wise.

Died: on Jun 19, in Portsmouth, Va, after a long & afflicting illness, Griffith B Grant, formerly of Wash City, aged 31 years, leaving a widow & 2 small children, with a large circle of friends, to lament his loss.

Died: on Wed last, in Wash City, Laura May, daughter of Wm & Mary M M Towers, aged 5 years. Her funeral is this morning at 10 o'clock.

SAT JUN 24, 1848
House of Reps: 1-Cmte of Claims: bill for the benefit of the legal reps of Jas C Watson, of Georgia: committed to the Cmte of the Whole. Same cmte: Bill for the relief of John F Ohl: committed. Same cmte: bills for the relief of Thos L Judge & for the relief of Satterlee Clarke: committed. Same cmte: adverse report on the ptn of Wm Armstrong: laid on the table. 2-Senate bill for the relief of Jose Argote Villalobos, Marie Rose, Frances Felix, Marqis de Fongeres, or their heirs of legal reps, was referred to the Cmte of Claims. 3-Cmte of Commerce: bill for the relief of Lewis H Bates & Wm Lacon: committed. Same cmte: bill for the relief of Wm Milford: committed. Same cmte: bill to authorize the issuing of a register to the schnr **James**: passed & sent to the Senate for concurrence. 4-Bill to incorporate the **Wash Gas Light Co**, with an amendment: passed. 5-Bills for the relief of Dr Adolphus Wislizenus, for the relief of Wm Parker, & for the relief of Joshua Barney, U S agent: were passed. 6-Bill for the relief of the personal reps of Wm A Slacum: referred.

The U S steamship **Portland** arrived at New Orleans on Jun 15, & brought over about 350 of the 13th Infty, with some convalescents & discharged teamsters. Remainder of that regt had embarked on the ship **Rhode Island**, & was ready for sea when the **Portland** left. The following ofcrs also returned on the **Portland**: Lt Gardner, bearer of dispatches from Mexico & of the ratified treaty; Col Bankhead, 2nd Artl; Lt Bankhead, U S Navy; Maj Manegault, Adj J C Monaghan, Quartermaster J R Page; Capts H L Clay & H H Higgins, 13th Infty; Capt Barnard & Lee, Lts Beauregard, E J Dammett, D G Wilds, S H Crumps & W F Reeves, Engineers; Capts E J Jones, H C W Clark, Lts R S Hayward, J C Marrast, J N Perkins, S S Fahnestick, E F Bagley, J M Ingle, G Simmons, J McBride, J W Smith, Reynolds, Vandorme, Curtiss, Dr Banks, Dr Vander Linden & family; Mr A S Forbes, with the bodies of Lt Col Baxter, Capts Pierson, Van Olinde & Barclay, Lts Chandler & Gallagher-all of the N Y Regt. Died at sea, Lt Bedford, [*or Bradford,] 14th Infty; Private H L Hancock, 13th Infty. *Copied as written. [Jul 17th newspaper: on Jul 16, Mr Forbes & 5 of the ofcrs of the N Y Regt, who fell in battle or died of wounds in Mexico, were removed to Greenwood Cemetery, where a lot has been set apart for their interment. A large procession & the bells of the Church were toiled, & minute guns were fired. There were probably in & around the Park 40,000 to 50,000 people. Eight pallbearers attending each hearse: Alex's S Forbes, Lt Col Chas Baxter, Capt Jas Barclay, Capt Chas H Pearson, Lt Chas F Gallagher, & Lt Edgar Chandler. Each hearse, as it passed by, bore on both sides the name of the deceased in large & distinct letters.]

The subscriber notifies his customers that bills will be made out up to Jul 1.
–P J Steer

Lt Washington A Bartlett, U S Navy, presented 2 bulbs of the Amole, or soap plant, of Calif, to the Farmers' Club of N Y at a late meeting. The bulbs are used for washing clothing in cold running water. The women cut off the roots of the bulbs & rub them on the clothes, & a rich & strong lather is formed, which cleanses most thoroughly. To propagate the plant the bulbs are set in a moist rich soil, & grow most luxuriantly in the soft bottoms of valleys on streams.

Senate: 1-Cmte of Claims: House bill for the relief of John P B Gratiot & the legal reps of Henry Gratiot. Same cmte: House bills without amendment: relief of Chas Ahrenfeldt & John F H Vogt; also, for the relief of the legal reps of Capt Geo Shoemaker. Same cmte: relief of the legal reps of David Gardner, of Southborough, Mass. 2-Cmte on Indian Affairs: bill to compensate R M Johnson for the erection of certain bldgs for the use of the Choctaw Academy.

Mrd: on Jun 22, by Rev Wm H Pitcher, Mr Wm Warder to Miss Cornelia M Sheriff, all of Wash City.

Died: yesterday, of scarlet fever, George Anna Virginia, in her 5th year, a twin dght of Jas & Sophia Davis. Her funeral is this morning at 10 o'clock, from the residence of her parents, near the corner of 6th st south & Pa ave west.

Died: yesterday, after a few hours' illness, Cornelius, son of Jeremiah & Mary Dacy, in his 4th year. His funeral is this afternoon at 3 o'clock, from the residence of the parents, corner of I & 4th sts

MON JUN 26, 1848
Senate: 1-Report on the claims of Father Mediore in relation to certain church lands at St Augustine, Florida. 2-Cmte on Pensions: adverse report on the memorials of Levi Wells, praying arrears of pension, & of Mary Francis Foot. 3-Bill for the relief of Geo Center: engrossed. 4-Bills passed-relief of: Russel Goss; Barclay & Livingston, & Smith, Thurgar & Co. Relief of Chas Richmond; of Wm B Stokes; of Saml Grice; of Geo V Mitchell; of Stalker & Hill; of H B Gaither; of Alfred White; of Benj Adams & Co & others. 5-Bills passed: pension to Bethia Healy, widow of Geo Healy, deceased. Bill to confirm to the legal reps of Jos Dutaille the location of a certain New Madrid certificate. Act to change the name of the steamboat **Charles Downing** to the steamboat **Calhoun**. 6-Bill for the relief of Fred'k Dawson, Jas Schott, & Elisha Dana Whitney was discussed at very considerable length, & its further consideration postponed. 7-Mr Dix moved to reconsider the vote by which the bill for the relief of Geo Center was lost. Senate adjourned.

House of Reps: 1-Ptn of E R Utter & others, citizens of Wisconsin, for the purchase of **Mount Vernon**. 2-Ptn of Mary Ann Ballan, widow of John Ballan, a soldier in the war of 1812-13, & who died from injuries received in the service.

Appointments by the Pres: 1-Isaac Toucey, of Conn, to be Atty Gen of the U S vice Nathan Clifford, resigned. 2-Stephen K Stanton, of N Y, to be Sec of the U S Legation to the French Republic, vice J L Martin, appointed Charge d'Affaires to the Papal State. 3-Robt Wallace, to be U S Marshal for D C, vice Alex'r Hunter, resigned. 4-Robt P Dunlap, Collector, Portland, Maine, vice John Anderson, whose commission expired. 5-Chas D Learned, Deputy Collector at Ship Island, Miss, new ofc. 6-Benett W Engle, Receiver of public moneys at Crawfordsville, Indiana, vice Philip E Engle, deceased.

Mr Edw Bromfield Phillips, a graduate at Harvard Univ in the class of 1845, 23 years of age, shot himself, in his room at the water-cure establishment at Battleborough, Vt, on Tue last. He was the son of the late Edw Phillips, of Boston, & had recently come into possession of property estimated at upwards of half a million of dollars. An affair of the heart is said to have been the cause of the act. [Jun 28th newspaper: Edw B Phillips bequeathed to Harvard Univ, for the purposes of the Cambridge Obseratory, the munificent sum of $100,000. He left property to the value of $900,000.]

The U S ship **Erie**, Lt Commanding Jas M Watson, arrived at N Y on Sat, in 48 days from Rio Janeiro. The **Erie** sailed from the U S on Jul 8, 1845, for the Pacific. The remains of the lamented Cmdor Alex'r J Dallas, who died on board the frig **Savannah**, in the harbor of Callao, Peru, on Jun 4, 1844, are on board the **Erie**. She also brings home 55 invalid men from the Pacific & Brazil squadrons. Lt Commanding Watson has in charge for the Gov't at Washington a treaty with Peru. Left at Rio the frig **Brandywine**, sloop **Plymouth**, & steamer **Alleghany**; the **Plymouth** to sail in a few days for the Cape of Good Hope. Following is a list of the ofcrs of the **Erie**: Lt Commanding Jas M Watson; Acting Lt John Rutledge; Purser, Chas Murray; Assist Surgeon, Edw Hudson; Acting Master, Chas W Hays; Midshipmen, Chas S Bell, Andrew W Johnson, Alex M De Bres, Robt R Carter; Capt's clerk, John H Poor, jr. Passengers: Capt Thos Crabre, frig **Brandywine**, Brazil station; Cmder Wm F Shields, sloop, Pacific station; Passed Mid J S Bohrer, sloop **Plymouth**, Brazil station; Capt's clerk, J M Wilder, frig **Brandywine**, Brazil station; Capt's Clerk, Eugene Lies, sloop **Preble**, Pacific station; Purser's Clerk, Chas Waterman, frig **Independence**, Pacific station; Acting Gunner, Danl Douglass, sloop **Cyane**; sailmaker, David Park, & Acting Boatswain, John J Young, from Brazil station, -Com Adv

Capt Judkins, of the steam-packet **America**, on leaving Liverpool for the U S on Apr 15, ordered his dinner to be ready at his hotel, on his returning from America, at 6 o'clock on May 22, & was there within 5 minutes of the time.

Recent death in England: Mrs Anderson, once known as the beautiful Josephine Bartolozzi, died on Jun 1 of consumption, at age 41 years.

The trial of Wm B Averett, late teller of the Branch Bank of Va in Lynchburg, on an indictment for embezzlement, was terminated on Tue last by a verdict of acquittal.

Liberal for return of strayed cow: E Wheeler, on south side Pa ave, between 6th & 7th sts: Hardware Store.

Orphans Court of the State of Delaware for Newcastle Co, of Feb Term, A D 1848. Upon the application of Isaac Ford, one of the heirs at law of Wm Ford, late of Christiana Hundred, in said county, deceased, who died intestate, as it has been represented to this Court by the ptn of the said Isaac Ford, in writing, it is, Feb 23, 1848, ruled that the other heirs at law of said deceased, to wit: Ann Conaway, Isaac Ford, Wm Ford, & Eliz Betts, children of Saml Ford, deceased, who was a brother of the said intestate: Julia Ann Ford, daughter of Abraham Ford, deceased, who was a son of said Saml Ford, deceased, who was a brother of the said intestate; Henry Armstrong, Saml Armstrong, Amanda Armstrong, & Chas Armstrong, children of Ann Armstrong, deceased, who was a daughter of the said Saml Ford, deceased, who was a brother of said intestate; Milner Ford, Enoch Ford, Benj Ford, Lydia Thatcher, Hannah Hill, Sarah Devou, Martha Gyer, Eliz Daily, & Mary Ann Backster, children of Benj Ford, deceased, who was a brother of the said intestate; & Wm S Ford, a son of Wm Ford, deceased, who was a son of the said Benj Ford, deceased, who was a brother of the said intestate; Abraham Smith, Eliz Miller, & Mary Rice, children of Eliz Smith, deceased, who was a sister of the said intestate; Wm F Husbands & Abraham Husbands, sons of Mary Husbands, deceased, who was a sister of the said intestate; & Wm R Husbands, a son of Mary Husbands, who was a dght of the said Mary Husbands, deceased, who was a sister of the said intestate, be & appear at an Orphans' Court of Newcastle Co aforesaid, on Sep 4 next, & then & there claim the preference due to them of accepting or choosing as they are successively entitled so to do the lands, tenements, & hereditaments of the said deceased as returned, surveyed, valued, & appraised under an order of the said Court heretofore made, to wit: 1-Farm in Christiana Hundred, on north side of the Kennett turnpike road, bounded by the said road, by a road leading from the turnpike road to Jos Bancroft's factory, & by the lands of said Jos Bancroft, Isaac Ford, & Mary Lovering, containing 62 acres or land, more or less, with a 2 story dwlg house, stone barn, & other improvements. 2-A lot of land in Christiana Hundred, bounded by the Kennett turnpike, by Gardner's Lane, & by the lands of Thomas & Philip McDowell, containing 6 acres of land, more or less, with a 2 story stone dwlg house & other improvements. 3-House & lot in the city of Wilmington on Ninta st, between Shipley & Orange sts, bounded by the lands of the late Jas Miller, Saml Wollaston, & others, with a 2 story frame dwlg house. 4-House & lot in city aforesaid, fronting on 10th st, between Shipley & Orange sts, bounded by lands of Nelson Cleland & Wm Murphy & lot 3, the improvements a stone dwlg house. 5-Lot of piece of marsh, in Brandywine Hundred, in Cherry Island marsh, bounded by the river Delaware & the Christiana river, & by lands of Wm Welden, John Thompson, & others, containing 20 acres of land, more or less, valued in the whole to the sum of $9,725.10; or show cause if any they have, why an order shall not be made for the sale of the said lands, tenements, & hereditaments of the said Wm Ford, deceased. –H H Thompson, Clerk of Orphans' Court of Newcastle Co, Delaware

Died: yesterday, after a protracted illness, Mrs Margaret Garet Hodgson, in her 55th year. Her funeral is from her late residence on 6th st, between G & H sts, this afternoon, at 4 o'clock.

Died: on Jun 10, at his residence in Buffalo township, Armstrong Co, Pa, after an illness of 2 weeks, Walter Monto Shelton, in his 44th year.

For rent: commodious house on the north side of Pa ave, between 3rd & 4th sts. –John Sinon

TUE JUN 27, 1848
Boots! Just received another lot of those fine Boots of McCauley's make, at prices from $3 to $6 per pair. Direct from the importer, French calf-skins, glazed & plain, which have been so much admired. –John Mills, 6th st, under Coleman's Hotel.

Books at auction: on Jun 28 & 29, by order of the Orphans Court of Wash Co, D C, the very valuable miscellaneous & Scientific private Library of the late Dr Thos P Jones, former Superintendent of the U S Patent Ofc. –W M Morrison, auctioneer

Superior household & kitchen furniture at auction: on Jun 30, at the residence of N P Trust, on F st, between 13th & 14th sts. -R W Dyer, auct

Mayor's Ofc: On Jul 3 I shall expose for sale, to the highest bidder all the Vegetable Stalls not previously sold & paid for in the Centre Market-house, for one year. Sale on Jul 5, of the Vegetable Stalls in the West Market-house; & on Jul 7, the Vegetable Stalls in the eastern Branch Market-house. -W W Seaton, Mayor -A Green, auctioneer

For rent: the very large & convenient house & premises on F, between 13th & 14th sts, occupied by me as a boarding-house for many years. Also for rent, the large adjoining house, now occupied by N P Trist. Apply at the house of Anna Cochran.

Senate: 1-Memorial from John T Sullivan, asking compensation for binding the laws & instructions of the Postmaster Genr'l for the use of the Dept. 2-Cmte on Private Land Claims: bill for the relief of Robt W Richardson, accompanied by a report. 3-Act passed for the relief of Wm Lawson. 4-Act passed for the relief of Edward Hickman, wife of Alex'r D Peck. [*wife of as written.]

Balt, Jun 26. Announcement of the death of Hon Stevenson Archer, Chief Judge of the High Court of Appeals of Md. He died this morning at his residence at Rock Run, in Harford Co, after an illness of about 2 weeks, having been first attacked with a bilious fever. The County Court room was filled by the members of the bar, drawn there by the melancholy tidings. Geo R Richardson, Atty Gen, announced the death of the distinguished jurist. The Court immediately adjourned.

Died: May 14th, at his residence, Woodville, Rappahannock Co, Va, in his 75th year, Zephaniah Turner, sen. He was extensively connected in business relations with the community in which he lived throughout almost his entire career, having served his county acceptably in the Legistrature of the State, & as a magistrate almost half a century. He has left a large family & a wide circle of friends to mourn his loss.

WED JUN 28, 1848
Laws of the U S, passed by the First Session 30th Congress. Act to provide for the purchase of the manuscript papers of the late Jas Madison, former Pres of the U S. That be sum of $25,000 be appropriated, out of any money in the Treasury not otherwise appropriated, to purchase of Mrs D P Madison, widow of the late Jas Madison, all the unpublished manscript papers of said Jas Madison now belonging to & in her possession. She shall be paid: $5,000 of the sum of $25,000, & the residue of $20,000 to Jas Buchanan, now Sec of State, John Y Mason, Sec of the Navy, & Richd Smith, of Wash City, to be held, put out to interest, vested in stocks, or otherwise managed or disposed of by them, or the survivor or survivors of them, as trustees for the said Mrs Madison, according to their best discretion & her best advantage, the interest or profit arising from the said principal sum to be paid over to her as the same accrues-the said principal sum to be & remain inalienable during her lifetime, as a permanent fund for her maintenance, but subject to be disposed of as she may please by her last will & testament.

Died: on Jun 27, Anthony Preston, aged 6 months & 14 days, only son of Jas M & Annie McKnight. His funeral is this afternoon at half past 4 o'clock, from the residence of Mrs Preston on 12th st.

Died: on Jun 18, at Vergennes, Vt, Wm Edmond.

Died: on Mar 18 last, at Manilla, in his 37th year, after an illness of only 6 days, Josiah Moore, U S Consul for the Philippine Islands.

House of Reps: 1-Leave was granted for the withdrawal from the files of the House of the ptn & papers of Enoch Baldwin; & the papers in the case of Saml Royer. 3-Ptn of Henry Bears: presented. 4-Ptn of Leoanrd Woods & 61 others, ofcrs & students of the Theological Seminary of Andover, Mass, praying that ordinary letter postage be reduced to two cents, & that the franking privilege now enjoyed by members of Congress be commuted for an increase of pecuniary compensation. 5-Ptn of Horatio Fitch, praying to have certain arrearages of pension which have been withheld from him paid over. 6-Ptn & papers of Wyott Eppes, asking the payment of a bill of cost allowed by the Dist Judge of the U S for the State of Miss. 7-Four memorials of the Hon Wm Cranch, Chas Wilkes, Jos H Bradley, & many other citizens of Wash, asking an appropriation to remove nuisances from the public grounds in Wash City. 8-Memorial of Wm Y Hansell, Wm H Underwood, & the reps of Saml Stockwell, deceased, attys & counselors for the Cherokee nation, praying that Congress do make provision, by law, for the early payment of their respective claims, according to the amounts awarded by the referees; which award was made under the authority of the U S Gov't.

Died: on May 28, at Norwalk, Ohio, after a lingering illness, Mrs Eleanor Thompson, widow of the late Hon John Thompson, formerly member of Congress from the State of N Y. Mrs Thompson was for many years prior to her late marriage a resident of Gtwn, D C, where she has left many friends & relatives.

Senate: 1-Memorial from Miss D S Dix, asking relief & support of the indigent insane in the several States of the Union.

$25 reward for runaway negro man Tom Shorter, about 26 years of age. Said slave has a wife now living on the estate of Mrs Jos Pearson, near Wash. –Edw Fenwick, near Wash [Jul 19th newspaper: $50 reward for runaway negro man Tom Shorter.]

For sale at the agency for the sale of <u>Goodyear's Rubber Goods</u>, between 4½ & 6th sts, Pa ave, Air Beds, Pillows, Cushions, Life Preservers, Parlor Balls, Baby Jumpers, Shower-bath Hose, & a great variety of other articles. –S Eddy

THU JUN 29, 1848
Wash Corp: 1-Ptn of Ulysses Ward & others: referred to the Cmte on Improvements. 2-Ptn from J E Thompson: referred to the Cmte on Schools. 3-Ptn of Robt B Clokey; Chas Shadd; & P Twomy; praying remission of fines: referred to the Cmte of Claims. 6-Resolved that the order of J L Henshaw upon the Register in favor of John France for 1 year's rent of the lot adjoinig the school-house in the 2nd Ward be referred to the Cmte of Ways & Means, to make provision for the payment of the same. 7-Ptn of Geo K Plant & others, for paving the alley in square 378: referred to the Cmte on Improvements.

On Sat last, Mr John Latts, Deputy Marshal, with a company of men, surprised the notorious outlaw Matt Gerring at the house of Ellis Starr, near Evansville. Gerring attempted to escape, when he was fired upon & killed. Eleven balls entered his body. On Sunday a party of about 60 Indians came upon Big Neck Ellis Starr, at the house of Dr Sloane, & killed him. On the evening of the same day the same company killed Wash Starr, & they are in pursuit of others of the same gang. These were all notorious outlaws & were refugees from the laws of Arkansas & the Cherokee Nation. Gerring was a white man, the Starrs were mixed blood Cherokee. The notorious Tom Starr is still at large. –Arkansas Intell of the 10th.

Senate: 1-Cmte of Claims: bill for the relief of Geo Poindexter. 2-Cmte on Pensions: House bill for the relief of Jonathan Slyter, & for the relief of Wm Parker. 3-Cmte on Pensions: adverse report on the memorial of Isaac Davenport. 4-Act for the relief of Wm Fitzwater: passed.

First arrival of troops from Mexico at New Orleans took place on Jun 16, in the ship **Russia**, from Vera Cruz. She anchored off Slaughter-house Point, below the city, with the following companies on board: Lr C R Perry, 4th Infty, commanding the detachment; Co A, 7th Infty, 92 men, with Lt J D Potter, 3rd Dragoons, & Lt J Neilly, 5th Infty; Co M, 4th Artl, 89 men, Lt E Murray, 2nd Infty, commanding, & Lt E Cook, N Y Volunteers, attached; Co G, 2nd Artl, 90 men, Lt J H Carlisle, 2nd Artl, commanding, & Lts E Underwood & J B Collins, 4th Infty, attached; Co C, 2nd Artl, 90 men, Lt R Hopkins, 9th Infty, commanding, & Lt R M Floyd, N Y Volunteers, attached.

The Mayor advises the Councils that he had this day appointed Chas B Cluskey to be Surveyor of Wash City, to supply temporarily the vacancy occasioned by the resignation of Randolph Coyle. The Mayor made the following nominations:

Jos Radcliff, for First Clerk Jos H Bradley, for Atty
Wm E Howard, for 2nd Clerk Jacob Kleiber, for Messenger
Chas A Davis, Jos Marshall, & Theodore Wheeler, for Com'rs of the Wash Asylum.
Benj E Gittings, for Intendant of the Asylum
Alex McWilliams, for Physician of the Asylum
Isaac Milstead, Inspector of Tobacco
Wm M McCauley, Sealer of Weights & Measures
Jacob Kleiber, Inspector of Flour & Provisions
Jas A Tait, Com'r Western Section of the Canal
Jos Cross, Com'r Eastern Section of the Canal
Caleb Buckingham, Inspector of Fire Apparatus

City Com'rs:
Geo W Harkness	F B Lord	John Magar
John Sessford	W A Mulloy	
C P Wannall	Ignatius Howe	

Police Constables:
F P Poston	J F Wollard	W A Mulloy
John Dewdney	E G Handy	Hanson Brown
John Waters	R R Burr	Ignatius Howe
O E P Hazard	J M Wright	John Magar

Com'r of the Centre Market:
Ignatius Mudd	Wm Orme	John H Goddard

Clerks of Markets:
Wm Serrin, West Market Peter Little, Eastern Market
John Waters, Centre Market Wm B Wilson, Northern Market
H B Robertson, Assist Clerk

Inspectors & Measurers of Lumber:
Wm G Deale	Benj Bean	John G Robinson
John W Ferguson	Wm Douglass	

Wood Corders & Coal Measurers:
Jas Gaither	Nathl Plant	John B Ferguson
Saml Kilman	Rich Wimsatt	John P Hilton

Gaugers & Inspectors:
Elixius Simms	Florian Hitz	

Measurers of Bran, & Shorts:
Jas Gaither	John B Ferguson	

Com'rs of West Burial Ground
Wm Wilson	John Wilson	John C Harkness

Sexton: Guy Graham

Com'rs of East Burial Ground:
John P Ingle	Jas Marshall	

Sexton: Thos J Barrett

Superintendents of Chimney Sweeps:
John Lewis	Roger Maffit	N B Wilkerson
Geo B Bowen	Jas Littleton	Isaac Stoddard

Scavengers:
G T McGlue	Jas Hollidge	John Cox
Luke Richardson	Saml Carson	Geo Evans
Jas Hollidge	Thos Greeves	
Wm Johnson	Jas Spurling	

To supply vacancies in the Board of Health:
Dr Richmond Johnson, vice Dr Magruder, who has forfeited his membership.
Dr Wm H Saunders, vice Dr May, who declines.
Dr A W Miller, to fill the existing vacancy.
W B Randolph, vice J W Jones, resigned
The Chair announced the appointment of the following standing cmtes, viz:
Of Claims: Messrs Orme, Clarke, & Drury
On Unfinished Business: Messrs Clarke & Scott
Of Improvements: Messrs Wilson, Towers, & Byington
Of Elections: Messrs Franklin, Adams, & Scott
Of Schools: Messrs Mudd, Wilson, & French
On Police: Messrs Towers, Drury, & Thornley
On Finance: Messrs Maury, Adams, & Byington
On the Canal: Messrs Franklin & Clarke
On Wharves: Messrs Thornley & Mudd
On Enrolled Bills: Mr Adams
On Money Transactions: Mr Orme
On the Accounts of the Register: Mr Maury
On the Asylum: Messrs Towers, Thornley, & Mudd

Laying of the cornerstone of the Washington Monument on Jul 4, 1848. Procession to form on D st, fronting to the north; other divisions will be arranged as to bring them all into column of march at the intersection of 5th st west & D st north. The line of march will be from D st, by 3rd st, to Pa ave, thence with the avenue to 14th st west; thence by 14th st to Monument square. The Masonic Order is charged with laying the corner-stone. Hymn, "With one consent let all the earth," to be sung by the whole concourse to "Old Hundred." For present the military will report to the Marshal. The firemen to Mr Geo S Gideon; the Masons to Mr B B French; the Odd Fellows to Mr W F Bayly; the Red Men to Mr C W Boteler, jr; the Rechabites to Mr Chas E Ball; the Sons of Temperance & Freemen's Vigilant Total Abstinence Asosictation to Mr A F Cunningham; the Wash Benevolent Society to Mr A J Joyce; the German Benevolent Society to Mr A Keese; all others to the Marshal.

FRI JUN 30, 1848
Senate: 1-Cmte of Claims: Joint resolution for the relief of Richd Field.

House of Reps: 1-Clerk of the House to pay to the administrator of Col Yell any money found to be due him for pay or mileage as a member of the 29th Congress.

Washington National Monument Ofc: Mr John Pettibone to permit any suitable person to erect a platform or platforms on the monument ground for the accommodation of ladies & gentlemen. Mr Joel Downer erected the platforms. –R Mills Architect -Jas Dixon [Tickets 25 cents.]

House of Reps: 1-Bill to vest the title of the U S in the purchasers of certain lands sold under execution against Gordon D Boyd: referred. 2-Bills referred-relief of: Alfred White; Stalker & Hill; Geo V Mitchell; Saml Grice; Wm B Stokes; Benj Adams & Co & others; & H B Gaither. Granting a pension to Bethiah Healy, widow of Geo Healy, deceased. Payment to Chas Richmond; confirm to the legal reps of Jos Dutaillis the location of a certain New Madrid certificate. 3-Concurrent resolution of the Senate for placing in the Library of Congress the portrait of Maj Gen Baron de Kalb, presented by his surviving family, was agreed to. 4-Memorial of the heirs of Col Seth Warner, for relief for Revolutionary services. 5-Ptn of John Frazer, for compensation for services in the erection of the N Y custom-house. 6-Ptn of Robt Morrison, a soldier in the first regt of heavy artl, U S Army, under Gen Brown, during the late war with Great Britain, praying for relief. 7-Memorial of Wm Brent, Danl Carroll, of Duddington, John S Mechan, & other citizens of Washington, asking an appropriation to remove nuisances from the public grounds.

Dr Owen D Leib, of Columbia Co, Pa, a member of the last Congress, but defeated for the present by the Hon Chester Butler, died at Catawissa on Sat week. His health had been declining ever since his return from Washington.

Hosea Hildreth Smith, convicted about 15 months ago at our Criminal Court of the crime of forgery, & sentenced to 8 years confinement in the penitentiary, was yesterday pardoned by the Pres & released from imprisonment.

For rent: desirable residence next to Mr Eberbach, on 8th st. Inquire of G C Grammer.

Mrd: on Jun 27, in Gtwn, D C, by Rev Mr Slicer, Jerome F Sanner to Miss Eliz Virginia Graham.

Died: on Jun 29, in Wash City, after an illness of 4 days, Robt W Dyer, in his 30th year, leaving a wife & 2 small children, with a large circle of friends, to mourn their premature bereavement. His funeral will take place from the residence of Mr John F Boone, near the Gen P O, tomorrow, at 11 o'clock.

Died: on Apr 11 last, suddenly, on board the U S brig **Porpoise**, off St Geo de Elmina, west coast of Africa, Passed Midshipman Fred'k P Wheelock, U S Navy.

Died: on Jun 15, at the residence of Col Tennille, Randolph Co, Georgia, after a severe illness of a few days, & in his 23rd year, Thos H Emory, of Wash City, son of Gideon & Caroline M Emory.

Died: on Jun 26, in his 42nd year, Capt Wm H Taylor, of Newark, N J, formerly of Newbern, N C, inventor of the sub-marine armor.

Died: on Jun 11, in Eliz City, N C, Ann D Shepard, wife of the Hon Wm B Shepard, & daughter of the late __siah Collins.

Died: on Jun 23, Jos Simms, only child of Walter M & Maria Amanda Clarke, aged 3 months & 17 days.

Complete Farrier & Horse Doctor: in the stable or on the road, with advise to purchasers. –R Farnham.

For rent: 2 story house on N Y ave, having extensive grounds. –John H Saunders, ofc La ave & 4½ st.

SAT JUL 1, 1848
Appointed Marshals for Jul 4th laying of the Washington Nat'l Monument cornerstone.

W D Addison	Z D Gilman	Wm Porter
Wm Barker	B Green	John R Queen
C W Boteler	Edw Hall	R Ray
A O Bowen	John A Hunnicutt	Col T J Robinson
D C Boyle	H N Henning	Frank Riley
P H Brooks	Saml Hanson	Jas Scott
Jno D Brown	A Harvey	D W Saunders
Wm Brown	Thos Kane	J H Smith
A H Clements	V E King	Wm J Stone
W B B Cross	John A Linton	Richd Sims
Edw M Clarke	K Lambell	Har Semmes
Wm Clarke	J H McBlair	B F Stewart
Reuben Clarke	A McIntire	Lem Towers
D Campbell	Jas Maguire	T P Tench
Robt M Combs	D W Middleton	C H Winder
W W Davis	W J McDonald	Jos Wilson
Dr Dove	Dr J E Morgan	Walter Warder
Wm P Elliot	John W Martin	W Wise
Saml M Edwards	H Nevitt	Maj A A Nicholson
John H Gibbs	Jas Nokes	Maj S R Hobbie
R Gott	John Potts	Capt J A Blake
Wm H Gunnell	Augustus Perry	
Aides of the Marshal:		
Maj Howie,	Capt Stuart	P B Key
Maj Lewis	W Lenox	

On Thu week, the Rev Thos C Dupont, Pastor of St Stephen's Chapel, in Charleston, S C, committed suicide while in a state of mental derangement.

Senate: 1-Cmte of Claims: bill for the relief of Thos W Chinn & others, with a report. 2-Cmte on Roads & Canals: bill for the relief of the legal reps of Moses Shepherd, with a report. 3-Bill for the relief of Chas M Gibson: passed. 4-Bill for the relief of Fred Dawson, Jas Schott, & Elisha Dana Whitney: postponed until tomorrow. 5-Bills passed- relief of: D A Waterson; Columbus Alexander & Theodosius Bernard; Moses White; the heir of John Wall, deceased; Mary Taylor, commonly called Polly Taylor; Jas C Carson; David Wilkinson; Stalker & Hill; H Fredieu, M Vercher, C Sanmiguel, N P Gagnon, V Caubarreux, & F Harbo, of La; of Wm W Wynn. 6-Bills laid on the table-relief of: David Myerlee; of Col Robt Wallace, aid-de-camp of Gen W Hull.

The Annual Meeting of the Alumni Association of the Columbian College, D C, will be held on Jul 12, in the Baptist Church, between 6th & 7th sts, at 8 o'clock.
–T B J Frye, Sec

Rough & Ready Line of Stages: a four horse stage coach will leave Washington 3 times a week for Upper Marlboro, PG Co, Md, starting on Tue, Thu, & Sat, at 6 o'clock; returning, will leave Upper Marlboro, on Mon, Wed, & Fri, at 11 o'clock. Ofc on Pa ave, at Massoletti's, where seats may be taken. Passengers will be taken up at their places of residence any where in the city. Fare $1.50. The line is owned & will be driven by J G & John House.

The partnership existing under firm of Corcoran & Riggs was dissolved on Jun 16. The business will be settled by either of the subscribers. –W W Corcoran, Geo W Riggs, jr
+
The business will be hereafter conducted by Wm W Corcoran & Elisha Riggs, jr, under the name of Corcoran & Riggs.

The following passengers have lately arrived at New Orleans from Mexico: By the English steamer **Trent**: Col Latham, Col Bonner, Capt Lytle, Capt Robertson, Capt Head & lady; Lts Fyffie, Kauffman, Pratt, Tucker, Gary, Thom & lady; Mrs Anderson, Mrs Sinclair, Mrs McKay, Mr McCorry, lady & child; Mr Ward & lady; Mr Glasscock & lady; Mr Gomez & lady & 3 dghts; Mr Hastings & lady & 2 children; Mr Slocomb & lady. By the schnr **Maria Burt**: Maj Wm H Polk, bearer of dispatches to Washington; Andrew J Dorn, Adj; Maj Winship; Capt J H Walker, of the voltigeurs; Capt J T Roland, Lt R H Rash, Lt D T Van Buren, Lt Stewart, Lt P V Hagner, Lt T T S Laidley, Lt C P Stone, Lt Maynard, U S Navy; Dr Stone, U S Army, & Dr Gaines, 5th Tenn volunteers. The steamer also brought over 400 discharged soldiers & quartermasters' men.

Charlestown, Va, Jun 29. Another child of Mr Francis Wentzell, of Harper's Ferry, died last week, making the 3rd within as many weeks, & on Fri evening, Mr Wentzell died suddenly. Mrs Wentzell & an infant are all that survive of a family of 6 when the month came in. –Free Press

MON JUL 3, 1848
Mr Alex'r Forbes, of N Y, died of the vomito at New Orleans on Jun 20th. He had in charge the bodies of Lt Col Chas Baxter, of N Y, Capt Pearson, of Brooklyn, & Van Olinda, of Albany. 1st Lt Floyd has taken charge of the bodies of the ofcrs, & also that of Mr Forbes, & is bringing them with him to N Y.

Mr E A Cook, a respectable merchant in Milk st, Boston, left his residence, at the Winthrop House, on Tue last, for N Y, having with him about $12,000 in money. Nothing has been heard of him since, & he cannot be traced to N Y. It is feared that he may have met with foul play.

The remains of Com Dallas have just been received in the U S, & deposited in their last resting-place in his native Pennsylvania with due honors, in the presence of his brother, the Vice Pres of the U S.

At Cape Map, on Thu, Mr O P Pearse, a much respected merchant of Phil, lost his life in the surf, having gone there to recover from a recent illness. He was with his sister-in-law, Mrs Wade, & they ventured out too far. She was able to float until picked up by a surf boat. Mr Pearse's body was not recovered.

Jos Boulanger, American & French Restaurateur: G st, near the War Dept, 1st Ward, Wash. [Ad]

Flags for sale at a low price by John Allen, Pa ave, near 10th st.

House of Reps: 1-Joint resolution for the relief of Richd Fields: referred to the Cmte of Claims. 2-Ptn of Mrs Mary Flowers, of Lawrence Co, Ill, praying that she may be permitted to purchase at the Gov't price that portion of the 16th section on which she resides.

In Chancery: John Thomson Mason, cmplnt, against John O Wharton & Eliz his wife, Abraham Barnes, Melcher B Mason, Thomson Mason, Virginia Mason, & Gen John Mason, dfndnts. The bill in substance states that John Thomson Mason, late of Wash Co, Md, died seized & possessed of part of lot 80, known & distinguished in the plan of Gtwn, D C: on Water st; that the wife of the said John Thomson Mason, deceased, has also departed this life; & that the cmplnt & Eliz, the wife of John O Wharton, Abraham Barnes, Melcher B Mason, & Virginia Mason are the only children of the said John Thomson Mason, deceased. The object of this bill is to have the property sold, & the proceeds divided between the cmplnt & his said brothers & sisters. The said dfndnts reside beyond the jurisdiction of the Court. Ordered that said dfndnts appear in this Court on or before the 2nd Mon in Nov next. –W Cranch -W Brent, clerk

Died: on Jun 30, in Wash City, Jane C Shyne, wife of Michl R Shyne, in her 28th year. May she rest in peace!

Died: on Jun 25, Mary Gale, daughter of F S & L A W Dunham, aged 11 months & 24 days.

TUE JUL 4, 1848

Corner-stone of the Washington Monument will be laid today, Jul 4. We are informed that Capt Josiah Sturgis, of the revenue cutter **Hamilton**, stationed at Boston, has in his possession the Masonic Apron of Maj Gen Warren, who fell at Bunker Hill in 1776. Gen Warren was Grand Master of the Grand Lodge of Mass. This apron was given by the heirs of Gen Warren to Maj Benj Russell, an ofcr of the Revolution, & subsequently Grand Master of the Grand Lodge of Mass, & for 45 years the well-known editor of the Boston Centinel. On his death it was given by his heirs to Capt Sturgis. It will be worn this day in the procession by him as a Knight Templar, with a hewel bearing date 1777.

Senate: 1-Cmte on Indian Affairs: House bill for the relief of the legal reps of Joshua Kennedy, deceased, without amendment.

House of Reps: 1-Resolved: that 2 brass field pieces captured from the enemy at the battle of Bennington, in Vt, in 1777, now in the possession of the U S, be well mounted & delivered to the Govn'r of Vt, to be hereafter holden as the property of said State.

Case of hydrophobia. About 3 weeks ago the 5 year old son of E L Snow, of N Y, was bitten by a dog running at large; the child expired Thu in a state of terrible suffering.
–N Y Com Advertiser

Mrd: on Sunday last, by Rev L F Morgan, Mr John H Johnson to Miss Sarah G Berry, all of Wash City.

Trustee's sale of valuable real estate: by decree of the Court of Chancery of Md: sale in Benedict, on Aug 4 next, all the real estate held in copartnership by Jas & Wm Morton at the death of Jas Morton, consisting of the following very productive Farms: 1-Tract of land in St Mary's Co, on Indian creek, containing 328 acres, more or less, being parts of 3 tracts of land called *Indian Creek, Truman's Hope,* & *Indian Creek with Addition*: with a good dwlg house, tobacco house, & other convenient houses. Also, a tract of land in Chas Co, on Swanson's creek, called *Wilford Meadows*, containing 120 acres, more or less; & a tract adjoining, called *The Mountains*, containing 210 acres, more or less. Also, another Farm, in Chas Co, on the road from Bryantown to Benedict; part of *Calverton's Manor*, & known as lots 19 & 30, one containing 220 acres, more or less: improvements are a dwlg house & other convenient houses. Also, that productive Farm called *Black Oak Thicket*, in Chas Co, containing 250 acres, more or less: with a dwlg house & other necessary bldgs thereon. Also, a small parcel of Land in Chas Co, being parts of tracts of land called *Cattle Grove* & *Four Brothers*, containing 23 acres more or less: woodland-very near Hughesville. Also, 2 tracts called *Hardship*, each containing 100 acres: near Gallant Greer, in Chas Co: with a dwlg house & other convenient houses on each place. Also, a lot in Benedict, designated as lot 9, with a convenient store-house; large tobacco house, 2 granaries, & salt house. –Gerard W Crain, Trustee: Port Tobacco, Md.

Valuable farm within 1½ miles of the Centre Market for sale: a Country Seat, in Wash Co, called *Jacksonville*, containing about 30 acres, with a commodious dwlg house & outbldgs thereon. This farm was purchased & improved by the owner with the intention of occupying it. Apply to Geo F Dyer, or the subscriber, Jas Maher, Wash.

Died: yesterday, Wm T Pettigrew, aged 25 years. His funeral is this morning at 9 o'clock, from the residence of his sister, on 14th st.

Died: Mon, of bronchitis, Henrietta Barnett, 2nd daughter of Jas B & Henrietta Dobson, aged 2 years & 3 months. Her funeral is tomorrow at 10 o'clock, from the residence of her parents on 6th st, between E & F sts.

Died: on Jun 27, at *Fruit Hill*, Jefferson Co, Va, Peyton Thompson, infant son of Jas E Yeatman, of St Louis, Mo, aged 15 months.

THU JUL 6, 1848
Atlantic & Ohio Telegraph: Annual Meeting, Jun 4, 1848. J K Moorhead, Pittsburg, Pres; Wm McKee, Phil, Sec & Treas; Jas D Reid, Phil, Superintendent. Dirs: Wm McKee, Wm Spering & M S Wickershan, of Phil; Henry O'Reilly, of N Y; J K Moorhead, Thos Bakewell, & Chas Avery, of Pittsburg; Alvah Strong, of Rochester, N Y; & Geo Dawson, of Albany, N Y.

Near Woodville, Miss, on Jun 10, a young lawyer, Benj M Cage, while separating fighting dogs, used the breech of his gun, & was shot through the body by the accidental discharge of the gun & died instantly.

Administration on the estate of Edw Green, late of Culpeper Co, Va, formerly of the county of Worcester, & Kingdom of Great Britain, having been granted to me, persons residing either in the U S or Great Britain are to make their claims known, that I may distribute the estate [$600] in my hands. –W A Griffin, adm

Leeches! Leeches! Leeches! Saml De Vaughan, Cupper, Leecher, & Bleeder, has a fresh supply of Swedish Leeches. His residence is now next door to the Temperance Hall, on E st, near 9th st.

House & lot for sale: house now occupied by me, on 7th st, between N & O sts. Apply on the premises for further information, B L Bogan.

Senate: Cmte on Indian Affairs: adverse report on the memorial of Saml Rusk & others, Choctaw com'rs.

Balt, Jul 5. Govn'r Thomas has appointed Judge Thos B Dorsey, Chief Justice of the High Court of Appeals of Md, & Wm Frick, of Balt, presiding Judge of the district composed of Balt city & county & Harford Co. These ofcs were made vacant by the lamented death of Judge Archer.

Died: on Jul 5, Richd Elliott, one of the oldest inhabitants of Wash City, aged 84 years. His funeral is this afternoon, at 4 o'clock, from his late residence on N Y ave, between 12th & 13th sts.

Died: yesterday, in Wash City, at the residence of his grandmother, Mrs Eliz E Page, near the Navy Yard, Danl Page, eldest son of Benedict & Martha Milburn, aged 5 years; from which place his funeral will take place this afternoon, at 4½ o'clock.

Died: on Jul 3, Edwin Duffield, son of John C & Ann D Franzoni, aged 6 months.

Geo Washington's education was in the common schools of Va; a land surveyor at age 16; he journeyed 41 days & 560 miles, from Williamsburg to French Creek, at age 21, as com'r from Gov Dinwiddie, to demand of the French forces their authority for invading the King's dominions. Bereft of his father at age 11 years, he had a mother left to whom the world can never over-estimate its debt. After Braddock's defeat he wrote to his venerated parent: "I have been protected beyond all human probability or expectation; for I had 4 bullets through my coat & 2 horses shot under me; yet I escaped unhurt, although death was leveling my companions on every side of me." Our Revolutionary fathers had many causes for adoring the invisible hand by which they were guided & guarded in their great struggle for liberty. In the war of the Revolution we see him the leader of our armies. In the formation of the Constitution we see him the Pres of our Councils. In the organization of the Federal Gov't we see him the Chief Magistrate of our Republic.

On Sat, at Asa White's establishment, in Boston, Leander Washburn, aged 19 years, was instantly killed by the bursting of a soda fountain which he was charging.

Jul 4th celebration & the laying of the corner-stone for the <u>Washington National Monument</u> on Jul 4, 1848. Military assemblage, commanded in chief, for the day, by Maj Quitman, U S Army, & Gen Cadwalader & Col May, commanding specially the infantry & cavalry troops respectively. [Col May is a very large man, with a great beard, who sits his horse so well.] Hon Robt C Winthrop, Speaker of the House of Reps, the appointed Orator of the day; followed by Mr B B French, Grand Master of the Masonic fraternity. The Procession was certainly one of the grandest & most imposing spectacles that was ever witnessed in the metropolis of the nation.

Fatal accident. Rev Mr Linthicum, while returning from a visit to a neighbor, while near Roxbury mill, in Howard District, was thrown from his buggy by the breaking of the coupling pin, & dragged some distance by the horse. His aged wife was the first to reach him, but he had ceased to breathe. Mr Linthicum was in his 88th year, & had been a local minister of the Methodist persuasion for upwards of 60 years.

FRI JUL 7, 1848
Senate: 1-Ptn from John P Williams, asking a confirmation of his title to a certain tract of land.

List of articles deposited in the Corner stone of the Washington National Monument on Jul 4, 1848.
Historical sketch of the Washington Nat'l Monument Society, since its origin, in MS.
Copy of the grant for the site of the Monument under the joint resolution of Congress.
Constitutions of the Washington Nat'l Monument Society, addresses, circulars, commissions, instructions, form of bond, from 1835 to 1848.
Large design of the W N Mounument, with the fac simile of the names of the Presidents of the U S & others. Lithographed.
Large design of the W N Mounment. Lighographed.
Portrait of Washington, from Stuart's painting, Faneuil Hall.
Small design of Monument & likeness of Washington, with blank certificates for contributors.
Constitution of the U S & Declaration of Independence: presented by Mr Hickey.
American Constitutions: by W Patton.
Plate engraved with the names of the officers & members of the Board of Managers.
Watterston's New Guide to Washington: by G Watterston.
Map of the city of Washington, by Jos Ratcliff.
Laws of the Corporation of Washington; by A Rothwell.
Statistics by John Sessford of the number of dwellings, value of improvements, assessments of the real & personal tax, in the city of Washington, from 1824 to 1848, print & manuscript: by John Sessford.
J B Varnum, jr, on the Seat of Gov't: by J M Varnum, jr.
The Statesman's Manual, containing Presidents' Messages from Washington to Polk, from 1789 to 1846, vols 1 & 2.
The Blue Book for 1847; Congressional Directory: by J & G S Gideon.
Message of the President of the U S & accompanying documents, 1847.
Morse's North American Atlas.
Appleton's Railroad & Steamboat Companion.
True Republican; the likenesses of all the Presidents to 1846, & inaugural addresses: by G Templeman.
Copies of the Union Magazine, Nat'l Magazine, Godey's Lady's Book, Graham's Magazine, & Columbian Magazine, for Jul, 1848: by Brooke & Shillington.
African Repository & Colonial Journal, 1848.
Thirty-first Annual Report of the American Colonization Society.
Coast Survey Document; Army Register for 1848.
Navy Register, 1848: by C Alexander.
Military Laws of the U S, 1846: by G Templeman.
Vail's Description of the Magnetic Telegraph: by A Vail.
Daguorreotype likenesses of Gen & Mrs Mary Washington, with a description of the Daguorreotype process: by John S Grubb, Alexandria, Va.
Silver Medal representing Gen Washington & the National Monument: by Jacob Seegar.
Report of the Joint Cmte on the Library, May 4, 1848, & an engraving: by M Vattemare.
Constitution of the Smithsonian Association, on the Island, instituted Nov 9, 1847.
Smithsonian Instiutution-Report of the Com'rs on its organization: Reports from the Board of Regents; by W W Seaton.
The Washington Monument-shall it be built? By J S Lyon.

Harer's Illustrated Catalogue: by S Colman
Guide to the Capitol, by R Mills: by R Mills.
Abstract Log for the use of American Navigators, by Lt M F Maury, U S N: by M F Maury.
American State Papers, 1832; National Intelligencer for 1846, [bound;] by Gales & Seaton.
American Archives, a Documentary History of the American Colonies to the present time, fourth series, vol 5: by Peter Force.
An American dollar; by Miss Sarah Smith, Stafford, N J.
Holy Bible, presented by the Bible Society, instituted 1816.
Report of Prof Bache, Superintendent of the Coast Survey: by Coast Survey Ofc.
Annual Report of the Comptroller of the State of N Y, Jan 5, 1848: Tolls, Trade, & Tonnage of the N Y Canals, 1847; State of N Y-first report of the Com'r, Practice & Pleadings; by Hon Washington Hunt.
Report of the Com'r of Patents, 1847: by Edmund Burke.
Fac simile of Washington's Accounts; by Michl Nourse.
U S Fiscal Dept, vols 1 & 2: by R Mayo, M D.
Specimens of Continental Money, 1776: by Thos Adams.
Walton's Vermont Register & Farmers' Almanac, 1848: by Hon Mr Henry.
Maps & Charts of the Coast Survey: by Survey Ofc.
Maury's Wind & Current Charts of the North Atlantic: by M F Maury.
Casts from the seals of the S of T & I O R M: by J W Ecklof.
A cent of 1783 of the Unity States of America: by W G Paine.
Claypole's American Daily Adveriser, Dec 25, 1799, & the Phil Gaz, Dec 27, 1799, containing a full account of the death & funeral ceremonies of Gen Washington, the official proceedings of Congress, Executive: by G M Grouard.
Publication No 1, Boston, 1833.
Letters of John Quincy Adams to W L Stone, & introduction; letters of J Q Adams to Edw Livingston, Grand High Priest; Vindication of Gen Washington, by Jos Ritner, Govn'r of Pa, with a letter to Daniel Webster, & his reply, printed in 1841; American Antimason, No 1, vol, Hartford, Conn, 1839, Maine Free Press; Correspondence Cmte of York, Pa, to Richd Rush, Apr 1831; his answer, May 4, 1841; Credentials of a Delegate from Jefferson Co, Missouri, & proceedings of a meeting of citizens to make the appointment of a delegate: by Henry Gassitt, Boston, Mass.
Astonomical Observations for 1845, made under M F Maury, at the Washington Observatory: M F Maury.
30th Congress & documents: by R P Anderson.
Census of the U S, 1840; Force's Guide to Washington & vicinity, 1848: by W Q Force.
Memoir of a Tour to Northern Mexico, 1846-'47: by R P Anderson.
Report on the organization of the Smithsonian Institute: by Prof Henry.
A list of the Judges of the Supreme Court of the U S, its Ofcrs, with the dates of their respective appointments: by W J Carroll, Clerk Supreme Court of the U S.
Drake's Poems: Catalogue of the Library of Congress, printed 1839; Catalogue from 1840 to 1847, both inclusive: by Joint Cmte on the Library of Congress.
Census of the U S from 1790 to 1848, inclusive.

Proceedings of the General Society of the Cincinnati, with the original institution of the order & fac simile of the signatures of the original members of the State Society of Pennsylvania: by Chas L Coltman.
Constitution & Genr'l Laws of the Great Council of the Improved Order of Red Men of the Dist of Col.
By-laws of Powhattan Tribe No 1, & Genr'l Laws of the Great Council of the same Order.
The Temple of Liberty, two copies, one ornamented & lettered with red. The letters are so arranged in each that the name of Washington may be spelled more than one thousand times in connexion: by John Kilbourn.
American Silk Flag: presented by Jos K Boyd, citizen of Wash, D C, on Jul 4, 1848.
Design of the Monument, small plate, produced by a process called electrotrype: by *Chas Fenderich, Washington. [*Jul 10th correction: the artist was Mr Selinar Siebert, of the Coast Survey ofc; not Chas Fenderich.]
A copy of the Constitution of the first organized Temperance Society in America: by L H Sprague, Jul 4, 1848.
Sons of Temperance in the District of Columbia.
Coat of Arms of the Washington family: by Mrs Jane Charlotte Washington, Jul 4, 1848.
All the coins of the U S, from the eagle to the half-dime, inclusive.
The Baltimore Sun of Jul 4, 1848, containing letters of Mrs Madison, Mrs Hamilton, Gen Cass, & Mr Fillmore: presented by Jas Lawrenson, jr, 6 years old, of Washington.
The Weekly Sun containing sundry notices of the Monument: presented by Richard Sewall Lawrenson, [the Doctor,] four & a half years old, of Washington.

Qualla Town, N C, is a name applied to a tract of 72,000 acres of land, in Haywood Co, which is occupied by about 800 Cherokee Indians & 100 Catawhas. Wm H Thomas is to become their business chief.

The citizens of Boston were much shocked on Mon to learn that the body of Hon Nathl P Russell had been found in the water at Nahant, under such circumstances as to leave no doubt that he had committed suicide. Mr Russell was the father of a numerous family, retiring & modest in his habits, but a gentleman of great worth. His age was about 68.

House of Reps: 1-Ptn of the heirs of Matthew Jack, late of Westmoreland Co, deceased, who was a captain in the 8th Pa line, in the Revolutionary war, praying for his commutation pay. 2-Remonstrance of Hosea Ilsley & 38 others, citizens of Suffolk Co, Mass, against the removal of the marine hospital in the town of Chelsea. 3-Ptn of John Osborn & others, citizens of Davies Co, Mo, praying establishment of a certain post route. 4-Ptn of Thos M Reade & others, citizens of Jefferson, N Y, praying the abolition of the franking privilege & the reduction of letter postage to the uniform rate of two cents.

For rent: a Schoolhouse on F st, between 5th & 6th sts, opposite the Wesley Chapel. Inquire of L Syfferly, corner of 6th & F sts.

Horse lost: escaped from my pasture: was formerly owned by Mr Derringer, of Wash City. Suitable reward to any one who will deliver him at my residence on F st, east of the Patent Ofc, Wash. –Amos Kendall

$10 reward for return of 2 horses that strayed away or were stolen from their owners; both were in good order. –Jos Miller, Butcher; Wm Thos Selby.

Public Notice: on Aug 1 I will sell at auction the entire stock of household furniture now in both my houses; one on 11 st & the other on Pa ave. After which I will offer for sale both the houses. My object is to pay my debts & keep the marshal from my door.
–Jos K Boyd

SAT JUL 8, 1848
Two ruffians, Gale Wagers & McGrat, part of a gang of villains, the authors of recent outrages committed near Mobile, were killed a few days ago at Red creek, Mo, near the Alabama line. –Mobile Advertiser

Accidents on the Fourth: 1-At N Y, John Scott had 2 of his fingers injured & then amputated; a son of Tobias Connor was run over by an omibus & very seriously injured. 2-At Boston, a son of Thos Dolliver was blown up by the explosion of powder in his powder-horn, & not expected to survive. Dr Wildes was severely injured by the premature discharge of a small cannon. A 12 year old son of Christopher Andrews was badly burnt by the explosion of gunpowder he was experimenting with. 3-At Manchester, Vt: Mr Albert Jorday had his left hand & wrist entirely blown away. Mr Fayette Battist had a part of one hand shot off & other injuries-feared mortal. 4-Morristown, N J: Henry Williams, a young man working in the Jerseyman ofc was shocking wounded by the bursting of a small cannon made from a musket barrel. It is thought he will recover. 5-At Buffalo, N Y: Jas E McKnight, teller of the Bank of Attles, was drowned in the Niagara river. A boat he was in with 4 others overturned.

A heavy storm visited Pittsburg on Sunday last, two men, of the names of Carey & Ryan, were killed by lightning near Birmingham. They had been teaching in St Paul's Sunday School & were killed instantly.

$5 reward for return of a Pistol, London make, twist barrel, about 10 inches long, with flint lock belinging to Maj J D Graham, U S Engineers: stolen from the shop of W G Bitner, 1st Ward, on Jul 3.

Wash Corp: 1-Ptn from J Crutchett: referred to the Cmte of Claims.

Senate: 1-Cmte of Claims: House bill for the relief of Archibald Beard & 21 other Tenn mounted volunteers, with an amendment. 2-Cmte of Claims: House bill for the relief of John W Hockett, without amendment. Same cmte: Senate bill for the relief of Bryan Callaghan.

House of Reps: 1-Cmte on Military Affairs: bill to provide for the payment of the companies of Capts Bush, Price, & Suarey for military services in Florida: committed.

Mrd: on Jul 5, at Balt, by Rev John M Duncan, D C, Thornton A Jenkins, Lt U S Navy, to Betty, daughter of Francis A Thornton, Purser U S Navy.

Died: on Jul 5, after an illness of 10 days, Richd S Black, in his 21st year.

Died: last evening, in Wash City, Ursula Christiana, infant child of Warren & Sarah Little, aged nearly 12 months. Her funeral is on Sunday, at 4 o'clock.

26th Anniversary Celebration of the Enosinian Society of the Columbian College, D C, will taken place on Tue next: oration by Wm B Webb, of Wash City.
–A F Scott, R H Griffith, A B Evans, cmte of arrangements.

The Evansville [Geo] Journal records the suicide of Miss Catherine Hall, who shot herself with a pistol because her parents refused her in marriage to a young man belonging to the army.

MON JUL 10, 1848
Died: on Jul 7, in Wash City, in her 4th year, Cornelia Reynolds, daughter of Jos & Mary L Reynolds.

Died: on Jul 9, in Wash City, Rose, daughter of John & Mary Ann Hands, aged 13 months & 8 days.

Died: on Jun 5, 1848, at Cedar creek Hundred, Sussex Co, near Milford, Del, Jacob Deputy, at the advanced aged of 117 years, 9 months & 15 days. He was born on Aug 20, 1730, in the Hundred aforesaid, & there lived as a cultivator of the soil up to the time of his death. His habits in life were said to be temperate, & health good. His mind, memory, & hearing were remarkable good to the last. His eyesight had failed him, but not to that extent as to prevent his walking about & attending to his ordinary business. Jacob Deputy was a colored man.

A letter received in Wash City yesterday announces the decease of a distinguished Matron, a relict of the era of the Revolution, in the person of Mrs Julia Rush, widow of the distinguished Dr Benj Rush, & mother of the Hon Richd Rush, now Minister of the U S to France. She died on Fri last, in her 90th year, at Sydenham, near Phil, [the residence of her son.] She was the sister of the late Hon Richd Stockton, of N J, & Grandmother of Com R F Stockton, U S Navy.

A son of Senator Baldwin, of Conn, died at the Round Hill Water Cure Establishment, in Northampton, on Thursday, of consumption. His age was about 30 years.
–Springfield Republican, Jul 7

Rev Oliver Wm Bourne Peabody, Pastor of the Unitarian congregation at Burlington, Vt, died there yesterday. He was at graduated from Harvard Univ in 1816; was a brother of Mrs Alex'r H Everett, & a twin brother of the late Rev W B O Peabody, of Springfield. Mr Peabody had been an able contributor to the North American Review, & for a time was connected with the editorial dept of the Daily Advertiser of Boston.
–Boston Transcript

List of articles deposited in the Corner-stone of the <u>Washington Nat'l Monument</u>, on Jul 4, 1848, by the R W Grand Lodge of D C:
A silver plate, containing on one side the name of the Grand Ofcrs of the R W Grand Lodge of D C, & on the other the names of the Cmte of Arrangements of said Grand Lodge, consisting of the W Master of each subordinate Lodge under its jurisdiction.
A roll of copper coin of the U S, 15 or 20 in number, obtained from the Mint at Phil, comprising all the early extant specimens of that coin.
Also, a cent of the coinage of 1783, presented by Bro W Hurst, to this Grand Lodge.
A metallic impress of the seal of the said Grand Lodge, a copy of its constitution, & a copy of its last published proceedings.
A parchment scroll, containing extracts from the ancient records of Fredericksburg Lodge, No 4, of Va, showing the initiation, passing, & raising of Bro Geo Washington by that Lodge; initiation of Nov 4, 1752; passing on Mar 3, 1753; & raising on Aug 4, 1753.
Also, a list of the present ofcrs & members of said Lodge.
A copy of the constitution & by-laws of Washington Lodge, No 22, of Alexandria, of which Bro Geo Washington was the W Master.
A copy of Bro Morris' Freemasons' Magazine, published at Boston, [No 8 of Vol 1,] containing the Masonic character & correspondence of Bro Geo Washington.
A copy of the constitution of the R W Grand Lodge of Texas.
A paper containing a list of the ofcrs & members of Mount Vernon Lodge, No 22, Georgia.
Another containing those of Washington Lodge, No 1.
Another containing those of Temple Lodge, No 11.
Another containing those of Lafayette Lodge, No 14.
Another containing those of Lafayette R A Chapter, all of Wilmington, Dela.
Another containing a list of the ofcrs of the Grand R A Chapter of the State of Delaware.
A printed copy of the Masonic Register for the State of Pa for the year 1848.
A copy of the Dry Goods Reporter of the date of Jul 1, 1848, published in N Y, Boston, & Phil.
A silver plate containing the names of the ofcrs of Washington Encampment, No 1, of D C.
A paper containing the by-laws & list of ofcrs of Wheeling Encampment, No 1, Va, together with resolutions & proceeding of said Encampment of Jun 15, 1848.
The foregoing articles were severally presented by the R W Grand Sec, C S Frailey, to the R W Grand Master, who, after announcing the same, handed them to the R W Grand Treasurer, Robt Clarke, by whom they were placed in a leaden box prepared therefore, & said box & contents then deposited within the cavity of the corner stone. Attest: Chas S Frailey, Grand Sec

The British steamer **Scourge** arrived at Bermuda on Jun 20th from Ireland, having on board John Mitchell, the condemnded Irishman, who was immediately transferred to the convict ship **Dromedary**.

For rent: large & commodious dwlg-house at corner of 8th & G sts, at present occupied by his excellency the Baron Gerolt, Minister of Prussia. Inquire of J Gideon, 9th st.

House of Reps: 1-Bills referred-relief of: Gamaliel Taylor [late marshal of Indiana] & his securities; Wm W Wynn; David Wilkinson; H Frediue, M Vetcher, C Sanmiguel, P U Gagnon, V Carbanaux, & F Harbo, of Louisiana; Mary Taylor; heirs of John Wall, deceased; heirs of Moses White; Columbus Alexander & Theodore Barnard; D A Watterston; Chas M Gibson; & Jas G Carson. 2-Ptn of Jas T Woodbury, of Acton, Mass, & 55 others, praying for the repeal of the franking privilege & the reduction of letter postage. 3-Ptn of the legal reps of Maj L P Montgomery.

Persons who have taken out licenses under the laws of the Corporation during the months of Mar, Apr, May, & June.

Cart license:

Adams, Robt
Anderson, John S
Ailer & Thyson
Adams, Caleb
Allen, Benj
Acton, Osborn-2
Batemen, Abr
Bayliss, Thos
Barnes, Elias
Baeschlin, John
Bruce, Chas
Barnes, John
Bridget, O
Brent, Elton
Bogle, John
Butler, John
Barr, Wm
Butler, M-2
Brown, Wm
Brooks, Hanson
Bean, Geo
Bean, C
Brown, Archer
Boone, J B
Bates & Co
Barrett, T J
Berkley, J S
Cissel, Wm

Chew, John
Chew, Phil
Casanave, Peter-2
Crowley, Wm
Coburn, W A
Campbell, Dan
Conlan, Peter
Casey, Pat-2
Davis, H C
Devers, Wm-2
Dent Bruce
Dick, Moses
Dunlop, G W
Delany, Adam
Day, D G
Dodd, Reuben
Davis, Elias
Einnis, Phil-2
Easby, Wm-3
Frye, Jos
Fletcher, John
Fitzgerald, John
Fletcher, John
Fowler, Jas
Ford, Wm
Fletcher, John
Fletcher, Wm
Fugitt, ___

Fields, Geo
Ferrity, Nicholas
Green, Patrick
Gillott, Jos
Giveney, Bern
Gatts, J N
Grinder, John-2
Green, Mant
Garnet, Primus
Goggin, Robt
Green, Edwin
Gunnell, W H & Co
Geyer, Bensn
Grupe, Wm
Gillespie, Alex
Harkness, G W
Hagerty, Wm
Hill, Isaac
Hanson, Chas
Hicks, Chas
Harvey, J S & Co
Howell, Thos
Hill, Isaac
Heitmiller, Ant
Hamilton, Martin
Haislep, Henry-2
Hoover, John
Iddins, Sam

Jackson, P
Jolly, John
Jones, Robt
Johnson, Townly
Jedt, J P
Kibball, Alex
Lauxman, M
Lewis, Thos
Lauxman, ___
Linkins, Jos
Lynch, Amb
Linkins, Walter
Lemman & Bro
Lee, Michl
Landrick, John
Lyons, Chas
Leddy, Owen
Linkins, Dan
Loveless, John
Lanahan, Mich
Lederer, C
Miller, Chas
Magruder, Field
Mohler, Fred
Madison, Cath
McGlue, G T
Mohun, Phil
Mulliken, J W
Mason, Jo
Mulliken, John
Mason, Jo
McNeeny, Thos
Moore, Wm

Wagon license:
Bohlayer, Jno
Barber, Geo
Brown, Thos
Burnett, Enoch
Bowen, Jas A
Butler, M
Bradey, M
Briscoe, Henry
Bates & Bro
Byrne, P A
Bird, Wm

Mitchell, Wm
Mister, Isaac
Noble, Martha
Neale, Levi
Nally, J T
Newton, Ben
Nepp, Dan
Noert, And
Neale, J C
Otterback, Phil
O'Donoghue, P & T
Payne, Sam
Prather, O J-2
Peterson, Henry
Plant, Nathan
Pulizzi, V
Purdy, John
Rhodes, Jas
Rison, Chas
Ragan, Dan-2
Redin, David
Redfern, Sam
Riley, Thos W-4
Richardson, Luke
Ready, John
Stott, Saml
Somerville, A
Simmons, John
Stewart, Chas jr-2
Semmes, J M
Stewart, Wm
Simmons, Aug-2
Stephenson, Jo

Barnes, Wm
Cook, L C
Colburn, Jas
Conner, John
Dyer, Henrietta
Dunlap, Henry
Donovan, Wm
Dyer, H U
Emmerson, G W
Fuller, E H
Fugitt, Jo

Smoot, Sam
Seitz, Geo
Selby, Thos
Stewart, Geo
Shepherd, Peter
Thomas, J G
Tyler, Robt
Thomas, Sam
Travers, M W-2
Thorn, Henry
Tinklen, Sam
Thyson, Paulus
Tinklen, Sam
Thomas, Chas
Tyler, Washington
Taylor, John H
Tinney, Chas
Uniack, John
Woods, John
Waters, Gust
Williamson, Thos
Wise, Wm-2
Wilson, W B-2
Wilson, John
Warder, Walter
Waters, Elkana-2
Walker & Peck-2
Walker, J F
Webster, Rezin
Williamson, Zad
Wood, Edw

Fitzgerald, David
Forshee, Moses
Hager, F
Haltmillar, Ant
Howard, John
Havenner, T & Son
Harvey & Lloyd
Hammersley, Edw
Henry, Jas
Horning, G D
Hatch, Well

Hager, Chas
Isaacs, Hester
Ingraham, Wash
Jones, Alfred-2
Krafft, John M-2
Key, Sam
Krafft, Geo
Knot, Geo
Miller, Chas
McCoubray, Thos
Milburn, T M & B
Moore, John
Miller, Mich
Mason, Jos
Nugent, Henry
Noerr, And
Otterback, Phil
O'Donoghue, P & T
Osborne, Jas
Owen, Edw
Owner, Jas
Purdy, John-2

Pearson, P M
Pettibone, J
Preston, O J & Co
Payne, Saml
Page, Geo
Rhodes, Jas
Reilley, John
Rywell, R R
Rodier, Julius-2
Rosenthall, C
Rawlings, D
Simmons, Benj
Shedd, W P
Shedd, J L
Stephonson, Jo
Semmes, J M
Semmes, Basil
Straub, Jos
Shaub, John & Co
Slade, Wm
Sibley, Jas
Smith, Thos

Seitz, Geo-2
Swaggert, Jo
Tyson, Paulus
Tinklen, Sam
Thomas, Chas
Tyler, Washington
Taylor, John H
Tinney, Chas
Van Reswick & Jones
Visser, J
Wright, Jas
Wunderlich, John-2
Wagner, John
Whaley, W H
Worcester, Giles
Walker, Wm
Wakeling, Ig
Wilson, Wm A
Willard, E & H
Young, John

Dray license:
Bacon & Co
Berry, J W
Jackson, B I & Bro
Middleton & Beall

O'Brien, J
Ober & Ryon
Parker, G & T
Pullen, Jas

Ryon, John T
Stephenson, Jo
Simpson, Pres
Wise, Chas J

Dog license:
Boyle, John
Banks, Michl
Bartley, Josiah
Brent, Elton
Bergman, H W
Bell, Wm
Barrett, T J
Brown, Thos B
Brunet, L L
Bell, Jas
Burke, G McD
Coffman, Geo
Clokey, John
Cunningham, J L
Cryer, Ben
Casanave, Peter

Croggon, Js
Chauncey, John
Collins, Wm
Dodson, J B
Datcher, Chas
Eaton, R M
Ehlen, J F
Evans, F S
Force, Peter-3
Fiensten, Peter
Fanning, W
Goings, Pat
Gannon, J P-2
Gray, Silvester
Hetzel, S S
Hess, Paul

Holmead, J B
Hazel, Zach-2
Isaacs, Hester
Jesup, Thos
Jones, Alfred
Johnson, Richd
Jenifer, Robt
Kutz, Geo
Key, P B
Keating, M
Kendall, J E
Korf, John
Little, Peter
Lefler, John
Linkins, Thos
McCoy, S M

Mount, Jas
May, J F
Mulloy, W A
Murray & Simms
Maryman, H R
Miller, Aug
Noland, Philip
Plant, J H
Plant, G H
Pumphrey, Jack
Peterson, W
Riddall, W C
Rappette, Jo
Ross, Jas

Smith, Milford
Smith, J C
Shedd, J I
Shaw, Richd
Spencer, C
Shadd, B
Stuart, F C
Stapper, And
Speaks, L
Stoke, J G
Simpson, Tobias
Shad, B
Simpson, E G
Sawyer, W B

Turpin, Thos
Thyson, J W
Van Reswick, Thos
Whitlock, W D
Wise, Wm
White, A D H
Washington, L Q
Williams, T J
Watterston, Geo
Williams, w H
Waters, D S
Washington, L Q
Wagoner, John
Young, M C

Hack license:
Birch, W H
Coates, Geo
Jones, Robt

King, Isaiah
Sutton, Robt
Turner, Henry

Wright, Jas
Yates, W H

Slave license:
Cooper, Sarah
Ford, J B
Gettings, Jed
Homiller, Chas

Isherwood, Robt
Muncaster, W J
Mattingly, F

Stewart, G W, for J Moore
Weems, Mary

Huckster license:
Collins, Sarah
Campbell, W W
Crampsey, Wm
Cobey, Hezekiah-transfer
Crump, Jas

Crump, John
Fenwick, F A
Humphreys, R
Hobbs, Isaac B
Lewe, Melch
Mills, R T

Oyster, D W
Semmes, J M
Wilson, J L
Wolland, H

Retail license:
Boyd, Robt
Earl, Robt
Fraunk, Jacob-transfer
Gross, Jas F
Hercus, Geo

Humes, John
Lewis, Mgt
Power, John
Phillips, Ann
Quinn, Bernard

Stewart, Wm-transfer
Webb, A J
Wall, W L & J T

Wood license
Brereton, John
Boone, J B
Beane, Geo

Casanave, Peter
Day, G D
McCutchen, John

Neale, John E

Grocery license:
Davy, Jas
Ingle, Jos
Malone, Law
Prentiss, W H
Simms, Samp
Wimsatt, Richd

Shop license:
Beute, Henry-transfer
Leopold, Augustus-transfer
Ritter, H G
Sweeny, Edw
Sanderson, Nich

Lumber license:
Fugitt, Jo
Gunnell, W H & Co
Harvey & Lloyd
Lenman & Bro
Pearson, P M
Preston, O J & Co
Purdy, John
Van Reswick & Jones
Webb, S B
Ward, Ulysses

Wood license:
Hill, Isaac
Haslop & Henry
Harvey & C
Wilson, John
Harvey & C
Jolly, John
Coal license:
Waters, Gust
Waters, E
Travers, J & Son
Thorn, Henry
Warder, Wm

Theatre license: Brown & Nichols-6; Heron, John
Slut license: Jackson, Pompey; Willingman, J
Shop, Fish wharf license: Butt & Storm; Goldin, Mgt-transfer; McGrann, Jas
Medicines license: Bates, J E; Davis & Bates; Davis, Chas E
Concert license: Dimpster, W R-3; Hutchinson Family; Heron, John
Hardware license: McGregor & Middleton; Quirk, Thos; Russell, T G & Co-transfer
Boots & Shoes license: Hoover, S D; King, Z M P-2; Magruder & Co; Wilson, Wm
Auctioneer license: McDevitt, John
Old iron license: Owen, Edw
Porter license: Rodier, Julius
Menagerie license: Van Amberg & Co
Dry goods license: Worthington & Curtain
Burning Moscow license: Young, W H
Wax figures license: Foster, Gideon-2
Confectionary license: Goodarsall, J
Ten Pins license: Farrar, J M
Tavern license: Cooke, Hatch
Nat curiosities license: Cobb, N F-2
Hardware license: Brown, Geo
Theatrical license: Brown & Nichols
Tavern license: Blackwell, C W

Persons fined during the months of Mar, Apr, May, & June, for failing to procure their licenses.

Alexander, C: dog
Anderson, G: dog
Adams, Robt: cart
Booth, Henry: dogs
Brown & Nicholls: theatre
Cloakey, R: dog
Coltman, C L: dog
Curry, Mary: dog
Colyear, Peyton: dog
Chase, Wm: dog
Carusi, Edw: huckstering
Cross, A C: wagon
Dowling, Wm: dog
Davis, Mrs: dog
Day, Spencer: dog
Dorsey, T: dog
Diggs, Susan: dog
Dowling, Wm: cart
Dowling, Wm: liquor
Dunlap, Mary: dog
Day, Spencer: liquor
Douglass, Henry: dog
Edtz, John P: dog
Finkman, C: dog
Frank, Mary: liquor
Fugit, Jas: wagon
Fuller, Edw: wagon
Fletcher, John: cart
Farrar, J M: bowling
Goodrich: dog
Goss, John: cider
Harris, Warner: dog
Harrison: dog
Howard, Eliz: dog
Hutchinson, Joshua: theatre
Hall, Edw: dray
Jesup, Thos S: dogs
Johnson, John: dog
Jacobs, Henry: cart
Jackson, B L & Bro: dray
Johnson, Edw: wagon
Knott, Geo: wagon
Kemble, Chas: dog
Lakemeyer, F: liquor
Leis, Thos: cart
Magune, Jas: doog
Mahon, A: dog
Mullen, John: hack
Magee, Saml: wagon
Middleton & Beall: dray
McGarvey, P: wagon
McKelden, John C: wagon
Mann, Chas: slut
Oshar, Geo: dog
O'Brian, John: dray
Pettibone, Wm: dog
Pierson, P M: wagon
Purdy, John: wagon & cart
Preston, O J: wagon
Quin, Barney: liquor
Riddle, W C: dog
Stewart, W T: dog
Simpson, Presley: dog
Saunders, Alex'r: wagon
Shadd, C: liquor
Shaw, Richd: wagon
Slade, Wm: wagon
Thompson, J E W: dog
Tree, L: dog
Triplett, T M: dog
Thomas, Jas: dog
Thomas, Frank R: cart
Woodward, John: dog
Williams, Lemuel: dog
Whitlock: dog
Woodland: dog
Williams, Mary: dog
Williamson, Jos: dog
Willard, W H & E D: wagon
Wilson, J L: huckstering
Wilson, Wm A: wagon
Wooster, Giles: wagon
Ward, U: wagon
Whaley, H H: wagon
Williams, Zadock: liquor
Words, John: dog
Young, John: wagon

TUE JUL 11, 1848
Appointment by Gen Kearny of civil ofcrs: being authorized by the Pres of the U S, for the gov't of New Mexico, a Territory of the U S. Appointed: Chas Bent, Govn'r; Bonsisano Vigil, Sec of the Territory; Richd Dallam, Marshal; Franics P Blair, U S District Atty; Chas Blummer, Treasurer; Eugene Seitzcodorfer, Auditor of Public Accounts; Joab Houghton, Antonio Jose Otero, Chas Beaubian, to be Judges of the Superior Court. Given at Santa Fe, the capital of the Territory of New Mexico, this 22nd day of Sep, 1846, & in the 71st year of the independence of the U S -S W Kearny, Brig Gen U S Army

Balt Life Ins Co [Md]: John I Donaldson, Pres; Richd B Dorsey, Sec. Chas W Pairo appointed Agent: ofc at the corner of F & 15th sts, Wash City.

France: Prince Louis Napoleon Bonaparte is expected to be elected cmder of the 3rd Legion of Nat'l Guards, & Prince Napoleon, son of the ex-King of Westphalia, was a candidate for the command of the 2nd Legion.

The copartnership existing between the undersigned, under the firm of E Pickrell & Co, was dissolved by mutual consent on Jul 3. Esau Pickrell & A H Pickrell will settle up the business of the late firm. –Esau Pickrell, A H Pickrell, John J Pickrell. The subscribers will continue the Grocery & Commission Business in Gtwn, under the firm of E Pickrell & Co. –Esau Pickrell, A H Pickrell

WED JUL 12, 1848
Army Order: Gen Orders No 37: War Dept, Adj Gen's Ofc: Wash, Jul 8, 1848. The following Non Commisioned Ofcrs have been attached by the Pres as Brevet 2nd Lts to the several regts of the regular Army below specified, to take rank from Jun 28, 1848.
1st Regt of Dragoons: Sgt David H Hastings, of the Company of Sappers & Miners.
2nd Regt of Dragoons:
Sgt Saml H Starr, of the Co of Sappers & Miners.
Sgt Maj Thos J McKean, of the 15th Regt of Infty.
Regt of Mounted Riflemen:
Sgt Wm B Lane
Sgt Caleb E Irvin
1st Regt of Artl:
Sgt Thornely S Everett, of the Co of Sappers & Miners.
Sgt John Dement, of the Regt of Mounted Riflemen.
2nd Regt of Artl:
Quartermaster Sgt Jas M Robinson
Sgt Henry Benson
3rd Regt of Artl: Sgt John H Heck
4th Regt of Artl: Sgt Maj Robt W Howard
1st Regt of Infty:
Sgt Henry Wilson, of the 2nd Regt of Artl
Sgt Chas N Underwood, of the Regt of Mounted Riflemen
Sgt Walter W Hudson, of the 15th Regt of Infty

2nd Regt of Infty:
Sgt Geo Bruce
Cpl Robt Bailey
Cpl Jas McGill, of the 15th Regt of Infty
3rd Regt of Infty:
Sgt Henry L Brown, of the Regt of Mounted Riflemen
Sgt Saml Boss, of the 15th Regt of Infty
4th Regt of Infty:
Sgt Hiram Dyer, of the Regt of Mounted Riflemen
Sgt Fortunatus Lilly, of the 15th Regt of Infty
5th Regt of Infty:
Sgt Jos Updegraff
Sgt Saml Archer
6th Regt of Infty:
Sgt Levi C Bootes, of the Regt of Mounted Riflemen
Cpl John L Tubbs, of the 12th Regt of Infty
7th Regt of Infty:
Quartermaster Sgt Wm S Bradford
Sgt Anthony S Sutton, of the 15th Regt of Infty.
8th Regt of Infty:
Sgt Maj Theodore Fink
Sgt Geo L Willard, of the 15th Regt of Infty
By order: R Jones, Adj Gen

Wash City News: the trial of Maj G Tochman for sending a challenge to fight a duel commenced yesterday. [Jul 14th newspaper: jury returned a verdict of not guilty, after about 20 minutes.]

Wash Corp: 1-Ptn of Fred'k Idelins, praying permission to raise a frame bldg adjoining a brick one: referred to the Cmte on Police. 2-Ptn of Edw Miller, praying payment of a balance due for work done on 2nd st east & Indiana ave: referred to the Cmte of Claims. 3-Ptn of Wm Lord, praying for a flag footway across the 55 feet alley on the west front of square 518: referred to the Cmte on Improvements. 4-Ptn of Wm Hughes, praying the graveling of G st north, between 1st & 2nd sts: referred to the Cmte on Improvements.

Senate: 1-Cmte on Private Land Claims: House bill for the relief of Lewis Benedict, without amendment, & recommending its passage. 2-Cmte of Claims: house bill for the relief of John B Rogers, without amendment, & recommending it do not pass. 3-Cmte on the Post Ofc & Post Roads: bill gives to Alex'r Vattemare, denominated in the bill the agent of the U S for international exchanges, the privilege of franking any letters, packages, books, & specimens of medals, not exceeding 3 pounds in weight. 4-Cmte on Military Affairs: asking to be discharged from the further consideration of the memorial of Ambrose R Davenport: which was agreed to.

Household & kitchen furniture, store fixtures, confectionary, horses, & bread cart at auction: on Jul 19, by deed of trust, at the residence of Mr Uriah Heeter, on I st, between 19th & 20th sts. –N Callan, trustee -Edw C & G F Dyer, auctioneers

By virtue of a writ of fieri facias issued by John L Smith, J P for Wash Co, D C, against the goods & chattels, lands & tenements of Richard Brooks, Danl Kelly, Edw McKenney, & Thos Kelly, at the suit of Clarke & Briscoe, to me directed, I have seized & taken in execution north half of lot 12 in square 1,000, with improvements, as the property of Edw McKenney, consisting of one frame house, which I shall proceed to sell on Aug 14, on the premises, for cash, to satisfy said execution. –Jno L Fowle, Constable

Orphans Court of Wash Co, D C. Letters of administration on the personal estate of Robt W Dyer, late of said county, deceased. –Stans Murray, adm

By virtue of 3 writs of fieri facias issued by John L Smith, J P for Wash Co, D C, against the goods & chattels, lands & tenements of John Holohon, Mary J Holohon, & Rose A Holohon, at the suit of Wm H English, to me directed, I have seized & taken in execution one two story brick dwlg-house, on 7th st, in Wash City, now occupied by said Holohon, which I shall proceed to sell on Aug 14, on the premises, for cash, to satisfy said execution. –O E P Hazard, Constable

House of Reps: 1-Ptn for the relief of Jesse Forsythe, of Knox Co, Mo: presented. 2-Ptn of Alonzo Chapin & others, of Abington, Mass, praying for the abolition of the franking privilege & for the reduction of postage.

For sale or lease: the undersigned being determined, should his life be spared, to retire from business in one year from this time, & wishing to put what little he has in the best situation to be available, offers the following for sale or lease: lot 5 in square 29; lots 20 & 21 in 70; part lot 5 & 6 & 7 in square 231; lots 1 thru 4 in square 294, with 5 small frame houses; half lot 4 in square 263, & small frame house; half lot in 325 & neat frame house; part of lot in 345 & frame house & back-bldg; parts of 6 & 7 in 374, & 3 story brick house & back-bldg; the whole of square 399; part of lot 8, opposite N L Market; 3 story brick house in square 427; lot 11 in square 448, frame house, unfinished; part lot 1 in square west of 484; 3 frame houses on Mass ave; lot on 6th st, in same square; lots 25 thru 29, 46 & 47 in 513, & 2 frame bldgs; part of lot 16 in square 453, with 2 three story brick houses; part of 12, in square south of 516, with frame house; part lot 1 in square 516, with neat frame house; lot 15, in square south of 562; lots 1 & 2 in square B, with 7 brick houses & back bldgs, which did rent for upwards of $2,000 per year; lots 4, 5, & 6 in square C, on Md ave; lots 28 & 29 in same square, fronting on the canal; lot 5 in square D, on Md ave; lot 24 in 584; lot 1, 15, & parts of 2 & 3 in 535; part of lot 4 in 575; 4 story brick, corner of Pa ave & 2nd st, now renting for $1,225 per year; also, lot 5 in same square, fronting 2nd st; lot 2 in 613; this is on the water, at the mouth of the Eastern Branch. –Ulysses Ward

The successors of Edw Dyer & Robt W Dyer, auctioneers of Wash City, lately deceased, beg leave to inform their friends that they will continue the Auction & Commission business at the old stand, corner of 10th & Pa ave. —Edw C Dyer, Geo F Dyer

THU JUL 13, 1848
All persons having claims against Jos Beardsley, deceased, are requested to present them to the subscriber for settlement on Thursday next. Claims should be approved by the Orphans Court of Wash Co, D C. —W Lenox

Senate: 1-Cmte of Claims: House bill for the relief of Elisha F Richards, with an amendment, accompanied by a report. Also, House bill for the relief of Lisur B Canfield. 2-Cmte on Private Land Claims: bill for the relief of Jos P Williams.

Notice. The Hydraulic Ram can be had at Mr J H Nevitt's, on Pa ave, opposite Willard's Hotel, Wash, who will furnish the necessary lead pipe & erect any wanted within a reasonable distance of the city. —J L Gatchel, Patentee, Elkton, Md

Mrd: on Jul 3, by Rev Mr Foley, Edmund F French, formerly of Chester, N H, to Miss Margaret A, eldest daughter of Peter Brady, of Wash City.

Mrd: on Jul 6, by Rev Mr Martin, Mr John H Gordon, of Balt, to Miss Clarissa S Maddox, of PG Co, Md.

The Hon Wm R King has been appointed by the Govn'r of Alabama to fill the vacancy occasioned by Mr Bagby's resignation of his seat in the Senate of the U S.

FRI JUL 14, 1848
John A Hellings, late landlord of the Steamboat Hotel, in South Trenton, accidentally shot himself on Sat last, on his farm, near Bristol, Pa. The unfortunate man had climbed the fence, &, in carelessly pulling the gun over afterwards, was shot entirely through the heart.

Mr Mordecai Cohen died at Charleston, S C, on Sat night last. He was one of the oldest inhabitants of that place, & enjoyed in a high degree the esteem & confidence of the community. He was in in 86th year.

Longevity: Mrs Mary Bacon, aged 108 years, died in Providence, R I, on Monday, at her residence on Westminster st. The accuracy of her age seems to be placed beyond controversy by the following record in the ofc of the city clerk: Mary Mathewson, daughter of John Mathewson & Phoebe his wife, was born at Providence the 10th days of June, 1740. She was married early in life, & was not long after left a widow. She had 2 children, both of whom died young. At the time of her death, she had no nearer blood relatives than the granchidlren of her brother, the late Col John Mathewson, who died in 1816, aged 73 years. He owned nearly all the land now known as *Point Pleasant*. Mrs Bacon enjoyed very tolerable health until a few weeks previous to her death.
—Providence Journal

Death of a veteran: old Ebenezer Clouth, whose face & silver shoe buckles have been familiar time out of mind to the oldest inhabitants of Boston, died on Jul 4. He was a true patriot & had never-failing veneration for the heroes of '76. He has left us in his 81st year. –Boston Transcript of the 5th.

House of Reps: 1-Cmte of Claims: bills for the relief of Thos H Noble; of John Howe; & of Orange H Dibble: committed. Same cmte: House bill for the relief of John P Converse, reported back with an amendment. Same cmte: adverse reports on the ptns of B I Heard, R C Prewitt, Wm Woodward, & S B Olmstead: laid on the table. Samt cmte: Senate bills for the relief of Richd Fields & for the payment to Chas Richmond: committed. Same cmte: Senate bills for the relief of J F Sothoron & for the relief of Saml Grice: committed. Same cmte: Senate bill for the relief of J W Nye, assignee of P Bargy & H Stewart: reported the same back to the House with the recommendation that it do not pass: committed. Same cmte: Senate bill for the relief of Jose Argote, Vallalobos, Marie Rose, Francois Felix, Marquis de Fongeres, or their heirs or legal reps, reported the same back to the House with an amendment. 2-Cmte of Claims: adverse report on the ptn of Anna Maria Baldwin: laid on the table. Same cmte: bills for the relief of the legal reps of John H Piatt; of B M Bonton; & of A H Patterson: committed. Same cmte: discharged from the ptns of Thos Copeland, Mary E Bunfoot, excx of John Clarke, deceased, Geo W Kidd, Jane Parker, & of the exc of John J Bulen, deceased: laid on the table. Same cmte: adverse report on the ptns of Jeremiah Carpenter & Danl G Garnsey: laid on the table. Same cmte: bill for the relief of Thos T Gammage: committed. 3-Cmte on Commerce: bill to compensate & reimburse the owner & crew of the whaling ship **Chandler Price** the losses & expenses incurred in ransoming the crew of the ship **Columbia**: committed. 4-Senate bill for the relief of Benj Adams & Co & others: committed. 5-Bill for the relief of Chas B Cluskey: committed. 6-Cmte on Public Lands: bill to confirm to the legal reps of Jos Dutailles the location of a certain New Madrid certificate: reported back without amendment. 7-Memorial of Isaac Garrason: presented in the House. 8-Ptn of Saml Coleman for a contract to prepare & publish an index to Congressional documents: presented.

Convicted: 1-Augustus Dutee, a French Canadian, was found guilty of murder, at Boston, on Sat, having shot Ellen Oakes, some time ago, so that she died. There had existed a very intimate relationship between them, but she refused to marry him. He was sentenced to be hanged on some day to be appointed by the Govn'r. 2-Jas Murphy, an Irishman, tried for the murder of his wife, was acquitted. A very good character was given to the prisoner, & the jury considered his wife's death the result of an accidental fall. She was intoxicated when the killing took place.

Died: on Jul 6, after a brief illness, Mrs Ann Gordon, wife of Mr John Gordon, aged 75 years, leaving an aged husband & a large number of children, grandchildren, & friends, mourning her departure.

Died: on Jul 9, in Wash City, Jacob Little, son of John E & Caroline Little, aged 1 year, 1 month & 13 days.

Died: on Jul 9, in Gtwn, D C, Kate, daughter of Thos A & Sarah A Lazenby, aged 12 months & 6 days.

Died: on Jun 26, at Baton Rouge, La, Maj H W Fowler, aged 48 years. He was well known in Wash, having served for 12 years in the Marine Corps; after which he was appointed to the Dragoons, in which he served 5 years in the Florida war & elsewhere. After which, resigning his commission in the Army, he filled for several years the ofc of Sheriff of East Baton Rouge. At the breaking out of the Mexican war he promptly raised a company & went to the Rio Grande, but his health failing him, he was obliged to resign his command & return home, where he gradually continued to sink beneath the inroads of disease until his death closed the scene of life.

Columbian College: annual commencement took place on Wed last. Order of Exercises: Music; prayer by the Pres, Dr Bacon. Orations by

Geo L Bosher, of King Wm Co, Va
W J H Carleton, Indian Springs, Ga
W S Christian, of Middlesex Co, Va
Andrew B Evans, of Middlesex Co, Va
J Mason Evans, of Middlesex Co, Va
J R Holliday, of Andalusia Ga
Francis Scott, Northampton Co, Va

S W Taylor, Cambridge, Mass
J Tilson, West Randolph, Vt
J H Wilson, Jefferson Co, Va
R H Woodward, Middlesex Co, Va
D J Yerkes, Haborough, Pa
Wentworth L Childs, Wash

Candidates for 2nd Degree:
Solomon C Boston, Va
W L Childs, D C
Christ'r B Jennett, Va

Jos B Pleasants, Va
Jeremiah L Sanders, Miss

SAT JUL 15, 1848

Senate: 1-Cmte of Claims: House bill for the relief of Joshua Barney, U S agent, without amendment. Same cmte: house bill for the relief of Jos E Doxey, with amendment. Same cmte: House bill for the relief of Chas Benne, with amendments.

Mrd: on Jun 13, by Rev Mr Lanahan, Wm Taylor to Julia Kalahan, both of Wash City.

Mrd: on Jul 12, by Rev Wm Friend, Wm T Swann, of Wash City, to Rosina Moore, daughter of Gustavus B Alexander, of Caledon, King Geo Co, Va.

Died: on Jul 14, in her 19th year, Mary, wife of Geo C Hanson, & daughter of Senator Barnes, of Ill. Her funeral is this afternoon at 6 o'clock, from her late residence, corner of D & 7th sts.

Died: on Thu last, Archibald Alexander, infant son of Rev R R Gurley.

Died: on Jul 6, at his residence at the head of St Clement's bay, in St Mary's Co, Md, Jas McWilliams, at the age of 78 years. He was affectionate as a husband & father, kind to his servants, & just to all. But, more than all, his Christian character was his brightest possession.

An address was delivered at Rahway, N J, on Jul 4, by Wm B Reed, on the occasion of the inauguration of a monument erected over the remains of Abraham Clark, one of the signers of the Declaration of Independence.

MON JUL 17, 1848
It has been reported that Kit Carson, celebrated as the guide & companion of Lt Col Fremont in his dangerous explorations of the West, has been killed on the plains by the Inidans. He left California, with dispatches for Washington, in Apr last, & should by this time have reached Independence, Mo. The rumor was brought to *Fort Independence* by an Indian.

Death in Maine on Jul 4. 1-The Norway Advertiser chronicles the death by drowning at Greenwood, of a son of Mr Saml Barker. 2-At Belfast, a son of Mr Jacob Ames, age 12 years, was thrown out of a wagon & almost instantly killed. 3-A Mr Herrick of Portland, had one of his legs blown off by the bursting of a cannon. 4-Howard M Trask, 11 years of age, was accidentally shot in the leg at Bangor, by some boys who were firing a cannon, & died the next day.

Amesbury, Mass: another died from eating clams at Black Rocks. On Wednesday Eliz Castles, age about 24 years died from eating the clams.

House of Reps: 1-Ptn of J W Nye, praying for payment for services rendered under a contract relating to the post ofc connected with the House of Reps.

Estray Red Cow came to the subscriber's about Jul 6: owner is to come for her, prove property, pay charges, & take her away. –Abner C Shoemaker, about 5 miles out on 7th st Turnpike

$5 reward for a large Durham Cow, that strayed from the subscriber, living on 8th st. –Henry N Young

Orphans Court of Wash Co, D C. Letters testamentary on the personal estate of Jas Day, late of said county, deceased. –Wm Ward, exc

TUE JUL 18, 1848
Senate: 1-Cmte ptn Public Lands: adverse report on the memorial of Agnes Slack.

Loudoun Farm for Sale: by authority of the last will & testatment of Chas Gassaway, deceased, the undersigned offer for sale the very valuable Farm, called The *Sugarland Farm*, purchased by deceased of Mrs Selden. It contains 678 acres. The bldgs are only ordinary for so large a farm. It will be shown by Mr Muse, the tenant. Apply to the undersigned, residing in Leesburg: C B Gassaway, F W Luckett, excx & exc of Chas Gassaway.

Balt: on Jul 16, Mr John S Lafitte, one of our citizens, formerly a wealthy merchant, committed suicide by drowning himself in the Spring Gardens.

Sale of part of lot 7 in square 633, in Wash City: by deed of trust from Chas Webster & wife, dated May 28, 1847, recorded in liber W B 136, folios 296 to 298, Wash Co, D C: will be sold at public auction on Aug 10: property is on First st west, between B & C sts north. -A Green, auctioneer

Montgomery Co Court, as a Court of Equity. Henry Slater, sen, obligee of Henry & Danl Slater, vs Thos Beall, of Danl, et al. This bill is to obtain a decree for the sale of the lands of the late John L Beall for the payment of his debts, upon an alleged insufficiency of personal assests. The original bill states that at Nov term, 1827, of said Court, the cmplnts, Henry & Danl Slater, recoverd judgment, in the name of the State, for their use, against the said John L Beall, which judgment was afterwards revived by scire facias at Mar term, 1832, as would appear from exhibit H D S No 1, filed with said bill; that John L Beall died intestate about 1833, leaving as his heirs-at-law Thos Beall of Danl, Mary Lazenby, the children of Mgt Lazenby, deceased, viz. Mary, Eliz, Ann, Catherine, [since intermarried with Jos Soper,] Edw, Martha, & Cornelia Lazenby; Rachel Beall, Sarah Perry, & Eliza Beall, of Montg Co, & Margaret, wife of Stephen Hooper, of Va; that Thos Beall of Danl administered on the estate of deceased, & the same was insufficient for the payment of the deceased's debts, as would appear from a copy of his first & only account, therewith filed, marked exhibit H D S No 2; that John L Beall died seized of real estate in Montg Co, which descended to the aforesaid persons as his heirs at-law; & prays that they be made dfndnts, & answer the same, & that the said lands be sold by a trustee, to be appointed for that purpose; & that an order of publication be passed, warning the non-resident dfndnts to appear & answer the premises. The bill revivor states the filing of the original bill on Feb 23, 1837; that one of the cmplnts, Danl Slater, hath since died, & his interest survived to the other cmplnts; that Sarah Perry, one of the dfndnts to the original bill, hath since died intestate, leaving Wm M, Augustus, Thos, Lewis, Sarah Jane, Amanda, & Joel C Perry, her heirs-at-law, all of whom reside out of this State, & the said Catherine Lazenby, one of the heirs of Mary Lazenby, hath intermarried with Jos Soper. The bill prays that the same be revised as to the said heirs-at-law of Sarah Perry, deceased, & the said Jos Soper & Catherine his wife. Absent dfndnts to appear in this Court on or before the 3rd Mon of Dec next. –T H Wilkinson

Died: on Jun 29, at Decatur, Ill, Mrs Rachel Ann Prather, consort of Wm Prather, & eldest daughter of the late Rev Jas Smith, of Md.

WED JUL 19, 1848
House of Reps: 1-Memorial of the heirs of Surgeon L A Wolpley, U S army, asking a pension. 2-Ptn of Thos Cockeron, Wm Campbell, & 49 others for a mail route from Harrisonburg to Nachitoches, via Rowesville, Desdemons, & Thompson's Springs, La.

New Orleans: letter dated Jul 8, states that the Hon Wm L Brent, formerly a member of Congress from La, died suddenly at St Martinsville, La, of apoplexy. He had just got into his carriage, when he was taken, & died immediately. Before his retiring from Congress, he was for many years a prominent member of the bar in Washington, &, under his auspices there, his son, Robt J Brent, of the Balt bar, embraced the profession. Mr Brent's late residence in Louisiana has been for about 5 years. -Sun

Orphans Court of Wash Co, D C. Letters of administration on the personal estate of Thos S Bingey, late of said county, deceased. –Saml Stott, adm

An accident took place yesterday on the front beach of Sullivan's Island. Four children, one a daughter of Dr Edmund Ravenel, & the others dghts of Col Edw Harelton, bathing in the surf, were carried by the ebbing tide beyond their depth. Miss Ravenel, aged 11 years, was drowned, & her body has not yet been recovered. The others were after great efforts saved. –Charleston News

Isaac Knight, of Camden Co, N J, was raking hay with a horse-rake on Wed, having thrown the reins over his shoulders that his hands might be free. The horse stumbles, & Mr Knight's breast was brought violently upon the head of the rake, which killed him.

Obit-died: on Jul 6, at **Round Hill**, Northampton, Mass, in his 26th year, Edw Law Baldwin, oldest son of Hon Roger Sherman Baldwin, U S Senator from Conn. He was a graduate of Yale College in 1843 with high standing as a scholar; removed to N Y C & qualified himself for practice in N Y; was soon after attacked by severe pulmonary disease, which drove him for relief to the south of Europe. On his return he renewed at New Haven the pursuit of his profession; a rapid decline terminated his life.

Died: on Jul 3, at the residence of Dr Hoffar, in Wash City, Miss Catharine Stonestreet, in her 27th year.

Died: on Jul 17, after an illness of 6 weeks, Saml L Wilson, of Princess Anne, Md. His funeral will take place from the residence of his sisters, on B st, today at 11 o'clock.

Died: on Jul 4, in Gtwn, Mrs Matilda Drummond, in her 55th year. She bore a long & painful illness with Christian fortitude. She was endeared by many virtues to a large number of friends & relatives.

Valuable property at auction: by deed of trust from John Sessford & wife to Jas Thrift, dated Jan 1, 1846, recorded in Liber W B # 124, folios 109 thru 111, of the land records of Wash Co, D C, & a subsequent decree of the Circuit Court of Wash Co, D C, sitting as a Court of Chancery, made in the cause of Nicolas Febrey vs John Sessford, & Jas Thrift, substituting me as Trustee in lieu of said Jas Thrift, I shall offer at auction, on Aug 19, in Wash City, lot 19 in square 293, on the west side of 12th st, south of Pa ave. –Wm R Woodward, trustee -Edw C & G F Dyer [Sep 25th newspaper: sale postponed until Oct 7 next.]

THU JUL 20, 1848
For sale: 3 story dwlg house at the corner of Bridge & Fred'k sts, Gtwn, opposite the residence of the subscriber. Also, a lot of ground fronting 147 feet on the south side of the Canal measured west from Market st. –Jno Marbury

Farm for rent: contains 230 acres, dwlg house, barns, & corn-house, 5 miles above Gtwn, near Rock Creek. Apply to Mrs Cartwright, on the premises, or to W H Godey, Gtwn.

Senate: 1-Cmte on Pensions: adverse report on the memorial of Mehitable Gibbs. Same cmte: adverse report on the memorial of Mary Coleman.

Obit-died: on Mon, in the Custom-house Store, in Pine st, Gen Robt Swarthwout, long known in the political & military circles of N Y, & recently elected Alderman of the 3rd Ward of that city, fell dead in an apoplectic fit. An ardent friend of Col Burr, he stuck with honorable fidelity to the fallen fortunes of the man whom in power he had approved. In the war of 1812 he was appointed a Quartermaster Gen of the Northern Army; & in the ill-conducted descent of the St Lawrence by the American army the command devolved upon Gen Swartwaout, [who had the rank of Brig,] in the bloody fight of Chrystlers Field. Pecuniary difficulties with the Gov't in the settlement of his accounts embarrassed his later years, yet did not break down his spirit or activity. –Courier & Enquirer

Appointments by the Pres: 1-Gideon J Pillow, of Tenn, [Brig Gen in the U S volunteer service,] to be Maj Gen, Apr 13, 1847, vice Benton, declined. 2-John A Quitman, of Miss, [Brig Gen in the U S volunteer service,] to be Maj Gen, Apr 14, 1847, vice Cummins, declined. 3-Caleb Cushing, of Mass, to be Brig Gen, Apr 14, 1847, vice Pillow, appointed Maj Gen. 4-Sterling Price, of Missouri, to be Brig Gen, Jul 20, 1847, vice Davis, declined.

Mrd: on Tue, at Balt, by Rev Dr Jones, Jno Wills to Rebecca Frances Toy, all of that city.

Mrd: on Thu last, at Portsmouth, Va, by the Rev John Henry Wingfield, Cmder Hugh Nelson Page, U S Navy, to Eliz Plume, daughter of the late Holt Wilson.

Casualties: 1-John T Palmer killed himself at Boston on Fri with a large dose of arsenic. He was 35 years of age, & leaves a wife & 4 children. No cause is assigned for the self-murder. 2-At Yarmouth, on Sun, Miss Hannah H Basset, aged about 60, committed suicide by drowning herself. She had been for some time partially insane. 3-Kelsey Van Aiken, of Hartford Landing, hung himself to a tree on Thu. He was in comfortable circumstances, had a wife & 2 children, & appeared contented with his position in life. 4-A German grocer, of N Y, by the name of Schroeder, was discovered on Mon suspended by a bedcord, & quite dead, with one end of the cord grasped firmly in his hands. 5-Augustus Naundorf, a German baker, unable to obtain work or business by which to support his wife, cut his throat in Phil on Thu. 6-Mary Scott died in Boston after taking an overdose of medicine. She took tea pills. 7-On Sun, at Boston, Jas S Wheeler, age 18 years, was drowned. Being an excellent swimmer, he ventured out too far. 8-On Sat, John Veber, a wheelwright, has an altercation near his shop with Edw Crosby, in relation to the payment of $2.50 which the latter claimed as wages due for labor. The dispute ended in Crosby's striking him 2 blows with his fist, knocking him down, & injuring him so seriously, that he died a few hours afterward. 9-On Fri, a Rochester, Henry Thos Padley, lately from Liverpool, England, was drowned while bathing in the canal. 10-At Montreal, on Wed, Private Jones, of the 19th Regt, shot Cpl Fitzgerald because the latter had threatened to report him for insolvent behavior.

Rittenhouse Academy, Indiana Ave, semi-annual examination of the pupils of this Institution will commence on Jul 20, -J E Nourse

WASH JUL 21, 1848
House of Reps: 1-Bill for the relief of Alfred White: reported. 2-Cmte on the Judiciary: bill for the relief of Messrs Cook, Anthony, Mahon, & others: committed. Same cmte: bill to provide compensation to Wm Woodbridge & Henry Chipman for services in adjusting titles to land in Mich & for other purposes: committed. 3-Cmte on Revolutionary Claims: adverse reports on the ptns of Nathl Tracy & of the heirs of Jonathan Hoge: laid on the table. Same cmte: discharged from the further consideration of the ptns of Lt Jona Smith, Mary Scott, admx of Lt John C Scott, deceased, Elijah W Brown, & of the heirs of Willis Wilson: laid on the table. Same cmte: bill for the relief of the legal reps of Capt Chas Smith & for the relief of the legal reps or heirs of Capt John Mountjoy: committed. Same cmte: bill for the relief of Mary M Telfair, heir & legal rep of Israel Pearce: committed. Same cmte: adverse report on the ptn of Dennis Purcell: laid on the table. 4-Cmte on Private Land Claims: Senate bill for the relief of Jesse Turner: committed. Same cmte: adverse report on the ptn of Geo W Kincaid: laid on the table. 5-Cmte on Indian Affairs: joint resolution of the Senate for the relief of H B Gaither: committed. 6-Cmte on Naval Affairs: bill for the relief of Jacob Boston: committed. 7-Ptn of John C P Edwards, of Portsmouth, Va, asking passage of an act to authorize him to sue the U S for damages. 8-Cmte on Invalid Pensions: bills for the relief of Susannah Prentiss; for the relief of Thos R Saunders; for the relief of Sylvanus Blodget; & for the relief of Aaron Stafford: all committed. Same cmte: bills for the relief of the heirs of Moses White; & for the relief of David N Smith: reported the same back to the House without amendment. 9-<u>Cmte on Revolutionary Pensions</u>: Senate bill granting a pension to Abigail Garland, widow of Jacob Garland, deceased: committed. Bill for the relief of Eve Boggs, widow of John Boggs: committed. Adverse report on the ptn of John England: laid on the table. Bills for the relief of Jos Dana, & for the relief of Hannah Kinney: committed. Bill for the relief of Mary Taylor: committed. Discharged from the ptns of Anne Royal, widow of Wm Royal, & Patience Corbin, & from the affidavit of Richd Pattison: laid on the table. Adverse reports on the ptns of the heirs of Danl Avery, Edw Shepherd, John M Rosebury, & Susannah Kimball: laid on the table. Bill for the relief of Matha Dameron, widow of Christopher Tompkins: committed. Discharged from the ptn of Jos Sloan: laid on the table. Adverse reports on the ptns of Andrew McKim & Robt Petty, heirs of Andrew Snyder, Abigail Edgerly, & Dickinson Lumpkin: laid on the table. Bill for the relief of Thompson Hutchinson: laid on the table. Bill for the relief of Welcome Parmenter: committed. Adverse report on the ptn of heirs of Jos Plumb: laid on the table. Discharged from the further consideration of the ptn of Eliz C Fitzhugh, widow of Pergrine Fitzhugh: laid on the table. Bill for the relief of Eliz Jones: laid on the table.

Senate: 1-Cmte on Public Lands: bill for the relief of Elias A Conway, assignee of Wm Barnett.

Eleazer Evans, the father of Hon Nathan Evans, of the House of Reps, died at his residence in Belmont Co, Ohio, on Jul 10, aged about 73 years.

SAT JUL 22, 1848
Senate: 1-Ptn from Louisa Catharine Adams, & other heirs of Joshua Johnson, deceased, asking the settlement of the accounts of the deceased consul & commercial agent at London, on the principles of equity, & the payment of any balance which may be found due for his services.

Wash Corp: 1-Ptn of Christopher Cammack, praying to be refunded the amount of certain licenses alleged to have been improperly paid to the Corp: referred to the Cmte of Claims. 2-Ptn of Chas Hebbs & others, praying for the improvement of 4th st, near the City Hall: referred to the Cmte on Improvements. Same for the ptn of J S Cunningham & others, for grading & gravelling M st, between 6th & 7th sts. 3-Ptn of H G O'Neale, for remission of a fine: referred to the Cmte of Claims. 4-Cmte of Claims: bill for the relief of John H Mullen: read twice.

By 2 writs of fieri facias issued by John L Smith, J P for Wash Co, D C, at the suit of T M Milburn & B Milburn, trading under the firm of T M & B Milburn, against the goods & chattels of Horatio R Maryman & Edmund Reilly, to me directed, I have seized & taken in execution all the right, title, & interest of Edmund Reilly, in & unto 54 pairs of boots & shoes: public auction on Jul 29, in front of the Centre Market House.
–U B Mitchell, Constable

For rent: the store & dwlg attached, on Pa ave, now occupied by B L Jackson & Bro: possession on Oct 1st. Inquire of Sarah T Hughes, F st, between 9th & 10th sts.

MON JUL 24, 1848
Agency for claims at Wash: Fredinand W Risque, Atty & Counsellor of Law, formerly of Lynchburg, Va, but more recently of St Louis, Mo, has opened an ofc in Wash City, in Lakemeyer's European Hotel, Pa ave, between 14th & 15th sts. .

Senate: 1-Ptn of John Lewis, a colored man of Phil, asking that the 5th section of the Oregon bill be so amended as to strike out "free white," so as to give the colored citizens of the U S an equal advantage with all others. 2-Cmte on Pensions: adverse report in the case of Henrietta Beddinger; also in the case of Leonard Gray.

House of Reps: 1-Memorial of the heirs of the late Joshua Johnson, of Md, asking for a settlement of his accounts as consul & commercial agent at London. 2-Claim of Capt F Schaffer, of Chicago, Ill, for refunding of certain moneys advanced by him when in the U S service. 3-Additional affidavits to accompany ptn of Edw Shepard for a pension.

Playing with Gunpowder. 1-S S Austin, of Uniontown, Pa, was killed at Pittsburg on Fri by the bursting of a Mexican swivel, which he was firing a salute with in honor of the returned volunteers. 2-At Cincinnati, on Wed, Geo Grodon & A A Attenborough were terribly lacerated by the premature discharge of a cannon while firing a salute.

Dr Lukenberg, of New Orleans, died at the Broadway Hotel, in Cincinnati, on Sat night.

Letter from the banks of the Genesse river says: "On arriving at Kingston on Jul 7, I was requested to see a dying stranger, Judge Saml Wilkeson, of Buffalo, N Y. I had heard of him. He had a daughter with him, on their way to visit his married daughter at Zelico Plains, 40 miles from this. The latter arrived to attend his funeral on the evening, the 9th. Bronchial erysipelas of 2 years' standing had caused gouty & rheumatic neuralgia in the lumbar & sciatic nerves, with other constitutional derangement. He was conscious of his approaching dissolution, & met it with the most perfect calmness & submission."

On Mon or Tue last a trifling land slide occurred on the levee, opposite the Ursuline Convent, in the 3rd Municipality, & a small frame bldg was partly submerged. A large number of persons assembled there to look at the chasm, when a considerable portion of the levee gave way, carrying with it a crowd of spectators. Those who are known to have fallen victims were: Mr Francois Andry, Madam Victorine Tromp & her child Gustave, aged 8 months; Felix Tromp, aged 21 years, & his 2 sisters, Louise & Fanny, the one 13 & the other 10 years of age; & Madam Charlotte Desaire, aged 22 years. Mr Paul Tromp, of all the family present, was alone saved, but so injured his recovery is doubtful. –New Orleans Bee, 15th inst.

Mrd: on Thu last, by Rev Mr Hamilton, P F Schleicker, of Norfolk, Va, to Miss A E Latimer, of Wash City.

The U S schnr **Mahonese**, Lt Commanding Wm D Porter, arrived at Norfolk on Thu. She brought home the body of Cmder Pinkney, who was drowned on the bar of Tuspan. It had been sent for the present to the Naval Hospital, whence it will be removed to Balt. She also brought over from Tuspan the remains of Cmder Harris, which were left at Pensacola.

Wash City News. A new company of citizen soldiers is about to be organized in the Northern part of this city, under John Y Bryant, as their commanding ofcr. The corps is to be styled the Walker Sharpshooters, in honor, we presume, of the late gallant Capt Saml H Walker, who fell on the plains of Mexico.

Mrd: on Mon last, at St Peter's Church, by Rev J Van Horning, Bernard Corrigan to Miss Mgt Carroll, all of Wash City.

Died: on Jul 16, in Wash City, Mrs Letitia Pollitt, a native of Md, aged 80 years.

Died: on Jul 12, at New Orleans, Mr Geo McCormick, a native of Wash City, & for the last 14 years a resident of New Orleans.

Died: on Jul 11, at his lodgings, in New Orleans, Maj Erastus B Smith, of Ky, Commissary of the U S Army. The deceased was returning home from the campaign of Mexico.

Died: on Jul 9, at Honesdale, Pa, Col Chas Niven, late of Newburg, Orange Co, N Y. He was also formerly sheriff of Orange Co, & subsequently in the Post Ofc Dept, Wash.

Died: on Jul 8, at Lake Scuppernoog, N C, Hon Ebenezer Pettigrew, in his 66th year. To the numerous friends of this estimable gentleman this announcement will cause sorrow deep & heartfelt. –Raleigh Reg

WASH JUL 25, 1848
The undersigned, being in possession of a correct list of our brave soldiers who have died of disease, or by wounds received in the several battles fought in Mexico, inform those interested that they will give the information of the time, place, & cause of death of each individual; without charge, provided the postage is paid. –Saml Stettinius, Gen Agent, Wash City; Wm M Fulton, Atty at Law, Richmond, Va; Geo W Stevenson, Atty at Law, 27 Beckman st, N Y.

Died: on Jul 23, at Petersburg, Va, aged 46 years, Weston Raleigh Gales, Proprietor & Editor of the Raleigh Register. He had arrived at Petersburg from Old Point Comfort the preceding day, then extremely ill. His remains, attended by a part of his afflicted family, were on Sunday conveyed to Raleigh, N C, the place of his nativity & of his residence. Our lamented friend was the only brother of one of the editors of this paper, & brother-in-law of the other. [Aug 5th newspaper: the Raleigh Times give his age as 47 years.]

Died: on Jun 8 last, at Saltillo, Mexico, Jas H Middleton, eldest son of E J Middleton, of Wash City, in his 21st year. The news of his death, which was the result of an accident, came upon his family & friends here like a thunderbolt from a cloudless day, at the very moment when his return was daily looked for. Although in a foreign land, he was surrounded by friends who did all that human aid could do to alleviate his sufferings.

Fred'k Co Court, Court of Equity, Feb Term, 1848. Barbara Spechten, vs John Schlotz, Michl Schmitt & others. The object of this suit is to obtain a decree for the sale of the real estate of which John Geo Badex, late of Fred'k Co, deceased, was the owner, for the payment of his debts. The bill states that Badex, late of said county, died in 1847, intestate, leaving real estate consisting of a house & lot, in Emmittsburg, Fred'k Co; that Joshua Motter obtained letters of administration from the Orphans' Court of Fred'k Co on the goods & chattels, rights & credits of said deceased, & that the personal assets of deceased were not sufficient to pay his debts. The cmplnt has a large debt against the deceased unpaid. The bill states that Badex died, leaving John Schlotz & Michl Schmitt his heirs-at-law, & also a number of other heirs whose names are unknown to the cmplnt, & the other creditors of said deceased. The bill states that all the heirs-at-law of the said deceased reside in Switzerland, in Europe, out of the State of Md, & beyond the reach of process of this Court. Notice is given to the absent dfndnts & heirs-at-law of the said John Geo Badex, to appear in this Court, in person or by solicitor, on or before the first Mon of Dec next. –Wm B Tyler, Clerk

Southampton, Jul 3. The Ocean Steam Navigation Company's ship **Hermann**, Capt E Crabtree, arrived in Cowes' Roads, late of Wight, last night, with the U S mails from Great Britian, France, & Germany.

Mrd: on Jul 11, in St Louis, Mo, by Rev Dr Potts, Dr Jas McDowell, late of Rockbridge Co, Va, to Miss Eliz L Brant, daughter of Col J B Brant, of St Louis.

Mrd: on Jul 18, at St Mary's Church, by Rev Mr Stanly, Wm N Loker, of St Louis, Mo, to Miss Anna A, 2nd daughter of Wm H Loker, of St Mary's Co, Md.

Mrd: on Jul 5, in Brunswick, Va, Capt Thos H Meredith to Miss Henrietta, daughter of Col Isham Trotter.

Died: on Jul 22, near the Navy Yard, of dropsy, Mary Handly, wife of Patrick Callaghan, born in the parish of Moycullen, Galway Co, Ireland, in her 53rd year.

Died: on Jul 23, Mrs Anna Maria Johnson, of consumption, in her 28th year, leaving a husband & 4 small children to mourn their irreparable loss.

Died: on Jul 14, at Kent Island, Md, aged 11 months, John Elliott, infant son of Jas L & Rachael E White, of Wash City.

Died: Jul 17, in Brunswick, Va, Mr Henry E Scott, formerly of Charlotte Co, aged 62 yrs.

Died: on Jul 24, John Bailey, aged 3 weeks, son of John S & Eliz Cunningham. His funeral is this afternoon at 5 o'clock, from the residence on M st, between 6th & 7th sts.

WED JUL 26, 1848
House of Reps: 1-Cmte of Claims: ptn of Jacob Housemen: laid on the table. 2-Cmte on Invalid Pensions: bill for the relief of Hector Perkins: committed. Same cmte: asking to be discharged from the further consideration of the ptn of Maj L P Montgomery: laid on the table. Same cmte: bills for the relief of Peter Myers, & for the relief of Capt Alex'r McEwen: committed. Adverse reports on the ptns of J W Knipe, Rezin Terris, & Ethel Bartis: laid on the table. Same cmte reported on the following-all committed: relief of Eliz S Cobbs; of Mary Ann Pollard; of Canfield Averill; & of the children of Lewis A Wolfley. 3-Cmte on Invalid Pensions: discharged from the further consideration of the ptn of Henry Powell: laid on the table. Same cmte: bill granting a pension to John Clark: committed. 4-Cmte of the Whole was discharged from the further consideration of the bill granting a pension to Wm Pittman. Same cmte reported a bill for the relief of Wm Kennedy: committed. 5-Cmte on Patents: bill for the relief of David Wilkinson: committed. Same cmte: bill for the relief of the heirs of Danl Pettibone: committed. Same cmte: discharged from the further consideration of the ptn of H I Thistle: laid on the table. 6-Resolved, that the Cmte of Accounts audit & pay the balance of the unsettled claim of John T Sullivan for stationery furnished the House of Reps in 1843.
7-Resolved-Cmte on the Library: the portrait of Maj Gen the Baron de Kalb, presented by his surviving family, be placed in the Library of Congress.

Gtwn College, D C: Annual Commencement was held on Jul 25, 1848.

Degree of A M was conferred on: Eliel S Wilson, of Md; Waldeman de Bodisco, of Russia

Degree of A B was conferred on the following students:
Henry J Forstall, of La
Henry B Leaumont, La
Alex'r A Allemong, S C
Bernard J Caulfield, D C
John C Riley, D C
I Valery Landry, La
Edmund R Smith, N Y
Casimire Dessaulles, Canada

Students awarded silver medals or premiums, or were honorably mentioned:
Henry J Forstall, of La
Alex'r A Allemong, S C
John C Riley, D C
Edmund R Smith, N Y
Henry B Leaumont, La
Bernard J Caulfield, D C
I Valery Landry, La
Casimire Dessaulles, Canada
Edmund A Deslonde, La
Pierre D Delacroix, La
J B Adrien Lepetre, La
Thos A Della Torre, S C
Alfred J Higgins, Va
Alfonso T Semmes, Ga
Alfred H Byrd, Va
Wm Mouton, La
John M Duncan, Ala
Edwin F King, D C
Hermogene Dufresne, La
F Matthews Lancaster, Md
Wm Wills, Md
Henry P Tricou, La
Lewis F Pise, N Y
Jules A Choppin, La
Louis E Deslonde, La
H Waring Brent, Md
Wm J Boarman, Md
Oscar P Tete, La
Wm H Duncan, Ala
Martin J Morris, D C
Francis P Fitnam, D C
Francis P Fulton, Tenn
J Buchanan Henry, Pa
Geo T May, D C
Pierre D Delacroix, La
Edmund A Deslonde, La
Edmund L Smith, Pa
Frederico Aldunate, Chili, S A
L John Carriel, Miss
Dominick A O'Bryan, Ga
Thos Della Torre, S C
Martin J Morris, D C
Henry P Trieou, La
Aristide L Aubert, Ala
Aleec A Atocha, La
Geo T May, D C
J Buchanan Henry, Pa
Julius C Eslava, Ala
Florence O'Donoghue, D C
Terenee Z Ranson, La
Raphael C Edelen, Md
Jerome Bres, La
Eugene A Shekell, D C
John L Love, D C
Jas C Middleton, Va
Francis Neale, Md
Wm H Duncan, Ala
Chas A Shafer, D C
Wm E Rickard, Ala
Wmos P Labarbe, N C
Thos H Dawson, D C
Augustus E Bass, La
Francis J Gasquet, La
Jos Adrien Hebert, La
Jules A Choppin, La
Wm P Freret, La
Edwin F M King, D C
Oscar P Tete, La
Zenon Freire, Chili, S A
Jas A Tillman, Ala

Manuel M Aldunate, Chili, S A
Amos P Labarbe, N C
Celestine C Pendergast, Md
Theliamar Gendry, La

Walter O Wynn, La
Isaac Pritchard, La
Wm Mouton, La
Lewis F Pise, N Y

For rent, the upper or dwlg part of that large bldgs on 7th st west, & Pa ave, over the stores of Shuster & Co & Messrs Hall & Brother, at present occupied by Mrs McCormick as a boarding house. For terms apply to Anne R Dermoth, residing in the house.

Senate: 1-Ptn from Capt Theodore Lewis, of the Louisiana volunteers, asking that bounty land might be allowed them. 2-Ptn from F F Aldrich, inventor of a new mode of propelling steam vessels intended for steam navigation, asking the Sec of the Navy be allowed to contract for the bldgs of a war steamer of 700 or 1,000 tons burden. The whole price not to exceed $200,000. 3-Cmte on Foreign Relations: bill for the relief of John B Hogan.

THU JUL 27, 1848
Senate: 1-Cmte on Pensions: House bill for the relief of Skelton Felton without amendment. Same cmte: adverse report on the House bill for the relief of Danl H Warren. 2-Cmte on the Post Ofc & Post Roads: asking to be discharged from the further consideration of the ptn of Jones & Boker.

For sale or trade: full-blooded Bay Horse, 7 years old. Also, a young Gray Mare & a good substantial Omnibus. Apply at the livery stable of Mr Earl, in the 1st Ward, Wash.

For rent: large & commodious house occupied for several years by the Brazilian Minister: located on the corner of 18th & K sts. Apply to Mrs D Walker, near the premises.

Died: on Jul 18, at his residence in Stafford Co, near Fredericksburg, Va, John Gray, in his 80th year. A native of Scotland, the deceased had resided in Va about 60 years.

Died: on Jul 2, at Greensborough, Ga, Mrs Frances Veazey, consort of Albert Veazey, & daughter of Sterling Gresham, for several years a resident of Wash City.

Penmanship. Chas Quin informs the citizens of Wash that he has opened a Writing School over Mr Krafft's confectionary, a few doors west of Brown's Hotel. Terms, $5 for the course of 10 lessons.

FRI JUL 28, 1848
Wash Corp: 1-Ptn of Saml Cromwell: referred to the Cmte of Claims. 2-Ptn of E H Fuller: referred to the Cmte of Claims: passed. 3-Ptn of P G Howle & others: referred to the Cmte on Wharves.

House of Reps: 1-Ptn of Hon Wm Jackson & 216 others, of Newton, Mass, praying for a law prohibiting the slave trade in D C.

Telegraphic dispatch from St Louis on Jul 25 gives the following items of news: The celebrated Kit Carson, whose death had been reported, arrived here today from Calif, in the capacity of a bearer of dispatches. He left Santa Fe on Jun 26. The accounts furnished by him confirm the death of Paymaster Spaulding.

A pleasure boat was capsized in Portland harbor, on Sat, by a sudden squall, & 8 persons lost their lives-the wife & 3 children of Mr Wm J Smith, & 4 children of Mr Whyley.

Academy of the Visitation, B V M. Gtwn D C: annual distribution of premiums took place on Jul 26. Premiums awarded to:

Eliz Roach, St Mary's Co, Md
Miss Eliz Griffin, Granville, Ohio
Harriet Lane, Lancaster, Pa
Rebecca Scott, Wash
Eleanora Gibson, Richmond, Va
Caroline King, Wash
Augusta Scott, Wash
Ada Benham, Alexandria, Va
Gertrude Fetterman, Pittsburg, Pa
Josephine Pleasanton, Phil
Mary Lufborough, Gtwn
Mary Ann Ennis, Wash
Glovinia Neale, Wash
Mary Ellen Brady, Wash
Julia Ewing, Phil
Catharine Templeman, Gtwn, D C
Clara Semmes, Gtwn
Catharine Cain, Wash
Christian Green, Montgomery
Emily Ward, Norfolk, Va
Felicie Sauve, New Orleans
Pauline Brock, New Orleans
Viginia Love, Gtwn, D C
Elara Mitchell, Balt
Josephine Briscoe, Wash
Eliz Donoghue, Wash
Rosa Ford, Wash
Amanda Clare, Wash
Matilda Devereux, Wash
Dora Murray, Gtwn
Mary E O'Neale, Gtwn
Adel Cutts, Wash
Odeide Mouton, New Orleans
Catharine Wheeler, Chas Co, Md
Ellen Roach, Gtwn
Marion Ramsay, Wash
Mathilde Mouton, New Orleans
Eliz Hanrahan, Greenville, N C
Sabina Semmes, Gtwn
Ann Gardner, Chas Co, Md
Catharine Corcoran, Wash
Catharine Lindsey, Gtwn
Isabel McLoskey, Batl
Jane Carroll, Gtwn
Julia Young, PG Co, Md
Harriet Thayer, Petersburg, Va
Catharine Tilghman, Eastern Shore, Md
Hannah Manly, Newbern, N C
Josephine Clements, Gtwn
Eliza Gwynn, PG Co, Md
Ann O'Donoghue, Gtwn
Rosa Queen, Wash
Mary C O'Donoghue, Gtwn
Jane Neale, Chas Co, Md
Georgiana Hill, Wash
Eliza Carrallo, Chili, S A
Celestia Neale, Chas Co, Md
Catherine Edelin, Wash
E Cissel, Wash
Virginia Magruder, PG Co, Md
Armantine Darcantel, New Orleans
Mary Peabody, Wash
Ellen Rose Matthews, Chas Co, Md
Mary Jane Jones, Wash
Geraldine Bellinger, Charleston, S C
Florence Greenhow, Wash
S Rainy, Wash
C Rochat, Wash
Virginia Davis, Gtwn
Elfrida Holland, Wash
Eliz Dodge, Gtwn
Christina Williams, St Augustine, Fla

Anna Waring, Montg Co, Md
E McCormick, Wash
Mary Jane Carroll, PG Co, Md
C Stoops, Gtwn
E J Donoghue, Gtwn
Mary Hagerty, Wash
Virginia Templeman, Gtwn
Emily Pierce, Gtwn
Ada Semmes, Gtwn
Rosa Porche, New Orleans
M Osborne, Gtwn
Pauline Clarke, Ky
C Barbarin, Gtwn
Frances Offutt, Gtwn
Anna King, Gtwn
Ellen Waring, Montg Co, Md
Cecelia Mouton, New Orleans
Mary Brooks, Gtwn
Josephine Meems, Gtwn
Sarah Fort, St Francisville, La
Mary Jane Briscoe, Wash
Josephine Laub, Wash
Mary Virginia Laub, Wash
Maria Louisa Devereux, Wash
Maraquita Seal, Rio Janeiro, S A

Emma Magruder, PG Co, Md
Victoria Brent, Chas Co, Md
Georgiana Morgan, Wash
Cora Dufour, St Mary's, Ga
Mary Catharine Donoghue, Gtwn
Louisa Gwynn, PG Co, Md
Cora Semmes, Gtwn
Bernadina Orme, Wash
Mary Adams, Wash
Maria Louisa Pierce, Montg Co, Md
Mary Ellen Mitchell, Gtwn, D C
Alida Gardner, Wash
A Snider, Phil
Delia Condry, Newburyport, Mass
Anna Bibb, Montg, Md
Francinia Berry, Wilmington, N C
Emily Fitzgerald, Wash
Rosa Hickey, Wash
Amanda Lepretre, New Orleans
Ellen Doland, Norfolk, Va
S O'Dell, Gtwn
Ernestine Blache, New Orleans
Irene Marshall, Norfolk, Va
Mary Barker, Wash

Gtwn College Annual Commencement was held on Tue in the spacious hall of the venerable institution. The band was under the direction of Prof Esputa. Public addresses were delivered by: [Jul 26th newspaper has more listings.]

Peter D D Delacroix	Edmund A Deslonde	Thos Della Torre
John C Riley	Jules Chappin	Edmund R Smith
Alfred J Higgins	Edmund L Smith	Jas C Middleton
Henry J Forstall	Bernard G Caulfield	John Duncan
Hermogene Dufresne	Ernest L Forstall	Benj E Green

Valedictory: Alex A Allemeng

Farm for sale: *Mellrose*, the farm on which she now resides, contains 225 acres; comfortable frame dwlg, & other necessary out-houses. Apply to S M Martin, near Bladensburg, Md.

Household & kitchen furniture at auction: on Jul 31, at the residence of Mrs Byrne, corner of Pa ave & 10th st. -Edw C & G F Dyer

Horse & carriage at auction: on Jul 29, by order of the Orphans Court of Wash Co, D C, in front of the auction store, the Horse & Jersey Wagon belonging to the estate of the late Robt W Dyer. -Edw C & G F Dyer

SAT JUL 29, 1848
Pennsylvania: on Wed Acting Govn'r Johnson arrived at the Capital at Harrisburg. Townsend Haines, of West Chester, has been appointed Sec of State. The Hon Jas Cooper, of Adams Co, will be tendered the Atty Generalship.

Senate: 1-Cmte on Revolutionary Claims: adverse report on the case of Haym M Salomon. 2-Cmte on Pensions: act granring a pension to Wm Pittman. Same cmte: adverse reports on the memorials of Jedediah Gray, Amos Doughty, & John Beetly, accompanined with a report in each case. 3-Cmte of Claims: bill for the relief of Geo L Brent & Jos Graham. 4-Cmte on Private Land Claims: bill for the relief of the heirs & legal reps of Jos McAlee, deceased.

Mrd: on Jul 27, in the 9th st Methodist Protestant Church, by Rev J Thos Ward, of Phil, Mr Oliver H P Donn to Miss Cecelia J Hipkins, both of Wash City.

Mrd: on Jul 27, by Rev Mr Lanahan, Thos H Phillips to Miss Mary R Gates, late of Loudoun Co, Va.

Died: on Jul 27, Jas O'Reilly, son of John O'Reilly, in his 24th year. His funeral is this evening at 4 o'clock, from the residence of Philip Gormly, on Jefferson st, Gtwn.

Died: on Jul 27, Wm Augustus Offutt, of Montg Co, Md, in his 31st year, after a short & painful illness.

Annual sale of Bucks, near Delaware City, Dela. Clayton B Reybold begs to inform the public that he will offer for unreserved sale, at auction, on Aug 2, about 25 long-wooled New Oxfordshire Yearling Bucks. -Marsh Mount

Landon Female Seminary, 7 miles from Fredericktown on the road to Wash, & 3 miles from the Ijamsville depot on the Balt & Ohio railroad. The Institution has been established for 6 years by the Rev Richd H Phillips. At present is under the care of Rev Mr Paterkin. Next session will commence on the 2nd Wed of Sep.
-Urbana, Fred'k Co, Md

Saml Greiner, son of Matthias Greiner & Barbara Mesert, left Presburg, in Hungary, [his native place,] several years ago, & is supposed to be now in the U S. His mother left him at her death some property, & he is requested to take possession of it. In case of his death it is desirable to receive a certificate of it. Any information concerning said Saml Greiner may be directed to the Austrian Legation, Wash.

Col Jas S Calhoun, lately commanding the Georgia mounted btln, arrived in Wash City yesterday, & is at Blackwell's Nat'l Hotel.

MON JUL 31, 1848
From Europe: the funeral of M de Chateaubriand took place on Jul 7, & was attended by nearly every literary person of any notice in Paris. By the will of M de Chateaubriand it is ordered that his memoirs, which he calls **d'outre tombe**, shall be published under the direction of his nephew, Louis de Chateaubriand, Hyde de Neuville, & 2 other gentlemen.

The latest from Vera Cruz, brought by the steamboat **New Orleans**, which sailed on Jun 18, represent that the mortality from yellow fever in Vera Cruz has of late been very great, & was rather on the increase. By this disease, Capt Gleason, Assist Quartermaster, met his death on Jun 16, & Lt Martin on the 12th. The latter died at the Nat'l Bridge, soon after his return from a short leave of absence to Vera Cruz. The troops are either all embarked, or have had transports assigned to them, except the 1st Regt of Artl, stationed in part in the castle & part in the town, as the garrison of the place; & the following companies of dragoons, composing the rear-guard of the army; Co D 1st Dragoons, Lt Gardner, commanding; Co F, do, Lt Noble, commanding; Co K, do, Lt Ewell, commanding; Co A, 2nd Dragoons, Lt Armstrong, commanding; Co I, Capt Sibley, do; Capt Duperu's Co, 3rd Dragoons, dismounted, embarked on the 17th inst; field battery, Co G, 4th Artl, Lt M Lovell, commanding, under orders to embark on the ship **Palmetto** on the 18th.

Mrd: on Jun 6, in Wash City, by Rev John Lanahan, Mr Jas A Thecker to Miss A Jane Brady, both of Gtwn, D C.

Died: on Jul 30, in Wash City, after a painful illness of 11 weeks, Sarah, wife of Rev G Bayley, in her 71st year. Her funeral will take place at the residence of Dr G Bailey, E & 8th st, this morning at 11 o'clock.

Died: on Jul 26, at the residence of her son, Henry Brewer, Mrs Eliz Brewer, widow of the late Jos Brewer, of Gtwn, in her 72nd year.

Cumberland Civilian: on Wed last, John Hicks, late from Cornwall, England, where he leaves a wife & child, was killed in the Eckhart mines, by coal falling & crushing his skull.

Senate: 1-Ptn from John A Brackenridge, vindicating his father from certain allegations charging him with a misapplication of the funds collected by him in the State of Missouri for the Washington Monument Society. 2-Ptn from Wm Archer & other citizens of D C, asking an appropriation for the removal of a nuisance on Pa ave. 3-Cmte of Revolutionary Claims: bill for the relief of the legal reps of David Hoban, deceased. 4-Private bills that were passed-relief of: John Manley; Sarah Stokes, widow of John Stokes; Benj White, Amzy Judd; Chas Chappell; Wm Culver; John Anderson; heirs of Matthew Stewart; E G Smith; Jonathan Moore, of the State of Mass; Robt Ellis; Catharine Fulton, of Wash Co, Pa; Bennett M Dell; Elijah H Willis; legal reps of Wm McKenzie, late a seaman on board the U S ship **Vincennes**; of Bent, St Vrain, & Company; & of J Throckmorton.

Dr Jos S Dellinger, formerly of Wash Co, Md, & late a resident of Pulaski, Mo, on Jun 26, whilst riding into Waynesville, was shot by a man named Horrell, & instantly fell from his horse & expired.

The Hon John I De Graff, of Schenectady, N Y, a very worthy gentleman, & formerly, [for 2 terms, at different times,] a Rep in Congress, died at his residence on Jun 26, of a disease which for some weeks had rendered his recovery almost hopeless.

Two ofcrs of the Ky Regt, just arrived at Louisville from Mexico, met at the Exchange Hotel, & had some altercation. R W Morrison threatened to shoot Lt Shackleford, & rushed upon him; when the latter drew a pistol & shot Morrison through the lungs. Morrison snapped a revolver several times, but the caps only exploded. The injury is supposed to be mortal.

TUE AUG 1, 1848
Gadsby's New Hotel, corner of Pa ave & 3rd st, near Railroad Depot, Wash, D C.

House, sign, & ornamental painting: dissolution of copartnership of Finch & Turner. The undersigned will continue the business of house-painting at the old paint-shop on La ave, next to the Bank of Wash. Cementing done on brick walls, warranted to stay on & keep the dampness out. –Chas Turner

Mrs D H Burr's French & English Seminary for Young Ladies, corner of E & 9th sts, Wash.

The firm of Van Riswick & Jones is this day dissolved by mutual consent. Mr Van Riswick will continue the business, at the Wash Planing Mill & Lumber Yard.
-John Van Riswick, J W Jones

Household & kitchen furniture at auction: on Jul 31, at the residence of Mrs Byrne, Pa ave & 10th st. -Edw C & G F Dyer

Senate: 1-Cmte on Pensions: adverse report on the ptn of Jos Hare. 2-Cmte of Claims: House bill for the relief of Chas R Allen. 3-Bills passed-relief of: Charity Harrington; of the legal reps of Thos J V Owen, deceased; & of Archibald Beard.

The Va Female Institute, Staunton, Va. Board of Trustees: Rt Rev Wm Meade, D D, Pres
Rev T T Castleman	F J Stribling, M D	Jas Pointe
Wm Kinney	N C Kinney	
T J Michie	R T Brooke	

Judge Shriver died at his residence in Fred'k, Md, on Sat, after a very short illness.

Died: yesterday, Jane Frances, daughter of John F & Jane E Tucker, aged 4 years. Her funeral will take place from her father's residence, near the Navy Yard, this evening at 3 o'clock.

On Sun Brian Frail was committed for trial by Justices Goddary & Drury to answer at the Criminal Court to the charge of killing on Sun last a boy named Maurice Connell, by striking the lad with a brickbat on the right side of the neck a fatal blow, which caused almost immediate death. [Sep 4th newspaper: the Pres of the U S granted a free pardon, on Thu last, to Bryan Frail, who was found guilty of manslaughter.

Indian massacre. Lake Superior News of the 21st ult learns from Lapointe that a savage encounter took place between a party of Chippewas & Siouxs near Sandy Lake. The Chippewas, about 80 of them, were out as a fishing party & unarmed, when they were surprised by a party of the Sioux, who massacred some 70 of the number, among whom was young Hole-in-the-day.

WED AUG 2, 1848
Wash Corp: 1-Communication from W H Gunnell, preferring a complaint against E G Handy, police constable of the 3rd Ward: laid on the table. 2-Bill for the relief of Edw Miller: referred to the Cmte on Improvements. 3-Referred to the Cmte of Claims-relief of: Richd Harrison; & of Caleb Dulany. Also, the ptns of Jas Hollidge, C W Blackwell; of Messrs Croggin & Cross. 4-Bill for the payment of the claim of Enoch Ridgway for repairing the City Hall: passed.

Died: yesterday, suddenly, after a short illness, Mrs Eliz Crutchett, wife of Mr Jas Crutchett, aged 31, deeply regretted by all who knew her. Her funeral is tomorrow morning, from the cottage, Capitol Hill.

Died: on Aug 1, in Wash City, of consumption, Mr Chas E Wilson, a native of Scotland, in his 51st year. His funeral is this afternoon, at 5 o'clock, from his late residence on M st, between 7th & 8th sts.

The mansion of John C Herbert, in Vansville district, PG Co, Md, was destroyed by fire on Jul 21. The house cost $10,000, & was insured for $5,000 in the Montg Mutual Fire Ins Co.

Lynchburg Virginian of Thu. At Nelson Courthouse on Mon last, a wealthy citizen of that county, Wyatt Hare, shot with a pistol & instantly killed Clayton C Harris, & by another shot wounded his brother so severely that there is no hope of his recovery. Jealousy was the cause. Hare surrendered to the ofcrs.

H G S Key appointed Chief Judge of the Orphans' Court of St Mary's Co, vice Richd M Miles, declined.

As Capt Allen, of the steamboat **John R Vinton**, of Providence, R I, was engaged on Fri in spreading an awning over the deck of his boat, he made a misstep & fell overboard, & was drowned. He was about 45 years of age, & leaves a widow.

Mrs Riggle, of Warren, Ohio, was crushed to death on Jul 10 while assisting her son to get a load of hay into the barn. The oxen became unmanageable & the wagon caught her & crushed her against the side.

A 14 year old boy in the employ of Mr A Boland, of Sharon, Conn, was taken with lockjaw. A physician was called & chloroform was given to relieve the pain, & the boy later aroused himself. In a few days he was almost entirely well.

Senate: 1-Ptn from Jas Harrington, asking to be indemnified for loss of time & expenses during illness contracted in the service of the U S. 2-Ptn from John Crawford, asking permission to locate for forfeited land. 3-Cmte of Claims: House bill for the relief of Peter Shaeffer, without amendment. Same cmte: adverse report on the claim of Littleton D Teackle.

THU AUG 3, 1848

The Mexican journals announce the death of Gen Antonio Gaona, aged 64 years, who died at Puebla on Jun 24. With the exception of Bustaments, he held the oldest commission in the Mexican army. When the war closed he had been 52 years in the Mexican service. When taken prisoner with his son apparently dying before him of a sword wound, he signalized the humanity of his disposition by one of the noblest acts which the war records. Col Childs, then Govn'r of Puebla, assumed the grave responsibility of his immediate release.

Nannie Wolcott died in Oxford, Maine, on Jul 17, aged 114 years.

Appointments by the Pres: 1-Nathan Clifford, of Maine, Envoy Extra & Minister Pleni of the U S to the Mexican republic. 2-Consuls of the U S in Mexico: John Black, for the city of Mexico: Franklin Chase, for Tampico; John A Robinson, for Guaymas; John Parrot, for Mazatlau; G W P Bissell, for San Blas; & F M Dimond, for Vera Cruz.

On Tue last the body of the gallant Capt Henry Fairfax, of Fairfax Co, was afforded our citizens. He died in Mexico whilst in command of the Fairfax Volunteers. The remains of the deceased were brought up in the steamboat **Oceola**. A funeral procession escorted the hearse to the Armory, where the corpse was deposited to be conveyed this morning to Falls Church. Appropriate remarks were made by Col C A Alexander, & an eloquent address delivered by Mr G W P Custis. –Alexandria Gaz

Strawberry plants for sale: the Deptlord-Pine & Alice Maud plants.
–John Slater, Alexandria, Va

Senate: 1-Cmte on Foreign Relations: House bill without amendment: relief of the legal reps of Cornelius Manning; & relief of Benj Hodges. Same cmte: bill for the relief of Robt M Harrison. 2-Cmte on pensions: adverse reports on the following bills from the House-relief of: Eliza S Roberts; of Francis Hutinack; of Aaron Tucker; & of Sarah Hildreth. Also, for the payment of arrearages of pension to Anthony Walton Bayard.

Plumbing & Gas-fitting Establishment opened on Pa ave, between 10th & 11th sts.
–J W Thompson

Mrd: on Jul 26, at **Bushwood**, the residence of Edmund J Plowden, in St Mary's Co, Md, by Rev Michl Dougherty, Jos Forrest to Henrietta Cecelia, only daughter of the late Wm H Plowden, all of said county.

FRI AUG 4, 1848
Arrived at Norfolk, the U S brig **Vesuvius**, Lt Mason. The remains of Assist Surgeon P Benson Delany, U S Navy, & Purser A D Crosby, both of whom died at Laguna, were brought home. -Beacon

Edmund Simpson, late manager of the Park Theatre, N Y, died there on Mon. He had control of the Park Theatre for 38 years, for which he paid the late John J Astor about half a million of dollars. A series of reverses in the latter period of his life left him poor at the time of his death.

Mr Geo W Matsell has been appointed chief of the police of N Y C for the next 2 years.

Mr Jas Cassady, of Cecil Co, Md, has a peach orchard of 30,000 trees of 28 varieties. They will yield this season about 60,000 baskets, half of which has been contracted for.

Mr Geo Campbell, foreman of the Oak Hall clothing establishment on Main st, Norfolk, was drowned in the surf at Old Point, on Sun last. His body was recovered. Mr Campbell leaves a wife & child, & aged parents, to mourn the sudden & unexpected sad bereavement. He was 26 years old. –Norfolk Beacon

SAT AUG 4, 1848
Nashville [Tenn] Whig, Jul 27. Announce the death of A P Maury, who died on Sat last, at his residence in Williamson Co, of typhoid fever. His death is a public loss not only to the county in which he resided, but to the State at large.

Chambersburg [Pa] Repository: died, suddenly, at his residence in this place, from paralysis, on Aug 2, the Hon Alex'r Thomson, aged about 63 years. He ranked as one of our most amiable & prominent citizens. [A true friend to D C, his portrait, painted for the Washington Corporation, now hangs in our City Hall.]

U S vs Danl Drayton: Drayton was found guilty yesterday with stealing slaves the property of Andrew Hoover. His trial on another indictment charged him with stealing slaves the property of W H Upperman was held yesterday.

Gen Riley, the veteran cmder of the 2nd Regt of Infty, passed through Cincinnati on Sat last. He has seen hard fights in the war of 1812, & the hardest fights in the war of 1846; & now he is about to march with his gallant regt to the wilds of Calif. With him go the best wishes of his country. –Cincinnati Atlas

Ofcrs of the U S frig **Brandywine**, bearing the broad pennant of Cmdor Geo W Storer, at Rio Janeiro on Jun 9, 1848-all well: Capt-Chas Boarman
Lts: John A Davis, 1st; Luther Stoddard, 2nd; Saml Larkin, 3rd; Thos T Hunter, 4th; John S Guthrie, 5th.

Fleet Surgeon: Benj F Bache Chaplain: John L Lenhart
Assist Surgeon: Philip Lansdale Marine Ofcr: John Contee Grayson
Purser: Jos C Eldredge
Passed Midshipmen: Jos M Bradford, Simeon S Bassett, Theodorick L Walker, Wm T Truxton, Thos W Broadhead, John T Barraud.
Midshipmen: Chas B Smith, John G Sproston, Wm Gwinn, Bayard E Hand, Robt T Chapman, John P Baker.
Cmdor's Sec: W H Parks Gunner: Thos P Venable
Capt's Clerk: R P Bryarly, jr Carpenter: Jos Cox
Boatswain: Wm Smith

Dr Luzenberg, an eminent physician of New Orleans died at Cincinnati on Jul 16.

Two Pa ave lots for sale: on one of the lots are the walls for building a 2 story house, with basement & cellars. Inquire of S Drury.

Mrd: on Aug 3, in St Patrick's Church, by Rev Mr Foley, Saml T Drury to Rachel Greer, daughter of Wm Greer, all of Wash City.

Died: a few days ago, Mrs Helen Lispenard Webb, wife of Col Jas Watson Webb, & daughter of the late A L Stewart, of N Y C.

College of St James: Wash Co, Md: next session will begin on Oct 2.
–John B Kerfoot, Rector

Household & kitchen furniture at auction: on Aug 8, at the residence of Mr Herbert Harris, on 13th st, near N Y ave, excellent lot of nearly new furniture.
A Green, auctioneer

Senate: 1-Ptn from J Thornton asking to be reimbursed for expenses incurred by the provisional gov't of Oregon in defending the citizens against Indian hostilities.
2-Cmte on Pensions: bill for the relief of Maj Jas M Scantlan: passed.

Orphans Court of Wash Co, D C. Letters of administration on the personal estate of Wm Beach, late of said county, deceased. –Catharine Beach, admx

MON AUG 7, 1848
Richd Barry, who resided at the Laurel Factory, met with a premature & horrible death on Sat. He had been drinking freely at the tavern between this city & Annapolis, & was run over by the cars advancing towards Balt. He died an immediate death.

The barque **Liberia** arrived at Balt on Fri last, having made the passage from Monrovia to the Capes of the Chesapeake in 26 days. The Packet brought home as passengers Judge Benedict, the Chief Justice of the republic of Liberia; Mr Russwurm, Govn'r of the Md colony at Cape Palmas, & his wife & dght; Jas B McGill & wife; Messrs Ball, Walker, Letcher, Merriweather, Zouce, Underwood, & Hooper.

The venerable Danl Wadsworth, one of the wealthiest citizens of Connecticut, died at Hartford last Fri, in his 77th year.

Died: on Aug 6, Miss Martha Lucinda Coburn, in her 15th year, the devoted daughter of Mr John Coburn, of Wash City. Her funeral is today at 10 o'clock, from the residence of her parents, 19th & G sts.

Public sale of 2 valuable tracts of limestone land: on Aug 31, in Howard District, Anne Arundel Co, Md, about 20 miles from Wash: on the direct road from Ellicott's Mills to Rockville, Montg Co: one tract of about 140 acres unimproved; the other about 60 acres.
–Pennel Palmer

TUE AUG 8, 1848
Army Genr'l Order: Gen Orders, #42: War Dept, Adj Gen Ofc, Wash, Jul 28, 1848.
Promotions:
3rd Regt of Dragoons:
1st Lt Danl Petigur, to Capt, Dec 23, 1847, vice Butler, deceased.
2nd Lt Hermann Thorn, to 1st Lt, to date from Jul 16, 1847.
2nd Lt J C D Williams, to 1st Lt, Jan 8, 1848, vice Cooke, resigned.
9th Regt of Infty:
Lt Col Henry L Webb, of 16th Infty, to Col, May 23, 1848, vice Withers, resigned.
1st Lt John H Jackson, to Capt, to date from Dec 4, 1847.
1st Lt Albert Tracy, to Capt, to date from Feb 23, 1848, to fill a vacancy occasioned by Capt Fitzgerald, Assist Quartermaster, vacating his Regt commission.
2nd Lt John Glackin, to 1st Lt, to date from Dec 4, 1847.
2nd Lt Robt Hopkins, to 1st Lt, to date from Jan 19, 1848.
2nd Lt Geo W May, to 1st Lt, to date from Feb 17, 1848.
2nd Lt Chas Simmons, to 1st Lt, vice Tracy, promoted.
2nd Lt Levi Woodhouse, to 1st Lt, Mar 16, 1848, vice Pierce, resigned.
2nd Lt Henry De Wolfe, to 1st Lt, May 6, 1848, vice Hodge, resigned.
10th Regt of Infty: Maj Ralph G Norvell, 16th Infty, to be Lt Col, Dec 3, 1847, vice Fay, promoted to 13th Infty.
Capt Danl Chase, 15th Infty, to Maj, May 23, 1848, vice Hamilton, promoted to 16th Infty.
1st Lt Saml R Dummer, to Capt, Jan 21, 1848, vice Collett, deceased.
1st Lt Francis M Cummins, to Capt, Mar 6, 1848, vice Wilkin, resigned.
1st Lt Robt C Morgan, to Capt, May 8, 1848, vice Postley, deceased.
2nd Lt Jas McKown, jr, to 1st Lt, Nov 19, 1847, vice Lewis, deceased.
2nd Lt Hiram Russell, to 1st Lt, Jan 21, 1848, vice Dummer, promoted.
2nd Lt Peter H Bruyere, to 1st Lt, Mar 6, 1848, vice Cummins, promoted.
2nd Lt Thos S Griffin, to 1st Lt, May 8, 1848, vice Morgan, promoted.

11th Regt of Infty:
2nd Lt Andrew H Tippin, to 1st Lt, Dec 6, 1847, vice Hannon, deceased.
2nd Lt Alonzo Loring, to 1st Lt, Dec 9, 1847, vice Samuels, deceased.
2nd Lt Geo B Fitzgerald, to 1st Lt, Jun 29, 1848, vice Haldeman, transferred to 8th Regt of Infty.
12th Regt of Infty:
1st Lt John J Martin, to be Capt, Dec 31, 1847, vice Hornsby, resigned.
1st Lt Chas Taplin, to Capt, Mar 31, 1848, vice Martin, resigned.
1st Lt John H H Felch, to Capt, May 23, 1848, vice Taplin, resigned.
2nd Lt Thos T Conway, to 1st Lt, Dec 22, 1847, vice Wilson, resigned.
2nd Lt Abner M Perrin, to 1st Lt, Dec 31, 1847, vice Martin, promoted.
2nd Lt Jas F Waddell, to 1st Lt, Mar 31, 1848, vice Taplin, promoted.
2nd Lt Christopher R P Butler, to 1st Lt, May 23, 1848, vice Felch, promoted.
13th Regt of Infty:
Lt Col John J Fay, 10th Infty, to Col, Dec 3, 1847, vice Echols, deceased.
Capt Eugene Van de Venter, 15th Infty, to Maj, Dec 22, 1847, vice Johnson, resigned.
1st Lt Jos A White, to Capt, Jan 31, 1848, vice Rice, resigned.
2nd Lt John N Perkins, to 1st Lt, Dec 31, 1847, vice Bradford, resigned.
2nd Lt Danl Kirkpatrick, to 1st Lt, Jan 31, 1848, vice White, promoted.
2nd Lt Nathl Grant, to 1st Lt, Feb 29, 1848, vice Ripley, resigned.
2nd Lt Edw J Dommett, to 1st Lt, Mar 31, 1848, vice Davis, resigned.
14th Regt of Infty:
Capt Chas Wickliffe, 16th Infty, to Maj, Feb 12, 1848, vice Wood, resigned.
1st Lt Geo W Morgan, to Capt, Dec 3, 1847, vice Beale, promoted to 16th Infty.
2nd Lt Saml B Davis, to 1st Lt, Dec 3, 1847, vice Morgan, promoted.
2nd Lt Wm H Seawell, to 1st Lt, Dec 21, 1847, vice Haynes, resigned.
2nd Lt John T Sanford, to 1st Lt, May 23, 1848, vice McAllon, resigned.
15th Regt of Infty:
1st Lt Thornton F Brodhead, to Capt, Dec 22, 1847, vice Van de Venter, promoted to 13th Infty.
1st Lt Diedrich Upmann, to Capt, May 6, 1848, vice Winans, resigned.
1st Lt Edw C Marshall, to Capt, May 6, 1848, vice Tanneyhill, resigned.
1st Lt Albert G Sutton, to Capt, May 23, 1848, vice Chase, promoted to 10th Infty.
2nd Lt Heman M Cady, to 1st Lt, Dec 22, 1847, vice Brodhead, promoted.
2nd Lt Cornelius Ketchum, to 1st Lt, Dec 31, 1847, vice Miller, resigned.
2nd Lt Saml E Beach, to 1st Lt, Feb 23, 1848, vice Cady, resigned.
2nd Lt Francis O Beckett, to 1st Lt, May 6, 1848, vice Upmann, promoted.
2nd Lt Thos B Tilton, to 1st Lt, May 6, 1848, vice Marshall, promoted.
2nd Lt Llewellyn Boyle, to 1st Lt, May 23, 1848, vice Sutton, promoted.
16th Regt of Infty:
Maj Fowler Hamilton, 10th Infty, to Lt Col, May 23, 1848, vice Webb, promoted to 9th Infty.
Capt Robt G Beale, 14th Infty, to Maj, Dec 3, 1847, vice Norvell, promoted to 10th Infty.
1st Lt John T Hughes, to Capt, Feb 12, 1848, vice Wickliffe, promoted to 14th Infty.
2nd Lt Burwell B Irvan, to 1st Lt, Feb 12, 1848, vice Hughes, promoted.
2nd Lt Alex'r Evans, to 1st Lt, May 13, 1848, vice Wilkinson, resigned.

Regt of Voltigeurs & Foot Riflemen:
2nd Lt Robt C Forsyth, to 1st Lt, to date from Sep 18, 1847.
2nd Lt Jas A Frost, to 1st Lt, Dec 31, 1847, vice Woolford, resigned.

Brevets:
"For gallant & meritorious conduct in several affairs with Guerrilleros, at Paso Ovejas, Nat'l Bridge, & Cerro Gordo, Mexico, on the 10th, 12th, & 15th Aug, 1847."

To date from-Aug 15, 1847.
Capt Frazey M Winans, 15th Infty, to Maj
Capt Wm J Clark, 12th Infty, to Maj
Capt Arthur C Cummings, 11th Infty, to Maj
"For gallant & meritorious conduct in the battles of Contreras & Churubusco, Mexico, Aug 20, 1847."

To date from-Aug 20, 1847.
Capt Theodore O'Hara, Assist Quartermaster, [Volunteer Staff] to Maj.
Capt Jos Daniels, Assist Quartermaster, [Volunteer Staff] to Maj.
Correction of dates-made by & with the advice & consent of the Senate:
1st Lt Wm Walker, 3rd Dragoons, to date from Dec 23, 1847, instead of Jul 16, 1847, & to take place in the Army Register, next below Lt Hermann Thorn.

Capt Lyman Bissell, 9th Infty, to date from Sep 8, 1847, instead of Sep 25, 1847.
Capt John B Slocum, 9th Infty, to date from Sep 25, 1847, instead of Oct 9, 1847.
Capt Chas J Sprague, 9th Infty, to date from Oct 9, 1847, instead of Dec 4, 1847.
Capt John H Jackson, 9th Infty, to date from Dec 4, 1847, instead of Feb 17, 1848.
1st Lt Asa A Stoddard, 9th Infty, to date from Sep 8, 1847, instead of Sep 25, 1847.
1st Lt John Glackin, 9th Infty, to date from Dec 4, 1847, instead of Jan 19, 1848.
1st Lt Robt Hopkins, 9th Infty, to date from Jan 19, 1848, instead of Feb 17, 1848.

Appointments:
3rd Regt of Dragoons: To 2nd Lt:
Jas D Potter, of N Y, Mar 3, 1848, vice Camp, resigned.
Hiram B Yeager, of Pa, Mar 29, 1848, vice Walker, promoted.
Frank Emerson, of Indiana, Mar 29, 1848, vice Williams, promoted.
Chas F Maguire, of Pa, Mar 29, 1848, vice Havilland, resigned.
John R Atkinson, of Missouri, to be Surgeon, May 16, 1848, vice Barton, resigned.

9th Regt of Infty: To 2nd Lt:
Nathl F Swett, of Maine, [late 2nd Lt,] Dec 17, 1847, re-appointed.
John Bedell, of N H, Dec 30, 1847, vice Cram, promoted.
Gustavus F Gardiner, of R I, Dec 30, 1847, vice Stoddard, promoted.
Nathl J Gill, of Mass, Dec 30, 1847, vice Pierce, promoted.
Thos Grey, of Conn, Dec 30, 1847, vice Gove, promoted.
Amos A Billings, of Maine, Mar 29, 1848, vice Crosby, promoted.
Albert G Barton, of Maine, Mar 29, 1848, vice Palmer, promoted.
Asa N Wyman, of Maine, Mar 29, 1848, vice Glackin, promoted.

10th Regt of Infty: To 2nd Lt:
Jas Easterly, of N Y, Dec 30, 1847, vice McGarry, promoted.
Alex'r P Ten Broeck, of N Y, Dec 30, 1847, vice Yard, deceased.
Wm S Truex, of N J, Dec 30, 1847, vice Griswold, resigned.
Henry A Perrine, of N J, Mar 3, 1848, vice Harte, resigned.
Wm H Hull, of N J, Mar 3, 1848, vice Russell, promoted.
Edw M Clitz, of N Y, Mar 3, 1848, vice Graham, transferred to First Dragoons.
11th Regt of Infty: To 2nd Lt:
Thos J Barclay, of Pa, Dec 30, 1847, vice Haldeman, promoted.
Thos Welsh, of Pa, Dec 30, 1847, vice Forster, promoted.
Wm A Todd, of Pa, Dec 30, 1847, vice McClelland, cashiered.
Wm Schoonover, of Pa, Dec 30, 1847, vice Mead, deceased.
Jos D Davis, of Pa, Mar 29, 1848, vice Tippin, promoted.
Chas M Stout, of Pa, Mar 29, 1848, vice Johnston, killed in battle.
Jacob Frick, of Pa, Mar 29, 1848, vice Brus, deceased.
Nathl E Cargill, of Va, May 10, 1848, vice Loring, promoted.
John P Brock, of Va, Jun 21, 1848, vice Scott, transferred to 4th Infty.
Jas Grimshaw, of Pa, to Assist Surgeon, Mar 29, 1848, vice Scott, resigned.
12th Regt of Infty: To 2nd Lt:
Manning Brown, of S C, Dec 30, 1847, vice Brooks, deceased.
Chas Manley, jr, of N C, Mar 3, 1848, vice Wherden, deceased.
Saml A Wilkins, of N C, Mar 3, 1848, vice Saunders, declined to accept.
John S Houston, of Ark, Mar 3, 1848, vice Perrin, promoted.
John C Peay, of Ark, Mar 3, 1848, vice Conway, promoted.
Jas M Perrin, of S C, Mar 3, 1848, vice Otterson, deceased.
Thos A Harris, of Missouri, May 31, 1848, vice Miller, resigned.
Danl R McKissack, of Ark, May 31, 1848, vice Magruder, resigned.
13th Regt of Infty: To 2nd Lt:
John M Inge, of Ala, Dec 30, 1847, vice Morrison, resigned.
John G Bush, of Ga, Mar 3, 1848, vice Reese, resigned.
Wm A Adams, of Ala, Mar 3, 1848, vice Perkins, promoted.
Philander Morgan, of Ala, Mar 3, 1848, vice Kirkpatrick, promoted.
John K McBride, of Ala, Mar 29, 1848, vice McClung, resigned.
Geo W Simmons, of Ala, Mar 29, 1848, vice Grant, promoted.
Ashley R Lentz, of Ala, Jun 27, 1848, vice Dummett, promoted.
Claiborne E Evans, of Ala, Jun 27, 1848, vice McMillion, resigned.
Thyos J Chilton, of Ala, to be Assist Surgeon, Mar 29, 1848, vice Malone, resigned.
14th Regt of Infty: To 2nd Lt:
Thos Cullen, of Tenn, Dec 30, 1847, vice Steele, promoted.
Robt B Wynne, of Tenn, Dec 30, 1847, vice Eastin, promoted.
Richd H Smith, of Tenn, Dec 30, 1847, vice Fitzgerald, promoted.
Saml C Scott, of La, Dec 30, 1847, vice Seawell, promoted.
Achille Berard, of La, Mar 3, 1848, vice Davis, promoted.
Thos Nichols, of La, Mar 24, 1848, vice Cheney, resigned.
Hamilton Montgomery, of Ala, Mar 29, 1848, vice Love, resigned.
Alvan Cullom, of Tenn, Jun 14, 1848, vice Tilman Cullom, deceased.

15th Regt of Infty: To 2nd Lt:
Isaac Harpster, of Ohio, Dec 30, 1847, vice Goodloe, resigned.
Oscar R Mitchell, of Ohio, Dec 30, 1847, vice Stuart, resigned.
John M Mount, of Ohio, Mar 3, 1848, vice French, promoted.
Saml Ramsey, of Ohio, Mar 3, 1848, vice Peternell, promoted.
Thos B Cunning, jr, of Mich, Mar 3, 1848, vice Wilkins, promoted.
Thos S Trask, of Ohio, Mar 29, 1848, vice Wiley, promoted.
Wellington C Burnett, of Mich, Jun 17, 1848, vice Doyle, deceased.
Allen T Welch, of Mich, Jun 17, 1848, vice Beach, promoted.
Marquis L Olds, of Ohio, Jun 17, 1848, vice Ketchum, promoted.
Herman M Cady, [late 1st Lt,] Jun 21, 1848.
David L McGugin, of Ohio, to be Surgeon, Mar 31, 1848, vice Slade, deceased.

16th Regt of Infty: To 2nd Lt:
Pythagoras E Holcomb, of Ill, Dec 30, 1847, vice Griffith, promoted.
Wm Osman, of Ill, Dec 30, 1847, vice Barry, promoted.
Wm B Reynolds, of Ill, Dec 30, 1847, vice Smith, deceased.
Jas T Young, of ___, Mar 3, 1848, vice How, resigned.
Thos H Taylor, of Ky, Mar 3, 1848, vice Irvan, promoted.
Zebulon M P Hand, of Ind, Mar 29, 1848, vice Carr, resigned.
John C Raily, of Ky, Jun 27, 1848, vice Young, declined.
Wm B Whiteside, of Ill, to be Assist Surgeon, May 31, 1848, vice Stuart, resigned.

Regt of Voltigeurs & Foot Riflemen: To 2nd Lt:
John W Graham, of Tenn, Dec 30, 1847, vice Vernon, resigned.
Thos H Gill, of Mass, Dec 30, 1847, vice Winder, deceased.
Wm R Depew, of N Y, Mar 29, 1848, vice Forsyth, promoted.
Glassop McQuire, of Pa, Mar 29, 1848, vice Gill, transferred to 9th Infty.
Wm H Fitzhugh, of Md, Mar 29, 1848, vice Frost, promoted.

Transfers:
2nd Lt Thos H Gill, Voltigeurs, transferred [Mar 24] to 9th Infty, to take place on the Army Register next below Lt Thos Grey.

Appointments & Transfers to the Regts of the old Army, made by the Pres, by & with the advice & consent of the Senate. Appointments:
2nd Lt Christopher R P Butler, 12th Infty, to 2nd Lt in the 2nd Regt of Artl, to take rank from Jun 27, 1848.
2nd Lt Jas E Slaughter, Voltigeurs, to be 2nd Lt in the 1st Regt of Artl, to take rank from Jun 27, 1848.
2nd Lt Richd H Smith, 14th Infty, to 2nd Lt in the 3rd Regt of Artl, to take rank from Jun 21, 1848.
2nd Lt Isaac W Patton, 10th Infty, to 2nd Lt in the 3rd Regt of Artl, to take rank from Jul 13, 1848.

Transfers:
2nd Lt Lorimer Graham, 10th Infty, transferred [Feb 2] to the 1st Regt of Dragoons, to take place on the Army Register next below Lt Evans.
Lt Horace Haldeman, 11th Infty, transferred [Jun 29] to the 8th Regt of Infty, to take rank from Apr 9, 1847, [the date of his former commission,] & to take place on the Army Register next below 2nd Lt Deaney.

2nd Lt Richd C Drum, 9th Infty, transferred [Mar 10] to the 4th Regt of Artl, to take place on the Army Register next below Lt Best.

2nd Lt Wm H Scott, 11th Infty, transferred [Mar 14] to the 4th Regt of Infty, to take place on the Army Register next below Lt Bussey.

2nd Lt Frank H Larned, Voltigeurs, transferred [Jun 29] to the 2nd Regt of Artl, to take place on the Army Register next below Lt Beall.

Appointments in the Quartermaster's, Commissary's, & Medical Depts:

Quartermaster's Dept:

Rush J Mitchell, of N C, to be Assist Quartermaster, with rank of Capt, Mar 3, 1848, vice Pender, deceased.

Chas H Pelham, of Ark, to be Assist Quartermaster, with rank of Capt, May 21, 1848, vice G P Smith, discharged.

Saml H Montgomery, of Pa, to be Assist Quartermaster, with rank of Capt, Jun 27, 1848. [Re-appointed.]

Commissary's Dept:

To be Assist Commissary with rank of Capt:

Alonzo W Adams, of Tenn, Feb 7, 1848, vice Clendenin, discharged.

Chas B Fletcher, of N H, Feb 14, 1848, vice T M Jones, discharged.

Wm S Brown, of Mich, Feb 14, 1848. [Original vacancy.]

Edmund R Badger, of Pa, Feb 23, 1848, vice Duerson, discharged.

Arthur Hood, of Ga, Jun 17, 1848, vice Hoyle, discharged.

Medical Dept:

To be Surgeon:

Francis M Hereford, of La, Mar 3, 1848, vice Dean, declined.

Fred'k W Miller, of Pa, [late Assist Surgeon,] Mar 3, 1848, vice McFarlane, resigned.

Griffin Smith, of Ill, Mar 3, 1848, vice Lane, discharged.

F W Todd, of Ill, Mar 3, 1848, vice Chamberlain, resigned.

Wm A Russell, of Tenn, [Assist Surgeon,] Jun 17, 1848, vice Irwin, resigned.

Thos J Buffington, of La, Jun 27, 1848, vice Hereford, declined.

To be Assist Surgeon:

Geo P Ogden, of La, Oct 20, 1847. [Original vacancy.]

J H Lyons, of Texas, Feb 14, 1848, vice Tucker, declined.

Jas S Gaines, of Tenn, Mar 3, 1848, vice W L Lyon, declined.

Francis B Thompson, of Ill, Mar 29, 1848, vice Ash, deceased.

Appointments in the Pay Dept.

Additional Paymasters:

Fred'k Lansing, of N Y, Dec 30, 1847.

Francis A Cunningham, of Ohio, Dec 30, 1847.

John C Bergh, of N Y, Mar 22, 1848, vice Lansing, declined.

Abram B Ragan, of Ga, Mar 29, 1848, vice Colquitt, resigned.

Geo C Hutter, of Va, May 10, 1848, vice Cloud, deceased.

Richd H Weightman, of the Dist of Columbia, May 10, 1848. [Original vacancy.]

Casualties: Resignations:

Col Jones M Withers, 9th Infty, May 23, 1848.

Maj Allen G Johnson, 13th Infty, Dec 22, 1847.

Maj John D Wood, 14th Infty, Feb 12, 1848.

Capt John W Rice, 12th Infty, Jan 31, 1848.
Capt Frazey M Winans, 15th Infty, May 6, 1848.
Capt Danl Bachelder, 9th Infty, Feb 17, 1848.
Capt C C Hornsby, 12th Infty, Dec 31, 1847.
Capt Alex'r Wilkins, 10th Infty, Mar 6, 1848.
Capt Wm S Tanneyhill, 15th Infty, May 6, 1848.
Capt John J Martin, 12th Infty, Mar 31, 1848.
Capt Chas Taplin, 12th Infty, May 23, 1848.
1st Lt Washington L Wilson, 12th Infty, Dec 22, 1847.
1st Lt Henry C Bradford, 13th Infty, Dec 31, 1847.
1st Lt Thos J Whipple, 9th Infty, Feb 23, 1848.
1st Lt Jas H Woolford, Voltigeurs, Dec 31, 1847.
1st Lt John B Miller, 15th Infty, Dec 31, 1847.
1st Lt Jas Hughes, 16th Infty, Jul 6, 1848.
1st Lt Wm B Cooks, 3rd Dragoons, Jan 8, 1848.
1st Lt Justin Hedge, 9th Infty, May 6, 1848.
1st Lt Preston G Haynes, 14th Infty, Dec 21, 1847.
1st Lt Joab Wilkinson, 16th Infty, May 13, 1848.
1st Lt A J McAllon, 14th Infty, May 23, 1848.
1st Lt Nicholas Davis, jr, 13th Infty, Mar 31, 1848.
1st Lt Fitz H Ripley, 13th Infty, Feb 29, 1848.
1st Lt Thos P Pierce, 9th Infty, Mar 16, 1848.
1st Lt Heman M Cady, 15th Infty, Feb 23, 1848.
2nd Lt Chas F Vernon, Voltigeurs, Dec 20, 1847.
2nd Lt Edw Cantwell, 12th Infty, Feb 21, 1848.
2nd Lt Jas P Miller, 12th Infty, Mar 31, 1848.
2nd Lt Wm J Magill, 3rd Dragoons, May 3, 1848.
2nd Lt Saml H Martin, 14th Infty, May 31, 1848.
2nd Lt David G Wilds, 13th Infty, Apr 18, 1848.
2nd Lt Hugh C Murray, 14th Infty, Mar 31, 1848.
2nd Lt Edw Harte, 10th Infty, Feb 3, 1848.
2nd Lt Lloyd Magruder, 12th Infty, Mar 31, 1848.
2nd Lt Mitchell Stever, 11th Infty, Jun 17, 1848.
2nd Lt Jas H Smythe, Voltigeurs, Jun 23, 1848.
2nd Lt Edwin R Merrifield, 15th Infty, Feb 17, 1848.
2nd Lt John V S Havilland, 3rd Dragoons, Dec 20, 1847.
2nd Lt Geo W Cheney, 14th Infty, Feb 23, 1848.
2nd Lt Louis W Templeton, 15th Infty, Jun 6, 1848.
2nd Lt John M Hatheway, 9th Infty, Mar 31, 1848.
2nd Lt Saml T Love, 14th Infty, Feb 8, 1848.
2nd Lt Marcus L McMillien, 13th Infty, Apr 27, 1848.
2nd Lt Purnell Lofland, 11th Infty, Feb 5, 1848.
2nd Lt Chas McClung, 13th Infty, Dec 31, 1847.
2nd Lt Saml D Stuart, 15th Infty, Dec 21, 1847.
2nd Lt Jas W Rhey, 11th Infty, Jun 14, 1848.
2nd Lt Elisha E Camp, 3rd Dragoons, Feb 4, 1848.

2nd Lt John C Reese, 13th Infty, Dec 30, 1847.
2nd Lt Thos J Barclay, 11th Infty, May 6, 1848.
2nd Lt Wm A Todd, 11th Infty, Jun 30, 1848.
2nd Lt Isaac Harpster, 15th Infty, May 6, 1848.
2nd Lt Geo W Simmons, 13th Infty, Jul 15, 1848.
2nd Lt Hamilton Montgomery, 14th Infty, Jun 14, 1848.
Surgeon Edw H Barton, 3rd Dragoons, Jan 29, 1848.
Assist Surgeon Franklin J Malone, 13th Infty, Dec 30, 1847.
Commission vacated under the provisions of the 7th section of the act of Jun 18, 1848,
[1.] Capt Edw H Fitzgerald, 9th Infty, Sep 8, 1847, Assist Quartermaster. [Regimental Commission [only] vacated.]
Declined:
2nd Lt John W Graham, Voltigeurs
2nd Lt Jas T Young, 16th Infty
2nd Lt Thos H Taylor, 16th Infty.
Deaths:
Col Robt M Echols, 13th Infty, at the Nat'l Bridge, Mexico, Dec 3, 1847.
Maj Jas M Talbott, 16th Infty, at ___ 1848.
Capt John Butler, 3rd Dragoons, at Mier, Mexico, Dec 23, 1847.
Capt Thos Postley, 10th Infty, at Camargo, Mexico, May 8, 1848.
Capt Joshua W Collett, 10th Infty, at Camargo, Mexico, Jan 21, 1848.
1st L Marshall Hannon, 11th Infty, at Carlisle, Pa, Dec 6, 1847.
1st Lt Wm C M Lewis, 10th Infty, at Matamoros, Mexico, Nov 19, 1847.
1st Lt Jos Samuels, 11th Infty, at Cabell Court-house, Va, Dec 9, 1847.
2nd Lt John J Wheeden, 12th Infty, at Raleigh, N C, Jan 14, 1848. [Of wounds received, Aug 12, in action at Nat'l Bridge.]
2nd Lt Wm D Gray, 13th Infty, at Vera Cruz, Mexico, Apr 7, 1848.
2nd Lt Michl P Doyle, 15th Infty, at Perote, Mexico, Oct 23, 1847.
2nd Lt John D Otterson, 12th Infty, in City of Mexico, Dec 26, 1847.
2nd Lt Edw McPherson, 3rd Dragoons, at Mier, Mexico, Mar 16, 1848.
2nd Lt Jacob Brus, 11th Infty, Perote, Mexico, Jul 3, 1847.
2nd Lt Whitfield B Brooks, 12th Infty, in City of Mexico, Oct 2, 1847. [Of wounds received, Aug 20, in battle at Churubusco.]
2nd Lt Gustavus F Gardiner, 9th Infty, at San Angel, Mexico, Mar 16, 1848.
2nd Lt Tilman Cullom, 14th Infty, City of Mexico, Jan 25, 1848.
Surgeon Jas B Slade, 15th Infty, in City of Mexico, Nov 30, 1847.
Dropped:
1st Lt Jas F Bragg, 9th Infty, Jan 19, 1848.
2nd Lt Edw N Saunders, 12th Infty, [there being no such person.]

Casualties-Volunteer Service:
Resignations:
Surgeon Jas S McFarlane, Jan 29, 1848.
Surgeon John Irwin, Feb 29, 1848.
Assist Surgeon John G McKibben, May 31, 1848.
Additional Paymaster Alfred H Colquitt, Jan 31, 1848.

Declined:
Capt Arthur Hood, Assist Commissary.
Surgeon Francis M Hereford.
Surgeon F W Todd
Surgeon Thos J Buffington
Assist Surgeon E Tucker.
Assist Surgeon Oliver M Langdon.
Assist Surgeon Washington L Lyon.
Additional Paymaster Fred'k Lansing.
Dismissed: Capt Saml H Montgomery, Assist Quartermaster, Feb 25, 1848.
Memorandum:
1-1st Lt Horace Haldeman, 11th Infty, vacated his 1st Lieutenantcy [Jul 1] to accept a transfer to the 8th Infty as 2nd Lt with his original date of commission in this grade.
2-The promotion of 2nd Lt Chas F Vernon, Voltigeurs, announced in Genr'l Orders, #36, of Dec 4, 1847, was revoked, & 2nd Lt Robt C Forsyth promoted in his stead.
3-2nd Lt Richd C Drum, 9th Infty, whose promotion to 1st Lt was announced in the Army Register, Feb, 1848, waived the promotion to accept a transfer to the 4th Artl, & 2nd Lt John Glackin, the next on the list, succeeded to the vacancy.

Died: yesterday, in Wash City, Mr Thos Collins, a native of Castle Hyde, Ireland. His funeral is this afternoon, at 4 o'clock, from his late residence, corner of M & 11th sts.

Died: on Aug 5, at Hampstead, Stafford Co, Va, the residence of his grandmother, Louisa Rose Potts, aged 14 months, daughter of John & Louisa Potts, of Wash City.

Senate: 1-Cmte on Private land Claims: bill for the relief of Shadrac Gillet & Geo Clark: passed. 2-Ptn from the widow of Alex H Everett, asking to be allowed, in the settlement of his accounts, certain items, expenses, & differences of exchange. 3-Memorial from W Hamilton & the citizens of the U S, asking the purchase of *Mount Vernon*. 4-Cmte on Pensions: adverse reports on the ptns of Sarah Tyler, of John Staner, & of Nancy Jillson. 5-Cmte on Commerce: bill granting a register to the barque **Mary Theresa**: passed. 6-Cmte on Foreign Relations: offered an amendment giving to Chas G Anderson the sum of $1,666.67 for acting as Charge d'Affaires, in the absence of Gen Cass from Paris. 7-Ptn from E Fitzgerald & others, asking to be paid for their attendance as witnesses in St Louis against a certain Garret Long. 8-Ptn from the legal reps of Robt P Carter, asking a settlement of the accounts of Roddy Carter & Jennings, contractors for provisions during the war of 1812. 9-Cmte on Pensions: adverse reports on the claim of Jos Barclay & Reuben M Gibbs. Same cmte: adverse report on House bill for the relief of Levi Colmus. Same cmte: asking to be discharged from the further consideration of the ptns of Mary Ann Bronaugh; of Catharine Hoffman; of Priscilla Decatur Twiggs, & of Sarah A Mackay. 10-Cmte on Private Land Claims: bill for the relief of John Crawford. 11-Mr Benton gave notice that he would, at the commencement of the next session of Congress, ask leave to bring in a bill to release the members of the late court martial whereof Brig Gen Brooke was Pres, & before which the ex-Lt Col of Mounted Rifles, J C Fremont, was tried, & the Judge Advocate, from their oath of secrecy, according to the precedent set by the British House of Commons in the case of Admiral Byng.

House of Reps: 1-Bills referred: bill to compensate R M Johnson for the erection of certain bldgs for the use of the Choctaw Academy. Bill for the relief of Ward & Smith. Bill for the relief of Shadrach Gillet & others.

Mrd: on Aug 3, by Rev Jas Read Eckard, Mr Ezra L Stevens to Miss Catharine S Durham, daughter of Jas H Durham, of Wash City.

Mrd: on Sabbath evening, by Rev John C Smith, Mr Benj C Wright to Miss Martha S Klopfer, all of Wash City.

Female Education: the subscriber announces his intention to establish, in connection with Robt Daniells, A M, a School for Young Ladies in Wash City. He has selected the 2 southern houses of the block fronting on capitol square, late the property of Gen Green, for occupancy by Sep 20. Prior to his pastoral connexion in Boston, he spent nearly 14 years as the head of the school in Phil, known as the Collegiate Institution for Young Ladies. [Daniells was late head-master of the St Andrew's School, Madras, & member of the Educational Institutes in Scotland.] -R W Cushman

Laws of the U S passed at the 1st Session 30th Congress: 1-Act to change the name of the steamboat **Charles Downing** to the steamboat **Calhoun**: owner Wm A Carson, to pay the usual fees. 2-Act to authorize the issuing of a register to the schnr **James**: formerly a British vessel, now owned by Timothy Carman, a citizen of South Oyster Bay, Queen's Co, N Y, & which vessel, having been wrecked & condemned on the south shore of Long Island, was purchased by him, & which he has caused to be repaired. 3-Act to incorporate the Wash Gas Light Co: that John F Callan, Jacob Bigelow, B B French, W H Harrover, M P Callan, W A Bradley, & W H English, & their present & future associates, are hereby declared to be a body, by the said name, & shall be able to sue & be sued, plead & be impleaded in all courts of law & equity in D C & elsewhere. The capital stock of this corporation shall not exceed $50,000; that a share in the same shall be $20.00.

By writ of fieri facias, at the suit of T M & B Milburn, against the goods & chattels of Wm Cooper, I have seized & taken in execution all the right, title, & interest of said Wm Cooper, in one frame dwlg house, on square 844, on Capitol Hill, on D st, between 5th & 6th sts, & will offer the said house for sale, for cash, to the highest bidder, on Aug 15. –U B Mitchell, Constable

By writ of fieri facias, I shall expose to public sale, in Wash City, 1 mahogany hair-seat sofa, 1 mahogany hair-seat lounge, 3 pair of Brass Andirons & 2 large mahogany tables, seized & taken in execution as the property of Thos M Haslep, & will be sold to satisfy a judgement in favor of Benj F Middleton & Benj Beall, trading under the firm of Middleton & Beall. –R R Burr, Constable

WED AUG 9, 1848
Col Riley, [Brig Gen by brevet,] of the 2nd Infty, has returned to his family in the city of Detroit.

Berkeley Springs: favorite watering place: the completion of Col Strother's Hotel, now presents a front of 125 feet, connecting 2 extensive wings. A new 9 pin alley has been constructed for this establishment. There are also billard rooms in the grove.
–Balt American

House of Reps: 1-Cmte on Invalid Pensions: discharged from the ptns of Abigail Williams, Isaiah Williams, Lettis Pond, Squire Ferris, Abigail Hamilton, Nancy Byrd, & Robt Allison: they were laid on the table. 2-Cmte on Revolutionary Pensions: discharged from the ptns of Nathl Bailey, Catherine Wilson, Solsbery Wheeler, heirs of Jas Taylor, Eliz Simpson, Ann Spencer, John T Parrish, administrator; Lemuel P Montgomery, Wm Sedford, Mrs Sally Ketchum, Josiah Hobbs, Lucretia & Mercy Demmon, Henry Bardan, Henry Haines, & Esther Fish, widow of John Ladd: & they were laid on the table. 3-Cmte on the Judiciary: discharged from the ptns of Morris Fosdick & Robt Graham: laid on the table. 4-Cmte on Patents: bill for the relief of Oliver C Harris: reported back without an amendment. Same cmte: bill for the relief of Ross Winans: committed. 5-Cmte on Foreign Affairs: Senate bill for the relief of the personal reps of Wm A Slacum, deceased: committed. 6-Cmte on Invalid Pensions: bill for the relief of Rebecca Freeman: committed. 7-Cmte on the Judiciary: discharged from the ptn of Wyatt Eppes: laid on the table. 8-Cmte on Revolutionary Claims: bills for the relief of the heirs of John Jackson; for the relief of the heirs of Willis Reddick; for the relief of the legal reps of Col John H Stone, an ofcr of the Revolutionary war: all committed. Same cmte: bill for the relief of the heirs of Capt Saml Ransom, an ofcr of the Revolutionary war, killed at Wyoming; & for the relief of Moses Van Campen: both committed. Same cmte: adverse reports on the ptns of the executors of Henry Pauling, heirs of Wm Cherry, & the heirs of Lt Micah Whitmarsh: laid on the table. 9-Cmte on Indian Affairs: discharged from the ptns of R C Gentry & others, Lawrence Taliaferro, late Indian Agent at St Peters, John Phagan, Jos Chaffee, Wm B Hart, assignee of Alex'r Anderson & others: laid on the table. Same cmte: Senate bill to compensate R M Johnson for the erection of certain bldgs for the use of the Choctaw Academy: committed. 10-Cmte on Military Affairs: Senate bill for the relief of the legal reps of Thos J V Owens, deceased: committed. 11-Cmte on Naval Affairs: adverse report on the ptn of C H Todd: laid on the table. 12-Cmte on Public Lands: adverse reports on the ptns of John Newton, John Ambrozine, & Wyatt Richards: laid on the table. Same cmte: bill for the relief of Wm J Price: committed. Same cmte: adverse reports on the ptn of citizens of Oregon Co, Mo, praying for a change of the location of a small tract of land; of Luke Lea & D Shelton, Nathl J Wyth, of the heirs of John Kendrick, Chas Bulfinch & others, Hall J Kelly, Luke Perry, & Jas Brownlee, & the citizens of Louisiana, for a grant of land: laid on the table. Same cmte: Senate bill for the relief of Wm W Wynn: laid on the table. 13-Cmte on Foreign Affirs: bill for the relief of the reps of John M Baker: committed. 14-Cmte on Invalid Pensions: adverse reports on the ptns of Robt & Henry Blow, Silas Chatfield, Jas M French, John Harrigan, & John Forrest: laid on the table. Same cmte: bill for the relief of Horatio Fitch: committed. 15-Cmte of the Whole: discharged from the further consideration of the bill of the Senate for the relief of David N Smith: returned to the Senate. 16-Cmte on Invalid Pensions: discharged from the further consideration of the ptns of Saml J Smith, of N Y, Wm Wallace, Sally S Crocker, & Chas Wilson: laid on the table. 17-Cmte on the Post Ofc & Post Roads: Senate bill for the relief of Geo V

Mitchell: committed. 18-Cmte on Invalid Pensions: discharged from the further consideration of the ptns of Jas Charles, John H Goolsby, & 19 others, & of Benj P Smith: laid on the table. Same cmte: bill for the relief of Wm Lynch: committed. 19-Cmte of the Whole: bill for the relief of Catharine Clark: passed. Same cmte: discharged from the further consideration of the bill for the relief of Jos D Ward: as directed by the Cmte on Invalid Pensions. 20-Cmte on Invalid Pensions: discharged from the further consideration of the ptns of Robt Ross, Jesse Ross, Aaron H Hoyt, Jos M Rhea, Joshua Russell, Benj Watson, Wm Murray, & Mrs C H Johnson: laid on the table.

We regret to record the death, on Fri last, in Brooklyn, of Lt Geo Wainwright, after a protracted illness. An *eleve* of West Point, where he graduated with distinction, he entered the army, & bore a part of the struggles in Mexico. In the terrible contest at Molino del Rey he was wounded twice & borne from the field, & the effects resulting from these injuries so weakened his system that he gradually sunk into death.
-N Y Courier & Enquirer

Died: on Aug 7, in Wash City, at his residence, on Capitol Hill, Mr Jas B Phillips, in his 31st year. His funeral is this afternoon, at 4 o'clock. In the loss of this estimable gentleman an aged mother has been deprived of an only son, 3 sisters of a brother, society of an ornament, his associates of a friend.

Household & kitchen furniture at auction: on Aug 16, at the European Hotel, kept by Fred'k Lachameir, on Pa ave, between 14th & 15th sts. –H Naylor, Trustee & Atty
-C W Boteler, auctioneer

Senate: 1-Memorial of Chas F Sibbald, asking that his claims may be adjusted under the direction of the Sec of the Treasury. 2-Cmte on Finance: House bill for the relief of David Thomas, of Phil, without amendment. 3-Cmte of Claims: adverse report on House bill for the relief of the legal reps of Amelia Brereton. 4-Cmte on Private Land Claims: asking to be discharged from the further consideration of the ptn of Villeneuve le Bland, & that the petitioner have leave to withdraw his papers. 5-Cmte on Pensions: asking to be discharged from the further consideration of the memorials of: Eliza A Mellon, of E P Hastings, of Candace Munn; also from the documents relating to the claim of John Ellis. 6-Bill for the relief of Gustavus Dorr: Mr Dorr originally belonged to the army, & was ordered to his post, which order he never obeyed, & was in consequence stricken from the rolls. Subsequently it was discovered that the disobedience was occasioned by insanity, & that he is now in the insane asylum. The object of the bill was to grant him a pension for his maintenance. Bill was passed without a dissenting voice.

Circuit Court of Wash Co, D C, Mar Term, 1848. 1-Levi Taylor vs Aetna Ins Co, garnishee of Hicks & Newton, #336, trials 13th Apr. Rule on plntf to employ new counsel. 2-Jas W Williams & W W Kennedy vs, Aetna Ins Co, garnishee of Hicks & Newton, #337, trials 15th Apr. Rule on plntf to employ new counsel. –Wm Brent, clk

Boarding: Mrs C Langton, on 7th st, one door south of E st: can accommodate with pleasant rooms.

N Y Chancery, Vol 2. Reports of cases argued & determined in the Court of Chancery of the State of N Y, by Oliver L Barbour, Vol 2, just published & this day received by F Taylor.

Trunks! Francis A Lutz, High st, near Gay, Gtwn. Large assortment of trunks of his own manufacture.

Farm for sale or exchange for city improved property. A farm of 215½ acres; with a 2 story frame house, with 9 rooms; stable & out-houses; 2½ miles from Montg Co courthouse, Md. Apply to Mr Bright, who lives there & will show the premises. Also, for sale or exchange: a farm of 119 acres in Alexandria Co; the house part log, part frame; stabling & out-houses; adjoining the estate of G W P Custis. Title indisputable & unencumbered. A lot of ground, in square 544, s w corner of M & 4½ sts south. A lot of ground, in square 788, Pa ave, Capitol Hill. Square east of 475; square north of 508; square north of 507, bounded by Boundary st, 5th st, R I & N J aves. Wanted immediately, a Servant Woman & Boy, either for a term of years or by the month, for a family. Apply to Louis Baker, Gen Agency & Intell Ofc, Pa ave, north side.

THU AUG 10, 1848
St Mary's Female Institute, near Bryantown, Chas Co, Md. Annual distribution of premiums took place on Aug 2, 1848. Premiums were awarded to:

Eleanor Downey
Eliza F Dyer, Wash, D C
Annie Downey, Chas Co, Md
Amelia D Thompson, Chas Co, Md
Mary F Mitchell, Chas Co, Md
Mary C Thompson, Chas Co, Md
Mary E Bowling, PG Co, Md
Mgt Queen, Chas Co, Md
Maria R Gwynn, PG Co, Md
Mary V Gardiner, Chas Co, Md
Henrietta M Dyer, Wash, D C
Rosalie Boone, Chas Co, Md
Mary J Boarman, Chas Co, Md
Mary E Fenwick, Wash, D C
Agnes Courtney, Balt, Md
Eleanor R Boarman, Chas Co, Md
Anna F Gardiner, PG Co, Md
Eliza A Fenwick, Wash, D C
Mgt H Gardiner, PG Co, Md
Maria L Murray, Wash, D C
Emily Boarman, Chas Co, Md
Rachel Shackelford, Port Tobacco, Chas Co, Md
Beatrice Gardiner, Chas Co, Md
Mary E Clements, PG Co, Md
Georgiana Davis, Wash, D C
Eliz Bowling, Chas Co, Md
Valinda Dent, Chas Co, Md
Martha Lorson, Chas Co, Md

Senate: 1-Select Cmte: bill for the relief of Wm Darby: to be printed. 2-Cmte on the Post Ofc & Post Roads: bill for the relief of Saml F Butterworth: to be passed. 3-Cmte on Pensions: asking to be discharged from the further consideration of the memorials of: Wm Parkeson, of Benj Miller, of Ellen F Smith, of Angel Spalding, of Wm Miller, of Sarah Overback, & of Wm Pennoyer. 4-Cmte on Private Land Claims: asking to be discharged from the further consideration of the ptn of of Lt Littleton Barclay. 5-The Senate took up House bill to confirm Eliz Burries, her heirs or assigns, in their title to a tract of land: passed.

Army Genr'l Order: Gen Orders, #43. War Dept, Adj Gen Ofc, Wash, Aug 7, 1848. The following named Cadets, constituting the First Class of 1848, having been adjudged by the Acaemic Staff, at the June examination, competent to perform duty in the Army, the Pres of the U S, has attached them as supernumerary ofcrs, with the Brevet of 2nd Lt, to the Regts & Corps below specified, to take rank from Jul 1, 1848. [All are "CADET"]

Brevet 2nd Lt attached to the Corps of Engineers:
1-Wm P Trowbridge
2-Andrew J Donelson
3-Jas C Duane
4-Walter H Stevens
6-Rufus A Roys

Brevet 2nd Lts attached to the Corps of Topographical Engineers:
5-Robt S Williamson
7-Nathl Michler, jr

Brevet 2nd Lt attached to the Dragoon Arm:
16-John Buford, jr: 1st Dragoons
23-Chas H Tyler: 2nd Dragoons
29-Chas H Ogle: 1st Dragoons
36: N G Evans: 1st Dragoons
37-Geo H Steuart: 2nd Dragoons

Brevet 2nd Lts attached to the Regt of Mounted Riflemen:
10-Wm E Jones
14-Thos S Rhett

Brevet 2nd Lt attached to the Artl Arm:
8-Jas M Haynes: Light Co B, 4th Artl
9-Jos C Clark, jr: Light Co C, 3rd Artl
11-John C Tidball: Light Co E, 3rd Artl
12-Wm G Gill: 3rd Artl
15-Jas Holmes: Light Co A, 2nd Artl
17-Truman K Walbridge 4th Artl
19-Grier Tallmadge: Light Co I, 1st Artl
22-Edw B Bryan: Light Co K, 1st Artl
24-John C Booth: Light Co M, 2nd Artl
25-Thos K Jackson 4th Artl

Brevet 2nd Lt attached to the Infty Arm:
13-Benj D Forsythe: 3rd Infty
18-Richd J Dodge: 8th Infty
20-Wm A Slaughter: 2nd Infty
21-Robt M Russell: 5th Infty
26-Geo H Paige: 6th Infty
27-Nathl H McLean: 7th Infty
28-A G Miller: 6th Infty
30-Wm N R Beall: 4th Infty
31-Ferdinand Paine: 4th Infty
32-Thos D Johns: 1st Infty
33-Wm T Mechling: 3rd Infty

34-Geo C Barber: 7th Infty
35-Danl Huston, jr: 8th Infty
38-Geo W Howland: 5th Infty
-R Jones, Adj Gen
After Order-transfers:
Cadet Thos S Rhett, from the Mounted Riflemen, to the 4th Artl, Light Co G
Cadet Thos K Jackson, from the 4th Artl, to the 5th Infty
Cadet Geo W Howland, from the 5th Infty, to the Mounted Riflemen
-R Jones, Adj Gen

Senate: 1-Select Cmte: bill for the relief of Wm Darby: to be printed. 2-Cmte on the Post Ofc & Post Roads: bill for the relief of Saml F Butterworth: to be passed. 3-Cmte on Pensions: asking to be discharged from the further consideration of the memorials of: Wm Parkeson, of Benj Miller, of Ellen F Smith, of Angel Spalding, of Wm Miller, of Sarah Overback, & of Wm Pennoyer. 4-Cmte on Private Land Claims: asking to be discharged from the further consideration of the ptn of of Lt Littleton Barclay. 5-The Senate took up House bill to confirm Eliz Burries, her heirs or assigns, in their title to a tract of land: passed.

LOST. Strayed or stolen from the residence of Gen Walter Jones, a white & liver-colored POINTER PUP, about 5 months old.

Rev John C Smith offers for sale his Family Horse & Carriage, with harness. They can be seen at the livery stable of Jas H Shreve, 7th st.

Madam A J Bujac's French & English Academy for Young Ladies, #11 Aisquith st, late McElderry's Mansion, Balt, Md: will resume on Sep 4.

FRI AUG 11, 1848
Wash Corp: 1-Ptn of Lawrence Callan: praying remission of a fine: referred to the Cmte of Claims. 2-Ptn of O J Preston & Co, praying remission of a fine: referred to the Cmte of Claims. 3-Ptn of Susanna Maryman, praying that certain geese seized by the police ofcr while going at large may be restored to her: referred to the Cmte of Claims.

Senate: 1-Cmte on Pensions: asking to be discharged from the further consideration of the ptns of Patrick Masterson, of Rebecca Robeson, & of W Ball. Same cmte: adverse report on the ptn of Eliza Buchanan. Same cmte: asking to be discharged from the further consideration of the House bill for the relief of Catharine Clarke, & that it be referred to the Cmte on Naval Affairs.

Naval: The ship **St Louis** sailed from Norfolk for Rio Janeiro on Tues last. The following is a list of her ofcrs: Cmder, Harrison H Cocke
Lt & Ex-Ofcr, John L Ring
Lts J R M Mullaney, Wm L Blanton, & Joshua D Todd
Purser: John F Steele   Acting Master: Thos L Dance
Acting Surgeon: S Wilson Kellogg   Assist Surgeon: John Ward

Passed Midshipmen: Wm C West, Chas Latimer, & John P Jones
Capt's Clerk: John Harrison
Acting Midshipmen: W A Weaver, C H Greene, W H Lyne, & S P Prickett
Boatswain: Chas Woodland   Yeoman: John Ferguson
Gunner: Eddin Ross   Purser's Steward: W J Willford
Carpenter: Danl James   Surgeon's Steward: C H Leistner
Sailmaker: Saml Tatem
Passengers for Rio: Mrs Todd, 2 children, & servant; Purser Edw Fitzgerald; Purser's Clerk, Elijah Goodrich.

Obit-died: a friend announces the death of Francis H Berry, late of Nanjemoy, Md, but who had joined the service of his country in Col Brough's Regt of Ohio volunteers, & served during the whole term of that brave corps. He was on his way to Cincinnati with his comrades to be discharged, when he fell a victim to diarrhoea on board the steamboat **Sarah Bladen**, & was buried at Ashmore's woodyard, about 50 miles below Helena, Ark. Every attention was paid him by his comrades & ofcrs. His bereaved mother & sister feel in his loss the bitterest calamity which war inflicts.

Mrd: on Aug 9, by Rev Mr Morgan, Wm Mitchell to Miss Sydney Virginia, daughter of Nicholas Travers, all of Wash City.

Mrd: on Aug 8, in Wash City, by Rev Dr Laurie, Lt Chas B Snow, late of the Texas Navy, to Miss Margareta W, daughter of the late Jos Mechlin, of Wash City.

Died: on Aug 10, Mrs Eliza Young, wife of Jas Young, of Wash City, after a lingering illness of 6 months. Her funeral is from her late residence, Capitol Hill, at 5 o'clock, on Aug 11.

Died: on Aug 7, Amanda M, only child of B O & Eliz C Greenwell, aged 10 months & 11 days.

Household furniture at auction: on Aug 11, at the residence of Mr Cummings, on D st, between 9th & 10th sts. -Edw C & G F Dyer

SAT AUG 12, 1848
Brookville Academy will commence on Sep 4: 23 weeks, $65. Reference may be had to the following patrons: Messrs Gales & Seaton; A Green; Jas Adams; Com'dr R H Poor: Wash, D C. E G Brown, Gtwn, D C. J H Orndorff; A Paine, Balt, Md. J O'Donnel; Arthur Fue; M D; T S Herbert, M D, Howard District, Md. H M Dungan, Morgan Co, Va. Address the Principal for particulars. –E J Hall, Brookville, Md

Senate: 1-Cmte of Claims: referring the papers of the reps of Robt Carter to the Auditors of the Treas to be examined.

Household & kitchen furniture at auction: on Aug 12, at the residence of a gentleman declining housekeeping, on Pa ave, near the corner of 21st st, next house to the residence of Dr Magruder, a lot of furniture. -A Green, auctioneer

House of Reps: 1-Cmte on Patents: ptn of Thos G Clinton, an assistant examiner in the Patent Ofc, preferring charges against Edmund Burke, Com'r of Patents, & the memorial of Edmund Burke, asking for an investigation of the charges preferred, made a report thereon: Resolved, that the cmte be discharged from the further consideration of the subject. 2-Cmte on Public Lands: bill for the relief of Wm Kingsbury, & for the relief of Elisha Hampton & others, of the State of Iowa: committed.

Household & kitchen furniture, pianos, & plated ware, at auction: on Aug 18, by order of the Orphans Court of Wash Co, D C: belonging to the estate of Robt W Dyer.
-Edw C & G F Dyer

MON AUG 14, 1848

House of Reps: Reported bills to the House without amemdment: 1-Act for the relief of Milledge Galphin, exc of the last will & testament of Geo Galphin, deceased. 2-Act authorizing the payment of a sum of money to Robt Purkis. Relief of: Purser Benj J Cahoone; of Anna J Hassler; of Eliz Pistole, widow of Chas Pistole; of David Currier; of Benj Adams & Co & others; of Messrs Cook, Anthony, Mahon & others; of Jesse Turner; of Mary Taylor; of Welcome Parmenter; of David Wilkinson; of D A Watterston; of Chas M Gibson; of Geo V Mitchell; of the legal reps of Thos J V Owens, deceased; of H B Gaither. Pension to Abilgail Garland, widow of Jacob Garland, deceased. Payment to Chas Richmond. Pension to John Clarke. 3-Cmte of the Whole: Act for the relief of John Lorimer Graham, late postmaster in N Y C; relief of Saml Grice; relief of Wm B Stokes; & relief of the widows & orphans of the ofcrs, seamen, & marines of the brig of war **Somers**. 4-Cmte of the Whole: discharged from the further consideration of the Senate bill to compensate R M Johnson for the erection of certain bldgs for the use of Choctaw Academy. 5-Cmte of Elections: resolution authorizing the Clerk to pay Jas Monroe for services as a member while contesting the seat of David S Jackson. Mr Vinton moved to amend the resolution so as to direct the Clerk to pay John M Botts for the time occupied in contesting the seat of John W Jones as a member from the State of Va in the 28th Congress. 6-Bill for the relief of Charity Harrington, as amended by the House, was concurred in.

Appointments by the Pres: by & with the advice & consent of the Senate. 1-Andrew J Donelson, of Tenn, to be Envoy Extra & Minister Pleni of the U S to the Federal Gov't of Germany. 2-Alfred H P Edwards, of Conn, Consul for the Phillipine Islands, vice H P Sturgis, resigned. 3-Fred'k V B Morris, Consul for the port of Batavia, in the Island of Java, vice Owen M Roberts, deceased.

The Wash Race Course has been laid out in avenues & divided into parcels of from 4 to 20 acres, by Mr Wm Holmead, the proprietor, to purchasers desirous of country residences within a convenient distance of Wash. We are glad that such an improvement of that valuable piece of land is to take place.

Marine Corps: promotions by brevet in the U S Marine Corps, made by the Pres, by & with the advice & consent of the Senate, Aug 8, 1848. [All by ***brevet***.]

1-1st Lt Arch H Gillespie to be capt from Sep 30, 1846, for distinguished services in Calif, & for meritorious conduct in the defence of the "Ciudad de los Angeles," when in command of a small party of volunteers, opposed by a force of Californians 800 strong, in Sep, 1848.

2-Capt A H Gillespie to be major from Dec 6, 1846, for gallantry & courage displayed in the battle of San Pascual, in Calif.

3-1st Lt Wm A Maddox to be capt from Jan 3, 1847, for gallant & meritorious conduct in the battle of Santa Clara, & in suppressing the insurrection at & around Monterey, while in command of a company of mounted volunteers operating in the middle district of Calif, in Dec, 1846.

4-Capt Jacob Zeilin to be major from Jan 9, 1847, for gallant & meritorious conduct displayed in the battles on the banks of the "Rio San Gabriel," & on the plains of the "Mesa."

For gallant & meritorious conduct at the bombardment & capture of the city of Vera Cruz, Mar 10, 1847:

1st Lt Addison Garland to be capt.

1st Lt Wm L Shuttleworth to be capt.

2nd Lt Geo Adams to be 1st Lt from Aug 12, 1847, for gallant & meritorious conduct at the Nat'l Bridge, while serving with the command of Maj Lally.

For gallant & meritorious conduct at the storming of Chapultepec, & at the capture of the city of Mexico, Sep 13, 1847. [By brevet.]

Capt John G Reynolds to be major.

1st Lt D D Baker to be capt.

1st Lt Wm L Young to be capt.

2nd Lt D J Sutherland to be 1st Lt.

2nd Lt Edw McD Reynolds to be 1st Lt.

2nd Lt Thos Y Field to be 1st Lt.

2nd Lt Chas G Macauley to be 1st Lt.

2nd Lt John S Nicholson to be 1st Lt.

2nd Lt Aug S Nicholson to be 1st Lt.

Capt Geo H Terrett to be major for gallant & meritorious conduct in the storming of the castle of Chapultepec, & in the capture of a redoubt on his advance upon the San Cosmo gate on Sep 13, 1847.

For gallant & meritorious conduct in the storming of the castle of Chapultepec, & in the capture of the San Cosmo gate, Sep 13, 1847.

1st Lt John D Simms to be capt.

2nd Lt Chas A Henderson to be 1st Lt.

1st Lt Robt Tansill to be capt from Nov 17, 1847, for gallant & meritorious conduct in the defence of the town of Guaymas, in Mexico, while in command of a small party of marines.

Mrd: on Jul 6, by Rev Saml C Kerr, Mr A T Hawkins Duvall, of Louisiana, to Miss Sarah S Williams, of Wilkinson Co, Miss.

Died: on Jul 23, at the Genr'l Hospital, Camp Carrollton, Louisiana, John T Hubbard, in his 21st year, son of Solomon Hubbard, of Wash.

By virtue of a writ of fieri facias, against the goods & chattels, lands & tenements of Richd Brooks, Danl Kelly, & Edw McKenney, & Thos Kelley, at the suit of Clarke & Briscoe, I have seized & taken in execution the north half of lot 12 in square 1000, with improvements, as the property of Edw McKenna, consisting of 1 frame house, which I shall sell on Aug 26, for cash. –Jno L Fowler, Constable

Criminal Court-Wash: Edw Sears charged with slave stealing: not guilty. [Chester English testified: he was one of the parties arrested & found on board the schnr **Pearl** at the time of her capture & imprisoned with Drayton & Sears ever since, being introduced against Sears.] [Aug 22nd newspaper: Chester English has been discharged, as there is no evidence to prove his participation in the design of abducting the slaves.]

TUE AUG 15, 1848
List of Acts passed at the First Session 30th Congress. Act for the relief of:

Heirs of John Paul Jones
Jos Wilson
Chas L Dell
Admx of Elisha L Kean, deceased
Legal reps of Geo Fisher, deceased
Edw Bolon
Jones & Boker
Richd Bloss & others
Fernando Fellanny
Peter Engels, sen
Tho Brownell
Oliver C Harris
Reynolds May
Alfred White
Heirs of Moses White
Christopher Cunningham
David N Smith
Gustavus Dorr
Charity Harrington
Jesse Turner
Ann J Hassler
Welcome Parmenter
David Currier
D A Watterston
Mary Taylor
David Wilkinson
Saml Grice
Wm B Stokes
Ward & Smith
Geo V Mitchell
Jas M Scantland
Benj J Cahoone-purser
B O Taylor
Richd Reynolds
Wm Pittman
Wm Triplett
Frederic Durrive
Wm Culver
Russel Goss
E G Smith
J Throckmorton
John Anderson
Alborne Allen
Amy Judd
Wm Ralston
Jos & Lindley Ward
John Mitchell
Silas Waterman
Bennett M Dell
John Manley
Stalker & Hill
Elijah H Willis
Jonathan Fitzwater
Saml Cony
Wm P Brady
Wm T Holland
Chas Cappel
Francis M Holton

Catharine Hoffman
John Farnham
Betsey McIntosh
H B V Gaither
Heirs of Mathew Stewart
Legal reps of John Snyder, deceased
Bent St Vrain & Co
Eliz Pistole, widow of Chas Pistole, deceased.
Legal reps of Thos J V Owen, deceased.
Robt Ellis, of Michigan
Benj Adams & Co & others
Catharine Fulton, of Wash Co, Pa
Edna Hickman, wife of Alex'r D Peck
Legal reps of Jas Brown, deceased
Mary Brown, widow of Jacob Brown
Sarah Stokes, widow of John Stokes

Jos Perry, a Choctaw Indian, or his assigns
Wm Hogan, adm of Michl Hogan, deceased
Saml W Bell, a native of the Cherokee nation
Abigail Garland, widow of Jacob Garland, deceased
Heris & widow of Francois Gramillion
Messrs Cook, Anthony, Mahony & others
John P B Gratiot & legal reps of Henry Gratiot
Barclay & Livingston, & Smith, Thurgar & Co
W B Slaughter, late Sec of the Terriroty of Wisconsin
John Lorimer Graham, late postmaster in N Y C
Phineas Capen, legal adm of John Cox, deceased, of Boston
John Black, late U S Consul at the city of Mexico
Walter Loomis & Abel Gay, approved Jul 2, 1836
Millidge Galphin, exc of the last will & testament of Geo Galphin, deceased
Jose Argote Villalobos, Marie Rose, Francois Felix, Marquis de Fougeres, or their hiers or legal reps
Widows & orphans of the ofcrs, seamen, & marines of the brig **Somers**.
Thos Scott, Register of the Land Ofc at Chillicothe, Ohio, for services connected with the duties of his ofc
Legal reps of Wm Mckenzie, late a seaman on board the U S ship **Vincennes**.
2-Payment to Chas Richmond. 3-Payment of sum of money to Robt Purkis. 4-Payment of claim of Walter R Johnson agasint the U S. 5-Settle the account of Jos Nourse, deceased. 6-Purchase of the manuscript papers of the late Jas Madison, former Pres of the U S.
7-Compensation to Saml Leech & for services in the investigation of suspended sale in the Mineral Point district, Wisconsin. 8-Confirm to the legal reps of Jos Dutaillis the location of a certain new Madrid certificate. 9-Compensate R M Johnson for erection of bldgs for use of the Choctaw Academy. 10-Benefit of Mrs Harriet Barney. 11-Benefit of Benj White. 12-Pension to Patrick Walker. 13-Pension to John Clark. 14-Franking privilege to Louis Catharine Adams. 15-Change the name of the steamboat **Chas Downing** to the **Calhoun**. 16-Act to change the name of Photius Kavasales to Photius Fisk. 17-Resolution granting to the Jackson Monument Cmte certain brass guns & mortars captured by Gen Andrew Jackson, & for other purposes. 18-Resolution in favor of David Shaw & Solomon T Corser.

Mrd: on Jul 27, at Beverly, by Rev John Corsdale, Edw P Pitts, of Accomac Co, Va, to Mary W, daughter of John U Dennis, of Worcester Co, Md.

Mrd: on Aug 3, by Rev Ulysses Ward, Geo M Oyster to Miss Rosa O'Bryon, all of Wash City.

Died: on Aug 11, at Newport, R I, Jane, wife of Capt Chas Wilkes, U S N. Her loss will be severely felt, not only by her immediate connexions, but by a large circle of friends in Wash City, to whom she was endeared by her worth & virtues.

The Court & Bar of St Mary's Co have passed resolutions testifying their regret at the death of the late Col Gerard N Causin, & their respect for his high character & worth.

The PG Agricultural Society have selected Gen Tench Tilghman & Dr Jas S Owners as their orators at the next fall exhibition.

WED AUG 16, 1848
Woman's Rights Convention organized a few days ago in the Unitarian Church. Ofcrs appointed:
Mrs Abigail Burr, Pres   Mrs Sarah L Hallowell, Sec
Mrs Laura Murray, Vice Pres   Mrs Mary H Hallowell, Sec
Mrs Catharine A T Stebbins, Sec
Wm C Nell read an essay upon Women's Rights. A letter from Gerritt Smith concurring in the objects sought to be accomplished. Mrs Eliz Stanton, of Seneca Falls, read the declaration adopted at the meeting. Mr Colton, of N Y, briefly stated his objections. Lucretia Mott wished to know what the speaker considered the proper sphere of woman. W C Bloss made some very humerous remarks, which were received with much applause. Mrs Sanford, of Michigan, made a forcible address. Eliz McClintock read a poetical composition, by Mrs Chapman, of Boston.

$5 reward for stayed or stolen black & white Cow. –Z Jones, exc of R I Jones, on 9th st, between L & M sts

Correspondent of the Albany Evening Journal, writing from Greene, in Chanango Co, on Aug 10: I reached home last night, but what changes have taken place since I left [2 weeks] here! There have been 24 deaths in this little village, & the cause baffles the skill of all our physicians in Binghamton, Oxford, & Norwich. R W Baker & Mrs E R Gray were buried yesterday. Several families have fled to the mountains.

Valuable real estate for sale. Wishing to remove to the West, I offer for sale the Farm on which I reside, near Warrenton, Fauquier Co, Va. It contains 233 acres; large & excellent dwlg-house, recently built; overseer's house, granary, stables, & other out-houses. Also, a tract of land on ***Dorrel's Run***, 18 miles below Warrenton: contains 600 acres: a new dwlg house & the usual farm houses are upon it. Also, a tract of 343 acres, lying on Sandy creek, in Pittsyvania Co. –Jas French

Died: yesterday, in Gtwn, D C, Mrs Deborah Heaton, formerly of England, aged 93 years. Her funeral will take place from the residence of Mrs C V Offley, on High st, Gtwn, today at 5 o'clock.

The Hon Millard Fillmore is one of the finest looking men in the nation, nearly 6 feet in height, a perfect model in his physical proportions, & his manners, movements & conversation exhibiting that happy union of dignity & affiability which gives assurance to all who come in contact with him that he is every inch a man & a gentleman. His arm has the strength of the blacksmith's, & his walk the freedom of the Indians.
–Boston Atlas. Newport, R I, Aug 11.

Coat found: apply to Ponpey Jackson, 4½ st, near Va ave.

Farm for sale: in Wash Co, D C: adjoins the land of Notley Moulden & the late Danl Kurtz, containing about 240 acres; formerly the property of Jas Calden, & now belongs to Mrs Eliz Cartwright. There is a small dwlg house, kitchen, stable, & 2 good barns.
–John Marbury

Alfred Lee has taken the house recently occupied by Mr L H Berryman, at 12th & C sts, as a Feed Store.

$30 reward for runaway negroes, Thos Bredon & his wife Suana. Thos is between 45 & 50 years of age, & Suana is about 33. They were formerly the property of Miss Tolson, of Prince Wm Co, Va. I purchased them from Dr Alex'r H Tolson, of PG Co, Md. I advertised for the same negroes on Mar 27 last.
–Zachariah Berry, **Blue Plains**, Alexandria, Va

THU AUG 17, 1848
For rent: nearly new 2 story frame house, with back bldg, on Vt ave. Inquire at the lumber yard on 12th st & canal. –Lenman & Brother

Appointments by the Pres, by & with the advice & consent of the Senate.
Francis H Merriman, U S Atty for the district of Texas, vice Gov W Brown, deceased.
Jas Shields, of Ill, to be Govn'r of the Territory of Oregon
Kintling Pritchett, of Pa, to be Sec for the Territory of Oregon
Wm P Bryant, of Indiana, to be Chief Justice of the U S Supreme Court for the Territory of Oregon
Peter H Burnett, of Oregon, to be an Assoc Justice of the U S Supreme Court for the Territory of Oregon
Isaac W R Bromley, of N Y, to be U S Atty for the district of Oregon
Jos L Meek, of Oregon, to be U S Marshal for the district of Oregon
John Adair, of Ky, to be Collector of the port for the district of Oregon, in the Territory of Oregon
Jas M Newell, to be Collector of the Customs at Bridgetown, N J, vice Lorenzo F Lee, deceased.
Danl S Macauley, Consul Genr'l at Alexandria, in Egypt
E S Offley, Consul for the port of Smyrna, vice D W Offley, deceased.
For the Navy Dept:
1st Lt Danl J Southerland, of the Marine Corps, to be Captain by brevet, for gallant & meritorious conduct in the assault upon the city of Mexico, to date from Sep 14, 1847.

Professors of Mathematics in the Navy:
John H C Coffin, of Maine   Wm Flye, of Maine
A G Pendleton, of Va   Wm Chauvenet, of Pa
Mordecai Yarnall, of Ky   Jas Major, of N Y
Wm Benedict, of Va   Jos S Hubbard, of Conn
Mark H Beecher, of N Y   Ruel Keith, of Vt
Henry H Longwood, of Dela   Arsene N Girault, of Md
Navy Agent: John Parrot, to be temporary Navy Agent at Mazatlan, in Mexico

The Hon A P Butler, U S Senator from S C, was arrested, on a warrant issued on Mon, on the oath of Mr Wallis, charged with being about to commit a breach of the peace, by fighting a duel with the Hon T H Benton, & on Tue he gave bail in the sum of $5,000 to keep the peace for the space of 12 months.

Mr Adam Alburger, the pyrotechnist, who was so dreadfully injured by the explosion in the laboratory of the U S Arsenal last Monday, died on Tuesday afternoon.

Mrd: on Tue, at Balt, by Rev Mr Atkinson, Hon D M Barringer, of N C, to Eliz, daughter of Lewin Wethered, of Balt.

Mrd: on Tue, by Rev John C Smith, Mr Aloysius Reeves to Mrs Martha Foanes, all of Wash City.

Died: on Aug 16, Mr Wm John Gallagher, aged 24 years. His funeral is today at half past 4 o'clock, from the residence of Mr Edw Doran, Navy Yard.

Montg Co [Md] Agricultural Society: appointed Delegates for the Convention to be held on Sep 5: A B Davis, Otho Magruder, Zachariah Waters, Geo W Dawson, Robt Dick, & Wm H Farquhar.

FRI AUG 18, 1848
Dr Presley H Craig, one of the oldest Surgeons in the U S service, died at the barracks below New Orleans on Aug 8.

Smith O'Brien, for whose arrest a reward of 500 pounds has been offered by the Lord-Lt of Ireland, has a brother, Sir Lucius O'Brien, in the House of Commons. The brother gave his vote in favor of the bill for suspending the habeas corpus act, knowing that his brother would be one of its first victims.

Tue last, a few miles of Albany, Mr Nelson Sanford, of Amsterdam, son of Hon John Sanford, of that place, while attempting to secure a cane which he had dropped from the train of which he was a passenger, was struck on the head by the side of a bridge under which he was passing & killed. He was in his 23rd year.

Appointed by the Pres: Jas Turney, of Ill, to be an Associate Justice of the U S Supreme Court for the Territory of Oregon.

The decision of the Naval Court in Inquiry recently convened at the Navy Yard, Brooklyn, in the case of the loss of the U S schnr **On-ka-hye**, exonerate Lt O H Berryman, commanding, from all censure.

Died: yesterday, in Wash City, Mr Bernard Quinn, in his 36th year. His friends & the members of Wash Benevolent Society are invited to attend his funeral this day, from his late residence on K & 15th sts.

Wash Corp: 1-Cmte of Claims: bill for the relief of Wm Campbell: passed. 2-Ptn from W H Harrover: referred to the Cmte on the Asylum. 3-Ptn of J B Edelin & others, praying for a flag footway across F st, on the east side of 12th st: referred to the Cmte on Improvements. 4-To be referred to the Cmte of Claims: the ptns of Geo Knott, Maria A Queen, Wm Fleming, Henry Turner, E D & H A Willard, C Finkman, Chas Kernan, Michl H Grymes, John Fitzgerald, J Lucchisi, Fred'k Lakemeyer, & Wm P Shedd. 5-Ptn of Jackson Edmonston & others, praying that the public alley in square 518 may be converted into a street: referred to the Cmte on Improvements.

Died: on Mon, near Balt, in his 48th year, Maj Thos Noel, of the 7th Regt U S Infty, after long & severe sufferings, the effect of a wound received by him while on active service in the late Florida war, & which he bore with the most Christian patience & fortitude.

The widow of the late Hon Roger M Sherman died at Fairfield, Conn, on Aug 3. In accordance with the united wishes of herself & husband, she has bequeathed her miscellaneous library, house, & homestead to the First Ecclesiastical Society of Fairfield, together with a fund of $2,500 for the purpose of keeping the same in repair; the law library of her late husband to Fairfield County, for the use of the law & courts of said county; $4,000 to the corporation of Yale College, on the condition that they pay an annuity of $200 to one of her nephews during his life; $2,000 to the Theological Institute of East Windsor; $4,000 to the American Home Missionary Society; $4,000 to the American Colonization Society; $4,000 to the Retreat for the Insane at Hartford; & $500 to the female Beneficent Society of Fairfield. –Connecticut Courant

At the late commencement of Amherst College, the degree of D D was conferred upon the Rev Thos Brainerd, of Phil, & that of L L D upon the Hon Rufus Choate & Prof C C Felton, of Harvard University.

SAT AUG 19, 1848

G C Grammer offers for rent that beautiful residence, with a large enclosure, lately occupied by Mr Randolph Coyle, situated on 8th st west, near the Gen Post Ofc. Immediate possession can be given. Also, for rent, the dwlg part of the 3 story brick house over Mr Brashear's store, opposite Brown's Hotel. Also, for rent, the 2 story frame house next to Apollo Hall. Possession next month. Apply to G C Grammer.

Wm C Lemon [of the late firm of John Anderson & Co} continues at the old stand, #4 Wall & 213 Duane sts, N Y: for sale Fine Cut Chewing & Smoking Tobacco, & Snuffs.

Wm W Corcoran, of the firm of Corcoran & Riggs, of Wash City, was among the passengers in the ship **America**, which sailed from N Y on Wed last for Liverpool.

Died: at Roxbury, Westmoreland Co, Va, the residence of his father, Col H T Garnett, Robt G R Garnett, in his 19th year. His affliction was protracted, painful & crushing to all his fondest hopes. He passed from earth to heaven. [No death date given-current item.]

Died: on Aug 17, at the residence of her son, Capitol Hill, Mrs Catharine A Owner, in her 64th year, after a severe illness of 4 weeks. Her funeral is today at 3 o'clock, from the residence of her son.

Died: on Aug 16, in Wash City, Mrs Catherine Quigly, aged 32 years, a native of the county of Roscommon, Ireland, leaving a husband & 2 children & many friends to mourn her loss.

MON AUG 21, 1848

A son, about 12 years of age, of Philip J Gray, editor of the Camden [N J] Mail, was accidentally drowned in the Delaware on Wed.

The Hon Reuben Booth died at his residence in Danbury, Conn, on last Mon. He was an able lawyer, & one of the most prominent men in the State, having been a member of both branches of the General assembly, Lt Govn'r of the State, & a Presidential Elector in 1840.

About a fortnight since, Hon Jas H Haines, of Burnham, Senator from Waldo Co, was suddenly called home from Augusta by the news that his son, about 18 years old, had become insane, wandered off into the woods, & could not be found. He returned about 6 days & nights later, his clothes tattered, & could give no account of where he had been. He is now well. –Portland [Maine] Argus

New place for a wedding: the other day Mr Jas S Kimball, of Stafford, Vt, & Miss Clara Partridge, of Templeton, Mass, teachers, were married on board the steamer **Maid of the Mist**, amidst the ascending spray, by Rev Mr Callahan.

Patent Ofc, Aug 3, 1848. Ptn of Thos J Goodman, of Balt, Md, for the extension of a patent granted to Thos J Goodman for an improvement in scalding hogs by steam, for 7 years from the expiration of said patent, which takes place on Feb 13, 1849. 2-Ptn of Carrington Wilson, of N Y C, for the extension of a patent granted to Carrington Wilson for an improvement in cooking stoves, for 7 years from the expiration of said patent, which takes place on Oct 10, 1848. –Edmund Burke, Cm'r of Patents

Mrd: on Aug 10, at Utica, N Y, Prof Morse to Sarah Eliz Griswold, of New Orleans.

Orphans Court of Wash Co, D C. Letters of administration on the personal estate of Thos Collins, late of said county, deceased. –John D McPherson, adm

TUE AUG 22, 1848

New Ice Cream Saloons: the subscriber having fitted up on Ice Cream Saloon in splendid style with gas lights, invites his customers & the citizens generally to pay him a visit. The Saloon is directly over his Confectionary, which is on the north side of Pa ave, a few doors west of Brown's Hotel. Profs Bergmann & Schell will give Instrumental Concerts every Mon & Thu: admission free. –Geo Krafft

New members of the 31st Congress:
Illinois:
Jos H Bissell	Thos L Harris	Edw D Baker
John A McClernand	John Wentworth	
Thos R Young	Wm A Richardson	

Missouri:
Jas B Bowlin	Jos S Phelps	Willard P Hall
Wm V N Bay	Jas S Green	

Iowa:
Wm Thompson	Shepherd Leffler

The cmder of the U S ship **Supply** [Lt Lynch] is the ofcr sent out to explore the Dead Sea. Ofcrs of the **Supply** at Genoa: Alex M Pennock, Lt Commanding; B N Westcott, Acting Master; John Y Mason, jr, Purser; J Thornley, Passed Assist Surgeon; W B Fitzgerald, Passed Midshipman; S P Quackenbush, Passed Midshipman. All hands well.

Trustee's sale of land: by decree of Chas Co Court sitting as a Court of Equity: public sale on Oct 3 next, at Port Tobacco, in said county, all that tract of land or farm called *Eutaw*, formerly the residence of the late Gen Philip Stewart, of Md, & sold for the purpose of partition amongst his legatees. The farm is in Chas Co, Md, on Mattawomen Swamp, & consists of 580 acres, more or less, a proportion of the land being swamp or bottom land. It has a dwlg, overseer's house, & the usual out-houses.
–F Stone, John W Mitchell, Trustees

From Oct 1st next, there will be, in Richmond, in my family & under my auspices, a small Select School for the education of Young Ladies: number will be limited to 12.
–B B Minor

Real estate at Public Sale: by decree of the PG Co Court, sitting in Chancery, in the case of Jas H M Dunlop, through his guardian, S S Williams, cmplnt, & Richd Estep, adm de bonis non of Henderson Magruder, dfndnt, I shall sell on the premises, on Sep 28, all that tract of land called *Brough*, in that part of PG Co, Md, called *The Forest*, containing about 125 acres, being the same of which said Henderson Magruder died seized & possessed. Improvements consist of a frame dwlg & tobacco houses. This property adjoins the lands of John Mitchell & Theodore Williams, & is now in the tenancy of the former. -S S Williams, trustee

WED AUG 23, 1848
To let, a 3 story brick dwlg house, with a bldg on the rear of the premises suitable for an ofc, on the north side of F st, between 12th & 13th sts, one door east of the residence of Wm Tyson. Apply to Mrs Ernis, 2nd door west of the premises. This property would be sold at a moderate price.

Chas Edw Antron, of N Y C, has been appointed Prof of Modern Languages in St John's College, Annapolis, Md.

The Zanesville [Ohio] Gaz of Aug 16 records the death of another of the race of the pioneers, Danl Convers, in his 74th year. He was born in the town of Thompson, Conn, in 1775, & emigrated to the West with his father, settling in the Ohio Company's purchase about the year 1790. In 1791 he was made captive by Indians, who carried him to the Wyandott towns on the Sandusky. He escaped in about 3 months, &, with the aid of traders & others, got back to his friends in Conn. He came to the West again in 1794, settling first at Marietta, & finally at Zanesville, [then called Woodbourne.]

The Pres has officially recognized Cesar Henrique Stuart de la Figaniere as vice consul of Portugal for the port of N Y, for other parts of the State of N Y, & for East Jersey.

Capt J P Breedlove died at New Orleans on Aug 12, of disease contracted in Mexico while serving as captain of one of the companies of the 14th Infty. He took an active part in the achievements of the Army in the valley of Mexico.

Criminal Court-Wash: yesterday the case of the U S vs Brian Frail was before the Court: Frail was charged with the murder of a boy named Maurice Conner, near Coltman's brickyard, not far from 14th st. The prisoner was indicted for manslaughter, & was defended by Messrs Ratcliffe & Green. The boys concerned in the affray said they saw Frail beat Conner with a brick bat on the neck & side.

Accident at Alexandria on Sunday night last. Mr Edw Smith, a clerk in the Treasury Dept, Wash, fell from a wharf and drowned. He was a worthy gentlemen, & a native of King Geo Co, Va. -Gaz

Died: on Aug 22, at his residence on Capitol Hill, Jas Moor, sen, in his 90th year, a native of Edinburgh, Scotland, & for the last 60 years a resident of this District. His funeral is tomorrow at 3 o'clock, from his late residence.

Died: on Aug 22, Jas R Lynch, son of Jas & Jane Lynch, aged 2 years, 2 months & 22 days. His funeral is today, from the residence of his grandmother, Mrs Philips, on Capitol Hill, at 3 o'clock.

Chas Astor Bristed, one of the heirs of John Jacob Astor, & a graduate of Yale, has made a donation of $1,350.00 to the College to endow a scholarship.

For rent: a good business stand, between 11th & 12th sts, north side, Pa ave, next to T Lewis' jewelry & W F Bayly's stationery stores. Also, the hall above said stores, 30 by 40 feet. Inquire of W M Lewis.

For rent: large 3 story brick house on 10th st & Pa ave. Apply to Michl Combs, on the premises.

Mrd: on Nov 13, 1847, in Phil City, by Alderman Mitchell, Mr Geo W Taylor to Miss Anna Draper, eldest daughter of Dr Alex C Draper, formerly of Phil, now of Washington.

Mrd: on Aug 15, by Rev J L Elliott, Wm Flinn, of Pittsburg, Pa, & Caroline Elliott, of Washington.

THU AUG 24, 1848
Miss M J Taylor's School, in C st, between 3rd & 4½ sts, will re-open on Sep 4.

For rent: the upper or dwlg part of that large bldg on 7th st west & Pa ave, & over the stores of Shuster & Co & Messrs Hall & Brother, at present occupied by Mrs McCormick as a boarding house. Apply to Anne R Dermott, residing in the house.

Miss Carroll, daughter of Ex-Govn'r Carroll, from Md, will open a Seminary for the education of young Ladies, in Wash, on the first Mon of Sep next. Location made known by subsequent notice.

Orphans Court of Wash Co, D C. Letters of administration de bonis non, with the will annexed, on the personal estate of Thos Burch, late of PG Co, Md, deceased.
–Zephaniah Jones, adm d b n with will annexed

Household & kitchen furniture at auction: on Aug 28, at the residence of Mrs Preston, on 12th st, between E & F sts, nearly opposite King's Painting Gallery. A good lot of furniture. -A Green, auctioneer

Criminal Court-Wash. 1-Brian Frail found guilty of manslaughter, & sentenced to be imprisoned 2 years at labor in the penitentiary, to take effect from Sep 1. 2-Danl Drayton, convicted of stealing negroes in 2 cases, sentenced to hard labor in the penitentiary for 20 years, being 10 years for each offence. 3-Edw Seyres guilty, in 74 cases, of transporting slaves on board the schnr **Pearl**, & sentenced to pay a fine of $160 in each case, one-half to go to the owners of said slaves & the other to the U S. 4-Wm Young guilty of an assault with intent to kill John Mockbee, was sentenced to be imprisoned 4 months in the county jail.

Sale of public property at Vera Cruz: U S ship **St Louis**, cost $20,000 when she sailed from Phil to Vera Cruz, sold for $500-let the Gov't deny it. The U S steamer **Mary Somers** [iron] cost the Gov't some $30,000, for which the purchaser paid some $12,000 of $13,000, & maybe less. The brig **Architect**, copper & copper fastened, which cost some four & five thousand dollars, was sold at $400.

Died: on Aug 23, Frances Marion, daughter of Wm S & Mary Ann Jackson, aged 3 years. Her funeral is this morning at 11 o'clock, from the residence of Henry Howison, on 9th st.

Engraver wanted, to execute map engraving at the ofc of the coast survey in Wash.
–A D Bache, Superintendent U S Coast Survey

FRI AUG 25, 1848

Orphans Court of Wash Co, D C. Letters of administration on the personal estate of Fred'k Liege, late of the U S Army, deceased. –John H Ballmann, adm

Wash Corp: 1-Cmte of Claims: act for the relief of Henry Jacobs; & an act for the relief of Michl Keller: passed. Same cmte: bill for the relief of Wm Jasper: recommitted to the same cmte. 2-Ptn of John C Harkness & others, praying the grading of 9th st, in front of squares 373 & 403: referred to the Cmte on Improvements. 3-Ptn of C Ailier & others, complaining of nuisances created by the deposites made by scavengers in the vicinity of 7th st west: referred to the Cmte on Police. 4-Cmte on Improvements: ptn of Geo H Plant & others, for grading & paving the alley in square 378: passed.

By the premature discharge of a cannon, in honor of the returned Volunteers of Pontiac, Mich, Luther Jones & Horace Budington were killed, & Peter Burke wounded. Burke was one of the returned volunteers.

Mr Chas Howell, an assist conductor on the Camden branch of the Southwestern Railroad, was accidentally knocked off the cars, on Sat last, as they were passing through the gate at Columbia, & instantly killed.

House of Reps refused to concur with the Senate in its amendment to the army bill, to retain the ofcrs & men of the Marine Corps which were to be dismissed at the end of the war. The Pres convened a board, [Col Miller & Majs Linton & Edelin,] to designate those who should be dismissed; which were Capts Ward Marston, Richd Donelan, Jos G Williams, Wm Lang; 1st Lts Jabez C Rich, Thos T Sloan, Edw L West, & John S Devlin; & 2nd Lts F Grundy Matson, Wm Butterfield, Wm E Perry, & Thos Y Field.
–Boston Post

The Lexington [Ky] Atlas brings us news of the death, on Aug 5, of Gen Jas Shelby, son of the late Govn'r Isaac Shelby. He was aged about 65 years, & was one of the most wealthy & respectable citizens of Fayette Co.

Dreadful explosion at Burkett's new flouring mill, north of Milton, Miani Co, Ohio, on Aug 14. David Curtis, about 22, was taken out dead; Washington Deacon, millwright, not expected to live; Mr Gilbert seriously injured, & his recovery doubtful; Jas Niles, thigh broken & toes mashed; Henry Clira & Thos Little slightly wounded.

Died: on Aug 23, Ann Foy, relict of the late Mordecai Foy, a native of Castlereagh, county Roscommon, Ireland, & for the last 20 years a resident of Wash City. Her funeral is this afternoon at 3:30 o'clock, from her late residence, between 4½ & 3rd sts.

Died: on Wed last, at *Spring Hill*, Fairfax Co, Va, Jas Beverly, infant son of Jas B & Henrietta Dodson. His funeral is this morning, at 10 o'clock, from the residence of his parents on 6th st, between E & F sts.

SAT AUG 26, 1848
Wash Hall Saddle, Harness, & Trunk Manufactory: s w corner of Pa ave & 6th sts. –Thos Fitnam [Ad]

Wash City lots to be sold for taxes on Nov 15. –A Rothwell, Collector
Andrae, Cornel: 1844 thru 1847: $90.75
Ault, Henry: 1844 thru 1847: $44.90
Acton, Osbourne: 1845 thru 1847: $6.66
Austin, Wm F: 1845 thru 1847: $9.21
Bull, John B: 1845 thru 1847: $27.48
Bond, Levi: 1844 thru 1847: $7.86
Bell, Otho B: 1845 thru 1847: $8.96
Bradley, Phineas: 1845 thru 1847: $102.38
Billing, Rebecca R: 1845 thru 1847: $41.82
Bacon, Saml: 1842 thru 1847: $14.76
Bank of Wash: 1843 thru 1847: $27.00
Bradley, Wm A: 1836 thru 1847: $194.87
Barnes, Wm H: 1842 thru 1847: $10.78
Bendick, Henry: 1836 thru 1847: $23.84
Breckenridge, John: 1845 thru 1847: $59.64
Barclay, Jas, & Jos Simpson: 1845 thru 1847: $21.54
Brady, John: 1845 thru 1847: $17.07
Bowen, Mary: 1845 thru 1847: $8.34
Bowie, Robt [in trust for the heirs of Geo French]: 1845 thru 1847: $18.90
Bulfinch, Thos: 1844 thru 1847: $8.80
Brady, Nathl, & Thos lae: 1844, 1846 & 1847: $37.04
Bickley, L W: 1846-1847: $29.53
Caden, Jas, & imp in name of J W Garner: 1844 thru 1847: $55.97
Carmack, Danl: 1845 thru 1847: $14.70
Carson, Geo: 1845 thru 1847: .90
Cowperchwart, J & others: 1845 thru 1847: $7.58
Clarke, Jos S: 1844 thru 1847: $47.50
Cross, Eli: 1844 thru 1847: $68.15
Columbian College: 1846-1847: $26.00
Crandall, Geo: 1845 thru 1847: $16.68
Coxe, Geo: 1845 thru 1847: $6.48
Craven, Isaac: 1844 thru 1847: $76.48
Costigan, Jos: 1837 thru 1847: $5.83
Clarke, M St Clair: 1837 thru 1847: $32.74
Clavelaux, Marc: 1845 thru 1847: .96
Carter, Maria: 1845 thru 1847: $21.60
Callahan, Thos: 1845 thru 1847: $26.27

Corcoran, W W: 1844 thru 1847: $105.57
Carroll, Wm: 1839 thru 1847: $6.48
Coxe, Wm W: 1845 thru 1847: $7.50
Clements, Wm A: 1845 thru 1847: $12.93
Digges, Cathrine: 1844 thru 1847: $129.39
Donohoo, Dolly Ann: 1845 thru 1847: $27.60
Dinex, Hanson: 1845 thru 1847: $12.90
Dulaney, Michl: 1844 thru 1847: $8.40
Davis, Richd: 1844 thru 1847: $15.66
Decamp, Sidney: 1844 thru 1847: $8.80
Donophon, Thornton A: 1839 thru 1847: $7.08
Dunlop, Eliz: 1845 thru 1847: $8.42
Doyle, John: 1845 thru 1847: $8.28
Doyle, Lawrence: 1845 thru 1847: $6.70
Davis, Richd: 1845 thru 1847: $2.78
Evans, F S: 1845 thru 1847: $26.34
Edmonson, Franklin: 1845 thru 1847: $9.12
Ellis, Chas F: 1836 thru 1847: $6.84
English & Nevins: 1838 thru 1847: $5.88
Foy, Mordecai: 1838 thru 1847: $106.98
Fischer, Wm, or Adam Villand: 1843 thru 1847: $80.11
Frazier, Simon: 1839 thru 1847: $206.81
Ferguson, Jas R: 1845 thru 1847: $2.16
Farland, John: 1845 thru 1847: $15.30
Forrest, Julius: 1845 thru 1847: $2.16
Fletcher, Thos: 1845 thru 1847: $78.21
Frazier, Thos: 1845 thru 1847: $36.75
Gratiot, Chas: 1845 thru 1847: $17.17
Garner. Jas W: 1844 thru 1847: $73.21
Gorman, John B: 1845 thru 1847: $7.86
Gardiner, John: 1845 thru 1847: $36.90
Gideon, Jacob: 1843 thru 1847: $58.27
Garretson, Remsen, & R J Dillon, adms of H T Garretson: 1845 thru 1847: $63.20
Griffin, Sarah A: 1845 thru 1847: $20.82
Griffin, Thos B: 1845 thru 1847: $25.08
Greer, Wm: 1844 thru 1847: $35.50
Gratiot, Chas, & A B McLean: 1845 thru 1847: $11.13
Greenleaf & Eliot: 1845 thru 1847: $29.89
Homans, Danl: 1845 thru 1847: $29.82
Hines, Henry: 1845 thru 1847: $71.85
Harman, J, jr: 1846-1847: $284.22
Hoover, John: 1845 thru 1847: $69.39
Higgins, John: 1845 thru 1847: $6.21
Handy, Mary G: 1845 thru 1847: $29.94
Holmes, Sylvanus: 1844 thru 1847: $32.11
Harkness, Saml: 1843 thru 1847: $202.28

Hogan, Thady: 1845 thru 1847: $53.25
Hughes, Thos: 1845 thru 1847: $32.31
Hewitt, Wm: 1842 thru 1847: $185.16
Hughes, Wm: 1845 thru 1847: $59.12
Hunt, Wm: 1842 thru 1847: $295.17
Houck, John: 1845 thru 1847: $9.66
Huntt, Saml, & John Patterson: 1845 thru 1847: $8.28
Hoover, Andrew: 1844 thru 1847: $208.88
Hyatt, Alpheus, & others: 1845 thru 1847: $83.25
Hibbs, Chas: 1845 thru 1847: $92.25
Harrison, Columbus: 1845 thru 1847: $7.38
Hall, David A: 1834 thru 1847: $665.63
Ingle & Lindsley: 1836 thru 1847: $76.62
Jarboe, Matthew: 1845 thru 1847: $23.88
Knox, Charlotte J: 1845 thru 1847: $4.26
Kuhn, J L: 1845 thru 1847: $35.96
Kelly, Jas: 1843 thru 1847: $85.74
Keyworth, Robt: 1845 thru 1847: $488.78
King, Henry: 1845 thru 1847: $19.44
King, John: 1845 thru 1847: $23.00
Knowles, Wm: 1845 thru 1847: $10.53
Lindenberger, Anna E: 1842 thru 1847: $91.30
Leddon, Benj: 1843 thru 1847: $10.13
Lawrence, John: 1845 thru 1847: $5.61
Law, Thos: 1842 thru 1847: $106.47
Lyons, Chas & N C Towle: 1842 thru 1847: $12.44
Mullikin, John: 1845 thru 1847: $25.65
McLeod, John: 1845 thru 1847: $92.43
Mudd, Ignatius: 1844 thru 1847: $157.26
Martin, Luther J & Mary J: 1845 thru 1847: $30.96
McQuay, Mary: 1845 thru 1847: $25.41
McGlue, Owen: 1845 thru 1847: $13.17
Matthew, Thos H: 1844 thru 1847: $2.44
Magnier, Thos: 1844 thru 1847: $91.99
McIntosh, Thos: 1844 thru 1847: $59.56
Morrow, Wm: 1845 thru 1847: $113.76
McGill, Wm: 1845 thru 1847: $2.11
Manning, Wilfred A: 1845 thru 1847: $2.85
Marshal, John & Jas, & Jas H Causten & W W Corcoran: 1846-1847: $27.28
McAleer, John: 1845 thru 1847: $13.96
Mackall, Leonard: 1845 thru 1847: $3.72
Maxcy, Virgil: 1845 thru 1847: $3.18
Munroe, Thos: interest from Nov 24, 1845, tax for paving 7th st: $291.78
Nicholson, A A: 1845 thru 1847: $128.97
Nally, Eliz: 1845 thru 1847: $87.34
Narden, Mary: 1844 thru 1847: $83.80

Nicholson, Mary Ann & Eliz: 1845 thru 1847: $8.28
Nicholls, Wm S: 1843 thru 1847: $10.35
Paris, Albert: 1845 thru 1847: $28.47
Peston, Anthony: 1840 thru 1847: $125.41
Parker & L O Cook: 1844 thru 1847: $152.00
Prather, Hugh D: 1845 thru 1847: $19.83
Patton, Lewis: 1845 thru 1847: $9.39
Passett, Peter: 1832 thru 1847: $161.64
Peter, America P: 1845 thru 1847: $2.61
Peter, Ann: 1845 thru 1847: $2.07
Pollard, Benj: 1844 thru 1847: $64.84
Peter, David: 1844 thru 1847: $31.12
Peter, Eliz, daughter of John: 1845 thru 1847: $6.54
Pratt, Henry, & others: 1844 thru 1847: $10.72
Peter, Mary: 1845 thru 1847: $1.83
Pairo, Thos W: 1844 thru 1847: $11.70
Phillips, Jas B: 1842 thru 1847: $582.52
Reynoldson, Catharine: 1845 thru 1847: $9.66
Roberts, John: 1845 thru 1847: $16.56
Reed, Thos: 1842 thru 1847: $22.07
Reynolds, Thos: 1845 thru 1847: $7.17
Richards, Wm & Thos: 1845 thru 1847: $5.10
Robinson, Saml: 1845 thru 1847: $100.23
Spence, Christopher: 1845 thru 1847: $8.43
Stewart, G W: 1844 thru 1847: $78.31
Smith, Geo B: 1845 thru 1847: $34.71
Smith, John: 1845 thru 1847: $8.68
Stroub, Jos: 1845 thru 1847: $141.75
Sinon, John: 1845 thru 1847: $17.73
Sweeney, Mary: 1845 thru 1847: $61.80
Sewall, Thos: 1845 thru 1847: $128.48
Semmes & Cox: 1844 thru 1847: $48.60
Seaver, Jonathan: 1835 thru 1847: $106.70
Shephard, Lodowick: 1844 thru 1847: $121.75
Sheriff, Mary C: 1845 thru 1847: $57.84
Sands, R C & Z Hazle: 1844 thru 1847: $62.87
Sands, Julia M: 1846-1847: $56.43
Thomas, Amelia: 1845 thru 1847: $40.62
Thruston, Buckner: 1841 thru 1847: $247.10
Taylor, Emily: 1845 thru 1847: $18.12
Thomas, Jas H: 1845 thru 1847: $21.09
Townsend, Lemuel: 1845 thru 1847: $8.75
Thompson, Richd: 1845 thru 1847: $60.43
Tompkins, Richd: 1845 thru 1847: $9.36
Thruston, Thos L: 1836 thru 1847: $139.38
Thompson, Wm: 1844 thru 1847: $67.92

Terry, Brooklin: 1845 thru 1847: $5.40
Tyler, Chas: 1845 thru 1847: $5.70
Turner, Henry: 1846-1847: $17.06
Tousard, Lewis: 1845 thru 1847: $2.07
Tayloe, B O: 1845-1847: $35.63
Van Ness, J P: 1842 thru 1847: $66.40

Boscage for sale: the subscriber, having determined to leave the county, offers for sale his Farm, immediately on the Brookville road, 5 miles from Gtwn, adjoining the farms of Robt P & Judge Dunlop, & is part of the ***Clean Drinking tract***: contains 300 acres, frame dwlg with 9 rooms finished in good style, barn, granary, blacksmith-shop, ice-house, & other necessary bldgs. –G M Watkins

Died: on Fri, Richd J Jones, a resident of Wash City, aged 37 years. His funeral is tomorrow at half past 9 o'clock, from the McKendree Chapel.

Died: on Aug 21, Sarah Ellen, infant daughter of Wm H & Sarah Ann Prentiss.

MON AUG 28, 1848
City Ordinances-Wash: 1-Act for the relief of Henry Jacobs: fine remitted for an alleged violation in regard to the licenses for carts: provided, he pay the costs of prosecution. 2-Act for the relief of Michl Keller: fine remitted, relative to grocery license: provided, he pay the costs of prosecution. 3-Act for the relief of Wm Campbell: fine remitted for an alleged violation relative to the harboring of dogs: provided, he pay the costs of prosecution.

Dr Litchfield, of Menaham, Conn, committed suicide by hanging himself in his barn. There was nothing in his circumstances, manners, & habits to account for this act, excepting that 3 years ago Dr Webb hung himself in the same barn & from the same beam. [No date given-current news item.]

TUE AUG 29, 1848
Teacher wanted: the Trustees of the Rockville Academy, Montg Co, Md, wish to engage a Teacher in the English dept-a gentleman well qualified to teach the English language & the higher branches of mathematics. The Teacher will receive $300 per annum from the State donation, in semi-annual payments, & the tuition fees accruing in his dept. By order, John Minis, Pres. –John Brewer, Sec pro tem

Eighth Street Academy will re-open on Aug 28: located on 8th st, near H. –A M Hushey, Principal. For information inquire of:

Rev R Gurley	Rev R T Berry	Mr C L Coltman
Rev N Bannatyne	Rev U Ward	Mr Jesse L Davis
Rev S D Finckel	Mr W W Seaton	Mr John Ferguson
Rev Mr Graiff	Mr Danl Leech	Mr John Wilson

Dublin Castle, Aug 8, 1847. A list of the political prisoners. Wm Smith O'Brien, M P for the county of Limerick; Chas Gavan Duffy, editor of the Nation; John Martin, proprietor of the Felon; Jos Brennan, sub-editor of the Felon; John Lawless, Sec of the Sandymount Club, Dublin; Francis Hawley, North Earl st, Dublin; Mr Nolan, supposed to be an American sympathizer, arrested at Thurles; Mr Fitzpatrick, Thurles; Mr Ryan, surgeon, Carrick-on-Suir; Mr O'Ryan, Cashel; Thos Witty, farmer or land owner, Wexford Co; Francis Strange, solicitor, Waterford, pres of the Felon Club there; Supple Glover, Waterford; Patrick McAuliffe, clothier, Waterford; Mr Fogarty, assist surgeon, Waterford; Thos Wm Condon, whitesmith, sec to the Wolfe Club, Waterford; Mr Taafe, barrister, Dublin; ___ Marron, editor of the Drogheda Argus; J S Barry, editor of the Cork Southern Reporter; Ralph Varien, Cork; Isaac Varien, Cork; 10 drapers' assistants from Messrs Pinns' establishment, Dublin; S J Meany, of the Irish Felon; Mr West surgeon, Dublin; M Carron, of America; Jas Bergen, ship broker, of N Y; Mr Butler, editor of the Gahway Vindicator; Mr Costigan, of Castlebar; Denny Lane, merchant, Cork, 21 countrymen from the neighborhood of Ballingary, in the county of Tipprary, charged with having assisted Smith O'Brien in the attack on the police. Parties against whom warrants are issued: Francis Morgan, solicitor to the Corporation, Dublin; Thos Francis Meagher, gentleman, Dublin; Michl Doheny, barrister, Tipperary; Richd O'Gorman, jr, barrister.

St Timothy's Hall, Catonsville, Md, 6 miles from Balt: pupils are received between 7 & 16 years of age at any time during the year. –Rev L Van Bokkelen

In virtue of 2 writs of fieri facias, I shall expose to public sale, on Sep 30 next, one house & lot, in square 729, lot 6, seized & taken in execution as the property of R L Homans, to satisfy a judgment due to Martin King; & at the same time one frame house in square 769, seized & taken in execution as the property of Matilda Wharton to satisfy a debt due to Robt Clark. Terms cash. –Wm A Mulloy, Constable

Trust sale of a valuable estate in Fauquier Co, Va: under the authority of a deed of trust, executed to me by Jas H Lufborough & Caroline S his wife, dated Sep 2, 1846, recorded in Fauquier Co, the purpose of which is to secure the payment of a sum of money therein mentioned to Thos Carter, I will offer for sale on the premises, on Oct 2, the tract of land in said county, near Salem, & adjoins the lands of John Baker, W M Morgan, & others. It contains 734 acres. Under the terms of the trust the sale is to be made for cash, but as less than $4,000 will pay the debt now remaining due & the expenses of the trust, it is supposed that a credit will be authorized by those interested, for the balance of the proceeds of the sale. –John E Page, Trustee, Clarke Co

Mrd: on Aug 28, by Rev Mr Morgan, Wm A Hacker, of Ill, to Angelica P, daughter of Isaac Holland, of Wash City.

Mrd: on Aug 28, by Rev Mr Vanhorseigh, Mr Saml Bridgeman to Miss Mary Thompson, all of Wash City.

Large sale of household & kitchen furniture: on Aug 29, at the residence of Mrs McDaniel, on 4½ st, a few doors above Pa ave. -Edw C & G F Dyer

WED AUG 30, 1848
Household & kitchen furniture at auction: on Sep 5, at the residence of Mrs Cochran, on F st, between 13th & 14th sts. -Edw C & G F Dyer

Orphans Court of Wash Co, D C. Letters of administration on the personal estate of Fred'k Sezd, late of the U S Army, deceased. –John H Ballmann, adm [See Sep 1, 1848 newspaper.]

Wash Corp: 1-Cmte of Claims: asking to be discharged from the further consideration of the ptn of Wm Johnson: discharged accordingly. 2-Relief of John Fletcher: referred to the Cmte on Improvements. 3-Cmte on Improvements: ptn of Geo Gibson, in relation to the filling up a certain lot in the First Ward, & a communication from S Drury relative thereto, asked to be discharged from the further consideration of the subject.

Official: Army Gen Order: Gen Orders, #47. War Dept, Adj Gen Ofc, Wash, Aug 24, 1848. Brevets conferred by the Pres, by & with the advice & consent of the Senate, during the recent session of Congress:
Capt Geo H Crossman, Assist Quartermaster [now Quartermaster,] to be Maj for gallant & meritorious conduct in the battle of Palo Alto, to date from May 8, 1846.
Brevets: for gallant & meritorious conduct in the battles of Palo Alto & Resaca de la Palma, Texas:
To date from May 9, 1846.
Brevet Maj Geo A McCall, Capt 4th Infty, [now Maj 3rd Infty,] to Lt Col
Brevet Capt Wm W S Bliss, Assist Adj Gen, to be Maj
1st Lt Leslie Chase, 2nd Artl, to be Capt
Brevet 2nd Lt Thos J Brereton, Ordnance, [now 2nd Lt,] to be 1st Lt
Brevet 2nd Lt Delos B Sacket, 2nd Dragoons, [now 2nd Lt 1st Dragoons,] to be 1st Lt
Brig Gen David E Twiggs, to be Maj Gen by Brevet, for gallant & meritorious service in the several conflicts at Monterey, Mexico, on Sep 21 thru 23, 1846, to date from Sep 23, 1846.
Brevets: for gallant & meritorious conduct in the several conflicts at Monterey, Mexico, on Sep 21 thru 23, 1846.
To date from Sep 23, 1846.
Brevet Maj Lorenzo Thomas, Assist Adj Gen, to be Lt Col
Majors by Brevet:
Capt Geo D Ramsay, Ordnance
Capt Henry Bainbridge, 3rd Infty, [now Maj 7th Infty.]
Capt Wm S Henry, 3rd Infty
Capt Lewis S Craig, 3rd Infty
Capts by Brevet:
1st Lt Wm A Mackall, 1st Artl, [now Brevet Capt & Assist Adj Gen.]
1st Lt Don Carlos Buell, 3rd Infty
1st Lt Wm T H Brooks, 3rd Infty

1st Lts by Brevet:
2nd Lt Schuyler Hamilton, 1st Infty, [now 1st Lt.]
2nd Lt Chas L Kilburn, 3rd Artl, [now 1st Lt.]
2nd Lt Saml G French, 3rd Artl, [now 1st Lt.]
Brevets: for gallant & meritorious conduct in the battle of Monterey, Mexico.
To Date from Sept 23, 1846.
Brevet Lt Col Jas Duncan, Capt 2nd Artl, to be Col
Capt Richd H Ross, 7th Infty, to be Maj
1st Lt John F Reynolds, 3rd Artl, to be Capt
2nd Lt Philip W McDonald, 2nd Dragoons, [now 1st Lt,] to be 1st Lt
2nd Lt Jos H Potter, 7th Infty, [now 1st Lt,] to be 1st Lt
Capt Geo G Waggaman, Commissary of Subsistence, to be Maj by Brevet, for for gallant & meritorious conduct in the battles of Palo Alto, Resaca de la Palma, & Monterey, Mexico, to date from Sep 23, 1846.
Brig Gen Stephen W Kearny, to be Maj Gen, for for gallant & meritorious conduct in New Mexico, & in Calif, to date from the battle of San Pasqual, Dec 6, 1846.
Capt Henry s Turner, 1st Dragoons, to be Maj, for gallant & meritorious conduct in the battles of San Pasqual, San Gabriel, & Plains of Mesa, in Calif, to date from Dec 6, 1846.
1st Lt Wm H Emory, Topographical Engineers, to be Capt, for gallant & meritorious conduct in the battle of San Pasqual, to date from Dec 6, 1846; & to be Maj, for gallant & meritorious conduct in the battles of San Gabriel, & the Plans of Mesa, to date from Jan 9, 1847.
1st Lt Wm H Warner, Topographical Engineers, to be Capt, for gallant & meritorious services in Calif, to date from Dec 6, 1846.
Brevets: for gallant & meritorious conduct in the conflicts at Embudo & Taos, New Mexico.
To date from Feb 4, 1847. 1st Lts by Brevet:
2nd Lt Alex'r B Dyer, Ordnance, [now 1st Lt.]
2nd Lt Rufus Ingalls, 1st Dragoons, [now 1st Lt.]
2nd Lt Clarendon J L Wilson, 1st Dragoons.
Brevet 2nd Lt Oliver H P Taylor, 1st Dragoons, [now 2nd Lt.]
Brevets: for gallant & meritorious conduct in the battles of Buena Vista, Mexico:
To date from Feb 23, 1847. Brig Genr'ls by Brevet:
Col Sylvester Churchill, Inspec Gen
Col Henry Whiting, Assist Quartermaster Gen
Brevet Col Wm G Belknap, Maj 8th Infty, [now Lt Col 5th Infty.
Cols by Brevet:
Brevet Lt Col Chas A May, Capt 2nd Dragoons
Brevet Lt Col John Monroe, Maj 2nd Artl
Brevet Lt Col Jos K F Mansfield, Capt Engineers
Lt Cols by Brevet:
Maj Roger S Dix, Paymaster
Brevet Maj Wm W S Bliss, Assist Adj Gen
Brevet Maj Braxton Bragg, Capt 2nd Artl
Maj John M Washington, 3rd Artl
Brevet Maj Lucian B Webster, Capt 1st Artl

Majors by Brevet:
Capt Thos B Linnard, Topographical Engineers
Capt Ebenezer S Sibley, Assist Quartermaster
Capt Amos S Eaton, Commissary of Subsistence
Capt Enoch Steen, 1st Dragoons
Capt Wm W Chapman, Assist Quartermaster
Capt Robt H Chilton, 1st Dragoons
Capt Thos W Sherman, 3rd Artl
Brevet Capt Jas L Donaldson, 1st Lt, 1st Artl, [now Assist Quartermaster.]
Brevet Capt Wm H Shover, 1st Lt, 3rd Artl, [now Capt.]
Brevet Capt Geo H Thomas, 1st Lt, 3rd Artl
Brevet Capt Robt S Garnett, 1st Lt, 4th Artl
Capt John P J O'Brien, Assist Quartermaster
Brevet Capt John F Reynolds, 1st Lt 3rd Artl
Capt Danl H Rucker, 1st Dragoons
Capt Jas H Carleton, 1st Dragoons

Capts by Brevet:
1st Lt Henry W Benham, Engineers, [now Capt.]
1st Lt Thos L Brent, 4th Artl
1st Lt Lorenzo Sitgreaves, Topographical Engineers
1st Lt Irvin McDowell, 1st Artl
1st Lt Reuben P Campbell, 2nd Dragoons
Brevet 1st Lt John Pope, 2nd Lt Topographical Engineers
Brevet 1st Lt Isaac Bowen, 1st Artl, [now 1st Lt.]
1st Lt Chas L Kilburn, 3rd Artl
Brevet 1st Lt Saml G French, 3rd Artl, [now 1st Lt.]
1st Lt Abraham Buford, 1st Dragoons.

1st Lts by Brevet:
2nd Lt Chas P Kingsbury, Ordnance, [now 1st Lt.]
2nd Lt Henry M Whiting, 4th Artl, [now 1st Lt.]
2nd Lt Wm B Franklin, Topographical Engineers
2nd Lt Jos H Whittlesey, 1st Dragoons, [now 1st Lt.]
2nd Lt Thos J Wood, 2nd Dragoons
2nd Lt Newton C Givens, 2nd Dragoons
Brevet 2nd Lt Francis T Bryan, Topographical Eng
2nd Lt Darius N Couch, 4th Artl
Brevet 2nd Lt Geo F Evans, 1st Dragoons, [now 2nd Lt.]

Brevets: for gallant & meritorious conduct in the battle of Sacramento, near Chiihuahua, Mexico, on Feb 28, 1847.
To date from Feb 28, 1847:
Capt Philip R Thompson, 1st Dragoons, to be Maj
1st Lt Chas F Wooster, 4th Artl, to be Capt

Brevets: for gallant & meritorious conduct in the affair of Medelin, [near Vera Cruz,] Mexico, Mar 25, 1847. To date from Mar 25, 1847.
Capt Wm H Hardee, 2nd Dragoons, to be Maj
Capt Henry H Sibley, 2nd Dragoons, to be Maj

1st Lt Henry B Judd, 3rd Artl, to be Capt
1st Lt Hachaliah Brown, 3rd Artl, to be Capt
2nd Lt Lewis Neil, 2nd Dragoons, [now 1st Lt,] to be 1st Lt
2nd Lt Owen Chapman, 1st Dragoons, to be 1st Lt
Brevet 2nd Lt Jas Oakes, 2nd Dragoons, [now 2nd Lt,] to be 1st Lt
Brevets: for gallant & meritorious conduct in the siege of Vera Cruz, Mexico, in Mar, 1847, to date from Mar 29, 1847, when the city surrendered under capitulation. To date from Mar 29, 1847:
Col Jas Bankhead, 2nd Artl, to be Brig Gen
Col Jos G Totten, Engineers, to be Brig Gen
Capt Benj Huger, Ordnance, to be Maj
1st Lt Henry W Halleck, Engineers, to be Capt, for gallant conduct in affairs with the enemy, on Nov 19 & 20, 1847, & for meritorious services in Calif, to date from May 1, 1847.
Brevets: for gallant & meritorious conduct in the battle of Cerro Gordo, Mexico, on Apr 17 & 18, 1847.
To date from Apr 18, 1847. Brig Gens by Brevet:
Brevet Col Bennet Riley, Lt Col 2nd Infty
Col Wm S Harney, 2nd Dragoons
Cols by Brevet:
Lt Col Jos Plympton, 7th Infty
Lt Col by Brevet:
Maj John L Smith, Engineers
Maj John L Gardner, 4th Artl
Maj Edwin V Sumner, 2nd Dragoons, [now Lt Col 1st Dragoons.]
Majors by Brevet:
Capt Thompson Morris, 2nd Infty, [now Maj 1st Infty.]
Capt Edmund B Alexander, 3rd Infty
Capt Francis Taylor, 1st Artl
Capt Robt E Lee, Engineers
Capt Geo W Hughes, Topographical Eng
Capt Danl P Whiting, 7th Infty
Capt Robt Allen, Assist Quartermaster
Capt John B Magruder, 1st Artl
Capt Jas W Penrose, 2nd Infty
Capt Geo W Patten, 2nd Infty
Capt Edw J Steptoe, 3rd Artl
Capts by Brevet:
1st Lt Peter V Hagner, Ordnance
1st Lt John P McCown, 4th Artl
1st Lt Jos A Haskin, 1st Artl
1st Lt Chas H Humber, 7th Infty
1st Lt Wm B Johns, 3rd Infty, [now Capt]
1st Lt Saml K Dawson, 1st Artl
1st Lt Andrew W Bowman, 3rd Infty
Brevet 1st Lt Franklin Gardner, 7th Infty, [now 1st Lt.]

1st Lt Napoleon J T Dana, 7th Infty
1st Lt Earl Van Dorn, 7th Infty
1st Lt Theodore T S Laidley, Ordnance
1st Lt Roswell S Ripley, 2nd Artl
1st Lt by Brevet.
2nd Lt Zealous B Tower, Engineers, [now 1st Lt.]
2nd Lt Gustavus W Smith, Engineers
2nd Lt Danl M Frost, Mounted Riflemen
2nd Lt Edmund K Smith, 7th Infty
2nd Lt Jas N Ward, 3rd Infty
2nd Lt Henry B Clitz, 3rd Infty
Brevet 2nd Lt Geo H Derby, Topographical Engineers
2nd Lt Jesse L Reno, Ordnance
2nd Lt Truman Seymour, 1st Artl, [now 1st Lt.]
Brevet 2nd Lt Dabney H Maury, Mounted Riflemen, [now 2nd Lt.]
Brevet 2nd Lt Alfred Gibbs, Mounted Riflemen, [now 2nd Lt.]
Brevet 2nd Lt Geo H Gordon, Mounted Riflemen, [now 2nd Lt.]
Capt Francis O Wyse, 3rd Artl, to be Maj, for gallant & meritorious conduct in the arrair with the enemy at Calaboso river, Mexico, to date from Jul 12, 1847.
Brevets: for gallant & meritorious conduct in an affair with the enemy at Mil Flores, Mexico.
To date from Aug 13, 1847.
Brevet 1st Lt Schuyler Hamilton, 1st Infty, [now 1st Lt,] to be Capt
2nd Lt Lorimer Graham, 10th Infty, [now 2nd Lt 1st Dragoons,] to be 1st Lt
Brevets: for gallant & meritorious conduct in the several affairs with Guerilleros, at Paso Ovijas, Nat'l Bridge, & Cerro Gordo, Mexico, on Aug 10, 12, & 15, 1847.
To date from Aug 15, 1847.
Capt Benj Alvord, 4th Infty, to be Maj
1st Lts by Brevet:
2nd Lt David A Russell, 4th Infty, [now 1st Lt.]
2nd Lt Henry B Sears, 2nd Artl, [now 1st Lt.]
2nd Lt Clinton W Lear, 5th Infty
Brevets: for gallant & meritorious conduct in an affair with the enemy at San Augustine, Mexico.
To date from Aug 20, 1847.
Brevet Maj Wm J Hardee, Capt 2nd Dragoons, to be Lt Col
2nd Lt Richd H Anderson, 2nd Dragoons, [now 1st Lt,] to be 1st Lt
Brevets: for gallant & meritorious conduct in the battle of Contreras, Mexico.
To date from Aug 20, 1847.
Brevet Lt Col John L Gardner, Maj 4th Artl, to be Col
Brevet Maj Richd H Ross, Capt 7th Infty, to be Lt Col
Brevet 1st Lt Edmund K Smith, 7th Infty, [now 2nd Lt,] to be Capt
Brevets: for gallant & meritorious conduct in the battles of Contreras & Churubusco, Mexico, Aug 20, 1847. To date from Aug 20, 1847.
Brevet Brig Gen Persifer F Smith, Col Mounted Riflemen, to be Maj Gen

Brig Gens by Brevet:
Brevet Col John Garland, Lt Col 4th Infty
Col Newman S Clarke, 6th Infty.
Cols by Brevet:
Lt Col Ethan A Hitchcock, 3rd Infty
Lt Col Francis S Belton, 3rd Artl
Brevet Lt Col Chas F Smith, Capt 2nd Artl
Brevet Lt Col John L Smith, Maj Engineers
Lt Cols by Brevet:
Maj Edmund Kirby, Paymaster
Brevet Maj Justin Dimick, Capt 1st Artl
Brevet Maj Harvey Brown, Capt 4th Artl
Maj Wm Turnbull, Topographical Eng
Brevet Maj Geo Wright, Capt 8th Infty, [now Maj 4th Infty.]
Maj Benj L E Bonneville, 6th Infty
Maj Abram Van Buren, Paymaster
Maj Henry Bainbridge, 7th Infty
Brevet Maj Lewis S Craig, Capt 3rd Infty
Maj Patrick H Galt, 2nd Artl
Maj Francis Lee, 4th Infty
Maj Carlos A Waite, 8th Infty
Maj Wm W Loring, Mounted Riflemen, [now Lt Col]
Brevet Maj Benj Juger, Capt Ordnance
Brevet Maj Edmund B Alexander, Capt 3rd Infty
Brevet Maj Robt E Lee, Capt Engineers
Majs by Brevet:
Capt Geo Nauman, 1st Artl
Capt Julius J B Kingsbury, 2nd Infty
Capt Wm Hoffman, 6th Infty
Capt Jos R Smith, 2nd Infty
Capt John B Grayson, Commissary of Subsistance
Capt Thos L Alexander, 8th Infty
Capt John McClellan, Topographical Eng
Capt Martin Burke, 2nd Artl
Capt Silas Casey, 2nd Infty
Capt Abraham C Myers, Assist Quartermaster
Capt Jefferson Van Horne, 3rd Infty
Capt John H Winder, 1st Artl
Capt Jas V Bomford, 8th Infty
Capt Wm Chapman, 5th Infty
Capt Henry C Wayne, Assist Quartermaster
Capt Winslow F Sanderson, Mounted Riflemen, [now Maj.]
Capt Geo B Crittenden, Mounted Riflemen,[since Maj.]
Capt Jacob B Backerstos, Mounted Riflemen
Capt Horace Brooks, 2nd Artl
Capt Danl Ruggles, 5th Infty

Capt Isaac V C Reeve, 8th Infty
Capt Danl H McPhail, 5th Infty
Capt Larkin Smith, 8th Infty
Capt Danl T Chandler, 3rd Infty
Brevet Capt Wm W Mackall, Assist Adj Gen
Brevet Capt Don Carlos Buell, 1st Lt 3rd Infty
Brevet Capt Wm T H Brooks, 1st Lt 3rd Infty
Capt Philip Kearny, jr, 1st Dragoons
Brevet Capt Geo Deas, Assist Adj Gen
Capt Henry L Scott, 4th Infty
Capt Henry W Wessells, 2nd Infty
Capt John S Hatheway, 1st Artl
Capt Geo W F Wood, Assist Quartermaster
Capt Justus McKinstry, Assist Quartermaster
Brevet Capt Edw R S Canby, Assist Adj Gen
Brevet Capt Earl Van Dorn, 1st Lt 7th Infty
Capt Jas L Mason, Engineers
Brevet Capt Francis N Page, Assist Adj Gen
Capt Jas G Martin, Assist Quartermaster
Capt Wm Austine, 3rd Artl

Capts by Brevet:
1st Lt Henry Prince, 4th Infty, [now Capt]
1st Lt John W Phelps, 4th Artl
1st Lt Lewis G Arnold, 2nd Artl, [now Capt]
1st Lt Wm H French, 1st Artl
1st Lt John Sedgwick, 3rd Artl
1st Lt Peter G T Beauregard, Engineers
1st Lt Arnold Elzey, 2nd Artl
1st Lt Isaac J Stevens, Engineers
1st Lt Thos Williams, 4th Artl
1st Lt Thos Hendrickson, 6th Infty
1st Lt Jos Selden, 8th Infty, [now Capt]
Brevet 1st Lt Franklin D Callender, Ordnance, [now 1st Lt]
1st Lt John H Gore, 4th Infty, [now Capt]
1st Lt Christopher S Lovell, 2nd Infty, [now Capt]
1st Lt Lewis A Armistead, 6th Infty
1st Lt Henry D Grafton, 1st Artl
1st Lt Richd S Ewell, 1st Dragoons
1st Lt Geo W Getty, 4th Artl
1st Lt Oliver H Shepherd, 3rd Infty, [now Capt]
1st Lt Delozier Davidson, 2nd Infty
1st Lt Wm Steele, 2nd Dragoons
1st Lt Sterne H Fowler, 5th Infty, [now Capt]
1st Lt Michl E Van Buren, Mounted Riflemen, [now Capt]
1st Lt Richd P Hammond, 3rd Artl
1st Lt Julius Hayden, 2nd Infty

1st Lt Henry J Hunt, 2nd Artl
1st Lt Albion P Howe, 4th Artl
1st Lt Pinkney Lugenbeel, 5th Infty
1st Lt Mortimer Rosecrantz, 5th Infty
1st Lt Israel B Richardson, 3rd Infty
1st Lt Geo Sykes, 3rd Infty
Brevet 1st Lt Philip W McDonald, 2nd Dragoons, [now 1st Lt]
Brevet 1st Lt Geo W Lay, 2nd Lt, 6th Infty
Brevet 1st Lt Lafayette B Wood, 8th Infty, [now 1st Lt]
1st Lt Nathl Lyon, 2nd Infty
1st Lt Jas Longstreet, 8th Infty
1st Lt Wm Hays, 2nd Artl
1st Lt John M Brannan, 1st Artl
1st Lt Geo W Rains, 4th Artl
1st Lt Danl H Hill, 4th Artl
1st Lt John J Peck, 2nd Artl
1st Lt Chas S Hamilton, 5th Infty
1st Lt Henry Coppee, 1st Artl
1st Lt Edw C Boynton, 1st Artl
1st Lt Thos J Jackson, 1st Artl
2nd Lt to 1st Lt by Brevet:
2nd Lt Ralph W Kirkham, 6th Infty
2nd Lt Jas W Schureman, 2nd Infty, [now 1st Lt]
2nd Lt Edmunds B Holloway, 8th Infty, [now 1st Lt]
2nd Lt Chas E Jarvis, 2nd Infty, [now 1st Lt]
2nd Lt Fred'k T Dent, 5th Infty, [now 1st Lt]
2nd Lt Simon B Buckner, 6th Infty
2nd Lt Winfield S Hancock, 6th Infty
2nd Lt Henry B Schroeder, 3rd Infty, [now 1st Lt]
2nd Lt Francis Collins, 4th Artl
2nd Lt John P Hatch, Mounted Riflemen
2nd Lt Patrick A Farrelly, 5th Infty, [now 1st Lt]
2nd Lt Jas G S Snelling, 8th Infty
2nd Lt Jas M Hawes, 2nd Dragoons
2nd Lt Gordon Granger, Mounted Riflemen
2nd Lt Thos G Pitcher, 8th Infty
2nd Lt Geo McLane, Mounted Riflemen, [now 1st Lt]
2nd Lt Julian May, Mounted Riflemen
2nd Lt Geo B McClellan, Engineers
Brevet 2nd Lt John G Foster, Engineers, [now __ Lt]
Brevet 2nd Lt Edmund L F Hardcastle, Topographical Eng
2nd Lt Albert L Magilton, 4th Artl
2nd Lt Marcus D L Simpson, 2nd Artl, [now 1st Lt]
2nd Lt Innis N Palmer, Mounted Riflemen
2nd Lt David R Jones, 2nd Infty
2nd Lt John D Wilkins, 3rd Infty

2nd Lt Jos N G Whistler, 3rd Infty
2nd Lt Nelson H Davis, 2nd Infty
2nd Lt Wm H Tyler, 7th Infty
2nd Lt Wm M Gardner, 2nd Infty
2nd Saml B Maxey, 7th Infty
2nd Lt Pickett, 8th Infty
2nd Lt Gustavus A DeRussy, 4th Artl
2nd Lt John B Gibson, 1st Artl, [now 1st Lt]
2nd Lt John H Lendrum, 3rd Artl, [now 1st Lt]
2nd Lt Saml L Gouverneur, 4th Artl
2nd Wm H Scott, 11th Infty, [now 2nd Lt 4th Infty.]
2nd Lt Thos Henry, 7th Infty
2nd Lt Arthur D Tree, 2nd Dragoons

Brevets: for gallant & meritorious conduct in the battle of Churubusco, Mexico, Aug 20, 1847. To date from Aug 20, 1847.
Brevet Maj Francis Taylor, Capt 1st Artl, to Lt Col
Brevet 1st Lt Lorimer Graham, 10th Infty, [now 2nd Lt 1st Dragoons,] to be Capt

Brevets: for gallant & meritorious conduct in the battle of Molino del Rey, Mexico, Sep 8, 1847. To date from Sep 8, 1847.

Cols by Brevet:
Brevet Lt Col Edwin V Sumner, 2nd Dragoons, [now Lt Col 1st Dragoons]
Brevet Lt Col Geo Wright, 8th Infty, [now Maj 4th Infty]
Brevet Lt Col Carlos A Waite, Maj 8th Infty

Lt Cols by Brevet: Brevet Maj:
Wm R Montgomery, Capt 8th Infty
Robt C Buchanan, Capt 4th Infty
Wm Hoffman, Capt 6th Infty
Martin Burke, Capt 3rd Artl
Jas V Bomford, Capt 8th Infty
Wm H T Walker, Capt 6th Infty
Isaac V D Reeve, Capt 8th Infty
Jas L Mason, Capt Engineers

Majs by Brevet:
Capt Robt Anderson, 3rd Artl
Capt Richd B Screven, 8th Infty
Capt Albemarle Cady, 6th Infty
Capt Collison R Gates, 8th Infty
Brevet Capt John C Pemberton, 1st Lt 4th Artl
Brevet Capt Wm A Nicols, 1st Lt 2nd Artl
Brevet Capt Henry Prince, 1st Lt 4th Infty, [now Capt]
Brevet Capt Lewis A Armistead, 1st Lt 6th Infty
Brevet Capt Jas Longstreet, 1st Lt 8th Infty
Brevet Capt John J Peck, 1st Lt 2nd Artl

Capts by Brevet:
1st Lt Edw Johnson, 6th Infty
1st Lt Leonidas Wetmore, 6th Infty

1st Lt Granville O Haller, 4th Infty, [now Capt]
1st Lt John D Clark 8th Infty
1st Lt Harvey A Allen, 2nd Artl
1st Lt Saml S Anderson, 2nd Artl
Brevet 1st Lt Jas Oakes, 2nd Lt 2nd Dragoons
1st Lt Fitz-John Porter, 4th Artl
Brevet 1st Lt Geo B McClellan, 2nd Lt Eng
Brevet 1st Lt John G Foster, 2nd Lt Eng
Brevet 1st Lt Edmund L F Hardcastle, Brevet 2nd Lt Topographical Eng
Brevet 1st Lt Hamilton L Shields, 2nd Lt 3rd Artl, [now 1st Lt]
1st Lt Geo P Andrews, 3rd Artl
2nd Lts to 1st Lts:
2nd Lt Henry M Judah, 4th Infty, [now 1st Lt]
2nd Lt Chas G Merchant, 8th Infty
2nd Lt Chas P Stone, Ordnance
2nd Lt Abram B Lincoln, 4th Infty, [now 1st Lt]
2nd Lt Delancy F Jones, 4th Infty, [now 1st Lt]
2nd Lt Thos R McConnell, 4th Infty
2nd Lt Maurice Maloney, 4th Inty, [now 1st Lt]
Brevets: for gallant & meritorious conduct in the battle of Chapultepec, Mexico, Sep 13, 1847. To date from Sep 13, 1847: Cols by Brevet:
Brevet Lt Col Edmund Kirby, Paymaster
Brevet Lt Col Wm W Loring, Maj Mounted Riflemen, [now Lt Col]
Brevet Lt Col Benj Huger, Capt Ordnance
Brevet Lt Col Robt E Lee, Capt Engineers
Lt Cols by Brevet:
Brevet Maj Thompson Morris, Capt 2nd Infty, [now Maj 1st Infty]
Brevet Maj John B Magruder, Capt 1st Artl
Brevet Maj Edw J Steptoe, Capt 3rd Artl
Brevet Maj Silas Casey, Capt 2nd Infty
Majs by Brevet:
Capt Gabriel R Paul, 7th Infty
Capt John S Simmons, Mounted Riflemen
Capt Stephen S Tucker, Mounted Riflemen
Brevet Capt Jos Hooker, Assist Adj Gen
Capt Benj S Roberts, Mounted Riflemen
Brevet Capt Peter V Hagner, 1st Lt Ordnance
Brevet Capt Jos A Haskin, 1st Lt 1st Artl
Capt Andrew Porter, Mounted Riflemen
Capt Edw H Fitzgerald, Assist Quartermaster
Brevet Capt Peter G T Beauregard, 1st Lt Engineers
Brevet Capt Isaac J Stevens, 1st Lt Engineers
Brevet Capt Jos Selden, 1st Lt 8th Infty [now Capt]
Brevet Capt Henry J Hunt, 1st Lt 2nd Artl
Brevet Capt Israel B Richardson, 1st Lt 3rd Infty
Brevet Capt Wm Hays, 1st Lt 2nd Artl

Capts by Brevet:
1st Lt Geo C Westcott, 2nd Infty
1st Lt Mansfield Lovell, 4th Infty
1st Lt Alex Morrow, 6th Infty
1st Lt Zealous B Tower, Engineers
Brevet 1st Lt Gustavus W Smith, 2nd Lt Eng
Brevet 1st Lt Jesse L Reno, 2nd Lt Ordnance
Brevet 1st Lt Geo McLane, 2nd Lt Mounted Riflemen, [now 1st Lt]
1st Lt Henry F Clarke, 2nd Atl

1st Lts by Brevet:
2nd Lt Fred'k Steele, 2nd Infty, [now 1st Lt]
2nd Lt Barnard E Bee, 3rd Infty
2nd Lt Robt M Morris, Mounted Riflemen, [now 1st Lt]
2nd Lt Francis S K Russell, Mounted Riflemen, [now 1st Lt]
Brevet 2nd Lt Jas Stuart, Mounted Riflemen, [now 2nd Lt]
2nd Lt Cadmus M Wilcox, 7th Infty
2nd Lt Richd C Drum, 9th Infty, [now 2nd Lt 4th Artl]
Brevet Maj John McClellan, Capt Topographical Engineers, to be Lt Col, for for gallant & meritorious conduct in the storming of Chapaltepec, Mexico, to date from Sep 13, 1847.

Brevets: for gallant & meritorious conduct in the battle of Huamantla, Mexico. To date from Oct 9, 1847.
Capt Saml P Heintzelman, 2nd Infty, to be Maj
Capt Geo Taylor, 3rd Artl, to be Maj
1st Lt Horace B Field, 3rd Artl, to be Capt
1st Lt Thos Claiborne, jr, Mounted Riflemen, to be Capt
2nd Lt Bedney F McDonald, 3rd Artl, to be 1st Lt

Brevets: for gallant & meritorious conduct in the defence of Puebla, Mexico, from Sep 13 to Oct 12, 1847.
To date from Oct 12, 1847:
Brevet Col Thos Childs, Maj 1st Artl, to be Brig Gen
Capt Henry L Kendrick, 2nd Artl, to be Maj
Capt John H Miller, 4th Artl, to be Maj
1st Lt Thos G Rhett, Mounted Riflemen, to be Capt
2nd Lt Geo Edwards, 2nd Artl, [now 1st Lt,] to be 1st Lt
1st Lt Henry C Pratt, 2nd Artl, [now Capt,] to be Capt, for for gallant & meritorious conduct in the affair at Atlixco, Mexico, to date from Oct 19, 1847.

Brevets conferred on ofcrs disbanded at the close of the war with Mexico:
Lt Col Jos E Johnston, Voltigeurs, to be Col, for gallant & meritorious conduct, to date from Apr 12, 1847, when he was severely wounded under the enemy's works at Cerro Gordo, Mexico, whilst on reconnoitering duty.

Brevets: for gallant & meritorious conduct in the several affairs with Guerilleros at Paso Ovejas, Nat'l Bridge, & Cerro Gordo, Mexico, on Aug 10, 12, & 15, 1847.
To date from Aug 15, 1847:
Maj Folliot T Lally, 9th Infty, to be Lt Col

Majs by Brevet:
Capt Frazey M Winans, 15th Infty
Capt Wm J Clark, 12th Infty
Capt Arthur C Cummings, 11th Infty
Capts by Brevet:
1st Lt John W Lee, Voltigeurs
1st Lt Chas M Creanor, 12th Infty
1st Lts by Brevet:
2nd Lt Wm D Wilkins, 15th Infty, [since 1st Lt]
2nd Lt Alonzo Loring, 11th Infty, [since 1st Lt]
Brevets: for gallant & meritorious conduct in the battles of Contreras & Churubusco, Mexico. To date from Aug 20, 1847:
Col Geo W Morgan, 15th Infty, to be Brig Gen
Maj John F Hunter, 11th Infty, to be Lt Col
Majs by Brevet:
Capt Danl Chase, 15th Infty, [since Maj 10th Infty]
Capt Nathl B Holden, 12th Infty
Capt Jas A Jones, 15th Infty
Capt Allen Wood, 12th Infty
Capt Wm H Irwin, 11th Infty
Capt E A Kimball, 9th Infty
Capt Presley N Guthrie, 11th Infty
Capt Moses Hoagland, 15th Infty
Capt Chas N Bodfish, 9th Infty
Capt Andrew T McReynolds, 3rd Dragoons
Capt Geo W Bowie, 15th Infty
Capt John Motz, 11th Infty
Capts by Brevet:
1st Lt John S Slocum, 9th Infty, [since Capt]
1st Lt Thornton F Brodhead, 15th Infty [since Capt]
1st Lt Chas J Sprague, 9th Infty, [since Capt]
1st Lt Geo Bowers, 9th Infty, [since Capt]
1st Lt Chas Taplin, 12th Infty, [since Capt]
1st Lt Thos F McCoy, 11th Infty
1st Lt John H Jackson, 9th Infty, [since Capt]
1st Lt Danl S Lee, 11th Infty
1st Lt Wm B Giles, 12th Infty
1st Lt John C Simkins, 12th Infty
1st Lt Hermann Thorn, 3rd Dragoons
1st Lt Columbus P Evans, 11th Infty
1st Lt Benj F Harley, 11th Infty
1st Lts by Brevet:
2nd Lt Thos P Pierce, 9th Infty, [since 1st Lt]
2nd Lt Saml B Davis, 14th Infty, [since 1st Lt]
2nd Lt Jas W Wiley, 15th Infty, [since 1st Lt]
2nd Lt Alpheus T Palmer, 9th Infty, [since 1st Lt]

2nd Lt Saml E Beach, 15th Infty, [since 1st Lt]
2nd Lt Andrew H Tippin, 11th Infty, [since 1st Lt]
2nd Lt Francis O Beckett, 15th Infty, [since 1st Lt]
2nd Lt Wm A Newman, 9th Infty
2nd Lt Alex'r E Steen, 12th Infty
2nd Lt John M Bronaugh, 12th Infty
Brevets: for gallant & meritorious conduct in the battle of Moline del Rey, Mexico. To date from Sep 8, 1847:
Lt Col Paul O Hebert, 14th Infty, to be Col
Maj Geo H Talcott, Voltigeurs, to be Lt Col
Brevets: for gallant & meritorious conduct in the battle of Chapultepec, Mexico, Sep 13, 1847. To date from Sep 13, 1847:
Brig Gen Geo Cadwalader, to be Maj Gen
Brig Gens by Brevet:
Col Timothy P Andrews, Voltigeurs
Col Wm Trousdale, 14th Infty
Cols by Brevet:
Lt Col Joshua Howard, 15th Infty
Lt Col Thos H Seymour, 12th Infty
Lt Cols by Brevet:
Maj Geo A Caldwell, Voltigeurs
Maj Saml Woods, 15th Infty
Majs by Brevet:
Capt Oscar E Edwards, Voltigeurs
Capt Chas J Biddle, Voltigeurs
Capt Nathl S Webb, 9th Infty
Capt Thos Glenn, 14th Infty
Capt John E Howard, Voltigeurs
Capt Jas M Scantland, 14th Infty
Capt Jas J Archer, Voltigeurs
Capt Moses J Barnard, Voltigeurs
Capts by Brevet:
1st Lt Jas Blackburn, 14th Infty, [since Capt]
1st Lt Thos H Freelon, 15th Infty, [since Capt]
1st Lt Wm S Walker, Voltigeurs
1st Lt Albert Tracy, 9th Infty, [since Capt]
1st Lt Edw C Marshall, 15th Infty, [since Capt]
1st Lt Albert G Sutton, 15th Infty, [since Capt]
1st Lt Danl French, 15th Infty
1st Lt Chas Peternell, 15th Infty
1st Lts by Brevet:
2nd Lt Robt C Forsyth, Voltigeurs, [since 1st Lt]
2nd Lt Asa A Stoddard, 9th Infty, [late 1st Lt]
2nd Lt Thompson H Crosby, 9th Infty, [since 1st Lt]
2nd Lt John Glackin, 9th Infty, [since 1st Lt]
2nd Lt Wm J Martin, Voltigeurs

2nd Lt Andrew J Isaacs, 14th Infty
2nd Lt Levi Woodhouse, 9th Infty, [since 1st Lt]
2nd Lt Platt S Titus, 15th Infty
2nd Lt John R Bennett, 15th Infty
2nd Lt John M Hatheway, 9th Infty
Capt Theodore F Rowe, 9th Infty, to be Maj, for for gallant & meritorious conduct in the defence of Puebla, Mexico, from Sep 13 to Oct 12, 1847, to date from Oct 12, 1847.
Brevets: for gallant & meritorious conduct in the battle of Atlixco, Mexico, Oct 19, 1847.
To date from Oct 19, 1847:
Capt Lemuel Ford, 3rd Dragoons, to be Maj
2nd Lt John W Martin, 3rd Dragoons, to be 1st Lt
Brevets conferred on General & Staff Ofcrs, provided for the organization of the Volunteer forces brought into the service of the U S, during the war with Mexico.
Brig Gen John A Quitman, [since Maj Gen in the Regular Army,] to be Maj Gen, for for gallant & meritorious conduct in the battle of Monterey, Mexico, to date from Sep 23, 1846.
Brig Gen Jas Shields, to be Maj Gen, for for gallant & meritorious conduct in the battle of Cerro Gordo, Mexico, on Apr 17 & 18, 1847, to date from Apr 18, 1847.
Brig Gen Jos Lane, to be Maj Gen, for gallant & meritorious conduct in the battle of Husamantla, Mexico, to date from Oct 19, 1847.
Capt Theodore O'Hara, Assist Quartermaster, to be Maj, for gallant & meritorious conduct in the battles of Contreras & Churubusco, Mexico, to date from Aug 20, 1847.
Capt Jos Daniels, Assist Quartermaster, to be Maj, for gallant & meritorious conduct in the battles of Contreras & Churubusco, Mexico, to date from Aug 20, 1847.
Ofcrs enumerated in the foregoing lists of Brevets, who may not now be in service, are requested to report their address to the Adj Gen, in order that their commissions may be duly forwarded to them. By order of the Sec of War: R Jones, Adj Gen

On Thu week, as Dr John Quigley, of Shepherdstown, Va, was riding horseback into the country, with one of his little daughters behind him, the horse became alarmed, & threw the child from her seat with such violence as to produce instant death.

Rooms to let: on 6th st, west side, 3 doors above D st, may be had with board.
–Wm Clare

A boy named Hickey, about 14 years of age, drowned Thu near the Bridge at Blagden's wharf.

Among the recent deaths in England we notice those of Capt Marryatt, author of Peter Simple, who died on Aug 9, at Laughrain, Norfolk, after a long & painful illness; Sir Nicholas Harris Nicholas, the compiler of Nelson's Letters & Despatches; & Mr Edw Baines, editor of the Leeds Mercury.

Farm for sale: 350 acres, on which are 2 dwlgs, a barn & saw-mill. For particulars call on Jos T Allen, who resides on the premises, about 18 miles south of Wash, & 8 miles east of Fairfax Court-house, Va.

Two frame houses & lot at auction: on Sep 4, lot 4 in square 997, corner of 11th st east & Georgia ave, belonging to the estate of Thos Gibson, deceased. –John Holroyd, exc -A Green, auctioneer

Rugby Academy, corner of Vt ave & L st: boarding & day School. Inquire of G F Morison, Principal. Almiricus L Zapponne, Prof of Ancient & Modern Languages. -Wm C Whitney, Tutor.

Mrd: on Aug 29, at the Church of the Epiphany, by Rev J W French, Capt Edw G Elliott, U S Army, to Miss Asenath M Miller.

Mrd: on Aug 28, in Wash City, by Rev J B Donelan, Mr Julius E Hilgard, of Ill, to Miss Katherine S, daughter of Capt Robt H Clements, of Wash City.

Died: on Aug 29, Mrs Rosannah Hays, aged 36 years, daughter of Michl Keller, late of Harrisburg, Pa. Her funeral is tomorrow at 5 o'clock, from the residence of her father, near 20th st, on Pa ave.

Died: on Aug 25, at Charlestown, Mass, Dr J Vaughan Smith, Surgeon U S Navy.

St John's Institute, a School for Boys, Mount Alban, near Gtwn, D C. –Visiter: The Bishop of the Diocese. Rector: The Rev Anthony Ten Broeck, A M

THU AUG 31, 1848
M A Tyson & Sister's Seminary, F st, between 12th & 13th sts, north side: will be resumed on Sep 18.

Boarding & Day School for Young Ladies, corner of 5th & Franklin sts, Shockoe Hill, Richmond, Va. Rev Moses D Hoge, Pastor of the 2nd Presbyterian Church, Principal. Commences on the 1st Mon in Oct.

For rent, the western House in *Gadsby's row*, for the last 6 years occupied by Mrs Cmdor Patterson. It has been painted & papered, & thoroughly repaired. Apply to Mrs Gadsby, or to J H McBlair.

Mrd: on Aug 29, by Rev Mr Morgan, Mr Wm Turpin, of Salisbury, Somerset Co, Md, to Miss Eliz Kerr Moore, of Wash City.

Mrd: on Jul 3, 1848, at the U S Consulate, Rio de Janeiro, Brazil, by Chaplain J L Lenhart, U S Navy, Purser Jos C Eldredge, U S Navy, to Miss Rebecca G, eldest daughter of Gordon Parks, U S Consul, Rio de Janeiro.

Died: on Aug 30, in Gtwn, after a few hours' illness, Mrs Mary Ann, consort of Peter Berry, in the 40th year of her age. Her funeral is today at half past 4 o'clock, from her late residence, Cherry st.

The situation of Principal of the Leesburg Academy became vacant, in consequence of the appointment of Mr Benedict to one of the Professorships in the Navy, & the Trustees of that institution are prepared to receive proposals for those who may desire the vacant place. –Wm H Gray, Pres of the Board of Trustees

The partnership lately subsisting between the subscribers, under the firm of Brooke & Shillington, was dissolved on Aug 1 by mutual consent. Gideon Brooke will continue the business at the old established stand at the corner of 15th st & Pa ave, & by Jos Shillington at the corner of Pa ave & 4½ st. A large assortment of new Books just received at both stores. –Gideon Brooke, Jos Shillington

Orphans Court of Wash Co, D C. Letters testamentary on the personal estate of Jas Moore, late of said county, deceased. –John P Ingle, Jos Ingle, excs

Horse shoeing. Jas Foy informs his friends & former customers, that he has again commenced business at the shop on B st, between 2nd & 3rd sts, in the rear of the Railroad Depot.

FRI SEP 1, 1848
Judge Henry St George Tucker died at his residence in Winchester on Aug 28. This gentleman has filled many of the most important posts in our State with distinguished ability & success. As a Rep in Congress, as Prof of Law at Winchester & the Univ of Va, as the author of valuable treatises on law, as Pres of the Court of Appeals, as a fine scholar of high literary taste. –Richmond Enquirer

Norfolk Beacon: a scene of touching interest at **Fortress Monroe** a few days ago. This was the return to the domicil of Col Walbach of the war-worn flag which had waved on to so many victories the gallant 4th Regt of Artl. It still clings to the staff, from which the spear-heard was torn away. Its bearer, shot through the heart, yielded it only with dying hands, to the brave Lt Benjamin, who planted it firmly on the memorable heights of Contreras.

Hon Geo W Lay, of Batavia, N Y, who was formerly Charge des Affaires to Stockholm, & a Member of Congress, died while on a visit to Avon Springs recently, of paralysis.

Boston, Mass, Aug 26, 1848. From our N Y Correspondent. **Mount Auburn**: beautiful "City of the Dead." The first tenant of the grounds, was Miss Hannah Adams. Among the dwellers who have come to rest are Story, & Channing, & Bowditch, with many others unknown to fame.

Mrd: on Aug 29, by Rev Wm Matthews, Mr Chas Muhler, of Paris, France, to Miss Caroline M Wiley, of Wash.

Mrd: on Aug 31, by Rev Wm Matthews, John M Sims, of Phil, to Miss Mary Jane Vermillion Rowley, of Wash City.

Orphans Court of Wash Co, D C. Letters of administration on the personal estate of Fred'k Seizd, late of the U S Army, deceased. −John H Ballmann, adm [See Aug 30th newspaper.]

SAT SEP 2, 1848
For rent: house on D st, between 6th & 7th sts, recently occupied by Mr McKean as a bindery. Apply to E Hunt, on La ave, between 6th & 7th sts.

Orphans Court of Wash Co, D C. Letters of administration on the personal estate of Mordecai Foy, late of said county, deceased. −Jas Foy, adm de bonis non

Mr Benj F Butler has received his dismissal from the post of U S District Atty, & Mr John McKeon is appointed his successor. −N Y Com Adv

Died: on Aug 21, at Buffalo, N Y, Agnes, daughter of Jas F & Katherine B Peter, aged about 17 months.

Died: on Aug 27, in Wash City, C W Birnie, after a short illness, in his 17th year.

Died: on Aug 24, at the NavyYard, of scarlet fever, Wm Arthur, in his 6th year. On Aug 25, Geo G Brooke, in his 4th year, & on Aug 26, Rachel Matilda, in her 9th year, children of Richd & Sarah Ann Carter. "Suffer little children, & forbid them not, to come unto me, for of such is the kingdom of heaven." [Balt papers will please copy.]

MON SEP 4, 1848
Naval: the Norfolk Beacon states that the frig **St Lawrence**, Capt Hiram Paulding has received sailing orders, & will proceed on her cruise in a few days, first to Bremen & to the Baltic, if the season will permit, & thence to her station in the Mediterranean as the flag ship. List of her ofcrs: Capt, Hiram Paulding. Lts: H K Hoff, Wm R Taylor, Chas C Barton, F B Renshaw, Edmund Lanier, Jos H Adams. Acting Master, Passed Midshipman F A Parker. Purser, F B Stockton. Surgeon, Geo Clymer
Assist Surgeons, John O'Connor Barclay, E F Carrington
Commanding Marines, 1st Lt B F Brooke & 2nd Lt A J Haves
Chaplain, Edwin Eaton. Passed Midshipmen, Saml P Carter, John E Hart, W M Gamble, Wm W Low, Marshal J Smith, F Scott Fillebrown, Watson Smith, Walter V Gilles, Wm K Mayor, Edmund W Henry, Jas E Jouette
Midshipmen, Saml Buell, Chas E Thorburn, Henry B Erbin, jr, John Irwin
Boatswain, Van Rensselaer Hall   Capt's Clerk, Chas Francis
Gunner, Saml G City   Purser's Clerk, Wm H Needles
Carpenter, Hugh Lindsay   Acting Master's Mate, Jas Patterson
Sailmaker, Jas Ferguson

Mr Norris Hibbard, a farmer from Delaware Co, Pa, was trampled to death on Wed by some fractious horses in the stable of a hotel in Market st, Phil, where he had been stopping. He died in great agony.

Missing Ship. Fears were entertained for the safety of the ship **Alice Gray**, of Boston, which sailed from Phil about the middle of Aug for Londonderry, where the last advice from there has her leaving there about 4 months ago. Capt Freeman S Nickerson, the master, was much respected; he is about 35 years old, & has left a wife & family in East Boston. Her first ofcr, Mr Saml Nickerson, belonged to Chatham, was about 22 years old, & unmarried. Mr Jonathan Twining, of Boston, 2nd ofcr, about 22, was unmarried. The seamen were shipped in Phil, & we have no knowledge of their age or residence. Their names were Jas Bishop, John Preston, John Miller, Jos Parsons, Jas Higginson, Otto Roemaer, & Michl Ryan. The following were passengers on board: Capt Jas C Ingleby, late of the British barque **Royal Saxon**, Thos Childs, Edw Williams, & John I Moore, late Seamen of the U S ship **Columbia**. –Boston Advertiser

Appointments by the Pres: 1-Chas McVean, of N Y, to be Atty of the U S for the southern district of N Y, vice Benj F Butler, removed. 2-Wm A Hall, of Missouri, to be Assoc Justice of the Supreme Court of the U S for the Territory of Oregon, vice Jas Turney, who declines to accept.

Mrd: on Aug 9, in St Matthew's Church, by Rev Jas B Donelan, Mr John O'Brien to Miss Sophia Moquest, all of Wash City.

Died: on Aug 30, in Greensville Co, Va, at the residence of Edmund Mason, Francis Key Mason, infant son of Hon John Y Mason, [Sec of the Navy,] aged 21 months.

TUE SEP 5, 1848

Obit-died: 0n Aug 9, 1848, at Roxbury, the summer residence of his father, Col H T Garnett, of Westmoreland, Va, Robt G R Garnett, in his 19th year. His last sickness was protracted for a period of 5 months, during which he made a profession of Christian faith, which became to him an anchor sure & steadfast. –A Near Friend [Union & Richmond papers.]

Meeting of the ofcrs present with the 8th U S Infty, Maj Montgomery called to the chair & Lt V G Pitcher appointed Sec: Resolved, that it is with feeling of deep regret & sorrow we have heard of the death of Lt Geo Wainwright, who shared with us the toils, discomforts, & perils of the recent arduous campaign in Mexico. –W R Montgomery, Brevet Maj 8th Infty; V G Pitcher, Lt 8th Infty, Sec. Jefferson Barracks, Mo, Aug 17, 1848

Governess: a Young Lady, who has considerable experience in teaching, wishes to engage as Governess to a private family at the South. She will teach, in addition to the English branches, the French language, the Piano Forte, & Drawing to beginners. Apply at the School Agency, 124 Nassau st, N Y C. –E H Wilcox

Mrd: on Aug 29, at the residence of the Misses Guild, in Phil, by Rev Dr A Barnes, Galbraith Stewart, of West Middletown, Pa, to Miss Ann Matilda Guild, of Phil.

Mrd: on Aug 31, at St Mary's Church, in Lancaster, Ohio, by Rt Rev Bishop Purcell, Philemon B Ewing to Miss Mary P Gillespie.

WED SEP 6, 1848
Wash Corp: 1-Cmte of Claims: passed: relief of Richd Harrison; of Caleb Dulany; of Louisa Collins; of Wm Wilson; & of Jas F W Thompson. 2-Cmte of Claims: asked to be discharged from the consideration of the ptn of Susanna Maryman.

Appointments by the Pres: 1-Arthur Johnson to be Postmaster at Ithica, N Y, vice Jacob McCormick, removed. 2-Hon Isaac Toucey, Atty Gen, to be acting Sec of State during the absence of Mr Buchanan.

A *Trappist Monastery* is about to be founded near Bardstown, Ky, where a tract of 1,200 acres of land has been bought for the purpose. About 80 of the members of the order are now on their way from Nantes, & the community will be organized next spring.

The Eagle Powder Mills, near the Cumberland river, below Nashville, Tenn, exploded on Aug 25, by which Colin S Hobbs, of the firm of Smith & Hobbs, of Nashville, was instantly killed.

The Methodists are now holding a Camp-Meeting at Federal Meeting house, in Montg Co, about 16 miles from Gtwn. A large number of persons were present last Sunday. Rev Sam Roszell preached a morning sermon that lasted about 2 hours. It was an extraordinary sermon. In the afternoon Rev Mr Morgan preached an excellent sermon.

Mr Calvin Barrett, jr, of Springfield, Mass, was filling a lighted spirit lamp, with the assistance of his wife, on Thu, when the flames caused the whole to explode. Mr Barrett was enveloped with flame, & died the next day. His wife escaped with no severe wounds than the burning of her hands.

On Wed Dr John B Walker left his residence to take a sail in the harbor. He procured a boat from Mr Manning, on Long Wharf, & has not been seen since. The boat was found on Fri, at Nantasket, with the coat, hat, & gloves of Dr Walker remaining in it, in a dry state. A piece of the boat's halyard had been cut off, & 56 pound weight of ballast was missing, which leads to the supposition that Dr Walker committed suicide. He was a young physician in good standing, & had a lucrative practice. His age was 25 years. -Boston Traveller

Some quite young lads of Goshen village, N Y, while on a hunting excursion on Sat last, came near the house of Mr Saml Beyes, when his 2 youngs sons went out to see the party, with whom they were well acquainted. While standing there, the elder of Mr Beyes' sons took the gun in his hand, when it accidentally discharged. It struck him in the head & he expired during the night. –Goshen [N Y] Democrat

Sudden death. Edw McGowan, a farrier by trade, & a person of intemperate habits, was found lying dead in Mr West's stable. The coroner held an inquest, & the jury rendered a verdict according to the evidence.

Mrd: on Sep 4, by Rev R W Hamilton, Jas R McAlister, of St Louis, Mo, to Miss Caroline, daughter of Mrs Ann H VanCoble, of Wash City.

Died: on Aug 22, Isabella, infant daughter of J J & M F Greenough.

Died: on Aug 29, in Gtwn, Susanna Coyle, aged 11 months, daughter of Jas Coyle & Susanna Turner.

Valuable brick house & lot at auction: on Sep 11, on the premises, house & lot in square 906, near the Navy Yard, now & for the last 10 years in the occupancy of Mr Jas Danforth, & used as a bakery. The lot fronts on Va ave. -A Green, auctioneer

Pittsburg Commercial Journal of Aug 31. Lt Col Clifton Wharton, whose remains were interred today, was a native of Phil, the son of Col Franklin Wharton, late of the U S Marines. While yet a youth he entered the U S Army as a Brevet 2nd Lt, serving first in the artillery, afterwards the infty, & subsequently in the first regt of U S Dragoons, in which arm of the service he continued from its formation in 1834 until Jul 12, 1848, when death terminated his earthly existence at *Fort Leavenworth*, leaving an affectionate wife & 4 children to lament their bereavement & loss. During the late war with Mexico, he was retained at *Fort Leavenworth*. He was buried in the Allegheny Cemetery, where the impressive burial rites of the Portestant Episcopal Church were performed.
–Pittsburg, Aug 30, 1848

THU SEP 7, 1848 .
We are adviced of a rencontre having taken place at Atlanta, Ga, on Sun last, in which it is feared the Hon Alex'r H Stephens was mortally wounded. He was traveling in the railroad cars, & got out at the tavern in Atlanta to dine. Here he was met by Mr Kone, late a circuit judge in Ga, who suddenly assaulted him with a dirk-knife, inflicting 5 severe wounds, 2 of which are in the breast, & one of them said to be mortal. [Sep 8th newspaper: Mr Stephens' condition on Wed improved, & his recovery was anticipated.]

Thos Meredith has been appointed Pres of the Commercial & Farmers' Bank of the city of Balt in the place of Elie Clagett, deceased.

I wish to sell a small farm, containing about 60 acres, in Fairfax Co, adjoining the lands of Dabney Ball & M C Fitzhugh, & now occupied by Franklin Hall.
–Jas Thrift, Fairfax Court-house, Va

History of the **Jesuits**, from their foundation to their suppression by Pope Clement XIV; their missions throughout the world; their educational system & literature; with their revival & present state. By Steinmitz: 2 vols. –F Taylor

By order of distrain from Ann R Dermott, against the goods & chattels of Hannah McCormick, I have seized & taken one negro girl, Rachael, the property of the said Hannah McCormick, to satisfy rent due & in arrears unto said Ann R Dermott; sale on Sep 14, in front of the jail in this county. –E G Handy, Bailiff

I certify that Mr John Lloyd, of Wash Co, D C, brought before me a stray bay horse, trespassing on his premises. –Jas Crandell, J P [Owner is to prove property, pay charges, & take him away. –John Lloyd, living at the end of the Navy Yard Bridge, on the south side.]

$5 reward for lost bay mare. –John Miller, near the Catholic graveyard, 7th st.

Orphans Court of Wash Co, D C. Letters of administration on the personal estate of Thos H Arny, alias Aymar, late of the U S Navy, deceased. –Fred'k W Eckloff, adm

In a suit for breach of marriage promise in Chautauque Co, N Y, Miss Phyloskey Smith recovered $500 from Mr C Johnson. The Phil Ledger says that a man that will deceive a woman with such a name deserves to be made to pay for it.

Thos McIlvain was killed on Sun by a mule that ran off with him on the tow-path of the Pa canal, above Manayunk. He was dragged by the animal for some distance, & received a fracture of the skull. He was about 45 years of age, & leaves a family.

A woman named Messick committed suicide 2 weeks since, by taking arsenic. She left 3 children, & was represented as a woman of excellent character. –Phil North American

Washington High School: having just learned that several of the late pupils would not return at present to this institution, their parents, who are Catholics, having determined to send them to the Catholic school about to be opened in this city, I inform that those who could not be admitted last year for want of room, can now be received, provided their application is renewed. –Edwin Arnold

FRI SEP 8, 1848
Mrd: on last evening, in Wash City, by Rev Mr Foley, Mr Jas Wm Johnson, of Wash City, to Miss Anna Maria Brookbank, daughter of Mr Thos Brookbank, of Chas Co, Md.

Capt Nazto Prouty, a most respectable citizen of Spencer, while walking the streets of Worcester, Mass, on Sat, was knocked down by the horses of a loaded coal from Brattleboro & the wheels passed over his chest. He died in less than a half hour afterwards. His wife, who was shopping, did not know of the disaster until her husband was dead. His age was 54.

Beltsville [Arkansas] Eagle of Aug 1 states that Mr Joshua Dillingham, of that vicinity, was bitten, while asleep, by a tarantula, or poisonous spider; his body swelling until the close of the 2nd day, when he died.

Valuable lot of land for sale: across the Navy Yard Bridge: contains 42 or 43 acres: offered for sale on Oct 4, at Good Hope. For information apply to S Pumphrey, Pa ave. –Rector Pumphrey

The Boonsboro Odd Fellow states that on Thu last, in Middletown, Fred'k Co, Md, a young lady named Spohn, visited the house of Mr Harbaugh, an aged man who was deranged, & scarcely had she entered before he seized a hatchet & gave her 3 blows in the head. Her recovery is doubtful. She is a relative of the old man.

By 4 writs of fieri facias, against the goods & chattels, lands & tenements, of Zachariah Hazel & Horatio R Maryman, superseder, to me directed, one at the suit of Jonathan Prout, one at the suit of R W Carter & Co, & 2 at the suits of E W Smallwood, use of O Whittlesey, I have levied on all the right, title, & interest & estate of said Zachariah Hazel, in the whole of lot 3 in square 784, with bldgs & improvements thereon; sale in front of the premises, on Oct 9. -Thos Plumsill, Constable

For rent, nearly new 2 story brick house on 16th st, opposite Cmdor Morris' & near Mr Corcoran's flower garden. Inquire of Jas Carrico, west of War Dept.

Harvard College is the oldest literary institution in the U S, having been founded in 1636- 16 years after the landing of the Pilgrims on Plymouth Rock. In 1638, the Rev John Harvard, of Charlestown, gave to the college, by his will, about 780 pounds in money, & more than 300 volumes of books. In 1640 the Rev Henry Dunster arrived from England, & was appointed the first Pres. He presided over the college 13 years, but fell under the suspicion of favoring the anti-pedobaptists, & was compelled to resign. He retired to Scituate, & shortly died afterwards. The bible that belonged to him is preserved as an interesting relic in the library. The 2nd Pres was Rev Chas Chauncey, of Scituate. During his presidency the only Indian who ever passed through the 4 years of college life took his degree. The 2 first Presidents of Harvard were educated in England, but all their successors in that ofc have been graduates of this University. These, in order of their administration, are, Leonard Hoar, Urian Oakes, John Rogers, Increase Mather, Saml Willard, John Leverett, Jos Sewell, Benj Colman, [the 2 last were elected to the ofc, but did not serve,] Benj Wadsworth, Edw Holyoke, [whose administration was the longest of any individual, being 32 years,] Saml Locke, Saml Langdon, Jos Willard, Fisher Ames, [elected, but did not serve,] Saml Webster, John T Kirkland, Josiah Quincy, & Edw Everett. In 1841 Benj Russy bequested an estate now valued at $320,000-one half to be devoted to a manual labor school on his estate in Roxbury, the other half to be divided between the Law & Theological Schools at Cambridge. In 1845 John Parker, jr, bequeathed $50,000; & in 1847 Abbott Lawrence gave $50,000. Some of the most considerable donations by individuals at earlier periods were: $28,000 by Count Rumford, in 1816; $20,000 by Abiel Smith; $20,000 by Saml Eliot; $20,000 by Jas Perkins; $10,000 by Nathan Dane; $20,000 by Joshua Fisher; $20,000 by John McLean; $10,000 by Sarah Jackson. In 1814 Israel Munson bequeathed $15,000. In 1831, Christopher Gore bequeathed an estate to the college which amounts to about $94,000. In 1846 Peter C Brooks gave $10,000 for erecting a house for the Pres. The present available property of the Univ is stated at about $700,000.

Executor's sale of valuable land in Fairfax Co, Va. The undersigned, exc of the last will & testament of Robt Thrift, deceased, will, on Oct 2 next, offer for sale, a tract of land, left by the said Robt Thrift, lying in said county, adjoining the lands of Geo Minor, Wm Nelson, & others, containing about 250 acres, with a convenient dwlg-house. Inquire at the law ofc of Swann & Swann, 5th st, Wash City, & of Geo & Wm Minor, near the premises. –Geo N Thrift, exc of R Thrift, deceased, Madison Court-house, Va.

For sale or rent: large commodious house on Pa ave, known as Congress Hall, lately in the occupancy of Mr P H King as a hotel & restaurant. Apply to Andrew Small.

Public sale of land: decree of the Circuit Superior Court of Law & Chancery for Fairfax Co, in the case of Hipkins, exc, against Hooe & others, & Buckner against Fowle & others, the undersigned, the Com'rs therein named, will sell, at Centreville, in said county, on Nov 4 next, the following tracts of land, to wit: 329 acres in Fauquier Co, allotted to Thos P Hooe, deceased, under a decree of the Superior Court of Prince Wm Co, in a suit in the name of Fowle against Hooe, describd as Lot #1, & known as part of **Hale's Tract**. Also, 624.3 acres, part of **Hale's Tract**, allotted in the aforesaid division to Wm H Fowle, described as lot #2, & conveyed by said Fowle & wife to Jacob Douglass, by deed dated Mar 3, 1835, recorded in the clerk's ofc of the county court of Fauquier on Apr 3, 1835. At the same time & place, 706.2 acres of land, allotted, in the division before mentioned, to Mgt S Hooe, & designated as Lot #3, being part of **Hale's Tract**, & conveyed to Jacob Douglass by Mgt S Hooe, by deed dated Sep 4, 1837, recorded Feb 27, 1838. Also, a tract of land in Prince Wm Co, called **Walnut Branch**, containing 473 acres allotted to Thos P Hooe, & conveyed by him to E B Evans, by deed dated Oct 23, 1834, now in possession of ___ Stone & Banks S Menifee, adjoining the lands of Elsha B Evans & others. Also, another tract of land, known as **Bull Run Quarter**, in Prince Wm Co, containing 107¼ acres, recently sold by Wm H Fowle to ___ Triplett, lies on Bull Run, adjoining the lands of T W Newman, Isaac Heath, & others. Another tract of land in Prince Wm Co, called **Cabin Branch**, adjoining **Bradley**, containing 140 acres, conveyed by Wm H Fowle to Wm Brawner, sen, by deed dated Jun 24, 1847, adjoining Wm Brawner's land on the n e & south, & **Bradley farm** on the west; no improvements on this tract. Also, a tract of land in Prince Wm Co, known as the **Purcell & Linton tract**, containing 406 acres, 10 acres of which was conveyed to Moses Lee by Thos P Hooe, deceased, by deed dated Feb 8, 1836. One other tract containing 54.1 acres, known as the **Linton & Larkin tract**, formerly belonging to Thos P Hooe, & sold by him or his excs to Strother Rennoe; lies just above Millford, on Broad Run, adjoining the lands of Thos W Beedle & others. Also, the **Bruce Tract**, containing 306 acres, formerly belonging to Thos P Hooe & now in possession of C C Marsteller; improvements on these parcels indifferent; the lands tolerably good, with sufficient timber. Also, a small tract of about 15 acres adjoining **Bradley**. The lands offered formerly belonged to Mrs E T Hooe, & will be shown by Mr Thos B Gaines, who resides near Haymarket, Prince Wm Co. –Francis L Smith, Alexandria -Thos R Love, Fairfax C H, Com'r of sale.

Household & kitchen furniture at auction: Sep 13, at the residence of Mr Jas Young, N J ave, Capitol Hill, near the south Capitol gate: a large lot of furniture. -A Green, auct

SAT SEP 9, 1848
W Baker's American & French Chocolate. Prepared Cocoa, Cocoa Paste, Broma, & Cocoa Shells. –Walter Baker, Dorchester, Mass

Auction on Sat in front of Centre Market, of a variety of second-hand furniture. Additions received till the hour of sale. –Martin & Wright, auctioneers

The packet-ship **Ocean Monarch**, Capt Murdock, of Boston, left Liverpool on Aug 24, with 360 steerage passengers, 6 in the first & 22 in the second cabin, &, with her crew, had on board 398 persons. She had not proceeded far before it was announced that the ship was on fire & she soon was in complete blaze. She was about 8 miles eastward of the great Armshead. Several vessels were in sight, which immediately sent their boats. The passengers & crew crowded forward to the jibboom; at length the foremast went overboard, snapping the fastings of the jibboom, which, with its load of human beings, dropped into the water, amidst the most heartrending screams. Many met with a watery grave. The Brazilian frig **Alfonzo** was out on a please excursion. She was commanded by the Marquis de Lisbon, & had on board the Prince de Joinville, his lady & suite, the Duke & Duchess of d'Aumale, the Brazilian Minister, De Chevalier de Lisbon, Admiral Greenfell & dghts, & others. The **Alfonzo** lost no time in lowering their boats. The Marquis de Lisbon leaped into one & Admiral Greenfell into another. They were untiring in their exertions to save the poor people. Of those on board the **Ocean Monarch** 32 were saved by the ship **Queen of the Ocean**, 100 by the **Alfonso**, 10 by a fishing vessel, & 17 by the ship **Prince of Wales**, being 225 saved, having 153 to be still accounted for.

For sale: property formerly occupied by Dr Penn, in the upper part of the village of Bladensburg. The premises & garden will be sold separate, or 15 acres of private prime meadow land will be attached to it if desired. Apply to Ammo Green, auctioneer, Wash, or to the subscriber, in Bladensburg. –C C Hyatt

Lene C Dickey has been nominated by the Whigs of Chester Co, Pa, as their candidate for Congress.

Gen Persifer F Smith, one of the most distinguished heroes of the late war, arrived in Wash on Wed. He will remain for several days.

MON SEP 11, 1848
The fine barque **Libera Packet**, Capt Goodmanson, left Balt on Thu on her 4th voyage to Liberia. Rev Messrs Beverly Wilson & Payne, both of whom have resided for many years in Liberia, are now returning after a brief visit to this country. –Balt American

John W Nash appointed a Judge of the Genr'l Court of Va, for the Petersburg district, in place of Judge Gholson, deceased.

Mr McClure, who acted as one of the sheriff's deputies during the late riot at the jail, died on Fri last, from injuries received, making the 5th victim to this mob usurpation.

Lt Geo F Ruxton, aged 38 years, of the 89th Regt British Army, died at St Louis, on Aug 29, of dysentery. He was the writer of the Blackwood series entitled "Life in the Far West." He arrived in St Louis a few weeks ago with another British ofcr, who, supposing him to be convalescing, proceeded with Gen Brooke for the Upper Mississippi.

Appointment by the Pres: Saml Grubb, to be a Justice of the Peace in Wash Co, D C.

In Alexandria, on Thu, a fine little boy, a son of Mr Patterson, living on Prince st, was accidentally struck by his mother with a leather strap. The blow was a slight one & the strap a small one, but the little boy fell, & died in a short time. He may have been injured in the fall. The grief of the afflicted parents is excessive. The family have the sympathy of all our citizens. –Alex Gaz

The application for divorce in Phil Courts by Mr Pierce Butler, against his wife Fanny Kemble Butler, is on the ground that she has deserted him for 2 years, having been abroad for that time in Europe. This case will be one of interest, as a large fortune is depending on its outcome.

Mrs Whitwell's house, on 4½ st, is open for reception of citizens or strangers by the day, week, or month.

Mrd: on Thu, Mr Wm H Brereton, of Wash City, to Miss Georgiana, daughter of Geo Taylor, of Wash Co, D C.

Mrd: on Sep 7, in Leesburg, Va, by Rev Geo Adie, John P Smart, of the above place, to Miss Charlotte A, daughter of the late Jas Orum, of N Y C.

Mrd: on Sep 4, by Rev Mr Flanagan, Mr Wm Devereaux, of the Indian Bureau, to Maria, eldest daughter of John Green, of **Rosedale**, near Gtwn, D C.

Died: on Sep 10, in Wash City, Mr John O'Leary, a native of the parish of Timolague, county of Cork, Ireland, aged 48 years. His funeral is today, at 3½ o'clock, from the residence of Mr Jeremiah Twomey, Md ave, near 4½ st.

Died: on Sep 10, in Wash City, Jas Frere, in his 66th year, a native of the town of Ross, in England, but a resident of Wash City for the last 30 years. His funeral is today at 4 o'clock, from his late residence on 20th st, near the West Market.

Died: on Aug 30, in Hudson, N Y, Mrs Julia A E Van Ness, wife of Capt Van Ness, U S Army, & daughter of Wm Yeaton, of Alexandria, Va.

Died: on Sep 6, of typhoid fever, Chas T Duley, of PG Co, Md, 2nd son of Thos A Duley.

Died: Sep 7, Anna Delia Lenmon, aged 1 year & 7 months, daughter of Chas & Martha E Lenmon.

Orphans Court of Wash Co, D C. Letters of administration to be granted to Jos Ehrmauntraut on the personal estate of Thos Dalton, late of the U S Navy, deceased. –Nathl F Causin -Edw N Roach, Reg o/wills

Interments in Wash City for the month ending Aug 31: 39 males & 32 females. –Thos Miller, M D, Pres of Board of Health

Fine parlor & chamber furniture at auction: on Sep 14, at the residence of Gen McCalla, on Indiana ave, between 3 & 4½ sts. -A Green, auctioneer

Public sale, on Oct 12, one frame house & lot, [the east half of lot 3 in square 730] seized & taken, under 3 writs of fieri facias, as the property of Z Hazel, 2 of which were issued by Jos W Beck, a J P for Wash Co, in favor of F M Jarboe, & the other in favor of Saml Entwizell, use of W J Wheatly, & another issued by J O Smith, a J P of Wash Co, in favor of Jos W Beck. –Wm A Mulloy, Constable

TUE SEP 12, 1848

Gtwn College, situated on the northern bank of the Potomac, commands a full view of Gtwn, Wash, the Potomac, & a great part of D C. On May 1, 1815, the College was raised by Congress to the rank of University. Annual pension for Tuition, Board & Lodging, washing & mending linen & stockings, Medical aid & Medicine is: $200. For Half-boarders: $125. For Day Scholars: $50. Graduation fees: $5. –Jas Ryder, Pres

Sale of valuable property: by deed of trust from John B Coddington & Camilla his wife, dated Aug 31, 1842, recorded in Liber W B #95, folio 49, in the land records of Wash Co, D C: public auction on Nov 18: lot 5 in reservation 11, fronting on B st, with a 2 story brick dwlg-house. –Wm M Morrison, auctioneer -P R Fendall, Trustee

Notice: I will sell my land in PG Co, Md, adjoining the lands of Dr Wm Gunton, H Tolson, & others: tract contains 335 acres. Apply to Dr W Gunton, of Wash. –Albert Gantt

Furnished rooms for rent. Apply to Mrs Sarah Murray, on 9th st, between D & E sts.

Household & kitchen furniture at auction: on Sep 15, at the residence of Mr Wm A Rawling, on 1st st south, near High st. -A Green, auctioneer

Valuable real estate at private sale: the subscriber having removed to the West offers his farm in Montg Co, Md, about 9 miles from Gtwn, containing about 300 acres, with a large & commodious brick dwlg, with all necessary outbldgs. Refer to my brother, Robt W Carter, residing near Rockville. –John A Carter

Died: on Sep 10, in Wash City, in his 54th year, Mr Wm Browne, a native of Newburyport, Mass, & for the last 35 years a resident of Wash.

WED SEP 13, 1848
To rent, a convenient 2 story brick house in *Pollard's row*. Inquire of C Bestor, Patriotic Bank.

For rent: frame dwlg house, containing 9 rooms, on 6th st, between, E & F sts. Inquire of Noah Fletcher.

The *White Mountains*, Conway, N H: located where 3 ways meet, & lead off in a fourth to the Notch in the Mountains. This place is famous as having been the birthplace of the celebrated Willet family, who in 1825 moved hence to the Notch, & opened a house for the accommodation of travelers, & who all [9 in number] perished on Aug 28, 1828, being overwhelmed by a tremendous avalanche. The bodies of 6 were found & brought to this place & buried.

At N Y, on Sun, previous to the consecration of a new Roman Catholic Church, by Bishop Hughes, the walls of the basement had been built, & the floor laid over the timbers. With from 800 to 1,000 persons on this floor, one of the walls gave way crushing Patrick Kelly, who soon died. Jane Burns had her right leg badly fractured. Hector McDougal had his right leg badly fractured. –Commercial Advertiser

Fire yesterday destroyed the carpenter's shop occupied by Mr Jas Free, on 9th st, between D & E sts. Mr Free is a poor & industrious mechanic, & has lost all his tools and $50 in work prepared to order. Some citizens have suggested that contributions be solicited in his behalf, & we hope the suggestion will be carried out.

Balt, Sep 12: serious accident occurred on the Balt & Ohio Railroad this morning. A portion of track had been taken up for repair & the train from Wash came in at full speed, not having received notice that the track had been taken up. Mr Costigan had his foot badly crushed; Mr Harding, attached to the Wash Navy Yard, had 2 or 3 of his fingers torn off; & Mr John Kelly had his feet & legs terribly injured These are all from the District. [Sep 14th newspaper: Mr Jas Kelly [not John, as erroneously stated] was found to be easy & comfortable. Mr Coster, [not Costigan, as erroneously stated] was seriously injured. Mr Hardy [not Harding, as erroneously stated,] had lost a thumb & 2 fingers of his right hand, which, it is thought, will forever disable him from working at his business as a strikesman in the smith's dept of the Navy Yard.]

Mrd: on Sep 12, by Rev P Vanhorsigh, Benj J Fenwick to Mary E Schwrar, all of Wash Co, D C.

Mrd: on Sep 11, by Rev Mr Morgan, Chas Howard, of Ohio, to Miss Ann V Williams, of Balt.

Died: on Sep 12, Mrs Louisa Padgett, aged 38 years, consort of Jos M Padgett. Her funeral is this afternoon, at 3 o'clock, from the residence of her husband, near the Navy Yard.

Died: on Mon last, at Bladensburg, Md, where he had been for the benefit of his health, Maj John W Williams, in his 52nd year. Friends & acquaintances are invited to accompany his remains to the steamer **Oceola**, from his late residence on 13th st, between A & B sts south, this morning at 8 o'clock.

Died: on Tue, of scarlet fever, after an illness of 72 hours, Jas William, son of Jas & Eliza J Lawrenson, aged 6 years & 4 months. His funeral is today at 10 o'clock.

THU SEP 14, 1848
Letters were received by the last steamer, announcing the death of Lt Dale, attached to the Dead Sea expedition.

For rent: the store & dwlg house on the corner of F & 13th sts, lately occupied by B W Reed as a grocery. Apply at the residence of Mrs S M Burche.

Business Stand for rent: fine brick store with new granite front, 7th & E sts. Apply: Raphael Semmes & Co.

Notice of Copartnership: subscriber had this day associated with him in business his brother, Thos E Baden, & will continue to conduct the Hardware Business at the old stand on Pa ave, under the name of J W Baden & Brother. –John W Baden, Pa av, south side, 3rd door from 6th st.

Trustee's sale: by an act of Congress, passed Jul 20, 1840, & of the decree of the Circuit Court of Wash Co, D C, & of the Orphans Court of Wash Co, D C, made in the case of Lewis G Davidson's heirs, & by authority from the heirs, I shall offer at auction, on Oct 5: lots 13 thru 15 in square 168, on Pa ave; lot 11 in square 168 on 18th st west; lots 3 & 4 in square 126, north I st, in the immediate neighborhood of Mrs Macomb's residence; lot 6 in square 163. Title indisputable. –Saml G Davidson, Trustee -Martin & Wright, aucts

$100 reward for runaway negro man Tom Shorter, about 25 years of age.
–Edw Fenwick, living in Wash.

Mutiny & murder on the High Seas: the ship **St Louis**, Capt Haley, left Vera Cruz on Aug 21 for New Orleans, with a crew of 8 men before the mast, 2 of them being Spaniards by birth, one named Antonio Sibelich, the other John Martinez. On Aug 28, at night, Sibelich stabbed & killed Mr Jas Chappell, a passenger, & then stabbed Capt Haley in the shoulder. The murderers were secured & put in irons, & given in charge to the U S Marshal on their arrival in New Orleans. –Bulletin

By the last overland mail from India advices were received of the decease of Jos H Webb, late of N Y C, merchant & U S Consular Agent at Singapore.

Irving House is a new & splendid Hotel, just opening N Y, by D D Howard, long & favorably known as the former proprietor of Howard's Hotel, from which he retired some 2 or 3 years since.

FRI SEP 15, 1848
Army Genr'l Order: Order #50. War Dept, Adj Genrl's Ofc, Wash, Sep 1, 1848.
Promotions & Appointments in the regular Army of the U S.
Promotions: Adj Gen Dept:
Brevet Capt Oscar F Winship, Assist Adj Gen to be Assist Adj Gen with the brevet rank of Major, Dec 26, 1847, vice McCall, who vacates his staff commission.
Corps of Engineers:
1st Lt Henry W Benham, to Capt, May 24, 1848, vice Welcker, deceased.
2nd Lt Horatio G Wright, to 1st Lt, Feb 28, 1848, vice Trapier, resigned.
2nd Lt Masillon Harrison, to 1st Lt, May 24, 1848, vice Benham, promoted.
Brevet 2nd Lt Chas E Blunt, to 2nd Lt, Feb 28, 1848, vice Wright, promoted.
Brevet 2nd Lt John G Foster, to 2nd Lt, May 24, 1848, vice Harrison, promoted.
Corps of Topographical Engineers:
1st Lt Andrew A Humphreys, to Capt, May 31, 1848, vice Mackay, deceased.
2nd Lt Wm R Palmer, to 1st Lt, May 31, 1848, vice Humphreys, promoted.
Brevet 2nd Lt Wm G Peck, to 2nd Lt, May 31, 1848, vice Palmer, promoted.
Ordnance Dept:
Lt Col Geo Talcott, to Col, Mar 25, 1848, vice Bomford, deceased.
Maj Henry K Craig, to Lt Col, Mar 25, 1848, vice Talcott, promoted.
Capt Wm H Bell, to Maj, Mar 25, 1848, vice Craig, promoted.
2nd Lt Jas G Benton, to 1st Lt, Mar 25, 1848, vice Walbach, promoted.
1st Regt of Dragoons:
Maj Edwin V Sumner, of 2nd Dragoons, to be Lt Col, Jul 13, 1848, vice Wharton, dec'd.
1st Lt Lucius B Northrop, to Capt, Jul 21, 1848, vice Turner, resigned.
2nd Lt John W Davidson, to 1st Lt, Jan 8, 1848, vice Northrop, dropped from the rolls.
2nd Regt of Dragoons:
Capt Marshall S Howe, to Maj, Jul 13, 1848, vice Sumner, promoted to 1st Dragoons.
1st Lt Washington I Newton, to Capt, Jul 13, 1848, vice Howe, promoted.
2nd Lt Lewis Neill, to 1st Lt, Dec 10, 1847, the date of 1st Lt Steel's appointment as Adj.
2nd Lt Richd H Anderson, to 1st Lt, Jul 13, 1848, vice Newton, promoted.
Brevet 2nd Lt Saml H Starr, to 2nd Lt, Jul 13, 1848, vice Anderson, promoted.
Regt of Mounted Riflemen:
Maj Wm W Loring, to Lt Col, Mar 15, 1848, vice Fremont, resigned.
Capt Winslow F Sanderson, to Maj, Jan 8, 1848, vice Burbridge, resigned.
Capt Geo B Crittenden, to Maj, Mar 15, 1848, vice Loring, promoted.
Capt John S Simonson, to Maj, Aug 19, 1848, vice Crittenden, cashiered.
1st Lt Llwellyn Jones, to Capt, Dec 31, 1847, vice Pope, resigned.
1st Lt Noah Newton, to Capt, Jan 8, 1848, vice Sanderson, promoted.
1st Lt Thos Duncan, to Capt, Mar 15, 1848, vice Crittenden, promoted.
1st Lt Wm W Taylor, to Capt, Aug 19, 1848, vice Simonson, promoted.
2nd Lt Robt M Morris, to 1st Lt, Jan 8, 1848, vice Newton, promoted.
2nd Lt Francis S K Russell, to 1st Lt, Mar 15, 1848, vice Duncan, promoted.
2nd Lt Julian May, to 1st Lt, Aug 19, 1848, vice Taylor, promoted.
Brevet 2nd Lt Alfred Gibbs, to 2nd Lt, Dec 31, 1847, vice 2nd Lt Hatch, appointed adj.
Brevet 2nd Lt Geo H Gordon, to 2nd Lt, Jan 8, 1848, vice Morris, promoted.
Brevet 2nd Lt Wm B Lane, to 2nd Lt, Aug 19, 1848, vice May, promoted.

1st Regt of Artl:
1st Lt Israel Vogdes, to Capt, Aug 20, 1847, vice Mackall, Assist Adj Gen, who vacates his regimental commission
1st Lt Bennett H Hill, to Capt, Jan 12, 1848, vice Aisquith, negatived by the Senate.
2nd Lt Truman Seymour, to 1st Lt to date from Aug 26, 1847.
2nd Lt Lewis O Morris, to 1st Lt, Dec 23, 1847, vice Green, deceased.
2nd Lt John B Gibson, to 1st Lt, Jan 12, 1848, vice Hill, promoted.

2nd Regt of Artl:
1st Lt Wm W Chapman, to Capt, Oct 27, 1847, vice Daniels, deceased.
1st Lt Francis Woodbridge, to Capt, Dec 8, 1847, vice Ridgely, resigned.
1st Lt Edw D Townsend, to Capt, Apr 21, 1848, vice De Hart, deceased.
1st Lt Henry C Pratt, to Capt, Apr 21, 1848, vice Townsend, Assist Adj Gen, who vacates his regimental commission.
2nd Lt Henry B Sears, to 1st Lt, Oct 27, 1847, vice Chapman, promted.
2nd Lt Richd H Rush, to 1st Lt, Dec 6, 1847, vice Woodbridge, promoted.
2nd Lt Jos S Totten, to 1st Lt, Apr 21, 1848, vice Townsend, promoted.
2nd Lt Anderson Merchant, to 1st Lt, Apr 21, 1848, vice Pratt, promoted.
Brevet 2nd Lt Jas M Robinson, to 2nd Lt, to fill a vacancy, to date from Jun 28, 1848, the date of his entry into the army.

3rd Regt of Artl:
2nd Lt John H Lendrum, to 1st Lt, Mar 24, 1848, vice Welch, deceased.
Brevet 2nd Lt John H Heck, 3rd Artl, to 2nd Lt, to fill a vacancy, to date from Jun 28, 1848, the date of his entry into the army.

4th Regt of Artl:
1st Lt Jos Roberts, to Capt, Aug 20, 1848, vice Smead, deceased.
2nd Lt John A Brown, to 1st Lt, Aug 20, 1848, vice Roberts, promoted.
Brevet 2nd Lt Robt W Howard, to 2nd Lt, Aug 20, 1848, vice Brown, promoted.

1st Regt of Infty:
Capt Thompson Morris, of 2nd Infty, to Maj, Jan 12, 1848, vice Hutter, negatived by the Senate.
1st Lt Alex'r W Reynolds, to Capt, Mar 15, 1848, vice Miller, promoted to 2nd Infty.
1st Lt Ferdinand S Mumford, to Capt, Mar 15, 1848, vice Reynolds, Assist quartermaster, who vacates his regimental commission.
2nd Lt Jos B Plummer, to 1st Lt, Mar 15, 1848, vice Reynolds, promoted.
2nd Lt Schuyler Hamilton, to 1st Lt, Mar 15, 1848, vice Mumford, promoted.
Brevet 2nd Lt Chas N Underwood, to 2nd Lt, Jun 28, 1848, date of his entry into the army.

2nd Regt of Artl:
Capt Albert S Miller, of the 1st Infty, to Maj, Mar 15, 1848, vice Allen, deceased.
1st Lt Justus McKinstry, to Capt, Jan 12, 1848, vice Morris, promoted to 1st Infty.
1st Lt Christopher S Lovell, to Capt, Jan 12, 1848, vice McKinstry, Assist Quartermaster, who vacates his regimental commission.
1st Lt Jas W Schureman, to 1st Lt, Jan 12, 1848, vice McKinstry, promoted.
2nd Lt Chas E Jarvis, to 1st Lt, Jan 12, 1848, vice Lovell, promoted.
2nd Lt Fred'k Steele, to 1st Lt, Jun 6, 1848, vice Tilden, resigned.
Brevet 2nd Lt Geo Bruce, to 2nd Lt, vice Steele, promoted, to date from Jun 28, 1848, the date of his entry into the army.

3rd Regt of Infty:
Capt Geo A McCall, of the 4th Infty, to Maj, Dec 26, 1847, vice Barnum, deceased.
1st Lt Oliver L Shepherd, to Capt, Dec 1, 1847, vice Dobbins, dismissed.
1st Lt Wm B Johns, to Capt, Dec 4, 1847, vice Smith, deceased.
2nd Lt John Trevitt, to 1st Lt, Dec 1, 1847, vice Shepherd, promoted.
2nd Lt Henry B Schroeder, to 1st Lt, Dec 4, 1847, vice Johns, promoted.
4th Regt of Infty:
Capt Lorenzo Thomas, to Maj, Jan 1, 1848, vice Cobbs, deceased.
Capt Geo Wright, 8th Infty, to be Maj, Jan 1, 1848, vice Thomas, Assist adj Gen, who vacates his regimental commission.
1st Lt John H Gore, to Capt, Dec 26, 1847, vice McCall, promoted to 3rd Infty.
1st Lt Edw G Elliott, to be Capt, Jan 1, 1848, vice Thomas, promoted.
1st Lt Granville O Haller, to Capt, Jan 1, 1848, vice Elliott, Assist Quartermaster, who vacates his regimental commission.
2nd Lt Abram B Lincoln, to 1st Lt, Nov 24, 1847, vice Ridgely, killed in action.
2nd Lt Thos J Montgomery, to 1st Lt, Dec 26, 1847, vice Gore, promoted.
2nd Lt David A Russell, to 1st Lt, Jan 1, 1848, vice Elliott, promoted.
2nd Lt Delancy F Jones, to 1st Lt, Jan 1, 1848, vice Haller, promoted.
2nd Lt Maurice Maloney, to 1st Lt, May 6, 1848, vice Beaman, deceased.
Brevet 2nd Lt Hiram Dryer, to 2nd Lt, Jul 31, 1848, vice Tobey, resigned.
5th Regt of Infty:
1st Lt Geo Deas, to Capt, Dec 2, 1847, vice Hooe, deceased.
1st Lt Sterne H Fowler, to Capt, Dec 9, 1847, vice Deas, Assist adj Gen, who vacates his regimental commission.
2nd Lt Wm Read, to 1st Lt, Dec 9, 1847, vice Deas, promoted.
2nd Lt Patrick A Farrely, to 1st Lt, Dec 9, 1847, vice Fowler, promoted.
7th Regt of Infty:
Capt Geo Andrews, 6th Infty, to be Maj, Aug 14, 1847, vice Noel, deceased.
8th Regt of Infty:
1st Lt Jos Selden, to Capt, Jan 1, 1848, vice Wright, promoted to 4th Infty.
1st Lt Arthur T Lee, to Capt, Jan 27, 1848, vice Kello, deceased.
2nd Lt Lafayette B Wood, to 1st Lt, Jan 1, 1848, vice Selden, promoted.
2nd Lt Alfred Crozet, to 1st Lt, Jan 7, 1848, vice Lee, promoted.
Brevet 2nd Lt Theodore Fink, to 2nd Lt, Aug 2, 1848, vice Wainwright, deceased.
Correction of Dates-made by & with the advice & consent of the Senate:
Deputy Paymaster Gen Danl Randall, Pay Dept, to date from Mar 3, 1847, instead of Mar 27, 1847.
2nd Lt Arthur D Tree, 2nd Dragoons, to date from Oct 18, 1847, the date of the Jr Brevet 2nd Lt [Evans] promoted in the Dragoon arm, instead of May 20, 1847, & to stand on the Army Register next below 2nd Lt W D Smith.
1st Lt Thos J Jackson, 1st Artl, to date from Aug 20, 1847, vice Vogdes, promoted, instead of Aug 26, 1847.
Capt Lewis G Arnold, 2nd Artl, to date from Oct 27, 1847, vice Chapman, Assist Quartermaster, who vacates his regimental commission, instead of Oct 19, 1847.
1st Lt Thos B J Weld, 2nd Artl, to date from Oct 19, 1847, vice Daniels, promoted, instead of Oct 27, 1847.

1st Lt Louis D Welch, 3rd Artl, to date from Sep 8, 1847, instead of Aug 13, 1847.
Capt Marcena R Patrick, 2nd Infty, to date from Aug 22, 1847, vice Anderson, deceased, of wounds received in battle, instead of Aug 20, 1847.
1st Lt Edw Murray, 2nd Infty, to date from Aug 22, 1847, vice Patrick, promoted, instead of Aug 20, 1847.

Appointments: Adj Genl's Dept.
1st Lt Don Carlos Buell, Adj 3rd Infty, to be Assist Adj Gen with the Brevet rank of Capt, Jan 25, 1847, vice Winship, promoted.

Quartermaster's Dept:
1st Lt Rufus Ingalls, 1st Dragoons, to Assist Quartermaster with the rank of Capt, Jan 12 1848, vice Churchill, deceased.
1st Lt [paper folded] Assist Quartermaster, with rank of Capt, Jan 12, 1848, vice Shover, who vacates his staff commission.
1st Lt Elias K Kane, 2nd Dragoons, to be Assist Quartermaster with rank of Capt, Jan 12, 1848, vice Armstrong, killed in battle.
1st Lt Napoleon J T Dana, 7th Infty, to Assist Quartermaster with rank of Capt, Mar 3, 1848, vice Irwin, deceased.
1st Lt Jos A Haskin, 1st Artl, to Assist Quartermaster, with rank of Capt, Aug 12, 1848, vice Cross, promoted.
Reuben M Potter, of Texas, to Military Storekeeper, Mar 23, 1848, vice King, cashiered.

Medical Dept:
To be Assist Surgeon: -original vacancy:
P G S Ten Broeck, of N Y, Dec 13, 1847.
John Campbell, of N Y, Dec 13, 1847.
John E Summer, of Va, Dec 13, 1847.
Chas H Smith, of Va, Dec 13, 1847.
Washington M Ryer, of N Y, Dec 13, 1847.
Lyman H Stone, of Vt, Dec 13, 1847.
John M Haden, of Miss, Dec 13, 1847.
Chas H Crane, of Mass, Feb 2, 1848, vice Suter, deceased.
Wm Hammond, jr, of Missouri, Mar 2, 1848, vice Glen, deceased.

Pay Dept: to be Paymaster:
John D Beatty, of N C, May 16, 1848, vice Bosworth, deceased.
Robt Strange, jr, of N C, Jun 14, 1848, vice Beatty, declined.
Jas W Spratley, of Va, Jul 13, 1848, vice Spark, deceased.

Regt of Mounted Riflemen:
John McL Addison, of D C, to be 2nd Lt, Jun 14, 1848, vice Russell, promoted.

1st Regt of Artl:
Jefferson C Davis, of Indiana, to 2nd Lt, Jun 17, 1848, vice Gibson, promoted.
Jas E Slaughter, of Va, [Lt in the Regt of Voltigeurs,] to 2nd Lt, Jun 27, 1848, vice Morris, promoted.
Danl Nickels, of Md, to 2nd Lt, Jul 13, 1848.

2nd Regt of Artl:
Jefferson H Nones, of Dela, to 2nd Lt, Dec 20, 1847, vice Edwards, promoted.
John McLean Taylor, of Ky, to 2nd Lt, Mar 3, 1848, vice Weld, promoted.
Lloyd Beall, of Mo, to 2nd Lt, Mar 28, 1848, vice Sears, promoted.

Paschal C Greeson, of Ga, to 2nd Lt, Mar 23, 1848, vice Simpson, promoted.
Wiley C Adams, of Ga, to 2nd Lt, May 31, 1848, vice Greeson, declined.
Caleb Smith, of Va, to 2nd Lt, Jun 21, 1848, vice Merchant, promoted.
Christopher R P Butler, of S C, [Lt in 12th Infty,] to 2nd Lt, Jun 27, 1848, vice Totten, promoted.
3rd Regt of Artl:
Chas C Churchill, of Pa, to 2nd Lt, Mar 3, 1848, vice Maury, transferred to the Mounted Riflemen.
Wm A Winder, of Md, to 2nd Lt, Mar 24, 1848, vice G T Andrews, promoted.
Richd H Smith, [Lt in 14th Infty,] to 2nd Lt, Jun 21, 1848, vice Minor, deceased.
Isaac W Patton, [Lt in 10th Infty,] to 2nd Lt, Jul 13, 1848, vice Lendrum, promoted.
1st Regt of Infty:
Edmund G Bradford, of Miss, to 2nd Lt, Jun 27, 1848, vice Plummer, promoted.
2nd Regt of Infty:
Thos W Sweeny, of N Y, to 2nd Lt, Mar 3, 1848, vice Schureman, promoted.
Wm W Johnston, of Ohio, to 2nd Lt, Jun 27, 1848, vice Jarvis, promoted.
3rd Regt of Infty:
Andrew Jackson, of Va, to 2nd Lt, Dec 30, 1847, vice McFerran, promoted.
Chas B Brower, of N Y, to 2nd Lt, Dec 30, 1847, vice O'Sullivan, resigned.
Lawrence W O'Bannon, of S C, to 2nd Lt, Mar 3, 1848, vice Trevitt, promoted.
Thos J Mason, of Fla, to 2nd Lt, Mar 3, 1848, vice Schroeder, promoted.
4th Regt of Infty:
To 2nd Lt:
Thos H Bussey, of Md, Dec 30, 1847, vice Judah, promoted.
Edmund Underwood, of Pa, Mar 3, 1848, vice Lincoln, promoted.
Wm C Tobey, of Pa, Mar 3, 1848, vice Montgomery, promoted.
Jos B Collins, of D C, Mar 29, 1848, vice Jones, promoted.
Columbus W Howard, of Ga, Jun 17, 1848, vice Maloney, promoted.
John C Bonneycastle, of Va, Jun 27, 1848, vice Bussey, cashiered.
5th Regt of Infty: to 2nd Lt:
John Neilly, of N Y, Mar 3, 1848, vice Read, promoted.
Benj Wingate, [Sgt, Co G, Mounted Riflemen,] Jun 14, 1848, vice Farelly, promoted.
6th Regt of Infty: to 2nd Lt:
Thos O Davis, of D C, Dec 30, 1847, vice Garnett, promoted.
Geo T Shackleford, of Va, Dec 30, 1847, vice Flint, promoted.
7th Regt of Infty: to 2nd Lt:
Robt R Garland, of Mo, Dec 30, 1847, vice Potter, promoted.
8th Regt of Infty: to 2nd Lt:
Wm A Merriwether, of Ky, Mar 3, 1848, vice Wood, promoted.
Jas A Deaney, of Pa, Mar 29, 1848, vice Crozet, promoted.
John Bold, of S C, Jun 27, 1848, vice Merriwether, declined.
Reappointments:
1st Regt of Dragoons:
Lucius B Northup, late 1st Lt, to 1st Lt, to fill a vacancy occasioned by the resignation of Capt Turner, to date from Jul 4, 1836, & to stand at the head of the list of 1st Lts, being his date & position at the time he was dropped from the rolls, Jan 8, 1848.

4th Regt of Artl:
Edw Deas, late of the 4th Artl, to Capt, todate from Feb 16, 1847, his former date.
Reappointments of ofcrs of the old army who received appointments in the additional regts raised for the war with Mexico.

Pay Dept:
Timothy P Andrews, [late Col Voltigeurs,] to be paymaster, to date from May 22, *1822, & to take place on the list of paymasters next below Paymaster C H Smith, being the date & position held by him under his former appointment in the pay dept. [*1822 as copied]

Corps of Topographical Engineers:
Jos E Johnston, [late Lt Col Voltigeurs,] to be Capt, to date from Sep 21, 1846, & to take place on the Army Register next below Capt T B Linnard being the rank & position held by him under his former commission in the Corps of Topographical Engingeers.

Ordnance Dept:
Geo H Talcott, [late Maj Voltigeurs,] to be Capt, to date from May 3, 1847, & to take place on the Army Register next below Capt R H K Whitney, being the rank & position to which he would nave succeeded in virtueof his former commission in the Ordnance.

2nd Regt of Dragoons:
Fowler Hamilton, [late Lt Col 18th Infty,] to be 1st Lt, to date from Aug 31, 1843, & to take place on the Army Register next below 1st Lt A Lowry, being the rank & position held by him under his former commission in the 2nd Dragoons.

2nd Regt of Infty:
Hermann Thorn, [late 1st Lt 2nd Dragoons,] to be 2nd Lt, to date from Oct 15, 1846, & to stand on the Army register next below 2nd Lt J M Henry, being the date & position held by him under his former commission in the 2nd Infty.

6th Regt of Infty:
Saml Woods, [late Maj 15th Infty,] to be Capt, to date from Feb 27, 1843, & to take place in his regt next below Capt W S Ketchum, & on the list of Capts of Infty next below Capt B R Alden, being the rank & position held by him under his former commission in the 6th Infty.

Transfers:
Brevet Maj Robt S Garnett, 1st Lt 4th Artl, transferred to the 7th Infty, to stand on the Army Register next below 1st Lt Humber.
1st Lt Richd S Smith, 7th Infty, transferred to the 4th Artl, to stand on the Army Register next below 1st Lt [paper folded.]
2nd Lt Dabney H Maury, 3rd Artl, transferred [Feb 19] to the Regt of Mounted Riflemen, to take his original position in said regt next below Lt G Granger.
2nd Lt Lorimer Graham, 10th Infty, transferred [Feb 2] to the 1st Regt of Dragoons, to take place on the Army Register nexr below Lt Evans.
Lt Horace Haldeman, 11th Infty, transferred [Jun 29] to the 8th Regt of Infty, to rank from Apr 9, 1847, [the date of his former commission,] & to take place on the Army Register next below 2nd Lt Deaney.
2nd Lt Richd C Drum, 9th Infty, transferred [Mar 10] to the 4th Regt of Artl, to take place on the Army Register next below Lt Best.
2nd Lt Wm H Scott, 11th Infty, transferred [Mar 14] to the 4th Regt of Infty, to take place on the Army Register next below Lt Bussey.

2nd Lt Frank H Larned, Voltigeurs, transferred [Jun 29] to the 2nd Regt of Artl, to take place on the Army Register next below Lt Beall.
2nd Lt Julian McAllister, 2nd Artl, transferred [Apr 13] to the Ordnance Dept, to take place in the Army Register next below Lt T M Whedbee.

Casualties: Resignations:
Brig Gen Franklin Pierce, Mar 20, 1848.
Lt Col John C Fremont, Mounted Riflemen, Mar 15, 1848.
Maj Geo S Burbridge, Mounted Riflemen, Jan 8, 1848.
Brevet Maj H S Turner, Capt 1st Dragoons, Jul 21, 1848.
Capt Henry C Pope, Mounted Riflemen, Dec 31, 1847.
1st Lt Jas H Trapier, Corps of Engineers, Feb 28, 1848.
Brevet 1st Lt Alex'r Hays, 2nd Lt 8th Infty, Apr 12, 1848.
1st Lt Bryant P Tilden, jr, 2nd Infty, Jun 6, 1848.
2nd Lt Wm C Tobey, 4th Infty, Jul 31, 1848.
2nd Lt Geo Bruce, 2nd Infty, Aug 19, 1848.
Assist Surgeon Grayson M Prevost, Jun 7, 1848.
Assist Surgeon John S Battee, Jul 28, 1848.
Paymaster Peter T Crutchfield, Jun 15, 1848.

Commissions vacated under the provisions of the 7th section of the act of Jun 18, 1846:
Maj L Thomas, 4th Infty, Jan 1, 1848, Assist Adj Gen. [Regimental commission (only) vacated.]
Brevet Maj G A McCall, Assist Adj Gen, Dec 26, 1847, Maj 3rd Infty. [Staff commission (only) vacated.]
Capt Robt Allen, 2nd Artl, Oct 19, 1847, Assist Quartermaster. [Regimental commission (only) vacated.]
Capt W W Chapman, 2nd Artl, Oct 27, 1847, Assist Quartermaster. [Regimental commission (only) vacated.]
Capt E D Townsend, 2nd Artl, Apr 21, 1848, Assist Adj Gen. [Regimental commission (only) vacated.]
Capt W W Mackall, 1st Artl, Aug 20, 1847, Assist Adj Gen. [Regimental commission (only) vacated.]
Capt Geo Deas, 5th Infty, Dec 9, 1847, Assist Adj Gen. [Regimental commission (only) vacated.]
Capt Justus McKinstry, 2nd Infty, Jan 12, 1848, Assist Quartermaster. [Regimental commission (only) vacated.]
Capt E G Elliott, 4th Infty, Jan 1, 1848, Assist Quartermaster. [Regimental commission (only) vacated.]
Capt A W Reynolds, 1st Infty, Mar 15, 1848, Assist Quartermaster. [Regimental commission (only) vacated.]

Disbanded, Jul 20, 1848, under requirements in Gen Orders #36, of Jul 7, 1848:
Maj Gen Gideon J Pillow
Maj Gen John A Quitman
Brig Gen Geo Cadwalader

Declined:
2nd Lt Wm A Merriwether, 8th Infty; 2nd Lt Paschal C Greeson, 2nd Artl;
Brevet 2nd Lt Thos J McKean, 2nd Dragoons; Paymaster John D Beatty

Deaths:
Col Geo Bomford, Ordnance, at Boston, Mass, Mar 25, 1848.
Brevet Lt Col G W Allen, Maj 2nd Infty, at Vera Cruz, Mexico, Mar 15, 1848.
Lt Col Clifton Wharton, 1st Dragoons, at *Fort Leavenworth*, Mo, Jul 13, 1848.
Maj W B Cobbs, 4th Infty, at Exeter, N H, Jan 1, 1848.
Maj Thos Noel, 7th Infty, near Balt, Md, Aug 14, 1848.
Brevet Maj A S Hooe, Capt 5th Infty, at Baton Rouge, La, Dec 9, 1847.
Maj E K Barnum, 2nd Infty, at Balt, Md, Dec 26, 1847.
Brevet Capt T Green, 1st Lt 1st Artl, at *Fort Monroe*, Va, Dec 23, 1847.
Capt J R Irwin, Assist Quartermaster, at the city of Mexico, Jan 10, 1848.
Capt W C De Hart, 2nd Artl, at Elizabethtown, N J, Apr 21, 1848.
Capt John Mackay, Topographical Engineers, at Savannah, Ga, May 31, 1848.
Capt W O Kello, 8th Infty, in Southampton Co, Va, Jan 27, 1848.
Capt R C Smead, 4th Artl, at *Fort Monroe*, Va, Aug 20, 1848.
Capt G L Welcker, engineers, at Savannah, Ga, May 24, 1848.
Capt T P Ridgely, 2nd Artl, in Balt Co, Md, Dec 6, 1847.
Capt J M Smith, 3rd Infty, at Encerro, Mexico, Dec 4, 1847.
1st Lt H Ridgely, 4th Infty, at the Pass of Galaxra Mexico, Nov 24, 1847. [Of wounds received in action.]
1st Lt Jenks Beaman, 4th Infty, at Tampico, Mexico, May 6, 1848.
1st Lt D G Rogers, 2nd Dragoons, at Vera Cruz, Mexico, Jul 21, 1848.
1st Lt L D Welch, 3rd Artl, at St Augustine, Fla, Mar 24, 1848.
2nd Lt Geo Wainwright, 8th Infty, at Brooklyn, N Y, Aug 3, 1848.
2nd Lt C J Minor, 3rd Artl, at Monterey, Calif, Aug 17, 1847.
Surgeon P H Craig, at New Orleans barracks, La, Aug 8, 1848.
Assist Surgeon A F Suter, at the city of Mexico, Dec 17, 1847.
Assist Surgeon J C Glen, at Matamoras, Mexico, Feb 14, 1848.
Assist Surgeon Robt Newton, at New Orleans barracks, La, Aug 9, 1848.
Paymaster W A Spark, at Selma, Ala, Jun 6, 1848.
Dropped: 1st Lt Lucius B Northrop, 1st Dragons, Jan 8, 1848.
Dismissed: Capt Edw Deas, 4th Artl, Apr 11, 1848;
Capt Stephen D Dobbins, 3rd Infty, Dec 1, 1847.
Cashiered: Maj Geo B Crittenden, Mounted Riflemen, Aug 19, 1848.
2nd Lt Thos H Bussey, 4th Infty, Apr 11, 1848.
Military Storekeeper T G King, Ordnance, Dec 23, 1847.
Negatived by the Senate:
Maj G C Hutter, 1st Infty, Jan 12, 1848.
Capt V E Aisquith, 1st Artl, Jan 12, 1848.
2nd Lt C Carson, Mounted Riflemen, Jan 28, 1848.
By order of the Sec of War: R Jones, Adj Gen
Memoranda: Reappointments:
Paymaster Chas H Smith, from Nov 24, 1847, when his former appointment expired.
Paymaster Edmund Kirby, from Aug 15, 1848, when his former appointment expired.
Paymaster Benj Walker, from Dec 17, 1847, when his former appointment expired.
Paymaster Eugene Van Ness, from Dec 18, 1847, when his former appointment expired.
Paymaster Lloyd J Beall, from Sep 13, 1848, when his present appointment will expire.

1-The nomimation of 1st Lt Jos A Haskin, 1st Artl, to be Assist Quartermaster, not having been confirmed till Aug 12, 1848, in consequence of the promotion of Capt Cross to be quartermaster, [on which it depended,] having been laid over for the consideration in the Senate, his appointment, as Assist Quartermaster necessarily dates from [line folded & missing] in the Army Register for Feb, 1848: & he accordingly takes place on the list of Assist Quartermasters next below Capt N J T Dana.

2-2nd Lt Colville J Minor, 3rd Artl, having died in Calif, Aug 17, 1847, [the notification of which was not received at the War Dept till Jan 27, 1848,] his promotion to be 1st Lt, to date from Sep 8, 1847, announced in Gen Orders #36, of Dec 4, 1847, is necessarily cancelled.

3-The appointment [announced as Gen Orders #37] of Sgt Henry Wilson & Cpl Robt Bailey, to be Brevet 2nd Lts in the 1st & 2nd Regts of Infty, respectively, to date from Jun 28, 1848, cancelled-it appearing by returns recently received that the said non-commissioned ofcrs died previous to the date of their appointment. -R Jones, Adj Gen

A telegraphic dispatch from N Y reports that Cmder Alex'r Slidell Mackenzie, of the U S Navy, is dead. He died at Sing Sing on Tue, of heart disease.

Mr Rufus Reed, a highly respected merchant of Portland, died there on Sat, of injuries received by having been thrown from a chaise a few days before. While descending a hill, some part of the harness gave way, causing the horse to take fright, & he was thrown violently to the ground.

The trial of Louisa Bremond for the murder of Pierre D Bremond, in Nassau st, N Y, in Jul, resulted in her acquittal on Fri. The Court semms to have charged favorably to the prisoner, who it was proved was married to the deceased, letters addressed by him to her & the marriage certificate being produced in Court.

City Ordinances-Wash: 1-Act for the relief of Louisa Collins: fine imposed for alleged violation relative to the use of firearms, is remitted: Provided, L Collins pay the costs of prosecution. 2-Act for the payment of the claim of W H Ward: for the sum of $54.97, balance due him for constructing a culvert across Mass ave, between 4th & 5th sts. 3-Act for the payment of Enoch Ridgway's claim for repairing the roof of the City Hall, in 1846 & 1847: sum of $30.70 to be paid to him. 4-Resolution for the relief of John Brown: in Intendent of the Asylum be required to surrender to John Brown the 3 hogs claimed by him & found at large in the city & taken to the poorhouse; he, the said Brown, paying the costs & charges attending their seizure & support. Approved, Sep 7, 1848.

John McGrail, a laborer, employed by the Camden & Amboy Railroad Co, was killed on Tue, near the Camden depot. While jumping upon a train of cars, employed in bringing dirt from an excavation, he slipped & fell beneath the wheels, killing him instantly.

An altercation took place in Easton, Md, on Thu last between Thos Ozment, of Jackson, Miss, formerly of Easton, who was on a visit for some months, & John A Catrup, of Talbot Co, which resulted in the death of Catrup, from a severe stab on the left side of the abdomen.

Mrd: on Sep 5, by Rev Wm Wickes, D D, Wm W Rennoe, of Chas Co, Md, to Mary Louisa, daughter of T M McIlhany, of Wash City.

Mrd: on Aug 22, by Rev Ulysses Ward, Mr Alfred McClellan to Miss Ruth Ann Haverstick.

Mrd: on Aug 14, by Rev Ulysses Ward, Mr Edw Sauls to Miss Nancy Bayliss.

Died: on Sep 2, at New Orleans, of apoplexy, in his 29th year, Columbus S Holmead, son of Jas B Holmead, of Wash City. He was a native of this place, & though almost from his boyhood a resident of the Southwest, kept up his association with the city of his birth by acts of courteous attention to its inhabitants whenever apportunities offered for rendering them. [St Louis papers will please copy.]

Died: on Sep 10, at Brooklyn, N Y, Passed Midshipman Geo B Bissell, U S Navy, son of Mr John Bissell, sen. He was a most promising young ofcr. After being wrecked in the brig **Truxton**, & taken prisoner by the Mexicans, he had been stationed at the scientific dept of the navy at Wash for the last 18 months. He joined the frig **Cumberland**, in the harbor of N Y as her Sailingmaster, on Aug 31. On Sep 3 he was taken ill, &, notwithstanding the best medical attendance, he expired, aged 24 years, 11 months & 25 days.

The Albany Argus contains a letter stating that at a meeting of the Free Soil party, held at Schroom Lake, Judge Tyrill was speaking for awhile and suddenly his voice fell, & he fainted. He expired instantly.

Wash Corp: 1-Bill for the relief of John Fletcher: passed. 2-Ptn of Presley Simpson: referred to the Cmte of Claims. 3-Cmte of Claims: bill for the relief of John Davidson: passed.

The U S ship **Albany** arrived. Lynnhaven Roads, Sep 12, 1848. The **Albany** arrived this day, after a passage of 22 days from Laguna: twice hit by lightning, which passed off without damage. List of Ofcrs:

John Kelly, Capt
A Gibson, Z Holland, & B S Gantt, Lts
John Wilkes, jr, Acting Master
R T Barry, Surgeon
W Sherman, Assist Surgeon
Geo F Cutter, Purser
Geo U Morris & J R Eggleston, Midshipmen
Geo Ingola, Capt's Clerk
John Bates, Boatswain
Wm Arnold, Gunner
J Stevens, Sailmaker
R L Sheffield, Carpenter

Mr Werden Cressen, U S Consul at Jerusalem, & the Rabbi Bucklore Cohen, of the same city, arrived at Boston on Monday last.

SAT SEP 16, 1848
Alex'r Slidell Mackenzie, while riding on his horse on Wed, at Sing Sing, fell in a fit of apoplexy & instantly expired. His connexion with the tragedy on board the brig **Somers**, is familiar to all. He was appointed to the command of the steam frig **Mississippi**, stationed in the Gulf of Mexico. He returned to Boston a short time since. He was brother of Mr John Slidell, late Minister to Mexico, & that was his name; but, in consequence of inheriting a fortune from a Mr Mackenzie, adopted that as his surname. He was also related to Cmdor Perry. Jury rendered his death from disease of the heart. –N Y paper

We learn from Capt Morehouse, of the steamer **Iowa**, from St Louis, that as he came past Cairo, Lt John D Clark, 8th Infty, came on board & registered as a passenger for Vicksburg, When opposite Helena, Ark, he jumped off from the hurricane deck & was drowned. –Picayune

Trustee's sale of valuable Cotton Factory: being the surviving trustee in a deed from the late Col Geo Bomford & others, to himself & Clement Cox, deceased, in execution of the trust created by the said deed, will offer at public sale, on Oct 17, part of lot 79, in the plan of Gtwn, D C, with the Cotton Factory thereon, recently erected by Col Bomford, with all the machinery, fixtures & furniture therein. The lot is bounded by Potomac st on the east, & runs of that width south about 190 feet to the Merchant Flour Mill erected by Alex'r Ray, including the Bark Mill occupied by B Crawford. The factory bldg is of brick, 40 feet by 110 feet. –John Kirtz, Gtwn, D C

Balt, Sep 15: the young man Coster, from your city, who was injured by the railroad accident of Sep 12, has been under the necessity of having his leg amputated- mortification having taken place.

For rent: pleasant frame dwlg house, on 6th st, between E & F sts. Inquire of Noah Fletcher.

For sale: at the Capitol Stables, a first-rate, large sorrel Horse, 7 years old. Apply to Jas Henry, in the post ofc House of Reps.

MON SEP 18, 1848
Govn'r Crittenden has appointed Orlando Brown, of Frankfort, Sec of State, & Henry C Harlan, Assist Sec.

The sloop of war **Marion**, which returned to Boston last week, left that port on Sep 4, 1845, & proceeded to the west coast of Africa: remained there until Jun 4, 1847, when she was ordered to visit the Mediterranean, to protect our commerce in that sea. During her absence the following deaths have occurred, namely: at Quitts, west coast of Africa, Dec 29, 1845, Purser John C Spencer, jr; at sea, Jan 11, 1846, Patrick Delan, private of marines; at Monrovia, Mar 30, 1846, Midshipman Jos T Bartlett; John Johnson, seaman, drowned by the capsizing of a boat on the bar; at sea, Jun 27, 1847, Wm Collins, capt of forecastle.

Davidson Co Court, Aug Term, 1848. Hon Wm K Turner, Presiding Judge. Hon Ephraim H Foster, at a meeting of the Nashville Bar, spoke of Jas Campbell, who died on Aug 20, 1848, at the close of his 54th year. He was born in Va, but most of his life a citizen of Tenn by adoption. The name he bore denoted a noble & gallant lineage. He was a profound statesman; an able jurist; devoted husband; a tender parent; a faithful friend; & an indulgent master. –Thos T Smiley, Clerk

Dwlg house & lots in square 27, fronting on Pa ave, formerly occupied by the late Hon John Forsyth, are now offered for sale. Apply to Rd Smith.

Trustee's sale: by a decree of the Circuit Court of Wash Co, D C, sitting as a Court of Chancery, made in the cause of Rosewell Woodward et al, vis, Wm H Ritter et al. Public auction on Oct 7, all that part of lot 38, of Old Gtwn, to wit: beginning at the s e corner of a 3 story brick house owned by the late Peter Ritter, westerly on the north line of Water st from stone #35, at the intersection of the north line of Water st with the west line of Duck lane. –Walter S Cox, Trustee -Edw S Wright, auctioneer

Trustees' sale of real estate: under a deed of trust from the late Patrick Moran, deceased, to the subscribers, dated Nov 19, 1845, duly recorded, they will expose to sale, for cash, by public auction, lots 9 & 10 in square 759, in Wash City, with improvements.
–Jas Adams, Thos Gunton, Trustees

Wash Co, D C. I certify that John Nally, of said county, brought before me as a stray, a red milch Cow. -Thos C Donn, J P [Owner will come forward, prove property, pay charges, & take her away. –Jno Nally, on Turnpike, near Spring Tavern.]

Some villain or villains, last Fri, broke into the dwlg of his excellency Mr Calderon, in the first Ward, & robbed him of some valuable articles.

Mrd: on Aug 10, near Louisville, Ky, by Rev Mr Chapman, Burton Randall, Surgeon U S Army, to Virginia, 3rd daughter of the late John Gibson Taylor, at the residence of her brother, F G Edwards.

Mrd: on Sep 12, by Rev Mr Myers, Jas T Smull, to Miss Virginia, daughter of J Huddleson, of Alleghany Co, Md.

Died: on Sep 10, at **Oak Wood**, Albemarle Co, Va, the residence of her nephew, Dr John W Gantt, Mrs Priscilla Gantt, widow of the late John Gantt, of Strawberry Vale, Fairfax Co, Va. The deceased was a consistent Christian, an esteemed member of the Methodist Church for 40 years. Though she died at a distance from the larger portion of her children, it may be consolotary to them to know that she was attended in her illness by warm friends & relatives, who did their utmost to relieve pain & prolong life.

Died: on Sep 5, in Balt, Catherine, wife of the Rev Chas Goodrice, & daughter of Benj Ogle, late of PG Co, Md.

Died: on Aug 24, of congestive fever, at her residence in Chickasaw Co, Miss, after a few days' illness, Mrs Tabitha Bowen, wife of Capt Geo Bowen, formerly from Waterloo, Laurens district, S C, in her 56th year, leaving a disconsolate husband & 8 children, with several grandchildren, & a large circle of friends to mourn her loss. [Sep 19th newspaper: Died: on Aug 24, of congestive fever, at her residence in Chickasaw Co, Miss, after a few days' illness, Mrs Tabitha Bowen, wife of Capt Geo Bowen, formerly from Waterloo, Laurene district, S C, in her 56th year, leaving a disconsolate husband & 8 children, with several grandchildren, & a large circle of special friends to mourn her loss.]

To the public: Patrick Moran, of Wash City, having asserted that he was never married to me, I ask the attention of my acquaintances & friends to the annexed certificate of the Rev Fr Matthews, Catholic minister in Wash City: To all whom is may concern: I, the under written, Rector of St Patrick's Church, Wash, do hereby certify that Patrick Moran & Susan Burnett were married by me the 8th day of Oct, 1837, in virtue of a licence to that effect from the Circuit Court of this District. –Wm Matthews, Wash, Sep 12, 1848.

TUE SEP 19, 1848
Household & kitchen furniture at auction on Sep 21, by order of the Orphans Court, at the late residence of Mr John Moore, on 1st st east, between B & C sts. -Edw C & G F Dyer
+
Horses, & farming utensils, at auction, by order of the Orphans' Court, on the farm of the late Mr John Moore, adjoining Mr Beale's & Mr J A Smith. -Edw C & G F Dyer

Teacher wanted: at the Fredericksburg Classical & Mathematical Institute. Address, post paid, Richd Sterling, Fredericksburg, Va.

Mrd: on Sep 14, in Balt, by Rev Mr Edwards, L E Massoletti, of Wash, to Miss Harriet St Clair, of Balt.

Mrd: on Sep 14, at the Wood Yard, PG Co, Md, by Rev Mr Woods, Dr John B Hereford, of Va, to Miss Mary Lloyd, only daughter of the late Richd West.

The late Gen Jas Shelby, of Ky: a protracted visit to his estate on the Mississippi led to fever, which developed itself on his return, & terminated so fatally in a week, on Aug 5. He was in his 65th year. His children, & his brothers & sisters, & a numerous connexion, mourn his loss. Gen Shelby was the eldest child of the late Govn'r Shelby, & was born, in 1784, upon the farm in Lincoln Co which was the first settlement & pre-emption granted in Ky. His father had been led to the selection of the tract of land by killing a buffalo while hunting at the Knob Licks to supply meat for the garrison & families at Boonesborough. The buffalo was killed at the spot upon which he erected his first cabin, & where the State had done herself honor by placing a Monument over his remains. Young Shelby established himself about 8 miles from the town. The companion of his bosom was a daughter of the late Dr R Pindell, then of Hagerstown, Md, who was the Surgeon of Lafayette at the battle of Brandywine, & dressed that great patriot's wounds on that memorable day. She was also the niece of Mrs Clay, whose illustrious husband was the intimate friend of the deceased.

Mrd: on Sep 18, in the Presbyterian Church, Gtwn, D C, by Rev Septimus Tustin, late Chaplain of the U S Senate, Rev Danl Motzer, of Pa, to Miss Eliz Bloomer, eldest daughter of the late Wm Williamson, & grand-daughter of the late Stephen B Balch, D D, of Gtwn, D C.

Died: on Sep 10, at his residence in Chambersburg, Pa, after a lingering illness, Thos G McCulloh, Pres of the Chambersburg Bank, aged 63 years. Several years ago he represented his district in Congress, & was afterwards repeatedly honored with a seat in the Legislature from his native county.

Died: on Aug 25, at the Red Sulphur Springs, Va, Judge Lafayette Saunders, of Clinton, La. He was a native of Tenn, but many years ago removed to La, in which State he was much respected. He has left a widow & several children to deplore his loss.

Died: on Sep 1, at his residence, Unionville, Westchester Co, N Y, Isaac G Graham, M D, aged 68 years. He had lived over 60 years upon the same delightful spot where he reared a numerous progeny. At an early period of life Dr Graham joined the army of the Revolution as an Assist Surgeon, & was attached to the command of Gen Washington, at West Point.

Household & kitchen furniture at auction: on Sep 29, at the residence of Mrs Robinson, on Pa ave, between 6th & 7th sts. -Edw C & G F Dyer

WED SEP 20, 1848
A case of slander was tried in a N Y Court of Common Pleas last week, brought by Chas H Carpenter against Henry Shelden, for asserting that the plntf had been guilty of issuing counterfeit money. This case grew out of the Kid salvage humbug. The jury gave a verdict of $9,375 damages.

The Ladies Furnishing Store, Pa ave, between 4½ & 6th st. –Mary Alice Murray, Agent

Knickerbocker for Sep. Paintings of Henry J Brent, who has recently returned to his native country from a prolonged residence abroad: the *Entrance to Rothsay Bay, on the Clyde*; *A Shipwreck on the Coast of Scotland; The Stag, an American Scene; & The Misty Morning.*

Mrd: on Sep 17, by Rev Mr Foley, Wm Stewart to Eliz Alby, all of Wash City.

Died: on Sep 19, in Wash City, Jos Ennals, son of Capt Maynadier, U S Army, aged 1 year.

Household & kitchen furniture at auction: on Sep 27, at the residence of Capt W Warder, on 12th st, between B & C sts south, [Island.] -Edw C & G F Dyer

THU SEP 21, 1848
Md Chancery Case: An agreement was made with Sullivan & Sons, by Robt W Bowie, of PG Co, Md, for advances, acceptances, on the crops of 1847, then growing. He died in Jan, 1848, before their delivery, & before the wheat crop was matured, leaving a personal estate insufficient for the payment of his obligation. The Chancellor decided that the executor should deliver the crops that were ready for market at the time of the death, & those that became ready afterwards; or, in other words, granted a specific performance of the agreement; so that the deficiency of the personal estate will not affect the merchant, as it would do if he had been left to seek his remedy by damages at law against the executor.

Gen Riley's Calif Brig [2nd Regt U S Infty] arrived in N Y C on Mon, & are making preparations to embark in the steamer **Edith** & the steamer **Mississippi** for their destination. The Regt numbers 700. Its cmder Gen Riley, distinguished himself in the battles between Vera Cruz & the city of Mexico. The ofcrs are as follows: 1st Lt Hayden, in command of regt, & commanding ofcr of Co H; Dr Turner, Surgeon; Adj Jones, commanding Cos C & G; 1st Lt A Sully, Regimental Quartermaster, Commissary, & commanding Co K; 1st Lt Murray, commanding Co I; 1st Lt Shureman, commanding Co A; 1st Lt Jarvis, commanding Co B; 2nd Lt Hendershot, commanding Co F; 2nd Lt Johnson, commanding Co E; 2nd Lt Sweeney, commanding Co D.

Rise of real estate in Cincinnati: Mr Wm V Barr, son of the late Wm Barr, owner of the **Barr Farm**, states that his father gave $33.30 per acre for this property in 1811, thus says Mr Barr, paying $355.50 for what at this day, on an average of $30 per foot, which is low, is worth $9,304,000.00, without reference to the bldgs.

Adolphe Durant St Andre has been appointed Consul of the French Republic for the Port of Phil.

We learn from Dr Fechtig, of Poolesville, Montg Co, Md, that a man named John Pym, of good address & plausible manners, stole from Dr Fechtig, on Sat last, a dark chestnut horse, a saddle, bridle, & martingel, also a patent lever gold watch & chain. Pym sold the horse on Capitol Hill, to a person who had since restored the horse to the owner, minus $35, the purchase money. The Gtwn ofcrs are in pursuit of the thief.

St Mary's County Court, Aug Term, 1848. In the matter of the petition of Danl Washington & others for the division of the real estate whereof Nathl Washington died seized, the com'rs made return that the same could not be divided without loss to all the parties interested, & the said report was confirmed by the Court. I t is therefore ordered that notice be given to Eliz Washington, Jas Washington, Danl Washington, Olevia Washingon, Margaret Washington, & Washington Washington, parties entitled to said estate, & who are out of the State of Md. Said parties to appear the first Mon of Mar next. –A C Magruder, Chief Judge of St Mary's Co Court. –Wm T Maddox, Clerk St Mary's Co Clerk.

County School for Boys, at Cold Stream, 2 miles from Balt, Md: under the superintendence of Mr J Harman Brown, will commence on the 1st Mon of Oct.

Catoctin Whig: Mr John Maught, [or Mock] a worthy farmer residing between Jefferson & Knoxville, on the Harper's Ferry road, was killed on Tue last, by being run over by a wagon loaded with flour.

Died: on Sep 19, Jos L Scholfield, aged 88 years. The deceased was one of the pioneers of Wash. His funeral will take place this afternoon, at half-past 2 o'clock, at the residence of Henry Janney.

Died: on Sep 15, Wm W Stewart, in his 39th year, after a long & painful illness, leaving a devoted wife & doating mother.

Mr Edw F Beale, Passed Midshipman, arrived in this city on Sat, from Cmdor Jones' squadron in the Pacific, & is said to have performed the most rapid journey that has ever been known from the Pacific to Wash. He left La Pax on Aug 1. He brings intelligence about the real El Dorado, the Gold region in Calif. His accounts of the extraordinary richness of the gold surface, & the excitement it had produced among all classes of people, among them seamen & soldiers. Mr Beale states that whalers had suspended their operations-the capts permiting their seamen to go to the gold region, upon condition that every ounce of gold the seaman obtained should be given to the capt for $10, making 6 or 7 dollars by the bargain.

U S Navy Agency, Monterey, Calif, Jul 1, 1848. I visited the south fork of the river American, which joins the Sacramento at *Suter's Fort*, or 2 miles from it. This river has its north & south forks, branching more than 20 miles from *Fort Suter*. On these 2 forks there are over 1,000 people digging & washing for gold. I do not think I am exaggerating in estimating the amount of gold obtained on the rivers at $10,000 a day for the last few days. In 2 weeks Monterey will be nearly without inhabitants. –Thos O Larkin. [Letter to Com Thos Ap C Jones.]

Mrd: on Sep 20, at St Matthew's Church, by Rev Jas Donelan, Claude D Blanchard, of New Orleans, to Meda A Anderson, of Wash.

Farm for sale: 24 acres, 1 mile north of the Capitol, adjoining the lands of Mr David Moore & Mrs Beale: excellent site for a bldg. Apply to Mr Geo Moore or Mr David Moore, adjoining the premises, or to the subscriber, at his grocery store on Capitol Hill. –Jos Ingle, Agent
+
For rent: the farm adjoining the above, containing about 80 acres, at present occupied by Mr Geo Moore: with an excellent dwlg-house & all necessary outbldgs. It adjoins the lands of Mr John A Smith & Mr Ephraim Gilman. Also for rent, the frame dwlg-house, with brick back bldgs, on Capitol Hill, recently occupied by Mr Jas Moore, deceased. Apply to Jos Ingle, Atty

FRI SEP 22, 1848
Rev John Wheeler, D D, has resigned the Presidency of the Univ of Vt, a station he has held for 14 years, on account of ill health in his family, which renders a voyage to Europe indispensable. Rev Washington Smith, D C, of St Albans, Vt, has been chosen to succeed him.

The Portsmouth [N H] Journal records the drowning of Miss Nancy J Underhill, at the Isle of Shoals, on Sep 11. Her friends remonstrated with her, when she ventured too far down the declivity of the rock, when a wave struck her, & in a moment she was dashed from their sight.

Helen Mar, daughter of Mr Chas Russell, of Bath, Maine, aged about 10 years, & Adelaide, daughter of Mr Robt B Rogers, of Chelsea, Mass, aged about 12 years, left the residence of Mr Russell, on Sep 8, to take a walk in the woods. They were found drowned in the Sewall stream, this morning, when they got beyond their depth.

Jacob Mann, committed suicide, in Phil, Tue, by blowing his brains out, it seems, in consequence of his arrest the day previous for some alleged offence in an estate, of which he was executor. He committed the deed in the house of the ofcr, where he had slept during the night. He was a widower, aged 57, & much respected.

Household & kitchen furniture, & piano forte, at auction: on Sep 2, at the residence of Mr Geo Stettinius, at the corner of 9th & D sts. -A Green, auctioneer

Mrd: on Wed, by Rev Mr Morgan, Mr Robt Ball, of Va, to Miss Eliz Ann McElwee, of Wash City.

Mrd: on Sep 16, by Rev Ulysses Ward, Mr Robt Ferguson to Miss Ann Kilbreth.

Mrd: on Sep 13, by Friends' ceremony, at the residence of Geo Shoemaker, Dr Saml E Tyson, of Wash, to Rachel Lukens, of Gtwn, D C.

SAT SEP 23, 1848
Balt Sun of yesterday. Affray at Havre de Grace on Wed, between a stranger, Aldridge, & a citizen, Wm Thomas, the latter said to be very respectably connected. A dispute arose at the gaming table, & the parties then went out, & Thomas shot Aldridge with a pistol, the wound expected to be fatal. Thomas fled, arriving at Bel Air yesterday, & took a room at Magraw's tavern, & soon after shot himself in the head. He is not expected to live. His friend, Geo Yellot found him lying in the agonies of death. Mr Thomas was the son of the late Abraham J Thomas, of Havre de Grace, & was a brother of the late Herman S Thomas, who sacrificed his life in a impetuous charge on one of the strongholds of the enemy at Monterey. Wm, after his brother's death, joined the Texas Rangers, & served in that gallant band with distinguished bravery, & was honorably discharged.

Th H Barron, being desirous of emigrating to the West, earnestly solicits all persons to whom he is indebted to bring forward their accounts for settlement without delay. Bills left with H Barron, Dentist, Pa ave, between 6th & 7th sts, will be thankfully received & punctually attended to.

In pursuance of a decree of the High Court of Chancery, the undersigned will sell, on Oct 14, all that beautiful Farm, in PG Co, at present occupied by Smith Thompson. The farm lies upon the railroad from Wash to Balt, adjoining the Muirkirk furnace, & contains 328+ acres; 1½ miles from Beltsville: comfortable frame dwlg, kitchen, stables, carriage-house, & all necessary outbldgs. –J Glenn, Trustee

Died: on Sep 21, in her 49th year, Mrs Mary Ann Fenwick, consort of Philip Fenwick. Her funeral is this morning, at 11 o'clock, from her late residence, *Oak Grove*.

For sale: beautiful farm of 133 acres in Farifax Co, Va, adjoining the estates of Com Jones, Messrs Ball, Sherman, & others. The dwlg house is finely situated, painted & papered, with an extensive basement. Apply at the farm, or by letter addressed to Langley Post Ofc to Chas K Hyde.

The following Bounty Land Certificates, addressed from Wash, D C, to Jas H Raymond, Austin, Texas, are believed to have been stolen from the mail on Aug 20 last. The below can be of no use to anyone but the owners: 1-Wm Stiles, Bailard's Company, #2,598, for 40 acres, dated Jul 25, 1848. 2-Wm Wooseley, Cooper's Company, Miss, # 20,600, for 160 acres, date Jul 25, 1848. 3-Whitfield Chalk, Ross' Company, #20,183, for 160 acres, dated Jul 24, 1848. 4-Certificate #5714, for $55.98, for pay due Thos alias Robt B Roberts, deceased, private of Capt Ross' Co of Texas Mounted Volunteers, payable to me as atty of John C Pool, guardian, by an Paymaster of the U S, & by me endorsed to said Raymond. –Jno Underwood, Wash

Applications will be received by the undersigned until Nov 1 for the appointment of a Steward at the Va Military Institute. Address, post paid, Francis H Smith, Superintendent Va Military Inst, Lexington, Va.

MON SEP 25, 1848
Furnished room wanted, not far from Willard's Hotel, in a house where there were few or no other lodgers. Address Chas Silliman, Post Ofc.

Dissolution of copartnership of E F Queen & Brother by mutual consent. The business will herafter be conducted by Chas S Queen, Wash, Sep 25, 1848.

The New Haven Journal states that within the last 3 years Mr Wm Goodwin, of that city, has watched with the sick 842 days. Mr Goodwin has a heart that leads him in the direction of the sick.

Lyman Trumbull, John D Caton, & S H Treat, have been elected Judges of the Supreme Court of Ill, under the New Constitution.

Information from Belair that Mr Wm Thomas, whose act we noticed yesterday, expired at about midnight from the effects of his wound. Young Aldridge, whom he shot on Wed, is likely to recover.

There appeared some years ago, in one of our Phil papers, an account of a monument in a church in Wiltshire, Eng, to the memory of an ancestor of Washington, Sir Lawrence Washington, who died in 1643. Mr Macready, the tragedian, & his eldest son, made a pilgrimage to this tomb. His letter is dated 5 Clarence Terrace, Regent's Park, London, Aug 25, 1848. We found **Garsdon**, distant from Malmsbury about 3 miles, by my best guess. It is situated in a church yard, the church being plain to absolute bareness, without one trace of decoration beyond 4 or 5 separate panes of stained glass still remaining in the small Gothic windows. The monument is a black marble oval tablet, encircled by a thick wreath of laurel in berry, set beneath a cornice of white marble surmounted by the family arms, on each side of which are 2 recumbent figures, resembling the sort of personage I should describe as Libitina. The monument is about 6 feet, & broad in proportion. This is a copy of the inscription:
To the memory of
Sr LAWRENCE WASHINGTON, Kt.
Lately Chelfe Register of the Chancery,
Of known piety, of charitye exemplarye,
A lovinge husband, a tender father, a Bountiful
Master, a constant reliever of the poore,
and to those of this parish
A perpetuall Benefactour, whom it pleased God
To take unto his peace from the fury
of the insuing warrs
Oxon May XIVto
Here interred XXIVto Ano Dmi 1643.
Aetat sum, 64.
Where allso Lyeth
Dame Ann his Wife, who deceased
Junii XIII to and was buryed
XVIto Ano Dmii. 1645.

Hic patrios cineres curavit filius urna
Condere, qui tumulo nune jacet ille pius.
The pious son his parent here inter'd,
Who hath his share in Urne for them prepar'd.
+
The Manor House on the opposite hill is a substantial feudal residence of about the time of Edward 4th. A stone slab, with the Washington arms, is in an old mansion, which is a very interesting bldg, still tenanted by respectable farmers of the name of Woody. In looking into the 1st volume Appendix of Washington's Life, by Sparks, I find a mention of this collateral branch of the family, though the crest is the same, the arms differ.
Believe me, my dear sir, your, very faithfully, W C Macready.

St Peter's Church, on Capitol Hill, of which the Rev Mr Van Horsigh is the esteemed pastor, is now undergoing a complete alteration. Is is one of the most spacious & neat church edifices in Wash City.

After the Convention at Atlanta a few day ago, while on his way to join his family at the Stone Mountain, the Hon John McP Berrien left by the regular train of cars, & was sent down after night by the agent on a dirt cart propelled by hands. This was met by the up-train, & dashed to pieces in a moment. Before the collision Mr Berrien jumped from the car, but, his cloak catching, threw him within a foot of the rail. In this position he remained until the locomotive had passed, when he was picked up & taken back to Atlanta. Two gentlemen with him were slightly injured. –Columbus Enquirer

The new Orphans' Asylum is about to be erected in Wash City & to be under the charge of the <u>Sisters of Mercy</u>. The large brick bldg in which the Asylum was formerly is now about to be reopened as a Seminary of learning, under the charge of the Rev John E Blox & other experienced teachers from Gtwn College.

Valuable property at auction: by deed of trust from John Sessford & wife to Jas Thrift, dated Jan 1, 1846, recorded in Liber W B 124, folios 109 thru 111, of the land records of Wash Co, D C, & a subsequent decree of the Circuit Court of Wash Co, D C, sitting as a Court of Chancery, made in the case of Nicolas Febrey vs John Sessford, & Jas Thrift: sale on

Died: on Sep 23, in Wash City, Francis Corday Labbe, in his 64th year. He was extensively known as a successful teacher of dancing. He was a native of L'Orient, in France, a nephew of that extraordinary woman, Charlotte Corday, whose daring hand relieved her country of one of the bloodiest scourges, Jean Paul Marat, a leader of the Mountain party in 1793. He was a midshipman in the French navy, & a prisoner of war to the English. Over 40 years he has been a citizen of the U S. His funeral is today at 11:30 o'clock, from his late residence on Pa ave, opposite Williard's Hotel.

From Texas. The Huntsville Banner reports a murder in Tyler Co: Jackson & Jas Cheshire, & their half-brother, got into a fight with a man named Pullam, which ended in the killing of the latter. The Cheshire party were seen to throw Pullam into the river & leave. His body was found with his throat cut, & his nose & both ears bit off. Jackson Cheshire has seen been apprehended. Large reward offered for the others.

Hon Wm T Senter, formerly a Rep in Congress from Tenn, died at his residence in Granger Co, Tenn, on Aug 28, aged 47 years.

TUE SEP 26, 1848
Household & kitchen furniture at auction: on Oct 3, at the residence of Dr W Brooke Jones, on L st, between 5th & 6th sts. -Edw C & G F Dyer

Notice: I wish to purchase of servant girl, 10 or 12 years old, of good character. I will give a liberal price for one. I would prefer one from the country. –A Lee, Washington

Wanted immediately, 2 or 3 first-rate hands to work at the Dress Making business. Also, a few apprentices. Inquire of Miss E Hill, south side Pa ave, next to Miller's Confectionary.

Recent accident on the Auburn railroad: some of the persons injured, as follows: Mr Duffer, of Wheeling, Ill, & Mr Hubbard, of Haffiday, Ill, were seriously injured; Isaac A Smith, of N Y, was cut on the head; E W Farrington, of Geneva, A H Brown, of Neward, & P W Clark, of Oxford, scalded, the last very severely; & Miss Ann Smith, of the Blind Asylum, N Y, slightly scalded & bruised.

Mrd: on Sep 21, by Rev L F Morgan, Mr Jas Frasier to Miss Mary Eliz Mullikin, both of Wash City.

WED SEP 27, 1848

Wash Corp: 1-Ptn of Jas A Wise & others for the improvement of M st, from 7th to 14th sts: referred to the Cmte on Improvements. 2-Cmte of Claims: act for the relief of Robt B Clokey: passed. 3-Cmte of Claims: bill for the relief of Presley Simpson: passed. Same cmte: relief of John Webster: passed. 4-Nominations for City Commissioners confirmed: Geo W Harkness, John Sessford, C P Wannall, F B Lord, W A Mulloy, Ignatius Mudd, & John Magar. For Police Constables: I F Wollard, E G Handy, & John Magar. Jas Gaither & John P Hilton, for Wood Corders & Coal Measurers. Jas Gaither, for Measurer of bran & shorts. Geo T McGlue, for Scavenger. 5-Ptn of John Boyle & others for improvement of 10th st west & R I ave: referred to the Cmte on Improvements. 6-Ptn of Patrick McGarvey, praying remission of a fine: referred to the Cmte of Claims.

The Capitol is about to receive its first coat of pain, to be executed under the supervision of the Com'r of Public Bldgs, who has engaged Messrs Offutt & Finch, 2 experienced painters of this city, to inspect the work & see to its faithful execution.

On Wed last the dwlg-house of Lawrence Harter, of Warren, Herkimer Co, N Y, was entirely destroyed by fire, & Jas Henry & David, the only children of Mr Harter, aged about 4 & 2 years, were consumed in the flames. Mr & Mrs Harter were absent on business, & had left the children in the care of Henry Miller, a young lad who was living in their family. He put the boys to sleep, & left the house, which was soon discovered to be all in flames.

Jesse Oakley, Clerk of the Superior Court of N Y, shot himself through the head with a pistol on Sat, in a water closet of the City Hall. He was about 55 years of age, a native of Poughkeepsie. His salary was about $3,000 per annum. He leaves no family of his own, but contributed to the support of a widowed sister.

Dr Jacob L Martin, American Charge d'Affaires at Rome, died at Rome about Sep 1, very suddenly, being found dead in his bed without any known preliminary illness. He was a native, we believe, of N Carolina.

Jas Russell, Jos Phelps, & Jas Williams were a few months ago convicted by the Phil Court of Sessions for robbing the house of Mr Kempton. A few days ago, Russell, who became dangerously ill, confessed he had perjured himself on the trial, & that Phelps & Williams were entirely innocent, 2 different men, who are at large, being his accomplices.

Newport News: the funeral of Mrs Martha Taber took place on Tue, at the North Captist Church, when a very appropriate address was delivered by Rev Dr Choules. The age of the deceased was 104 years & 6 months. She had a sister at the funeral whose age is 93 years, & a niece aged 78 years.

Late from Santa Fe, Aug 1. Our volunteer troops had another severe fight with the Apaches & Eutaws on Jul 18. They were pursued beyond the Ratone mountains by Capt Roake, of the Missouri mounted regt & 60 men. The Indians retreated, leaving behind some 32 head of horses & mules. Maj Reynolds followed with 150 men, joined the advance, & with Williams, Fisher, Mitchell, & Kirker, mountaineers, as guides, continued the pursuit, & came up with a detachment of some 400 Indians. A fight ensued, the Indians retreating, leaving 25 of their number dead on the field. Two of our men were killed & 6 wounded. Capt Salmon, & Old Bill Williams, the mountaineer, were wounded.

Since my removal to Gtwn, residence & ofc west end of 1st st, opposite *Coxe's Row*, many of my Wash patients have called on me, & those who wish to avail themselves of my professional services may do so by calling as early in the day as convenient.
–Wm P McConnell, Surgeon Dentist

Fatal re-encounter between 2 of our estimable citizens: Henry A Crabbe & John Jenkins, one of the editors of the Sentinel, at the political meeting of Tue. Yesterday the 2 gentlemen met on Washington st; words ensued; Mr Jenkins stabbed Mr Crabbe, when the latter presented a pistol & shot Jenkins in the heart, killing him almost instantly. Mr Crabbe is mortally wounded. Mr Jenkins leaves an estimable lady & several children. Both of them have always been regarded as peaceful men. –Vicksburg Whig, 16th.

On Sep 16, Col Francis Lee, 4th Regt U S Army, & his lady, were going from Jefferson barracks to St Louis in a buggy. As they descended the hill by the barracks hospital, the harness having been improperly put on, the buggy ran upon the horse, the animal became frightened, & broke off in a desperate rate up the road. Col Lee was thrown upon the ground, his head stunned for some time. The horse dragged Mrs Lee in the carriage over every obstacle that presented itself. A young man, Dousberger, 1st Sgt of Co H, 8th Regt Infty, sprang forward & seized the reins near the horse's mouth. The horse rushed on, &, as he plunged, the end of the shaft penetrated Mr Dousberger's body several inches, below the breast, & he fell instantly dead. Mrs Lee remained in the carriage & escaped unhurt. Sgt Dousberger was about 22 years of age; served with honor throughout the Mexican war, & was in the most of the principal battles. -Republican

The work of filling up the low ground on the north side of Indiana ave, has been under the supervision of Mr Wm Dowling.

Mrd: on Sep 26, by Rev Mathias Alig, of St Mary's Church, Mr Jos Leo Schneider to Appolonia Polluck, both of Wash City.

Died: on Sep 25, Mrs Mary Hanson, relict of the late Col Saml Hanson, of Saml, at an advanced age. Her funeral is tomorrow, at 12 o'clock, from the residence of Miss Hanson, on La ave, near 6th st.

Died: on Sep 16, at Rockville, Md, Dr Thos Patterson, aged 74, formerly a resident of Wash City, & well known as a skillful practioner. He had for many years suffered from mental & physical debility. He leaves his widow & children to mourn his loss.

Died: on Sep 15, at Pascagoula, Miss, after a short illness of congestive fever, Mr Dennis Velmillion, in his 51st year. He was long a resident of Wash City.

Died: on Sep 26, in Gtwn, D C, in her 29th year, after a long & painful illness, Ann C, daughter of the late Jas & Mary G Belt, & wife of Richd L Mackall, leaving a husband & 4 little children to deplore their irreparable loss. Her funeral is today at 4 o'clock, from the residence of her husband, on Washington st.

THU SEP 28, 1848
The following will show the time when the "New States," or those not included in the "Old Thirteen," were admitted into the Union:
Vermont originally was part of N Y, & admitted into the Union, Jun 1, 1791.
Ky, formerly a part of Va, admitted into the Union Jun 1, 1792.
Tenn, formed of territory ceded to the U S by the State of N C: admitted into the Union Jun 1, 1796.
Ohio, formed of part of the territory northwest of the Ohio: admitted into the Union Nov 29, 1802.
Louisiana, formed out of part of the territory ceded to the U S by France: admitted into the Union Apr 8, 1812.
Indiana formed out of a part of the Northwest Territory ceded to the U S by Va: admitted into the Union Dec 11, 1816.
Mississippi, formed out of a part of the territory ceded to the U S by the State of S C: admitted into the Union Dec 10, 1817.
Illinois, formed out of part of the Northwester Territory: admitted into the Union Dec 3, 1818.
Alabama, formed out of a part of the territory ceded to the U S by S C & Ga: admitted into the Union Dec 15, 1818.
Maine, formed out of a part of Mass: admitted into the Union Mar 15, 1820.
Missouri, formed out of a part of the territory ceded by France by treaty of Apr 30, 1803: admitted into the Union Aug 10, 1821: after the adoption of the noted compromise line excluding slavery from all territory north of 36 degrees west of the Mississippi, saving States or Territories already formed.

Arkansas, formed part of the same territory: admitted Jun 15, 1838.
Michigan formed part of the territory ceded to the United States by Va: admitted into the Union Jan 26, 1837.
Florida, formed out of the territory ceded by Spain to the United States by treaty of Feb 22, 1819: admitted into the Union Mar 3, 1845.
Texas, an independent republic: admitted into the United States by a joint resolution of Congress, approved Mar 28, 1847.
Iowa, admitted into the Union, Dec 26, 1846.
Wisconsin: an act was passed on Mar 3, 1847, to admit this Territory into the Union upon the condition that the people adopt the constitution passed Dec 16, 1846. This constitution was rejected; but the people having subsequently agreed upon a constitution, the State was admitted into the Union by act of Congress May 29, 1848.
Territories-Nebraska, Bill reported to fix boundaries Jan 7, 1845; but no action on the subject.
Oregon: Bill to establish a Territorial Gov't passed House of Reps Jan 16, 1847; no final action on the subject in the Senate during that session. In 1848 a bill passed both Houses of Congress, & was approved by the Pres on Aug 14, establishing a Territorial Gov't.
Minnesota: Bill to establish a Territorial Gov't passed the House Feb 17, 1848; referred to Judiciary Cmte in Senate. No further action on the subject.

For rent: the brick house, with furniture, if desired, at the corner of F & 20th sts, First Ward. Inquire on the premises, or of Saml Stott.

Passed Midshipman Edw Fitzgerald Beale recently arrived from the Western coast, brings news of the discovery, now at last, at the western base of the Sierra Nevada, of the real Dorado. [The account of his travels is covered in 2 columns in the paper.]

The 25th Annual Session of the Alexandria Boarding School will commence on Oct 2. For further particulars see circulars. –Benj Hallowell, Alexandria

Georgia Journal & Messenger: after proceeding as far as Griffin, on his way to attend his appointments in Wilkinson Co, the Hon Alex'r H Stephens was obliged to desist, & return home. His hand had grown extremely painful, & the general debility of his system increased so, that it was advisable that he abandon all idea of further engaging in the fatigues of the campaign.

Court of Oyer & Terminer of N Y: on Sat, Thos Hayes, convicted of murder, [killing his wife,] & Jacob Haifler, convicted of manslaughter in the 2nd degree, [killing Patrick Cogan,] was put to the bar. Hayes was sentenced to be hung on Nov 17. Haifler was sentenced to the State prison at Sing Sing for 7 years.

Superior Court of Dinwiddie, Va: Judge Nash presiding: on Mon week. Dandridge Epes, charged with the murder of Adolphus F Muir. Trial commenced on Tue last, & a jury was procured on Thu. [Sep 30th newspaper: the jury have brought in a verdict of guilty. Epes is sentenced to be hung on Dec 2.]

For rent: 2 fine houses in ***Carroll Place***, Capitol Hill. Also, valuable City Lots for sale. Inquire of Ben E Green, ofc C st, between 4½ & 6th sts.

Household & kitchen furniture, & brick house & lot at auction, in Gtwn, on Oct 3, at the residence of Mr W King, on Jefferson st, near Bridge st, Gtwn. -A Green, auctioneer -P S-also, a good milch Cow will be sold immediately after the sale of the furniture.

Mrd: on Sep 27, in Wash City, by Rev Thos Foley, Mr Peter Follain, of France, to Miss Terese Caroline Wills, of Grand Coteau, La, daughter of Fred'k & Terese Wills.

Died: on Wed, Robt B, only son of Wm D & Isabella A Brackenridge, aged 20 months & 5 days. His funeral is on Fri, at 10 o'clock, from the family residence, on 6th st, between G & H sts.

Died: on Sep 25, at his residence, Richland, near Fredericktown, Md, Mr Chas S Hammond, in his 33rd year. He leaves a bereaved widow & a large circle of dead friends.

Died: on Sat last, in Gtwn, in her 21st year, Mrs Martha E Read, consort of Mr Igns Davis Read, & lately of Montg Co, Md.

$100 reward for runaway negro man Patrick Marlow, about 27 years old. His ears are pierced for ear-rings, which he usually wears. –Philip Stone, living in Montg Co, Md.

FRI SEP 29, 1848
We observed mechanics & laborers busily employed painting the Capitol on the outside, & improving the open lots facing the western front of the bldg, between the ***Tiber creek*** & the foot of the Capitol.

City Ordinances-Wash. 1-Act for the relief of John Fletcher: to be paid the sum of $452.23, being the balance due him for gravelling 4½ st from Indiana ave to Pa ave.

Mrd: Sep 20, in Balt, by Rev J P Donelan, Wm P Mohun to Miss Mary M, only daughter of Jos Baker, of Balt, Md.

Died: yesterday, in Wash City, in her 21st year, Emily Ann, consort of Saml C Espey. She bore a lingering pulmonary illness with a fortitude only known to those who place their reliance in the will of an all wise Provicence, into whose hands she calmly resigned her soul. Her funeral is tomorrow at 2 p m. from the residence of her father, Mr Fielder Burch, on 14th st, near F st.

Died: at the residence of Edw Watts, Roanoke Co, Va, Miss Catherine L Turpin, of Wash, D C, in her 24th year, by that dreadful malady, consumption. May she rest in peace. [No death date given-current item.]

Whig celebration of the battles of Monterey were celebrated in Wash City on Fri last. W W Seaton presided; introduced Francis L Smith, of Alexandria. Coleman Yellott, of Balt, was next introduced. Geo Wash Parke Custis, the venerable & only surviving member of Gen Washington's family, was introduced. In his own rich full-toned voice the old orator addressed the attentive crowd, for three quarters of an hour. Col John A Rogers, of Pa, who was with Gen Cass is a capt in the regular army in the war of 1812, was next introduced. Col Sherman, of Wash City, being loudly called for by the crowd, next stepped forward.

SAT SEP 30, 1848
Orphans Court of Wash Co, D C. Letters of administration on the personal estate of Thos Dalton, late of the U S Marine Corps, deceased. –Jos Ehrmanntrant, adm

Kosciusko's Estate, Circuit Court of D C, in Chancery. John F Ennis, adm de bonis non of the estates of Jos Zolkowski, & others, vs Jonathan B H Smith, adm of the estate of Geo Bomford; Lewis Johnson, adm de bonis non of Gen Thadeus Kosciusko, [Kosciuszko,] deceased. The bill states that said Gen Thadeus Kosciusko, a native of Lithuania, formerly a part of Poland, now a province of Russia, was in his lifetime & at the time of his death possessed of a large personal property in the U S of America & in various parts of Europe. He made & executed 4 wills or testaments; first, on or about May 5, 1798, in this country, by which he named the late Thos Jefferson as exc, & bequeathed to him all his personal property in the U S, for certain charitable purposes; second, on or about Jun 28, 1806, at Paris, in France, by which he bequeathed to a certain Kosciusko Armstrong $3,704, & for so much revoked the first will; third, bearing date of Jun 4, 1816, made & executed at Soleure, in Switzerland, by which he bequeathed certain legacies to Thadea Emilie Wilchelmine Zeltner, Marie Charlotte Julie Marqueritte Zeltner, & Bonnissant Pere, directed that they should be paid over out of his funds being in France in the hands of Mr Hottinger, or out of any other if that should not be sufficient, & revoked all the wills or testaments which he might have previously made; fourth, bearing date of Oct 10, 1817, made & executed also at Soleure, in Switzerland, by which he bequeathed certain legacies to Gen Baszkoyski, Emelie Zeltner, Mr & Mrs Zavier Zeltner, Mr & Mrs Edw Zeltner, Zavier Amieth, adm of said will, Miss ___ Wagnery, Dr ___ Schurer, & Miss Ursula Zeltner, & directed that they should be paid over out of his funds being in England & Switzerland, leaving the will or testament of Jun 4, 1816, aforesaid, unrevoked & in full force, except as regards the last mentioned legacies. The bill then charges that all said legacies by the will of Jun 4, 1816, & of Oct 10, 1817, have been fully paid & satisfied out of the funds specified therein, which said Kosciusko left in France, England, & Switzerland; that he made no other will of any kind in relation to personal property, & died intestate as to the property left in the U S on or about Oct 15, 1817; & that France was his permanent residence, though he happened to die in Switzerland. It then goes on to show that said Gen Kosciusko died unmarried & without issue; that he had a brother, Jos, who died before him without issue, & 2 sisters, Anna & Catherine; that his sister Anna married Peter Estko; that she survived her husband & died intestate before her brother, said Thadeus Kosciusko, leaving 3 children, viz: Roman Estko, Louisa Narbut born Estko, & Martina Estko, which last mentioned died in 1840, unmarried, intestate, & without issue, & Stanislaus Estko, who survived his mother, said

Anna, & his uncle, said Kosciusko, & died in 1820, leaving one son, Hippolitus Estko. That said Catharine married Chas Zolkowski, survived him, & died also before her brother, said Kosciusko; that she had 7 children, viz: Jos, John, Ignatius, Carolina, Bregida, Anna, & Helena, who all survived her except Ignatius; that said Jos Zolkowski survived his uncle, & died married & without issue, leaving a will, whereby he devised his share in the estate of Kosciusko, one-half to Hippolitus Wankowiez & Vladislaus Wankowiez, another half to Michl Szyrma; that said John Zolkowski survived also his uncle, was married to Eliz Bychowice, whom he also survived, & then died without issue, having previously assigned his portion in said estate to Adam Bychowice; that said Ignatius Zolkowski died before his mother, wife, & uncle, leaving one dght, Isabella, who was married to Ignatius Wankowiez, survived him & her uncle, said Kosciusko, left 2 children, viz: Hippolitus Wankowiez & Vladislaus Wankowiez, & died intestate; that said Carolina, Bregida, & Anna Zolkowski survived their uncle, said Kosciusko, & died unmarried, without issue, & intestate; that said Helena Zolkowski was married to a certain Korosof, whom she survived; she also survived her said uncle, & died intestate & without issue. The bill then shows & charges that, by the laws of Lithuania, & also by the laws of France in force at the time of Kosciusko's death, the succession to the whole estate which he left in the U S was cast upon the descendants of his said sisters representing the parents living at the time of his death; & it further charges that the cmplnts, together with said Roman Estko & Louisa Narbut born Estko are the only next of kin entitled to the distribution of Kosciusko's estate in portions aforesaid. It then admits that Hippolitus Estko assigned his portion to Catharine Estko, but avers that she has now no right thereto nor interest therein. The bill further shows that said Thos Jefferson declined the executorship given to him by the first testamentary paper; that before the exhibition & probate of the other 3 testamentary papers, letters of administration, cum testamento annexe, were granted to the Orphans' Court of the District of Columbia to a certain Benj L Lear; that he died without having made distribution of any part of the estate; & that after his death, on Dec 28, 1832, administration de bonis non of Kosciusko's estate was granted to Geo Bomford; that the several persons who became security for said Bomford, in his first administration bond, died, & the bond became barred by limitation, in consequence of which said Bomford, administrator, at the instance of some of the cmplnts, & under orders of the Court, gave 2 other bonds, which were duly executed & filed in the Orphans Court of D C, one on May 7, 1846, & the other on Jan 4, 1847, giving Jas Carrico, Saml Stott, & Geo C Bomford as sureties in one bond, & Jacob Gideon, Ulysses Ward, & Jonathan B H Smith as sureties in another bond; that said Geo Bomford executed a certain deed of trust to the said Jonathan B H Smith to secure his sureties; that in his lifetime, as administrator of Kosciusko's estate, he, said Bomford, possessed himself of a very large amount of the estate, to the value of $58,000, which he converted to his own use, & died insolvent on or about Mar 27, 1848, without having made distribution to any part of the estate amongst the cmplnts; that, in consequence of his death, administration de bonis non of Kosciusko's estate was granted by said Orphans' Court to Lewis Johnson; that Jonathan B H Smith obtained letters of administration upon said Geo Bomford's estate. And it appearing to the Court that several dfndnts in this case, viz: said Roman Estko, Louisa Narbut born Estko, Catharine Estko, Thadea Emilie Wilchclmine Zeltner, Maria Charlotte Julis Marqueritte Zeltner, Bonnissant Pere, General Baszkoyski, Emilie Zeltner,

Mr & Mrs Zavier Zeltner, Mr & Mrs Edw Zeltner, Zavier Amieth, Miss Wagnery, Dr Schurer, & Miss Ursula Zeltner do not reside in the U S, but, so far as it appears to the Court, some of the said dfndnts reside in Poland under the Gov't of Russia, some in France, & some in Switzerland; it is, therefore, by this Court, on motion of the Solicitor of the cmplnts, G Tochman, ordered, this 26th day of Sep, 1848, that said absent dfndnts be & appear before this Court, in person or by solicitors, on or before Mar 1, 1849, to answer the cmplnts' said bill, or to show cause why a decree should not be passed as prayed by said bill, otherwise the same will be taken pro confesso against them. –Jas S Morsell, Assoc Judge of the Circuit Court of D C. –W Brent, clerk

Mrd: on Sep 27, by Rev E C Bittinger, Richd Thompson, M D, of the city of Mexico, to Miss Mary E Lyon, daughter of Levi Lyon, of Fairfield, Conn.

Mrd: on Sep 27, by Rev E C Bittinger, Chas Oliver Joline, of Chilicothe, Ohio, to Miss Mary E Hoffman, daughter of Dr Hoffman, of Sing Sing, N Y.

Mr Fillmore's origin: Millard Fillmore is a native of N Y: born in Cayuga Co, at a place called *Summer Hill*, on Jan 7, 1800. His father, Nathl Fillmore, was born in Burlington, Vt, 1771; he emigrated in early life to the western part of N Y, then a wilderness, & in 1819 purchased a farm in Erie Co, which he still cultivates. At age 19, young Fillmore met the late Walter Wood. Judge Wood, a lawyer, possessed a good library & a handsome fortune. He prevailed unpon Fillmore to quit the trade of wool-carding & take to the study of law. In 1821 he removed to Erie Co, & entered a lawyer's ofc in Buffalo. Mr Fillmore is in his 49th year, a fine lusty looking man, with a sanquine temperament, a tall commanding presence, & a grave but good-natured countenance. He is an excellent specimen of a genuine Northern Yankee, as Old Rough & Ready is of the Southern breed.

The N Y papers announce the death of the Hon Michl Hoffman, formerly of Herkimer Co, but for the last few years past Naval Ofcr for the port of N Y. He died at Brooklyn on Wed, at the advanced age of 60. -Journal of Commerce

Wm A Leidesdorff, lately Vice Consul at San Francisco, Calif, died there on May 18, after a short illness. He was a Dane by birth, but was formerly well known as a sea captain in the ports of New Orleans & N Y. He was much esteemed in Calif, & every demonstration of respect to his memory was made by the residents of San Francisco.

The Arkansas Intelligencer reports that Martin Benge, son of Capt John Benge, murdered Geo Fields, both Cherokees, in the Cherokee Nation, on Aug 31. It was a cold-blooded, desperate affair. The father & friends of Benge held Fields while Benge plunged a bowie-knife into him; he died on the spot. The difficulty grew up at a horse race. Young Benge is said to be a perfect desperado, who has often been screened by his father's influence from punishment. The old man has been arrested.

For rent: a comfortable 2 story brick house on 13th st, near Md ave. Apply to Mrs Cheshire, 19th st, a few doors north of Pa ave.

Patrick Coonan, assistant barkeeper at Willard's Hotel, died suddenly there on Wed night, or early on Thu morning. He had been sick a day or two, & a dose was prescribed for him, by mistake, of 15 grams of morphine instead of so much quinine. Patrick had a wife & 2 children living in the State of N Y.

On Wed the dead body of a German, Danl Miller, aged about 35 years, was found floating in the Potomac near the Long Bridge. He had been missing for several days, & his neighbors considered him of unsound mind. Coroner's verdict was rendered that the deceased was found drowned in the Potomac.

The N Y Tribune, edited by Horace Greeley, appeared this morning, Sep 29, with the Taylor & Fillmore flag at the head of its columns in bold characters.

Lands for sale: a tract of 25 acres near the farm of John Agg, north of the Capitol: no improvements. Also, a tract of about 90 acres in Alexandria Co, Va, about 5 miles from the Centre Market-house. –W A Bradley

New Store under Brown's Hotel, for the sale of Gentlemen's Furnishing Goods. –T Bastianelli & Co

MON OCT 2, 1848

City Ordinance-Wash. Act for the relief of John Webster: that $19 be paid for the claim of Webster, for repairing the culvert at Va ave & 3rd sts east. Approved: Sep 28, 1848.

Maj John P Gaines, who has been seriously if not dangerously ill at his residence in Boone Co, Ky, is now rapidly recovering.

The wife & 4 children of Mr Wm Lamoreaux, who keeps the ferry on the Schoharie creek, near Sloansville, N Y, have, within a week or two, all fallen victims to a disease which has prevailed to an alarming extent in that vicinity. The youngest of the children was but 2 months, the eldest about 13 years. The disease is pronounced by the physicians to be a malignant dysentery.

Fatal Leap. A young man by the name of Munn jumped over the bank of the Genesee river, about 200 feet down, at Mount Morris, on Sun, & was instantly dashed to pieces.

Orphans Court of Wash Co, D C. Letters of administration on the personal estate of John W Williams, late of said county, deceased. –Wm F Purcell, adm

Foreign Items: Dr James & his wife, missionaries from the U S, were recently lost in a vessel off Hong Kong.

Mrd: on Sep 21, at Newmarket, by Rev Joshua Peterkin, Dr Jas T Johnson, jr, to Nannie, daughter of Dr E W Mobelly, all of Fred'k Co, Md.

Mrd: on Sep 27, at St Peter's Church, by Rev Jos Van Horsigh, Mr Wm E Short, of Alexandria, Va, to Miss Eliz A Bright, of Wash City.

Died: on Sep 30, Ann Willamina Sengstack, daughter of Chas P Sengstack, in her 23rd year. Her funeral is on Oct 2, at the residence of her father, at 11 o'clock.

Died: on Sep 30, in Wash City, of disease of the heart, Mrs Ann Wason, consort of Mr Edw Wason, in her 64th year, leaving a devoted husband & a numerous family of children to mourn their irreparable loss. Her funeral is on Oct 3, at 2 o'clock, from her late residence, near the Navy Yard.

TUE OCT 3, 1848
The handsome church edifice, St Paul's English Lutheran Church, was dedicated Sun. Amongst those present was noticed the Pres of the U S & the Sec of State. Rev Mr Conrad, of Hagerstown, delivered the sermon; Rev Doct Morris, of Balt, preached in the evening. Nearly $1,000 was collected towards the bldg expenses.

In Jul last a little daughter of Mrs Williams, of Laporte, Sullivan Co, Pa, disappeared, & was lost in the wilderness in that county. On Sep 16 some of the remains were accidentally found about a mile north of Laporte. The clothes were identified by the mother.

On Oct 3, 2 boats upset at the Quebec Regatta, & Mr Theodore Martin, a clerk in the firm of Messrs Patterson, Young, & Co, drowned. Several others also perished.

Phil, Oct 2. Com Jas Biddle, late cmder of the East India squadron, died last night in Phil. He distinguished himself in the naval service in the war of 1812.

Mrd: on Sep 28, in Gtwn, by Rev N P Tillinghast, Dr Jas F Harrison, of the U S Navy, to Miss Amanda Gwynn Noble, of Gtwn.

Died: on Sep 30, in Wash City, at her father's residence, Mrs Ann Eliz Rawlings, wife of Wm A Rawlings, of Gtwn, D C, & daughter of John & Eliz Brown, in her 23rd year. She has left a husband & child to mourn her loss.

Died: on Fri week, at his residence near Jackson, Miss, of congestive chills, after a short illness, Mr Wm Gahan, in about his 68th year. He was a native of the town of Enniscorthy, county of Wexford, Ireland, but had been a resident of the U S for more than 30 years, about 26 of which were passed in Wash City. He raised & educated in a liberal manner 2 sons & 2 dghts, who, with an affectionate wife, survive to deplore & lament his loss. –Jackson Southron

Died: on Sep 24, at his residence, near West Rushville, Ohio, our venerable old friend Edw Murphy, in his 77th year, who has left a wife & a large circle of friends to mourn their irreparable loss.

Valuable 3 story brick house & lot at auction: on Oct 9, located on 12th st, between F & G sts, being the house built by Mr Isaac C Smith. Title indisputable. -A Green, auctioneer

Valuable land at auction: 92½ acres, in Fairfax Co, Va, fronting on the west side of Little Falls turnpike road, a short distance from the Chain Bridge or from Gtwn. The property belonged to Mr Isaac C Smith; surrounded with the best society, being in the immediate neighborhood of Messrs Wagaman & Slade. -A Green, auctioneer

Good 2 story frame house & lot at auction: on Oct 5, on H st, between 6th & 7th sts, being the house belonging to Mr D S Waters. Title indisputable. -A Green, auctioneer

WED OCT 4, 1848
Wash Corp: 1-Act for the relief of Wm P Shedd & others: reported without amendment. 2-Cmte of Claims: act for the relief of E D & H A Willard: read. 3-Communication was received from Amos Holton, offering himself as a candidate for the ofc of police magistrate of the 2nd Ward: laid on the table. 4-Bill for the relief of J E Thompson & others: referred to the Cmte on Public Schools. 5-Act for the relief of Saml Cromwell: referred to the Cmte of Claims. 6-Act for the relief of Jas Crutchett: referred to the Cmte of Claims. 7-Act for the relief of P Simpson: referred to the Cmte of Claims. 8-Ptn of Geo Humes & others: for a railroad route along K st & a depot near K st & 7th: referred to the Cmte on Improvements. 9-Ptn of Anthony Holmead & others for the extension of the Centre Market on La ave, between 9th & 10th sts: referred to the Cmte on Police.

On Sep 22, the 7 year old son of Mr Jas Sheetz, residing on the Phil turnpike, near Reading, fell into a boiling kettle of soap just taken from the fire, & died in a few hours.

<u>Persons who have taken out licenses under the laws of the Wash Corp during July, Aug, & Sep:</u>

Alexander, John: dog
Adams, J G: cart
Adams, R H: huckster
Blagden, Thos: dog
Burrell, John: dog
Boarman, S B: dog
Burns, C: dog
Bailey, J R: dog
Brereton & Bro: dog
Brosnaham: retail
Bowen, Jas A: hack-transfer
Blagden, Thos: lumber
Butler & Thomas: huckster
Baylies & Skidmore: huckster-3
Boteler, Chas W: auction
Brown & Nicholls: theatre
Brereton & Bro: cart
Burke, Wm H: cart

Conner, John: tavern
Callon, Lawrence: shop
Cronin, John: retail
Creutschel, G P: confectionary
Cruit, Jas: huckster-transfer
Casparis, Jas: tenpins
Dowling, Wm: shop
Donavan, W: retail
Dyer, E C & G F: retail-transfer
Donaldson, W: hack
Dowling, W: cart-2
Dobbyn, G W: huckster
Davis, A: huckster
Dyer, E C & G F: auction-transfer
Ellis, Richd: huckster
Edelen, C: slave
Fitzhugh, Clem't: dog
Fuller, Edw H: tavern

Frazier, Geo W: retail
Fasnaught, Geo: cart
Fearson, J C: huckster
Foley, John: huckster
Grainger, Peter: dog
Grymes, J M: dog
Garner, C W: dry goods
Gildermeister, H: cart
Gill, John: cart
Gross, J W: huckster
Henning, Stephen: dog
Honethamp, H: shop
Holden, F: retail
Hall, John: cart
Horseman, Elijah: huckster
Hamilton, P H: slave
Holroyd, Jno: dog
Jones, Peter: cart
Jones, Andrew: cart
Johnson, W P: cart
Jost, B: tenpin alley-2
Keiser, A: dog
Knott, G A: dog
King, Elijah: cart
King, Martin: cart
Klopfer, F A: huckster
Kinner, E: slave
Kehrer, Michl: shop
Lewis & Elisha: huckster
McDonald, W J: dog-2
Meehan, J M: dog
McIntyre, Walter: shop
Milstead, Robt: retail
Mortimer, J T: dry goods
Murray & Semmes: dray
Morell & Miller: wagon
Martin & Wright: auction
Milstead, Thos: retail

Martin, Wm: cart
Nally, Jas T: shop
Nardin, Mary: [blank-Charge was $40.]
O'Dell, T Thos: dry goods
Owens, John: cart
Page, Quincy L: hack
Peirce, J M: wagon
Powers, Jacob: huckster
Page, Miss: slave
Ross, Danl: dog
Renehan, Martin: retail
Rosenstock, M: dry goods
Robinson & Co: circus
Slade, Wm: dog
Semmes & Co J H: retail
Slade, Wm: dry goods
Seinzheimer & Co L: dry goods
Semmes & Co, R: dray
Shad, B: wood
Sherwood & Son, T: huckster
Smith, Eliz: retail
Shaub, Jno: cart
Turton, J B: dog
Twomy, Jeremiah: retail
Tate, J B & A: dry goods-transfer
Vonderlher, Jacob: dog
Valentine, Wm: hack
Wilkerson, Eliz: dog
Wert, J P: cart-2
Williams, Z: cart
Wendall & Van Benthuysen: wagon
Wakeling, Ignatius: huckster-transfer
Wollard, H: huckster-2
Walker, J F: huckster
Wagoner, N: huckster
Welch, Rufus: equestrian
Welch, Thos: retail
Young, Alex'r: huckster

Geo W Boteler, of the 2nd Ward, was fined $10 within the above period, for selling liquor without a license. -Wm J McCormick, Register

John Trimble, a young man of Flanders, Morris Co, N J, treed a coon last week, & climbed the tree a considerable height, when he fell to the ground. After being conveyed home, it was discovered that the spine of his back was broken, & the lower part of his body was dead. He lies in a hopeless state. –Newark Advertiser

Balt Sun: 1-On last Sat, an explosion of powder took place at a blacksmith's shop, near Woodbine, near the line of the Balt & Ohio railroad. Mem employed in blasting rock in the stone quarry of Mr Patrick Crowley, were returning from their labors, when, overtaken by a shower of rain, entered a blacksmith shop, also owned by Mr Crowley. Whilst there some of them amused themselves by placing heated coals upon the anvile, striking them with a sledge-hammer, which produced sparks which caused the powder in 3 or 4 kegs to explode. Instantly killed was Alex'r Mozetta. Patrick Waldran, of this city, was picked up dead some distance from the scene by his brother. Mr Henry Crowley, son of the proprietor, & Mr Jas Morgan, from New Market, Fred'k Co, are seriously maimed & injured as to give no hopes of recovery. Thos Newman, from Balt, was thrown some distance & had his back & 2 ribs broken; Thos McGivney, also from this city, was injured but is doing well. The remains of Patrick Waldan were conveyed to the city in charge of his brother, & will be interred today. The unfortunate men did not know there was any powder in the shop. 2-Sykesville, Oct 1, 1848. Henry C Crowley, son of the contractor, & Jas Morgan, blacksmith, died this morning. Thos Newman & Thos McGivney, very badly hurt. Dr Gustavus Riggs, of Howard District, one of our most eminent physicians in the State, has hopes for the last 2. In haste, very respectfully, Henry W Hunt. [The remains of the son of Mr Crowley having been brought to this city, the funeral will take place today at 10 A M, from the residence of Mr J Gideon, on 7th st.]

Cornelius S Bogardus, formerly assist Collector, has been appointed naval ofcr for the port of N Y, in place of Michl Hoffman, deceased.

Capt John Gwinn has been ordered to the command of the frig **Constitution**, now fitting out at Boston, & destined to the Mediterranean.

The railroad disaster of Sep 12, proved a serious misfortune to 2 industrious citizens of Wash, who have become crippled for life, through the culpable neglect of the company's agent in Balt. We hope the Railroad Co will take the destitute condition of the 2 principal sufferers, Messrs Costar & Hardy, into immediate consideration, & afford them the means of permanent support, for themselves & their families.

Mrd: on Oct 2, by Rev Mr Graeff, Jas Owner, of Wash, to Miss Sarah Eliz Stuck, of Va.

Small pox has appeared in some sections of Wash City & it is of such a contagious character, it is liable to spread. All infected portions of the city should be avoided; all communication with those affected by the disease should be guarded against; persons so affected should be kept as much isolated as possible; all persons who have not been vaccinated should immediately resort to that preventive. By order of the Board: Thos Miller, M D, Pres

THU OCT 5, 1848
Wash City Savings Bank removed to the north side of C st, into the new rooms one door east of the Bank of Wash. –Lewis Johnson, Treasurer W C S B

Pianos, Organs, & Music for sale: Richd Davis, Pa ave, Wash.

$15 reward for runaway negro boy Ben, aged about 18 years. –Salvadora McLaughlin, F st, between 19th & 20th sts.

The last of the N Y Merchants of the past age has departed, in the death of Nehemiah Rogers, aged 95 years. His companions & contemporaries, the Leroys, the Bayards, Archd Gracie, the Winthrops, the Ludlows, the Gouverneurs, the Kembles, & other well-known respected names, the merchants of the last century, have all long since passed away.

A child, of about 6 months old, of Mr Washington Howe, Boston, was exercising in a baby jumper, a few days since, when the hook to which it was attached in the ceiling gave way, &, falling upon the child's head, penetrated the brain, & caused its death in a short time.

Louisville Journal of Sep 28. The Hon Wm J Graves died at his residence in this city yesterday, after a long & very painful illness. He was well known throughout the Union as an able, enthusiastic, & devoted advocate of the Whig cause. From 1837 to 1841 he represented this district in Congress. Mr Graves has left a wife & children. His funeral will take place this morning from his late residence on Walnut st. His body will be carried to Henry Co, where he formerly resided, for interment.

Destructive fire at Pensacola, on Mon week, consumed the houses of G W Barkley, J Quigles, J Forsyth, The Globe House, J Borsnaham, F Tio, the Florida House, J Innerarity, & several others.

Capt Jas Biddle, of the Navy, died in this city on Sat last. He was a native of Phil, where he always resided when not actively employed in the service. He was one of the oldest Post Capts upon the naval register, on which he holds the 6th place. He was the son of Chas Biddle, of Phil, & was born in Feb, 1783, being 65 years old at the time of his death. He entered the service as a Midshipman in 1800. He was on the ship **Philadelphia** at the time it fell into the hands of the Algerines, & was confined a prisoner in that country for 18 months. On his release he was promoted to a Lt. In 1806 he made a voyage to China as captain of a merchantman. In 1810 he took charge of the sloop-of-war **Syren**. In 1812 when the war broke out, he joined the ship **Wasp**, Capt Jones, & after the capture of the sloop-of-war **Frolic**, was ordered to take charge of the prize, but her crippled condition made her & the **Wasp** an easy capture to a British 74-the **Poietiers**, which hove in sight. On his exchange he was promoted to master commandant, & commanded the gunboats in the Delaware. He was appointed to the command of the sloop-of-war **Hornet**. From 1838 to 1842 he was in charge of the Naval Asylum on the Schuylkill. He recently was in command on the Pacific station, & returned to Phil in Mar last, in bad health. He was a man of slight frame & delicate constitution, but of an indomitable spirit, which sustained him through trials & hardships.

Lt J F Schenck, U S N, bearer of dispatches from the Pacific to our Gov't, arrived at Phil on Sat in the barque **Emily**, from Kingston, Jamaica.

Mr M H Hough, the manager & proprietor of the Museum in Manchester, N H, was accidentally shot on Fri last. He was with a party of gentlemen in the woods of Candia & Derry hunting. The gun of one of the others accidentally fired. Mr Hough lingered until evening, when he died in great suffering.

Two sons of Mr Jas Harrison, keeper of the Western Hotel, Courtland st, N Y, were seriously injured on Sat, near their father's residence, on Bergen Hill. The younger of the two threw a bottle of camphene on a flame to make it more brilliant. A terrible explosion ensued burning both of the young men.

Julius A Fay's Boarding School For Boys, Elizabethtown, N J, will commence on the 1st Mon of Nov. References:

Lt G W Gillis, Wash
Rev J N Danforth, Alexandria
Rt Rev Dr Johns, Richmond
Hon David Stewart, Balt
Rev S Tustin, Hagerstown

Rev Dr Lord, Phil
Hon D S Gregory, Jersey City
Rev Dr Baird, N Y
G G Howland, N Y

Five cents reward for runaway, [about Jun 1,] Offy Gray, a negro boy, an indented apprentice. It is supposed he was taken from this place on board a vessel which left Blagden's wharf. –John Pettibone

Balt, Oct 4. The election for Sheriff is progressing very slowly. The candidates are: Col Geo P Kane, John Mitchell, Augustus P Shutt, Jas Hance, John Young, & S R Waters, Independents, & Chas F Cloud, Locofoco nominee.

FRI OCT 6, 1848
Portland, Maine, Sep 29, 1848. On the elevated land at each end of the city is a cemetery. The one in the northeast is much the oldest, being almost coeval with the earliest settlement of the place. Here beneath a neat marble monument lies the remains of Cmdor Edw Preble, who, in 1804, added lustre to the fame of the American navy by his gallant service before the walls of Tripoli. The Cmdor died shortly after his return home, Aug 25, 1807, aged 46 years. Another marble monument is erected here to the memory of the gallant band who voluntarily sacrificed their lives in that memorable service. It bears the following inscriptions: "In memory of Henry Wadsworth, Lt in the U S Navy, who fell before the walls of Tripoli on 4th of Sep, 1804, in his 20th year, by the explosion of a fire-ship, which he with others gallantly conducted against the enemy. Capt Richd Somers, Lt Henry Wadsworth, Lt Jos Israel, & 10 brave seamen, volunteers, were the devoted band." The Cmders of the **Enterprise** & **Boxer**, so memorable in the last war between the U S & Great Britain, lie here side by side, beneath 2 marble tablets bearing the following inscription: "Beneath this stone moulders the body of Wm Borrows, late Cmder of the U S brig **Enterprise**, who was mortally wounded on the 5th day of Sep 5, 1813, in an action which contributed to increase the fame of American valor by capturing his Britannic Majesty's brig **Boxer**, after a severe contest of 45 minutes, aged 28 years. A passing stranger has erected this monument of respect to the manes of a patriot, who in the hour of peril obeyed the loud summons of an injured country, & who gallantly met,

fought, & conquered the enemy." There epitaph of the British Cmder is as follows: "In memory of Capt Samuel Blythe, late cmder of his Britannic Majesty's brig **Boxer**. He nobly fell on the 5th day of Sep, 1813, in an action with the U S brig **Enterpise**. In life honorable, in death glorious. His country will long deplore one of her bravest sons. His friends long lament one of the best of men. Aged 29 years." "The surviving ofcrs of his crew offer this feeble tribute of admiration and regard."

Mrd: on Oct 3, at Trinity Church, in Wash City, by Rev C M Butler, Otis W Marsh, of Batavia, N Y, to Miss Harriet Eliza Haliday, of Wash City.

Mrd: on Oct 4, at the Church of the Ascension, by Rev L J Gilliss, John R Ashby, of Va, to Ellen G, daughter of the late S J Todd, of Wash City.

Mrd: on Oct 4, at Warrenton, Fauquier Co, Va, by Rev Geo H Norton, S S Fahnestock, U S A, to Miss Caroline, daughter of the late Thos O Jennings.

It was reported that all the volunteers attached to Co B, Capt Nagle, 1st Regt of Pa, were opposed to the election of Gen Zachary Taylor for Pres, we, the undersigned, members of said company, do declare said report to be false, & we will give Gen Taylor our united & undivided support for said ofc. He is a man that never surrenders, nor will we.

Peter Douty	Danl Schappel	G W Garret	Saml Shadman
Henry Fisher	Jas W Sands	Jas Cochran	Lt Edw Rehr
John Meyers	Reuben Stamm	Alex McDonald	Thos W Gilpin
Seth Price	Benj Shell	Michl Sands	Franklin
Chas Serimshaw	John Hays	John Kepple	Seitsinger
Singleton	Wm Wollinger	Jacob W Shoup	
Kimmel	Levi Elper	Nelson Berger	

Another of those ministering angels of mercy, the Sisters of Charity, who pursue their practical piety & truly Christian benevolence even to the death. Sister Julia Shink, a native of Balt, about 58 years of age, died yesterday of yellow fever in the Charity Hospital. For several years she was connected with the hospital, cheerfully bearing her share of the labors that devolve on the members of her order.
-New Orleans Delta of Sep 27th.

The full vote given to the several candidates for the ofc of Sheriff of the city of Balt, Md, on Wed last, is as follows: Chas F Cloud-9,086; John Mitchell, 11,206: Democrats. Geo P Kane, 8,919; Aug P Shutt, 597; Jas Hance, 890: Whigs. Democratic majority: 800. Norman B Harding, Whig, was elected Sheriff of Fred'k Co by a majority of from 400 to 500. Jas Crew, Whig, was chosen Sheriff of PG Co, Md. Hanson S Webb, Whig, was elected Sheriff in Carroll Co by a majority of 127 votes. Robt McGaw, Whig, was elected Sheriff in Harford Co by 170 majority.

Died: on Oct 3, at N Y, Mr Edmund Burke, in his 37th year, leaving a fond wife & 3 children. He was the former Editor of the New England Washingtonian, published at Boston, & for many years a resident of Wash.

Died: on Oct 4, in Wash City, after a very short illness, Mary Ann, wife of Isaac H Robbins, lately of the Post Ofc Dept.

City Ordinance-Wash: Act for the relief of H G O'Neale, that fine imposed relative to the keeping of dogs, be remitted: provided, he pay the costs of prosecution. Approved: Oct 5, 1848.

Millinery: Mrs L Allen will open on Sat: Pa ave, between 9th & 10th sts, Wash.
$20 reward for runaway negro boy Ben Bell, about 16, belonging to the estate of the late Lt John T McLaughlin, U S N. Apply to the Magistrate of the First Ward.
–S McLaughlin, admx

New Store: Saml T Drury has taken the old stand, well known as the N Y Cheap Lace Store, between 10th & 11th sts, Wash, & is now opening a large stock of Bonnets, Ribands, Laces, & Flowers.

SAT OCT 7, 1848
Patrick Miller was shot in Cincinnati on Fri last, by a German, Bernard Strutsman, who mistook the man for a burglar trying to get into his house, when he was only intoxicated & mistook the house. He died instantly.

Fruit trees for sale: John Perkins, Proprietor, Morristown, N J.

The ship **Lancaster**, lately commanded by Capt Corvell, sailed from New Bedford, Jun 24, for the Pacific Ocean, & returned Sep 30, in consequence of the loss of her Capt, who died on Sep 1. Capt Corvell was standing on the quarter deck leaning over the rail, when a men employed upon the mizzen top-sail yard missed his hold & fell upon the back of Capt Coveell, injuring him so severely internally that he survived the accident about 8 hours. The man had only a slight wound on the arm. Mr Wm T Faxon, of Boston, late U S naval storekeeper at Port Praya, took passage in the **Lancaster** for home, & died on Wed last.

Miss Emery, whose sudden death was in the Globe Mill, at Newburyport, was in the habit of chewing large quantities of cloves, & this was no doubt an indirect, if not direct cause of her death. –Boston Journal

Mr Geo Collamore sailed from Boston to Halifax on Sep 17, in his beautiful schnr rigged yacht **Brenda**, of 37 tons, with his wife, 2 children, waiting-maid, steward, & boat-keeper. No tidings have been received of the **Brenda**, & it is feared she has perished at sea, with all on board.

MON OCT 9, 1848
Rudd; the ship **Warren**, Cmder Long; the ship **Southampton**, Lt Com Thorburn; the ship **Lexington**, Lt Com Chatard, was at La Paz Jul 28. The **Congress**, after visiting San Bias, would return home.

Died: Geo W Crump, the late Chief Clerk in the ofc of the Com'r of Pensions, died after a protracted disease of several months' standing, aged 62 years & 5 days. For a long time past he has suffered seriously by his attack, & some weeks since was removed to Va by his relatives, among whom he breathed his last on Oct 1, in Powhatan Co. In his native State, Va, he had ranked high as a man of talents. –Union

The Pacific squadron, under command of Cmdor Thos Ap Catesby Jones, consisting of the flag-ship **Ohio**, Capt Taylor; the ship **Congress**, Capt Elie; the ship **Dale**, Cmder

Mr John P Kennedy, a citizen of Harper's Ferry, Va, took his life on Thu week, by taking laudanum. He was about 38 years of age & leaves a wife & children. Mortification at having broken the pledge, after once reforming, is supposed to have been the cause.

As the passenger train of cars on Sat last, from Winchester to Harper's Ferry, was going down, the main passenger car upset, & Maj Wm B Thompson, of Charlestown, & Mr A J Stoffer, of Martinsburg, were among the most badly injured.

The British ship **Peels' Own**, from Liverpool, for Richibucto, N B, struck on Capt North, N S, on Sep 18, & 14 lives lost. The ship had on board Capt Francis, crew, & passengers of the schnr **Valena**, of St John, N B, from St John's, N F, for Pictou, which she had run into that day, & injured her so much that she was abandoned. 8 persons were lost from the schnr, & 6 from the ship. The **Valena** was insured in N Y for $3,200.
–St John N B paper

Mrd: on Oct 7, by Rev Mr Martin, Maj Geo T Howard, of Texas, to Miss Mary Frances, daughter of Hugh McCormick, of Wash City.

Mrd: on Oct 5, at St Mary's Church, by Rev Mr Alig, Mr Antonia Lehmann to Miss Barbara Ruppert, both of Wash City.

Died: on Oct 4, Mary Ann, wife of Isaac H Robbins, of Wash City. She leaves a large circle of friends, besides her 5 children & husband, to deplore their loss. –O

Died: in Wash City, near the Navy Yard, after a few hour's illness, Mary Eliz Brown, only child of Jas & Rosela Brown, aged 20 months. [No death date given-current item.]

Died: on Sat last, Chas Granville, 2nd son of W H & Martha Ann Winter, aged 19 months & 17 days.

For sale: Goods & Fixtures in the Grocery Store under Jackson Hall. Inquire at the store of Wm W Birth.

Col Jas G Berret has been appointed Chief Clerk in the Pension Ofc, vice Dr Geo W Crump, deceased.

On Tue, a U S Dragoon, Lewis Jones, who was one of a detachment of recruits of that arm of the service destined for Calif, was drowned in the Delaware near the Navy Yard, in an attempt to swim ashore from the barque **Hermione**. The recruits had come from N Y, & were going to New Orleans. Jones failing to obtain permission to see his family, who resided in Southwark, made the hazardous attempt to do so, contrary to orders, & thus perished. He was a printer, & is spoken of as an excellent man, & leaves several children. His wife died a few months ago. In the Mexican war he served in Capt Scott's company of the 1st Pa Regt.

TUE OCT 10, 1848
Trustee's sale of household & kitchen furniture: on Oct 11, by bill of sale from Henry Howison, recorded among the land records of Wash Co: auction at the dwlg of the said Howison, on 9th st, between E & F sts. -Richd Wallach, Trustee -C W Boteler, Auct

Hon Chas C P Hastings died of apoplexy, on Sep 25, in Mendon, Mass, aged 44 years. He was a graduate of Brown Univ, of the class of 1825, & was a son of the late Hon Seth Hastings, of Mendon, formerly a Member of Congress, & the Judge of the Court of Sessions; & the only brother of the Hon Wm S Hastings, who died at the Red Sulphur Springs, in Va, where he had gone for the improvement of his health.

Notice to physicians. A young gentleman of good literary & scientific acquirements is desirous of a situation as a private Tutor in the family of a Physician. He would refer those desirous of his services to contact H C McLaughlin, Principal of the Upper Marlboro Academy, PG Co, Md.

Gen Henry Burbeck died on Oct 2, 1848, aged 94. He was born in Boston Jun 8, 1754, & reared in his native place, spending the early aprt of his life in Castle William, now *Fort Independence*, in Boston harbor; his father being an ofcr of the ordnance dept in the service of Great Britain. He had just attained his majority when the war of Independence broke out. His father promptly took part with the popular cause, & entered into the service of the country. He also joined the American Army, & his first commission, as a lt in a company of which his father had commanded, is dated at Cambridge 18th of May, 1775, & signed by Gen Jos Warren. He received the commission of a capt in a regt of artl of the Massachusetts line 12th of Sep, 1777, & continued in that regt & line till the close of the war. In 1775 he was with the army in Cambridge, Mass; in 1777 he joined the army of Pa under Gen Washington, & was in the bloody conflicts of Brandywine & Germantown, & in the deprivations of the winter at Valley Forge. He was present at the battle of Monmouth, & continued in service until the close of the war in 1783, when the army was disbanded. He again entered the service & was for several years engaged in the Indian wars along the Western frontier under Gen Wayne. His death has left Gen Solomon Van Rensselaer the only surviving ofcr of Wayne's army. Gen Burbeck was one of the original members of the Society of Cincinnati, & was the last survivor of those whose names were first subscribed to the articles of association. At the time of his decease he was Pres of the Cincinnati of Mass. --New London Chronicle

Mrd: on Thu last, at the Church of the Epiphany, in Wash City, by Rev Jas T Johnston, of Alexandria, Va, Capt Delozier Davidson, U S Army, to Henrietta Maria, daughter of T Hartley Crawford, of Wash City.

Mrd: on Oct 6, at *Fortress Monroe*, Old Point Comfort, Va, by Rev Mr Chevers, Lt Isaac F Quimby, U S A, to Eliz Greenbury, daughter of Col John L Gardner.

Died: on Sun, in Wash City, Henry M Prevost, in his 35th year. His funeral is today at 12 o'clock, frim the residence of his mother-in-law, Mrs Susan B Hough, on 9th st.

Died: on Oct 9, suddenly, Martha Ellen, daughter of John F & Martha E Bradley, aged 3 years & 9 months. Her funeral is this afternoon at 3 o'clock, from the residence of her parents, 13th & Md ave.

Died: on Oct 9, of congestive fever, Eleanor Penelope, aged 8 years & 11 months, only child of J B & Jane J Wingerd. Her funeral is today at 3 o'clock, from the residence of her grandfather, Wm Anderson.

Died: on Sep 28, at the house of Mrs Hamill, near Frankford, Pa, Mrs Esther Pepper, widow of M Pepper, in her 86th year.

John Fillmore, the great grandfather of Millard Fillmore, & the common ancestor of all of that name in the U S, was born about 1700 in one of the New England States, & at age 19 went on board a fishing vessel which sailed from Boston. The vessel was captured by a noted pirate ship, commanded by Capt Phillipe, & young Fillmore was kept as a prisoner for 9 months, when, with 2 others, made an attack upon the pirates, killed several, took the vessel & brought it into Boston harbor. John Fillmore settled in Franklin, Conn, where he died. His son, Nathl Fillmore, settled at an early day in Bennington, Vt, then called the Hampshire Grants, where he lived until his death in 1814. He served in the French war, & was a true Whig. Nathl Fillmore, his son, & father of Millard, was born at Bennington in 1771, & early in life removed to what is now called *Summer Hill*, Cayuga Co, where Millard was born Jan 7, 1800. He was a farmer, & soon after lost all his property by a bad title to one of the military lots he had purchased. About 1802 he removed to Sempronius, now Niles, in Cayuga Co, & resided there until 1819, when he removed to Erie Co, where he still lives, cultivating a small farm with his own hands.

Died: on Oct 9, of congestive fever, Eleanor Penelope, aged 8 years & 11 months, only child of J B & Jane J Wingerd. Her funeral is today at 3 o'clock, from the residence of her grandfather, Wm Anderson.

Died: on Sep 28, at the house of Mrs Hamill, near Frankford, Pa, Mrs Esther Pepper, widow of M Pepper, in her 86th year.

Masonic: meeting of Federal Lodge #1 today at 4:30 p m. -J Goldsborough Bruff, Sec

WED OCT 11, 1848
Rough & Ready Club of Spalding district, PG Co, Md: meeting held on Oct 9: Saml Arnold called to the chair; John T Naylor appointed sec. Cmte appointed:

Dr John H Bayne	Thos Brooks
H Dyer	Thos Grimes
Saml Arnold	Henry Bowlin
Col Wm M Maddox	E Ferguson
J T Naylor	Jesse Ridgway, sr
W D Addison	Jesse Ridgway, jr
M Brooke	Jos Soper
Warren Waugh	N Soper
J F Brown	Wm Gray
Jos Kimble	Thos Ryan
Judson Naylor	Geo Walker
Dr Robinson	John Addison
Henry Brooks	

For rent: comfortable 2 story brick house on 6th st, between G & H sts. Apply to Gregory Ennis.

Wash City News: Geo A Davis, formerly a cabinetmaker, & lately employed as a fireman at the Navy Yard, came to his death yesterday. He was trying to break a horse for the purpose of drawing a cart, &, while in the attempt to drive the unruly animal, the horse became restiff & ran away. Mr Davis was thrown out of the cart, & the wheel passed over his body, causing his death a few hours afterwards.

Mrd: on Oct 9, by Rev Smith Pyne, Mr John J Kidwell to Miss Mary Jane Nalley, both of Wash.

Mrd: on Sep 5, in Boonville, Oneida Co, N Y, by Rev Shepherd Wells, of Tenn, Mr John E F Carlin, of Wash City, to Mrs Helen M Whalen, of Milton, Saratoga Co, N Y.

Mrd: on Oct 10, by Elder R C Leachman, of Va, John A Ruff to Dorothy A, daughter of Jos Bryan, of Wash.

Died: on Oct 10, Calvin Goddard, in his 28th year. His funeral is on Wed, from the residence of his father, Capt Goddard, at 3 o'clock.

Died: on Oct 9, Maria Josephine, only child of B Jost, at the age of 5 years. Her funeral is today at 11 o'clock, at the parent's residence.

THU OCT 12, 1848
Dr John C Weaver, lately Prof of Ancient & Modern Languages in Strasburgh Academy, Pa, offers his services. Apply to himself, at Mr Noerr's Nat'l Bakery, 11th st, or to Rev Mr S Finckle & Rev Mr Graeff.

On Aug 12 last, the anniversary of the birthday of the Grand Duke, the christening of the infant son of the Hereditary Grand Duke & Duchess of Mecklinburg Strelitz took place in the palace at Strelitz, in the presence of the relatives of the illustrious house, & a large assembly of the nobility, amongst whom were the Earl of Westmoreland & Count Kniphausen, & the Hanoverian Minister of the Court of Berlin, who acted as prozy for the King of Hanover, one of the godfathers. The names of the Prince-Geo Adolphus Frederic Augustus Victor Adelbert Ernest Gustavus Wm Wellington. –London paper

For sale, household furniture, & house for rent: on Oct 16, at the residence of Richd B Lloyd, who intends removing to the country. –A J Fleming, Alexandria, Auctioneer [The commodious house is opposite the Market-house, containing upwards of 25 rooms, restaurant, ice-house, green-house, bath-house, cistern, vaults under ground for coal or liquors, a bowling saloon, stable, & carriage-house.]

Liberal reward for returning to me a strayed blue Bull Terrier Pup, about 6 months old. Return to C W Heydon, a few doors east of Coleman's Hotel.

Public auction: by deed of trust from Owen Connolly to the subscriber, dated Mar 7, 1848, recorded in Liber W B #143, in the land records of Wash Co, D C: auction on Oct 21, lot 18, in square 407, Wash City. -W Lenox, Trustee -C W Boteler, Auct

Valuable property for rent: **Holmes' Island**, or **Jackson City**, on the south end of the Potomac Long Bridge. Address the subscriber at Clearspring, Wash Co, Md. -Wm Dodge, Agent.

Orphans Court of Wash Co, D C. Letters of administration on the estate of Adam Alburger, late of said city, deceased, have been obtained by Emily Alburger, of Wash City, Admx.

Naval. The U S ship **Cyane**, Cmder S F Du Pont, from the Pacific, arrived at Norfolk on Mon, after 62½ days from Valparaiso. List of her ofcrs: Cmder, S F Du Pont; Lts, S C Rowan, Geo L Selden, Geo W Harrison [acting,] A Mchae; Surgeon, Danl Egbert; Purser, W A Christian; Master, D McN Fairfax; Passed Midshipman, Reuben Harris; Midshipmen, E Vanderhorst, Albert Allmand, Edmund Shepherd, R F R Lewis, Jos Parrish, A Rich Simmons, Benj F Wells, W Mitchell; Cmder's Clerk, Albert B Ashton; Acting Boatswain, John Collins; Carpenter, M M Dodd; Sailmaker, Robt Hunter.

FRI OCT 13, 1848
City Affairs-Wash. Visit to the Eastern Burial Ground of Wash City, is nearly in the centre of a cornfield, & the access to it from Md ave is through a pond ankle deep in water. The square, 1,026, assigned by the com'rs in 1798 as a grave-yard has been, ever since Wash was incorporated, under the control of the Corp, has fallen into a condition so rude & wild as to shock the sensibility of all who cance to visit it. Many of the original inhabitants of the city sleep the long sleep of death here. –An Old Citizen

Dancing Academy: Robt H Crozier, at the Odeon Saloon, corner of 4½ st & Pa ave. He has been engaged in the instruction of Dancing for the last 4 years in Alexandria & Gtwn.

Services in the Park st church, Boston, on Sabbath evening last, preparatory to the departure of missionaries to the Tamil mission, under the A B C F M. Rev Mr Poor was the speaker. Their destinations are as follows: Rev John W Dules & wife, with Mrs Winslow on her return, to the Madras mission; Dr Chas S Shelton & wife to the Madura mission; & Rev Jos T Noyes & wife, Rev Cyrus T Mills & wife, & Mr Thos S Burnell & wife, to the Ceylon mission. They sailed in the ship **Bowditch**, for Madras, on Tue. Rev Wm Ireland & wife are destined to the South African mission, & will sail in a few days. Another similar meeting was held in the Bowdoin square Baptist church the same evening. Missions there took their departure, under the charge of the American Baptist Missionary Union, as follows: Rev Lyman Jewett & wife, designated to *Teloogoo Mission, Madras Presidency; Rev Henry L Van Meter & wife, to Burman & Arracan Mission; Rev Calvin C Moore & wife, Karen & Arracan Mission; Rev Judson Benjamin & wife, Karen mission Tavoy, Tenaasserim. The Rev S S Day, of the *Teloogo Mission, & Mr & Mrs Jewett, for Madras, sailed in company with missionaries of the A B C F M. The others, with Mrs Brown, of Assam Mission, expect to sail on Oct 17 for Calcutta, in the ship **Cato**. [2 spellings of Teloogoo: Teloogo.]

Col Washington's expedition to Calif has proceeded 420 miles with a train of 150 wagons, heavily loaded in the space of 21 days, & was then encamped near Maperne, in the State of Durango. They have been treated with great kindness by the Mexicans. -New Orleans Delta

For rent: commodious house in **Carroll Place**, on Capitol Hill, fronting east Capitol garden. Also, valuable City Lots for sale. –Benj E Green, ofc on C st, between 4½ & 6th sts.

Died: on Sep 22, at Point Isabel, of yellow fever, Capt Jas H Prentiss, of the 1st U S Artl. He entered the service on graduating at the U S Military Academy, West Point, in 1830, as a Brevet 2nd Lt of Artl: served with honor in the Indian war, known as the Black Hawk campaign. In 1839 he was advanced to an Assist Adj Gen, with the rank of Capt, which he held until the Mexican war, when he took the choice of Captaincy in the line & the command of a company of artillery. He entered the field war with the column of Gen Wool, & held the post of honor at Rinconada during the operations at Buena Vista. Peace to his ashes.

Mrd: on Sep 29, by Rev Mathias Alig, in St Mary's Church, Mr Geo Gineman to Miss Louisa Barber, both of Wash City.

Mrd: on Oct 10, by Rev Mr Thomas, of Rockville, Md, Thos L Maccubbin, of Md, to Eliz, daughter of David Shoemaker, of Wash Co, D C.

SAT OCT 14, 1848
Mrd: on Oct 12, in the city of Balt, by Rev Mr Peck, S Asbury Sheppard, of Wash, late of the Balt Bar, to Miss Margaret L Armstrong, of the former place.

Died: on Sep 23, after a lingering illness, Mr Henry Birch. His funeral is this afternoon at 3 o'clock, from the residence of his mother, on Massachusetts ave, between 5th & 6th sts.

Died: on Oct 13, in Wash City, Fred'k Hagar, aged 36 years. His funeral is on Oct 15, at 3 o'clock, from his late residence on F st, near the white warehouse.

Accident on Sep 18 at Mount Pleasant, Mo, when a number of persons were engaged in raising the cupola of the Congregational Church. The scaffold gave way & 7 men fell to the ground. Mr Pixley was seriously mangled; Mr N Lathrop's right shoulder dislocated; L G Palmer's face cut; T V Toft & T F Newton were injured by the falling timber. E Tine & H Higgins were also injured, but not seriously.

MON OCT 16, 1848
Ladies with letters in the Wash Post Ofc, Oct 15, 1848:

Butler, Miss Ann R	Chase, Miss Milka A	Jenkins, Mrs Sarah
Bayliss, Mrs C	Dunkin, Mrs Eliz	Jackson, Mrs Sarah
Beander, Bertha	Dougherty, Miss El	Lawrence, Harriet
Butler, Miss Caro	Dunlop, Ellen	Lawrason, Miss A C
Berry, Mrs C M	Dolphin, Mrs E	Morgan, Mrs Caro
Barnard, Mrs Rach	Duer, Mrs Lucy A	Miller, Miss Eliza
Beans, Mrs Harriet	Dor-ey, Mrs Maria	Melvin, Miss
Berry, Mrs Mildred	Duvall, Miss Mar E	Manly, Mrs Mary
Burgears, Mrs	Davis, Miss Mary	Martier, Mrs Sarh
Banks, Miss Mary	Dixson, Mrs Mary	McHenry, Mrs H
Brown, Rachael	Drinker, Ruth	McPherson, Mrs A
Benjamin, Susan M	Drummond, Mrs N'h	McNew, Miss Mar S
Bantum, Sarah	Evans, Miss Fanny	Newlin, Miss C
Battaile, Sarah	Elbert, Miss Fanny	Nottingham, Miss E
Barber, Miss Cath	Eisennery, Mrs Mary	Norvell, Mrs Marg
Brown, Miss Frances	Farr, Mrs Sarah A	Neale, Miss Mary J
Boyer, Miss Mary A	Fitzgerald, Miss Ann	Peters, Mrs Louisa
Bryant, Patty [col'd]	Gautt, Mrs E C-3	Phelan, Mrs
Baltimore, Mrs Han	Grey, Miss Mary	Perry, Mrs
Currbey, Mrs Fran	Green, Miss Rosalie	Parker, Miss Marg-2
Cole, Miss Nelly	Graham, Mrs Danl	Richards, Miss A R
Corum, Miss Susan	Herbert, Miss Allen	Russell, Charlotte
Crook, Miss Matilda	Hall, Mrs Anna M	Rose, Miss Patsy
Clarke, Miss Martha	Homoun, Louisa	Stewart, Mrs Com
Canan, Mrs [formerly Mrs Higgins]	H-ll, Mary George	Smith, Mrs Jane
Carrall, Miss Rosa'a	Harry, Miss Sarah A	Salomon, Mrs K
Cunningham, Miss S J	Hodgkins, Miss Mary	Sprague, Mrs Mary
	Jackson, Mrs Lue'a	Thompson, Mrs M H

Thompson, Mrs M G	Woodward, Miss J	Williams, Miss Anna
Todd, Mrs Frances G	Williams, Mrs M S	Williams, Mrs Betty
Washington, Miss Anna M	Warren, Mrs Maria	Wise, Mrs Josephine
Wagoner, Mrs Cath	Wilson, Miss Sarah	Young, Mrs Amelia T
West, Eleanor	Wiley, Miss Virginia	-C K Gardner, P M
	Wright, Francis R-3	

Mons Julian Montandon, having gone South for a few weeks, those persons who left watches with him to be repaired will please call this day, Oct 16, for them. Watches not repaired yet will be attended to shortly by Mr A C Hugenin, from Switzerland, who is authorized to attend to Mr Montandon's affairs during his absence. The shop will be closed for about one week, until Mr Hugenin returns from the North.

Furnished house to rent: the house the subscriber now resides in, with its furniture. –Smith Pyne

Mrd: on Oct 8, by Rev L J Morgan, Mr John Q Wilson to Miss Frances O Masters, all of Wash City.

TUE OCT 17, 1848
In the Circuit Court held at Newburgh, N Y, last week, Gilbert W Oliver recovered a verdict of $8,000 against the N Y & Erie Railroad Co, as compensation for severe injuries sustained by him 4 years ago, making him a cripple for life, by an accident to the train in which he was. A defect in one of the wheels, which broke, caused the cars to be thrown into a gully.

Mrd: on Oct 12, by Rev J W French, Alex'r McIntire to Mrs Mary M Ellis, both of Wash City.

Mrd: on Oct 15, by Rev Mr Morgan, Mr Geo L Kite to Miss Martha Ann Koontz, both of Page Co, Va.

Extensive sale of nearly new & well kept furniture: on Oct 25, at Tyler's Hotel, [he being about to remove to Boston,] his entire stock of furniture. –Martin & Wright, auctioneers

WED OCT 18, 1848
Information was received in the Navy Yard at Wash that the widow & children of the late Geo S Davis, who was accidentally killed on Mon, were in great distress, when quickly $115 was subscribed by the mechanics & workingmen of the Yard, for the relief of the unfortunate family. –News

Nauvoo. The <u>Mormon Temple</u> is in ruins from the fire on Oct 9. The fire is supposed to have been set by an incendiary.

Died: on Oct 15, after a short & severe illness, Emma, youngest child of I A & Eliz Newton, aged 5 years.

Died: on Oct 16, at Phil, at the residence of Jas R Smith, Jas Lawrence, son of Wm G W White, of Wash City. His funeral is this morning at 11 o'clock, from the residence of his father, on 4½ st.

Penitentiary for D C, Wash, Oct 5, 1848. We, the undersigned, ofcrs employed at the Penitentiary for D C, do hereby certify that the present Warden, Mr C P Sengstack, has not at any time employed the convicts of this prison either in making or painting Democratic or other transparencies, to be used for electioneering purposes in this city or any other quarter. Neither has he had them folding or directing documents for any political purpose. –Craven Ashford, John A Young, Jas Parsons, Wm H Clark, Benj Stees, Richd Pierce, Michl Nash, & Chas Fraelar. Sworn to on Oct 10, by each of the deponents before Saml Grubb, J P.

Marshal's sale: by 2 writs of fieri facias: sale for cash on Nov 16: lot 9 in square 323, in Wash City, beginning from the n e corner of D st; said lot in the occupancy of Patrick Davy, as specified in the deed of conveyance from Cornelius McDermott Roe to John Sessford, recorded in Liber S #18, folio 48. Also, the south part of lot 13 in square 431, fronting on 7th st west, running back as specified in the mortgage deed of John Sessford to Jonathan Seaver, recorded in Liber W B #47, folio 374, with improvements; seized & levied upon as the property of John Sessford, & sold to satisfy judicials 11 & 12 to Oct term, in favor of Wm Chestnut. –Alex'r Hunter, late Marshal D C

THU OCT 19, 1848
Wash Corp: 1-Cmte on Police: bill for the relief of Thos J Barrett: passed. 2-Nomination of Josias Adams, as additional police ofcr for the 6th Ward: confirmed. 3-Cmte of Claims: asked to be discharged from the further consideration of the ptn of Geo Knott.

Extensive sale of new & second-hand furniture at auction: on Oct 24, in the Ware Rooms of Messrs T M & B Milburn, on 7th st, opposite the ofc of the Nat'l Intell.
-Edw C & G F Dyer

Valuable real estate for sale by subscriber: in Spottsylvania, heretofore occupied by him as a summer residence, **Mountain Way**, consisting of about 200 acres of land, about 4 miles from the town of Fredericksburg, on which is an excellent dwlg-house & all other necessary outhouses. Apply to the overseer, Mr Bloxton, who resides on the premises; for terms of sale, apply to me in Wmsburg, or to Mr John M Herndon, in Fredericksburg.
–Robt P Waller

Sep 29. The news of the morning is that the Duchess of Montpensier has given birth to a daughter; & that the Carlists have been defeated in Catalonia.

Mrd: on Oct 17, by Rev Mathias Alig, of St Mary's Church, Mr Richd G Ennis to Miss Mary, daughter of Patrick Donoghue, both of Wash City.

Died: on Monday last, after a few days' illness, Philip Edward, son of Philip & Sarah Cronin, aged 10 years & 7 months.

Died: on Oct 18, Juliet Ann Caroline, daughter of Thos & Emily MacGill. Her funeral is this morning at 10 o'clock, at their residence, corner of 7th & G sts.

In Chancery. Murray Barker against David Riley, heir at law of Catherine Campbell. The creditors of Cath Catherine Campbell, deceased, are to file their claims with the subscriber, duly vouched, on or before Nov 1 next. –W Redin, auditor

For rent: house on north side of Pa ave, between 9th & 10th sts, over the dry goods store of Mr G F Allen. Entrance on D st, 2nd door from 10th st. Rent: $150 per annum. Apply to S H Hill, 8th & Pa ave.

Stray horse taken up trespassing on my premises, a dark colored Horse, with a white spot on the forehead. The owner can have said horse by proving property & paying charges. –Henry D Gunnell, near the Arsenal

Fire yesterday, destroyed a wooden stable occupied by Alfred Kiger, a colored man. A frame dwlg, in front of the German Catholic Church on 5th st, was also destroyed. Mr Langfelt was the owner of the dwlg. The dwlg of Mr Bernard Giveney was also partially injured.

Obits-died: 1-Hon Jeremiah Mason, one of the oldest & most eminent lawyers in the country, died on Sat, of an apoplectic stroke, with which he was visited on Wed, aged 82 years. He was a member of the U S Senate from N H, many years ago, but for the last 20 years had resided in Boston. 2-Mr Wm Lawrence, a brother of Messrs Amos & Abbott Lawrence, like them distinguished for mercantile enterprise & success, died on Sat, at the age of 65, having been for more than a year disabled by paralysis. –Commercial Adv

FRI OCT 20, 1848

A day on **Rock Creek**, Wash, Oct, 1848. Rock Creek rises in the central portion of Montg Co, &, after running a distance of some 15 miles, finally empties into the Potomac, between Wash & Gtwn. We struck the creek just without the limits of the city, & the first object that attracted our attention was Decatur's tomb. This memorial of a departed naval hero occupied the summit of a picturesque hill. It is built of bricks, which are painted white, & resembles in shape a small Grecian temple without its columns, & is without any inscription. The remains of the Cmdor were originally deposited here, but his ashes have been removed to Phil & deposited in his family vault. This land is called **Kalorama**, & belongs to an estate originally owned by Joel Barlow, which fact is alone sufficient to give it a reputation; but it is somewhat more interesting to known that it was upon this spot of earth that Robt Fulton first tried his experiments while studying out the science of steam navigation. This was at the time when Barlow & Fulton were on the most intimate terms of friendship, & **Kalorama** was Fulton's principal home. I was informed that the parlor walls of **Kalorama** were once ornamented with fresco paintings, executed by Fulton at the request of his friend Barlow. Our next halting place was at an old mill in a secluded glen. This beautiful place is associated with the late John Quincy Adams, who became its purchaser many years ago, & to whose estate [as I believe] it now belongs. We passed along the road that took us from Adams' Mill further up the stream. There we met a colored boy who told us: "I'm gwine down to Mr Pierce's." We reached Pierce's Plantation & found the ruins of an old saw-mill. Rock Creek church lies somewhere between 1 & 2 miles eastward of the stream from which it derives its name. The original Rock Creek chapel was founded in 1719, & the bricks employed in its construction were brought from England. It became a parish church in 1726, at which time the glebe land amounted to 100 acres. It was rebuilt in 1768, & improvements added in 1808. The first rector of the Church was the Rev Geo Murdock, who officiated for 34 years; his successors were Rev Alex'r Williamson, Rev Thos Read, Rev Alfred Henry Dashields, Rev Thos G Allen, Rev Henry C Knight, Rev Levin I Gills, Rev Edw Waylen, & the present incumbent, Rev Wm A Harris. Of Mr Read it is recorded that he presided over the church for 40 years, during the whole of which time he was absent only 30 months; & with regard to Mr Waylen, he compiled an interesting history of the Parish, which was published in 1845. The church as it now stands is simply that of an old fashioned but very comfortable brick church, on a gentle hill, surrounded by tombs & grave-stones. I came upon one which read: "Grant, Lord, when I from death do wake, I may of endless life partake. J R 1802 Tarry with me a few moments at the elegant mansion of a certain retired banker. So much for a vagabondizing day on Rock Creek.

Among the passengers from Liverpool in the steamer **Britannia** were Mr Wm W Corcoran, of Wash City, & the Hon John Davis, of Mass.

Died: on Oct 5, at the residence of his son, John M Chilton, of Vicksburg, Miss, Wm Chilton, at the ripe age of 74 years & 8 months. The deceased was a native of Fauquier Co, Va, & resided till fall of 1846 in Loudoun Co, Va, where for many years he served ably as Commonwealth Atty, & for several years was a member of the Legislature of Miss. He was one of a troop of horse that was revived by Gen Washington & went to **Fort Pitt** to aid in suppressing the disturbances, known in history as the Whiskey Insurrection, & was also a capt in the Va militia during the last war in active service at & near Norfolk, till peace was declared. He was a Federal Republican of the Washington school.

Parts of **Woodley** for sale: by decree of the Circuit Court of this District, passed in a cause wherein Geo Lowry is cmplnt, & the heirs at law of the late Lazare Kervand & others are dfndnts, will be sold at auction on Nov 21, in Wash City, at the auction rooms of Martin & Wright, certain portions of the tract of land called **Woodley**, lately owned by said Kervand, lying in Wash Co, on the west side of Rock Creek, about 2 miles from Wash & Gtwn. The part now proposed to be sold has been divided into 5 fields of from about 5 to 40 acres, in all about 130 acres. A plat of the portions now offered for sale can be seen at the ofc of the subscriber, where, & of Mrs Kervand, residing at Woodley, further information can be obtained. The creditors of said Lazare Kervand are notified to file their claims duly vouched. –W Redin, trustee -Martin & Wright, auctioneers.

Mrd: on Oct 15, by Rev P B O'Flanegan, Josepa Duval to Theodosia, eldest daughter of Jas Colburn, all of Gtwn.

In Chancery. Circuit Court of Wash Co, D C. Richards, Bassett & Abom, plntfs, vs Sylvanus Holmes, A H Harper, Philip R Fendall, Jas E Southworth, Electus B Litchfield, Jas R Beach, & Cornelia S Dwight, dfndnts. The bill alleges that Sylvanus Holmes executed to Geo A Dwight, now deceased, of whom the dfndnt, Cordelia, is heiress, a deed of trust on lots of land #s 14 & 15 in square 297 in Wash City, to secure to the dfndnts, Southworth, Litchfield & Beach, the payment of a note fo $3,000, bearing date Feb 9, 1846, payable 4 months after date at the Bank of America, in N Y; that, on Jan 14, 1847, the said Southworth, Litchfield & Beach assigned to the plntfs, Richards, Basset & Abom, the said note for $3,000 & the deed of trust, representing the said note to be due & unpaid; that the lien for security of the same was valid & subsisting on the said lots of land, & engaging that the plntfs should be entitled to the first proceeds of sale of the lots; that said Holmes executed another deed of trust of subsequent date, on the same lots, to Philip R Fendall, to secure to A H Harper the payment of $2,800; that Harper & Fendall had notice of the prior deed of trust; that the trustee, Geo A Dwight, alleged that Holmes had paid to Southworth, Litchfield & Beach the debt for which the deed of trust was executed to him, & therefore refused in his lifetime to sell the lots of land; that said Dwight is dead, & that Cordelia S Dwight is his sole child & heiress at law; that Holmes, Fendall, & Harper allege that the debt to Southworth, Litchfield & Beach had been paid & satisfied, & that the lien on the lots for satisfaction of the debt to Harper is valid, subsisting, & superior to the claim of the plntfs as assignee of Southworth, Litchfield & Beach; that the said assignors admit they received from Holmes, after the deed of trust & before assignment to the plntfs, moneys to the sum of the said notes to them, but that they applied the money to subsequent demands, which they, Southworth, Litchfield & Beach, had against Holmes, & that they had the right so to apply the payment. The bill prays that the dfndnts may interplead & litigate those matters, & that upon a final hearing the plntfs may have a decree for sale of the lots to satisfy the debt assigned by Southworth, Litchfield & Beach, or, if that shall not be found proper, & that the dfndnt, Harper, hath the superior lien, than that the plntfs may have a decree against the assignors, Southworth, Litchfield & Beach, & for general relief. And it appearing to the satisfaction of the Court that the dfndnts, Sylvanus Holmes, Cordelia S Dwight, Jas E Southworth, Electus B Litchfield, & Jas R Beach, are absent from D C, & residing in other parts of the U S, & they, the absentees, not having answered the bill nor entered an appearance to the said suit, & the plntfs [by their counsel] having prayed an order of publication against the aforesaid absentees, warning them to appear & answer, it is thereupon ordered, upon this 17th of Oct, 1848, that the 1st Mon in Apr next be assigned for the appearance of said Sylvanus Holmes, Cordelia S Dwight, Jas E Southworth, Electus B Litchfield, & Jas R Beach. By order of the Court. Test: Wm Brent, clerk. Geo M Bibb, of counsel for cmplnts

Trustee's sale: by decree of the Circuit Court of Wash Co, D C, sitting as a Court of Chancery, made in the cause of Robt W Dyer et al vs Sarah G Stewart et al, I will offer at public auction, on Nov 11, the following: lots 7 & 8 in square 316; lot 3 in square 321; lots 11 in square 348; & east half of lot 12 in square 348. –Walter S Cox, trustee
-Edw C & G F Dyer

SAT OCT 21, 1848
Nat'l Medical College, 7th st between E & F sts, Wash. Faculty:
Thos Miller, M D, Prof of Anatomy
John M Thomas, M D, Prof of Physiology & Medical Jurisprudence
Wm P Johnston, M D, Prof of Obstetrics & Diseases of Women & Children
Chas G Page, M D, & Leonard D Gale, M D, Professors of Chemistry
Joshua Riley, M D, Prof of Materia Medica & Therapeutics
John Fred May, M D, Prof of Surgery
Grafton Tyler, M D, Prof of Pathology & Practice of Medicine
R King Stone, M D, Adj Prof of Anatomy
Johnson Eliot, M D, Demonstrator of Anatony
Clinical Lectures twice a week, with operations. Fee for a full course of Lectures $105-Demonstrator ticket $10. Good board can be procured at from $2.50 to $3.00 per week.
Wm P Johnston, M D, Dean

By 2 writs of fieri facias, at the suits of Saml Bacon & Peter F Bacon, under the firm of Saml Bacon & Co, & Raphael Semmes & Stanislaus Murray, late trading under the firm of Semmes & Murray, against the goods & chattels, lands & tenements, rights & credits of Chas Baum: I have seized the property of said Baum-lot 18 in square 453, with bldgs, & will expose it for sale on Nov 22. –H R Maryman, constable

West Point, Sep 14, 1848. Seven flag staffs taken by the U S Army in the campaign commenced at Vera cruz & terminated in the capital of Mexico. Four other staffs, captured with the strong works, viz: the entrenched camp of Contreras, the convent of Churubusco, the bridge-head of Churubusco, & the citidel of Mexico, were divided into small individual trophies by our ofcrs & men. All captured flags & colors were, as nat'l trophies, sent to Wash.
The following have been placed on the respective objects:
1-Part of the flag-staff of the Castle of San Juan de Ulus, Vera Cruz, taken by the American army Mar 29, 1847.
2-Part of the flag-staff at *Fort San Iago*, Vera Cruz, taken by the American army Mar 29, 1847.
3-Part of the flag-staff of *Fort Conception*, Vera Cruz, taken by the American army Mar 29, 1847.
4-Part of the flag-staff of Cerro Gordo, taken by the American army Apr 18, 1847.
5-Part of the flag-staff of the Castle of Perote, taken by the American army Apr 23, 1847.
6-Part of the flag-staff of the Castle of Chapultepec, taken by the American army Sep 13, 1847.
7-Part of the flag-staff of the Nat'l Palace of Mexico, taken by the American army Sep 14, 1847. -Winifield Scott to Capt Henry Brewerton, Superintendent U S Military Academy

Mrd: on Oct 17, by Rev Thos Reese, Mr Wm S Lewis to Martha, daughter of the late John Espey, all of Wash City.

Died: yesterday, of scarlet fever, John H, son of Wm & Eliz Dennesson, aged 5 year & 8 months. His funeral is this afternoon, at 4 o'clock, on G st, between 5th & 6th sts.

The late firm of Owen, Evans & Co has been dissolved by the death of Evan Evans. Edw Owen is authorized to settle all business concerning the said late firm. –Wm B Magruder, exc of Evan Evans. -E Owen, S W Owen [The latter two will continue the business at the old stand, under the firm & name of Edw Owen & Son.]

In Chancery. Circuit Court of Wash Co, D C. Nicholas Febrey vs John Sessford & Jas Thrift. Wm R Woodward, trustee, exposed to sale, for cash, on Oct 7, the following property, in Wash City, to wit: south half of lot 19 in square 293, on west side of Pa ave; that, at such sale, Wm B Todd was the highest bidder for the same, & became the purchaser at the price or sum of $326.66 2/3, & has complied with the terms of the sale. –W Brent, clerk

Died: yesterday, of scarlet fever, John H, son of Wm & Eliz Dennesson, aged 5 year & 8 months. His funeral is this afternoon, at 4 o'clock, on G st, between 5th & 6th sts.

Died: yesterday, in Wash City, Mr Jeremiah T Loockerman, in his 35th year, a native of Annapolis, Md, but for several years past a resident of this city.

Masonic Funeral. Members of Federal Lodge #1 will meet Oct 22, at 10 o'clock, to follow to the grave the remains of their late Brother Jeremiah T Loockerman. –J Goldsborough Bruff, sec

MON OCT 23, 1848

Orphans Court of Wash Co, D C. Letters of administration on the personal estate of Benj Burch, late of Wash Co, deceased. –C H Wiltberger, adm de bonis non

Board of Naval Surgeons now in session at the Naval Asylum, near Phil, for the examination & promotion of Assist Surgeons, & also for the examination of candidates for admission into the service. The Board members are Surgeons Jas Cornish, [Pres,] Jas M Greene, G R Horner, Robt J Dod, & Saml Barrington.

Miss M A Jack has received her Fall Patterns & is prepared to make Visites, Mantillas, Cloaks, & Dresses, in the latest style. 4½ st, a few doors south of Pa ave.

In Chancery. Jas McIntosh against Sarah McIntosh & others. The creditors of Thos McIntosh are notified to file their claims against his estate, duly vouched, with me, at my ofc in the City Hall, Wash, or in Gtwn, on or before Nov 1 next. –W Redin, auditor

The subscribers, Trustees of primary School #3, Vansville, PG Co, Md, with to employ a Teacher for said school. –R I Duvall, J T Clark, Richd Isaac, of Jos: trustees

Mrd: on Oct 22, in Wash City, by Rev Mr Prettyman, Mr Richd Francis, of Portugal, to Miss Sarah Ann Robey, of Wash.

The large imposing structure on the corner of F & 17th sts is approaching completion. It was built by Wm H Winder, of Phil, & will cost him nearly $150,000. It was built under the superintendence H D Cooper & R A Gilpin, & the principal contractors were Chas L Coltman; carpenter A D Caldwell; marble mason, Wm Dougherty; brick mason, Thos Lewis; & painter, Jas O'Bryon. It is heated by hot water pipes. Of the public ofcrs who have moved into it, may be mentioned the Surveyor Genr'l, the Paymaster Genr'l, Second Auditor, & heads of several bureaus connected with the War & Navy Depts.

Died: on Oct 21, at her residence, in Wash City, after a long & painful illness, Mrs Eliz Ross, in her 52nd year, relict of the late Richd Ross, of Montg Co, Md. Her funeral will take place today at 11 A M, from her late residence on 7th st, opposite the City Post Ofc.

TUE OCT 24, 1848
$5 reward for fine Cashmere Shawl taken either by mistake or stolen, at a Cotillon Party of the United Club, Oct 18. Return to my residence-corner 6th & H sts. –Jno S Finch

To Let: 3 story house on Mass ave, in the block of 5, containing 11 rooms, located between 6th & 7th sts. -Jas B Phillips

To teachers: wanted, a Lady to take charge of a large class of little girls.
–C D Elliott, Nashville Female Seminary

Mrd: on Oct 23, in Wash City, by Rev Mr Ballantyne, E Jaquelin Smith, of Winchester, to Ella Alice, daughter of the late Richd B Buckner, of Fauquier Co, Va.

Mrd: on Thu, at Norfolk, by Rev Mr Anderson, Passed Midshipman E Lloyd Winder, U S Navy, to Miss Ellen, daughter of the late Jas D Thornburn, of that city.

Died: on Oct 22, in Gtwn, after a long illness, Mary E Barron, in her 35th year, wife of Henry Barron, of PG Co, Md, leaving a husband & 4 children to mourn their loss. Her funeral is from the residence of her father, Chas Dean, on West st, today, at 2 o'clock.

Died: on Oct 15, at his residence on Short Creek, John J Jacob, one of the Justices of the Peace of Ohio Co, Va, in his 58th year. –Wheeling paper

Notice: Mr Ould has no right in law or equity to advertise the Gtwn Iron Works for sale, either as trustee or otherwise. He has no claim whatever to or on my furnaces, & can give no valid title or claim on the furnaces or the personal property on the premises.
–John Rynex [See following Notice.]
+
WED OCT 25, 1848
Notice: The property which I am authorized & required to sell, in virtue of a deed of trust from John Rynex, on Nov 2, is described by metes & bounds in the advertisement of sale, & improvements intended to be disposed of are those, or such parts, erected on lots or parts of lots embraced within said limits. –Robt Ould, Trustee [See the above Notice.]

The Fair of the PG Co Agricultural Society was held at Upper Marlborough on Wed & Thu last. Dr Bayne & Thos Duckett: splendid assortment of vegetables. Address delivered by Gen Tench Tilghman, of Talbot Co. Geo Washington Parke Curtis, who had quit his quiet retreat at Arlington, attended. Dr Payne made a report on Farming, in which Col Capron's farm was highly complimented, & received the 1st premium on farms. The 2nd premium was awared to Col John D Bowling, the third to Mr Jas Somerville. Best mutton premium award to W W Bowie. Addresses made by Hon Mr Jenifer, C Calvert, W W Bowie, T F Bowie, & other gentlemen.

Died: on Oct 24, at his residence near the Marine Garrison, Mr Jos A Blagrove, aged 27 years, after an illness of a few days of bilious fever. He leaves a young wife & aged father to mourn his loss. His funeral is this afternoon, at 3 o'clock.

Died: on Oct 24, in Wash City, Mrs Rose Smith, aged about 75 years, a native of Old Castle, county Meath, Ireland. Her funeral is this evening at 3½ o'clock, from the residence of her daughter-in-law, on the corner of 8th & H sts.

Died: on Oct 24, Francis Lombardi, in his 36th year. His funeral is this day, at 3 o'clock, from his late residence on 11th st.

Wanted: a Teacher to take charge of a female school in Chestertown, Md. Apply to Geo B Westcott.

Trustee's sale: by deed of trust from Wm Langfitt & Mary Ann his wife, dated Mar 23, 1847, recorded in Liber W B 133, folio 233: auction on Nov 27, in front of lot 24 in square 486, in Wash City. –W Redin, trustee -Martin & Wright, auctioneers

Trustee reported a sale on Oct 19, of the real estate of Lewis G Davidson, to Columbus Alexander of lots 13 thru 15 in square 168, for $1,321.96; to Jas Carrico lot 6 in square 163, for $87.66; & both have complied with the terms of the sale. –Nathl P Causin -Ed N Roach, Reg of Wills

Geo McNeir, Notary Public & Gen Agent: Ofc-4½ sts, Wash.

By order of distrains, from John Miller, against the goods & chattels of Geo Garner, I have seized the following goods of Garner, to satisfy rent due & in arrears to John Miller, to wit: furniture, washstands, buckets, clothes horse, stove, blinds, & andirons. Public auction on Oct 28 in front of the centre Market-house. –J F Wollard, Bailiff

In Chancery. Wm Dowling adm of Greenfield & John Maguire, against John F Ennis, adm, & others, heirs at law of Bernard Kelly. The creditors of Bernard Kelly, deceased, are to file their claims, duly vouched, with me, at my ofc, in the City Hall, Wash, or in Gtwn, on or before Nov 4. –W Redin, auditor

THU OCT 26, 1848
Missionaries left Boston on Sat for India, under the care of the American Baptist Union, namely, Rev Messrs H L Van Meter & Judson Benjamin, with their wives, & Mrs E W Brown.

American soldiers for the Mexican Army. [From the New Orleans Delta, of Oct 15.] Col Geo W White, late a Capt in the Louisiana regt serving in Mexico, left last evening in the brig **Harriette**, Capt Martin, for Sisal, in command of 125 men. The following ofcrs of the regt also went down with Col White: Capt Robt J Kelly, Capt Linton, Lts Beresford, Campbell, H S Boyle, Bassint, Puhl, Strauss, & Tiedger. On arrival at Sisal, they proceed to Merida.

For rent: commodious 2 story brick dwlg on the corner of Washington & West sts, lately occupied by Mr R L Mackall. For terms apply to Mr R L Mackall, 4th Auditor's ofc, Wash, or to J W Belt, Bridge st, Gtwn.

Died: on Oct 7, at Ypsilanti, Michigan, of disease contracted during the Mexican war, Brevet Capt Mortimer Rosecrants, of the 5th infty, in his 30th year. He graduated at the Military Academy, West Point, in 1841, & was promoted to the 5th infty as a brevet 2nd Lt. In 1845 he went with his regt to Corpus Christi, & from thence marched with the army under Gen Taylor to the Rio Grande. His gallantry in the conflicts of Palo Alto, Resaca de la Palma, & Monterey was worthy of his own character. In Jan, 1847, he joined the columns under Gen Scott in his operations against Vera Cruz. He was the first to volunteer to accompany the storming parties from his regt, both at Molino del Rey & Chapultepec.

Died: Sep 17, at his residence, **Phoenix Hall**, Chas Co, Md, Col John Hughes, after a short illness of 4 days.

Notice is given to the men of the late companies of volunteers commanded by Capt Corse & Capt Thrift, who were discharged in Mexico, & the heirs of those who died in service, that Maj Spratley, Paymaster U S Army, will be in Alexandria on Oct 30, for the purpose of paying them the 3 months' extra pay provided for under the 5th section of the Act of Congress approved 19th Jul, 1848.

Ice-house for rent: recently occupied by Messrs Burd & Gunnell, 11th & Va ave. Inquire of Wm B Todd.

Household & kitchen furniture at auction: on Oct 29, at the residence of J E Millard, on 2nd st, Capitol Hill, 2 doors north of St Peter's Church. -A Green, auctioneer

FRI OCT 27, 1848
Wash Corp: 1-Ptn of J C Crusor, praying remission of a fine: referred to the Cmte of Claims. 2-Ptn of Saml De Vaughan & others, in reference to the grade of E st north: referred to the Cmte on Improvements. 3-Ptn of John Becksler, praying the remission of a fine: referred to the Cmte of Claims.

Washington Light Infty to give a Military & Civic Ball at Odd Fellows Hall on Nov 20. Managers:

Capt Jos B Tate	Henry D Cooper	Jos Mitchell
Lt John F Tucker	Jas H Mead	T O Sparrow
Lt Wm H Clark	Geo Becker	Thos B Duvall
Lt Jas Y Davis	Wm Garner	Thos Laxen
Sgt Hiram Richey	Benj F Beers	John Hutchinson
Sgt Jas Kelly	Wm M Payne	Chas F McCarty
Sgt Edw Varden	Peter M Dubant	Jas Burdine
Sgt Wm Morgan	Wm S Lewis	Franklin Benter
Q M Serg W E Morcoe	Thos Mitchell	Geo Payne John
Judson O Warner	John S Finch	Browers
Jas Booth	Edw B Duvall	Wm S Kerr
Jas Powers	Alex'r Garret	John Pie
Andrew J Joyce	Wm S Burch	Jos McCuen
Jas Bouseau	S Henry Warner	Ensign John W Mead
Patrick H King	Henry Khul	

The Hon Dixon H Lewis, U S Senator from Alabama, died on Oct 25, at the Nat'l Hotel, in this city. He arrived in N Y 2 or 3 weeks since with his wife, & has been ill most of the time. –N Y Express

Applications for taverns & ordinaries in Wash: Mayor's ofc, Oct 26, 1848.

A Favier, square 119, 19th st
E H Fuller, square 322, Pa ave & 12th st
Jas Maher, square 256, E & 13½ sts
Abraham Butler, square 254, F st
E D & H A Willard, square 225, Pa ave
Andrew Hancock, square 292, Pa ave
C Finkman, square 292, Pa ave
W H Campbell, square B, Pa ave
John Connor, square 407, 8th st
H Cook, square 407, D & 8th sts
J H Eberbach, square 467, 8$^{th\,\&}$ E sts
J R Hendley, square 431, 7th & E sts
John Foy, square 378, D st
Thos Baker, square 432, D & 8th sts
Fred Stutz, square 408, 9th st
Patrick Moran, square 407, D & 8th sts
W H Campbell, square 431
P W Dorsey, square 428, 7th & H sts
C W Blackwell, Pa ave
Hall & Scott, Res 10, Pa ave
Wm Gadsby, Res 10, Pa ave & 3rd st
Jas Fitzgerald, Res 10, Pa ave
Geo Topham, Res 10, Pa ave
John West, square 461, 7th st
Wm Benter, square 491, Pa ave
P H King, square B, Pa ave
B O Sheckell, square 461, 7th st
Ellen Sweeting, square 490, C st
Jas Long, square 460, Pa ave & 6th st
Lucy H Laskey, square 461, 7th st
T P & M Brown, square 460, Pa ave
J H Clarvoe, square 461, 7th st
Rand & Williams [no other information]
John Foy, square 638, Pa ave
Jas Casparis, square 688, A st
Patrick Magarvey, Pa ave
Jno Donovan, Pa ave
B Shad, B & 2nd st
Jno A Golden, square 928, 8th st
R H Harrington, square 930, 8th st
Wm Thomas, sq 267, 13½ st & Md ave
Job Corson, square 355, Water st
Peter Jones, square 356, Water st

Premises examined, certified, & recommended by:

Saml Redfern	B O Sheckell	Michl McDermott
Thos Smith	Taphael Jones	Michl McCarty
Geo Kraft	Thos Donoho	Thos Young
Saml Stott	Jos Harbaugh	Stans Murray
F Schneider	Wm T Steiger	John Kelly
Chas A Schneider	John F Boone	J P Pepper
Wm Fischer	John Foy	F Cudlip
David Munroe	H Thorn	Seth Hyatt
John France	F Mattingly	Thos Pursell
Augustus Lepreux	Saml Bacon	Z D Gilman
Geo A W Randall	Robt S Patterson	Chas Stott
J Aigler	Edw B Stelle	A Coyle
Joel Downer	Vincent Massi	T P Brown
Wm Morrow	C Buckingham	A F Kimmell
Jas McColgan	S P Franklin	Levi Pumphrey
Nicholas Travers	R Jones	R Wallach
Abraham Butler	Patrick Moran	Jas Dixon
C P Sengstack	F Schlegel	Andrew Small
E Simms	Geo Wilner	Wm A Bradley
McC Young	Thos Cookendorfer	Jos H Bradley
Allison Nailor	W H Harrover	Jos Peck
Jas Larned	John Donohoo	H S Fitch
Michl Nourse	John Walker	J H Clarvoe
John J Joyce	Jas H Shreeve	J B Iardella
S R Hobbie	B F Morsell	N N Iardella
Thos Miller	Thos B Brown	A B Thruston
J W Clery	Geo C Siebel	Chas T Iardella
Jas H Causten	P Thyson	S A Iardella
Geo Lamb	J M Peerce	J B Gardner
E Evans	B F Middleton	W S Wheatley
Nathl Plant	Benj Beall	Simeon Brown
Enoch Ridgway	Geo Parker	A B Thruston
C Uttermohle	John W Maury	N C Towle
C Eckloff	Wm H Winter	Jos F Brown
John M Farrar	J M Johnson	Chas Lee Jones
J M Johnson	W H Upperman	Wm Greason
John H Buthman	Jas Fitzgerald	B Shadd
Jas Kelcher	R E Simms	Jno T Kilmon
S Pumphrey	P W Browning	J B Phillips
S Hyatt	John F Coyle	N Acker
Thos Baker	Edw Simms	J T Kilmon
Edw Sweeny	John A Smith	John Bohlayer
John R Hendley	A J Duvall	R M Combs
Michl Talty	W B Kibby	J R Queen
J H Eberbach	P W Browning	F S Walsh

Thos Bayne	J S Harvey & Co	Geo Mattingley
Antonio Catalano	Peter Casanave	K H Lambell
Philip Otterback	John Pettibone	J W Martin
Jas Tucker	Jno H Taylor	L Thomas
Wm M Ellis	D Johnson	Richd Wimsatt
Thos Kelly	John Laskey	Wm C Bamberger
Jas Rhodes	Jas Mitchell	Geo Hercus
J M Pagett	Richd Wimsatt	Peter Hepburn

Mrd: on Oct 18, at Gardiner, Maine, by Rt Rev Bishop Burgess, Maj F T Lally to Miss Ellen L Evans, daughter of the Hon Geo Evans.

Died: yesterday, of scarlet fever, Agnes Elizabeth, daughter of Wm & Eliz Dennisson, aged 3 years. Her funeral is this afternoon, at 4 o'clock, from the residence of her parents on G, between 5th & 6th sts.

Household & kitchen furniture at auction: on Nov 1, at the residence of his Excellency Baron Gerolt, Prussian Minister, at 8th & G sts, his very superior household furniture. –Edw C & G F Dyer

Persons lost by the burning of the steamer **Piney Woods**: Mr Duncan, whose body was found; Mr McNeil & wife, of New Orleans; Mrs Nicol & 2 children; 2 young daughters of Mr J H Harvey; the father also of Mrs McNeil & Mrs Nicol; 2 negro girls belonging to Mr Harvey; Mr Brown, of Clinton; The little boy who swam so well & was saved, was the son of Mr Harvey. New Orleans Com Bulletin of Oct 12

SAT OCT 28, 1848
Household & kitchen furniture at auction: deed of trust from Isaac H Robbins, dated May 26, 1847, recorded in Liber W B 134, folio 388, at the late residence of Robbins, on C st south, between 12th & 13th sts, on the Island, near Md ave, a good assortment of furniture. –Chas S Wallach, trustee -A Green, auct

Valuable house for rent or sale: now occupied by the Rev Mr Pyne, commonly known as the De Menon Bldgs. –H M Morfit, on 4½ st. Possession can be had in Nov.

A child of Mr Upham, who keeps a confectionary shop on Winthrop st, in this town, was smothered to death on Fri. The child, about a year old, was left on a bed, & forgetful of the fact, the father turned the bed up. In about half an hour the bed was taken down, & the child was found dead. –Hallowell Gaz

Dog lost. Finder liberally rewarded on leaving him with J B Chubb, 15th & F sts.

Mrd: on Oct 26, in Gtwn, D C, by Rev Mr Gassaway, Benj Stoddert Gantt, U S Navy, to Margaret Carrol, youngest daughter of the late Clement Smith, of Gtwn.

Mrd: on Oct 25, by Rev Jas S Donelan, Mr John B Floyd, of N Y, to Mrs Mary A Charles, of Wash City.

Mrd: on Oct 26, by Rev Wm Hamilton, Franklin Ford, of Bourbon Co, Ky, to Rebecca Louisa, eldest daughter of Presley Simpson.

Died: on Oct 26, of croup, Joseph, youngest child of John H & Eliz Smoot, in his 4th year. His funeral is from the residence of the parents, on 7th st, near the Navy Yard, on Sunday, at half-past 2 o'clock.

Died: on Oct 26, Charles Henry, son of Benj F & Lucinda Duvall, aged 6 months & 10 days.

Death of Lt Perry & others. By the New Orleans Mercury, of the 17th of the arrival of the ship **Suvial**, from the Balize, on the 5th instant, for N Y, having on board the 4th Regt of Infty, from Pascagoula, under command of Brevet Maj B Alvord. She encountered a severe storm in the Gulf, lost her rudder, & compelled to put back. On the 8th instant, while the storm was raging, Lt Christopher R Perry, of the 4th Infty, & 6 of the men, died on board, & 1 man was washed away. Lt Perry was a son of the late celebrated Com Oliver H Perry, & was a gallant ofcr.

For rent: the Cottage occupied by the subscriber, on Capitol Hill, 2nd door from St Peter's Church. Possession immediately. Apply to J E Millard, on the premises.

MON OCT 30, 1848
For rent: capacious house & premises lately occupied by the Hon H S Fox. Apply to Corcoran & Riggs.

Albany, N Y, Oct 27. The iron covering of the immense tank in process of erection in the city fell in today, & Giles Frederick, of N J, was killed. Injured: Philip P Dalley, of Phil, thigh & arm broken; Mr Davis, Mason, arm broken; Mr Gannon, badly injured.

The Queen has conferred the honor of knighthood on Mr Chas Lyell, late Pres of the Geological Society. -English papers

The handsome vessel **Lawrence** lately built by Capt Easby, under an order from the U S Gov't, is lying at the Arsenal, in the Potomac, until Nov 1 when she sets sail for Norfolk. Much credit to Mr Valentine Harbaugh, who furnished & arranged the medicine chest. Ofcrs attached to **Lawrence**: Alex'r V Fraser, Cmder; J S S Chaddock, E C Kennedy, W R Pierce, R H Bowling, & A J Gwin, Lts; J T Overstreet, Surgeon; Jas Walker, Boatswain; Jas Rankin, Gunner; Benj Brown, Carpenter; & John Adams, Sailmaker.

Died: on Oct 25, after a severe & protracted illness, at the residence of Mr Wm Ferguson, near Charlestown, Va, Miss Eliza, youngest daughter of the late Simon Summers, of Alexandria Co, in the full expectation of a blessed immortality.

Died: yesterday, in Wash City, in his 65th year, Capt John D Scott, late of Gtwn, whose execellence of character may be comprised in one short line, " An honest man is the noblest work of God." His funeral is this evening at 4 o'clock, at the Catholic Church, in Gtwn.

TUE OCT 31, 1848
The death of Martin Duralde, a once distinguished citizen of Louisiana, was lately announced. He was born of an affluent family in Attakapas, extensively connected, augmenting his hereditary fortune by successful investments, married to a daughter of the Hon Henry Clay, who was then at the zenith of his popularity & power. Reverse overtook him; city property rapidly ran down; his wife died; his friends diminished with his fortune. He recently embarked on a trading schnr at Tampico, to return home. The deadly fever of that coast swept off every one of the crew but a small boy, & when the vessel, after beating about in the Gulf, finally made the bar of the river with a signal of distress, the capt was found dead on a pallet, & Duralde by his side in the last agonies, no water, no medicine, with scarcely a ration of food on board. [Dec 5th newspaper: Martin Duralde, sr, had 2 beautiful daughters; one of whom was the 2nd wife of Chas Cole Claiborne, Govn'r of La; the other became Mrs John Clay. They were both married in their father's house & on the same day.]

Trustee's sale of real estate. By deed of trust from Thos Lowe, jr, to the subscriber, recorded in Liber W B, folios 59 thru 62, of the land records of Wash Co: auction on Nov 9 of lots 6, 7, & 8 in square north of square 743, with improvements. –Jas Adams, trustee -Edw C & G F Dyer

Valuable real estate for sale: the undersigned offer about 230 acres of land, lying on the west side of the road from Bladensburg to Rockville. It lies in PG Co, Md. Apply to the subscribers, residing near Bladensburg, or of D C Digges, Atty at Law, Upper Marlboro, PG Co, Md. –Norah Digges, Geo A Digges

WED NOV 1, 1848
The new schnr **Arlington**, named in honor of G W P Custis, lately built in Connecticut for Messrs F & A Dodge, of Gtwn, was to sail from N Y last Sat. She is intended to run between N Y & the port of Gtwn.

The Boston papers announce the decease on Sun last, of the Hon Harrison Gray Otis, at the advanced age of 83 years. He was a descendant of John Otis, who came from England to this country & settled in Hingham, Mass, in 1830; & a nephew of the celebrated Jas Otis, of Revolutionary memory, to whose eloquence the cause of American Independence was so lately indebted. Mr Otis was born in Boston, Oct 8, 1765, & was in his 84th year. He graduated at Harvard University in 1783. He was appointed District Atty under John Adams, member of the Hartford Convention, Pres of our State Senate, Judge of the Boston Court of Common Pleas, & 3rd Mayor of Boston

Mrd: on Oct 31, by Rev Wm Collier, Mr C F P E Greer to Miss Mary C Carr, of Wash.

Circuit Court: Hugh McElrath vs Sec of the Treasury. On Sat last, this case was up. It was a bill filed on the equity side of the Court in the following case: it appears that Betsy McIntosh, who resided among the Indians, beyond the Mississippi, had in May, 1847, awarded her $7,500 in commutation for 640 acres of land, under the treaties of 1817 & 1835 with the Cherokee tribe of Indians. She gave a power of atty to Hugh McElrath to receive & receipt for what was coming to her from the U S, & covenanted therein to give him one half for his services, should he obtain her claim. McElrath employed J H Eaton, who presented her claim, & demanded the amount due of the Sec of the Treas, who refused to pay it over. The effect of the bill is to enjoin the money in the hands of the Sec. Chancellor Bibb for cmplnt, & D A & Mr Gillet, Solicitor of the Treasury, for the U S. Further consideration of the case was postponed until next Sat.

Wash Corp: 1-Ptn of J C Hall & others, for straightening & enlarging the sewer between 9th & 10th sts, from Pa ave to the Canal: referred to the Cmte on Improvements. 2-Cmte of Claims: bill for the relief of Thos J Barrett: passed. Same cmte: act for the relief of Benj F Middleton: passed. Same cmte: bill for the relief of Caleb Dulany: passed. 3-Ptn of M Rozenstock, for remission of a fine: referred to the Cmte of Claims.

Died: on Oct 30, after a short illness, Mrs Catharine Anne Hayre, daughter of Richd & Susan Burch, of Wash City. Her funeral is this afternoon, at 3 o'clock, from her late residence, the *Van Ness Mansion*, 17th st.

Died: on Oct 30, of consumption, Wm H Wright. His funeral is from the residence of Jos H Nevett, Pa ave, between 14th & 15th sts, on Thu, at 12 o'clock.

A new book store, on Pa ave, near 9th st, is to be opened this day by 2 of our worthy young townsmen, Messrs Hudson Taylor & C B Maury. We cheerfully commend these young aspirants to our readers.
+
Hudson Taylor & Chas B Maury have associated themselves under the firm of Taylor & Maury, Booksellers & Stationers. Their store is under the ofc of Dr J C Hall, Pa ave, 5 doors west of 9th st.

Circuit Court of D C, sitting in Wash. Susan M Burch, cmplnt, vs Robt Craig, Geo Craig, Thos Craig, Chas Craig, Wm McCreary & Martha McCreary, children of John McCreary & Harriet, his wife, late Harriet Craig, & others, descendants & heirs at law of Geo Craig, late of Gtwn, D C, deceased, dfndnts. Bill of cmplnt sets forth that, in 1818, Jeremiah W Bronaugh & others filed their bill of cmplnt in said Court against Ann Craig, widow, & Louis, Robt, Geo, Henry, Chas, Washington, & Thos Craig, children & heirs at law of Geo Craig, late of Gtwn, D C, deceased, in which they charged that Geo Craig had died indebted to them & others, & that his personal estate was insufficient to pay his debts, & prayed a decree for the sale of so much of his estate as might be necessary, in addition to his personal estate, to pay the debts due to the cmplnts & to such others of the creditors of said Geo as might come in & contribute to the expenses of the said suit; &

such further proceedings were had in said cause, that, on Jun 27, 1818, the said Court decreed that lots 226, 255, & 268, & part of lot 54, in Beall's addition to Gtwn, part of the real estate of said Geo Craig, deceased, should be sold for the purpose aforesaid, & that Nicholas Hedges, now deceased, should be trustee to make such sale; that Hedges reported to the Court he had sold the said part of lot 54 to Ann Craig, for $590; that the said Court, on Jun 11, 1822, passed an order that the sale so made & reported should be ratified & confirmed, unless good cause to the contrary be shown to the Court on or before Oct 1 next; said Ann Criag afterwards sold her interest in the premises so acquired to John A Wilson, on certain terms, which were fully complied with by Wilson, & since his death by the cmplnt; that she said Wilson, in his lifetime, paid the said purchase money, & the said trustee & the said Ann Craig, by a certain deed executed by them & filed with the said bill of cmplnt, conveyed the said part of lot 54 to the said Wilson, his heirs & assigns; that John A Wilson made his last will & testament, & devised the premises to the cmplnt, & hath died without revoking or altering the same; that the said trustee, so far as appears by the proceedings in the suit, did not cause the said provisional order of ratification to be published as was required, & no file of said paper is accessible to the cmplnt, so that she cannot prove the publication of the same; the object of cmplnts' bill is to obtain a further order of the said Court, in the said original cause, for the ratification of the said sale, & for the appointment of a trustee in the place of the deceased Nicholas Hedges, to convey to her the said premises. The bill states that Ann Craig & Henry Craig, have died intestate, the latter without issue; that Robt & Geo Craig left the U S more than 20 years past, & have never been heard from, & are supposed to be dead, intestate & without issue; that Thos Craig removed more than 10 years since to the State of Alabama, is supposed to be dead, not having been heard of for 8 years. Chas Craig lives in the State of Ohio; Louis Craig is dead intestate, leaving a widow, named Nancy Ann Craig, & 4 sons, his heirs at law, viz: John H Craig, Geo W Craig, Chas E Craig, & Wm Craig; that Washington Craig is still living; that Harriet McCreary is dead, leaving 2 children her heirs at law, namely, Wm McCreary & Marthy McCreary, all of whom are named dfndnts to the cmplnt's bill. It appears to the Court that the said Robt Craig, Geo Craig, & Thos Craig, if living, & Chas Craig, Wm McCreary & Martha McCreary are not inhabitants of D C, & cannot be found therein, it is ordered that the said absent dfndnts appear in this Court by the 3rd Mon of Mar next. –Wm Brent, clk [*2 spellings of Marthy-Martha.]

THU NOV 2, 1848
For rent: that handsome 2 story frame house corner of 13th & K sts, lately occupied by J S Reed. Inquire of the subscriber, on F st, between 14th & 15th sts, or to Mr John Y Laub, 1st Comptroller's Ofc, Treas Dept. -Eliz A Laub

Mrs Armitage, the English giantess, is dead. She weighed 31 stone, was 4 feet round the waist, 6 feet round the bust, 7 feet 1 inch round the hips, & 22 inches round the arm above the elbow.

The late fire in Alexandria, La, consumed about 70 bldgs. The principal sufferers are Messrs S Mead, S A Henarie, O W Nalley, D E Goodwin, Jacob Walker, J McFeely, Lawrence Fehrer, Biossat, H M Hams, & R Chew.

Telegraphic dispatch dated yesterday at St Louis: the gallant Gen Kearny, who served his country so faithfully during the war, & who endured so many hardships while in Calif, died in this city yesterday, after a lingering illness.

Died: on Oct 31, Mrs Susanna Derrick, aged 81 years. With simplicity & Godly sincerity she had her conversation in the world.

Died: on Oct 26, Mary Ellen, daughter of Wm G & Cecilia Jones, aged 3 years, 11 months & 26 days.

For rent: 2 story brick house on B st, nearly opposite Gadsby's Hotel. Apply to Simms & Son, Pa ave. -Edw Simms

For rent: 2 well furnished rooms, a parlor, & a chamber, in a private family, near the State Dept. Inquire of B Reiss, G st, between 14th & 15th sts.

The subscriber, wishing to change his business, will dispose of his interest in that well-known Tavern stand on La ave, adjoining *Copp's Pavilion*. Inquire on the premises.
–John Douglas

FRI NOV 3, 1848
City Ordinances-Wash: 1-Act for the relief of Thos J Barrett: sum of $37.51 be paid to him, being the balance due him on settlement of his accounts as police ofcr of the late 4th Ward. 2-Act to reimburse Benj F Middleton the amount paid by him in the case of smallpox on La ave in 1846 to prevent the spreading of the disease: the sum of $30 is appropriated. 3-Act for the relief of Caleb Dulany: refund of $10, being the amount of a fine. 4-Act for the relief of Saml Cromwell: fine imposed for an alleged violation of an ordinance relative to fast driving his omnibus, is hereby remitted. 5-Act for the relief of E D & H A Willard: fine imposed for an alleged violation of law relative to baggage wagons: hereby remitted.

The corner stone of the **Roman Catholic Cathedral**, to be built at Cleveland, Ohio, was laid, with impressive religious ceremonies, on Oct 22. Bishop Timon officiated.

Last summer, a young daughter of Mr Corcoran, [of the firm of Corcoran & Riggs] of Wash, was playing with some friends on a wharf in the rear of the grounds of Capt Chas Williams, at Stonington, Conn, & stepped into a boat which loosed & drifted from shore. The child, frightened, jumped overboard. Mr Gurdon Smith, a boat builder, who was near by, swam in & rescued her at the last moment of struggling. Mr Corcoran was in Europe on business. Last week a letter from Mr Corcoran to Mr Smith, expressing his gratitude, had $1,000 enclosed as a testimony of his gratitude. This was an unexpected reward.

Mrd: on Nov 1, by Rev L J Gilliss, John H Thompson to Harriet Jane, youngest daughter of Gustavus Waters, all of Wash City.

Mrd: on Oct 26, by Rev Dr Ryder, Pres of the Gtwn College, Dr Thos J Villard, of Gtwn, to Miss Caroline C Bryan, of Wash City.

Died: on Nov 2, Mrs Harriet E Clarke, in her 59th year. Her funeral will take place from her late residence, on 8th st, between L & M sts, at 3 o'clock this Fri evening.

Died: on Oct 31, Mrs Susanna Derrick, aged 81 years. Her friends & acquaintants, & those of her daughter, Mrs Ulrick, are requested to attend her funeral at St John's Church, this day, at one o'clock.

Died: on Oct 18, at New Orleans, after a short but fatal attack of yellow fever, Jas McKim, first mate of the ship **James Titcomb**, & eldest son of Mr John McKim, of Wash City, aged 27 years.

All persons are notified that I will not be responsible for debts hereafter contracted on my account, unless with me personally, or by my written order. –B Chambers [Balt Sun]

SAT NOV 4, 1848
Died: on Nov 2, Mrs Eliz Thompson, in her 38th year, relict of the late Geo C Thompson. Her funeral is on Nov 5, from her late residence on 2nd st south, Capitol Hill. [No time given.]

Died: yesterday, Mr Wm Gulager, in his 60th year. His funeral is this afternoon, at 2 o'clock, from his late residence on 12th st, between Pa ave & E st.

Died: on Nov 3, Jane Frances, infant daughter of Alice, widow of Patrick Moran, deceased. The funeral will take place from the residence of Mrs A Moran, Water st, Gtwn, on this evening, at 4 o'clock.

Trustee's sale: by order of Montg Co Court as a Court of Equity, in the case of Adam Robb & others vs Henry Harding, adm of Thos F W Vinson & others, the subscriber, as trustee, will offer at public sale all the real estate of which said Thos F W Vinson died seized, to wit: on Dec 16, sale on the premises of *The Resurvey on Corsbasket* & *The Resurvey on Blantire*, containing 524 acres of land, 265 acres of which are assigned as the widow's dower, & will be sold subject to her interest therein. This land lies within 2 miles of Poolesville, Montg Co, Md. On Dec 18, will sell at the Courthouse door, in Rockville, the farm, with improvements thereon, in said county, called *Addition to Ray's Adventure*, containing 134 acres of land, as conveyed by deed from Wm N Austin, trustee of Wm O'Neale, jr, to said Thos F W Vinson, bearing date of Dec 17, 1842, recorded in Liber B S 12, folio 115, of the land records of Montg Co, & is the same land upon which Philip Duvall now resides. The subscriber will also sell, at the time & place last mentioned, the house & lot in Rockville, fronting the Courthouse square, in which the said Thos F W Vinson resided at the time of his death, being part of lot 2; & also the lot known in said plot as lot 3, lying between the lots respectively occupied by Mr Wm Baker & Dr Anderson. –Robt W Carter, Trustee

Watches & watch repairing: place of business is removed to Todd's bldg, 4 doors west of Brown's Indian Queen Hotel, between 6th & 7th sts, Pa ave. —Chauncey Warriner

Mrd: on Nov 1, at Martinsburg, Va, by Rev Wm Love, John Blair Hoge to Anna Creighton, daughter of the late John K Wilson.

MON NOV 6, 1848

On Oct 25 the coast of Florida was visited by a severe storm, which caused the loss of life & considerable property damage. Several vessels are known to have been lost, one one of which the following passengers perished: Mr Wm Gamble, son of Col John G Gamble, of Tallahassee; Mr Bushnell, resident on one of the Keys, but lately of Illinois; Mrs Butler, a lady under his protection; & a sailor, name not known.

In Chancery. Jos Edmund Law, cmplnt, against Jas Adams, Lloyd N Rogers & others, dfndnts. Persons claiming to be creditors of Thos Law, late of Wash City, deceased, to present & prove their claims with me. -W Redin, adm

Railroad collision on Thu at the Marblehead junction, in Mass. Killed: Saml Manning, of Marblehead, a young married man; Nathl W Roundy, of do; John Geo Stevens, of do; John Cross, of do, about 15 years of age, the son of a widow; Henry Trefry, about 20, son of the cashier of the Marblehead Bank; & a lad by the name of Russell. Wounded: son of Capt B Brown, who had both legs cut off; Moses Hill, of Marblehead; & others whose names we have not heard.

European Intelligence: Gen Rachis, cmder of the 5th division of the army of the Alps, was killed by being thrown from his horse against a tree. He was 69 years old.

Mrd: on Nov 2, by Rev Francis Vinton, D D, Rector of Emanuel Church, David H Vinton, Major U S Army, & Eliza A, 2nd daughter of D H Arnold, of Brooklyn.

Died: on Nov 5, in Gtwn, Mr Gustavus Harrison, in his 56th year. His funeral is from his late residence, on Prospect st, this afternoon, Nov 6, at 3½ o'clock.

Died: on Nov 5, of dropsy of the brain, after an illness of 18 days, Lewis Philip, son of Henry & Hannah Janney, aged 13 months & 11 days. His funeral is today at 2 o'clock.

For rent: 3 story brick dwlg, on F st, between 12th & 13th sts. In the rear is a brick bldg 24 feet square, in which the Misses Tyson recently kept their Female Seminary. For terms, apply to J M Krofft's Bakery, on the corner near & east of the premises.

Mr Owen Conolly, one of the ofcrs at the Capitol, was seriously injured on Sat. He was unlocking the ponderous iron gate, weighing probably 8 cwt, & the gate got off the hing, fell upon him, & so fixed him under it that he was unable to extricate himself, until he was discovered by Mr McCarthy, the carrier of the Nat'l Intell, who, with the help of another person, released the sufferer. Mr Conolly's collar-bone is broken & he is much injured in the back & side.

House for rent: the subscriber has for rent the dwlg part of his 3 story brick house, opposite Brown's Hotel, Pa ave. It has an alley outlet to Canal st. Apply for terms to G C Grammer.

TUE NOV 7, 1848
Valuable lands at auction: under the authority of the last will & testament of the late proprietor: public auction, on Dec 1, the farm on the Eastern Branch of the Potomac, now in the occupation of Mr Geo Marbury: 130 acres to be sold in sub-divisions or lots as follows: 1-25 to 30 acres bounded on the east by the old Bladensburg road, on the west by the Eastern Branch, & lies between Mr Danford's land & the old Ferry road. 2-Lot of about 15 acres in the rear of Webster & Ball's property. 3-Lot of about 15 acres, between #2 lot & Danford's land. 4-Lot of about 30 acres, fronts on the main road from the Navy Yard bridge. 5-Lot of about 30 acres, that fronts on the Navy Yard road.
--John Marbury, trustee -Edw C & G F Dyer

Orphans Court of Wash Co, D C. Letters of administration on the personal estate of Francis Lombardi, late of Wash Co, deceased. –Caroline Lombardi, admx

The proprietor of the *Anacostia Bridge*, having, under the late act of Congress, sold his bridge to the U S, we are authorized to state that it is now free. [Nov 8 newspaper: the Sec fixed the Anacostia bridge at $10,000.]

Mrd: on Nov 5, by Rev O B Brown, Mr Wm S Groves to Miss Willie Ann Donnelly, both of Wash City.

I hereby certify that John O Harry, of Tenallytown, Wash Co, D C, brought before me 2 stray bright bay horses. –Chas R Belt, J P [Owner to prove property, pay charges, & take them away. –John O Harry]

For rent: a genteel Dwlg-house, suited to a small family: on the north side of the West Market square. Apply to Maj Geo Bender, living near the premises.

Mrs J B Hills will open Winter Millinery on Nov 9: south side of Pa ave, between 9th & 10th sts.

WED NOV 8, 1848
Louis Napoleon Bonaparte: the Courrier des Etats Unis: Paris, Oct 12, 1848. Last Thu, in the church of Rueil, the annual service was celebrated to the memory of the Empress Josephine & Queen Hortense, the grandmother & mother of citizen ex-Prince Louis Napoleon Bonaparte, representative of the people. The absence of the family was owing to the excessive care of Prince Louis to withdraw himself from public view. He had come to Rueil the day before with his uncle, the ex-King Jerome, & his 2 cousins, & they made their devotion privately in the church, where the clergy awaited them. They visited Malmaison, which is rich in reminiscence, & which now belongs to Maria Christina, Queen Dowager of Spain.

Wanted an Overseer, to take charge of a farm about 4 miles north of the centre Market. No objection to a Scotchman or Englishman. Inquire of John H Buthman, Wine Merchant, opposite Coleman's Hotel.

The Mississippi Jacksonian of Oct 25 states the death of ex-Govn'r A G McNutt, who died within 20 miles of Holly Springs on Oct 22. He was one of the Democratic Electors of the State at large.

Phil Sun of Mon: Murdered in our city on Fri, Alfred Coleman, between 19 & 20 years old, son of Mr Nathan Coleman, who with 2 lads, Geo W Roberts & Thos Marple, stood watching a Democratic torchlight procession. John Agen is charged with being the striker of the blow that killed Coleman. David McAleer has been arrested, charged with other Democrats, of the crime of assaulting Danl Copehart the same night.

Death from Hydrophobia. Mr Mathias Duke, Issuer in the Commissariat, died in Kingston, Canada, a few days since. He received, about a month ago, a bite from a cat which it is presumed caused his malady.

The Earl of Carlisle, who died at his seat at Castle Howard on the 7th instant, in his 96th year, was one of the com'rs appointed by the British Gov't in 1778 to treat with the American colonies. He was the uncle of Lord Byron. The Earl's son was the gallant Howard who fell at Waterloo, whose memory is preserved in the well-known stanzas of Childe Harolde, where the poet confesses that he "did his sire some wrong."

Died: on Oct 21, at the residence of Mrs Eliza Ashton, Fauquier Co, Va, after a protracted illness, Miss Peggy Ashton, late of Alexandria, Va, at an advanced age, a lady of exemplary piety & benevolence.

For rent: the dwlg part of a 3 story brick house on Pa ave, between 9th & 10th sts. Possession given immediately. Inquire of Mary H Alexander, 12th st, below the avenue.

The dwlg house of Mr John Hooe, Mayfield, Prince Wm Co, Va, was entirely consumed by fire on Nov 1. Every kindness has been offered to the family by the neighbors.
–Alexandria Gaz

A skeleton was discovered in removing the foundations of Trinity College Church, in Edinburgh, which was supposed to be the remains of the Queen, Mary Gueldress, wife of the Second James, foundress of the chapel. The bones were conveyed with considerable pomp to the royal vault at Holyrood, & deposited with the kingly dead of Scotland. A few weeks later another skeleton was discovered, which the antiquarians believed to be the true remains, & it too was buried in a royal style.

THU NOV 9, 1848
Died: on Nov 8, Helena Josephine, daughter of Seraphin & Catharine Masi, aged 2 years & 10 months. Her funeral is this afternoon, at 4 o'clock.

Mrs Ellet's new work, "The Women of the Revolution." The wife of Benedict Arnold was Margaret Shippen, of Phil. One of her ancestors, Edw Shippen, who was mayor of the city in the beginning of the 18th century, suffered severe persecutions from the zealots in authority at Boston, for his Quakerism; but in his business, he amassed a large fortune, & had the biggest house & carriage in Phil. His mansion was called the *governor's house*. Edw Shippen, afterward Chief Justice of Pa, was the father of Margaret. The youngest of his daughters, only 18 years of age, full of spirit & gayety, was the toast of the British ofcrs while their army occupied Phil. She became the object of Arnold's admiration. Mrs Arnold survived her husband 3 years, & died in London in 1804, at the age of 43. Hannah, the sister of Arnold, possessed great excellence of character; but no particulars have been obtained by which full justice could be done her.

Notice is hereby given to the heirs of Saml Leonard, late of Chestertown, Kent Co, Md, that I have administered on the estate of the said deceased; & that they are to appear before the Orphans' Court of Kent Co, on or before Apr 7 next. –Peregrine Wroth, adm of S Leonard, deceased.

Mrd: on Tue last, by Rev J F Cook, Mr Wm P Parke to Miss Virginia Norris, both of Wash City.

Mrd: on Nov 8, by Rev Mr Morgan, Geo McCauley to Miss Susan, daughter of the late Jas Shields, of Wash.

Trustee's sale: by decree of the Circuit Court of D C, passed in a cause wherein Jacob Snider, jr, is cmplnt, & the heirs at law of the late John Vaughan are dfndnts: auction on Nov 20: lots 14 & 16 in square 583; lots 6, 11 & 16, in square 585; lots 11 & 16 in square 587; lots 14 thru 18 in square 589; & lots 3, 7 thru 11, & 16, in square 643, in Wash City. –D A Hall, trustee -A Green, auctioneer

FRI NOV 10, 1848
Pastry & Cakes of superior quality. -Thos Havenner & Son, C st, between 4½ & 6th sts.

The steamship **Edith**, of the Quartermaster's Dept, Coulyard master, sailed from N Y on Nov 7, bound for San Francisco, Calif. Passengers on board: Capt F B Shaeffer, U S Army, J Keller & W P Humphreys, U S Coast Survey.

The gas pipes being laid on both side of Pa ave is for the purpose of lighting it with Solar Gas. It is expected that by Dec 1, Pa ave & the Pres' House will receive the benefit of the solar lights.

Mrd: on Tue last, by Rev Mr Alig, Mr Wm H Howell to Miss Sarah Ann Paugett, both of Chas Co, Md.

For rent: brick dwlg house on N Y ave, near 14th st, lately occupied by Geo W Young, with the large lot adjoining. Apply to Mr James, next door, or to Jas Larned, 13th st.

By deed of trust from Wm Coale to the subscriber, dated Apr 10, 1848, recorded in Liber A B 142, folio 175, of the land records of Wash Co, I shall sell at public auction, on Nov 20, at the store recently occupied by said Coale, on 7th st, between I & N Y ave, all his stock in trade of groceries & store fixtures, & goods of every description.
–Edw Swann, trustee

Public sale of highly valuable personal property: by order of the Orphans' Court of Montg Co: sale on Nov 23, at the late residence of John P C Peter, late of said county, deceased: horses, cattle sheep, & hogs, being raised by Mr Reybold, of Delaware, & purchased of him by Mr Peter. Also, a large collection of farming utensils. Also, the household & kitchen furniture. –Eliz Jane Peters, admx

Orphans Court of Wash Co, D C. Letters of administration on the personal estate of Jas Frerer, late of Wash Co, deceased. –Eliz M Frerer, admx

SAT NOV 11, 1848
The Electoral returns which we publish this morning proclaim that Zachary Taylor has been elected Pres of the U S. The fourth of Mar, 1849, will revive the heroic age of the Republic.

For rent: 2 story brick house on the island, south F st. Apply to Mrs A T Young, on 8th st, between G & H.

Orphans Court of Wash Co, D C. Letters testamentary on the personal estate of Eliz A Thompson, late of said county, deceased. –Wm J Wheatly, exc

D H Branch & Co, late of Petersburg, Va, have within a few days past undertaken the management of the U S Hotel, on Pa ave between 3rd & 4½ sts, in Wash

Thaddeus B Wakeman, the founder of the American Institute, died in this city yesterday, aged about 70 years. He was a graduate of Yale College, & Judge Meigs was his old friend & class-mate.

Md Agricultural Exhibition: in the city of Balt, on Nov 9. Horace Capron, of PG Co, has a Durham bull, 8 years old, & weighs no less than 1,900 pounds. C B Calvert exhibited his collection of Alderney & Durham cows. His display of horses & oxen is highly creditable. J H McHenry, of Balt, displayed a Canadian stallion. Other cow exhibitors: Col Atlee, of Carroll Co; Dr Troup, of Balt Co; A Clement, of Phil, Pa; B Reybold, of Delaware; Mr Goldsborough, of Talbot Co; W B Dobbin & John Gibson, of Chester Hill. Thos Blagden, of Wash, had the sleekest yoke of oxen. Award for hogs goes to Jas G Coxe & Wm Jessup; in for sheep-Col Ware, of Va, & Geo Patterson, of Carroll Co.

Orphans Court of Wash Co, D C. Letters of administration on the personal estate of Henry M Prevost, late of said county, deceased. –Sophia Prevost, admx [Jas H Hamilton is authorized to receive accounts & receipt for money.]

MON NOV 13, 1848

Franklin Camper, of Balt, & John Rady, of Wash City, were committed, on Wed last, to jail, charged with outrageously assaulting Aquila Allen & John Brady on Nov 7, near the Whig Congressional Cmte Room on Pa ave.

Improvements on the island. A handsome brick dwlg has been erected on the corner of 12th st & Md ave for Mr Bird; another bldg erected for Mr Emory is now occupied as a grocery store by Mr Myers. Mr Jones has made considerable improvements in his hotel at the Steamboat wharf.

Information wanted of his son Edw Boulanger, who is said to be in Mobile, any person who knows where he is will confer a very great favor by addressing a line to Jos Boulanger, G st, near the War & Navy Depts, Wash, D C.

For sale: improved & unimproved property in Wash. Apply to Middleton & Beall, or to the subscriber, J Boulanger.

Circuit Court of Wash Co, D C: made in the cause wherein Wm Dowling, adm of Greenfield, & others, are plntfs, & John F Ennis, adm de bonis non of Bernard Kelly & others, are dfndnts: on Nov 27, I will proceed to sell on the premises, lot 1 in square west of 1, with a 2 story brick house long used as a tavern. Also lot 11 in square 1, with the improvements. This property is on K st north, opposite the Wash Brewery.
–Jas W Sheahan, trustee -A Green, auctioneer

In Chancery. Saml Smoot, cmplnt, against Mary Jane Smoot, widow, & Saml C Smoot, Luther Smoot, John Waggerman & Lydia his wife, Jos Pleasants & Rosa his wife, & Araminta Smoot, heirs of Chas H Smoot, dfndnts. The creditors of Chas H Smoot, deceased, to file their claims on or before Nov 17, at my ofc, in the City Hall, Wash.
–W Redin, auditor

Mrd: on Oct 31, at *Fruit Vale*, by Rev Wm F Lockwood, Col Jas Thrift to Lucretia M, youngest daughter of Col John Reid, all of Fairfax Co.

Mrd: on Nov 7, at Berkeley Springs, by the Rev Wm Love, Jas Lingan Randolph to Emily, daughter of John Strother, of Martinsburg, Va.

Cincinnati papers. Gen Jas Taylor died at his residence in Newport, Ky, on Nov 7. He was born in 1769, in Caroline Co, Va, & emigrated to Ky in 1792. He was Quartermaster Gen of the Northwestern Army during the last war with England. He preserved his faculties to the last hour. He had the satisfaction of casting his vote for his friend & relative, Gen Zachary Taylor, for Pres of the U S. The Judges of the Election went to his chamber to receive his vote. Gen Jas Taylor was the oldest inhabitant of Campbell Co, & was in his 80th year.

Died: on Nov 12, in her 5th year, Sophia Bache, only daughter of Maj Wm H Emory, U S Army.

Died: yesterday, in Wash City, after a protracted illness, Mr John H Wade, one of the oldest & most highly esteemed printers of this city, in his 58th year. He was a native of England, but for the last 40 years a resident in this District. His funeral is Tue, at 11 o'clock, from his late residence on 6th st, between G & H.

TUE NOV 14, 1848
Jonathan Harrington, of Lexington, the last survivor of the battle of Lexington, who is now about 90 years of age, walked 1½ miles on Tue, & deposited the first vote for Zachary Taylor in that town.

Mr Wm A Bardwell, son of Rev Mr Bardwell, of Oxford, Mass, died yesterday of hydrophobia. He was bitten by a strange dog on Jul 29. He was about 18 years of age.
–Lowell Courier

Relative rank of Generals. An ofcr of the war of 1812, who amuses himself with such matters, has compiled the following:
Maj Generals: Scott, Gaines, Jesup, Taylor, [Butler, Patterson,] Worth, Twiggs, [Quitman,] Kearny, [dead,] Wool, [Pillow, Shields,] Persifer Smith, [Cadwalader, & Lane.]
Brig Generals: Brady, Brooke, Gibson, Arbuckle, Roger Jones, Towson, [Marshall,] Churchill, Whiting, Belknap, Pierce, Bankhead, Totten, [Cushing,] Riley, Harney, [Price,] Garland, Clark, [Morgan, Andrews, Trousdale,] Chiled. Those in parentheses are disbanded.

Inquest was held over the body of Jas Pearce, about 35 years of age, & a native of Ireland. He left his boarding house & when near the 7th st bridge he suddenly fell & expired. He had served his country faithfully in Mexico, & was well known here.

Napoleon Crossing the Alps painted by Paul Delroche, now on exhibition in Wash City, is a work of art of much merit. Napoleon is dress in his gray coat, seated on a plodding mule.

Mrd: on Nov 13, at St Mary's Church, by Rev Mathias Alig, Mr Xaver Wild to Miss Eliz Raab, both of Wash City.

Died: on Nov 10, the Rev John Hodges, in his 39th year.

Died: on Sun, in Wash City, suddenly, of disease of the heart, Robt Stuart, aged about 65 years. Thus has fallen, in the full meridian of his usefulness & in the ripeness of his years, an honorable upright man. He was by birth a Scotchman, but emigrated to this country at an early age. He has filled various official stations in Michigan, & as Indian agent did much to better the condition & improve the hearts of the Red Men among whom he was thrown. At about age 20, he was one of the party sent out by the American Fur Co which made the settlement & established a trading house at the mouth of the Columbia river, in Oregon. -Chicago Journal, Nov 6

Public sale, at his residence in Queen Ann district, on Dec 14, his entire personal property, consisting of negroes, horses, cattle, sheep, hogs, crop of tobacco, & corn, together with household & kitchen furniture. –Richd C Bowie

Farm on Paint Creek: subscriber offers his Farm in the Turnpike road at the crossings of Paint Creek, 16 miles west of Chillicothe, for sale: 388 acres.
–J Woodbridge, Chillicothe, Ohio.

Superior Family Groceries: 15th & I sts, opposite Mrs Madison's. –Z M P King

Trustee's sale: by decree of the Circuit Court of Wash Co, D C, in Chancery, in the cause of Henry Barker et al, vs David Riley, the only heir at law of Catharine Campbell, deceased: I will offer at public auction, Dec 14, lot 8 in square 16, in Wash City- improved real estate. –Dan Radcliff, trustee -Martin & Wright, aucts

Capt Korponay, who commanded one of the companies of the Missouri volunteers with so much credit in Mexico, has been appointed teacher of cavalry tactics in the U S Academy at West Point.

The Lachine Railroad has been purchased by Sir Geo Simpson for $120,000. It cost $600,000.

In Chancery. Edmund Hanly's excs & others vs Susan D Shepherd & Alex'r R Shepherd & others, admx & heirs of Alex'r Shepherd, deceased. Creditors to file their claims.
–Hamilton Lufborough, Special Auditor

Runaway committed to the jail of Wash Co, a negro man John Minor, about 25 years of age. Says at one time he belonged to Hanson Prock, at Falmouth Mills, Spottsylvania Co, Va, & others that he is free. Owners of said negro is to prove his property, pay charges, & take him away. –Thos Martin, Sheriff

Household & kitchen furniture at auction, on Nov 21, at the residence of Maj Gen Winfield Scott, on the corner of F & 15th sts. -Edw C & G F Dyer

WED NOV 15, 1848
The paintshop of Mr A W Purdy on 3rd st, between C & Pa ave, was destroyed by fire yesterday.

Wash Co: 1-Wm A Robinson as superintendent of chimney sweeps for the 4th Ward, in place of Jos Littleton, resigned, was confirmed.

Appointments by the Pres: 1-Jos Graham, of Ohio, to be Consul of the U S for Buenos Ayres, vice Geo I Fairfield, deceased. 2-Geo F Shepley, to be U S Atty for the district of Maine, vice Augustine Haynes, resigned. 3-Lucian Barbour, to be U S Atty, for the district of Indiana, vice Danl Mace, resigned.

The steamer **Massachusetts** sailed from N Y on Fri, for Oregon, with U S troops. The command consists of companies L & M of the 1st Regt of U S Artl, numbering about 160 men, & the following ofcrs: Maj J S Hathaway, 1st Artl, commanding the btln; Capt B H Hill, 1st Artl, commanding Co M; 1st Lt John B Gibson, 1st Artl; 1st Lt T Talbot, 1st Artl; 2nd Lt T J Woods, 1st Artl; 2nd Lt Jas B Fry, 1st Artl; 2nd Lt Grier Tallmadge, 1st Artl; 2nd Lt John Dement, 1st Artl. Assist Surgeon Holden, U S A, accompanies the command.

$100 reward for runaway negro man Gassaway, called by the servants Wm Burgess: aged 22 years old, left home on Nov 10. –Thos Clagett, near Upper Marlboro, PG Co, Md.

In Friday's Albany journal is reported the trial of Titus Foster, at the Wash Oyer & Terminer, for the murder of his son on Mar 10. Foster had been freely drinking when his wife & son set off together. The old man quarreled with his wife & the son grappled with his father, who stabbed him. Verdict, manslaughter in the 3rd degree. Punishment, 4 years in State prison.

Franklin's resting place. In the corner of the burying ground, best known as <u>Christ's Church yard</u>, Phil, repose the remains of the philosopher Franklin. Inscription: Benjamin & Deborah Franklin. –Baptist Record

On Nov 4, at Troy, N Y, Mr Calvin Symmes became caught in his factory, while the drum was revolving, & his skull was fractured, & most of his bones in his body were broken by violent strokes against the floor.

<u>Ladies with letters in the Wash Post Ofc, Nov 15, 1848.</u>

Adams, Mrs Cath	Dunking, Mrs E	Jackson, Miss H
Alexander, Mrs E	Dover, Miss Mary	Jones, Miss Mary
Anderson, Mrs E	Delano, Miss Susan	King, Mrs Sarah S
Ball, Miss Amanda	Edwards, Mrs Anne	Lewis, Miss M C
Beall, Miss Ann E	Ewell, Miss Mil E	Laurason, Miss A C
Blanche, Miss C	Freeman, Miss Ann	Lindsay, Miss Cath
Burton, Miss Cath	Finnegan, Mrs C	Laurason, Mrs E
Butler, Miss Emily	Foulkes, Mrs E A	Laracy, Miss R A
Beyer, Miss Hen	Fairbanks, Miss F	Locke, Mrs S A
Beach, Miss Jane C	Foushee, Mrs Isa	Morton, Mrs M-2
Burch, Miss M P	Fitzgerald, Mrs Jas	Morse, Mrs Edw
Brawner, Miss M	Groce, Miss Indiana	Moffitt, Mrs E
Bell, Miss Matilda	Gary, Mrs Louisa	Marshall, Miss E A
Bruce, Mary F	Gibson, Mrs M J	Miles, Miss M E
Bell, Miss Sophia	Hobbs, Mrs Ann H	Mitchell, Mrs M A
Crier, Miss Emily	Hebron, Amelia	Murray, Mrs M H
Coke, Mrs Emily	Herbert, Miss Allen	Martin, Miss M S
Childs, Mrs M G-2	Hall, Mrs Geo W	Marrow, Mrs Susan
Duvall, Mrs C H	Henning, Mrs Hen	McPherson, Miss M
Davis, Mrs Cath	Hall, Miss Maria	Richards, Miss A R
Dyer, Mrs Cath	Hays, Miss Vir	Rump, Mrs

Shepherd, Kate	Sturgeon, Mrs	Wise, Mrs Harriet
Sewell, Caroline	Smith, Mrs M A	Wilkins, Mrs Jane
Scott, Miss Ellen S	True, Ann Eliza	Wilson, Miss Lou
Scott, Miss H L	Thornton, Miss E	Wood, Mrs Mat A
Sinclair, Miss	Tangle, Nancy	Williams, Mrs V
Smith, Mrs Jane E	Vann, Mrs Annette	
Smith, Mrs R V	Washington, Betsy	

I forewarn all persons from harboring, secreting, or employing my indented servant, Isaac Whitlow, a colored boy, who absconded fom my service about Jun 10, 1847, as I am determined to enforce the penalty of the law against all persons so offending. –J H Eberbach

Wash [Pa] Examiner: Mr Wm Adams, a soldier of the Revolution, died at the good old age of 100 years. He served during the whole war, & was attached to the Flying Camp, so termed. [No death date given-current item.]

Affray at Yellville, Marion Co, Ark, a few days ago, in which a man named Sinclair killed Simeon Everett.

Died: on Nov 13, after a long & painful illness, Edw J Plunkett, in his 35th year. His funeral is today at 11 o'clock, from the residence of his mother, Mrs Jane Taylor, on Pa ave, between 4½ & 6th sts.

Died: on Nov 8, at Dayton, Ohio, of pulmonary disease, after an illness of several months, Mrs Anna Delano, wife of W J Delano, aged 27 years.

Died: on Nov 13, Mrs Lavinia, consort of Henry B Robinson. Her funeral is this day at 2 o'clock, from the residence of her son-in-law, Mr Hansell, on 8th & I sts.

Died: on Nov 13, in Wash City, Annie Josephine, infant daughter of Benj Harrison & Annie Cheever, aged 6 months & 21 days.

THU NOV 16, 1848
Ofc of the Secretary of State, City of Jackson, Miss, Nov 1, 1848. I acknowledge the receipt, by the hands of Hon Jefferson Davis, a piece of the corner-stone of the <u>Washington National Monument</u>, presented by the Board of Managers. It will be placed in the archives of the State. –Saml Stamps, Sec of State to Geo Watterston, Sec of the W M Society.

By an order of distrain from E G Handy, atty for E G Handy, of Indiana, to me directed against the goods & chattels of ____ Campbell, I have seized said goods to satisfy house-rent due & in arrears to said E G Handy: public auction in front of the Centre Market on Nov 18. –J F Wollard, Bailiff

At a late Court of Common Pleas at Zanesville, Mary McClelland recovered a verdict of $3,000 against John Vandervert, for a breach of promise of marriage. Paying pretty dear for a few months' courting.

N Y, Nov 15. Capt G P Hopkins, of the steamer **Capt W Young**, was almost instantly killed this morning while assisting to fend off the Express steamer **Newsboy**. He was struck on the head by an instrument termed the tender, & died in a few minutes. He was a gentleman highly esteemed.

Mrd: on Nov 15, at the Second Presbyterian Church, by Rev J R Eckard, Mr David McClelland & Miss M Eliz Gilman, both of Wash City.

Died: on Nov 3, near Bladensburg, James W, son of John & Caroline Veitch, in his 20th year.

Died: on Oct 12, at her residence in Davies Co, Ky, Mrs Clara Hawes, relict of Richd Hawes, & the mother of the Hon Richd Hawes & Hon A G Hawes.

Farm for sale on the waters of the West Fork of Ohio Brush creek, Adams Co, Ohio, containing about 400 acres, with 2 comfortable dwlgs: the late residence of Mahlon Purcell, deceased. –Hector Osborn, Norvall Osborn, excs of Mahlon Purcell, deceased.

Valuable property for sale: by deed of trust from John B Coddington & Camilla his wife, to the subscriber, dated Aug 31, 1842, recorded in Liber W B 95, folio 49, of the land records of Wash Co, D C: public auction on Nov 18, on the premises, of lot 5 in reservation 11, fronting on B st, with a 2 story brick dwlg house & other improvements thereon. –Wm M Morrison, auctioneer -P R Fendall, trustee

FRI NOV 17, 1848
Fatal accident at Rose, Wayne Co, Nov 11. As Mr Abel Howard was about firing a blast, a lighted cigar fell from his mouth into the blast, causing it to explode & blowing him 10 feet into the air. He died instantly.

A miracle was effected by the genius & perserverance of Dr Howe, in the well known case of Laura Bridgman, a young girl born deaf & dumb & blind, through the sense of touch; & it was not only achieved in her case but at a recent number of a Boston periodical, an engraving representing Laura Bridgman engaged in teaching another unhapply being like herself, a young man named Oliver Caswell. Laura was brought into the institution 11 years ago, at age 8 years, when Dr Howe took her in charge to educate her.

On Nov 7 at Dundas, Canada West, John Carrel was grinding an axe on the stone in the axe factory of Mr Leavett, when the stone burst, & the head of Mr Carrel was struck from his body.

Md Historical Society met last month. A note from Dr Wm J Barry, late Surgeon 11th Regt U S Infty, was read, accompanying 3 interesting Mexican maps of the battles of Buena Vista & of the Valley of Mexico. The Pres read 2 letters from G W P Custis, giving the details of the uniform & equipments of the ofcrs & men of the Revolutionary army of the U S. He mentions that he is engaged on a picture of the battle of Monmouth, fought Jun 28, 1778, in which several distinguished Revolutionary cmders are introduced.

Mrd: on Nov 15, at the Church of the Epiphany, by Rev Mr French, Wm H Gilman to Maggie C, only daughter of the late Geo E Dyson, of Wash City.

Died: on Nov 15, Simeon, son of Isaac & Adalin Bassett, aged 2 years, 8 months & 21 days. His funeral is today at 3 o'clock, from his father's residence, 2nd st, Capitol Hill.

New Millinery: Miss M J Colfar, Pa ave, between 17th & 18th sts, over Mr Heaney's clothing store.

Fred'k Md, Nov 15. The gable end of the new back bldg on Patrick st, owned by Mr Seth S Nichols, gave way this afternoon, & in falling buried under the ruins Mr N Haller, Mr Weddell, a German workman, & a colored man engaged as a bricklayer. The colored man was killed & Haller & Weddell badly injured.

The subscriber will open the Irving Restaurant, on Pa ave, corner of 10th st, on Nov 18. –Michl R Combs

Valuable farm, 8 miles from Wash or Gtwn, at auction: on the premises, on Nov 30, the farm that formerly belonged to Mr Webb, deceased, but now occupied by & belonging to Mr J H Knott: contains 373½ acres: good dwlg house & all necessary outbldgs. -A Green, auctioneer

Caution. The public are cautioned against receiving an endorsed note drawn by the subscriber for $40, payable at 30 days after date, & dated Nov 15, the said note having been lost. –N Mullikin

SAT NOV 18, 1848
The fine ship **Fanny Forester**, Capt Sweetlin, sailed from N Y on Wed for Monterey, Calif, having on board Co M, 3rd Artl. Ofcrs: Brevet Capt Geo P Andrews, commanding; Lts John H Lendrum, Horatio G Gibson, & Wm G Gill. Also, a detachment of recruits in charge of Lt John Hamilton, 3rd Artl; Dr H S Hewitt, surgeon; W H Chever & J R Daniels, passengers. The U S steamship **Edith**, which sailed on Nov 8, took out a portion of the Regt under command of Gen Riley. The barque **Whiton**, under the command of Capt Gelston, will leave N Y about Tues for the Sandwich Islands, Calif, & Oregon. –Com Adv

Mrd: on Nov 15, at St John's Church, by Rev Dr Pyne, Robt H Leslie, of Balt, Md, to Ellen Louisa, daughter of Alex'r Ray, of Wash City.

Mrd: Nov 14, by Rev Mr Boteler, John B Clagett to Margaret, eldest daughter of W H Gunnell, all of Wash City.

Mrd: on Nov 16, in Wash City, by Rev Smith Pyne, Lt W Decatur Hurst, U S Navy, to Mary Lang, daughter of the late Lt Col J M Gamble, U S Marine Corps.

Mrd: on Nov 14, by Rev Mr Murphy, Mr Jas T Fry, of Wash, to Miss Eliz Moore, of Chas Co, Md.

Mrd: on Nov 14, at N Y, in the Church of the Ascension, by Rev Mr Irving, Jno Fred'k May, M D, of Wash, to Sarah Maria, daughter of P L Mills.

Died: on Nov 10, of a protracted illness, in her 36th year, Mrs Harriet Ann Garrett, wife of Wm Garrett, & only daughter of Mr Warren Washington, late of King Geo Co, Va.

Servant for sale. A good cook & washerwoman for sale. Inquire of Gilson Dove.

At a Circuit Court of Law & Chancery held for the County of Loudoun, Va, on Oct 28, 1848. On the motion of John K Littleton, one of the execs named therein, who offered for probate a paper purporting to be the last will & testament of Enoch Furr, deceased, as the true last will & testament of said decendent. It is ordered that summonses be issued by the Clerk of this Court, directed to the Sheriff or other ofcr of any county or corporation where the parties may be found, requiring said Sheriff or ofcr to summon Saml Berkeley & Tacey his wife, Charity Wills, Newton Furr, Bersheba Morehead, Sarah A Furr, an infant child of Edwin Furr, deceased, Maaziah Thomas & Eliz his wife, Hannah Littleton, Wm G Furr, Jeremiah C Furr, to appear on the first day of the next term of this Court to shaw cause, if any there be, why the said will & testament should not be admitted to probate. It appearing to the Court that Saml Berkeley & Tacey his wife, Sarah A Furr, infant daughter of Edwin Furr, deceased, Jeremiah C Furr, Maaziah Thomas, have no known place of residence within this Commonwealth, it is further ordered that they appear on the first day of the next term of this Court, for the purpose aforesaid. –Thos P Knox, Clerk Court

Mr Clency, of Germantown, Ohio, has reached the advanced age of 105, & on Nov 7 voted for Taylor, probably his last vote.

MON NOV 20, 1848
The Hon Alex'r Dromgoole Sims, one of the Reps in Congress from the State of S C, died at Kingstree, S C, on Thu last, Nov 16. [Dec 15th newspaper: Mr Sims was born in Brunswick Co, Va, on Jun 12, 1803. His parents had 2 of their sons attain eminence & distinction. The deceased, was a gentleman of excellent intellect. His brother [late a prof of Alabama Univ] was an eminent divine & ripe scholar. Mr Sims studied law in the ofc of his uncle, the late Gen Dromgoole.]

The Hon John W Davis, U S Com'r to China, arrived at Macao Aug 15, in the U S sloop-of-war **Plymouth**.

The ship **Mary & Adeline** sailed from N Y for Calif on Nov 9, with companies A & F of the 2nd Regt. Ofcrs on board: Capts Day, Davidson, & Lowell; Lts Hendershot, Schureman, & De Russey; Assist Surg Dr Deverle. Passengers, Geo Hyslop & Saml Kip.

The Hon Peter J Borst expired at his residence in Middleburg, N Y, on Nov 14, &, as is supposed, of a disease of the heart. He formerly represented the Greene & Schoharie district in Congress.

Eaton [O] Register: Geo McCabe, a young man, was accidentally killed when attempting to load a rifle. He left a wife & family, & was an esteemed & respectable citizen.

A sail boat that plies between Buffalo & Dunnville [C W] was found beached a few miles above Point Abino, on Monday last. In the boat the captain, Robt Marsh, & his son, aged about 14 years, were found locked in each other's arms, dead-having in all probability, perished in the late snow storm. –Buff Com Adv

Alfred Kiger takes this opportunity to thank all his kind friends who in the time of his loss by fire, came forward & contributed to his aid. Mr John Payne, coach maker, of Gtwn, D C, has let him have another carriage on convenient & easy terms.

Trustee's sale of valuable property, by deed of trust dated Jan 27, 1831, recorded in Liber W B 34, folios 444 thru 447, of the land records of Wash Co, D C: sale on Nov 30, of lot 3 in square 690, with a 3 story brick house, fronting on south C st, between N J ave & I st east. –R C Weightman, John H Riely, trustees -Edw C & G F Dyer

For rent: the desirable residence, so long occupied by the Brazilian Minister, M Lisboa, at K & 19th sts. Inquire a few door this side, of Mrs Dorcas Walker, Agent.

Died: on Thu last, at Balt, Littleton Dennis Teackle, of Somerset Co, Md, in his 72nd year.

TUE NOV 21, 1848
There died in Boston on Wed an eccentric individual named Wm G Baylies, aged 68 years, leaving a fortune estimated at over $200,000. For 6 months past the deceased has confined himself entirely to his room, refusing to see any one-even his own brother-but the lady at whose house he boarded.

Mrd: on Nov 15, by Rev Mr Forbes, Danl, eldest son of the Hon Danl Jenifer, to Miss Mary E, only daughter of Dr Risteau, of Balt Co, Md.

In Chancery. Esau Pickrell & Co & Saml Wolff, & others, against Stanislaus Murray, adm, & Wm L, Francis, & Catharine Corcoran, heirs at law of Hannah G Corcoran, deceased. The creditors of Hannah G Corcoran are to file their claims, duly proved, on or before Nov 27. –W Redin, Auditor

Died: Nov 18, in Gtwn, Saml C, eldest child of Lewis J & Jane Knight, aged 2 years, 4 months & 9 days.

Subscriber wishes to procure a gentleman who has had some experience in teaching & who is well qualified, to take charge of a small school in his family. Salary of $300 per annum, together with board & washing, will be given. —W J Morgan

WED NOV 22, 1848
Fatal election row in New Orleans: on election day, Nicholas Dignan was stabbed & killed. J F Duganny, charged with the deed, was so injured that he died the next day. The latter was formerly an ofcr in the French service, & served under Napoleon.

Jas & Wm Diffin, of Clay, N Y, have been arrested for causing the death of Mr Abbot, by pouring rum down his throat while intoxicated.

The following is a list of the ofcrs of the British army who were killed & wounded during the operations against Moultan, in India: Killed-Lt Col R T R Pattoun & Quartermaster G Taylor, her Majesty's 32nd foot; Maj G S Montizambert, 10th foot; Ensign C O Lloyd, 8th native infty, & Lt T Cubitt, 49th native infty. Wounded: Lt Col T H Franks, C B, Capt M McGregor, Lts H A Hollinsworth & J S Herbert, her Majesty's 10th foot; Lt Col F Markham, Capt A L Balfour, Lts C T King, J Swineburn, & W A Birthwhistle, her Majesty's 32nd foot; Maj Napier & Lt Lake, engineers; Lt Binney, horse artl; Lt E C Vibart, 11th cavalry; Lt W Christopher, I N, Indus flotilla; Capt F Wroughton, Lts A Trunbull & H R Drew, & Ensign F H Kennedy, 8th native infty; Lts J F Richardson, T H Plumer, & W Irwin, 49th native infty.

Mrd: on Nov 20, by Rev W Hodges, Mr John Shelton to Miss Henrietta Sanderson, both of Wash City.

Died: on Nov 20, of croup, Wm Henry, son of Saml & Ellen Grubb, aged 4 years. His funeral is today at 10 o'clock, from the residence of his father, on C st, between 12th & 13th sts, on the Island.

Died: on Sep 30, at his residence in Fauquier Co, Va, Maj Seth Combs, in his 67th year. In the death of Maj Combs an aged & pious mother has been made to mourn the death of an only son.

Wash Corp: 1-Ptn of Basil Simms, praying remission of a fine: referred to the Cmte of Claims. 2-Ptn of Jas H Moore, & of Saml & Perry Riggs, praying the restoration of certain hogs taken up by the police ofcrs for being found going at large: referred to the Cmte of Claims.

New Confectionary Establishment: corner of F & 9th sts, will open on Nov 27.
–Henry Eckardt

In Chancery. Circuit Court of Wash Co, D C. Sarah Cruikshank, surviving admx of John Cruikshank, vs Wm Morton & wife & Jas Thomson, heirs at law of Geo Thomson. The creditors of Geo Thomson, deceased, late of Gtwn, to file their claims, duly proved, on or before Dec 4. –J B H Smith, Special Auditor

Orphans Court of Wash Co, D C. Letters testamentary on the personal estate of Eliz Ross, late of said county, deceased. –Richd L Ross, exc

THU NOV 23, 1848
Naval: ofcrs of the U S ship **Yorktown**, now lying off the Boston navy Yard, & which will sail next week for the coast of Africa: Benj Cooper, cmdor; John Marston, cmder; Thos K Rootes, C F M Spotswood, Jas Madison Frailey, & Chas E Fleming, Lts; Wm Johnson, fleet surgeon; Thos M Potter, passed assist surgeon; Jas A Seinple, purser; Chas H B Caldwell, acting master; _____ Pettit, cmdor's sec; Wm H Parker, Edw A Selden, Jos A Seawell, & David Colemen, passed midshipmen; Jos P Fyffe, Edw J Means, Jas Bruce, Jas Parker, midshipmen; J Farnesworth, capt's clerk; John J Young, boatswain; Chas B Oliver, gunner; Nicholas Mager, carpenter; Henry W Franklin, jr, sailmaker.

Died: on Nov 14, at Balt, in his 74th year, Benj Tanner, sen, formerly an eminent Engraver of Phil. In 1816-17 Mr Tanner engraved & published a large print of the Surrender of Cornwallis at Yorktown, & large prints of the Naval Victories on Lakes Erie & Champlain.

Valuable farm at auction, at Elil Palmer's tavern, on Dec 20, the farm formerly the property of Basil Barnes, in PG Co, Md, Piscataway district, adjoining the lands of Messrs Robt Hunter, John H Lowe, & Elil Palmer, & now in the occupation of John S Edelen: 175 acres with a good dwlg & all necessary out-houses. Information can be obtained from Horatio Dyer, P G Co. -Edw C & G F Dyer

Mrd: Nov 20, by Rev Mr Jos Guest, Ignatius M Knott, of Wash, to Miss Mary D Seeders, of Leesburg, Va.

Trustee's sale: by deed of trust dated Oct 15, 1845, recorded in Liber W B 121, folio 340, executed by Hopeful Toler to me, to secure a debt due to Gen Archibald Henderson, & at the request of the latter. Sale on Nov 25, at the jail in Wash City, a negro woman named Polly, aged about 36, & her daughter, Mary Ann, aged about 16 years.
–Jos H Bradley, trustee -A Green, auctioneer

Circuit Court of Wash Co, D C. John Drill, cmplnt, against Jas Ross & Anna Maria his wife, Martha Ann Ross, & John Marbury & Harriet H his wife, dfndnts. The above named Jas Ross & his wife conveyed unto the above named Harriet H Marbury part of lot 10 in Gtwn, & gave, in the deed of conveyance, an erroneous description thereof, making the same being at the n e corner of Thos Jackson's house, instead of the n w corner thereof; that Mr & Mrs Marbury conveyed the same, by the same erroneous description, to Susan L Howard; that the above named Martha Ann Ross conveyed her part of the lot ot Susan L Howard by the same erroneous description; & that Mrs Howard sold & conveyed the whole of the premises to the cmplnts. Object of this bill is to correct the said error. Jas Ross & Anna Maria his wife, & Martha Ann Ross, do not reside in this District. Same to appear in this Court by the 4th Mon of Mar next. –Wm Brent, clerk -Richd W Redin, for cmplnt

Died: on Nov 16, at *Sidney*, near Wash City, Eliz, aged about 10 months, daughter of Eramus J & Ellen Middleton.

Splendid assortment of flowering Plants, bearing Orange & Lemon Trees at auction: on Nov 28, at the residence of Mrs Lenon, on E st between 9th & 10th sts.

SAT NOV 25, 1848
Fruit & ornamental trees at the Nursery at *Linden Hill*, near Wash. –Joshua Pearce

Hon Isaac Wilson died at Batavia, Ill, on Oct 25. He was for many years first Judge of Genesee Co, N Y. During the war of 1812 he commanded a company of cavalry, & was in some of the severest actions on the Northern frontier.

$5 reward for 2 double-barrel Guns stolen from my shop on Tue. –C H Munck, Gunsmith & Cutler, D st.

On Sat the steamboat train of cars for Boston ran over a Mr Gassite, at New Worcester, killing him instantly. He was 69 years of age, & a resident of New Worcester. In order to escape from an approaching freight train, he stepped upon the other track.

Fred'k Whitmore, about 13 years of age, a son of Gen John C Humphreys, was drowned in Brunswick, Maine, last Sat. The ice broke through while he was skating with other lads. –Portland Adv

Orphans Court of Wash Co, D C. Letters testamentary on the personal estate of Walter Smith, late of said county, deceased. –Rd Smith, exc

Circuit Court of Wash Co, D C–in Chancery. Henry Naylor, cmplnt, vs Jas Carland & Eliz his wife, Thos Murray & Sarah his wife, & Jos Foyles & others, dfndnts. Edw W Clarke, deceased, in his lifetime, was indebted to the Bank of Wash & the Bank of the Metropolis in large sums of money, to secure which he made 2 deeds, each bearing date Sep 29, 1821; & by one conveyed part of lot 11 in square 688, in Wash City, to Thos Foyles & his heirs, to secure the debt due to the Bank of Wash; & by the other conveyed the same premises to Alex'r Kerr & his heirs, to secure the debt due the Bank of the Metropolis. The bill further states that the said debts have been somewhat reduced, & that a large balance on each remains still due & unpaid; that the said banks have assigned their respective debts to the cmplnt, & said balances are due to him; that the said Thos Foyles & Alex'r Kerr, the said named trustees, are both dead, & that the above named dfndnts are some of the heirs at law of said Thos Foyles, & live out of D C. The object of the bill is to obtain the appointment of a trustee in the place of Foyles & Kerr, & a decree for the sale of the said property to pay the debts mentioned in the said deeds. It appears that Jas Carland & Eliz his wife, Thos Murray & Sarah his wife, & Jas Foyles, jr, do not reside within D C. Same to appear on or before the 4th Mon in Mar next.
–Wm Brent, clerk

Died: on Nov 21, in Gtwn, D C, Edwin, infant son of Dr Chas H & Mary Cragin, aged 5 months & 23 days.

Died: in Oct last, on Staten Island, N Y, Julia Dallas, eldest daughter of the Rev F S Miner & grand-daughter of A B Lindsely, late of Wash City, aged 15 years.

Died: on Nov 24, Mary E, infant daughter of Wm H & Eliz A Dennesson, aged 6 months. Her funeral is tomorrow at 3 o'clock.

MON NOV 27, 1848

Appointment by the Pres: O C Pratt, of Ill, to be Assist Justice of the Supreme Court of the U S for the Territory of Oregon, in the place of Wm A Hall, declined.

Chas White, of Vassalboro, who will be 99 years old next Feb, went to the polls on Nov 7, & voted for the Taylor & Fillmore ticket. His first vote was for Geo Washington. Mr White was in the army of the Revolution, & is a native of Lunenburg, Mass, where there are now a great number of very old people. —Maine Journal

N Y, Nov 24. 1-Jonathan Goodhue, principal of the firm of the Goodhue & Co, died this morning, in his 66th year: affection of the heart. The flags of the shipping & on the Merchants' Exchange hang at half mast, as a token of mourning. —Journal of Commerce 2-Death from hydrophobia: David Burchell, about 14 years of age, residing in Yorkville, N Y, died on Wed, having been bitten 3 months before.

Lyne Stabling, one of the original proprietors of the soil on which the city of Columbus is located, & among its earliest inhabitants, died on Nov 21, after a protracted disease. He was one of the most wealthy men of the State. The Medical College in this city bears his name. He was 70 years of age. —Columbus [O] Journal

Late storm at the East. The British schnr **Olive**, Oliver, wrecked near point Alderton. All lost. She had 5 or 6 persons on board. The ship **Clars**, of Portsmouth, Capt Penhallow, from Cadiz, Oct 1, went ashore on Truro Beach, on Mon. Capt Penhallow was lost overboard. The remainder of the crew was saved.

Mr Wm H Soper, of the firm of Soper & Co, auctioneers, South Chas st, Balt, died on Fri when he stepped backward down a trap-door, which had been opened a few moments before without his knowledge, falling from the 1st floor into the cellar, his head striking the floor first. He died in the evening. —Balt American

Mrd: on Nov 23, by Rev J B Donelan, Mr Wm A Flaherty, of Wash, to Miss Eliza Stone, of Gtwn.

Mrd: on Nov 21, by Rev Jas Keen, Jas Gordon Allison to Mrs Jane P Ratliffe, daughter of S Daniel, all of Fairfax Co, Va.

Died: on Nov 23, in Gtwn, in her 69th year, Mrs Mary Chapman, relict of the late Henry H Chapman, of Md. Her funeral is on Nov 27, at 3½ p m, from her late residence on Dunbarton st.

Died: on Nov 23, at Ashburton, near Balt, Mrs Eleanor S Gittings, wife of Mr John S Gittings.

TUE NOV 28, 1848
Presidential elections.
In 1789: 10 States were entitled to 73 votes. Geo Washington received 79, which were all the votes cast, as some of the States were not represented in full. John Adams was chosen Vice Pres.
In 1792: 15 States were entitled to 135 votes, of which Geo Washington received 133, all the votes cast. John Adams again Vice Pres.
In 1796: 16 States were entitled to 138 votes, of which John Adams received 71, & Thos Jefferson was chosen Vice Pres.
In 1800: 16 States were entitled to 188 votes, of which Thos Jefferson & Aaron Burr received each 73. No choice by the people. The House of Reps, after balloting 6 days, on the 36th ballot elected Thos Jefferson Pres & Aaron Burr Vice Pres.
In 1804: 17 States were entitled to 176 votes, of which Thos Jefferson received 162. Geo Clinton Vice Pres.
In 1808: 17 States & 176 votes. Jas Madison received 122 votes, & was chosen Pres; Geo Clinton Vice Pres. Geo Clinton had received electoral votes at every election since the organization of the Gov't.
In 1812: 18 States & 218 votes. Jas Madison received 128 as Pres, & Elbridge Gerry 131 as Vice Pres.
In 1816: 19 States & 221 votes, of which Jas Monroe received 183. D D Tompkins Vice Pres.
In 1820: 24 States & 232 votes. Jas Monroe received 231. D D Tompkins Vice Pres.
In 1804 to 1820 the successful candidates had been nominated by a caucus of the Democratic party in Congress. Since that time, 1820, all parties have nominated in Nat'l Conventions.
In 1824: 24 States & 261 votes. Andrew Jackson received 99 for Pres, & John Q Adams 84 as the Whig candidate. John C Calhoun, Vice Pres, had 188 votes.
In 1828: 24 States & 261 votes. Jackson received 178, a majority over Adams of 95 electoral votes. Calhoun Vice Pres.
In 1832: 25 States & 288 votes. Jackson received 219, a majority of 170 over Clay. Martin Van Buren Vice Pres.
In 1836: 26 States & 294 votes. M Van Buren received 170, a majority of 97 over Wm H Harrison. R M Johnson Vice Pres.
In 1840: 26 States & 294 votes, of which Gen Harrison received 234, a majority of 174 over Van Buren. John Tyler Vice Pres.
In 1844: 26 States & 275 votes, of which Jas K Polk received 170, a majority over Mr Clay of 64. G M Dallas Vice Pres.
The popular vote since 1828 for Pres has been as follows:
1828: 1,162,418 votes

1832: 1,290,498 votes
1836: 1,501,298 votes
1840: 2,402,658 votes
1844: 2,702,549 votes

By virtue of 2 writs of fieri facias at the suit of Thos M Milburn, against the goods & chattels of John Corbett, I have seized & taken under execution, one 4 wheeled carriage, the property of said Corbitt, to satisfy the same. Auction in front of the Centre Market on Nov 30. –J F Wollard, Constable

Furnished rooms & house for rent: inquire at the Grocery Store of the subscriber, Pa ave & 20th st, who will show the premises. –David Hines

Boston Traveller of Nov 25. The venerable relic of the Pilgrims, the old Pear Tree at Eastham, planted by Gov Prince, of Plymouth Colony, more than 2 centuries ago, was blown down during the late gale. It had stood on the farm of Mr Freeman, in Eastham, once the dwlg place of Gov Prince, by whose hand the tree is said to have been planted.

A Reminiscence: from the Providence [R I] Journal. The burning of the old *Seaver House* the other night produces recollections of long past. The house is supposed to have been built more than 100 years ago by Mr Seaver, who inhabited it during his long life, & left it to his son Obed & a sister. Obed was what was called a paper money man. $1.00 in silver would buy $5 in paper. Chas Lippitt had a shop on Whitman's land, & Obed went there to buy a jackknife. Lippitt said he did not take paper money. Seaver went to Court the next Mon. The Judge had gone down to Tockwotton to look for his cow that had run away. The Court was adjourned. This was the only case under the penal law in the county of Providence. –Old Times

Washington Academy, Rappahannock Co, Va: in the town of Washington, will open on Jan 8, 1849. Additional information by addressing the Principals: G W Grayson, H W Maertens, A M.

Ptn of Aaron Stedman, of Annsville, N Y, praying for the extension of a patent granted to him for an improvement in a machine for making bedsteads for 7 years from the expiration of said patent, which takes place on Jan 16, 1849.
–Edmund Burke, Com'r of Patents

Mrd: on Nov 16, by Rev C W Butler, Mr Marvin Percival Fisher, formerly of Boston, to Miss Mary Elizabeth, eldest daughter of Henry D Gunnell, of Wash City.

Notice: to the heirs & reps of the late Miss Eleanor McCormick, deceased, of Wash Co, Md. After paying the debts of her estate, & the heirs of Hugh & John McCormick, there is in my hands above $400, besides a small amount uncollected, which will be paid to any one legally authorized to receive it. –Chas Kemper, adm de bonis non of Eleanor McCormick, deceased. Near Warrenton, Fauquier Co, Va.

Trustee's sale: decree of the Circuit Court of Wash Co, D C, in Chancery: in the cause of Saml Smoot et al vs Mary Jane Smoot, Saml C Smoot, Luther Smoot, John Waggerman & Lydia his wife, Jos Pleasants & Ross his wife, & Araminta Smoot, the only reps & heirs of Chas H Smoot, deceased, I will offer at public auction on the premises, on Dec 29, the undivided 3rd part of a 2 story brick house & lot, being lot 2 in square 4, & 2 small tenements & lots, in the western part of the city, & a lot in Gtwn, being lot 11 in Deaken's, Lee, & Cazenove's addition. –Danl Ratcliffe, Trustee

Died: on Nov 19, aged 22 years, Calhoun Barbour, son of the Hon John S Barbour, of Culpeper Co, Va.

Died: on Nov 23, in Alexandria, Va, Mrs Jane Allen Ramsay, in her 81st year, widow of the late Col Dennis Ramsay. Mrs Ramsay was born in Belfast, Ireland, & was brought by her father to Alexandria in 1778, where she has resided ever since.

Died: on Nov 17, Laura P Jones, aged 2 years, 3 months & 5 days, the only remaining child of Wm & Lucipia Ann Jones.

WED NOV 29, 1848
Monterey, Sep 15, 1848. Messrs Grinnell, Minturn & Co. All hands have left me but two. All the ships at San Francisco have stripped & laid up. A sailor will be up at the mines for 2 months, work on his own account, & come down with from two to three thousand dollars, & those who go in parties do much better. It is impossible for me to give you any idea of the gold that is got here. –Christopher Allyn, Capt of the ship **Isaak Walton.**

The N Y Journal of Commerce announces the death of Wm L Prall, long connected with the press of that city as a reporter, aged 60 years. Also, of Col Alden Spooner, aged 65, long connected with the press of Brooklyn. The Gospel Messenger, published at Utica, is in mourning for the loss of its editor, the venerable Rev John C Rudd, D D, who died on Wed last.

In Hanover, Polk Co, Pa, on Wed, a little girl named Sarah, aged about 3 years, daughter of the Rev Jacob Sechler, fell into a tub of hot water, scalding herself so badly that she died in 30 hours.

Mrd: on Nov 28, by Rev Mr S D Finckel, Mr John P Boss to Miss Caroline S C, 2nd daughter of Mr Chas Pettit, all of Wash City.

Died: on Nov 21, in her 44th year, after a lingering illness, Mrs Lucy D Bruce, consort of Mr Chas Bruce, of Wash City, & daughter of the late Jos Dunlap, for many years a resident of PG Co, Md.

Died: yesterday, Miss Margaret Anderson. Her funeral is this afternoon, at 3:30 o'clock, from the residence of Mr John Hughes, on High st, a few doors below Bridge st, Gtwn.

Valuable house for rent or for sale: now occupied by Rev Mr Pyne, commonly known as one of the De Menou Bldgs. Inquire on the premises, or at the ofc of H M Morfit, on 4½ st. Possession immediately.

THU NOV 30, 1848
Died: on Nov 27, Jeremiah Hughes, in his 66th year, late editor of Niles' Nat'l Register.

Cumberland Co, Pa: last week was tried the case of Catharine Oliver & others, of Md, against Danl Kaufman, of Cumberland Co, for aiding the escape & harboring 13 slaves, claimed as the propery of the plntfs. The slaves were brought on Oct 24, 1847, to the barn of Kaufman, & after staying there a few nights, were taken in his wagon across the Susquehanna river. The jury returned a verdict of $2,000 damages for the plntfs.
–Balt Patriot

Geo Beltzhoover, extensively known among the great traveling community, for many years, as the proprietor of the Fountain Inn, in Balt, died at his residence near that city, on Sat, in his 75th year.

Rev John W Douglass & Rev Saml H Wiley have been appointed missionaries of the American Home Mission Society for Calif. The latter for Monterey & the former for San Francisco. The American Baptist Home Mission Society has appointed Rev O C Wheeler, of Jersey City, as a missionary to San Francisco.

The St Jos Gaz of Nov 10 announces they have received information that Maj Singer, Paymaster in the U S army, had a few days previous been murdered & robbed in Saline Co, Missouri. Maj Singer's wife & sister, who were with him, both shared the same fate. The Major had $160,000 with him, & was proceeding to the upper part of this State to pay the 3 months' extra pay to those volunteers that were entitled to it. No clue thus far as to who perpetrated the foul deed, other than a supposition that the soldiers who had acted as his escort were the murderers. Maj Singer was married but a short time since.

Wash Corp: 1-Act for the relief of Walter Linkins: referred to the Cmte on Improvements. 2-Act for the relief of Wm B Wilson: passed. 3-Ptn from Wm Rupp: referred to the Cmte of Claims. 4-Ptn of E G Handy, police ofcr, praying payment of a claim against the Corp: referred to the Cmte of Claims. 5-Ptn of Lawrence Callan: Cmte of Claims asking to be discharged from the further consideration of the same.
6-Elected Trustees of the Public Schools:

Robt Farnham	Thos Donoho	John M Roberts
Jas F Haliday	Peter F Bacon	Jas E Morgan
Geo J Abbott	Geo Watterston	Wm Ashdown
Valentine Harbaugh	Jonas B Ellis	Ignatius Mudd

7-Elected Police Magistrates:

Saml Drury	John L Smith	Jos W Beck
Saml Grubb	Thos C Donn	Jas Crandell
J P Van Tyne	Benj K Morsell	Craven Ashford
Thos Donoho	Jas Marshall	Wm F Purcell

On Sat, in Richmond, Mr Jas Butterworth, a very worthy citizen, lost his life by falling through a trap-door of the new house now being constructed near Messrs Fry's store, on 14th st. Mr Butterworth was engaged in fixing the gutters of the house.

Died: on Nov 8, at Phil, at the advanced age of 91 years, Mrs Ann Hodge, relict of the late Andrew Hodge, of that city, & the revered mother of the editor of the New Orleans Bulletin.

Died: on Nov 4, at sea, on board the ship **Pioneer**, of Alexandria, Va, while on her passage from Liverpool, 2nd Mate Jas F Kerr, of Wash City, in his 28th year.

Died: on Nov 23, in Wash City, Mrs Eliz Benter, aged 68 years, relict of the late Wm Benter, of Alexandria, Va.

Died: on Nov 17, at his residence in Fairfax Co, Va, suddenly, of a disease of the heart, Hiram Harrover, in his 56th year, leaving a large family to mourn their loss. The deceased had been for the last 32 years a leading member of the Baptist Church, & had gained the affections of all who knew him.

Notice: I hereby forbid J F Wollard from selling any Carriage of mine, as I do not owe T M Milburn legally or equitably the amount which he demands, & whoever purchases by virtue of such levy will buy a lawsuit. -J Corbett

In Chancery. Chas Thomas, Octavia Clark, Josephine Clark, Sarah A Thomas, Jas Thomas, Mary Ann Thomas, & A Green, petitioners for sale of real estate. Saml S Williams, trustee in the above cause, reported the sale of the lot of ground in said cause to Geo U Stewart, for $255, being part of lot 1 in square 317, in Wash City, D C. –W Brent, clk

FRI DEC 1, 1848
Balt Clipper: Jeremiah Hughes, of this city, died on Mon after a brief illness, of consumption. He was about 65 years of age, & for more than a quarter of a century has been associated with the newspaper press of the State. For many years he was editor of the Annapolis Republican, & printer for the State. After the death of Hezekiah Niles, he became the editor & proprietor of the Niles Register. He leaves a large family.

Dr Devine, imprisoned at Poughkeepsie for the murder of Richd Wall, cut his throat on Sat night, & was found dead in his cell next morning. He had been tried once for the murder, but the jury did not agree.

Improvements about the Pres' House: the paving is progressing with vigor; the wooden fence in front of the State & War dept is being replaced with an iron fence. The builder of the fence is Mr M P Coons, of Lansingburg, N Y, who receives only $1.50 per foot, or $900 for 600 feet of work. The iron & the castings are from the foundry of B Arnold & Son, of Poughkeepsie, N Y, & reflect much credit to their work.

Ladies with letters in the Wash Post Ofc Dec 1, 1848:

Allair, Miss Maria A
Anderson, Miss Anna
Adams, Miss Eliz
Ashwood, Miss
Beall, Miss Eliza B
Bell, Miss Eliz
Barrat, Mrs Laura
Ball, Mrs Leatheana
Blake, Mis M M
Beall, Miss Martha Ann
Barcley, Mrs Eliz
Ball, Miss Joannah
Clinton, Mrs A W
Clarke, Mrs Annie
Coke, Mrs Emily
Cross, Lydia B
Clevenger, Mrs Am
Colder, Mrs J R
Davis, Mrs Caroline
Day, Mrs Eliz
Davis, Mrs Jefferson
Dixon, Mrs Mary
Dixon, Mrs Nelly
Danford, Miss Ann E
Dodson, Miss Marg't
Donnelly, Miss Mary E
Evans, Miss Anna E
Elliott, Mrs Jon'tn D
Fish, Miss Eliz L
Fowler, Miss Eliz
Flood, Mrs Pris'a C
Green, Miss Cons'ee
Gray, Sarah
Gasbey, Mrs Sarah
Gantt, Mrs Eliz C-2
Gartland, Miss Eliz
Graham, Mrs Lawrence
Hall, Miss Amanda
Haskins, Mrs Marg
Hunt, Miss Mary E
Hemming, Mrs Mary
Hull, Miss Rebecca
Ingle, Mrs Mary
Johnson, Mrs Am M
Jackson, Miss H
Jacob, Mary
King, Mrs Eliza A
Kaufman, Mrs Jane
Kingsbury, Joanna
Kerr, Mrs Sarah
Kroft, Mrs Catharine
King, Mrs Henrietta
Lust, Miss Ann
Little, Mrs Barbara
Lawrence, Mrs Jane
Lewis, Mrs Dixon H-2
Lemoyne, Miss Annie
Morse, Mrs Eliz K
Mulloy, Miss Francis T
McCeeney, Harriet
McBane, Mrs M E
Macready, Mrs Mary
North, Mrs Stephen
Ott, Miss Mary
Parker, Margaret
Picket, Mrs Mary
Parsons, Mrs Eliz
Reyes, Miss Andora De
Reed, Miss Anna M
Robinson, Miss Ellen
Robinson, Miss Mary
Smith, Mrs Ann
Stelle, Mrs Anna M
Scott, Miss Eliz S
Sanders, Mrs
Stakes, Mrs Sarah
Spanton, Sarah
Smith, Miss Susan J
Scott, Miss Lavina L
Sorrell, Miss Lucinda L
Sorrell, Mrs Henrietta
Scrivener, Mrs El'nr
Stewart, Mrs Com-2
Thompson, Mrs Eliz D
Taylor, Miss Louisa C B
Thompson, Mrs Letty
Thomear, Miss Eliz
Whitall, Mrs Capt
Williams, Mrs Ann
Watkins, Mrs Jane
White, Mrs Sarah
Wood, Mrs
Williams, Mrs V
Watson, Miss Martha J
Woodward, Mrs Sarah
Wise, Miss Bettie
Warren, Miss Martha Jane
Young, Mrs Amelia T
-C K Gardiner, P M

The U S transport ship **Rhode Island** arrived at N Y on Wed from New Orleans, having on board companies A & E, 1st, & E of 2nd Artl, with the following ofcrs & passengers: 1st Lt Jas B Ricketts, 1st Artl, commanding; Assist Surgeon R H Coolidge, U S A; Brevet Maj J F Reynolds, 3rd Artl; 1st Lt A Doubleday, 1st Artl; 2nd Lt D M Beltzhoover, 1st Artl; 2nd Lt O H Tillinghast, 1st Artl, A C S; Brevet 2nd Lt J C Tidball, 3rd Artl; Mrs Dr Coolidge & children.

The oldest voter in America, Mr Hughes, a Revolutionary soldier, in his 107th year, was taken to the polls at Rockbridge Co, Va, at the late election, by a friend in a carriage drawn by 4 horses.

The Wheeling Times is for sale by its present publisher Jas G Wharton.

Boston Daily Adv: the King of Denmark has directed the Comet Medal, founded by one of his predecessors, to be awarded to Miss Maria Mitchell, of Nantucket, for her discovery of the <u>telescopic comet</u> of Oct 1, 1847. Miss Mitchell's comet was first seen in Europe by Father De Vice, at Rome, on Oct 3, 1847.

A coroner's inquest was held at N Y on Mon on the body of Rachael Gedney, aged 107 years, who died suddenly on Sun, at 91 Seventh ave. A grand-daughter of the deceased testified that her grandmother was born at Manaroneck, Westchester Co, in 1741; that her parents were Indians; her father belonged to the Tappan tribe, & her mother was a Mohegan. The deceased married a Malay, by whom she had 2 children, one of whom is mother of the witness, & is still living, at age 77 years. The mother of the deceased lived to the age of 107. The deceased has lived, during her long life, in various parts of this & neighborhing States, & when 90 years old she went from Haverstraw to new Haven, & remained there a short time. About a fortnight since she came to this city to see her daughter. She had perfect possession of her faculties; her sight was perfect; deceased was a Christian. In her childhood she encamped & cooked meals in what is now called the Battery. -Jour of Com

Mr Morris, one of the proprietors of an extensive foundry in Galena, Ill, became involved with some creditors who were about to push him. As Mr Harris was passing the foundry recently, Mr Morris shot him dead; then rushed into the foundry & shot Mr Ross. Morris then fled to his house & shot himself dead.

Died: on Nov 29, in Wash City, of pulmonary consumption, in her 19th year, Miss Catharine, daughter of Mr John Smallwood. Her funeral is today, at 2:30 o'clock, from the residence of her father, near the Navy Yard.

City Ordinance-Wash. Act for the relief of John E Thompson & others: for a balance of compensation as assist teacher: $41.67. For balance of compensation by Mrs Henshaw, as assist teacher: $132.62½. For balance of compensation by Mrs Emma Southworth, as assist teacher: $76.45. Approved: Nov 30, 1848.

SAT DEC 2, 1848
The Roll of Electoral Votes for Pres & Vice Pres of the U S will be as follows:
Total number of electoral votes 290; necessary to a choice 146. Zachary Taylor & Millard Fillmore have a majority of 36 votes. [For Taylor & Fillmore: 163. For Cass & Butler: 127.]

Died: on Oct 30, at the *Vineyard*, in his 5th year, of croup, Henry H, son of Henry H & Anna Maria Dent. His funeral is tomorrow, at 2 o'clock.

Mr Jos J Kessler, lately from Vienna, leaves N Y & will establish himself as a Prof of the Piano & Singing. Apply at Mrs Anderson's Music Store, Pa ave.

Trustee's sale: by decree of PG Co Court, [Md] as Court of Equity, public sale on Dec 21, at the late residence of Geo Kirby, deceased, the real estate of which he died seized & possessed: ***Bachelor's Harbor***, about 300 acres; ***Warburton Manor***: about 132 acres, lying on the Potomac river: with every necessary bldg for farming operations.
–N C Stephen, Trustee

Trustee's sale: by decree of the High Court of Chancery of Md: sale on Dec 9, all that farm called ***Locust Grove***, in Montg Co, Md, composed of 2 tracts of land: ***Peace & Plenty & Quince Orchard***, containing about 226 acres, adjoining the lands of Judge Bibb, F C Clopper, & the late Savon Offutt, which have lately been bought by Mr Chefaly, of Wash. Improvements consist of a new & handsome frame dwlg & out bldgs. This farm was formerly the residence of C H W Wharton, & lately of Mrs Eliza M Scott. The title is good. –T Parkin Scott

Walnut St Female Seminary, 254 Walnut st, Phil. Miss H M Phelps, Principal

MON DEC 4, 1848
The steamship **Falcon**, under command of Capt Thompson, sailed from N Y on Fri. She touches at Savannah, Havana, New Orleans, & is bound to the Pacific. Passengers: for Chagres: Maj Fitzgerald, E Woodruff, J W Douglass, S H Willey, W F Tilghman, E G Elliott & lady, Lt Gibbs, Persifer Frazier, O C Wheeler & lady, Rev Mr Woodbridge, J Voorhees-special agent, W P Bryant, Chief Judge K Prichett, Loyd Brooks, R W Heath, Geo E Tyler, W H Peise, Levi Stowell, H F Williams, Wm S Burch, John Joyce, & John Morse.

By decree of the Circuit Court of Wash Co, D C, in Chancery, passed in a cause wherein Esau Pickrell & others are cmplnts, & Stanislaus Murray adm, & others, heirs at law of Hannah G Corcoran, deceased, are dfndnts, I shall proceed to sell, on Dec 19, lot 10 in square 218, with 2 story frame house, nearly new. Property is between 14th & 15th sts, one square immediately north of St Matthew's Church. –John F Ennis, Trustee
-A Green, auctioneer

Jas Bailie's New Wine Store: 85 Chestnut st, next door to Congress Hall Hotel, Phil.

Wash Co, D C: I certify that Malachi B Farr brought before me as an estray, a light bay mare. –J L Smith, J P [Owner to prove property, pay charges, & take her away.
–Malachi B Farr, over the Anacostia Bridge]

TUE DEC 5, 1848
Mules just arrived from Ky, for sale low. They can be seen at the subscriber's farm, just west of the Anacostia free-bridge. –Henry Miller

Zachary Taylor proves to be a very old name, as the N Y Sun says that in the list of emigrants from Gravesend, who embarked for Va Jan 6, 1635, on board the ship **Thomas & John**, Richd Lambard master, occurs the name Zachary Taylor, aged 24.

Trustee's sale of valuable property: deed of trust from Jas Young, to the subscribers, dated Jan 27, 1831, recorded in Liber W B 34, folios 444 thru 447, of the land records of Wash Co, D C: sale on Dec 12, of lot 3 in square 690, with improvements-a good 3 story brick house, fronting on N J ave, between B & C sts south. –R C Weightman, John H Riely, trustees. -A Green, auctioneer

Criminal Court for D C-Dec term. Sworn to serve upon the Grand Inquest:

Peter Force, foreman	John Pickrell	Judson Mitchell
John Boyle	Zachariah Walker	Chas R Belt
Geo W Riggs	G C Grammer	Benj K Morsell
Thos Brown	Wm Gunton	Thos Carbery
John Kurtz	Evan Lyons	Thos Blagden
R C Weightman	R S Patterson	Geo Mattingly
G W Young	Joshua Peirce	Ignatius Mudd
Henry Haw	Isaac Clarke	Lewis Johnson

Mrd: on Nov 23, by Rev Dr Plumer, at the Franklin st church, Balt, Md, a Ross Ray, of Wash, to Eliza A S Leslie, daughter of Capt Leslie, of the former city.

Mrd: on Nov 22, at Rose Bank, Fauquier Co, Va, by Rev Mr Atkinson, Geo M Green, of Frankfort, Ky, to Miss Bettie Ashby, daughter of the late Turner Ashby.

Mrd: on Dec 3, at St Matthew's Church, by Rev Mr Donelan, Mr Bernard Mulrany to Mrs Ann Steele, both of Wash.

Died: on Dec 1, at Staunton, Ill, Mrs Lucy G Walsh, wife of Michl Walsh, merchant, formerly of Wash, aged 24 years, after a severe illness of 6 weeks, leaving a husband, an infant daughter, & many relatives & friends.

Died: on Dec 3, in Wash City, Sarah Bond, infant daughter of Alex'r H & Jane Lawrence.

Rooms to let, furnished. Also, his Grocery Store & Fixtures. –Jas McColgan, Pa ave, between 12th & 13th.

WED DEC 6, 1848
Rev H W Ellis, the learned slave, liberated by subscriptions in the Presbyterian Synod of Louisiana & Alabama, has commenced his labors in Africa with zeal. –Norfolk Herald

Hon Ela Collins died suddenly, of apoplexy, on Thanksgiving Day, at Lowville, Lewis Co, N Y, where he had resided since 1808. The present Rep in Congress, Hon Wm Collins, & Lt Collins, of the U S Army, are sons of the deceased. –Albany Ev Jour

Mrs Nixon, of Medina, Orleans Co, N Y, who was riding to Albion, with her husband, last Thu, called at a drug store for morphine to relieve a toothache. The lad gave her strychnine, a fatal poison. She died almost immediately after applying it.

Board: J T Frost, Carroll Pl, Capitol Hill, is prepared to accommodate a small Mess of Members of Congress. The best attendance is assured.

A vigorous effort is now in operation in Brooklyn to erect a monument to the memory of Gen Nath'l Woodhull, a hero & martyr of the Revolution. It is to be erected on <u>Cypress Hill</u>, where a new & extensive cemetery of more than 100 acres has recently been laid out, & was opened a few weeks ago. Gen Woodhull was born on Long Island, Dec 30, 1722; at age 36 he entered the army as Major under Gen Abercrombie, in the French war; distinguished himself at Ticonderoga, & Frontinac; in 1760 was Col of the N Y Provincials engaged in the conquest of Canada. He was in the disastrous battle of Long Island & taken prisoner. He was commanded to say "God save the King." His calm reply was "God save us all!: This brought down upon him savage blows from his captors. He was thrown into one of the British prison ships, where his arm was amputated, & after lingering a short time, he died.

Mrd: on Nov 22 last, at the residence of Dr E T Lynan, Warrenton, Ga, Joshua Nicholls, of D C, to Mrs Mary A Faber, of Charleston, S C.

Died: yesterday, in Wash City, Bernard Martin, aged 30 years. His funeral is today at 3 o'clock, from his late residence on Capitol Hill.

Died: on Dec 3, Mr Thos Hall, of PG Co, Md, aged 68 years, after a severe illness of 6 days, leaving 8 children & many relatives & friends to mourn his loss.

THU DEC 7, 1848
Senate: 1-The ptns & papers on the files of the Senate in the case of Peter A Carnes; in the case of Thos Fillebrown; in the case of Sydney J Bowen; & in the case of John Crawford & wife: were all withdrawn.

On Sat last, while Mr Jas D Sigler was passing the corner of Broadway & Chambers st, N Y, one of the awning posts snapped in two & struck him on the head, fracturing his skull. He died in about an hour. He was a native of N J, & his family reside at Paterson.

New & Fashionable watches & jewelry, at Heydon's Store, 13, east of Coleman's Hotel, Pa ave, Wash. —C W Heydon

Wash Corp: 1-Ptn of Jas Fitzgerald: referred to the Cmte of Claims. 2-Ptn of Geo Mattingly & others: referred to the Cmte on Improvements. 3-Act for the relief of Wm B Wilson: referred to the Cmte on Improvements. 4-Cmte of Claims: bill for the relief of Thos Bevan: passed.

Died: yesterday, in Wash City, Mrs Bridget Herrity, in her 98th year, a native of Galway, Ireland, & for the last 50 years a resident of Wash City. Her funeral will take place from the residence of her son-in-law, Mr Wm Hughes, at the corner of 2nd & G sts, this afternoon, at 3 o'clock.

FRI DEC 8, 1848
Senate: 1-On the 26th day of Oct last, in his 47th year, Dixon H Lewis, a Senator from the State of Alabama, breathed his last in N Y C. He was interred in Greenwood cemetery, on Long Island. Mr Lewis was a native of Ga, & received his education at the college of S C. He then removed to Alabama, became a student in a law ofc, & soon qualified for the bar. In 1829 he represented the Congress of the U S & in 1844 was appointed Govn'r of Alabama. He was chosen, during last winter, by the Legislature for the full term of 6 years. [House of Reps: He leaves the companion of his youthful days; the mother of his children; she who bends lowliest beside his bier.]

Boarding School for Young Lads has been for a year past in progress under the care of the Misses Quincy, too long known as teachers in Wash City. It is located in Franklin Row.

Hon Robt C Schenck, Rep from Ohio, has been called home from Congress by the sudden death of one of his children, & the illness of Mrs Schenck.

Moses Y Beach, the senior editor & proprietor of the N Y Sun has retired to private life.

House of Reps: 1-Ptn of Abram Van Ingen, only surviving son & heir of Dr Dirk Van Ingen, praying Congress to authorize the payment to him of a loss he sustained in continental money.

A letter in the Tribune announces the death of Thos J Farnham, on Sep 13, at San Francisco, Calif; formerly principal of the academy in Jefferson Co, N Y; then a lawyer in Ill.

Mrd: on Nov 30, in Gtwn, D C, by Rev Mr Collier, Wm Jewell, jr, of Va, to Miss Cordelia B Holtzman, of the former place.

During my absence I have left my establishment with Mr A C Huguenin, from Switzerland, who is perfectly able to repair all kinds of Watches, Clocks, & Chronometers. –J Montandon

Donations to aid in the erection of a new orphan asylum will be thankfully received by Sister De Sales, at St Vincent's Orphan Asylum, in 10th st, between F & G sts, or by either of the Lady Managers, viz:

Mrs Newman, 1st Directress Mrs Susan Graham
Mrs Talbot, 2nd Directress Mrs Janet M C Riggs
Mrs Ann S Hill, Treas Mrs Feran
Mrs Ellen A Lee, Sec Mrs Clark
Mrs Stubbs

For rent: the large dwlg-house & store at 13th & F sts, lately occupied by B W Reed as a grocery. Apply to Mr John Wilson, 17th st, between H & I sts, or at the residence of Mrs S M Burche.

By order of distrain, I shall sell for cash, on Dec 11, furniture, & sundry other items, the property of Thos Stevenson, to satisfy rent due to R A Cruit. –John Dewdney, Bailiff

SAT DEC 9, 1848
Wm G Boggs, who has been connected with the N Y Evening Post for 12 years past, has retired from the concern. His interest in the establishment has been purchased by John Bigelow.

The Gov't steamer **Waterwitch**, returned to our navy yard after some 2 years. The engine was from a design by C H Haswell, Engineer-in-chief, & has been unremittingly employed in the Gulf of Mexico, & is very superior to any other now in use. This reflects great credit on Wm M Ellis, the Engineer of the yard, under whose superintendence it was constructed.

$100 reward for runaway negro Thos Jackson, about 30 years old. –Washington J Beall, living near Upper Marlboro, PG Co, Md.

Land at public sale: on Dec 19, on the premises, the Farm of the late Thos Hall, deceased, near Good Luck Post Ofc, PG Co, Md: contains about 450 acres: with a comfortable dwlg house & other necessary outbldgs. Title indisputable, & possession given immediately. –Absalom A Hall, Agent for the heirs.

$50 reward for the conviction of the thief who broke into my shop on E st, on Nov 28, & stole shop tools. -Jos K Boyd

Mrd: on Dec 5, by Rev Mathias Alig, of St Mary's Church, Mr Jos R Rehy to Catherina Schmitt, both of Wash City.

The following Assist Surgeons in the Navy, examined by the Medical Board recently convened at the Naval Asylum, Phil, have been found qualified for promotion, & passed, viz:
Andrew A Henderson, Passed Assist Surgeon, to rank after Passed Assist Surgeon J Hopkinson.
Elisha K Kane, Passed Assist Surgeon, to rank next after Passed Assist Surgeon J Wilson, jr.
Edw Hudson, Passed Assist Surgeon, to rank next after Passed Assist Surgeon E K Kane.
Of the candidates examined for admission into the service as Assist Surgeons, the following have been found qualified, viz:

1-Francis M Gunnell, of D C
2-Jas Suddam, of Pa
3-Robt Carter, of Va
4-S Allen Engles, of Pa
5-Edw Shippen, of Pa
6-Gerard Alexander, of Ky
7-Benj Vreeland, of N Y
8-Walter Hore, of Va
9-Carthen Archer, of Va
10-Richd B Tunstall, of Va
11-Chas H Williamson, of Va
12-Jas F Heustiss, of La
13-Arthur M Lynch, of S C

Died: on Dec 7, in Wash City, Zachariah George, son of Mr Zachariah Dent, of Chas Co, Md, in his 14th year. His funeral is to take place from Mr Geo Richards, his brother-in-law, on B st south, between 6th & 7th sts, this day at 10 o'clock.

Died: on Dec 7, at Milton, Montg Co, Md, Nathan Lufborough, in his 77th year, for many years before & after the acquaintance of the Editors of his paper with Wash City, Chief Clerk in the then ofc of Comptroller of the Treasury. He retired some 25 or 30 years ago, to rural life & pursuits. His funeral is at *Milton*, his late residence, tomorrow at 2 o'clock, & the interment at Grassland at 3½ p m.

MON DEC 11, 1848

Jas Butterfield, of Tyngsborough, Mass, was shockingly killed on the Concord railroad, in Chelmsford, on Mon, when he stepped from one track to the other to avoid a coming train. He leaves a wife & children.

A note from Capt Geo H Tobin, dated "Bark Florida, off the Balize, 28th Nov," says: "All well under Col White. Men behaving admirable." The following is a list of the ofcrs of Col Geo W White's regt of Yucatan volunteers, on board the bark **Florida**, now on her way to Sisal: Col G W White; Lt Col L A Besancon; Majors D S McDowell & F McHenry; Capts Jas Edmonston, John Freeland, R P Mace, Danl Clark Briggs, Geo H Tobin, J G Molloy, & Solis; 1st Lts McKeever, H C Young, [Act Adj,] Fred Sevier, W O Whitmen, J S McCreary, J D Gallagher, Juan Corrille, & J J Gaines; 2nd Lts Ed Dessomines, Corlis, Loftes, McDonald, Juan Eliza Cooper, Hicks, Burgess, & Brown. -New Orleans Delta

At the studio of Mr Chas Miller, in this city, a friend of ours was furnished with the particulars of an equestrian statue of Andrew Jackson, which was ordered by a party of Democratic subscribers about 6 months ago. The statue is to consist of a rearing horse mounted by the Gen in full military costume, to be of bronze, & one third larger than life. It will cost, exclusive of the pedestal, about $16,000, $12,000 of which is to be paid to the artist, & is to occupy the centre of Lafayette Square, in front of the Pres' House. According to the artist the Statue will be completed & placed in Lafayette Square in Jan, 1850.

Mr B Franklin Coston, in his 28th year, lately died at Phil. He was formerly a resident of Wash. Mr Coston invented the ingenious apparatus for the generation of the sylvic gas light. He recently disposed in New England of the patent-right for his gas apparatus for the sum of $!0,000. He has left a widow & 4 children.

Public sale of valuable Wash City lots: under deed of trust from Richd Thompson & wife to Wm Prout, dated 14th Oct, 1837, recorded in Liber W B #65, folio 458, of the land records of Wash Co, D C: the subscriber, [substituted as trustee in the place of said Prout, deceased, by the decree of the Circuit Court of Wash Co, D C,] will sell at public auction, all the right, title & interest of said Thompson & wife, in lots 2, 6, & 8, in square 518: located north of the jail. Sale on Jan 18 next. –Cassius F Lee, Trustee

Farm near Washington for sale: about 170 acres, with a new, commodious & handsome dwlg, & all necessary outbldgs. Fifty head of stock can be wintered on accommodating terms, by application to Robt Chas Jones, at *Clean Drinking*, or to the subscriber at *Norwood*, near Gtwn. –John C Jones

Mrd: on Dec 8, in Gtwn, by Rev Mr Berry, Mr Leoline Jenkins, of N Y, to Miss Rosa Louisa Beeler, daughter of Lewis Beeler, of Wash.

Mrd: on Jul 19, 1848, at *Sutter's Fort*, in Upper California, by John Sinclair, Alcalde for the District of Sacramento, Lamford W Hasting, Atty & Counsellor at Law, to Charlotte Catherine Toler, daughter of H Toler, late of Wash.

Mrd: on Dec 10, at *Sonoma*, by L W Boggs, Chief Magistrate of the District of Sonoma, Mr John L Tanner, of Va, to Miss Mary Tabor, daughter of Mr J D Tabor, of Monterey.

Orphans Court of Wash Co, D C. Dec 8, 1848. Upon motion of Geo S Watkins & Caroline his wife, administrators of Henry Ashton, deceased, [late Midshipman in the U S Navy,] it is ordered that Jan 10 next be assigned to make a pro rata dividend & distribution of the assets collected of said intestate among the creditors.
–Nathl Pope Causin -Ed N Roach, Reg/o wills

TUE DEC 12, 1848
Circuit Court of Wash Co, D C, in Chancery. Bladen Forrest & Mary H Forrest his wife, cmplnts, vs Anderson Kieth & Catharine C Kieth his wife, & others, dfndnts. Jas Kieth, late of said county, departed this life, leaving a last will & testament, in which he gave to Catharine C Kieth an annuity of $200 per annum as long thereafter as she shall live, which said annuity, as well as others, settled on other persons mentioned in the said will is thereby charged on all the estate of the said testator, & subject to the said charges the testator devised his estate to Thos R Kieth, his heirs, excs, & adms, in trust for the sole use & benefit of Mary H Forrest, the cmplnt, & her children; & the bill further states that the said Thos R Kieth refuses to take upon himself the trust of the said will; the object of the said bill is to obtain a decree of the said Court of the appointment of a suitable person trustee in the place of the said Thos R Kieth, with power to manage & execute the said trusts as the said Thos R Kieth might have done if he had accepted the ofc of trustee under the said will. It appears that Anderson & Catharine Kieth do not reside in D C but beyond the reach of this Court. Absent dfndnts to appear in this Court on or before the 3rd Mon in Apr next. -Wm Brent, clerk

Trustee's sale of valuable property on Pa ave: by authority of 3 deeds of trust, one dated 11th Nov, 1840, recorded in Liber W B 83, folios 391; the other dated 3rd Dec, 1841, recorded in Liber W B 90, folios 319; the other dated 18th Oct, 1843, recorded in Liber W B 103, folios 411: all of the land records of Wash Co, D C. Public auction on Jan 10, 1849, on the premises: part of lot 7 in square 491, with improvements: located adjoining the Nat'l Hotel. –Jourdan W Maury, trustee -A Green, auctioneer

House of Reps: 1-Election of Rev R R Gurley as Chaplain of the House.

Garallan Farm for sale: in Loudoun Co, Va, a part of that tract of land upon the Potomac river well known as ***Douglas' Bottom***: lies east of the Catocton Mountain, in the Limestone Valley, between Leesburg & the Point of Rocks, & contains 417 acres. The dwlg-house, now occupied by the tenant & family, but lately erected, is a 2 story log house. Sale on the 2nd Mon of Feb next, before the Court-house. Also, at the same time, a large Asbestos Safety Chest will be sold. --Robt W Gray, Asher W Gray, excx of Jno Gray, deceased.

WED DEC 13, 1848

Fire at Utica, N Y, on Thu destroyed Owen O'Neils' extensive copper, tin, & sheet-iron factory.

Deaths from fighting. 1-A son of Mr Saml Harris was killed on Thu near Glasgow, Cecil Co, Md, by a blow on the head from a gun in the hands of another boy. 2-A colored boy named Jas Bostick was killed at Elkton on Tue in a fight.

The house of a colored woman, Celia Butler, at a place called ***Beggar's Neck***, in St Mary's Co, Md, was destroyed by fire on Sat week, & her 4 children, the eldest 9 years of age, perished in the flames. The mother was absent at a husking feast.

The 7 year old son of Capt Alex'r Myers, of Havre de Grace, died on Fri, after being scalded on Wed, by upsetting a stove on which was a kettle of boiling lard.

Senate: 1-Ptn of Jos Holden, asking the right of pre-emption to a certain tract of land: referred to the Cmte on Private Land Claims. 2-Ptn of Jos Walker, asking the confirmation of certain land claims: referred to the Cmte on Private Land Claims. 3-Ptn of Wm C Sterrett, asking a pension: referred to the Cmte on Pensions. 4-Ptn of Benj Simson, asking payment of the amount due for the charter of the brig **Orion** as a storeship by the U S: referred to the Cmte of Claims. 5-Ptn of Mary, the widow of Benj Hassell, asking a pension: referred to the Cmte on Pensions. 6-Ptn of Ruth Kerr, widow of a Revolutionary soldier, asking a pension: referred to the Cmte on Pensions. 7-Ptn of Thos M Taylor, a purser in the navy, praying to be released from liabilities for certain moneys which were lost in consequence of the failure of the bank in which they were deposited: referred to the Cmte on Naval Affairs. 8-Ptn of Chas Colburn, asking compensation for his services as yeoman in the navy: referred to the Cmte of Claims. 9-Memorial of Chas M Keller & others, on behalf of a convention of inventors, asking that certain defects in the patent laws may be remedied: referred to the Cmte on Patents & the Patent Ofc. 10-Ptn of Saml Colt, asking that he may be authorized by law to furnish repeating firearms for the Gov't: referred to the Cmte on Military Affairs. 11-Ptn of Jos Raynes, asking confirmation of his title to a certain tract of land: referred to the Cmte on Private Land Claims. 12-Ordered that the ptn of Azel Spaulding, & the documents relating to the claim of Caroline Mack, on the files of the Senate, be referred to the Cmte on Pensions. 13-Ordered that the ptn of Erskine & Eichelberger, on the files of the Senate, be referred to the Cmte of Claims. 14-Ordered that the ptn of John McColgan be taken from the files of the Senate & referred to the Cmte on Commerce. 15-Ordered that the ptn of the heirs of Jos Watson, deceased, on the files of the Senate, be referred to the Cmte of Claims. Also, that of Horsee Southmayd & Son, Sarah Crandall, Jas Wormsby, & the heirs of Saml Beach, have leave to withdraw their petitions & papers. 16-Leave was granted to withdraw from the files of the Senate the petition & papers of Asa Anderson. 17-The following adverse reports made at the last session of Congress were taken up & severally concurred in: Cmte on Pensions: on the ptns of Elijah Buchanan, Sarah Tyler, Amos Doughty, Jos Hair, Henrietta Bedinger, Mary Coleman, Mehitable Gibbs, Reuben M Gibbs, John Stannert, Nancy Jillson, Isaac Davenport, Judediah Gray, Hector St John Beetley, Jos Barclay, Leonard Gray, & Mary Morris Foote. Cmte on Naval Affairs: on the memorials of John Baldwin, Ann Kellogg, widow of Danl Kellogg, John Ericson, & Abel Gregg. Cmte of Claims: on the claims of Arnold Naudain, Littleton Dennis Teackle, & Amos Holton. Cmte on Indian Affairs: on the memorials of Saml Rusk, Wm Tyler & Geo S Gaines, late Choctaw Com'rs of the Seneca, Onondaga & Cayuga Indians, citizens of Rochester, N Y, in behalf of the Tonowanda band of Seneca Indians. Cmte on Public Lands: on the memorial of Isaac Slacke, & the heirs of D Reperiligny. 18-The adverse report made last session by the Cmte of Claims upon the memorial of C B Calcott, was recommitted to the Cmte of Claims. 19-The adverse report made by the Cmte on Revolutionary Claims on the case of Haym Soloman, was concurred in: recommitted to the Cmte on Revolutionary Claims.

Two hogs raised by Mr Danl Mumms, of Hagerstown, weighed 975 pounds. Mr Job Eldridge, of Cecil Co, sent to Balt a few days ago a hog, which was only 19 months old, that weighed 800 pounds.

Fire broke out yesterday in the hay loft over the brick stable of Rev Mr McLain, on C st, & was partially destroyed. The horse was got out & saved. The general impression is that the stable was set on fire.

Criminal Court for this District now in session: U S vs Wm James, free negro. Found guilty of stealing a box of candles & a box of soap, the property of Bates & Brother. Judge Crawford sentenced him to suffer 18 months in the Penitentiary.

Rooms to Let: a good parlor & bedroom adjoining can be had at Mrs Dixon's, corner of F & 11th sts; breakfast & tea could be furnished if desired.

After the death of the late Jonathan Goodhue, a letter was found, written by him only a few months before, & addressed to his family. "Born on the 21st of Jun, 1783, I am now well advanced on my 65th year." For 2 years past I occasionally found an oppression of the chest-some derangement of the heart. He expresses his gratitude for the blessings of his domestic ties, & the happiness of his home. I have often mentioned that, among my associates in my native town, Salem, I scarcely ever heard a profane word. I wish to advise my children against every thing like extravagance. Things comfortable, if they can afford it. In reference to the closing scene in this world, it would be my desire that none but the immediate relatives & friends should be called together when the usual religious services should be performed, & that not more than a single carriage should follow the hearse to the cemetery. I pray Heaven to receive my parting spirit.
-Jonathan Goodhue

Mrd: on Dec 5, by Rev Wm Prettyman, John H Kidwell to Miss Sarah K Bradley, both of Wash.

Mrd: on Dec 11, at Trinity Church, by Rev C M Butler, Jas H Payne, of Westmoreland Co, Va, to Miss Farinda F Washington, of Wash City.

Mrd: on Nov 30, at N Y, by Rt Rev Bishop Hughes, Frederick Francis De La Figaneira, Attache to the Portuguese son of Her Most Faithful Majesty's Minister in the U S, to Josephine, only daughter of Saml I Hunt, of that city.

Mrd: on Dec 7, at Balt, by Rev Dr Atkinson, John Stewart to Henrietta R, daughter of Geo R Gaither.

Died: on Nov 16, at the residence of her son, Stockley Donelson, [in the vicinity of Nashville, Tenn,] Mrs Mary Donelson, relict of the late Capt John Donelson, in her 86th year.

Died: on Mon last, in her 4th year, Florence Drayton, daughter of Peter F & Eliz C Bacon. Her funeral is today at 10 o'clock.

Died: on Dec 11, in Wash City, Chas William, youngest child of Benj Owen & Sarah Ann Shekell, aged 17 months & 19 days. His funeral is today at 2 o'clock, from the residence of his parents, on D, between 9th & 10th sts.

Hon John McClellan was one of the Taylor electors of the State of Conn: a resident of Woodstock, Windham Co, & has arrived at the good old age of 82 years. He voted for the first Pres of the country, the great & good Washington. –New Haven Palladium

In Talbot Co Court, [Md] last week, negro Ben Thomas, belonging to Wm H Golt, was convicted of enticing & assisting 4 slaves to run away. He was sentenced in 15 years & 6 months' labor in the penitentiary. In the same Court Jas E Work was convicted of abducting 2 slaves.

Last evening the express train from Lowell run over Chas White, near Bacon's Bridge, Medford, & killed him instantly. Mr White was 26 years old, & leaves a widow & one child. He was a turner by trade, & worked in Medford. –Bee

House of Reps: 1-Resolved that John B Frye, who acted as clerk in the ofc of the Sgt-At-Arms at the last session of Congress, be paid the same amount of extra compensation as was allowed to the assist clerks in the Clerk's ofc. 2-Mr Asa Whitney's proposed plan of a railroad from Lake Michigan to the Pacific ocean: laid on the table. 3-Memorial of John H Goldsby, & papers, be withdrawn from the files, & referred to the Cmte on Invalid Pensions. 4-Bill for the relief of Jos Decret.

City Ordinances-Wash: 1-Act for the relief of Wm B Wilson: to be paid $8.24 the balance due him for laying flag footways, Nov 11, 1848. 2-Act for the relief of Thos Bevan: fine relative to bread, remitted. Provided he pay the cost of prosecution.

Wash Corp: 1-Bill for the relief of Robt B Cluskey: referred to the Cmte of Claims. 2-Cmte of Claims: bill for the relief of Wm Rupp: recommitted to the same cmte. 3-Cmte of Claims: act for the relief of E G Handy was read. 4-Cmte of Claims: asking to be discharged from the further consideration of the ptn of Christopher Hager.

Marshal's sale: writ of fieri facias, on scire facias under the lien law, public sale, for cash, on Jan 10, of 5 two story frame dwlg-houses, on part of lots 4 & 5 in square 369, in Wash City, the property of Sylvanus Holmes, & sold to satisfy Judicials 34, to Mar term, 1849, in favor of Ulysses Ward. –Robt Wallace, Marshal of D C

THU DEC 14, 1848
For Calif: the U S ship **Fredonia** sailed from N Y on Mon for the Pacific. Although merely ordered to the Pacific, she is going to Calif to protect the interests of the people & Gov't of the U S in that quarter. The following are the ofcrs, viz: F A Neville, Lt Commanding; Abner Reed, Acting Master; Jas F Harrison & F M Ringgold, Assist Surgeons; A F Monroe, L H Lyne, & Ed Renshaw, Passed Midshipmen; Jas B Coskery, Surgeon's Steward; Robt Kearney, Acting Master's Mate.

Baton Rouge. Encounter took place today between Dr J G Byrd, of this town, & Dr Edw Skillman, of Opelousas. Dr Skillman attacked Byrd in his ofc & shot at him. A scuffle ensued in which Dr Skillman received a wound in the right breast, causing his death in about half an hour. Dr Byrd received 3 wounds, one of which was severe. Dr Byrd, it seems, acted in self-defence.

Senate: 1-Memorial of Mr John D Emerson, asking compensation for the use, by the U S, of an improvement in the steam engine, of which he is the inventor & patantee: referred to the Cmte on Patents & the Patent Ofc. 2-Memorial of Jas G King & others, of N Y, asking the removal of obstructions to the Hurlgate channel & N Y harbor: referred to the Cmte on Commerce. 3-Ptn of Ward Marston & others, late ofcrs in the U S Marine Corps, asking to be reinstated in their position in the corps, from which they were dropped in consequence of its reduction on the termination of the war with Mexico: referred to the Cmte on Naval Affairs. 4-Ptn of R L Baker, an ofcr in the army, asking to be allowed brevet pay & emoluments, which, with the papers on file, was referred to the Cmte on Military Affairs. 5-Ptn of the heirs & legal reps of Jos Crockett, deceased, late marshal of the district of Ky & collector of district taxes & internal revenue, asking an equitable settlement of his accounts: referred to the Cmte of Claims. 6-Ptn of Margaret W Fisher: referred to the Cmte on Military Affairs. 7-Mr Johnson, of Md, asked leave to withdraw from the files of the Senate the memorial of John S Skinner, & that it be referred to a special cmte. Not agreed to. Memorial of Mr Skinner was then referred to the Cmte on Agriculture.

FRI DEC 15, 1848
Col H D Peire died at New Orleans on Dec 2, in his 69th year. He was a distinguished ofcr of the regular army in the war of 1812, & was conspicuous as major commandant of the 44th Infty at the capture of Pensacola, in 1814, by Gen Jackson.

Senate: 1-Memorial of Isaac S Keith Reeves, of the U S Army, asking that his allowances as adjutant of the Military Academy may be made the same by law as those of an adjutant of a regt of dragoons. 2-Ptn of Jas Foy & others, employed in the Quartermaster's dept, praying that bounty land & 3 months extra pay may be allowed to them, the same as others engaged in the war with Mexico: referred to the Cmte on Military Affairs. 3-Ptn of Danl Webb, praying that he may be allowed arrears of pension: referred to the Cmte on Pensions. 4-Ptn of A J Grinnan & other heirs of Andrew Glossell, deceased, praying indemnity for French spoliations prior to 1800: referred to the Cmte on Foreign Relations. 5-Ptn of Rosanna Maury, praying a pension: referred to the Cmte on Pensiona. 6-Ordered, that the ptn of the administrator of Francis Cazeau be taken from the files & referred to the Cmte on the Judiciary. 7-Ordered, that the memorial of Jos Radcliff & the ptn of John Bruce, on the files of the Senate, be referred to the Cmte on Claims. 8-Ordered, that the ptn of Benj Miller & the documents relating to the claim of Wm Parkinson be taken from the files & referred to the Cmte on Pensions. 9-Ordered, that Aaron Carman have leave to withdraw the documents accompanying his petition. 10-Ordered, that Pierson Cogswell have leave to withdraw his petition & papers. 11-Ordered, that the ptn of Amasa Dana, praying an increase of pension for Jesse Young, be taken from the files & referred to the Cmte on Pensions. 12-Cmte on Military Affairs: memorial of Wm H Aspinwall & others, relative to the construction of a railroad across the Isthmus of Panama, reported the following bill: that the Sec of the Navy be authorized to enter into a contract on behalf of the U S Gov't, for a period not exceeding 20 years, with Wm H Aspinwall, John L Stevens, & Henry Chauncey, all of N Y C, [regarding the aforesaid construction.] 13-Cmte on Pensions: to inquire into a bill for the confirmation of the claim of Benj F Bosworth for bounty lands.

The Rev W W Hill, of Louisville, received a letter conveying that Rev Danl Baker, who has been laboring under the care of the Presbyterian Board of Missions for some months past in Texas, was murdered in cold blood by the Camanche Indians, on his way from San Antonio de Bexar to Victoria. He was also scalped by the savages. Mr Baker was for a number of years Pastor of the 2nd Presbyterian Church in this city, whence he removed to Frankfort, Ky, to take charge of the church there. [See Dec 18, 1840.]

The Walker Sharpshooters announce their 1st Annual Ball to be given at the Odd Fellows' Hall, on Dec 18. Managers:

W W Seaton	Capt J H Goddard	Jas King
Walter Lenox	Washington Adams	O F M Powell
Jos A Bradley	B B Edmonston	John Wallis
John W Maury	Josiah Essex	H H McPherson
Hugh B Sweeny	Nelson Henning	W H Winter
Dr W B Magruder	Wm McCollum	____ Goodrick
Dr A Holmead	Jas Ellis	

Walker Sharpshooters:
Lt E M Chapin   Sgt J Tabler   Cpl B H Hurst
Lt B F Morsell   Sgt J S Chew   E C Eckloff
Lt M Birkhead   Cpl Geo Kennedy   J H Goddard, jr

Light Infty:
Capt Tate   Lt Clark
Lt Tucker   Lt Davis

Nat'l Grays:
Capt Bacon   Lt Mohum
Lt Tait   Lt Tucker

Independent Grays:
Lt Upperman   Lt Waugh   Lt Griffin

As the train from Boston was approaching the depot, on Wed, Mr Jos M Bradley attempted to cross the track & was run over by the train & instantly killed. He was about 40 years of age, & leaves a wife & 3 or 4 children. –Concord [N H] Patriot

City property & farm for sale: about 9 acres, with good house & outhouses, at the junction of Balt & Marlborough roads. Also a lot with a brick & a frame house, on 8th st, now in the occupancy of Henry Janney. –Jos Scholfield, exc -A Green, auctioneer

Trustee's sale of valuable household furniture: by deed of trust executed to me by the late E W Smallwood, dated Sep 15, 1847: sale on Dec 27, at the late residence of said Smallwood, on East Capitol st. –John Pickrell, trustee -Martin & Wright, auctioneers

Mrd: on Dec 12, in Wash, by Rev Mr Martin, Mary Louisa Dunlap & Wm Henry Daingerfield, of Bellemont, PG Co, Md.

Mrd: on Dec 11, in Trinity Church, by Rev C M Butler, Jas H Payne, of Westmoreland Co, Va, to Fairinda, daughter of Perrin Washington, of Wash City. [*Republished in order to correct it-Editors note.]

Died: on Dec 10, in Wash City, Mrs Mary Ann Potter, in her 28th year. Mrs Potter was a devoted & affectionate wife, a firm friend, & a sincere Christian.

Died: on Dec 14, of croup, Wm Henry Harrison, 2nd son of Wm M & Mary Ann Ellis, aged 7 years & 9 months. His funeral is on Sat at 2 o'clock. [Balt Sun & Phil Ledger please copy.]

Died: on Dec 9, John Wm, only son of Jerome R & Jane Wroe, aged 3 years, 4 months & 28 days.

SAT DEC 16, 1848

Mr Philip S Lanhan, of St Louis, had been bedridden for 5 months, with an affection of the spine. His friends placed him on a bed & conveyed him to the asylum of Mr Keely, the magnetizer. Being magnetized, Mr Keely raised the patient to his feet & told him to walk, which he did freely, without pain.

Mr Jos Cutting, direct from the gold mines of Calif, arrived at New Orleans on Dec 7, leaving San Francisco on Oct 11, taking the overland route via the city of Mexico & Vera Cruz. He was one year in Calif, & nearly 6 weeks in the gold digging, without mining materials or assistance of any kind. He used a butcher knife, pickaxe, shovel, & a pan to wash the dirt. He collected upwards of $1,500 of the pure metal. Gold has been discovered in the neighborhood of Los Angeles. The editor of the Californian, in his paper of Oct 7, announces: "Really we dread the digging of a well or the grading of a street in our neighborhood."

Maj T M Leavenworth has been elected alcalde, & B R Backelew & Barton Mowry councilmen of San Francisco. Cmte to draft a memorial to the U S Congress, urging the necessity that exists for the speedy establishment of a branch mint at San Francisco. Cmte consists of: C V Gillespie, Judge G Hyde, Dr John Townsend, Capt J L Folsom, & Saml Brannan, who have prepared & published a memorial.

The Mormons of Calif have laid claim to a large portion of the gold territory, & demand 30% of the ore taken therefrom. The demand is expected to lead to trouble.

Rhode Island Historical Society meeting at Providence on Dec 5. Mr Geo W Greene read an account of the papers of Gen Nathl Greene, which he has in his possession & is preparing for publication. The collection is very large, from two to three thousand letters of most of the eminent men of the American Revolution period. One of the letters read was of Jan 4, 1776, written at the camp on Prospect Hill to Gov Ward, then in Congress. The other letter was addressed to Robt Morris, & gives a very gloomy account of the financial embarrassments both of the army & the country. Several original letters were also shown from Washington, Lafayette, Steuben, St Clair, Marion, Sumter, Lee, Williams, & Putnam. Also the original report of the battle of the Cowpens.
–Prov Journal

The Gen Court of Va has refused to allow a new trial in the case of Wm Dandridge Eppes, convicted of the murder of F Adolphus Muir, in Dinwiddie. He is sentenced to be hanged on Dec 22, & will be executed, unless the Govn'r should pardon him. The Gen Court also refused to grant a new trial to John _ Blevins, who was convicted of stealing slaves. His sentence will be for life, he having been confined in the Penitentiary under prior sentences for upwards of 23 years. The Gen Court also refused to grant a new trial to Allen Ewing, who was convicted of aiding slaves to escape from their masters, & sentenced to 5 years imprisonment in the Penitentiary.

A new county in the southern portion of the State of Arkansas has been named Ashley County, in respect to the memory of the late Senator of that name.

Red River Republican announces the death of the venerable Seth Lewis, of Rapides, La, in his 85th year. He was a District Judge of La for many years. –Bee

Hon Christopher C Scott & Hon David Walker have been elected by the Legislature to be Judges of the Supreme Court of Arkansas.

The most remarkable of all the ancient bldgs in the Northern Neck, Va, is that of Stratford, County of Westmoreland, on the bank of the Potomac, for a long time the property of the Lees. It was built by Mr Thos Lee, father of Richd Henry Lee. He is known by the name of Pres Lee, or Govn'r Lee, having been Pres of the King's Council, & Govn'r of Va, while a Colony. While Govn'r, his house was burnt down, & either the British Gov't or the merchants of London built this house for him at great expense. The brick were brought from England. The walls of the first story are 2½ feet thick; of the 2nd story, 2 feet. The late Gen Henry Lee, of the Revolution, took down some of the partitions. –Southern Churchman

A new Post Ofc was established yesterday at **Fort Washington** & Lt F S Everett is appointed postmaster.

Mrd: on Dec 14, at the residence of her father, in Gtwn, D C, by Rev D S Finkle, Robt G McCreary, of the bar of Gettysburg, Pa, to Miss Louisa A E, daughter of Capt John & Mary C Moore, formerly of Loudoun Co, Va.

Died: yesterday, in Wash City, after a severe & painful illness, Mrs Marie Antoinette Estelle Johnston, wife of Edw W Johnston. Her funeral is today at 2 o'clock, from her late residence.

Died: on Thu, Col Wm Brent, Clerk of the Circuit, & District, & Criminal Courts of this District, in his 74th year. Descended from the earlier of the settlers on the shores of Md, & from ancestors of great worth, no shade has ever rested on the rectitude & honor of our deceased friend. He leaves behind him a family who will long lament the loss of the kindest of fathers & the best of friends. His funeral is at 10:30 today, at his late residence on Capitol Hill, whence his remains will be taken to the Family Burial-ground at Rock Creek Catholic Church, in Montg Co, Md.

For rent: brick dwlg house on N Y ave, near 14th st, lately occupied by Geo W Young. Apply to Mr James, next door, or to Jas Larned, 13th st.

MON DEC 18, 1848
The rumor of the murder of Rev Danl Baker, an esteemed Presbyterian Missionary in Texas, is contradicted, letters having been received from him at Princeton, N J, stating his escape from the perils to which he was exposed among the Indians, & his safe return to Victoria.

Madame de Montjoie, a faithful friend of the ex-Queen of France, who followed her into exile, has lately died.

The prize of $100 for the best tale written for the N Y Organ has been awarded Mrs C W Denison, of Boston. It is entitled Gertrude Russel, & is already commenced in the Organ. [Weekly paper.]

Lord Melbourne, the former Whig Premier of Great Britain, is dead.

Mrd: on Dec 14, at Ingle Side, Chester Co, Pa, by Rev Mr Dubois, Bronaugh M Deringer, of Wash, to Estalina P Woodland, of Wilmington, Delaware.

Mrd: on Dec 12, by Rev Jos Hammitt, Mr J J Biggs, of Raleigh, N C, to Miss Isabella A, 2nd daughter of Mr Israel E James, of the city of Phil.

Died: on Dec 11, in Jacksonville, Fla, where he had gone for his health, Richd B Nalley, in his 33rd year. His funeral is this day at 3 o'clock, from his late residence, G st near 9th st.

New Fancy Goods & Toys: Mrs H Clitch, Pa ave, between 9th & 10th sts, 4 doors from 10th.

TUE DEC 19, 1848

Senate: 1-Memorial from Geo Wilkes, of N Y C, asking the construction of a railroad by the Gov't from the Missouri river to the Pacific: referred to the Cmte on Roads & Canals. 2-Memorial from Henry O'Rielly, asking authority & assistance of Congress to enable him to establish a telegraphic communication between the Mississippi valley & Calif & Oregon: referred to the Cmte on Territories. 3-Ptn of Eliz Morse & others, heirs of Dewry Ragsdale, asking commutation pay: referred to the Cmte on Revolutionary Claims. 4-Ptn of Jas Disturnell, asking that an appropriation may be made for collecting, in connexion with the taking of the 7th census, statistical information relating to North America & the West India Islands: referred to Select Cmte. 5-Mr Johnson, of Md, presented the ptn of Julia Martin, asking a pension for her brother Luther Martin, late a midshipman in the navy: referred to the Cmte on Pensions. 6-Memorial from John Collins, claiming difference of pay between boatswain & a boatswain's mate: referred to the Cmte on Naval Affairs. 7-Ptn of Wm H Shover, capt & brevet major in the U S army, asking for arrears of pay: referred to the Cmte on Military Affairs. 8-Memorial from Leonidas Wetmore, asking compensation for 2 horses lost in the military service of the U S: referred to the Cmte on Military Affairs. 9-Memorial of Jas M Scantling, asking an increase of pension or a donation: referred to the Cmte on Pensions. 10-Ordered, that the ptn & papers in the case of Isabella Stout, now on file, be taken therefrom & referred to the Cmte on Private Land Claims. 11-Ordered, that the ptn & papers in the case of Rev John John E Tucker, now on file, be taken therefrom & referred to the Cmte on Military Affairs. 12-Ordered, that the papers on file in the case of Robt Sewall be referred to the Cmte of Claims.

Our news from Italy commences with the death of the Prime Minister of the Pope of Rome, Count Rossi, by the dagger of an assassin. He was unpopular with the lower classes of the citizens. The assassin is known, but has escaped.

Orphans Court of Wash Co, D C. Letters testamentary on the personal estate of Mary Hanson, late of said county, deceased. –Ann Hanson, excx

Mrd: on Dec 5, at Baton Rouge, La, by Rev John Bache, Bvt Lt Col W W S Bliss, U S A, to Betty, youngest daughter of Maj Gen Z Taylor.

Mrd: on Dec 12, by Rev Mr Busey, Mr Benj Brooke Edmonson to Miss Martha A Willis, all of Wash City.

Mrd: on Aug 27, by Rev Mr Vanhorsigh, Jules Marie, of Paris, France, to Lucie Tisseuil, of the same place.

Died: yesterday, after a lingering illness, Mary E, daughter of John T Sullivan, of Wash City. Her funeral is today at 2 o'clock, from the residence of her father.

Died: Dec 18, Mrs Ellen Wilson, aged 64 years, wife of Jas Wilson, & daughter of the late Thos Lee Mitchell, of PG Co, Md. Her funeral is on Dec 20, at 10 o'clock, from her residence on B st, fronting the Capitol square.

WED DEC 20, 1848
Senate: 1-Ptn of John A Ragan, proposing to drain the inundated public lands in the valley of the Mississippi river, on condition that the U S will grant him every alternate section of the land so drained: referred to the Cmte on Public Lands. 2-Ptn of Thos Linard, asking compensation for forage furnished for the use of certain mounted volunteers in the Mexican war: referred to the Cmte of Claims. 3-Ptn of Talcott Reed, a Revolutionary soldier, asking to be allowed a pension: referred to the Cmte on Pensions. 4-Ptn of Mary Wilkinson, widow of John Wilkinson, late a sailing-master on board the private armed schnr **Nonsuch**, Capt Lovely, of Balt, in the late war with England, & slain in battle by the enemy, asking to be restored to the pension roll & for the arrears of pension: referred to the Cmte on Pensions. 5-Ptn & documents of Wm H Burns, master's mate in the U S Navy, asking compensation for services rendered: referred to the Cmte on Naval Affairs. 6-Ptn of Asa Lift, praying for a law to change the name of the vessel **Kestrie** to **Annie Lift**: referred to the Cmte on Commerce. 7-Ptn of Hiram Smith, Register of the Land Ofc at Champagnote, Ark, asking to be allowed compensation for certain expenses in connexion with his ofc: referred to the Cmte on Public Lands. 8-Ptn of Jas L Lillard & others, heirs & legal reps of Jos Spencer, asking bounty land & commutation pay: referred to the Cmte on Pensions. 9-Cmte on Military Affairs: joint resolution for the relief of Maj R L Baker, of the ordnance corps: passed to a 2nd reading. 10-Cmte on Indian Affairs: reported a bill to authorize the Sec of War to make reparation for the killing of a <u>Caddo boy</u> by volunteer troops in Mexico. The Indian agent & Col Bell, who commanded upon that frontier, concluded a treaty with these Indians. The Indians agreed to take $500 to keep the peace, according to their custom: bill was passed.

Lt Newman, late in service in Mexico, is forming a company in Vermont for Calif. Capt Simmons is also recruiting a company in the Green Mountains.

House of Reps: 1-Ordered that the ptn & papers of Saml Reed, of Pike Co, Ohio, be withdrawn from the files & referred to the Cmte of Claims. 2-Ordered, that leave be given to withdraw the papers in the case of Capt John Oldham. 3-Resolved, that leave be given to Thos Chaney to withdraw his ptn & other papers now on file. 4-Resolved, that Nancy G Van Rensselaer, widow of the late Capt Henry Van Rensselaer, have leave to withdraw her ptn & papers [praying for a pension] from the files of this House. 5-Resolved, that leave be granted to withdraw the papers on the files of this House in the case of Minard Harden, in order that the same may be placed before the Postmaster General. 6-Resolved, that the Clerk of this House pay to the widow, or her order, of the late Hon John M Holley the expense of removing the remains of her late husband to the place of his former residence, in the State of N Y, providing said expense shall not exceed the sum of $300. 7-Resolved, that leave be granted for the withdrawal of the memorial & vouchers of Benedict J Heard. 8-Memorial of Isaac S K Reeves, 1st Lt in the regiment U S Artl, & adjutant of the Military Academy, in relation to his allowances: referred to the Cmte on Military Affairs. 9-Memorial of Archibald R Bogardus, praying that his pension for disability may be made to commence from the date of the said disability: referred to the Cmte on Naval Affairs. 10-Ptn of Eugene H Abadie, assist surgeon in the U S Army, praying compensation for services rendered in Florida in 1838, heretofore presented. 11-Ptn of L B Harbour, praying compensation for a horse taken by public authority & converted to public use, heretofore presented. Which was referred to the Cmte of Claims. 12-Notice of bills: bill for the relief of W O Walker. 13-Cmte on Private Land Claims: bill from the Senate entitled an act for the relief of the heirs of Jean F Perry, Josiah Bleakley, Nicholas Jarrot, & Robt Morrison, reported the same back to the House without amendment: bill was passed & returned to the Senate. Same cmte: bills for the relief of Sidney Flower, of La, & for the relief of Amelia Covillion, of La: committed. Same cmte: bill from the Senate for the relief of the heirs of John Wall, deceased: committed. 13-Cmte on Revolutionary Pensions: Senate bill granting a pension to Bethiah Healy, widow of Geo Healy, deceased: committed. 14-Cmte on Invalid Pensions: bill for the relief of John McIntosh: committed. Same cmte: adverse reports on the ptns of Wm Slocum & John H Goolsby: laid on the table. Same cmte: bill for the relief of Levi M Roberts: committed.

All persons having claims against Thos Y Conly, for bldg or furnishing Fuller's Hotel, 12th & Pa ave, are to call at the lumber ofc of Messrs O J Preston & Co, 14th st bridge, where they will find papers appointing the undersigned trustees to liquidate & settle, on certain specified terms, all such claims. –B Willet, O J Preston, trustees

Died: on Sunday, at Balt, Geo Law, an old, respected, & useful citizen.

New Establishment: Wholesale & Retail Tobacco, Snuff, & Cigar Depot, #3, Elliot's bldgs, Pa ave, between 3rd & 4½ sts. F H Williams has taken the store lately occupied by N E Tyson.

For rent: store room now occupied by A Hoover & Son, on Pa ave, between 6th & 7th sts. Possession given on Jan 1. Inquire of B L Jackson & Brother.

Wash Corp: 1-Ptns from J A Williams & J A Williams & others, praying a modification of the law levying a tax upon livery stables: referred to the Cmte on Finance. 2-Ptn from Geo Seitz for the remission of a fine: referred to the Cmte of Claims. 3-Cmte of Claims: report a bill for the relief of C Gautier. 4-Cmte of Claims: asking to be discharged from the further consideration of the ptn of Wm Rupp: so decided. 5-Act for the relief of Saml Cromwell: passed. 6-Cmte of Claims: act for the relief of M Rosenstock. 6-Bill for the relief of Emily G Jones, excx of the late Thos P Jones, was referred to the delegation from the 2nd Ward. 7-Ptn of J Thomas, praying remission of a fine: referred to the Cmte of Claims. 7-Bill for the relief of E G Handy: passed.

City Ordinance-Wash. 1-Act for the relief of Jas H Moore & Saml & Perry Biggs: that the Intendant of the Asylum be required to surrender to Jas H Moore 3 hogs, & to Saml & Perry Biggs 2 hogs, claimed by them & found going at large in the city, & taken to the Poor House; the said Moore & Biggs paying the cost & charges attending their seizure & support. Approved, Dec 13, 1848.

THU DEC 21, 1848

Senate: 1-Ptn of Saml D Davis, a Revolutionary soldier, asking to be allowed an increase of pension: referred to the Cmte on Revolutionary Claims. 2-Ptn of John A Webber, U S military storekeeper at Watertown, Mass, asking to be allowed compensation for extra service: referred to the Cmte on Military Affairs. 3-Memorial of J W Nye, asking compensation for certain public lots occupied by him & now required to be surrendered: referred to the Cmte on the Public Bldgs. 4-Memorial from Benedict J Heard, asking compensation for the destruction of his property by the enemy in 1814: referred to the Cmte of Claims. 5-Ptn of Wm Hunley, register, & Geo S Galladay, receiver of public lands in Mississippi, asking that commissions may be allowed on entries of military land warrants: referred to the Cmte on Public Lands. 6-Bill for the relief of Geo Poindexter was recommitted to the Cmte of Claims. 7-Ptn & papers of Hugh Wallace Wormley taken from the files & referred to the Cmte on Pensions. 8-The Senate considered the adverse report of the Cmte of Claims upon the ptn of Arnold Naudain: which was concurred in. Also, to the consideration of the adverse report of the Cmte of Claims upon the ptn of Gustavus C Horner: which, was passed over for the present. 9-Cmte of the Whole: considered the bill for the relief of Philip J Fontane: passed. [This man was a contractor with the Gov't for the performance of certain work, viz the bldg of a lighthouse, & he executed a larger amount of work. The auditor reported that he ought to be paid the amount claimed; but the contractor, being anxious for a speedy settlement, consented to accept $1,000, which was one-third less than his claim, although the auditor has assented to the justness of the whole. The cmte have reported only $1,000, & I presume he will be willing to accept it.]

The Hon Andrew Stewart, of the House of Reps, has been for the last week, confined to his rooms in Cumberland, Md. It is his intention to proceed to Wash City as soon as his health will permit.

House of Reps: 1-Bill for the relief of Martin O Walker: referred to the Cmte on the Post Ofc & Post Roads. 2-Bill for the relief of Jos Decret: referred to the Cmte on Military Affairs.

Maryland Family Hams: just received & for sale. -Geo & Thos Parker

Mrd: on Dec 19, by Rev Mr Ballentine, Mr David McQueen, of N Y, & Christiana Jane, daughter of Mr Geo Hercus, of Wash City.

FRI DEC 22, 1848
House of Reps: 1-Ordered, that the papers of Henry Haines relative to his application for a pension be taken from the files & referred to the Cmte on Revolutionary Pensions. 2-Resolved, that the papers in the application of Jos Ross for a pension be taken from the files & referred to the Cmte on Pensions. 3-Resolved, that the heirs of Capt John Slaughter have leave to withdraw their papers from the Clerk's ofc, & that their ptn, with the accompanying papers, be referred to the Cmte on Revolutionary Claims.

Senate: 1-Ptn of John B White, only surviving child of Capt Robt White, an ofcr of the Revolution, asking that the pension claimed to be due to his father may be paid: referred to the Cmte on Revolutionary Claims. 2-Ptn of John Dickey & 130 other citizens of Vt, asking for a mail route from Corinth to Wash, by East Orange, in Vt: referred to the Cmte on the Post Ofc & Post Roads. 3-Ptn of John S Develin, adm of Maj Weed, late quartermaster of marines, asking that the accounting ofcrs of the Treasury be authorized to settle the accounts of said Weed upon equitable principles: referred to the Cmte of Claims. 4-Mr Yulee presented the remonstrance of the wardens & vestry of Trinity Church, Fla, against the claim set up by Mr Medeore, vicar genr'l of Fla, to the lot on which said church is built, together with other papers, which they request may be printed: referred to the Cmte on Private Land Claims. 5-Ptn of Hugh W Dobbin, an ofcr in the last war with Great Britain, asking remuneration for his military services; which, with the papers on file in the Senate in relation to the said claim, were referred to the Cmte on Military Affairs. 6-Ordered, that the memorial of Thos L K Brent, on the files of the Senate: be referred to the Cmte on Foreign Relations. 7-Ordered, that the ptn of C G Gunter, on the files of the Senate, be referred to the Cmte on Private Land Claims. 8-Cmte on Revolutionary Claims: adverse report upon the ptn of the legal reps of Saml Beach, which was laid on the table. Same cmte: to be discharged from the further consideration of the ptn of Catharine O'Neal, that it be referred to the Cmte on Revolutionary Pensions. 9-Cmte on Patents: bill for the relief of Jas Henley: committed. 10-Cmte on Foreign Affairs be discharged from the further consideration of the memorial of Joshua P Powers, & that it be referred to the Cmte of Claims. 11-Bill for the relief of Houghton A Fletcher, introduced. 12-Bill for the relief of John P Montgomery & other soldiers in the late war with Mexico: introduced. 13-Bill for the relief of Henry D Garrison: considered as in the Cmte of the Whole. The whole amount granted by the bill was about $50,000, & that is was derived from the sale of lands which had been obtained from the Indians. Bill was postponed. 14-Mr Yulee request the Senate to take up, though not in its order, a bill for the relief of the captors of the frig **Philadelphia**. It is a case of long standing, & a very meritorious one. The bill was taken up. It proposes to give the sum of $100,000, under the direction of the Sec of the Navy, to the ofcrs & crew of the ketch **Intrepid**, commanded by Stephen Decatur, who were engaged in the capture & destruction of the frig **Philadelphia**, in the harbor of Tripoli, on Feb 16, 1804, to be distributed pro rata among the ofcrs & crew, according to the rates fixed by the 6th section of the act of Apr 23, 1800, for the better gov't of the U S Navy. The sum specified in the bill appears to have been regarded as one half of the estimated value of the frigate. [So annoying to our squadron, the then Lt Stephen Decatur, conceived the bold idea of recapturing the **Philadelphia** with his vessel, the U S schnr **Enterprise**, which he then commanded, & communicated his plan of operation to Cmdor Preble, who approved the plan.] Here are 2 laws, passed in quick succession, in 1813: the first is an act rewarding the ofcrs & crew of the frig **Constitution** & the ofcrs & crew of the **Wasp**, & others. It authorizes the Pres of the U S to have distributed as prize money to Capt Isaac Hull, of the frig **Constitution**, his ofcrs & crew, the sum of $50,000 for the capture & destruction of the British frig **Guerriere**; & the like sum in like manner to Capt Wm Bainbridge, his ofcrs & crew, for the capture & destruction of the British frig **Java**; & the sum of $25,000 in like manner to Capt Jacob Jones, of the sloop of war **Wasp**, his ofcrs & crew, for the capture of the British sloop of war **Frolic**; & the sum of $125,000 was approved for these purposes. The second act was an act to reward the ofcrs & crew of the sloop of war **Hornet**, & Lt Elliott & his ofcrs & companions; & it authorizes the Pres of the U S to have distributed as prize money, to Capt Jas Lawrence, late of the sloop of war **Hornet**, his ofcrs & crew, & their widows & children, the sum of $25,000 for the capture & destruction of the British brig **Peacock**; & to Lt Elliott & his ofcrs & companions, & their widows & children, the sum of $12,000 for the capture & destruction of the British brig **Detroit**; & the sum of $37,000 was thereby appropriated for those purposes.

The New Orleans paper of Dec 11 announces the death of Jo Landie, an eminent & influential merchant of that city.

Appointments by the Pres: 1-O C Pratt, of Ill, to be an Associate Justice of the Supreme Court of the U S for the Territory of Oregon, vice Wm A Hall, declined. 2-John Rayburn, to the U S Marshal for the northern district of Mississippi, vice Andrew A Kincannon, deceased. 3-Matthew F Rainy, Receiver of Public Moneys at Champagnole, Ark, vice Thos L Mulholland, deceased. Attys for the U S: 1-Andrew K Blythe, for the northern district of Mississippi, vice Oscar F Bledsoe, resigned. 2-Franklin H Merriman, for Texas, vice Geo W Brown, deceased. 3-Geo F Shepley, for Maine, vice Augustine Haines, resigned. 4-Lucian Barbour, for Indiana, vice Danl Mace, resigned.

The paper mill of Mr J H Hunter, near Cockeysville, Balt Co, Md, was burnt to the ground on Monday last. Loss $15,000, & insurance said to be but partial.

Mrd: on Dec 21, by Rev J C Smith, Mr Thos Caton to Miss Ariana, daughter of Geo Dale, all of Wash City.

Died: on Dec 19, in Gtwn, Lucy, daughter of the Hon Wm Duer, one of the Reps in Congress from the State of N Y, aged 4 years & 1 month.

Letters in the Dead-letter ofc at the Fair for the Benefit of the Union Benevolent Society, at Odd Fellows' Hall, 7th st.

Adams, Hull, C S
Adams, John, U S N
Ashmun, Hon Mr
Astaburnags, Mr Chilian legation
Bach, R, U S N
Barringer, Hon Davl
Buchanan, Hon Jas
Cass, Lewis, jr-3
Chubb, Munroe-2
Cutts, Richd C S
Cramer, Mr Russian Legation
Crampton, Mr English Legation
Clements & McClery, Messrs-3
Cross, Wm-2
Coyle, Leonidas
Clingman, Hon T L-3
Cabell, Hon E C
Corcoran, W W
Donald, Hon Mr
Dixon, Hon Mr
Dayton, Hon Mr
Emory, Lt Col, U S A
Foltz, Dr, U S N
Farley, Mr, U S A
Goldsborough, John, U S N-3
Goldsborough, H
Green, Benj
Grinnell, Hon J
Green, Hon Mr
Hulsemann, Mr Austrian Legation
Haswell, Chas, Engineer in Chief
Hill, Richd
Hall, Dr
Haskill, Dr, U S A
Jones, C Lee
Jay, Mr Brentwood
King, Hon Butler
Key, Barton
Linton, John
March, Clement C-2
Maddox, Mr, U S M C-2
May, Wm, U S N-2
Markoe, Mr F-1
Nicholson, G, U S M C-2
Patterson, Dr-2
Patterson, H, U S N-2
Porter, Humes-2
Rogers, G, Coast Survey-2
Ritchie, Dr
Roberts, Jno, Coast Survey-2
Schenck, Francis-2
Sitgreaves, Mr, U S A
Selden, Miles-2
Shiray, Capt, U S A
Saunders, John
Saunders, Dr Wm
Stoechel, Russian Legation
Thorn, Capt Geo-3
Tayloe, Benj Ogle
Taylor, Hudson
Wallach, Richd
Walker, Capt W C, U S A
Winder, Chas
Williamson, Mr, U S A
Walker, J Kox
Wolfe, John

SAT DEC 23, 1848
The subscriber offers for sale the extensive plantation in Arkansas, formerly belonging to & occupied by the late Govn'r Kent, of Md, containing 2,383½ acres of land. It is in Philips Co & Crittenden Co, in Walnut Bend, on the Mississippi river. Apply to Wm B Perine, Balt, Md.

The Boston papers announce the death by consumption of Mr D S Dickinson, proprietor of an extensive printing establishment, long celebrated for the neatness & beauty of the work produced at it. He was the publisher of the Boston Almanac.

Senate: 1-Memorial of Ephraim F Gilbert, of Erie Co, N Y, asking that Congress make provision by law for the settlement of his accounts & payment of his claims against the Gov't: referred to the Cmte of Claims. 2-Ptn of Nathan Weston, jr, an additional paymaster in the army, asking the extra pay of 3 months granted by Congress for services in the Mexican war: referred to the Cmte on Military Affairs. 3-Ptn of Chas J Burgess, asking bounty land & 3 months' extra pay for services in the Mexican war: referred to the Cmte on Military Affairs. 4-Ordered, that the papers on file in the case of Thos Fillebrowne be referred to the Cmte on the Judiciary. 5-Ordered, that the papers on file in the case of Archibald Williams & Chas Griffin be referred to the Cmte on Claims. 6-Ordered, that the papers on file in the case of Mrs Sally Ross, widow of Wm Ross, be withdrawn. 7-Cmte of Claims: bill for the relief of John B Smith & Simeon Darden, reported with an amendment. 8-Cmte of the Whole, the consideration of the bill for the relief of Reuben Perry & Thos Ligon was passed. 9-Bill for the relief of John P Baldwin: postponed. 10-Bill for the relief of Cadwallader Wallace now stands on the calendar as a proposition lying on the table. This is a claim for $75,000, founded upon a land claim in the survey of what is called the Virginia military lands, or the Virginia reservation, in the State of Ohio. In 1784, the State of Va, transferred her right to the whole Northwestern Territory to the U S. About 1789, the State of Va proposed to give to her military ofcrs & soldiers a certain amount of bounty land. Troops were the Continental establishment & the Va State line. In 1802 the Executive Gov't authorized a surveyor, Ludlow, well known in this country, to run a direct line distinguishing the boundary of the Congress lands from the military lands. 11-Cmte of the Whole: bill for the relief of Chas Waldron: passed.

House of Reps: 1-Bills to the House, viz: relief of; the grandchildren of Maj Gen Baron DeKalb; Zachariah Lawrence, of Ohio; Legal reps of Bernard Todd, deceased; Wm Fuller; John Campbell; Legal reps of Capt Saml Jones, deceased; Legal reps of Jos Savage, deceased; Chas A Barnitz, husband of Mgt Barnitz, the only surviving heir of Lt Col David Grier, of the army of the Revolution; Legal reps of Wm McFarland, deceased; John J Young, a cmder in the U S Navy; joint resolution for the relief of Saml T Anderson, without amendment. 2-Bills for the relief of Wm Blake, & for the relief of the heirs of Joshua Eddy, deceased, with amendments. 3-Bill for the relief of Wm DeBuys, late postmaster at New Orleans. 4-Bill to refund to Chas A Kellett the tonnage duties & light money paid on the Chinese Junk Keying, & a bill for the relief of Jeremiah Moore; when the same was ordered to be engrossed, & sent to the Senate for concurrence.

Appointments by the Pres: 1-Jos Lane, of Indiana, Govn'r of Oregon, vice Jas Shields, declined. 2-Chas McVean, U S Atty for the southern district of N Y, vice Benj F Butler, removed. 3-Pierre Auguste Bertrand, melter & refiner of the branch mint at New Orleans, vice John L Riddel, removed. Land Ofcrs: 1-John Gardner, register, Winathac, Indiana, reappointed. 2-Lunsford R Noel, receiver, Danville, Ill, reappointed.

Reward of $5 for return of a roan Mare stolen on Tue from my stable.
–John Ray, 4th st, near the new Jail.

Died: on Mon, at Raleigh, N C, Mrs Dobbin, wife of the Hon Jas C Dobbin, one of the Reps of N C in the last Congress.

Died: on Wed, at N Y, Chas McVean, U S District Atty for the southern district of N Y, aged 46 years & 2 months. At the time of his decease he was Surrogate of N Y C & Co. –Com Advertiser

Died: on Dec 23, Martha Ellen, only daughter of Wm Henry & Ann Maria Upperman, aged 8 years & 6 months. Her funeral is this morning at 10 o'clock.

MON DEC 25, 1848

The Cincinnati papers state that Mr Hathaway, a wealthy resident of that city, has been declared by a commission de lunatico inquirendo, incompetent to manage his estate, which is landed, & valued at $750,000. It has passed into the hands of guardians for the benefit of his children. Mr Hathaway purchased this property in 1840 for $1,100!

The celebrated & learned Jesuit Astronomer, Francis De Vico, died in England on Nov 15, where he went on business connected with the Gtwn College. –Gtwn Advocate

Natchez Free Trader. Mrd: on Dec 11, in the court house, by Rev Jo Bell, Mr Wm Peevy to Miss Caroline Hudspeth, all of this county. The minister has just been elected brig general of this brigade, when called upon to officiate at the marriage ceremony.

Ptn of Jas Harley, of Pittsburg, Pa, praying for the extension of a patent granted to him for an improvement in casting chilled rollers, for 7 years from the expiration of said patent, which takes place on Mar 3, 1849. -Edmund Burke, Com'r of Patents

New Billard Saloon: on Pa ave, between 11th & 12th sts. –H N Roby

At Aberdeen, Miss, Col Francis Inge, in his 52nd year. Col Inge was a native of Granville Co, N C. He resided for many years in Alabama, in which he was an active merchant, & always a conspicuous citizen. [No other information. Could be a death notice!]

Wesley Goodwin, a canal capt at Albany, has been sent to the penitentiary for 2 years for abusing his wife & infant child.

House of Reps: 1-Bill for the relief of the legal reps of Antonio Pacheco: bill provides for the payment to the legal reps of Pacheco of $1,000, the value of a slave taken by the Seminole Indians from Fla to the west of the Mississippi river.

Mrd: on Dec 24, in Wash City, at Trinity Church, by Rev Dr Butler, Col Geo C Thomas, of Wash, to Fannie, daughter of H W Gray, deceased, of Balt, Md.

Mrd: on Dec 23, by Rev Mr Lanehan, Danl P Cover to Meline Kanaris Throop, eldest daughter of J V N Throop, all of Wash City.

Died: on Dec 21, at his residence in Newcastle, Dela, in his 90th year, the Hon Kensey Johns, senior, ex-Chancellor of Delaware.

Died: on Dec 12, at his late residence in Anne Arundel Co, Md, Capt Christopher L Gantt, in his 67th year.

Died: on Dec 11, at Jacksonville, Fla, in his 34th year, Richd B Nalley, of Wash City. He was one of the firm of D Clagett & Co. He was known as a tender husband & an affectionate father. In order to reclaim his declining health he started in Nov last for the South, in company with his physician, but, overcome by the fatigue of travel, he was unable either to return home to his family, or to proceed further than Jacksonville. Beside a large circle of relatives & friends, he leaves an aged mother, a disconsolate wife, & 3 small children to lament his early demise. May he rest in peace! -C

Shocking murder. From the Cleveland Herald: Mr David Johnson, of that city, was lately robbed & murdered in Marion Co. The landlord of a tavern where he stopped was arrested & put in jail.

WED DEC 27, 1848
The Court yesterday sentenced Joshua Batemen, found guilty of aggravated assault, to pay a fine of $100.

Senate: 1-Memorial of Wm Plummer, legal rep of Wm A Turner, deceased, asking to be released from a judgment in favor of the U S against the deceased, which he alleges has been satisfied: referred to the Cmte on the Judiciary. 2-Ordered, that the ptn of Jas Harvey, on the files, be referred to the Cmte on Patents & the Patent Ofc. 3-Ordered, that the ptn & papers of the legal reps of John G Mackall, deceased, be taken from the files, & referred to the Cmte on the Judiciary. 4-Memorial of Peter Von Schmidt, proposing a plan for rendering the gold mines in Calif productive: referred to the Cmte on the Territories. 5-Bills from the House of Reps: referred to the Cmte of Claims: relief of-the legal reps of Bernard Todd, deceased; of Zachariah Lawrence, of Ohio; of Jeremiah Moors. 6-Bills referred to the Cmte on Revolutionary Claims: relief of: legal reps of Jos Savage, deceased; of legal reps of Capt Saml Jones, deceased; of Chas A Barnitz, husband of Mgt Barnitz, only surviving heir of Lt Col Grier, of the army of the Revolution; of the grandchidlren of Maj Gen Baron De Kalb; of the heirs of Joshua Eddy, deceased. 7-Bills referred to the Cmte on Naval Affairs: relief of Saml T Anderson; of John J Young, cmder in the U S Navy. 8-Bill for the relief of John Campbell: referred to the Cmte on Pensions. 9-Referred to the Cmte on the Judiciary: act for the relief of Wm Fuller; of John P Skinner & the legal reps of Isaac Green. 10-Bill for the relief of the legal reps of Wm McFarland, deceased: referred to the Cmte on Private Land Claims.

Mrd: on Sabbath evening, by Rev John C Smith, Mr Richd H Adamson to Miss Mary Ann Crown, all of Wash City.

Mrd: on Sunday last, by Rev Mr Samson, Franklin Edmonston, of Wash City, to Miss Eliz T Gatewood, of Richmond, Va.

Died: on Dec 22, Jas Woodward, only son of Aaron W & Julia Miller, aged 1 month & 16 days.

Dandrigde Eppes was hung at Dinwiddie Court-house on Fri last for the murder of F Adolphus Muir.

The steamship **Falcon**, sailed from New Orleans for Chagres on Dec 16, was crowded with passengers. Only a few of the names which we find in the list of persons who went in her: Persifer F Smith, Govn'r of Calif, lady & 2 servants; Geo Adair, Collector for the port of Astoria, wife & 6 children; Judge W P Bryant, Chief Justice of Oregon; R Prichett, Sec of State of Oregon; W Van Voorhees, U S Mail Agent in Calif; Maj Fitzgerald, U S A; Maj Ogden, U S A, & lady; Maj Canby, U S A, & lady; Capt E G Elliott, U S A, & lady; Isaac Bronson, Mail Agent in Oregon; Capt J McDougall, lady & child; Lt Gibbs; Capt R Waterman; Rev Mr Woodbridge; Rev Mr Douglass; Rec O C Wheeler& lady.

A man by the name of Skimmons, of West Troy, was killed at the railway crossing in Broadway Dec 23. He was driving a cutter. His horse took fright at the locomotive, & drew him on the track, when the engine passed over him.

THU DEC 28, 1848

Senate: 1-Memorial of John P Brown, asking compensation for his services as Charge d'Afaires of the U S at the Sublime Port during the absence of the Minister resident: referred to the Cmte on Foreign Relations. 2-Ptn of Sashel Woods, asking to be allowed certain mining privileges in Calif & New Mexico: referred to the Cmte on Public Lands. 3-Ptn of the heirs of Wm Flanigan & Wm Parsons, asking indemnity for losses sustained in the execution of a contract for bldg a frig in 1813: referred to the Cmte on Naval Affaires. 4-Ptn of John P Duval, asking compensation for services as acting Govn'r of the Territory of Fla: referred to the Cmte on Territories. 5-Ordered, that the documents on the files relating the claims of the excs of Henry King, be referred to the Cmte on Revolutionary Claims. 6-Additional documents submitted to enable the settlement of the accounts of the legal reps of Moses Shepherd, deceased. 7-Ordered, that the ptn of Guire & McLaughlin, on the files of the Senate, be referred to the Cmte on the Post Ofc & Post Roads. 8-Mr Jones gave notice of his intention to bring in a bill for the relief of Saml J Bayard, late receiver of public moneys in Iowa. 9-Mr Dodge, of Iowa, to being in a bill for the relief of Elisha Hampton & others, of Iowa: referred to the Cmte on the Public Lands.

Mrd: on Dec 26, by Rev J C Smith, Mr Reuben B Clarke, formerly of N H, to Miss Margaret E Thomas, of Wash City.

Mrd: on Dec 27, by Rev Vanhorsigh, Saml Ker Dashiell, formerly of Somerset Co, Md, to Ellen Maria, daughter of Geo Hamilton, of Howard District, Anne Arundel Co, Md.

Mrd: on Dec 20, at *Spy Hill*, by Rev W A Baynham, Dr Thos S Garnett, of Westmoreland Co, Va, to Miss Emma L, only daughter of Col Thos B B Baber, of King Geo Co, Va.

Mrd: on Dec 25, by Rev Mr Lanahan, Mr Robt Goggin to Miss Sarah E Gardiner, all of Wash City.

Mrd: on Dec 11, in Phil, by Rev Christian Wiltberger, Mr Thos L Hewitt, of Wash City, to Julia, daughter of Maj Wm M Evans, of Phil.

Died: on Dec 24, in Wash City, Miss Kezziah Burgess, after an illness of 5 months, in her 66th year. She was a native of Fred'k Co, Md, but for the last 30 years a resident of this District.

Liberal reward for return of a black Mule that strayed away. –Edwin Green, corner of Pa ave & 11th st

Valuable farm at private sale: 100 acres of land formerly belonging to the estate of A Shepperd, deceased, adjoining the farm of Col Walker: about 4 miles from Wash, fronting on the Rock Creek Church road: good dwlg, with other out-houses. Apply to A Green, auctioneer.

FRI DEC 29, 1848

Senate: 1-Bills passed-relief of: Elisha Thompson; of Jas P Sexton; of Simon Rodrigues. 2-Act for the relief of Marcus F Johnson: &, without disposing thereof. The Senate adjourned.

House of Reps: 1-Cmte of Claims: adverse report on the ptn of Geo W Farmer: laid on the table.

A new Roman Catholic Church in N Y, called St Nicholas, was dedicated on Sunday last. It was erected for the German congregation, & cost $30,000.

In N Y, on Mon, Henry H Seymour, aged 25 years, a young physician of great promise, put an end to his life by jumping out of a second story window.

Mr Wm J Snelling, [late editor of the Boston Herald,] died at his residence in Chelsea, yesterday. His age was 44 years. It is a singular fact that Mr Simon Jordan, 65 years of age, & father-in-law of Mr Snelling, died very suddenly in the same house yesterday. Mr Jordan was in his usual good health until after his son-in-law expired.
–Boston Daily Adv

Col R L Weakley, the head of a numerous & interesting family was killed on Sun in an encounter with a man named Bowman, who is in custody. A pistol was used to commit the deed. -Nashville

Three children of Mr Wm W Snow, of this city, living on Lenant road, while sliding down hill during the recess at school, fell into a channel cut in the ice & were all swept under the ice & drowned. The father was in the market with his team.
–Bangor Whig, 19th.

Senate: 1-Memorial of J W Mason, deceased, & others, settlers & occupants of the Maison Rouge grant, in the State of Louisiana: referred to the Cmte on Private Land Claims. 2-Ptn of Jacob Wilcox, asking the repayment of money advanced to the late republic of Texas: referred to the Cmte of Claims. 4-Ptn of N B Hill, adm of Gilbert Stalker, asking compensation for the use of a steamboat in transporting U S troops during the Seminole war: referred to the Cmte of Claims. 5-Ptn of Wm D, & Julia Achen reps of Wm Yool, deceased, a master's mate in the navy, asking to be allowed a pension: referred to the Cmte on Pensions. 6-Ordered, that the ptn of Alex'r Murdock, on the files of the Senate, to be referred to the Cmte on Finance. 7-Ordered, that the papers of Thos P McBlair, on the files of the Senate, be referred to the Cmte on Naval Affairs. 8-Ordered, that the memorial of John A Rogers be referred to the Cmte of Claims. 9-Ordered, that the ptn of David L White, on the files of the Senate, be referred to the Cmte on Commerce. 10-Cmte on Private Land Claims: favorable report in the case of John Holden: to be printed.

Appointment by the Pres: Wm F Purcell, of Wash, to be Judge of the Orphans Court of Wash Co, D C, in place of Nathl P Causin, resigned.

Mrd: on Dec 28, by Rev J R Eckard, Mr Oliver Whittlesey to Miss Eliz McClelland, both of Wash City.

Mrd: Dec 24, by Rev Mr Van Horsigh, Mr Richd Wood, of Wash, to Miss Mary E Edelin, also of Wash.

Died: on Dec 17, at her residence, **Mount Pleasant**, St Mary's Co, Md, of a short & painful illness, Mrs Catharine Hebb, in her 64th year, relict of the late Jas Hebb, deceased.

Died: on Dec 28, of croup, Geo Washington, 4th son of Wm M & Mary Ann Ellis, aged 3 years & 11 months. His funeral is on Sat at 2 o'clock.

SAT DEC 30, 1848
Col Drayton Jones, a respectable citizen of Wayne, Ohio, lately came to a dreadful death. He fell through the scaffolding in the loft to the floor of his barn where he was thrown across the threshing machine, which was in motion. He lingered 5 days in the most excruciating agony, when he expired.

By deed of trust from Archibald Ludlow to the subscriber, dated Nov 20, recorded among the land records of Wash Co, D C, I shall sell, on Dec 30, horses & lumber wagon, cart, carryall, & 2 large piles of manure & a lot of corn fodder. All sums under $30 cash.
–Wm W Farr, trustee

Mrd: on Dec 28, in Wash City, by Rev Dr Jas Laurie, John Moody, of N Y C, to Miss Eliz A Steele, of Fairfax Co, Va.

Mrd: on Thu last, by Rev N J B Morgan, of Balt, Mr Chas L Coltman to Miss Rebecca McClelland, both of Wash City.

Mrd: on Dec 21, in Reading, Pa, by Rev E J Richards, Jas Lesley, jr, of Phil, to Kate Kennedy, grand-daughter of John McKnight, of the former city.

A

Abadie, 443
Abbot, 196, 415
Abbott, 153, 199, 422
Abeel, 78, 95
Abel, 5, 88
Abercrombie, 36, 428
Abert, 57
Abom, 386
Achen, 453
Acken, 167
Acker, 393
Ackley, 17
Acklin, 101
Acton, 96, 243, 304
Adains, 31
Adair, 296, 451
Adalt, 66
Adam, 42, 78
Adams, 5, 8, 18, 39, 55, 61, 62, 64, 65, 66, 67, 68, 69, 70, 72, 75, 78, 81, 88, 90, 102, 104, 114, 128, 149, 153, 171, 181, 199, 202, 206, 222, 229, 230, 238, 243, 248, 253, 260, 267, 278, 280, 290, 291, 292, 294, 325, 326, 342, 349, 368, 383, 384, 395, 396, 401, 409, 410, 419, 424, 437, 447
Adamson, 450
Addams, 78
Addis, 132
Addison, 29, 39, 80, 153, 191, 205, 231, 341, 378
Addition, 150
Addition to Ray's Adventure, 400
Adie, 334
Adkins, 189
Adler, 110
Agen, 403
Ager, 1, 105, 123
Agg, 366
Aguiel, 78, 141
Ahrenfeldt, 104, 140, 222
Aigler, 153, 393
Aiken, 5, 75, 139, 180

Aileir, 153
Ailer, 243
Ailier, 303
Aisquith, 289, 339, 345
Albert, 153
Albertson, 192
Albro, 182
Alburger, 297, 379
Alburtis, 121
Alby, 351
Alden, 343
Aldrich, 136, 265
Aldridge, 354, 356
Aldunate, 264, 265
Alexander, 22, 36, 96, 109, 212, 232, 237, 243, 248, 254, 272, 313, 315, 368, 390, 403, 409, 430
Alexander the Great, 148
Alhambra, 152
Alig, 360, 375, 380, 383, 404, 407, 430
Allair, 424
Allan, 6
Allemeng, 267
Allemong, 264
Allen, 4, 6, 13, 16, 32, 36, 39, 48, 53, 60, 78, 104, 107, 140, 141, 171, 179, 197, 214, 233, 243, 270, 271, 293, 313, 319, 323, 339, 344, 345, 374, 384, 385
Allison, 92, 194, 285, 418
Allmand, 379
Allyn, 421
Almond, 49
Alvord, 314, 395
Ambrozine, 5, 285
Ames, 112, 182, 255, 331
Amieth, 363, 365
Anacostia Bridge, 402
Analostan Island, 118
Anderson, 6, 10, 11, 16, 32, 36, 42, 44, 48, 66, 88, 94, 111, 112, 121, 125, 127, 141, 144, 153, 169, 223, 232, 238, 243, 248, 269, 283, 285, 293, 298, 314, 318, 319, 338, 341, 353, 377, 389, 400, 409, 421, 424, 425, 434, 448, 450

Andorff, 49
Andrae, 304
Andre, 177
Andrew, 153
Andrews, 35, 63, 70, 147, 163, 240, 319, 322, 340, 342, 343, 407, 412
Andry, 261
Angus, 17, 42, 124
Anthony, 163, 177, 178, 179, 220, 259, 291, 294
Antietam Iron Works, 132
Antron, 301
Apart, 149
Appleton, 29, 107, 109, 125, 143, 237
Applewight, 131
Aram, 79, 83
Arbuckle, 407
Archer, 29, 225, 235, 250, 269, 322, 430
Argote, 136, 221, 253
Aristotle, 149
Armistead, 121, 149, 316, 318
Armitage, 398
Armor, 71
Armstead, 149, 151
Armstrong, 44, 56, 71, 120, 140, 164, 193, 203, 221, 224, 269, 341, 363, 381
Arnett, 23
Arnold, 44, 56, 62, 78, 107, 150, 172, 316, 340, 347, 378, 401, 404, 423
Arny, 330
Arthur, 194
Artificer, 32
Ash, 280
Ashard, 120
Ashards, 89
Ashbridge, 92
Ashburton, 193
Ashby, 128, 427
Ashdown, 196, 200, 422
Ashe, 65
Ashford, 187, 196, 200, 383, 422
Ashley, 142, 143, 166, 172, 213, 439
Ashmun, 447
Ashton, 379, 403, 432
Ashwood, 194, 218, 424
Askew, 191, 217

Aspinwall, 137, 437
Asquith, 172
Astaburnags, 447
Astor, 106, 109, 273, 301
Astor's will, 113
Athery, 35
Atkins, 88, 111, 153
Atkinson, 113, 277, 297, 427, 435
Atlantic & Ohio Telegraph, 235
Atlee, 405
Atocha, 264
Aubert, 264
Auger, 172
Augustia, 37
Ault, 304
Austen, 218
Austin, 8, 217, 260, 304, 400
Austine, 316
Averett, 223
Averill, 263
Avery, 49, 134, 171, 235, 259
Aymar, 330
Ayres, 10, 44

B

Baber, 452
Bach, 447
Bache, 76, 114, 154, 238, 274, 303, 406, 442
Bachelder, 281
Bachelor's Harbor, 426
Backelew, 439
Backerstos, 315
Backster, 224
Backus, 23
Bacon, 6, 32, 44, 112, 196, 200, 218, 245, 252, 254, 304, 387, 393, 422, 435, 438
Baden, 337
Badex, 262
Badger, 99, 122, 123, 280
Baers, 73
Baeschlin, 243
Bagby, 212
Bagley, 221

Bailey, 2, 216, 250, 263, 269, 285, 346, 368
Bailie, 426
Baily, 6, 199, 200
Bain, 119
Bainbridge, 136, 173, 310, 315, 446
Baines, 323
Baird, 372
Baker, 2, 5, 6, 31, 40, 60, 76, 110, 124, 129, 138, 140, 150, 153, 181, 184, 195, 216, 274, 285, 287, 292, 295, 300, 309, 333, 362, 392, 393, 400, 436, 437, 440, 442
Bakewell, 235
Balantine, 29
Balch, 351
Baldwin, 6, 39, 46, 51, 60, 128, 132, 180, 212, 226, 241, 253, 257, 434, 448
Balfour, 415
Ball, 78, 104, 194, 229, 275, 289, 329, 354, 355, 409, 424
Ballan, 222
Ballantine, 76
Ballantyne, 389
Ballard, 32
Ballentine, 445
Balley, 154
Ballmann, 303, 310, 326
Balner, 50
Baltimore, 381
Balum, 7
Bamberger, 144, 394
Bancroft, 214, 224
Baner, 49
Bangs, 213
Bankhead, 121, 177, 221, 313, 407
Banks, 221, 245, 381
Bannatyne, 308
Bantum, 381
Barber, 100, 154, 244, 289, 380, 381
Barbour, 287, 408, 421, 446
Barclay, 36, 59, 139, 177, 196, 199, 221, 222, 278, 282, 283, 287, 289, 294, 304, 326, 434
Barcley, 424
Barcroft, 154

Bardan, 285
Bardwell, 407
Barea, 2
Bargy, 146, 151, 213, 220, 253
Baring, 193
bark **Florida**, 431
Barker, 45, 68, 91, 207, 217, 231, 255, 267, 384, 408
Barkley, 371
Barlow, 384
Barnard, 93, 168, 221, 243, 322, 381
Barnes, 14, 56, 62, 233, 243, 244, 254, 304, 327, 416
Barnett, 6, 235, 259
Barney, 5, 24, 36, 42, 48, 49, 83, 118, 124, 129, 254, 294
Barnheart, 32
Barnhill, 154
Barnitz, 84, 448, 450
Barnum, 340, 345
Baron d'Hautville, 115
barque **Emily**, 371
barque **Hermione**, 376
barque **Libera Packet**, 333
barque **Liberia**, 275
barque **Margaret Hugg**, 28
barque **Mary Theresa**, 283
barque **Royal Saxon**, 327
barque **Whiton**, 412
barque **Wilhamet**, 47
Barr, 243, 352
Barr Farm, 352
Barrand, 76
Barrat, 424
Barraud, 274
Barrett, 2, 24, 78, 207, 219, 228, 243, 245, 328, 383, 397, 399
Barringer, 297, 447
Barrington, 388
Barron, 35, 136, 355, 389
Barrow, 97
Barrowman, 81
Barry, 67, 73, 98, 109, 124, 172, 274, 279, 309, 347, 412
Barthon, 50
Bartis, 263

457

Bartlett, 64, 73, 95, 109, 136, 153, 222, 348
Bartley, 245
Bartolozzi, 223
Barton, 8, 10, 13, 32, 79, 277, 282, 326
basque **Kirkland**, 25
Bass, 264
Basset, 258
Bassett, 76, 274, 386, 412
Bassint, 391
Bastianelli, 366
Baszkoyski, 363, 364
Batemen, 243, 450
Bates, 42, 58, 154, 171, 172, 176, 221, 243, 244, 247, 347, 434
Battaile, 381
Battee, 90, 344
Battist, 240
Battle, 148
Baudenin, 107
Baudonin, 140
Baughman, 167
Baum, 387
Bawyer, 188
Baxter, 221, 233
Bay, 300
Bayard, 5, 36, 42, 57, 89, 99, 272, 451
Bayards, 371
Bayes, 193
Bayles, 32, 107
Bayless, 140, 165
Bayley, 269
Baylies, 368, 414
Bayliss, 153, 243, 347, 381
Bayly, 136, 153, 154, 229, 302
Bayne, 79, 378, 390, 394
Baynham, 452
Beach, 274, 276, 279, 322, 386, 409, 429, 434, 445
Beady, 154
Beal, 73
Beale, 43, 145, 154, 191, 276, 350, 353
Beall, 8, 17, 19, 29, 33, 35, 74, 82, 84, 154, 161, 170, 217, 245, 248, 256, 280, 284, 288, 341, 344, 345, 393, 406, 409, 424, 430

Beaman, 340, 345
Beams, 194
Bean, 23, 69, 73, 228, 243
Beander, 381
Beane, 246
Beans, 42, 381
Bear Camp, 149
Bear Wallow, 150
Bearbout, 6
Beard, 6, 20, 22, 32, 84, 173, 183, 240, 270
Bearden, 4
Beardon, 41, 48, 71
Beardsley, 252
Bears, 226
Beasely, 27
Beasley, 4, 10, 37, 154
Beattie, 152
Beatty, 12, 149, 150, 190, 341, 344
Beatty's Plains, 150
Beaubian, 249
Beaugrand, 16
Beaulieu, 197
Beauregard, 221, 316, 319
Bechtel, 187
Bechtor, 81
Beck, 53, 108, 197, 200, 206, 335, 422
Becker, 392
Beckett, 9, 276, 322
Becksler, 391
Beckwith's Disappointment, 152
Beddinger, 98, 149, 260
Bede, 153
Bedell, 16, 97, 277
Bedford, 221
Bedinger, 434
Bee, 320
Beebe, 50
Beecher, 297
Beeckman, 16
Beedle, 332
Beef & Chickens, 151
Beeler, 129, 432
Beers, 392
Beetley, 434
Beetly, 268

Begbie, 83
Beggar's Neck, 433
Begnam, 56, 154
Behn, 101
Belknap, 25, 172, 311, 407
Bell, 5, 25, 41, 70, 81, 129, 146, 154, 176, 183, 194, 195, 223, 245, 294, 304, 338, 374, 409, 424, 442, 449
Belle Plain, 163
Bellevue Estate, 208
Bellinger, 22, 266
Bellsville, 6
Belt, 29, 38, 41, 125, 211, 218, 360, 391, 402, 427
Belton, 108, 112, 116, 205, 315
Beltzhoover, 422, 424
Bemis, 22
Bend, 125
Bender, 402
Bendick, 304
Benedict, 30, 250, 275, 297, 325
Benge, 365
Benham, 56, 62, 82, 101, 174, 266, 312, 338
Benj Ray Tract, 96
Benjamin, 79, 325, 380, 381, 391
Benne, 254
Bennett, 58, 78, 88, 101, 194, 323
Benns, 17, 36, 76
Benson, 153, 249
Bent, 16, 249
Benter, 154, 161, 392, 423
Bentley, 42
Benton, 28, 39, 61, 66, 258, 283, 297, 338
Berard, 278
Berd, 193
Beresford, 391
Bergen, 309
Berger, 373
Bergh, 280
Bergman, 18, 189, 245
Bergmann, 300
Berkeley, 14, 413
Berkeley Springs, 285
Berkley, 110, 243

Bernard, 16, 21, 31, 168, 171, 232
Berowski, 73
Berret, 375
Berri, 81
Berrien, 56, 357
Berris, 143
Berry, 35, 56, 104, 123, 124, 128, 141, 145, 168, 213, 219, 234, 245, 267, 290, 296, 308, 324, 381, 432
Berryman, 153, 296, 298
Bertach, 50
Bertrand, 448
Besancon, 431
Bessee, 30, 119
Bessie, 76
Best, 103, 280, 343
Bestor, 140, 336
Betbel, 164
Bethany, 219
Bettincourt, 87
Betts, 224
Beute, 247
Bevan, 428, 436
Beverley, 14
Bewley, 186
Beyer, 409
Beyes, 328
Bibb, 267, 386, 397, 426
Bickler, 154
Bickley, 304
Bicknell, 56
Bicksler, 153
Biddle, 77, 322, 367, 371
Bierns, 63
Big Elk Lick, 96
Bigelow, 128, 284, 430
Biggs, 441, 444
Bill, 180
Billing, 304
Billings, 277
Bingey, 133, 257
Bingham, 20, 84, 193
Binney, 144, 415
Biossat, 398
Birch, 141, 153, 154, 167, 211, 246, 381
Bird, 32, 148, 187, 197, 201, 244, 406

Birkhead, 438
Birnie, 326
Birth, 195, 196, 375
Birthwhistle, 415
Biscoe, 79, 129
Bishop, 56, 61, 81, 183, 327
Bissell, 272, 277, 300, 347
Bitner, 240
Bittinger, 365
Blache, 267
Black, 18, 58, 59, 76, 88, 93, 108, 112, 124, 138, 140, 154, 167, 206, 241, 294
Black Oak Thicket, 234
Black Range, 150
Blackburn, 322
Blackford, 84, 118, 120
Blackiston, 2
Blackson, 2
Blackwell, 26, 105, 247, 268, 271, 392
Bladen, 134
Blagden, 110, 111, 154, 323, 368, 405, 427
Blagrove, 116, 390
Blair, 121, 249
Blake, 46, 49, 54, 154, 175, 196, 199, 200, 201, 231, 424, 448
Blake, 102
Blakelee, 214
Blakely, 121, 164, 212
Blanchard, 27, 67, 353
Blanche, 409
Blanding, 8, 123
Blane, 141
Blaney, 65
Blangy, 163
Blanton, 289
Bleakley, 54, 220, 443
Blecker, 63
Bledsoe, 446
Blevins, 439
Bliss, 100, 173, 174, 208, 310, 311, 442
Blodget, 259
Blodgett, 29
Bloom, 16, 83
Bloomer, 351
Bloomfield, 164

Bloomsbury, 28, 58
Bloss, 16, 35, 42, 71, 193, 293, 295
Blow, 285
Blox, 357
Bloxton, 383
Blue, 140
Blue Plains, 296
Blum, 90
Blumer, 51
Blummer, 249
Blunt, 213, 338
Blythe, 171, 373, 446
Boardman, 182
Boarman, 16, 34, 44, 153, 194, 264, 274, 287, 368
boat **Verona**, 214
Bock, 30, 216
Bodfish, 321
Bodisco, 19, 197
Bogan, 57, 161, 235
Bogardus, 370, 443
Bogart, 139, 167
Bogert, 111
Boggs, 259, 430, 432
Bogle, 243
Bogue, 78, 194
Bohlayer, 56, 74, 154, 244, 393
Bohrer, 13, 154, 218, 223
Boker, 14, 49, 83, 193, 265, 293
Boland, 164, 272
Bold, 342
Bolen, 15
Boles, 43
Bolon, 45, 48, 183, 293
Bomford, 106, 141, 170, 204, 211, 315, 318, 338, 345, 348, 363, 364
Bonaparte, 249, 402
Bond, 112, 304, 427
Bondurant, 26, 137
Bonham, 116
Bonner, 6, 232
Bonneville, 315
Bonneycastle, 342
Bonton, 38, 253
Bonum, 6
Book, 127

Booley, 140
Boone, 122, 230, 243, 246, 287, 393
Boot Yard, 150
Bootes, 168, 250
Booth, 217, 248, 288, 299, 392
Boothe, 2, 128
Borland, 128, 153, 196, 199
Borrows, 196, 199, 372
Borsnaham, 371
Borst, 414
Borum, 6
Boscage, 308
Bosely, 151
Bosher, 254
Boss, 250, 421
Bosse, 154
Bossot, 164
Bostick, 433
Boston, 254, 259
Boswell, 78, 141
Bosworth, 341, 437
Boteler, 137, 153, 154, 229, 231, 286, 368, 369, 376, 379, 413
Botts, 291
Bouchard, 4, 41
Bouck, 60
Boudinot, 2
Bouion, 81
Boulanger, 153, 233, 406
Bouldings, 208
Bouseau, 392
Bousefard, 95
Bowditch, 325
Bowen, 30, 90, 119, 144, 229, 231, 244, 304, 312, 350, 368, 428
Bower, 116
Bowerman, 23, 49
Bowers, 321
Bowie, 10, 26, 54, 126, 134, 219, 304, 321, 352, 390, 408
Bowlin, 60, 300, 378
Bowling, 154, 287, 390, 395
Bowman, 2, 57, 313, 452
Bowyer, 23, 209
Boyd, 5, 6, 24, 50, 66, 78, 90, 107, 119, 154, 230, 239, 240, 246, 430

Boyden, 141
Boyer, 381
Boyle, 46, 103, 141, 154, 187, 199, 200, 201, 218, 231, 245, 276, 358, 391, 427
Boynton, 317
Brackenridge, 269, 362
Brackett, 184
Bradbury, 96, 218
Braddock, 61, 188, 236
Bradey, 244
Bradford, 8, 58, 70, 76, 145, 221, 250, 274, 276, 281, 342
Bradish, 211
Bradley, 30, 51, 55, 68, 134, 153, 154, 164, 172, 211, 226, 228, 284, 304, 332, 366, 377, 393, 416, 435, 437, 438
Bradley farm, 332
Bradly, 62
Bradshaw, 14, 51, 116
Brady, 49, 99, 103, 122, 154, 186, 252, 266, 269, 293, 304, 406, 407
Bragdon, 104, 140, 216
Bragg, 174, 282, 311
Braiden, 79
Brainerd, 298
Braintree, 65
Branch, 405
Brandon, 6
Brandy, 73
Brandywine Chalybeate Springs, 135
Brannan, 317, 439
Brant, 149, 263
Brant's mill, 149
Brashear, 154, 298
Brashears, 153, 204
Brauguard, 32
Brawner, 332, 409
Break, 42
Breckenridge, 304
Bredon, 296
Breedlove, 301
Breese, 64
Breeze, 58
Bremond, 346
Brenan, 32
Brener, 153

Brennan, 309
Brenner, 2, 154, 161
Brent, 4, 46, 70, 84, 110, 122, 147, 154, 170, 171, 174, 185, 230, 243, 245, 256, 264, 267, 268, 286, 312, 351, 416, 440, 445
Brereton, 17, 42, 77, 94, 153, 154, 173, 246, 286, 310, 334, 368
Bres, 264
Bressie, 204
Breuil, 96
Brevoort, 177
Brewer, 20, 29, 114, 269, 308
Brewerton, 387
Brewster, 168
Briasmade, 194
Brice, 149
Briceland, 8
Bridel, 139
Bridgeman, 309
Bridgeport, 152
Bridget, 243
Bridgman, 2, 411
Briel, 154
brig **Adams**, 50
brig **Architect**, 302
brig **Bontemps** to **Palmetto**, 74
brig **Boxer**, 372
brig **Caledonia**, 50
brig **Caroline**, 64
brig **Charles Grey**, 133
brig **Detroit**, 446
brig **Diana**, 207
brig **Dolphin**, 14
brig **Douglas**, 40
brig **Enterprise**, 372
brig **Evelina Sandel**, 133
brig **Harriette**, 391
brig **John Enders**, 27
brig of war **Somers**, 209, 291
brig **Orion**, 433
brig **Peacock**, 446
brig **Philadelphia**, 38
brig **Porpoise**, 25, 230
brig **Restaurador**, 209
brig **Smithfield**, 212

brig **Somers**, 51, 189, 294, 348
brig **St Petersburg**, 179
brig **Truxton**, 347
brig **Vesuvius**, 273
Brigg, 182
Briggs, 431
Brigham, 118, 120
Bright, 2, 46, 128, 141, 287, 367
Brinker, 41, 175
Brisco, 79
Briscoe, 89, 137, 189, 244, 251, 266, 267, 293
Bristed, 301
Bristow, 35
British 74-the **Poietiers**, 371
Broadbent, 95
Broadhead, 274
Broadwaters, 150
Brock, 266, 278
Brockwa, 127
Brockway, 209
Brodback, 153
Brodbeck, 153
Brodhead, 12, 76, 196, 200, 276, 321
Brodie, 2
Brogan, 150
Brognerd, 14
Bromley, 296
Bronaugh, 12, 96, 116, 154, 213, 283, 322, 397
Bronson, 451
Brook, 67
Brookbank, 330
Brooke, 60, 65, 78, 86, 128, 132, 154, 194, 205, 237, 270, 283, 325, 326, 334, 378, 407
Brookes, 102
Brooks, 2, 21, 32, 33, 47, 72, 81, 173, 219, 231, 243, 251, 267, 278, 282, 293, 310, 315, 316, 331, 378, 426
Broom, 90
Broome, 24
Brosnaham, 368
Brotherly Love, 152
Brough, 290, 300
Brower, 342

Browers, 392
Brown, 2, 12, 17, 19, 20, 27, 29, 30, 34, 36, 37, 41, 46, 49, 55, 59, 63, 67, 71, 73, 78, 81, 85, 86, 90, 104, 128, 136, 139, 140, 153, 154, 161, 172, 173, 176, 177, 183, 194, 208, 213, 218, 219, 220, 228, 230, 231, 243, 244, 245, 247, 248, 250, 259, 265, 278, 280, 290, 294, 296, 298, 300, 313, 315, 339, 346, 348, 353, 358, 366, 367, 368, 375, 378, 380, 381, 391, 392, 393, 394, 395, 401, 402, 427, 431, 446, 451
Brown's Garden, 43
Browne, 45, 48, 335
Brownell, 21, 125, 146, 176, 183, 293
Browning, 154, 393
Brownlee, 285
Bruce, 58, 96, 104, 150, 243, 250, 339, 344, 409, 416, 421, 437
Bruff, 377, 388
Brugere, 139
Brulon, 20
Brunet, 1, 38, 245
Brunett, 195
Brunot, 176
Brus, 278, 282
Brush, 25, 139, 165
Bruss, 50
Bruyere, 275
Bryan, 17, 32, 48, 70, 77, 99, 102, 104, 124, 125, 133, 139, 154, 174, 196, 199, 209, 217, 288, 312, 378, 400
Bryand, 49
Bryant, 10, 67, 79, 83, 89, 123, 171, 174, 194, 199, 261, 296, 381, 426, 451
Bryarly, 274
Bryden, 42
Bryles, 2
Buamyer, 152
Buchanan, 31, 58, 65, 136, 151, 213, 226, 289, 318, 328, 434, 447
Buck Shooting, 149
Buck's Bones, 152
Buckingham, 8, 171, 174, 207, 228, 393
Buckland, 33

Buckles, 113
Buckley, 38, 46, 70, 131, 153, 154
Bucklore, 347
Buckner, 108, 168, 307, 317, 332, 389
Bucks, 63
Budington, 303
Buel, 32, 90
Buell, 15, 108, 173, 310, 316, 326, 341
Buffalo Tract, 96
Buffington, 280, 283
Buford, 217, 288, 312
Bugbee, 22
Bujac, 289
Bukey, 136
Bulen, 253
Bulfinch, 285, 304
Bull, 35, 99, 112, 140, 202, 304
Bull Run Quarter, 332
Bullen, 210
Bulmocke, 81
Bulwer, 83
Bump, 72, 88
Bumpton, 149
Bunfoot, 253
Burbank, 44
Burbeck, 376
Burbridge, 338, 344
Burch, 2, 6, 56, 63, 144, 146, 153, 167, 302, 362, 388, 392, 397, 409, 426
Burche, 28, 39, 70, 85, 152, 166, 337, 429
Burchell, 418
Burd, 391
Burdine, 392
Burgan, 2
Burgears, 381
Burgess, 154, 198, 394, 409, 431, 448, 452
Burgoyne, 110
Burham, 216
Burhans, 63
burial ground, 178
Buriss, 119
Burk, 63

Burke, 25, 44, 95, 149, 153, 183, 238, 245, 291, 299, 303, 315, 318, 368, 373, 420, 449
Burkett, 303
Burnell, 380
Burnes, 163
Burnett, 244, 279, 296, 350
Burnham, 89, 176
Burns, 5, 84, 153, 336, 368, 442
Burnt Mill seat, 150
Burr, 11, 33, 43, 67, 102, 146, 154, 156, 184, 201, 228, 258, 270, 284, 295, 419
Burrell, 368
Burries, 287, 289
Burris, 99
Burriss, 48
Burrows, 23, 73, 109, 141
Burton, 194, 409
Burwell, 14, 44, 276
Busey, 98, 442
Bush, 4, 38, 56, 59, 154, 180, 241, 278
Bushman, 153
Bushnell, 212, 401
Bushwood, 273
Bussey, 280, 342, 343, 345
Bustaments, 272
Buthman, 393, 403
Butler, 8, 11, 27, 28, 34, 58, 71, 79, 116, 133, 141, 154, 164, 177, 191, 193, 202, 203, 212, 230, 243, 244, 275, 276, 279, 282, 297, 309, 326, 327, 334, 342, 368, 373, 381, 392, 393, 401, 407, 409, 420, 425, 433, 435, 438, 448, 449
Butt, 179, 202, 247
Butterfield, 303, 431
Butterworth, 287, 289, 423
Buttolpk, 177
Butts, 167
Byar, 194
Bychowice, 364
Byington, 196, 200, 229
Byng, 283
Byrd, 264, 285, 436
Byrne, 154, 204, 206, 244, 267, 270
Byrnes, 33

C

Cabin Branch, 332
Caddo boy, 442
Caden, 130, 155, 304
Cadwalader, 97, 115, 236, 322, 344, 407
Cady, 34, 276, 279, 281, 318
Caffey, 35, 99
Cage, 235
Cahoone, 34, 178, 209, 291, 293
Cailleux, 95
Cain, 31, 33, 47, 266
Cairmell, 151
Calahan, 169
Calcott, 434
Calden, 296
Calderon, 349
Caldin, 63
Caldwell, 15, 18, 51, 56, 84, 107, 120, 121, 125, 146, 155, 166, 202, 210, 212, 322, 389, 416
Calhoun, 66, 268, 419
Callaghan, 96, 240, 263
Callahan, 299, 304
Callan, 51, 53, 122, 154, 162, 196, 199, 251, 284, 289, 422
Callender, 316
Callon, 368
Calvert, 67, 154, 184, 390, 405
Calverton's Manor, 234
Cameron, 201
Camlin, 215
Cammack, 96, 154, 180, 260
Camon, 32
Camp, 277, 281
Campbell, 14, 24, 28, 40, 70, 71, 127, 136, 137, 139, 141, 155, 175, 184, 188, 194, 231, 243, 246, 256, 273, 308, 312, 341, 349, 384, 391, 392, 408, 410, 448, 450
Camper, 114, 406
Canal, 191
Canal & Railroad, 151
Canan, 381
Canby, 115, 316, 451
Caneau, 55
Canfield, 30, 71, 193, 252

Cannon, 58, 154
Canonge, 37
Cantwell, 8, 281
Capa, 41
Capella, 41, 48, 71
Capello, 4
Capen, 19, 27, 59, 294
Caperton, 213
Capo, 4, 48, 71
Cappel, 71, 93, 293
Capron, 44, 81, 111, 390, 405
Carbanaux, 243
Carbery, 128, 172, 196, 427
Carey, 73, 240
Cargill, 278
Carl, 32
Carland, 417
Carleton, 254, 312
Carlin, 32, 154, 378
Carlisle, 204, 227
Carlton, 70, 81
Carmack, 304
Carman, 14, 59, 187, 284, 437
Carmichael, 32, 58
Carnes, 169, 428
Carney, 164
Caro, 164, 207
Carothers, 34, 94, 161
Carpenter, 20, 58, 77, 85, 110, 133, 172, 212, 213, 218, 253, 351, 395
Carper, 49
Carr, 22, 125, 146, 149, 171, 279, 396
Carrall, 381
Carrallo, 266
Carrel, 411
Carrico, 331, 364, 390
Carriel, 264
Carrington, 71, 85, 118, 145, 188, 326
Carroll, 27, 151, 154, 161, 194, 196, 200, 230, 238, 261, 266, 302, 305
Carroll Place, 362, 380
Carrollville, 152
Carron, 309
Carson, 91, 102, 229, 232, 243, 255, 266, 284, 304, 345

Carter, 2, 13, 17, 63, 77, 79, 80, 154, 176, 223, 283, 290, 304, 309, 326, 331, 335, 400, 430
Cartwright, 202, 257, 296
Carty, 70
Carusi, 18, 248
Casanave, 243, 245, 246, 394
Casement, 95
Casey, 9, 243, 315, 319
Cash, 77, 155, 161
Casparis, 155, 161, 368, 392
Cass, 9, 58, 213, 239, 283, 363, 425, 447
Cassady, 140, 273
Cassedy, 220
Cassell, 196, 200
Cassin, 29, 54, 59, 202
Castleman, 270
Castles, 255
Caswell, 411
Cat Point, 151
Catalano, 155, 394
Catchcart, 199
Cathcart, 154, 187, 196
Catholic Church, 336
Catholic school, 330
Catipidam, 62
Caton, 21, 38, 355, 446
Catrup, 346
Cattle Grove, 234
Caubarreux, 232
Caulfield, 264, 267
Causin, 295, 335, 390, 453
Causten, 306, 393
Cavallier, 144
Cazean, 71
Cazeau, 40, 59, 437
Cazenova, 14
Cecil, 79
Cenobio, 131
Center, 18, 222
Cevans, 146
Chaddock, 395
Chaffee, 138, 285
Chaflin, 95
Chalk, 355
Chamber, 167

Chamberlain, 40, 128, 280
Chambers, 24, 168, 189, 400, 428
Champlin, 19, 76, 84, 124
Chance, 176
Chandler, 221, 316
Chaney, 173, 443
Channing, 325
Chapin, 251, 438
Chapman, 13, 22, 29, 30, 76, 77, 98, 110, 152, 174, 207, 219, 274, 295, 312, 313, 315, 339, 340, 344, 349, 419
Chappel, 33
Chappell, 269, 337
Chappin, 267
Charles, 286, 395
Charm, 177
Charnon, 139
Chase, 2, 22, 77, 95, 103, 120, 248, 272, 275, 276, 310, 321, 381
Chatard, 374
Chateaubriand, 269
Chatfield, 115, 285
Chatman, 50
Chatteras, 164
Chaules, 141
Chauncey, 40, 53, 58, 69, 245, 331, 437
Chauvenet, 297
Cheethan, 62
Cheever, 70, 125, 146, 165, 410
Chefaly, 426
Cheney, 278, 281
Cherry, 285
Cherry Hill, 152
Cheseltine, 155
Cheshire, 357, 365
Chester, 101, 140
Chestnut, 383
Chestnut flat, 150
Chevallie, 121
Chever, 412
Chevers, 377
Chew, 79, 205, 243, 398, 438
Chezum, 57
Chezun, 129
Chichester, 119, 163
Chief Black Dog, 153

Childers, 50
Childs, 138, 146, 172, 212, 254, 272, 320, 327, 409
Chiled, 407
Chiles, 216
Chilolmwood, 117
Chilton, 121, 278, 312, 385
Chiney, 62
Chinn, 127, 232
Chipman, 7, 54, 212, 220, 259
Chism, 129
Chittenden, 95
Choate, 136, 211, 298
Choice, 152
Choppin, 264
Choules, 359
Chouteau, 14, 120
Chrisman, 73
Christian, 7, 13, 170, 254, 379
Christian year, 75
Christians, 188
Christie, 88
Christopher, 415
Chubb, 155, 394, 447
Church, 204
Churchill, 17, 27, 173, 205, 311, 341, 342, 407
Chuston, 49
Cinque Foil, 152
Cissel, 243, 266
City, 326
City of the Dead, 325
Claborn, 112
Claflin, 216
Clagett, 190, 329, 409, 450
Claiborne, 109, 320, 396
Clamorgan, 122, 127
Clampett, 170
Clancy, 6
Clapp, 135
Clapper, 36, 42
Clapper's Hollow, 151
Clare, 79, 266, 323
Clarence, 215
Clark, 5, 8, 41, 62, 71, 79, 83, 107, 109, 112, 135, 167, 171, 176, 212, 215,

216, 217, 220, 221, 255, 263, 277,
283, 286, 288, 294, 309, 319, 321,
348, 358, 383, 388, 392, 407, 423,
429, 438
Clarke, 11, 30, 42, 44, 54, 64, 74, 77,
102, 113, 116, 141, 146, 154, 155,
161, 184, 194, 204, 211, 218, 221,
229, 231, 242, 251, 253, 267, 289,
291, 293, 304, 315, 320, 381, 400,
417, 424, 427, 451
Clarks, 32
Clarkson, 29, 92
Clarvoe, 392, 393
Clavadetscher, 208
Clavelaux, 304
Clay, 41, 88, 120, 127, 214, 221, 350, 396, 419
Claypole, 238
Clayton, 149
Clean Drinking, 432
Clean Drinking tract, 308
Cleandrinking, 129
Cleland, 224
Clement, 32, 174, 188, 405
Clementon, 139
Clements, 2, 8, 9, 37, 73, 79, 105, 149, 154, 174, 231, 266, 287, 305, 324, 447
Clency, 413
Clendenin, 280
Clephane, 195, 196, 199
Clermon, 175
Clery, 393
Cleveland, 83
Clevenger, 424
Click, 216
Clifford, 79, 93, 141, 213, 223, 272
Clingman, 447
Clinton, 13, 92, 291, 419, 424
Clira, 303
Clitch, 441
Clitz, 44, 56, 62, 155, 278, 314
Cliver, 141
Cloakey, 248
Clokey, 227, 245, 358
Clopper, 8, 426
Closkey, 103

Cloud, 280, 372, 373
Clouth, 253
Club, 112
Cluskey, 228, 253, 436
Clymer, 326
Coal & iron banks, 150
Coal in Store, 150
Coale, 405
Coates, 246
Cobb, 2, 22, 49, 78, 247
Cobbs, 207, 263, 340, 345
Coberly, 5
Cobey, 246
Coburn, 22, 243, 275
Cochran, 13, 41, 56, 137, 140, 153, 225, 310, 373
Cochrane, 198
Cocke, 13, 112, 289
Cockerille, 21
Cockeron, 256
Coddington, 335, 411
Coe, 140
Coffin, 79, 297
Coffman, 245
Cogan, 361
Coggill, 95
Coglan, 32
Cogswell, 22, 141, 175, 216, 437
Cohen, 31, 57, 122, 154, 252, 347
Cohoone, 177
Coincidence, 150
Coke, 13, 409, 424
Colbert, 192
Colbey, 215
Colburn, 214, 244, 385, 433
Colby, 183
Colden, 67
Colder, 92, 424
Coldwell, 118
Cole, 6, 15, 65, 74, 88, 98, 110, 128, 144, 146, 154, 155, 161, 216, 381
Coleman, 26, 41, 63, 100, 111, 112, 131, 225, 253, 258, 379, 403, 428, 434
Colemen, 416
Colfar, 412
Collamore, 374

Collard, 154, 171, 200
Collet, 59
Collett, 275, 282
Collier, 154, 155, 396, 429
Collingsworth, 10
Collins, 20, 31, 38, 43, 154, 165, 190, 196, 210, 227, 231, 245, 246, 283, 299, 317, 328, 342, 346, 348, 379, 427, 441
Collis, 144
Colman, 238, 331
Colmary, 185
Colmus, 107, 140, 283
Colonization Society, 28
Colquitt, 280, 282
Colston, 194
Colt, 155, 433
Coltman, 91, 239, 248, 301, 308, 389, 454
Colton, 295
Columb, 144
Columbus, 1
Colville, 95
Colyear, 248
Comas, 155
Combs, 24, 89, 231, 302, 393, 412, 415
Commercial Mart, 151
Comora, 104
Conant, 18, 71, 193, 209
Conaway, 224
Condon, 309
Condry, 45, 267
Cone, 48
Conelly, 15
Coney, 99
Conger, 83, 118
Congress Burial Ground, 189
Congressional Burial ground, 69
Congressional Burial Ground, 93
Congressional Burying ground, 24
Congressional Burying Ground, 81, 201
Congressional Cemetery, 28
Conklin, 73
Conkling, 19
Conlan, 182, 243
Conley, 17, 42, 124

Conly, 443
Connell, 271
Conner, 148, 244, 301, 368
Connick Farm, 54
Connolly, 42, 43, 103, 182, 379
Connor, 49, 103, 240, 392
Connors, 32
Conolly, 401
Conrad, 115, 197, 367
Consilvi, 95
Constitution Vale, 152
Convent of the Visitation, 78
Convers, 301
Converse, 16, 24, 71, 118, 122, 193, 253
Conway, 6, 35, 37, 123, 124, 259, 276, 278
Cony, 49, 122, 293
Cook, 57, 79, 95, 124, 129, 141, 148, 154, 155, 177, 178, 227, 233, 244, 259, 291, 294, 307, 392, 404
Cooke, 2, 25, 33, 70, 247, 275
Cookendorfer, 154, 393
Cooks, 281
Cooley, 60
Coolidge, 103, 104, 183, 424
Coombs, 51, 179
Coon, 22
Coonan, 366
Coons, 423
Cooper, 2, 70, 74, 96, 187, 246, 268, 284, 389, 392, 416, 431
Cope, 150
Copehart, 403
Copeland, 253
Copp, 154, 161
Copp's Pavilion, 399
Coppee, 317
Copperwalt, 150
Copway, 179
Corbett, 420
Corbin, 22, 259
Corcoran, 65, 130, 232, 266, 299, 305, 306, 331, 385, 395, 399, 414, 426, 447
Corday, 357
Corder, 50
Corey, 109

Corley, 4
Corlis, 431
Cornell, 1, 182, 183
Cornice, 31
Cornish, 155, 388
Cornwall, 151
Cornwallis, 202
Coromandel, 150
Corrigan, 261
Corrille, 431
Corsdale, 294
Corse, 391
Corser, 5, 18, 71, 193, 294
Corson, 62, 175, 183, 392
Corum, 381
Corvell, 374
Corwin, 5
Cory, 216
Coskery, 177, 436
Cosley, 44
Costar, 50, 370
Costard, 43
Costello, 155
Coster, 336, 348
Costigan, 154, 304, 309, 336
Costin, 155
Costney, 141
Coston, 141, 431
Cotter, 165
Couch, 174, 312
Coudas, 8
Coulter, 52
Coulyard, 404
Coumbe, 155
Count Rossi, 441
Courtney, 127, 287
Coventry, 79
Cover, 449
Coville, 5
Covillion, 443
Cow Pasture, 151
Cowell, 87
Cowperchwart, 304
Cox, 17, 19, 27, 36, 41, 42, 51, 59, 77, 84, 105, 109, 114, 142, 210, 212, 213, 229, 274, 294, 307, 348, 349, 386

Coxe, 7, 20, 41, 48, 69, 71, 95, 134, 304, 305, 405
Coxe's Row, 359
Coxeaden, 141
Coxen, 79
Coyle, 46, 111, 154, 197, 199, 200, 201, 228, 298, 329, 393, 447
Crabbe, 76, 359
Crabre, 223
Crabtree, 263
Cragin, 418
Craig, 121, 213, 220, 297, 310, 315, 338, 345, 397
Crain, 108, 234
Craitzer, 163
Craken, 141
Cram, 277
Cramer, 447
Crampsey, 246
Crampton, 447
Cranch, 122, 177, 185, 207, 226, 233
Crandall, 304, 434
Crandell, 46, 122, 187, 200, 330, 422
Crane, 205, 212, 341
Cranston, 112
Craven, 304
Crawford, 22, 66, 80, 110, 154, 175, 272, 283, 348, 377, 428, 434
Creanor, 321
Creighton, 401
Cressen, 347
Cressey, 136
Creutschel, 368
Crew, 373
Crier, 79, 409
Crigan, 144
Cripps, 154, 216
Crittenden, 109, 315, 338, 345, 348
Crocker, 285
Crockett, 211, 436
Crockwell, 213
Crofoot, 32
Croggin, 271
Croggon, 1, 245
Cromwell, 265, 368, 399, 444
Cronin, 368, 383

Crook, 77, 147, 183, 381
Crooked Billet, 150
Crookes, 62
Crooks, 108
Cropley, 213
Crosby, 7, 125, 176, 258, 273, 277, 322
Cross, 127, 154, 155, 184, 194, 200, 228, 231, 248, 271, 304, 341, 346, 401, 424, 447
Crossman, 41, 216, 310
Crotia, 152
Crowell, 208
Crowley, 243, 370
Crown, 88, 450
Crowther, 155
Crozet, 340, 342
Crozier, 380
Cruikshank, 142, 415
Cruit, 56, 59, 368, 430
Cruitt, 154
Crump, 77, 246, 375
Crumps, 221
Crusor, 391
Crutchett, 42, 98, 155, 182, 184, 240, 271, 368
Crutchfield, 172, 344
Crutzfeldt, 154, 155
Cryder, 45
Cryer, 245
Cubitt, 415
Cudlip, 393
Cull, 196, 200
Cullen, 278
Cullom, 278, 282
Culonne, 144
Culver, 36, 42, 94, 269, 293
Culverwell, 206
Cumberland, 185
Cummings, 97, 121, 277, 290, 321
Cummins, 258, 275
Cummisky, 62
Cunning, 279
Cunningham, 6, 20, 44, 118, 122, 140, 152, 229, 245, 260, 263, 280, 293, 381
Curran, 110, 179
Currbey, 381

Currier, 48, 177, 178, 216, 291, 293
Curry, 248
Curtain, 247
Curtenius, 25
Curtin, 92
Curtis, 303
Curtiss, 221
Curts, 172
Cushing, 63, 172, 258, 407
Cushman, 50, 147, 153, 284
Custis, 93, 103, 194, 272, 287, 363, 396, 412
Cut & Come Again, 149
Cuthbert, 37
Cutter, 172, 347
cutter **Hamilton**, 234
Cutting, 110, 439
Cutts, 266, 447

D

d'Aligre, 220
D'Israeli, 52
D'Olier, 62
Dacy, 222
Dade, 136
Daily, 224
Daingerfield, 168, 438
Dale, 32, 337, 446
Daley, 104
Dall, 65
Dallam, 249
Dallas, 135, 169, 223, 233, 419
Dalley, 395
Dalton, 4, 13, 27, 37, 155, 335, 363
Daly, 98, 105, 138
Dameron, 259
Dammett, 221
Damrell, 88
Damrow, 216
Dan's Mountain, 150
Dana, 259, 314, 341, 346, 437
Dance, 58, 289
Dane, 331
Danford, 424
Danforth, 329, 372
Daniel, 45, 57, 66, 125, 418

Daniells, 284
Daniels, 30, 32, 44, 277, 323, 339, 340, 412
Darby, 26, 35, 287, 289
Darcantel, 266
Darden, 87, 137, 152, 448
Darling, 178
Darlington, 7, 186
Dashields, 385
Dashiell, 97, 451
Datcher, 245
Davenport, 48, 54, 99, 124, 206, 216, 227, 250, 434
Davey, 55
David, 2
Davidge, 5
Davidson, 29, 92, 152, 171, 316, 337, 338, 347, 377, 390, 414
Davis, 1, 6, 10, 32, 46, 52, 55, 56, 59, 64, 76, 77, 82, 86, 92, 107, 112, 123, 129, 134, 135, 136, 141, 147, 148, 152, 155, 175, 177, 189, 222, 228, 231, 243, 247, 248, 258, 266, 274, 276, 278, 281, 287, 297, 305, 308, 318, 321, 341, 342, 368, 370, 378, 381, 382, 385, 392, 395, 409, 410, 413, 424, 438, 444
Davy, 247, 383
Dawson, 18, 222, 232, 235, 264, 297, 313
Day, 141, 186, 212, 216, 220, 243, 246, 248, 255, 380, 414, 424
Dayton, 447
De Bres, 223
De Buys, 71
de Chateaubriand, 269
De Courcy, 163
de Fongeres, 221, 253
de Fougeres, 294
De Graff, 270
De Hart, 138, 339, 345
de Kalb, 47, 147, 230, 263
De Kalb, 450
De Kay, 206
De La Figaneira, 435
De La Rache, 30

de la Roche, 76
de La Roche, 124
De la Roche, 11
De Leon, 108, 109
De Liessielin, 48
De Lirac, 147
De Menon, 394
De Menou, 422
de Montjoie, 440
de Neuville, 269
De Russey, 414
De Saules, 155
De Selding, 205
De Smet, 192
De Vaughan, 235, 391
De Vice, 425
De Vico, 449
De Wolfe, 275
Deacon, 303
Deakin, 96
Deakins, 96
Deale, 228
Dean, 35, 72, 280, 389
Deaney, 279, 342, 343
Dearborn, 80, 91, 180
Dearey, 6
Dearing, 131
Dearment, 83
Deas, 115, 181, 184, 220, 316, 340, 343, 344, 345
Deaver, 107
Debaugh, 33
DeBuys, 22, 193, 448
Decamp, 305
Decatur, 22, 38, 39, 89, 136, 283, 384, 446
Decret, 435, 445
Dedman, 50
Deeble, 19, 195, 196, 199, 200, 201
Deer Park, 148
Deer Park Resurveyed, 151
Degges, 73
Degroot, 88
Dehart, 32
DeKalb, 448
DeKay, 103

Delacalia, 152
Delacey, 32
Delacroix, 264, 267
Delafield, 60
Delan, 348
Delano, 201, 409, 410
Delany, 38, 155, 243, 273
DeLirac, 41, 99
Delius, 95
Dell, 41, 48, 71, 76, 104, 193, 267, 269, 293, 369
Dellinger, 270
Delmotte, 42
Delroche, 407
Delshy, 31
Demar, 155
Dement, 155, 195, 249, 409
Demmon, 285
Deneale, 155
Denison, 2, 441
Dennesson, 388, 418
Dennisson, 394
Denny, 108
Dent, 155, 243, 287, 317, 425, 431
Depew, 279
Depot, 151
Depuison, 88
Deputy, 241
Derby, 314
Deringer, 441
Dermoth, 265
Dermott, 2, 155, 302, 330
Derrick, 399, 400
Derringer, 240
DeRussy, 318
Desaire, 261
Desellum, 8
Deslonde, 264, 267
Desmond, 155
Dessaulles, 264
Dessnell, 161
Dessomines, 431
Devaughan, 134
Deveal, 216
Devecmon, 148
Develin, 445

Devereaux, 334
Devereux, 266, 267
Deverle, 414
Devers, 243
Devine, 140, 423
Devitte, 32
Devlin, 54, 103, 135, 303
Devore, 150
Devou, 224
Dewar, 11
Dewdney, 129, 228, 430
Dewey, 107
Dews, 131
Dexter, 20, 63
Dibble, 42, 77, 116, 253
Dick, 29, 243, 297
Dickerson, 151
Dickey, 16, 333, 445
Dickins, 44, 69
Dickinson, 8, 28, 88, 158, 447
Dicks, 96
Dickson, 35, 74, 79, 84, 200
Didlake, 24
Differt, 171
Difficult creek, 96
Diffin, 415
Digges, 51, 139, 305, 396
Diggs, 248
Dignan, 415
Dillingham, 172, 330
Dillon, 305
Dimick, 315
Dimond, 272
Dimpster, 247
Dinas, 32
Dincan, 49
Dinex, 305
Dingle, 31
Dinwiddie, 236
Disbrow, 33
Disturnell, 441
Divernois, 41
Dix, 174, 222, 227, 311
Dixon, 92, 129, 139, 180, 230, 393, 424, 434, 447
Dixson, 381

Dobbin, 7, 36, 41, 111, 217, 405, 445, 449
Dobbins, 340, 345
Dobbyn, 368
Dobin, 49
Dobson, 235
Dod, 388
Dodd, 15, 243, 379
Dodge, 12, 29, 74, 95, 136, 213, 217, 266, 288, 379, 396, 451
Dodson, 141, 155, 245, 304, 424
Doheny, 309
Dolan, 73
Doland, 112, 267
Doll, 98
Dolliver, 240
Dolphin, 183, 381
Dommett, 276
Donald, 447
Donaldson, 37, 82, 128, 148, 174, 249, 312, 368
Donally, 141
Donan, 90
Donavan, 368
Donelan, 1, 13, 36, 37, 76, 119, 164, 167, 185, 303, 324, 327, 353, 362, 395, 418, 427
Donellan, 213
Donelson, 217, 288, 291, 435
Doniphan, 191, 217
Donn, 84, 117, 268, 349, 422
Donnellan, 213
Donnelly, 402, 424
Donnet, 115
Donoghue, 155, 244, 245, 264, 266, 267, 383
Donoho, 393, 422
Donohoo, 305, 393
Donophon, 305
Donovan, 155, 244, 392
Dooley, 155
Doolittle, 60
Door, 32
Dor, 381
Doran, 297
Dorby, 42

Dorn, 232
Dorr, 40, 103, 124, 286, 293
Dorrel's Run, 295
Dorset, 199
Dorsett, 196
Dorsey, 142, 155, 178, 235, 248, 249, 392
Doss, 128
Dossett, 30
Doty, 82
Doubleday, 424
Dougherty, 31, 273, 381, 389
Doughlass, 144
Doughty, 80, 195, 268, 434
Douglas, 2, 33, 82, 125, 146, 155, 189, 399
Douglas' Bottom, 433
Douglass, 3, 24, 32, 54, 194, 196, 199, 209, 223, 228, 248, 332, 422, 426, 451
Dousberger, 359
Douty, 373
Dove, 46, 147, 155, 196, 199, 200, 231, 413
Dover, 409
Dow, 77, 80, 100, 196, 199
Dowell, 155, 161
Dowling, 182, 199, 207, 248, 360, 368, 390, 406
Downer, 155, 230, 393
Downey, 57, 67, 88, 116, 123, 130, 133, 144, 146, 287
Downing, 200
Downs, 19, 146, 155, 216
Dowson, 93
Dowson's Row, 118
Doxey, 16, 42, 254
Doyle, 155, 279, 282, 305
Drake, 1, 46, 77, 128, 187, 238
Drane, 1, 84
Draper, 130, 302
Drayton, 77, 132, 273, 293, 302, 435
Drew, 211, 415
Driggs, 79
Drill, 416
Drinker, 381
Drum, 280, 283, 320, 343

Drummond, 103, 257, 381
Drummond tract, 149
Drury, 141, 155, 185, 194, 196, 197, 199, 210, 229, 271, 274, 310, 374, 422
Dry Hill, 151
Dryer, 340
Du Pont, 379
Duane, 217, 288
Dubant, 392
DuBarry, 136
Dublin Castle, 309
Dubois, 441
Dubs, 8
Duchess of Montpensier, 383
Duckett, 390
Ducouren, 163
Dudley, 39, 86, 121
Due, 146
Duer, 45, 381, 446
Duerson, 280
Duff, 212
Duffer, 358
Duffield, 92, 236
Duffy, 309
Dufour, 267
Dufresne, 264, 267
Dugan, 31
Duganny, 415
Duke, 403
Duke of Lucca, 31
Duke of Orleans, 93
Duke of Richmond, 142
Dulaney, 305
Dulany, 2, 24, 136, 165, 194, 199, 271, 328, 397, 399
Dules, 380
Duley, 126, 334
Dulton, 70
Dumas, 110
Dumbleton, 155
Dumbolton, 18
Dummer, 275
Dummett, 278
Dumphy, 155
Dunawin, 119
Dunbar, 183

Duncan, 6, 16, 48, 95, 130, 141, 172, 217, 241, 264, 267, 311, 338, 394
Dungan, 92, 290
Dunham, 23, 234
Dunkin, 381
Dunking, 409
Dunlap, 223, 244, 248, 421, 438
Dunlop, 2, 47, 110, 243, 300, 305, 308, 381
Dunn, 77, 79, 129, 168, 189, 194
Dunne, 49
Dunnington, 141, 155
Dunster, 331
Dunwell, 155
Duperu, 269
Dupont, 64, 231
Duralde, 396
Durand, 151
Durff, 68
Durham, 31, 284
Durrire, 48
Durrive, 99, 293
Dury, 62
Dusenbury, 62
Dutaille, 222
Dutailles, 253
Dutaillis, 70, 230, 294
Dutee, 143, 217, 253
Dutton, 140, 203
Duval, 385, 451
Duvall, 155, 292, 381, 388, 392, 393, 395, 400, 409
Dwight, 39, 386
Dye, 35, 209
Dyer, 22, 88, 122, 155, 162, 169, 195, 198, 215, 230, 235, 244, 250, 251, 267, 287, 291, 311, 368, 378, 409, 416
Dyer, 155
Dyson, 155, 412
Dyvenau, 155

E

Eagan, 85
Earl, 246, 265
Earl of Carlisle, 403
Earl of Westmoreland, 379

Earle, 155, 183
Easby, 196, 199, 243, 395
Easley, 121
Eastep, 134
Easterly, 278
Eastern Burial Ground, 379
Eastin, 278
Eastland, 62
Easton, 144
Eaton, 9, 60, 88, 123, 155, 174, 190, 210, 245, 312, 326, 397
Eberbach, 230, 392, 393, 410
Echols, 276, 282
Eckard, 284, 411, 453
Eckardt, 415
Eckeher, 164
Eckel, 110
Ecklof, 238
Eckloff, 330, 393, 438
Eddy, 227, 448
Edelen, 264, 368, 416
Edelin, 36, 155, 266, 298, 303, 453
Eden's Paradise Regained, 148
Edes, 213
Edgan, 206
Edgerly, 259
Edgerton, 155
Edmond, 226
Edmondson, 89
Edmonson, 168, 305, 442
Edmonston, 298, 431, 437, 450
Edtz, 248
Edwards, 2, 22, 25, 32, 39, 90, 120, 121, 128, 141, 144, 155, 231, 259, 291, 320, 322, 341, 349, 350, 409
Egan, 27, 59
Egbert, 379
Eggleston, 172, 347
Ehlen, 51, 245
Ehrmanbrent, 155
Ehrmanntrant, 363
Ehrmauntraut, 335
Eichelberger, 433
Eichorn, 155
Einnis, 243
Eisennery, 381

Eitchie, 136
Elbert, 381
Eld, 141
Elder, 35
Eldred, 31
Eldredge, 274, 324
Eldridge, 434
Elias, 155
Elie, 375
Eliot, 331, 387
Elk Garden, 152
Elk Lick, 152
Elkins, 32
Ellet, 404
Elli, 56
Ellicott, 148
Ellington, 163
Elliot, 17, 135, 146, 155, 195, 201, 231
Elliott, 26, 79, 125, 171, 198, 236, 302, 324, 340, 344, 389, 424, 426, 446, 451
Ellis, 27, 30, 37, 46, 59, 76, 79, 81, 97, 155, 187, 196, 200, 269, 286, 294, 305, 368, 382, 394, 422, 427, 430, 437, 438, 453
Elmer, 83
Elper, 373
Elston, 65, 107
Elverton Hall, 103
Elzey, 44, 62, 316
Elzy, 56
Emerson, 34, 88, 103, 116, 277, 436
Emery, 28, 44, 62, 374
Emmerich, 41, 72
Emmerson, 244
Emmert, 155
Emmons, 36, 42, 76, 102
Emory, 57, 230, 311, 406, 447
Empress Josephine, 402
Enbels, 76
Engels, 16, 118, 293
Engils, 84
England, 259
Engle, 223
Engles, 69, 430
English, 74, 132, 151, 218, 251, 284, 293, 305

Enlow, 149
Ennals, 351
Ennis, 27, 49, 86, 95, 100, 155, 172, 173, 187, 266, 363, 378, 383, 390, 406, 426
Entwistle, 155
Entwizell, 335
Epes, 91, 361
Ephraim, 163
Eppes, 226, 285, 439, 451
Erbin, 326
Erickson, 80
Ericson, 434
Ernis, 301
Erskine, 433
Erving, 205
Erwin, 127
Escandon, 139
Esher, 194
Eslava, 264
Espey, 362, 387
Esputa, 267
Espy, 13, 17, 68, 212
Essex, 437
Estaureson, 62
Estep, 300
Esters, 143
Estes, 143
Estko, 363, 364
Etheredge, 100
Etherington, 42
Eutaw, 300
Evans, 20, 21, 28, 49, 79, 83, 86, 97, 99, 114, 116, 119, 125, 129, 217, 220, 229, 241, 245, 254, 259, 276, 278, 279, 288, 305, 312, 321, 332, 340, 343, 381, 388, 393, 394, 424, 452
Everett, 10, 242, 249, 283, 331, 410, 440
Everhart, 6
Eversfield, 155
Everson, 33
Ewell, 121, 194, 269, 316, 409
Ewing, 8, 139, 212, 217, 266, 328, 439
Eytinge, 164

F

Fabens, 124
Faber, 428
Factories tract, 150
Faherty, 86, 103
Fahnestick, 221
Fahnestock, 373
Fair, 216
Fairbanks, 409
Fairchild, 6
Faire, 167
Fairfax, 35, 72, 96, 108, 212, 272, 379
Fairfax tract, 152
Fairfield, 10, 21, 79, 194, 408
Fairy, 44
Fallofield, 164
Falls, 122, 150
Faly, 130
Fanelly, 62
Fanning, 141, 245
Faragut, 136
Farelly, 342
Far-enough, 151
Faris, 109
Farland, 305
Farley, 447
Farmer, 452
Farnesworth, 416
Farnham, 105, 140, 155, 183, 196, 202, 231, 294, 422, 429
Farquhar, 297
Farquharson, 148
Farr, 381, 426, 453
Farragut, 64
Farrar, 156, 161, 247, 248, 393
Farrell, 50, 56
Farrelly, 44, 317
Farrely, 340
Farrington, 30, 216, 358
Farrow, 41
Fasnaught, 369
Fassett, 31
Favier, 156, 210, 392
Faxon, 374
Fay, 275, 276, 372
Fearney, 110

Fearson, 37, 156, 369
Febiger, 77
Febrey, 126, 257, 357, 388
Fechtig, 352
Feeney, 88
Fehrer, 398
Felch, 135, 187, 276
Felix, 136, 221, 253
Fell, 66
Fellanny, 293
Fellany, 16, 76, 84, 193
Felt, 166
Felton, 11, 71, 193, 265, 298
Fendall, 335, 386, 411
Fenderich, 239
Fenton, 137
Fenwick, 7, 15, 227, 246, 287, 336, 337, 355
Feran, 429
Ferguson, 144, 228, 290, 308, 326, 354, 378, 395
Ferguson, 305
Fernando, 32
Ferrah, 107
Ferral, 92
Ferrell, 206
Ferriere, 113
Ferris, 285
Ferrity, 243
Fetterman, 266
Fevan, 165
Ficket, 141
Ficklin, 37, 60
Field, 39, 229, 292, 303, 320
field pieces, 234
Fields, 233, 243, 253, 365
Fiensten, 245
Fiesco, 123
Fifth survey, 151
Figaniere, 19, 301
Fillebrown, 326, 428
Fillebrowne, 448
Fillmore, 213, 239, 296, 365, 366, 377, 418, 425
Finch, 30, 32, 35, 45, 99, 112, 194, 270, 358, 389, 392

Finckel, 13, 125, 308, 421
Finckle, 378
Findlay, 14, 95
Fink, 250, 340
Finkle, 130, 440
Finkman, 156, 248, 298, 392
Finkmann, 174
Finley, 195
Finnegan, 73, 85, 409
Finney, 178
Fischer, 46, 155, 305, 393
Fish, 285, 424
Fisher, 6, 7, 14, 51, 70, 92, 120, 163, 194, 293, 331, 359, 373, 420, 436
Fisk, 214, 294
Fister, 156
Fitch, 8, 16, 216, 226, 285, 393
Fitnam, 103, 156, 264, 304
Fitton, 156
Fitzgerald, 10, 44, 62, 121, 155, 156, 213, 243, 244, 258, 267, 275, 276, 278, 282, 283, 290, 298, 300, 319, 381, 392, 393, 409, 426, 428, 451
Fitzhugh, 122, 259, 279, 329, 368
Fitzpatrick, 32, 104, 309
Fitzwater, 49, 99, 114, 227, 293
flag staffs, 387
flag-ship **Ohio**, 375
Flaherty, 38, 418
Flanagan, 89, 334
Flanagin, 140, 183
Flanegan, 139, 202, 385
Flanigan, 451
Fleming, 4, 25, 123, 144, 298, 379, 416
Flemming, 156
Flenner, 156, 161
Flesher, 6
Fletcher, 6, 86, 107, 171, 190, 194, 199, 207, 243, 248, 280, 305, 310, 336, 347, 348, 362, 445
Flinn, 302
Flint, 103, 342
Flood, 23, 216, 424
Flournoy, 58, 144
Flower, 443
Flowers, 233

Flowery Mead, 149
Flowery Meads, 150
Floyd, 56, 62, 227, 233, 395
Flye, 297
Foal, 6
Foanes, 297
Fogarty, 191, 309
Foley, 147, 206, 252, 274, 330, 351, 362, 369
Follain, 362
Follansbee, 156
Folsom, 439
Foltz, 106, 447
Fongeres, 136
Fontain, 209
Fontane, 173, 183, 444
Foot, 7, 71, 112, 222, 277
Foote, 141, 434
Forbes, 31, 116, 221, 233, 414
Force, 32, 147, 196, 199, 200, 201, 218, 238, 245, 427
Ford, 8, 79, 141, 156, 209, 224, 243, 246, 266, 323, 395
Foreman, 17, 80, 218
Forge Seat & Mill Seat, 150
Forrest, 74, 156, 213, 273, 285, 305, 432
Forshaw, 80
Forshee, 244
Forstall, 264, 267
Forster, 278
Forsyth, 277, 279, 283, 322, 349, 371
Forsythe, 217, 251, 288
Fort, 267
Fort Ann, 110
Fort Atkinson, 205
Fort Brown, 19, 181
Fort Columbus, 97
Fort Conception, 387
Fort Duquesne, 61
Fort Erie, 50
Fort Gibson, 50
Fort Grenville, 30
Fort Hamilton, 205
Fort Independence, 255, 376
Fort Leavenworth, 16, 329, 345
Fort Mackimac, 205

Fort McHenry, 28, 71, 205
Fort Miller, 110
Fort Monroe, 205, 212, 345
Fort Moultrie, 205
Fort Pike, 101
Fort Pitt, 385
Fort San Iago, 387
Fort Smith, 89
Fort Snelling, 55
Fort Washington, 440
Fort Watson, 188
Fort Wayne, 189
Fortress Monroe, 325, 377
Forwell, 74
Fosdick, 285
Foster, 71, 99, 167, 247, 317, 319, 338, 349, 409
Fotherill, 42
Fougeres, 110
Fougieres, 122
Foulkes, 409
Fountain Park, 143
Four Brothers, 234
Fournier, 95
Foushee, 409
Fouty, 151
Fowle, 251, 332
Fowler, 6, 58, 150, 155, 156, 165, 216, 243, 254, 293, 316, 340, 424
Fowler's lot, 150
Fox, 47, 52, 76, 82, 204, 395
Fox Chase, 151
Foy, 86, 103, 111, 139, 155, 303, 305, 325, 326, 392, 393, 437
Foyles, 64, 417
Fraelar, 383
Frail, 271, 301, 302
Frailey, 242, 416
Fraiser, 2, 148, 155
Fraler, 156
France, 49, 106, 227, 393
Frances, 2
Francis, 33, 326, 375, 388
Francisco, 209
Frank, 248

Franklin, 31, 79, 113, 156, 181, 190, 229, 312, 373, 393, 409, 416
Franklin Row, 128
Franklin's Progress, 108
Franks, 415
Franzoni, 212, 236
Fraser, 9, 86, 163, 395
Frasier, 40, 156, 358
Fraunck, 156
Fraunk, 246
Frazer, 144, 230
Frazier, 16, 305, 369, 426
Frederich, 72
Frederick, 31, 137, 395
Fredieu, 106, 232
Frediue, 243
Free, 336
Freeland, 112, 431
Freelon, 322
Freeman, 48, 129, 136, 175, 216, 285, 409, 420
Freire, 264
Frekle, 112
Fremont, 60, 61, 255, 283, 338, 344
French, 28, 45, 66, 69, 77, 79, 93, 115, 139, 173, 174, 196, 200, 229, 236, 252, 279, 284, 285, 295, 304, 311, 312, 316, 322, 324, 382, 412
French Revolution, 134
Frere, 334
Frerer, 405
Freret, 264
Frick, 235, 278
Friend, 23, 254
Friendship, 105, 148
Friendship tract, 150
Fries, 141, 156
frig **Alfonzo**, 333
frig **Alliance**, 190
frig **Brandywine**, 22, 44, 76, 223, 274
frig **Constellation**, 53
frig **Constitution**, 5, 53, 55, 370, 446
frig **Cumberland**, 347
frig **Cyane**, 64
frig **Guerriere**, 446
frig **Independence**, 223

frig **Java**, 446
frig **Macedonian**, 206
frig **Mississippi**, 348
frig **Philadelphia**, 89, 119, 136, 445
frig **Portsmouth**, 64
frig **Savannah**, 223
frig **St Lawrence**, 326
Frink, 135
Frost, 277, 279, 314, 428
Fruit Hill, 235
Fruit Vale, 406
Frunk, 156
Fry, 121, 126, 187, 199, 409, 413, 423
Frye, 196, 232, 243, 435
Fryer, 208
Fue, 290
Fugate, 71, 193, 219
Fugit, 248
Fugitt, 243, 244, 247
Fuller, 24, 68, 71, 119, 155, 156, 161, 175, 185, 193, 210, 215, 244, 248, 265, 368, 392, 448, 450
Fuller's Hotel, 443
Fulmer, 196, 200
Fulton, 30, 34, 76, 97, 193, 262, 264, 269, 294, 384
Furr, 413
Fyffe, 416
Fyffie, 232

G

Gaar, 187
Gadsby, 3, 40, 156, 270, 392
Gadsby's row, 324
Gadsden, 191, 217
Gage, 205
Gagnon, 232, 243
Gahan, 194, 367
Gaines, 15, 101, 104, 232, 280, 332, 366, 407, 431, 434
Gainnie, 11
Gainsborough, 204
Gaither, 7, 53, 85, 91, 222, 228, 230, 259, 291, 294, 358, 435
Galabrun, 103, 170
Gales, 99, 238, 262, 290

Galladay, 444
Gallagher, 221, 431
Gallaher, 219
Gallatin, 109
Galligan, 190
Galloway, 148, 151
Galphin, 27, 71, 291, 294
Galplin, 27
Galt, 116, 121, 156, 315
Gamble, 192, 326, 401, 413
Gamlin, 195
Gammage, 253
Gander, 112
Gannon, 73, 245, 395
Gansevoort, 35
Gantt, 18, 172, 335, 347, 349, 394, 424, 450
Gaona, 272
Garallan Farm, 433
Garber, 219
Gardiner, 16, 141, 277, 282, 287, 305, 424, 452
Gardner, 24, 35, 79, 99, 133, 144, 156, 161, 166, 212, 216, 219, 221, 222, 266, 267, 269, 313, 314, 318, 377, 382, 393, 448
Garland, 21, 22, 125, 199, 205, 259, 291, 292, 294, 315, 342, 407
Garlick, 136
Garner, 86, 304, 305, 369, 390, 392
Garnet, 243
Garnett, 121, 128, 174, 220, 299, 312, 327, 342, 343, 452
Garney, 176
Garnsey, 83, 129, 209, 253
Garrason, 253
Garret, 50, 156, 373, 392
Garretson, 305
Garrett, 87, 125, 192, 413
Garrison, 167, 187, 445
Garsdon, 356
Gartland, 424
Gary, 232, 409
gas pipes, 404
Gasbey, 424
Gaskins, 177

Gasquet, 264
Gassaway, 19, 117, 140, 192, 215, 255, 394, 409
Gassite, 417
Gassitt, 238
Gaston, 81
Gatchel, 252
Gates, 2, 79, 194, 268, 318
Gatewood, 450
Gatts, 243
Gautier, 444
Gautt, 381
Gay, 15, 45, 48, 99, 164, 183, 294
Gayon, 62
Geddersen, 163
Gedney, 82, 425
Geer, 177
Gellen, 186
Gelston, 412
Gen Duff Green's Iron & Ore lands, 150
Gendry, 265
Gentry, 30, 37, 285
George, 163
Gerard, 184
Gere, 136
Germon, 18
Gernsel, 25
Gerolt, 243, 394
Gerring, 227
Gerry, 419
Gertrude Russel, 441
Gess, 156
Gettings, 246
Getty, 316
Geyer, 243
Gholson, 333
Gibbons, 138
Gibbs, 7, 17, 45, 53, 79, 82, 132, 156, 231, 258, 283, 314, 338, 426, 434, 451
Gibson, 15, 66, 83, 92, 104, 156, 163, 172, 219, 232, 243, 266, 291, 310, 318, 324, 339, 341, 347, 405, 407, 409, 412
Gideon, 16, 42, 67, 68, 196, 200, 229, 237, 243, 305, 344, 364, 370

Giffin, 193
Gilbert, 107, 131, 183, 303, 448
Gilbreath, 6
Gilchrist, 215
Gildermeister, 369
Giles, 321
Gill, 139, 217, 277, 279, 288, 369, 412
Gillaspie, 23
Gilles, 326
Gillespie, 11, 24, 64, 75, 91, 243, 292, 328, 439
Gillet, 13, 38, 129, 283, 284, 397
Gillis, 118, 157, 372
Gilliss, 20, 42, 97, 115, 128, 373, 399
Gillott, 156, 243
Gillow, 95
Gills, 385
Gilman, 231, 353, 393, 411, 412
Gilmer, 123
Gilpin, 47, 373, 389
Gineman, 380
Ginters, 31
Girard, 30
Girault, 297
Gitt, 47
Gittings, 228, 419
Given, 78, 201
Giveney, 2, 243, 384
Glackin, 275, 277, 283, 322
Gladen, 141
Gladman, 156
Glancy, 27
Glass, 60
Glasscock, 232
Gleason, 269
Glen, 210, 341, 345
Glendy, 17
Glenn, 58, 78, 322, 355
Gloscester, 42
Glossell, 437
Glover, 67, 73, 309
Glynn, 17, 42, 124, 169
Gobbs, 104
Goddard, 156, 161, 228, 378, 437, 438
Goddary, 271
Godeon, 139

Godey, 237, 257
Godfrey, 30
Godman's Level, 150
Goggin, 134, 243, 452
Goings, 245
Goins, Sarah, 141
Golden, 209, 392
Golder, 46
Goldin, 156, 247
Golding, 156
Goldsberry, 194
Goldsborough, 82, 156, 405, 447
Goldsby, 435
Golman, 150
Golt, 435
Gomez, 232
Goodarsall, 247
Goodell, 5
Goodenough, 48
Goodhall, 156
Goodhue, 151, 418, 434
Gooding, 156
Goodloe, 77, 147, 279
Goodly lands, 148
Goodman, 299
Goodmanson, 333
Goodrice, 349
Goodrich, 5, 8, 67, 151, 156, 172, 215, 248, 290
Goodrick, 437
Goodwin, 41, 56, 355, 398, 449
Goodyear's Rubber Goods, 227
Goolsby, 286, 443
Gorden, 156
Gordon, 25, 32, 45, 47, 49, 56, 139, 145, 163, 195, 207, 210, 213, 216, 252, 253, 314, 338
Gore, 316, 331, 340
Gorham, 70
Gorman, 71, 305, 309
Gormley, 190
Gormly, 268
Gorsuch, 189
Goss, 5, 36, 48, 212, 222, 248, 293
Gostenhoffer, 42
Got, 183

Gott, 129, 140, 202, 231
Gough, 29, 156, 167
Gould, 15, 194
Goulding, 140
Gouverneur, 318
Gouverneurs, 371
Gove, 136, 277
governor's house, 404
Goyne, 210
Gracie, 371
Gracy, 107
Grady, 49, 80, 170
Graeff, 64, 370, 378
Graeve, 79
Grafton, 62, 316
Graham, 2, 4, 7, 8, 26, 28, 38, 41, 77, 79, 84, 90, 114, 119, 121, 133, 146, 156, 190, 193, 209, 214, 228, 230, 237, 240, 268, 278, 279, 282, 285, 291, 294, 314, 318, 343, 351, 381, 408, 424, 429
Graiff, 308
Grainger, 369
Gramillion, 48, 294
Gramillon, 99
Grammer, 230, 298, 402, 427
Grand Duke, 379
Grandy, 58
Grange, 37
Granger, 317, 343
Graninger, 77
Grant, 221, 276, 278
Granville, 375
Grapnell, 183
Grason, 141
Gratiot, 146, 183, 222, 294, 305
Gravel, 139
Graven, 131
Graves, 146, 371
Gray, 56, 71, 87, 89, 90, 95, 109, 112, 151, 171, 172, 186, 193, 219, 245, 260, 265, 268, 282, 295, 299, 325, 372, 378, 424, 433, 434, 449
Grayson, 48, 55, 76, 156, 212, 274, 315, 420
Greason, 393

Greeley, 366
Green, 4, 15, 26, 32, 42, 45, 47, 60, 79, 101, 111, 147, 150, 156, 166, 174, 178, 231, 235, 243, 266, 267, 284, 290, 300, 301, 333, 334, 339, 345, 362, 380, 381, 423, 424, 426, 427, 447, 450, 452
Green Meadows & Deep Creek, 148
Green's Row, 211
Greenan, 81
Greenbury, 377
Greene, 217, 290, 388, 439
Greenfell, 333
Greenfield, 57, 390, 406
Greenhow, 10, 266
Greenleaf, 29, 111, 145, 305
Greenough, 329
Greenwell, 164, 290
Greenwood, 210
Greenwood cemetery, 429
Greenwood Cemetery, 221
Greer, 17, 29, 34, 41, 133, 216, 234, 274, 305, 396
Greeson, 342, 344
Greeves, 156, 229
Gregg, 15, 84, 107, 186, 434
Gregory, 48, 202, 372
Greiner, 268
Gresham, 265
Grey, 137, 277, 279, 381
Grice, 80, 222, 230, 253, 291, 293
Grier, 84, 129, 140, 448, 450
Griffen, 15
Griffin, 13, 71, 150, 187, 202, 235, 266, 275, 305, 438, 448
Griffith, 156, 241, 279
Grigg, 183
Griggs, 15
Grimeke, 95
Grimes, 56, 156, 378
Grimshaw, 278
Grindage, 149
Grinder, 11, 243
Grinnan, 437
Grinnell, 421, 447
Griswold, 108, 166, 169, 212, 278, 299

482

Groce, 409
Grodon, 260
Groove, 149
Groper lot, 151
Grose, 171
Groshoby, 81
Gross, 37, 246, 369
Grossman, 39, 95
Grouard, 238
Groupe, 156
Grove, 97, 137
Groves, 402
Grubb, 237, 334, 383, 415, 422
Grupe, 243
Grymes, 298, 369
Gtwn College, 335
Gueldress, 403
Guernsey, 1
Guest, 98, 177, 416
Gugniard, 95
Guild, 206, 327
Guillow, 77
Guists, 156
Gulager, 400
Gumaer, 46
Gunnell, 80, 156, 231, 243, 247, 271, 384, 391, 413, 420, 430
Gunston, 81
Gunston estate, 81
Gunter, 445
Gunton, 14, 156, 218, 219, 335, 349, 427
Gurley, 68, 254, 308, 432
Gurner, 73
Gushire, 8
Guthrie, 76, 274, 321
Guyer, 150, 156
Gwin, 76, 395
Gwinn, 274, 370
Gwynn, 121, 266, 267, 287
Gyer, 224
Gyles, 86

H

Haberstein, 31
Habs, 42
Hacker, 309

Haddock's Hills, 162
Hadduck, 135
Haden, 341
Hagadorn, 73
Hagan, 24
Hagar, 381
Hager, 157, 244, 245, 436
Hagerty, 156, 243, 267
Haggard, 110, 118
Haggler, 56
Hagner, 116, 157, 232, 313, 319
Hague, 109
Haifler, 361
Haige, 49
Haille, 56
Haines, 156, 285, 299, 445, 446
Hainman, 31
Hair, 123, 434
Hairmiller, 157
Haislep, 243
Haislip, 157
Haldee, 62
Haldeman, 276, 278, 279, 283, 343
Hale, 44, 63, 121
Hale's Tract, 332
Haley, 8, 337
Half Moon, 151
Half Small Meadows, 152
Haliday, 80, 196, 199, 373, 422
Hall, 31, 35, 56, 62, 70, 77, 81, 84, 89, 107, 141, 144, 146, 156, 157, 184, 185, 186, 206, 231, 241, 248, 265, 290, 300, 302, 306, 327, 329, 369, 381, 392, 397, 404, 409, 418, 424, 428, 430, 446, 447
Hallack, 113
Halleck, 313
Hallenbach, 202
Hallenbeck, 71
Haller, 56, 319, 340, 412
Hallowell, 95, 166, 295, 361
Hallstead, 33
Halstead, 140, 183
Halsted, 202
Haltmillar, 244
Halverson, 183

Hamberlin, 49
Hamborough, 150
Hamersley, 72
Hames, 49
Hamill, 377
Hamilton, 35, 41, 45, 48, 50, 88, 89, 98, 125, 157, 173, 191, 202, 217, 239, 243, 261, 275, 276, 283, 314, 317, 329, 339, 343, 369, 395, 412, 451
Hammersley, 156, 244
Hammitt, 441
Hammond, 15, 28, 82, 216, 316, 341, 362
Hampton, 58, 88, 157, 207, 291, 451
Hams, 398
Hamtramck, 87
Hance, 372, 373
Hancock, 38, 199, 221, 317, 392
Hand, 40, 76, 274, 279
Handley, 79
Handly, 263
Hands, 196, 199, 200, 201, 241
Handy, 91, 139, 157, 228, 271, 305, 330, 358, 410, 422, 436, 444
Hank, 98
Hanly, 408
Hannon, 276, 282
Hannwalk, 149
Hanrahan, 266
Hansell, 50, 226, 410
Hanson, 35, 44, 83, 89, 94, 98, 164, 231, 243, 254, 360, 442
Hapham, 84
Haralson, 82
Harbaugh, 15, 46, 67, 135, 156, 157, 187, 331, 393, 395, 422
Harbo, 232, 243
Harbour, 443
Hard Bargain Resurveyed, 152
Hardcastle, 317, 319
Hardee, 44, 56, 312, 314
Harden, 6, 150, 443
Harding, 26, 81, 118, 336, 373, 400
Hardship, 234
Hardy, 6, 54, 156, 166, 336, 370
Hare, 172, 203, 270, 271

Harelton, 257
Harer, 238
Hargrave, 219
Harkness, 65, 80, 156, 171, 196, 197, 199, 200, 228, 243, 303, 305, 358
Harlan, 348
Harley, 138, 321, 449
Harlon, 22, 49
Harman, 49, 183, 219, 305
Harmanson, 112
Harmon, 31
Harmony, 107, 119
Harness, 96
Harney, 313, 407
Harper, 21, 24, 210, 386
Harpham, 140
Harpster, 279, 282
Harrel, 25
Harrendon, 66
Harrigan, 71, 285
Harrington, 18, 102, 270, 272, 291, 293, 392, 407
Harris, 17, 41, 77, 84, 88, 90, 98, 125, 127, 129, 134, 146, 152, 156, 157, 187, 193, 195, 248, 261, 271, 274, 278, 285, 293, 300, 379, 385, 425, 433
Harrison, 5, 36, 42, 77, 85, 131, 135, 162, 178, 199, 248, 271, 272, 290, 306, 328, 338, 367, 372, 379, 401, 410, 419, 436, 438
Harrover, 284, 298, 393, 423
Harry, 381, 402
Hart, 37, 56, 62, 71, 84, 88, 98, 105, 110, 133, 138, 157, 164, 176, 186, 193, 216, 285, 326
Harte, 278, 281
Harter, 358
Hartstene, 56
Harvard, 331
<u>Harvard College</u>, 331
Harvey, 68, 94, 125, 157, 187, 231, 243, 244, 247, 394, 450
Haskett, 135
Haskill, 447
Haskin, 313, 319, 341, 346
Haskins, 424

Haslep, 284
Haslop, 247
Haslup, 56
Hassell, 433
Hassitt, 163
Hassler, 15, 41, 177, 178, 216, 291, 293
Hastie, 2
Hasting, 432
Hastings, 71, 93, 100, 193, 219, 232, 249, 286, 376
Haswell, 430, 447
Hatch, 244, 317, 338
Hatfield, 32
Hathaway, 409, 449
Hatheway, 281, 316, 323
Hatinack, 112
Hatten, 112
Haughey, 114
Haughrey, 32
Haup, 176, 183, 202
Haven, 70
Havenner, 175, 244, 404
Haves, 326
Havilland, 277, 281
Haw, 33, 43, 173, 176, 218, 427
Hawes, 56, 62, 317, 411
Hawkins, 136, 149, 156, 157
Hawks, 28
Hawley, 20, 134, 309
Hawly, 50
Hawson, 93
Hay, 139
Hayden, 6, 22, 316, 352
Haydon, 47
Haye, 109
Hayes, 361
Haynes, 217, 276, 281, 288, 408
Hayre, 397
Hays, 13, 112, 223, 317, 319, 324, 344, 373, 409
Hayward, 221
Haywood, 64, 239
Hazard, 129, 228, 251
Hazel, 11, 245, 331, 335
Hazelton, 79
Hazle, 307

Head, 232
Head of Frazier, 124
Heady, 84
Heald, 105
Healey, 70
Healy, 214, 222, 230, 443
Heaney, 412
Heap, 113
Heard, 135, 253, 443, 444
Heath, 332, 426
Heaton, 295
Hebb, 69, 111, 453
Hebbard, 186
Hebbs, 260
Hebert, 109, 264, 322
Hebron, 141, 409
Heck, 249, 339
Heckett, 36
Hedge, 281
Hedges, 398
Heeter, 11, 251
Heffernan, 104
Heighan, 81
Heintzelman, 320
Heise, 218
Heiss, 134, 179
Heitmiller, 243
Helevman, 79
Hellemes, 194
Hellings, 252
Hemming, 424
Hemple, 1
Henarie, 398
Henck, 156
Hendershot, 56, 352, 414
Henderson, 6, 20, 79, 89, 94, 141, 171, 211, 214, 292, 416, 430
Hendley, 392, 393
Hendrickson, 96, 316
Hening, 217
Henley, 156, 157, 194, 445
Henly, 157
Henman, 164
Henner, 33
Henning, 73, 102, 231, 369, 409, 437
Henrie, 73, 74, 104

Henry, 44, 56, 62, 70, 99, 173, 188, 216, 238, 244, 247, 264, 310, 318, 326, 343, 348
Henshaw, 46, 227, 425
Hensley, 117, 156
Henson, 157, 194
Hepburn, 46, 78, 141, 156, 179, 197, 200, 201, 394
Herald, 157
Herbert, 103, 138, 194, 271, 274, 290, 381, 409, 415
Herbrailt, 139
Herchy, 32
Hercus, 246, 394, 445
Hereford, 280, 283, 350
Hernander, 63
Herndon, 383
Herold, 70, 88, 105, 110
Heron, 139, 247
Herrick, 255
Herrington, 202
Herrity, 428
Herron, 50
Hersey, 16
Hervey, 7, 62
Heskinson, 32
Hess, 33, 156, 157, 245
Hesselin, 151
Hettick, 151
Hettleson, 66
Hetzel, 179, 245
Heustiss, 430
Hewitt, 28, 97, 141, 306, 412, 452
Hewlett, 87
Hewlings, 51
Hewson, 62
Heydon, 156, 379, 428
Hibbard, 326
Hibbert, 71, 193
Hibbs, 193, 306
Hickerson, 157
Hickey, 51, 237, 267, 323
Hickley, 214
Hickman, 84, 118, 120, 157, 215, 225, 294
Hicks, 157, 243, 269, 286, 431

Higbee, 216
Higgins, 163, 168, 221, 264, 267, 305, 381
Higginson, 10, 327
High, 171
Hightower, 199
Highway, 62
Hilbert, 219
Hildebrand, 31
Hildreth, 49, 99, 230, 272
Hilgard, 324
Hill, 2, 30, 31, 76, 85, 104, 106, 109, 117, 157, 164, 193, 194, 196, 199, 205, 222, 224, 230, 232, 243, 247, 266, 293, 317, 339, 358, 384, 401, 409, 429, 437, 447, 453
Hillary, 12, 17, 36, 135
Hilliard, 65
Hilliary, 42, 76
Hillman, 17, 23
Hills, 402
Hillyard, 156
Hilton, 37, 228, 358
Himes, 67
Hinckson, 6
Hinds, 175
Hines, 179, 197, 199, 305, 420
Hinton, 18, 135, 194
Hipkins, 268, 332
Hise, 107, 109
Hitchcock, 42, 95, 178, 315
Hitner, 92
Hitz, 46, 157, 228
Hix, 17
Hoagland, 66, 321
Hoar, 331
Hoban, 269
Hobbie, 134, 156, 231, 393
Hobbs, 103, 246, 285, 328, 409
Hockett, 17, 42, 240
Hodge, 63, 156, 275, 423
Hodges, 17, 68, 272, 407, 415
Hodgkins, 381
Hodgman, 130
Hodgson, 224
Hoe, 95

Hoff, 326
Hoffar, 257
Hoffman, 11, 14, 44, 72, 106, 140, 183, 186, 202, 283, 294, 315, 318, 365, 370
Hoffman's Delight, 150
Hogan, 15, 17, 30, 36, 41, 42, 76, 265, 294, 306
Hoge, 259, 324, 401
Hogeboom, 69, 137
Hoggat, 15
Hoggatt, 48
Hogmire, 45
Hogue, 140
Holbernan, 62
Holbrook, 157
Holcomb, 58, 279
Holden, 24, 321, 369, 409, 433, 453
Holey, 146
Holgate, 30
Holladay, 140
Holland, 16, 49, 99, 100, 140, 147, 156, 172, 176, 213, 266, 293, 309
Hollenbeck, 193
Holley, 83, 443
Holliday, 254
Hollidge, 157, 161, 171, 229, 271
Hollinsworth, 415
Hollister, 203
Hollohan, 204
Hollohon, 153
Holloway, 317
Holmead, 105, 156, 245, 291, 347, 368, 437
Holmes, 12, 23, 71, 79, 187, 217, 288, 305, 386, 436
Holmes' Island, 379
Holohon, 251
Holroyd, 324, 369
Holt, 33, 171
Holton, 21, 80, 107, 139, 164, 186, 293, 368, 434
Holtzman, 429
Holyoke, 331
Homan, 72
Homans, 46, 305, 309
Homer, 157

Homiller, 246
Homoun, 381
Hone, 152
Honethamp, 369
Hood, 32, 143, 280, 283
Hooe, 82, 121, 332, 340, 345, 403
Hooker, 115, 319
Hooper, 28, 256, 275
Hoover, 31, 98, 104, 198, 214, 243, 247, 273, 305, 306, 443
Hope, 5, 151
Hope tract, 150
Hopkins, 33, 49, 63, 71, 124, 127, 227, 275, 277, 411
Hopkinson, 430
Hore, 430
Horn, 6
Hornbeck, 26
Horner, 163, 388, 444
Horning, 157, 244, 261
Hornsby, 276, 281
Horrell, 270
Horseman, 369
Horton, 31, 209
Hottinger, 363
Houck, 189, 306
Hough, 156, 195, 372, 377
Houghton, 249
House, 217, 232
Housemen, 263
Houssaye, 50
Houston, 77, 278
How, 279
Howard, 18, 21, 22, 41, 56, 62, 79, 88, 94, 141, 150, 157, 163, 182, 195, 196, 213, 228, 244, 248, 249, 322, 336, 337, 339, 342, 375, 403, 411, 416
Howe, 4, 91, 141, 157, 210, 228, 253, 317, 338, 371, 411
Howell, 42, 150, 156, 161, 243, 303, 404
Howie, 231
Howison, 68, 303, 376
Howland, 217, 289, 372
Howle, 157, 265
Howze, 101
Hoye, 87

Hoye's Coal, Iron, & Lime Discovery, 150
Hoye's Fortune, 150
Hoyle, 280
Hoyt, 56, 88, 286
Hubbard, 98, 118, 131, 139, 216, 293, 297, 358
Huber, 23
Huddleson, 349
Huddleston, 157
Hudson, 34, 48, 88, 95, 104, 186, 223, 249, 430
Hudspeth, 449
Huffington, 35
Huffman, 157
Huffnagle, 10
Hugenin, 382
Huger, 101, 172, 313, 319
Hughes, 2, 24, 63, 66, 73, 112, 140, 156, 168, 213, 250, 260, 276, 281, 306, 313, 336, 391, 422, 423, 424, 428, 435
Huguenin, 429
Hull, 41, 98, 99, 112, 172, 232, 278, 424, 446, 447
Hulsemann, 447
Humber, 313, 343
Humes, 246, 368, 447
Hummer, 21
Humphreys, 24, 61, 139, 141, 246, 338, 404, 417
Hunley, 444
Hunn, 192
Hunnicutt, 231
Hunt, 23, 60, 93, 110, 112, 168, 198, 238, 306, 317, 319, 326, 370, 424, 435
Hunter, 9, 17, 24, 30, 64, 82, 83, 112, 113, 123, 150, 156, 187, 223, 274, 321, 379, 383, 416, 446
Hunting ground, 152
Huntington, 125, 146
Hunton, 79
Huntoon, 109
Huntt, 79, 306
Hurburt, 194
Hurdle, 165
Hurdorp, 137

Hurley, 87, 92
Huron, 149
Hurray, 162
Hurst, 121, 242, 413, 438
Hurt, 101
Hurtscamp, 157
Husbands, 224
Hushey, 308
Husks, 25
Hussey, 45, 46, 170
Huston, 217, 289
Hutchinson, 22, 71, 90, 125, 146, 247, 248, 259, 392
Hutinach, 84
Hutinack, 102, 118, 272
Hutter, 207, 280, 339, 345
Hutton, 50
Hyams, 74, 80
Hyatt, 80, 101, 306, 333, 393
Hyde, 120, 355, 439
Hyman, 81
Hyslop, 414

I

Iardella, 67, 202, 393
Ibottson, 81
Iddins, 243
Idelins, 250
Illins, 95
Ilsley, 239
Indian Creek, 234
Indian Creek with Addition, 234
Indian massacre, 271
Ingalls, 311, 341
Inge, 278, 449
Ingersoll, 27, 66, 95, 103, 212, 214
Ingle, 80, 129, 153, 157, 200, 202, 221, 228, 247, 306, 325, 353, 424
Ingleby, 327
Ingola, 347
Ingolls, 172
Ingraham, 206, 216, 245
Ington, 149
Innerarity, 371
Internal Improvements, 149
Ipso, 149

Ireland, 87, 380
Irons, 31, 44, 125
Irvan, 279
Irvin, 249
Irvine, 92
Irving, 97, 109, 413
Irwin, 44, 47, 63, 121, 280, 282, 321, 326, 341, 345, 415
Isaac, 388
Isaacs, 245, 323
Isacks, 87, 112
Isherwood, 104, 218, 246
Israel, 372

J

Jack, 239, 388
Jackson, 2, 8, 40, 63, 71, 73, 78, 79, 88, 95, 101, 105, 110, 111, 112, 121, 123, 125, 142, 157, 165, 174, 182, 193, 194, 209, 213, 217, 244, 245, 247, 248, 260, 265, 275, 277, 285, 288, 289, 291, 296, 303, 317, 321, 331, 340, 342, 381, 409, 416, 419, 424, 430, 431, 437, 443
Jackson City, 379
Jackson Monument Cmte, 294
Jacksonville, 235
Jacob, 28, 389, 424
Jacob's Ladder, 151
Jacobs, 137, 151, 184, 248, 303, 308
Jamaison, 141, 194
James, 34, 162, 192, 290, 366, 404, 434, 440, 441
Jamieson, 157
Jamiseon, 219
Janney, 42, 123, 353, 401, 438
Janpear, 33
Jarboe, 98, 306, 335
Jarrot, 48, 54, 212, 220, 443
Jarvis, 9, 317, 339, 342, 352
Jasper, 43, 123, 157, 161, 165, 303
Jay, 20, 103, 447
Jedt, 244
Jefferies, 74
Jefferson, 14, 15, 166, 202, 217, 363, 364, 419, 424

Jell, 95
Jenifer, 245, 390, 414
Jenkins, 124, 157, 165, 179, 199, 241, 359, 381, 432
Jenkins' Deer Park Resurveyed, 151
Jenks, 178
Jenne, 17
Jennett, 254
Jennings, 5, 49, 85, 157, 194, 283, 373
Jesetr, 83
Jessup, 405
Jesuit missionary, 192
Jesuits, 329
Jesup, 245, 248, 407
Jett, 137
Jevons, 144
Jewell, 89, 149, 213, 429
Jewelry, 149
Jewett, 46, 88, 380
Jillard, 72
Jillson, 164, 283, 434
Joff, 73
John, 447
Johns, 111, 144, 217, 288, 313, 340, 372, 450
Johnson, 2, 4, 5, 6, 9, 17, 18, 24, 28, 32, 35, 36, 40, 42, 44, 48, 57, 60, 73, 76, 79, 80, 82, 84, 86, 92, 99, 108, 118, 121, 127, 136, 137, 141, 144, 145, 148, 157, 162, 164, 165, 174, 176, 181, 185, 190, 193, 194, 196, 199, 200, 209, 222, 223, 229, 234, 244, 245, 248, 260, 263, 268, 276, 280, 284, 285, 286, 291, 294, 310, 318, 328, 330, 348, 352, 363, 364, 366, 369, 370, 393, 394, 416, 419, 424, 427, 436, 441, 450, 452, 507
Johnston, 6, 77, 79, 120, 121, 145, 188, 278, 320, 342, 343, 377, 387, 440
Johnstone, 121
Joice, 62
Joline, 365
Jolly, 244, 247
Jolys, 144
Jonas, 90

Jones, 8, 9, 11, 14, 22, 26, 36, 37, 40, 41, 42, 44, 46, 49, 51, 60, 61, 66, 70, 71, 74, 75, 81, 83, 87, 89, 98, 99, 101, 103, 107, 113, 118, 125, 129, 135, 138, 140, 141, 144, 145, 146, 148, 157, 162, 166, 168, 169, 170, 176, 182, 184, 190, 193, 194, 196, 200, 205, 206, 212, 217, 220, 221, 225, 229, 244, 245, 246, 247, 250, 258, 259, 265, 266, 270, 280, 288, 289, 290, 291, 293, 295, 302, 303, 308, 317, 319, 321, 323, 338, 340, 342, 345, 346, 352, 353, 355, 357, 369, 371, 375, 376, 392, 393, 399, 406, 407, 409, 421, 432, 444, 446, 447, 448, 450, 451, 453
Jonny cake creek, 96
Jordan, 8, 45, 103, 452
Jorday, 240
Jordine, 157
Jos' Dream, 151
Jos' Dreqam, 151
Joseph, 144
Joseph Park, 129
Josiah, 110
Jost, 157, 369, 378
Jouette, 326
Joy, 79
Joyce, 2, 5, 88, 103, 116, 184, 199, 229, 392, 393, 426
Jubax & Syphax, 150
Judah, 319, 342
Judd, 17, 42, 269, 293, 313
Judge, 38, 221
Judkins, 8, 223
Juger, 315
Julian calendar, 75
junk **Keying**, 104
Junkins, 150
Juricks, 79
Justice, 60

K

Ka-ge-ga-gah-bowh, 179
Kahl, 123
Kalahan, 254

Kalorama, 384
Kambrick, 152
Kanaley, 157
Kane, 231, 341, 372, 373, 430
Karmer, 88
Karouse, 95
Kauffman, 232
Kaufman, 422, 424
Kaumick, 73
Kavasales, 294
Kay, 42, 164
Kealey, 197
Keally, 200
Kean, 293
Kearney, 58, 69, 140, 436
Kearns, 198
Kearny, 34, 123, 249, 311, 316, 399, 407
Kearon, 65
Kearsley, 4
Keating, 30, 245
Keeler, 43, 50
Keely, 439
Keen, 4, 5, 18, 19, 76, 418
Keenan, 10, 86, 103
Keenan's Fancy, 151
Keene, 81, 193
Keener, 175
Keep, 18, 116
Keer, 17
Keese, 229
Keeton, 83
Keffer, 77
Kehrer, 369
Keim, 13
Keiser, 369
Keith, 297
Kelcher, 157, 393
Kellar, 136
Kelleher, 133
Keller, 20, 62, 65, 79, 98, 157, 172, 203, 303, 308, 324, 404, 433
Kellet, 104
Kellett, 448
Kelley, 40, 95, 140, 293
Kello, 53, 340, 345
Kellogg, 289, 434

Kelly, 26, 98, 106, 109, 149, 172, 186, 251, 285, 293, 306, 336, 347, 390, 391, 392, 393, 394, 406
Kemble, 248, 334
Kembles, 371
Kemp, 23
Kemper, 169, 420
Kempton, 359
Kenan, 1
Kendall, 240, 245
Kendig, 73
Kendrick, 10, 72, 285, 320
Kengla, 72
Keniford, 32
Kenline, 6
Kennally, 40
Kennan, 157
Kennedy, 8, 12, 41, 142, 149, 185, 213, 234, 263, 286, 375, 395, 415, 438, 454
Kennerly, 70
Kenney, 42, 148
Kennison, 80
Kenny, 82
Kent, 447
Keokuk, 208
Kepler, 157
Kepplar, 219
Kepple, 373
Kerfoot, 274
Kern, 210
Kernan, 298
Kerner, 28
Kerr, 131, 144, 292, 392, 417, 423, 424, 433
Kervand, 385
Kessler, 425
ketch **Intrepid**, 446
Ketchum, 30, 276, 279, 285, 343
Key, 178, 231, 245, 271, 447
Keyworth, 93, 157, 161, 306
Khul, 392
Kibball, 244
Kibben, 39, 65
Kibby, 393
Kidd, 253
Kidwell, 70, 80, 91, 378, 435

Kieth, 432
Kiger, 384, 414
Kilbourn, 239
Kilbreth, 354
Kilburn, 173, 174, 311, 312
Kilgour, 117
Killion, 161
Kilman, 228
Kilmiste, 157
Kilmon, 393
Kimball, 54, 167, 186, 259, 299, 321
Kimble, 378
Kimmel, 373
Kimmell, 119, 393
Kincaid, 259
Kincannon, 446
Kinchy, 91
King, 1, 2, 32, 77, 83, 93, 96, 97, 100, 104, 105, 109, 117, 136, 141, 142, 144, 152, 157, 170, 175, 176, 213, 231, 246, 247, 252, 264, 266, 267, 302, 306, 309, 332, 341, 345, 362, 369, 392, 408, 409, 415, 424, 436, 437, 447, 451
King's Sorrow, 151
Kingman, 150, 157
Kingman's Discovery, 150
Kingsbury, 32, 136, 144, 215, 291, 312, 315, 424
Kingsland, 220
Kingsley, 53, 69, 174
Kinner, 369
Kinney, 126, 157, 216, 259, 270
Kinsley, 157
Kintzing, 58
Kinzie, 14
Kip, 414
Kirby, 108, 157, 315, 319, 345, 426
Kirdwood, 161
Kirk, 38, 39, 194
Kirker, 359
Kirkham, 317
Kirkland, 331
Kirkpatrick, 6, 276, 278
Kirkwood, 121, 171, 203, 207
Kirtz, 49, 348

Kite, 382
Kleiber, 78, 228
Kleindenst, 157
Klemm, 95
Klingenden, 144
Klopfer, 284, 369
Knaggs, 30
Knapp, 112
Kneads, 58
Knepper, 32
Knickerbocker, 177
Knight, 6, 22, 30, 42, 73, 89, 107, 139, 165, 183, 257, 385, 414
knighthood, 395
Knipe, 263
Kniphausen, 379
Knot, 105, 245
Knott, 41, 107, 248, 298, 369, 383, 412, 416
Knowles, 306
Knowlton, 104
Knox, 184, 306, 413
Koeger, 163
Koley, 131
Koons, 72
Koontz, 11, 152, 382
Korf, John, 245
Korosof, 364
Korponay, 408
Kosciusko, 190, 363, 364
Kosciusko's Estate, 363
Kosciuszko, 363
Kowen, 126
Krafft, 157, 245, 265, 300
Kraft, 393
Krantz, 73
Krebs, 150
Krofft, 401
Kroft, 424
Kubanks, 32
Kuhn, 157, 306
Kuntz, 141
Kurtz, 105, 185, 218, 296
Kutz, 245
Kuydendall, 125
Kuykendall, 21, 146, 152

Kyle, 194

L

La Jeunesse, 48
La Reintree, 114, 147
La Vallette, 64
Labarbe, 264, 265
Labbe, 357
Lachameir, 286
Lachance, 84
Lackett, 24
Lacon, 221
Ladd, 6, 55, 70, 75, 216, 285
Lafayette, 55, 60, 68, 123, 242, 350, 439
Lafayette Square, 431
Lafitte, 255
Lafontaine, 86
Laidley, 121, 232, 314
Lake, 415
Lakemeyer, 86, 103, 248, 260, 298
Lale, 56
Lally, 292, 320, 394
Lamb, 6, 393
Lambard, 426
Lambell, 158, 231, 394
Lambelle, 151
Lambert, 69
Lamborn, 38
Lambright, 161
Lamme, 122
Lamoreaux, 366
Lamothe, 204
Lanahan, 98, 114, 185, 244, 254, 268, 269, 452
Lancaster, 16, 41, 71, 158, 163, 194, 264
Land of the Living, 151
Land off, 151
Landais, 113
Landen, 194
Lander, 217
Landie, 446
Landis, 33, 92
Landrick, 158, 244
Landry, 264

Lane, 1, 10, 62, 97, 109, 112, 129, 141, 157, 249, 266, 280, 309, 323, 338, 407, 448
Lanehan, 449
Lang, 213, 303, 413
Langdon, 283, 331
Langfelt, 384
Langfitt, 390
Langley, 45
Langloid, 144
Langton, 286
Langworthy, 74
Lanham, 2
Lanhan, 439
Lanier, 326
Lanman, 56
Lansdale, 76, 274
Lansdown, 140
Lansing, 95, 280, 283
Larabee, 53, 191
Laracy, 409
Larewso, 151
Lariston, 1
Larkin, 76, 91, 274, 316, 353
Larned, 77, 158, 280, 344, 393, 404, 440
Larner, 164
Larrabee, 217
Lasby, 34
Laskey, 205, 392, 394
Lasky, 158
Lassiter, 7, 89
Last Shift, 151, 152
Latham, 3, 232
Lathan, 158
Lathrop, 381
Latimer, 261, 290
Latts, 227
Laub, 103, 158, 267, 398
Lauck, 205
Laughery, 3
Laughlin, 26, 107
Lauless, 32
Laurason, 409
Laurel Milk, 157
Laurie, 13, 20, 91, 93, 95, 290, 454
Lauxman, 158, 244

Lavender, 157, 158
Laverty, 203
Law, 43, 158, 203, 306, 401, 443
Lawler, 115
Lawless, 309
Lawrason, 381
Lawrence, 48, 70, 107, 136, 152, 172, 210, 306, 331, 381, 384, 424, 427, 448, 450
Lawrenson, 239, 337
Lawson, 42, 158, 225
Lawton, 133
Laxen, 392
Lay, 121, 139, 317, 325
Lazarus, 4, 43, 46, 98, 157, 161
Lazenby, 254, 256
le Bland, 286
Le Casse, 118
Le Grand, 71, 118, 145
Le Roy, 206
Lea, 80, 285
Leach, 158
Leachman, 378
Leake, 55
Leakin, 148
Lear, 20, 148, 198, 208, 314, 364
Learned, 223
Leary, 204
Leatherwood Bottom, 150
Leaumont, 264
Leavenworth, 439
Leavett, 411
Leavitt, 191
Leckie, 215
Ledden, 125
Leddon, 306
Leddy, 157, 158, 244
Lederer, 244
Lederin, 96
Lee, 1, 2, 17, 20, 38, 62, 68, 71, 79, 81, 93, 108, 112, 119, 121, 124, 128, 129, 135, 141, 142, 144, 158, 167, 170, 187, 188, 212, 221, 244, 296, 313, 315, 319, 321, 332, 340, 359, 429, 431, 439, 440
Leech, 21, 36, 99, 107, 142, 294, 308

Leeds, 3
Lees, 440
Leffler, 300
Lefler, 157, 245
Leggett, 31, 137, 152
Lehman, 79
Lehmann, 375
Leib, 230
Leidesdorff, 365
Leigh, 31, 121
Leis, 248
Leistner, 290
Lemman, 244
Lemon, 158, 298
Lemoyne, 424
Lendrum, 318, 339, 342, 412
Lenhart, 76, 274, 324
Lenman, 44, 247, 296
Lenmon, 334
Lenon, 417
Lenox, 196, 200, 211, 231, 252, 379, 437
Lentz, 278
Lenze, 31
Leonard, 404
Leopold, 247
Lepetre, 264
Lepretre, 267
Lepreux, 158, 393
Leroys, 371
Lesban, 33
Lesenfalt, 31
Lesley, 454
Leslie, 412, 427
Lester, 10
Letcher, 275
Leucks, 46
Leveagne, 139
Leverett, 41, 216, 331
Lewe, 246
Lewis, 2, 31, 38, 43, 77, 79, 85, 125, 140, 141, 144, 146, 158, 194, 197, 200, 209, 219, 229, 231, 244, 246, 260, 265, 275, 282, 302, 369, 379, 387, 389, 392, 409, 424, 429, 440
Libbey, 211

Libby, 74, 145
Lick, 151
Liege, 303
Lies, 223
Lift, 442
Liggon, 104
Ligon, 30, 76, 112, 448
Lillard, 442
Lillett, 141
Lilly, 250
Limestone, 150
Linard, 442
Lincoln, 4, 8, 124, 135, 319, 340, 342
Linden, 221
Linden Hill, 417
Lindenberger, 306
Lindon, 32
Lindsay, 2, 90, 326, 409
Lindsely, 418
Lindsey, 49, 266
Lindsley, 79
Linkins, 34, 244, 245, 422
Linnard, 9, 174, 312, 343
Linthicum, 29, 80, 98, 213, 236
Linton, 231, 303, 391, 447
Linton & Larkin tract, 332
Linville, 135, 216
Liomin, 158
Lippitt, 420
Lipscomb, 106
Lisboa, 414
Lissam, 6
Litchfield, 308, 386
Little, 9, 41, 80, 111, 135, 146, 187, 194, 198, 228, 241, 245, 253, 303, 424
Littleton, 98, 133, 216, 229, 408, 413
Livingston, 36, 107, 124, 133, 205, 222, 238, 294
Lloyd, 176, 196, 200, 244, 247, 330, 350, 379, 415
Loats, 79
Lock Valley, 150
Locke, 202, 331, 409
Locker, 58
Locks, 103
Lockwood, 62, 187, 406

Locust Grove, 426
Lodge, 139
Lofland, 281
Loftes, 431
Logsdon, 150
Logsdon's estate, 150
Loker, 69, 263
Lomax, 55
Lombardi, 133, 390, 402
London, 217
Long, 11, 37, 60, 133, 145, 157, 176, 283, 374, 392
Long Old Fields, 47
Longden, 158
Longstreet, 317, 318
Longwood, 297
Looby, 158
Loockerman, 388
Look Up, 151
Loomis, 15, 32, 45, 48, 88, 92, 99, 194, 294
Lord, 109, 157, 158, 216, 219, 228, 250, 358, 372
Lord Byron, 403
Loring, 276, 278, 315, 319, 321, 338
Lorrain, 149
Lorson, 287
Lost Glove, 152
Louisen, 42
Loupean, 33
Loury, 70
Love, 8, 139, 264, 266, 278, 281, 332, 401, 406
Lovejoy, 65
Loveless, 244
Lovell, 115, 269, 316, 320, 339
Lovely, 442
Lover, 158
Low, 326
Lowber, 82
Lowe, 86, 157, 198, 396, 416
Lowell, 72, 414
Lowndes, 198
Lowry, 19, 80, 146, 158, 184, 343, 385
Loyal, 64
Lucas, 141, 157, 164

Lucchisi, 298
Luce, 20, 77, 145, 219
Luckett, 167, 215, 255
Luddington, 151
Ludlow, 448, 453
Ludlows, 371
Ludwig, 153
Luechese, 63
Lufborough, 266, 309, 408, 431
Luffborough, 80
Luftborough, 218
Lugenbeel, 124, 317
Lukenberg, 260
Lukens, 354
Lumpkin, 112, 259
Lumpkins, 133
Lund, 64
Lusby, 89, 158
Luse, 81
Lust, 424
Lutz, 287
Luzenberg, 274
Lyell, 395
Lyle, 6
Lymch, 100
Lynan, 428
Lynch, 103, 144, 203, 244, 286, 300, 301, 430
Lynde, 42
Lyne, 290, 436
Lynn, 40, 71
Lyon, 41, 101, 164, 169, 198, 213, 217, 237, 280, 283, 317, 365
Lyons, 25, 74, 101, 190, 194, 218, 244, 280, 306, 427
Lytle, 232

M

Mabley, 176
Macafee, 164
Macauley, 292, 296
Maccubbin, 380
Macdaniel, 54
Mace, 408, 431, 446
MacGill, 384
Macgregor, 2

Machlin, 140
Macintosh, 147
Mack, 433
Mackall, 30, 115, 173, 210, 306, 310, 316, 339, 344, 360, 391, 450
Mackay, 176, 201, 283, 338, 345
Mackenzie, 346, 348
Mackinson, 1
Macomb, 337
Macomdry, 95
MacRae, 59
Macready, 356, 424
Maddox, 51, 77, 123, 252, 292, 352, 378, 447
Madeore, 46
Madison, 1, 8, 18, 69, 92, 169, 188, 226, 239, 244, 294, 419
Madisons, 188
Maertens, 420
Maffit, 229
Magar, 122, 228, 358
Magarvey, 392
Magee, 85, 158, 179, 201, 248
Mager, 32, 416
Magill, 86, 178, 281
Magilton, 317
Magnier, 306
Magruder, 8, 51, 102, 108, 121, 122, 129, 141, 149, 158, 188, 195, 196, 199, 200, 201, 229, 244, 247, 266, 267, 278, 281, 291, 297, 300, 313, 319, 352, 388, 437
Maguire, 86, 103, 231, 277, 390
Magune, 248
Maher, 6, 158, 235, 392
Mahon, 177, 178, 248, 259, 291
Mahoney, 70
Mahony, 294
Mahue, 79
Main, 50
Maitland, 144
Major, 297
Majores, 64
Mallicoat, 11
Malone, 247, 278, 282
Maloney, 319, 340, 342

Malster, 111
Mandeville, 209
Manegault, 221
Maney, 109, 112
Manice, 175
Manifold, 95
Mankin, 158
Manley, 76, 89, 269, 278, 293
Manly, 2, 24, 119, 266, 381
Mann, 101, 114, 151, 248, 354
Manning, 17, 42, 188, 272, 306, 328, 401
Mansfield, 173, 311
Mansion-House Farm, 8
Manypenny, 23
Maples, 97
Marantette, 9
Marat, 357
Marberry, 149
Marble, 31, 49
Marbury, 107, 142, 207, 257, 296, 402, 416
March, 447
Marchand, 49
Marcole, 164
Mardus, 2
Marias, 95
Marie, 442
Marion, 439
Markell, 148
Markham, 415
Markland, 79
Markle, 92
Markoe, 58, 447
Marks, 158, 194
Marll, 14
Marlow, 362
Marple, 403
Marquis de Lisbon, 333
Marr, 55
Marrast, 221
Marraulette, 166
Marron, 309
Marrow, 409
Marryatt, 323
Marsh, 6, 186, 373, 414

Marshal, 84, 306
Marshall, 2, 46, 59, 115, 175, 177, 197, 228, 267, 276, 322, 407, 409, 422
Marsteller, 332
Marston, 303, 416, 436
Marsutette, 22
Martier, 381
Martin, 2, 22, 46, 49, 68, 71, 79, 85, 101, 107, 108, 109, 112, 121, 136, 143, 158, 167, 206, 216, 223, 231, 252, 267, 269, 276, 281, 306, 309, 316, 322, 323, 333, 358, 367, 369, 375, 382, 391, 394, 408, 409, 428, 438, 441
Martineau, 139
Martinez, 337
Marvin, 7, 15, 48, 51
Maryman, 43, 96, 118, 153, 204, 246, 260, 289, 328, 331, 387
Masi, 68, 158, 403
Mason, 79, 81, 84, 121, 149, 158, 161, 163, 218, 233, 244, 245, 273, 300, 316, 318, 327, 342, 384, 453
Mass, 163
Massi, 393
Massoletti, 232, 350
Masters, 142, 382
Masterson, 145, 289
Mastin, 37
Maston, 63
Mather, 331
Mathew, 217
Mathews, 50, 67, 70, 107, 194
Mathewson, 252
Mathias, 33
Matlock, 126
Matsell, 273
Matson, 303
Matthew, 158, 306
Matthews, 7, 29, 42, 103, 104, 163, 209, 210, 264, 266, 325, 350
Mattingley, 394
Mattingly, 58, 133, 158, 246, 393, 427, 428
Maught, 353
Mauran, 8

Maury, 77, 110, 121, 144, 158, 164, 211, 229, 238, 273, 314, 342, 343, 393, 397, 432, 437
Maxcy, 306
Maxey, 150, 318
Maxwell, 4, 74, 76, 158
May, 34, 48, 122, 125, 146, 172, 175, 183, 229, 236, 246, 264, 275, 311, 317, 338, 387, 413, 447
Maynadier, 351
Maynard, 232
Mayo, 81, 238
Mayor, 326
Mays, 17, 42, 124
Mayson, 80
McAlee, 268
McAleer, 306, 403
McAlister, 88, 329
McAllistar, 71
McAllister, 146, 344
McAllon, 276, 281
McArthur, 81
McAuliffe, 309
McAvey, 42
McAvoy, 17, 36, 76
McBane, 424
McBee, 25
McBlair, 40, 231, 324, 453
McBrayar, 220
McBride, 221, 278
McCabe, 208, 414
McCall, 173, 310, 338, 340, 344
McCalla, 103, 335
McCallan, 172
McCam, 48
McCarthy, 103, 401
McCarty, 392, 393
McCary, 32
McCaskey, 129
McCauley, 136, 196, 200, 225, 228, 404
McCawley, 220
McCeeney, 424
McCerren, 63
McClain, 187, 189
McClean, 3
McClellan, 315, 317, 319, 320, 347, 435

497

McClelland, 32, 194, 278, 411, 453, 454
McClermand, 112
McClernand, 300
McClery, 158, 447
McClintock, 295
McClung, 8, 209, 218, 278, 281
McClure, 333
McCobb, 152, 180
McColgan, 106, 393, 427, 433
McCollum, 98, 437
McColough, 6
McComas, 8
McConkey, 49
McConnell, 319, 359
McCorgan, 32
McCorkle, 29
McCormack, 33
McCormick, 46, 52, 63, 84, 119, 169, 194, 195, 196, 199, 200, 201, 261, 265, 267, 302, 328, 330, 369, 375, 420
McCorry, 101, 232
McCoubray, 245
McCowan, 8
McCown, 313
McCoy, 95, 245, 321
McCrackin, 150
McCreary, 397, 431, 440
McCubbin, 15, 152
McCuen, 392
McCulloh, 152, 351
McCullough, 80
McCurdy, 149
McCuskey, 110
McCutchen, 148, 246
McDaniel, 5, 48, 310
McDaniels, 191, 217
McDermott, 38, 89, 123, 136, 138, 158, 169, 383, 393
McDermut, 77
McDevitt, 43, 247
McDonald, 6, 23, 35, 49, 79, 134, 231, 311, 317, 320, 369, 373, 431
McDonnell, 4, 13, 70, 91
McDougal, 336
McDougall, 104, 124, 451

McDowell, 9, 28, 101, 120, 174, 224, 263, 312, 431
McDuell, 38, 78
McElderry, 289
McElrath, 129, 397
McElroy, 32, 172
McElvaine, 23, 214
McElwee, 354
McEwen, 193, 263
McFarland, 84, 448, 450
McFarlane, 280, 282
McFeely, 398
McFerran, 342
McGarry, 278
McGarvey, 103, 193, 248, 358
McGava, 32
McGaw, 373
McGee, 98, 165
McGhee, 137
McGill, 250, 275, 306
McGilvay, 192
McGinnis, 83, 158
McGivney, 370
McGlue, 229, 244, 306, 358
McGowan, 11, 329
McGrail, 346
McGrann, 247
McGrat, 240
McGraw, 43
McGregor, 137, 153, 247, 415
McGugin, 279
McGuire, 49, 86, 137, 179
Mchae, 379
McHaney, 131
McHenry, 74, 381, 405, 431
McIlhany, 347
McIlvain, 330
McIntire, 158, 231, 382
McIntosh, 5, 44, 45, 51, 71, 128, 294, 306, 388, 397, 443
McIntyre, 134, 369
McKain, 218
McKay, 66, 232
McKean, 249, 326, 344
McKee, 104, 176, 179, 235
McKee;, 104

McKeever, 431
McKelden, 248
McKelly, 214
McKenna, 293
McKenney, 80, 106, 251, 293
McKenny, 2, 184
Mckenzie, 32, 294
McKenzie, 11, 44, 47, 99, 106, 269
McKeon, 326
McKibben, 107, 282
McKim, 187, 213, 259, 400
McKinley, 60
McKinstry, 139, 316, 339, 344
McKissack, 278
McKizzick, 50
McKnight, 70, 158, 161, 194, 226, 240, 454
McKonkey, 141
McKoun, 32
McKown, 275
McLain, 8, 434
McLanahan, 64, 127
McLane, 77, 317, 320
McLaughlin, 60, 152, 219, 371, 374, 376, 451
McLawghlin, 192
McLean, 22, 66, 95, 217, 288, 305, 331
McLeod, 175, 306
McLoskey, 266
McMakin, 143
McMasters, 42
McMillan, 215
McMillien, 281
McMillion, 278
McNair, 138
McNamee, 103, 170
McNaughten, 86
McNeeny, 244
McNeil, 394
McNeill, 216
McNeir, 390
McNemar, 96
McNew, 381
McNorton, 158
McNulty, 106
McNutt, 403

McPeake, 171
McPhail, 316
McPherson, 10, 123, 282, 299, 381, 409, 437
McQuay, 158, 306
McQueen, 445
McQuire, 279
McRae, 14
McRea, 76, 107
McReynolds, 321
McShane, 171
McTavish, 139
McVean, 327, 448, 449
McWade, 31
McWilliams, 158, 228, 254
Md Historical Society, 412
Mead, 42, 167, 214, 278, 392, 398
Meade, 17, 31, 42, 168, 270
Meagher, 309
Means, 14, 416
Meany, 309
Meare, 120
Meashun, 158
Mechan, 230
Mechlenburg, 152
Mechlin, 146, 148, 199, 290
Mechling, 217, 288
Mecklin, 158
Medary, 60
Medeore, 445
Mediore, 222
Meehan, 158, 369
Meek, 180, 296
Meekins, 44
Meems, 267
Megowan, 70
Meigs, 405
MeKelden, 158
Melbourne, 441
Meley, 149
Melish, 26
Mellon, 16, 107, 139, 202, 286
Mellow, 30
Mellrose, 267
Melton, 88
Melvin, 381

Mendeville, 26
Menifee, 332
Mercer, 2, 158
Merchant, 97, 208, 319, 339, 342
Merean, 50
Meredith, 69, 132, 263, 329
Meridian Hill, 114
Merrick, 138, 185
Merrifield, 281
Merrill, 44, 56, 81
Merriman, 296, 446
Merritt, 89
Merriweather, 275
Merriwether, 88, 342, 344
Merry, 141
Mesert, 268
Messick, 330
Metcalf, 50, 66
Metclear, 161
Meyers, 373
Michie, 270
Michler, 217, 288
Michlin, 196
Middleton, 2, 20, 79, 80, 82, 98, 140, 158, 161, 197, 200, 231, 245, 247, 248, 262, 264, 267, 284, 393, 397, 399, 406, 417
Milam, 89
Milan, 84
Milburn, 40, 50, 91, 99, 100, 158, 210, 236, 245, 260, 284, 383, 420, 423
Milby, 62
Mildmay, 193
Miles, 71, 111, 271, 409
Milford, 221
Millard, 391, 395
Miller, 2, 6, 20, 23, 31, 32, 42, 49, 50, 51, 63, 76, 79, 80, 84, 95, 105, 108, 130, 132, 136, 140, 141, 144, 146, 151, 152, 158, 161, 170, 176, 197, 212, 216, 217, 224, 229, 240, 244, 245, 246, 250, 271, 276, 278, 280, 281, 287, 288, 289, 303, 320, 324, 327, 330, 335, 339, 358, 366, 369, 370, 374, 381, 387, 390, 393, 426, 431, 437, 451

Miller's Chance, 151
Milligan, 176
Millis, 73
Mills, 2, 26, 36, 82, 158, 194, 225, 230, 238, 246, 380, 413
Millstone Point, 150
Millwood, 207
Milstead, 138, 228, 369
Milton, 431
Miner, 418
Minis, 308
Minnix, 144, 185
Minor, 37, 121, 129, 133, 143, 300, 332, 342, 345, 346, 408
Minot, 13
Minturn, 421
Mister, 244
Mitchell, 18, 22, 27, 42, 63, 73, 76, 89, 108, 144, 169, 194, 204, 209, 218, 222, 230, 243, 244, 260, 266, 267, 279, 280, 284, 286, 287, 290, 291, 293, 300, 302, 359, 372, 373, 379, 392, 394, 409, 425, 427, 442
Mix, 71, 74, 123
Mixter, 74
Mobelly, 366
Mock, 353
Mockbee, 302
Moeler, 35
Moffitt, 409
Mohldr, 129
Mohler, 158, 244
Mohum, 438
Mohun, 179, 191, 244, 362
Molloy, 431
Molrudge, 63
Monaghan, 221
Monotonical Speller, 63
Monroe, 31, 49, 105, 118, 121, 173, 208, 291, 311, 419, 436
Montague, 14
Montandon, 382, 429
Montgomery, 64, 110, 124, 263, 278, 280, 282, 283, 285, 318, 327, 340, 342, 445
Montizambert, 415

Moody, 140, 454
Moon, 16, 220
Moor, 21, 41, 301
Moore, 20, 30, 49, 51, 76, 79, 81, 88, 89, 97, 133, 138, 140, 141, 158, 181, 195, 196, 216, 220, 226, 244, 245, 246, 254, 269, 324, 325, 327, 350, 353, 380, 413, 415, 440, 444, 448
Moorefield, 96
Moorhead, 235
Moors, 450
Moquest, 327
Morales, 67
Moran, 21, 158, 164, 349, 350, 392, 393, 400
Morcoe, 392
More, 2, 95
Moreau, 141
Morehead, 209, 413
Morehouse, 348
Morell, 158, 369
Morfit, 394, 422
Morgan, 3, 10, 25, 27, 60, 70, 77, 98, 99, 127, 133, 135, 136, 142, 147, 179, 185, 231, 234, 267, 275, 276, 278, 290, 309, 321, 324, 328, 336, 354, 358, 370, 381, 382, 392, 404, 407, 415, 422, 454
Morison, 54, 324
Mormon Temple, 382
Mormons, 439
Moro, 50
Morris, 2, 58, 66, 119, 136, 158, 169, 171, 172, 191, 194, 217, 242, 264, 291, 313, 319, 320, 331, 338, 339, 341, 347, 367, 425, 439
Morrisette, 140
Morrison, 16, 30, 33, 49, 63, 71, 76, 118, 122, 158, 211, 212, 220, 225, 230, 270, 278, 335, 411, 443
Morrow, 78, 306, 320, 393
Morse, 2, 30, 194, 237, 299, 409, 424, 426, 441
Morsell, 59, 199, 200, 201, 365, 393, 422, 427, 438
Mortimer, 117, 158, 369

Morton, 29, 66, 79, 84, 118, 142, 145, 171, 186, 234, 409, 415
Moseley, 26
Moses, 153
Mosher, 132
Mosley, 167
Most, 149
Mott, 295
Motter, 262
Motz, 321
Motzer, 351
Moulden, 296
Moulder, 113, 165
Moulon, 16, 76
Mount, 246, 268, 279
Mount Airy, 148
Mount Alban, 111
Mount Auburn, 325
Mount Clear, 149
Mount Holly Cemetery, 213
Mount Hope Resurveyed, 150
Mount Ida, 176
Mount Misery, 151
Mount Oak, 219
Mount Pleasant, 150, 151, 453
Mount Vernon, 25, 61, 62, 127, 132, 135, 178, 211, 222, 283
Mountain Island, 55
Mountain Way, 383
Mountjoy, 55, 259
Mouton, 264, 265, 266, 267
Mowry, 439
Mozetta, 370
Mud Lick Mine, 150
Mud Spring, 149
Mudd, 195, 196, 199, 200, 201, 228, 229, 306, 358, 422, 427
Mudge, 64
Muhler, 325
Muir, 91, 144, 361, 439, 451
Muirkirk, 355
Mulholland, 446
Mullaney, 289
Mullen, 82, 144, 148, 158, 161, 220, 248, 260
Muller, 42

501

Mulliken, 122, 244
Mullikin, 158, 219, 306, 358, 412
Mullin, 158
Mulling, 144
Mulloy, 85, 228, 246, 309, 335, 358, 424
Mulrany, 427
Mumford, 339
Mumms, 434
Muncaster, 246
Munck, 417
Munger, 72
Munkins, 158
Munn, 186, 286, 366
Munroe, 144, 146, 187, 306, 393
Munson, 331
Murcheson, 48
Murdock, 104, 333, 385, 453
Murphy, 2, 79, 158, 217, 224, 253, 367, 413
Murray, 8, 15, 19, 33, 43, 50, 73, 109, 111, 135, 158, 223, 227, 246, 251, 266, 281, 286, 287, 295, 335, 341, 351, 352, 369, 387, 393, 409, 414, 417, 426
Muse, 1, 28, 158, 255
Mustin, 46, 56, 63, 161
Myerhaffer, 73
Myerle, 5, 42, 102
Myerlee, 93, 124, 232
Myers, 3, 31, 73, 79, 107, 136, 166, 211, 263, 315, 349, 406, 433

N

Nadal, 133
Nagle, 373
Nailor, 158, 393
Nalley, 378, 398, 441, 450
Nally, 244, 306, 349, 369
Napier, 415
Napoleon, 31, 180, 249, 407, 415
Napton, 107
Narbut, 363, 364
Narden, 306
Nardin, 369
Nash, 119, 204, 333, 361, 383
Naudain, 133, 216, 434, 444

Naughton, 194
Nauman, 315
Naundorf, 258
Naylor, 35, 196, 200, 214, 286, 378, 417
Neale, 181, 244, 246, 264, 266, 381
Needles, 77, 94, 326
Neely, 70, 83, 140
Neff, 63
Negroes, 6
Neil, 23, 313
Neill, 121, 338
Neilly, 227, 342
Nell, 295
Nelligan, 198
Nelson, 150, 152
Nepp, 159
Nepp, 244
Neth, 148
Netle, 159
Nettleton, 2
Neville, 436
Nevins, 305
Nevitt, 231, 252
New Addition, 152
New States, 360
Newbold, 128
Newcomb, 135
Newell, 16, 53, 98, 171, 296
Newkirk, 135
Newlin, 381
Newman, 79, 135, 162, 194, 315, 322, 332, 370, 429, 442
Newsman, 42
Newton, 2, 5, 36, 38, 48, 77, 79, 159, 179, 194, 212, 244, 285, 286, 312, 338, 345, 381, 382
Nicholas, 16, 132, 323
Nicholls, 248, 307, 368, 428
Nichols, 8, 12, 29, 31, 63, 153, 158, 166, 216, 247, 278, 412
Nicholson, 73, 213, 231, 292, 306, 307, 447
Nickels, 341
Nickerson, 327
Nicol, 394
Nicols, 318

Niles, 10, 123, 303, 423
Niven, 262
Nixon, 5, 83, 427
Noad, 139
Noble, 159, 194, 244, 253, 269, 367
Nock, 25, 46
Noel, 298, 340, 345, 448
Noell, 99
Noerr, 159, 245, 378
Noert, 244
Nokes, 158, 231
Nolan, 309
Noland, 64, 158, 246
Nones, 341
Norbeck, 158
Nordeck, 152
Nored, 79
Norfleet, 35
Norris, 24, 186, 404
North, 188, 424
Northrop, 338, 345
Northup, 143, 342
Norton, 10, 373
Norvell, 275, 276, 381
Norwood, 129, 432
Norwood Farm, 149
Nottbeck, 95
Nottingham, 54, 381
Nourse, 15, 35, 83, 134, 149, 158, 184, 238, 259, 294, 393
Nowland, 83, 217
Noyes, 104, 197, 200, 380
Nugent, 159, 161, 245
Nunnally, 140
Nusby, 2
Nutter, 137
Nye, 146, 213, 220, 253, 255, 444
Nyne, 112

O

O'Bannon, 342
O'Brian, 63, 248
O'Brien, 132, 174, 245, 297, 309, 312, 327
O'Bryan, 264
O'Bryon, 295, 389

O'Donnel, 290
O'Donnell, 56
O'Hara, 277, 323
O'Leary, 334
O'Neal, 123, 132, 445
O'Neale, 104, 105, 123, 159, 161, 216, 218, 260, 266, 374, 400
O'Neil, 32, 50
O'Neils, 433
O'Reidy, 181
O'Reilly, 76, 235, 268
O'Rielly, 441
O'Ryan, 309
O'Siris, 71
Oak Grove, 355
Oak Hill, 180
Oak Wood, 349
Oake, 171
Oakes, 143, 253, 313, 319, 331
Oakley, 191, 358
Ober, 159, 165, 245
Offield, 74, 104
Offley, 295, 296
Offutt, 8, 267, 268, 358, 426
Ogden, 64, 101, 180, 186, 280, 451
Ogilby, 144
Ogle, 159, 217, 288, 349
Oglesby, 38, 216
Ohl, 221
Old Men's Follies never cease, 151
old Pear Tree, 420
Old style, 75
Oldham, 216, 443
Oldhan, 216
Olds, 214, 279
Olinger, 48
Oliver, 32, 85, 382, 416, 418, 422
Olmstead, 253
oodward, 176
Opie, 219
Ordendorff, 55
Orear, 19, 89
Ormas, 32
Orme, 74, 82, 174, 184, 189, 196, 199, 204, 207, 213, 228, 229, 267
Orndorff, 290

Orr, 120, 159
Orum, 334
Osbin, 73
Osborn, 33, 74, 213, 239, 411
Osborne, 10, 42, 245, 267
Osburn, 194
Oshar, 248
Osma, 69
Osman, 279
Osmur, 123
Otero, 249
Otey, 9
Otis, 396
Ott, 148, 424
Otterbach, 159
Otterback, 80, 102, 147, 165, 244, 245, 394
Otterson, 278, 282
Oubre, 206
Ould, 12, 29, 165, 202, 213, 389
Overback, 287, 289
Overing, 168
Overshiner, 20
Overstreet, 24, 395
Owen, 29, 62, 66, 79, 164, 245, 247, 270, 294, 388
Owens, 159, 285, 291, 369
Owings, 124, 218
Owner, 38, 53, 118, 159, 245, 299, 370
Owners, 295
Oxen Hill, 39
Oyster, 10, 159, 246, 295
Ozias, 193
Ozment, 346

P

Paca, 152
Pacheco, 48, 449
Packer, 64
packet-ship **Mediator**, 164
Paddy, 107, 140, 165
Padgett, 43, 79, 336
Padley, 258
Page, 7, 32, 35, 36, 79, 82, 115, 121, 159, 194, 220, 221, 236, 245, 258, 309, 316, 369, 387
Pageot, 130
Pagett, 394
Paige, 27, 217, 288
Paine, 47, 116, 118, 176, 184, 217, 238, 288, 290
Paintings, 351
Pairo, 249, 307
Palmer, 32, 37, 100, 108, 162, 258, 275, 277, 317, 321, 338, 381, 416
Pancost, 93
Pardoe, 81
Parhall, 32
Paris, 131, 307
Parish, 216
Park, 223
Parke, 404
Parker, 2, 6, 7, 10, 28, 58, 81, 100, 107, 117, 122, 133, 136, 140, 149, 153, 159, 161, 173, 182, 216, 218, 221, 227, 245, 253, 307, 326, 331, 381, 393, 416, 424, 445
Parker's Row, 210
Parkeson, 122, 287, 289
Parkinson, 437
Parks, 76, 274, 324
Parmanter, 35
Parmele, 111
Parmenter, 48, 178, 259, 291, 293
Parmeter, 177
Parris, 159
Parrish, 285, 379
Parrot, 272, 297
Parsons, 73, 76, 152, 327, 383, 424, 451
Parton, 164
Partridge, 164, 299
Passett, 307
Paterkin, 268
Patriarch, 1
Patrick, 341
Patten, 9, 90, 313
Patteron's Creek Warehouse, 151
Patterson, 17, 23, 29, 32, 49, 86, 115, 121, 126, 144, 191, 202, 218, 253, 306, 324, 326, 334, 360, 367, 393, 405, 407, 427, 447
Pattison, 98, 259

Patton, 5, 123, 144, 188, 237, 279, 307, 342
Pattoun, 415
Paugett, 404
Paul, 319
Paulding, 326
Pauling, 285
Pavilion, 6, 203
Paxton, 159
Payne, 9, 38, 121, 159, 244, 245, 333, 390, 392, 414, 435, 438, 507
Paynes, 214
Peabody, 242, 266
Peace & Plenty & Quince Orchard, 426
Peall, 161
Pearce, 57, 149, 191, 259, 407, 417
Peard, 139
Pearse, 233
Pearson, 20, 32, 63, 67, 85, 110, 112, 145, 161, 195, 196, 199, 200, 201, 221, 227, 233, 245, 247
Peath, 33
Peay, 278
Peck, 29, 80, 84, 118, 120, 159, 225, 244, 294, 317, 318, 338, 381, 393
Peddicord, 194
Peerce, 393
Peetach, 37
Peetch, 46, 116
Peevy, 449
Peirce, 128, 165, 172, 218, 369, 427
Peire, 437
Peise, 426
Pelfrey, 136
Pelham, 280
Pell, 18
Peltier, 84
Peltzer, 69
Pemberton, 8, 318
Pender, 280
Pendergast, 265
Pendleton, 297
Penhallow, 418
Penly, 88
Penn, 13, 333
Pennell, 81

Pennock, 300
Pennoyer, 287, 289
Penot, 37, 105
Penrod, 118, 119
Penrose, 313
Pense, 45
Pepper, 377, 393
Perces, 186
Percival, 55, 71, 77, 118, 124
Pere, 363, 364
Perham, 89
Perine, 163, 447
Perkins, 45, 46, 107, 140, 159, 163, 165, 187, 191, 221, 263, 276, 278, 331, 374
Perra, 62
Perrigo, 140
Perrin, 276, 278
Perrine, 278
Perry, 29, 30, 49, 54, 76, 79, 104, 108, 114, 135, 164, 176, 183, 184, 202, 212, 214, 220, 227, 231, 285, 294, 303, 348, 381, 395, 443, 448
Pertch, 123
Pestch, 161
Peston, 307
Peter, 307, 326, 405
Peterkin, 28, 366
Peternell, 279, 322
Peters, 159, 162, 381
Peterson, 54, 107, 204, 244, 246
Petigur, 275
Petrie, 81
Petry, 4
Pettibone, 118, 230, 245, 248, 263, 372, 394
Pettigrew, 235, 262
Pettipau, 67
Pettit, 41, 159, 416, 421
Petty, 17, 48, 71, 259
Peyton, 141
Phagan, 176, 285
Phelan, 381
Phelps, 49, 55, 56, 62, 66, 88, 89, 194, 216, 300, 316, 359, 426
Philippe, 93, 180, 208
Philips, 134, 195, 301

Phillipe, 377
Phillips, 38, 95, 159, 164, 176, 199, 200, 201, 223, 246, 268, 286, 307, 389, 393
Phoenix Hall, 391
Phyloskey, 330
Piatt, 118, 253
Pic, 96
Picken, 159, 192
Pickering, 128
Picket, 424
Pickett, 32, 121, 318
Pickney, 58
Pickrell, 29, 74, 215, 218, 249, 414, 426, 427, 438
Pie, 392
Pierce, 8, 13, 159, 164, 165, 267, 275, 277, 281, 321, 344, 383, 385, 395, 407
Pierson, 123, 221, 248
Pifer, 128
Pig Iron, 150
Pigg, 70
Pike, 7, 176, 183, 202
Pilcher, 209
Pilgrims, 420
Pilling, 13
Pillow, 172, 258, 407
Pilsbury, 133
Pilson, 6
Pinckney, 193
Pindell, 350
Pine, 216
Piney Bottom, 152
Piney Point, 203
Pinkham, 175
Pinkney, 195, 216, 261
Pinns, 309
Piper, 29
Pipon, 144
Pirtle, 100
Pise, 264, 265
Pistole, 16, 125, 146, 216, 291, 294
Pitcher, 8, 98, 206, 222, 317, 327
Pitchlynn, 192
Pitkin, 2
Pitman, 138
Pittman, 112, 165, 216, 263, 268, 293

Pitts, 294
Pix, 26, 84, 118
Pixley, 381
Plant, 98, 105, 159, 161, 174, 179, 191, 197, 199, 227, 228, 244, 246, 303, 393
Plate, 95
Plater, 29, 69
Platter, 6
Pleasant Hill, 73, 74
Pleasant Vale, 151
Pleasanton, 159, 266
Pleasants, 1, 121, 254, 406, 421
Plimpton, 50
Plowden, 273
Plowman, 2
Plumb, 259
Plume, 258
Plumer, 13, 415, 427
Plummer, 212, 339, 342, 450
Plumsell, 15, 51
Plumsill, 159, 331
Plunkett, 127, 131, 410
Plympton, 109, 112, 313
Poe, 29, 100, 162
Poindexter, 53, 77, 227, 444
Point Isabel, 27
Point Pleasant, 252
Pointe, 270
Points, 13
Poisal, 20
Poland Sugar Camp, 150
Polk, 10, 61, 66, 112, 167, 232, 237, 419
Pollard, 117, 263, 307
Pollard's row, 336
Pollard's Row, 117
Pollitt, 261
Pollock, 46, 167
Polluck, 360
Polly & Addition to Polly, 148
Pompey, 247
Pond, 17, 285
Pool, 23, 48, 49, 71, 99, 355
Poole, 88
Pooler, 10
Poor, 6, 23, 87, 223, 290, 380

Pope, 2, 112, 174, 185, 312, 338, 344, 432
Pope Clement XIV, 329
Poplar Ridge, 103
Porche, 267
Porter, 5, 10, 16, 35, 47, 62, 71, 95, 103, 119, 141, 163, 231, 261, 319, 447
Porterfield, 70, 83, 99, 214
Posey, 27, 80
Post, 80
Postley, 59, 186, 275, 282
Poston, 159, 228
Potsdamm, 95
Potter, 23, 69, 111, 227, 277, 311, 341, 342, 416, 438
Potts, 150, 231, 263, 283
Powell, 2, 68, 115, 159, 263, 437
Power, 136, 246
Powers, 2, 32, 48, 79, 369, 392, 445
Pracole, 164
Prall, 421
Prather, 41, 159, 165, 199, 244, 256, 307
Pratt, 49, 164, 171, 232, 307, 320, 339, 418, 446
Preble, 53, 101, 372, 446
Prentiss, 39, 177, 178, 247, 259, 308, 380
Prescott, 191, 217
President Jefferson, 150
Preston, 159, 178, 188, 212, 226, 245, 247, 248, 289, 302, 327, 443
Pretty Prospect, 150
Prettyman, 72, 98, 139, 388, 435
Preuss, 168
Prevost, 344, 377, 405
Prewitt, 253
Price, 205, 241, 258, 285, 373, 407
Price's Desire, 149
Prichard, 139
Prichett, 426, 451
Prickett, 290
Prince, 8, 316, 318, 420
Prince de Joinville, 333
Princess Adelaide, 42
Princess Sophia, 211
Prindergart, 62

Pringle, 58
Pritchard, 109, 216, 265
Pritchett, 296
Pritchett's Purchase, 105
privateer **Gen Armstrong**, 102
Prock, 408
Prollett, 62
propeller **Sarah Sands**, 163
Prospect, 152
Prospect Hill, 34, 151
Prosser, 161
Prouan, 144
Prout, 81, 166, 331, 431
Prouty, 330
Pryer, 32
Pugh, 109, 112
Puhl, 391
Pulizzi, 159, 244
Pullam, 357
Pullen, 245
Pumphrey, 159, 201, 220, 246, 331, 393
Pumroy, 135, 143
Purcell, 259, 328, 366, 411, 422, 453
Purcell & Linton tract, 332
Purdy, 161, 203, 244, 245, 247, 248, 408
Purgentt, 150
Purkis, 174, 187, 291, 294
Purnell, 91
Purrington, 29
Pursell, 159, 393
Purviance, 92
Putnam, 31, 439
Pyatt, 22
Pye, 33, 136
Pyles, 141
Pym, 352
Pyne, 20, 28, 67, 81, 168, 177, 378, 382, 394, 412, 413, 422
Pyron, 63
Pywell, 159

Q

Quackenboss, 125, 146
Quackenbush, 108, 300
Qualla Town, 239
Quarter, 130

Quartier, 124
Quarts, 150
Queen, 2, 11, 68, 69, 141, 159, 174, 184, 196, 200, 231, 266, 287, 298, 355, 393
Queen Dowager, 402
Queen Hortense, 402
Quesenbury, 194
Quigles, 371
Quigley, 4, 159, 161, 170, 323
Quigly, 53, 299
Quimby, 97, 377
Quin, 248, 265
Quincy, 151, 331, 429
Quinn, 5, 36, 124, 246, 298
Quirk, 85
Quitman, 236, 258, 323, 344, 407
Quynn, 58

R

Raab, 407
Rabbit, 159
Rabbit's Walk, 150
Rachis, 401
Radcliff, 66, 159, 228, 408, 437
Rade, 98
Rady, 406
Ragan, 141, 244, 280, 442
Ragsdale, 441
Railroad & canal, 151
Raily, 279
Rainals, 214
Rains, 317
Rainy, 266, 446
Rall, 97
Ralston, 17, 36, 42, 76, 120, 207, 293
Ramey, 70
Ramsay, 9, 55, 97, 159, 161, 173, 191, 202, 208, 209, 210, 215, 266, 310, 421
Ramsden, 95
Ramsey, 29, 121, 140, 151, 183, 217, 279
Rand, 79, 111, 392
Randal, 172
Randall, 7, 71, 340, 349, 393
Randolph, 14, 101, 103, 159, 173, 229, 406
Rankin, 50, 124, 395
Ransom, 1, 8, 141, 285
Ranson, 264
Rappette, 246
Rash, 232
Ratcliff, 141, 237
Ratcliffe, 301, 421
Ratliffe, 418
Raub, 128, 141, 147
Ravenel, 257
Ravens, 73
Rawling, 335
Rawlings, 116, 138, 159, 245, 367
Ray, 195, 231, 348, 427, 448
Ray's Discovery, 150
Rayburn, 446
Raymond, 33, 49, 140, 149, 355
Raynes, 433
Raywood, 191
razee **Independence**, 64
Rea, 22, 38
Read, 22, 141, 186, 191, 342, 362, 385
Reade, 239
Ready, 3, 144, 162, 244
Rease, 149
Reddall, 146
Reddick, 285
Redfern, 65, 100, 159, 244, 393
Redfield, 191, 217
Redfren, 173
Redin, 111, 244, 384, 390, 401, 406, 414, 416
Redman, 6
Redstrike, 159
Reed, 11, 17, 83, 102, 115, 124, 139, 169, 183, 255, 307, 337, 346, 398, 424, 429, 436, 442, 443
Reeder, 16, 42, 108, 118, 145
Reedin, 95
Reefanyder, 165
Reeks, 48
Reese, 1, 16, 78, 98, 128, 278, 282, 387
Reeside, 88
Reeve, 316, 318
Reeves, 144, 221, 297, 437, 443
Regan, 119

Regnal, 36, 42, 76
Rehr, 373
Rehy, 430
Reid, 42, 235, 406
Reifsnyder, 139
Reiley, 124
Reilley, 245
Reilly, 159, 260
Reisnyder, 107
Reiss, 399
Reitz, 162
Renard, 10, 81
Renault grant, 204
Renehan, 369
Renick, 55
Reniger, 49
Renner, 49, 183, 216
Rennoe, 332, 347
Reno, 56, 121, 314, 320
Renshaw, 3, 64, 77, 326, 436
Rentzel, 3
Reperiligny, 434
Republican Bonam, 148
Request, 152
Resurvey on Blantire, 400
Resurvey on Corsbasket, 400
Resurvey on Three Springs, 151
Reuben's Desire, 151
Reverton tract, 150
Reybold, 268, 405
Reyes, 424
Reyno, 31
Reynolds, 34, 42, 71, 112, 118, 145, 173, 174, 221, 241, 279, 292, 293, 307, 311, 312, 339, 344, 359, 424
Reynoldson, 307
Rhea, 98, 286
Rheem, 13
Rhett, 217, 288, 289, 320
Rhey, 281
Rhind, 185
Rhinoceros, 152
Rhode Island Historical Society, 439
Rhodes, 5, 7, 18, 30, 80, 159, 244, 245, 394

Rice, 9, 21, 35, 79, 176, 207, 224, 276, 281
Rich, 63, 82, 109, 123, 174, 184, 207, 303
Rich Glades, 152
Richard, 63, 136
Richards, 41, 49, 159, 183, 252, 285, 307, 381, 386, 409, 431, 454
Richardson, 11, 28, 35, 50, 73, 79, 89, 109, 136, 159, 177, 197, 216, 225, 229, 244, 300, 317, 319, 415
Richey, 392
Richie, 152
Richmond, 22, 65, 222, 230, 253, 291, 294
Rickard, 264
Ricker, 50
Rickets, 15
Ricketson, 83
Ricketts, 159, 424
Riddall, 98, 116, 246
Riddel, 448
Riddle, 94, 136, 152, 184, 209, 248
Ridgely, 10, 43, 45, 53, 74, 76, 122, 125, 148, 172, 339, 340, 345
Ridgley, 36, 42, 213
Ridgway, 153, 271, 346, 378, 393
Ried, 159
Riell, 145
Riely, 414, 427
Rife, 17
Riggle, 272
Riggles, 153
Riggs, 138, 232, 299, 370, 395, 399, 415, 427, 429
Rights of Man, 148
Rignald, 135
Riley, 105, 193, 207, 231, 264, 267, 273, 284, 313, 352, 384, 387, 407, 408, 412
Riley, 244
Ring, 289
Ringgold, 148, 198, 220, 436
Rinker, 48
Rinter, 196
Riordan, 159
Ripley, 137, 172, 276, 281, 314

Rison, 244
Risque, 29, 260
Risteau, 414
Ritchie, 103, 112, 130, 148, 447
Ritner, 238
Ritter, 37, 159, 247, 349
Rives, 80, 159, 162, 177, 208, 215, 218
Rizer, 149
Roach, 73, 95, 96, 130, 159, 177, 204, 266, 335, 390, 432
Roake, 359
Roane, 159
Roanoke tract, 152
Robb, 29, 59, 400
Robbins, 35, 374, 375, 394
Robbs, 129
Robert, 107, 163
Roberts, 5, 19, 22, 27, 49, 56, 73, 79, 84, 118, 140, 159, 168, 195, 272, 291, 307, 319, 339, 355, 403, 422, 443, 447
Robertson, 39, 56, 77, 79, 125, 144, 159, 202, 206, 228, 232
Robeson, 97, 289
Robey, 159, 388
Robinett, 5
Robinson, 3, 36, 42, 59, 62, 77, 79, 101, 118, 141, 147, 159, 175, 185, 194, 199, 220, 228, 231, 249, 272, 307, 339, 351, 369, 378, 408, 410, 424
Roby, 166, 449
Roby's Adventure, 148
Rochat, 159, 266
Roche, 67, 194
Rock Creek, 384
Rock Creek Catholic Church, 440
Rock Point, 151
Rockwell, 112, 212
Rocky Point, 151
Rodgers, 33, 51, 53, 58, 122
Rodier, 245, 247
Rodman, 77, 182
Rodrigues, 48, 99, 452
Roe, 383
Roemaer, 327
Roeris, 79
Rogassi, 67
Rogers, 13, 58, 70, 79, 81, 99, 101, 120, 128, 186, 194, 250, 331, 345, 354, 363, 371, 401, 447, 453
Roland, 232
Rollan, 6
Rollin, 58
Rollins, 194
Roman Catholic Cathedral, 399
Roman Catholic Church, 52, 452
Rooney, 20
Rootes, 416
Roper, 23
Ropping, 28
Rose, 33, 79, 136, 197, 221, 253, 294, 381
Rose Buds, 150
Rose Hall, 33
Rosebury, 259
Rosecrants, 391
Rosecrantz, 317
Rosedale, 334
Rosenstock, 369, 444
Rosenthall, 245
Ross, 31, 38, 43, 63, 74, 109, 112, 144, 159, 246, 286, 290, 311, 314, 355, 369, 389, 416, 421, 425, 445, 448
Rossiter, 63
Roszell, 328
Rothwell, 37, 122, 195, 196, 199, 200, 201, 237, 304
Roucard, 79
Round Hill, 257
Roundy, 401
Roura, 212
Row, 159
Rowan, 10, 82, 100, 126, 379
Rowe, 323
Rowland, 25
Rowlett, 73
Rowley, 325
Roy, 139, 142
Royal, 259
Royce, 31
Royer, 226
Roys, 217, 288
Rozenstock, 397

Rucker, 312
Rudd, 374, 421
Rudersell, 49
Rudman, 144
Rudolph, 188
Ruff, 2, 159, 164, 378
Ruggles, 56, 315
Rugglesworth, 198
Rumford, 331
Rump, 409
Rumyon, 70
Rupert, 32
Rupp, 422, 436, 444
Ruppert, 375
Ruschenberger, 15, 82
Rush, 77, 238, 241, 339
Rushton, 88
Rusk, 235, 434
Russell, 5, 6, 25, 56, 64, 76, 95, 101, 103, 114, 129, 139, 194, 206, 209, 217, 234, 239, 247, 275, 278, 280, 286, 288, 314, 320, 338, 340, 341, 354, 359, 381, 401
Russworm, 114
Russwurm, 275
Russy, 331
Rustie's Hat, 150
Ruth, 32
Rutledge, 223
Rutlidge, 6
Ruxton, 334
Ryan, 144, 240, 309, 327, 378
Ryder, 171, 335, 400
Ryer, 341
Rynes, 12
Rynex, 389
Ryon, 159, 245
Rywell, 245

S

Sacket, 310
Sackett, 173
Sadler, 79
Sagar Camp, 151
Sage, 96
Sager, 186

Sailling, 171
Sales, 186
Salisbury, 32, 180
Salmon, 359
Salomon, 137, 268, 381
Saltmarsh, 24, 87, 185, 193
Salts, 84
Sammi, 81
Sampson, 55, 74, 105, 107
Samson, 450
Samuels, 159, 276, 282
Sanca Panca, 149
Sanchez, 114
Sanders, 6, 86, 186, 254, 424
Sanderson, 41, 247, 315, 338, 415
Sandiford, 185
Sands, 25, 66, 307, 373
Sandy, 29
Saner, 160
Sanford, 10, 162, 276, 295, 297
Sanger, 11, 30, 76, 124, 135
Sanmiguel, 232, 243
Sanner, 230
Sanns, 20
Santa Anna, 126, 134
Sapp's Neglect, 150
Sargent, 145
Sarint, 42
Sartori, 56
Satinere, 50
Sauger, 176
Saulsbury, 73
Saunders, 12, 46, 95, 152, 160, 229, 231, 248, 259, 278, 282, 351, 447
Sauve, 266
Savage, 83, 107, 140, 165, 448, 450
Savoy, 3
Sawyer, 4, 84, 130, 207, 246
Sayres, 132
Scaggs, 160
Scanlon, 94
Scantlan, 274
Scantland, 8, 293, 322
Scantling, 441
Schaeffer, 73
Schaffelin, 129

Schaffer, 260
Schappel, 373
Schell, 300
Schenck, 371, 429, 447
Schenley, 144
Schlacher, 144
Schlegel, 393
Schleicker, 261
Schlem, 171
Schley, 65, 150
Schlotz, 262
Schlutter, 152
Schmitt, 262, 430
Schmucker, 92
Schnebel, 83
Schneider, 13, 360, 393
schnr **Albatross**, 26
schnr **Arlington**, 396
schnr **Daniel**, 135
schnr **Enterprise**, 446
schnr **Franciscan**, 73
schnr **Independence**, 64
schnr **James**, 187, 221, 284
schnr **Mahonese**, 195, 261
schnr **Maria Burt**, 232
schnr **Nonsuch**, 442
schnr **Olive**, 418
schnr **On-ka-hye**, 298
schnr **Pearl**, 293, 302
schnr **Robert Henry**, 48
schnr **Robt Henry**, 46
schnr **Ticonic**, 120
schnr **Valena**, 375
Schoennewolf, 73
Schofield, 32, 123
Scholfield, 7, 38, 110, 353, 438
Scholl, 18, 69
Schoonover, 97, 278
Schott, 89, 222, 232
Schrack, 73
Schroeder, 1, 258, 317, 340, 342
Schuermann, 175
Schult, 95
Schureman, 3, 317, 339, 342, 414
Schurer, 363, 365
Schussler, 3

Schutt, 3
Schuyler, 50, 311
Schwartze, 163, 170
Schweitzer, 160
Schwrar, 336
Schyder, 33
Scolley, 17
Scott, 2, 3, 8, 11, 17, 18, 20, 23, 30, 42, 44, 62, 63, 68, 93, 104, 122, 127, 139, 144, 156, 159, 160, 175, 179, 216, 229, 231, 240, 241, 254, 258, 259, 263, 266, 278, 280, 294, 316, 318, 343, 376, 387, 391, 392, 396, 407, 408, 410, 424, 426, 440
Screven, 318
Scrivener, 424
Seakly, 89
Seal, 267
Searing, 24
Searle, 90
Sears, 4, 115, 122, 158, 162, 293, 314, 339, 341
Seaton, 66, 99, 196, 199, 200, 201, 225, 237, 238, 290, 308, 363, 437
Seaver, 180, 307, 383, 420
Seaver House, 420
Seawell, 100, 276, 278, 416
Seay, 9
Sechler, 421
Second James, 403
Sedford, 285
Sedgwick, 160, 316
Seeders, 416
Sefton, 3
Seger, 3
Segui, 51
Seibert, 110
Seinple, 416
Seinzheimer, 369
Seitsinger, 373
Seitz, 20, 160, 244, 245, 444
Seitzcodorfer, 249
Seizd, 73, 326
Selby, 240, 244
Selden, 121, 130, 141, 176, 255, 316, 319, 340, 379, 416, 447

Seldon, 77
Selfridge, 64
Selvey, 12
Semmes, 9, 79, 124, 158, 198, 231, 244, 245, 246, 264, 266, 267, 307, 337, 369, 387
Sengstack, 105, 367, 383, 393
Senter, 357
Serrin, 228
Sessford, 126, 171, 197, 199, 218, 220, 228, 237, 257, 357, 358, 383, 388
Setter, 171
Setzer, 32
Seven Springs, 151
Sevier, 90, 123, 213, 431
Sevoige, 164
Sewall, 169, 307, 441
Sewell, 120, 160, 331, 410
Sexsmith, 128
Sexton, 48, 99
Seymour, 3, 96, 314, 322, 339, 452
Seyres, 302
Sezd, 310
Shackelford, 32, 97, 287
Shackleford, 121, 270, 342
Shad, 246, 369, 392
Shadd, 31, 227, 246, 248, 393
Shadman, 373
Shaeffer, 272, 404
Shafer, 6, 107, 264
Shaffer, 49, 193
Shane, 6
Shanks, 46, 171, 191
Shannon, 160
Sharp, 58, 74
Sharpe, 140
Sharples, 144
Shaub, 245, 369
Shaw, 3, 5, 8, 18, 71, 102, 112, 160, 193, 246, 248, 294
Sheahan, 185, 199, 200, 201, 406
Sheckell, 159, 392, 393
Shedd, 160, 245, 246, 298, 368
Sheehy, 62
Sheetz, 368
Sheffield, 172, 347

Sheflett, 209
Sheid, 1
Shekell, 264, 435
Shelby, 303, 350
Shelden, 128, 351
Shell, 373
Shelton, 80, 85, 160, 225, 285, 380, 415
Shepard, 139, 231, 260
Shepawney, 192
Shephard, 307
Shepherd, 104, 210, 232, 244, 259, 316, 340, 379, 408, 410, 451
Shepherd's Park, 150
Shepley, 408, 446
Sheppard, 52, 160, 381
Shepperd, 452
Sheriff, 80, 222, 307
Sherman, 172, 174, 298, 312, 347, 355, 363
Sherwood, 101, 159, 369
Shewerman, 95
Shields, 103, 109, 121, 223, 296, 319, 323, 404, 407, 448
Shiflet, 71
Shiflett, 193
Shiles, 197, 201
Shillingburg, 96
Shillington, 86, 237, 325
Shiner, 160
Shink, 373
ship **Queen of the Ocean**, 333
ship **Abraham H Howland**, 116
ship **Albany**, 172, 347
ship **Alice Gray**, 327
ship **America**, 213, 220, 299
ship **Arcole**, 90
ship **Bon Hommer Richard**, 190
ship **Bowditch**, 380
ship **Cato**, 380
ship **Chandler Price**, 185, 253
ship **Christiana**, 97
ship **Clars**, 418
ship **Columbia**, 253, 327
ship **Congress**, 64, 375
ship **Creole**, 24
ship **Cumberland**, 195

ship **Cyane**, 379
ship **Dale**, 64, 375
ship **Dromedary**, 243
ship **Eliza Caroline**, 180
ship **Erie**, 223
ship **Etna**, 56
ship **Fanny Forester**, 412
ship **Fredonia**, 436
ship **Germantown**, 58, 122
ship **Hermann**, 263
ship **Hibernia**, 191
ship **Independence**, 114
ship **Iowa**, 164
ship **Isaak Walton**, 421
ship **Ivanhoe**, 81
ship **James Mitchell**, 136
ship **James Titcomb**, 400
ship **Lancaster**, 374
ship **Lexington**, 374
ship **M Howes**, 90
ship **Mary & Adeline**, 414
ship **Mississippi**, 81
ship **North Carolina**, 130
ship **Ocean Monarch**, 333
ship of the line **Columbus**, 77
ship **Ohio**, 169
ship **Palmetto**, 269
ship **Peels' Own**, 375
ship **Philadelphia**, 371
ship **Pioneer**, 423
ship **Preble**, 169
ship **Prince of Wales**, 333
ship **Rhode Island**, 221, 424
ship **Russia**, 227
ship **Southampton**, 374
ship **Speed**, 86
ship **St Louis**, 289, 302, 337
ship **Supply**, 100, 300
ship **Thomas & John**, 426
ship **United States**, 211
ship **Vincennes**, 47, 99, 106, 269, 294
ship **Warren**, 374
ship **Wasp**, 371
ship **Wenham**, 180
ship **West Point**, 126
ship **Yorktown**, 416

ship-of-the-line **Ohio**, 25
Shippen, 137, 404, 430
ships **Caledonia & Detroit**, 95
Shiras, 191
Shiray, 447
Shirley, 160
Shocco Springs, 184
Shoemaker, 41, 222, 255, 354, 380
Shoewalter, 6
Short, 31, 367
Shorter, 4, 160, 165, 227, 337
Shoumo, 81
Shoup, 373
Shover, 174, 312, 341, 441
Shran, 50
Shreeve, 393
Shreve, 5, 36, 42, 102, 159, 160, 168, 174, 289
Shriver, 270
Shroder, 210
Shubrick, 20, 56, 64
Shureman, 352
Shurtliff, 136
Shuster, 42, 265, 302
Shutt, 372, 373
Shuttleworth, 90, 292
Shyne, 233
Sibbald, 286
Sibelich, 337
Sibley, 9, 63, 112, 172, 174, 245, 269, 312
Sickles, 130, 145
Sidlinger, 171
Sidney, 417
Sidway, 79
Siebel, 393
Siebert, 239
Siege of Acre, 152
Sigler, 428
Sill, 128
Silliman, 355
Silver, 33
Simington, 165
Simkins, 321
Simmes, 79

Simmons, 32, 46, 56, 80, 88, 91, 140, 144, 202, 221, 244, 245, 275, 278, 282, 319, 379, 442
Simms, 15, 46, 80, 113, 159, 160, 162, 187, 228, 231, 246, 247, 292, 393, 399, 415
Simonds, 69
Simons, 77, 79, 95, 183
Simonson, 109, 338
Simonton, 48, 125, 130, 164
Simpson, 38, 81, 159, 187, 220, 245, 246, 248, 273, 285, 304, 317, 342, 347, 358, 368, 395, 408
Sims, 29, 231, 325, 413
Simson, 433
Sinclair, 73, 126, 148, 232, 410, 432
Singer, 422
Singleton, 148, 373
Sink, 83
Sinon, 225, 307
Sioussa, 160, 180
Sister De Sales, 429
Sister Mary Agnes, 78
Sister Mary De Chantal, 111
Sister Mary Dennis, 50
Sister of Charity, 208
Sister Victorine Kenny, 208
Sisters of Charity, 14, 373
Sisters of Mercy, 357
Sitgreaves, 9, 174, 312, 447
Sith, 194
Skidmore, 107, 153, 165, 368
Skillman, 436
Skimmons, 451
Skinner, 26, 47, 80, 162, 436, 450
Skipton, 151
Skirving, 124
Slabaugh, 149
Slack, 255
Slacke, 434
Slacum, 164, 219, 221, 285
Slade, 8, 245, 248, 279, 282, 368, 369
Slate Cabin Tract, 96
Slater, 171, 256, 272
Slaughter, 4, 7, 17, 44, 56, 62, 185, 193, 213, 217, 279, 288, 294, 341, 445

Slavin, 140
Sleator, 168
Sled, 83
Slicer, 20, 98, 180, 230
Slicer's Lands, 150
Slidell, 348
Slight, 160
Sliker, 73
Sloam, 50
Sloan, 50, 95, 119, 187, 259, 303
Sloane, 227
Slocomb, 232
Slocum, 62, 277, 321, 443
sloop **Ceres**, 215
sloop **Cyane**, 223
sloop of war **Hornet**, 446
sloop of war **Marion**, 348
sloop of war **Wasp**, 446
sloop **Plymouth**, 223
sloop **Preble**, 223
sloop-of-war **Erie**, 53
sloop-of-war **Frolic**, 371
sloop-of-war **Hornet**, 371
sloop-of-war **Peacock**, 219
sloop-of-war **Plymouth**, 82
sloop-of-war **Plymouth.**, 413
sloop-of-war **Saratoga**, 64
sloop-of-war **Syren**, 371
Slothower, 114
Slyter, 139, 227
Small, 332, 393
Small pox, 370
Smallbeck, 32
Smallwood, 70, 73, 141, 159, 160, 196, 200, 331, 425, 438
Smart, 49, 334
Smead, 339, 345
Smiley, 210, 349
Smith, 1, 3, 4, 5, 8, 15, 17, 19, 20, 22, 24, 27, 32, 33, 36, 37, 42, 44, 49, 50, 56, 58, 61, 62, 64, 66, 67, 72, 76, 79, 85, 87, 92, 94, 95, 96, 97, 106, 107, 109, 115, 117, 118, 121, 124, 130, 131, 132, 134, 137, 139, 140, 141, 142, 148, 152, 160, 162, 163, 169, 171, 177, 185, 191, 192, 193, 196,

199, 200, 204, 208, 209, 211, 212,
216, 217, 220, 221, 222, 224, 226,
230, 231, 238, 245, 246, 251, 256,
259, 260, 261, 264, 266, 267, 269,
274, 278, 279, 280, 284, 285, 286,
287, 289, 293, 294, 295, 297, 301,
307, 313, 314, 315, 316, 320, 324,
326, 328, 330, 331, 332, 333, 335,
340, 341, 342, 343, 345, 349, 350,
353, 354, 355, 358, 363, 364, 368,
369, 381, 383, 389, 390, 393, 394,
399, 407, 410, 415, 417, 422, 424,
426, 442, 446, 448, 450, 451
Smoot, 79, 142, 160, 194, 244, 395, 406, 421
Smull, 349
Smyth, 8
Smythe, 281
Sneider, 182
Snelling, 317, 452
Snethen, 220
Snider, 185, 404
Snow, 204, 234, 290, 453
Snowden, 31, 220
Snyder, 17, 42, 59, 73, 92, 213, 259, 294
Soldier's lot, 150
Solis, 431
Soloman, 434
Solomon, 79, 194
Somers, 3, 216, 372
Somerville, 10, 25, 58, 244, 390
Sonoma, 432
Soper, 102, 160, 173, 256, 378, 418
Sorrell, 424
Sothoron, 160, 212, 213, 220, 253
Southard, 33
Southerland, 296
Southmayd, 434
Southron, 42, 367
Southworth, 4, 20, 46, 56, 59, 386, 425
Spaier, 49
Spalding, 73, 74, 78, 185, 186, 287, 289
Spark, 9, 341, 345
Sparking Camp, 151
Sparks, 30, 32, 356
Sparrow, 392

Spaulding, 54, 266, 433
Spaus, 107
Speakman, 165
Speaks, 246
Spear, 31
Spechten, 262
Speiden, 48, 99, 124
Speiser, 160
Spellman, 3
Spence, 307
Spencer, 10, 90, 92, 194, 211, 246, 285, 348, 442
Spenser, 31
Spering, 235
Spignal, 160
Spignull, 160
Spillman, 79
Spohn, 331
Spohr, 175
Spooner, 421
Spoor, 176
Sportsman's Field, 151
Spotswood, 416
Sprague, 11, 49, 169, 239, 277, 321, 381
Spratley, 341, 391
Sprigg, 160, 211
Spring Hill, 304
Springman, 159, 160
Sproston, 76, 274
Sprouts, 6
Spurling, 229
Spy Hill, 452
Sryock, 104
St Andre, 352
St Clair, 350, 439
St Vincent's Orphan Asylum, 429
St Vrain, 16, 42, 76, 110, 294
Stabler, 166
Stables, 170
Stabling, 418
Stacy, 41
Stafford, 55, 183, 259
Stairs, 114
Stakes, 424
Stalker, 30, 76, 85, 104, 222, 230, 232, 293, 453

Stallings, 160
Stamm, 373
Stamps, 410
Stanburcher, 164
Staner, 283
Stanert, 15, 22
Stanley, 507
Stanly, 263
Stannert, 434
Stanton, 32, 223, 295
Stanwood, 18
Staples, 10, 62
Stapper, 246
Starr, 227, 249, 338
Starrit, 99
Staser, 60, 175
Steam Mill, 151
steamboat **A N Johnson**, 6
steamboat **Admiral**, 198
steamboat **Calhoun**, 70, 82, 222, 284
steamboat **Charles Downing**, 70, 222, 284
steamboat **Chas Downing**, 82, 294
steamboat **H Kenney**, 197
steamboat **Halifax**, 184
steamboat **John R Vinton**, 271
steamboat **New Orleans**, 269
steamboat **Oceola**, 272
steamboat **Price**, 210
steamboat **Sarah Bladen**, 290
steamboat **Yallabusha**, 36
steamer **Alleghany**, 223
steamer **Benjamin Rush**, 193
steamer **Blue Ridge**, 20, 51
steamer **Britannia**, 81, 385
steamer **Capt W Young**, 411
steamer **Clarksville**, 197
steamer **Edith**, 352
steamer **Fanny**, 63
steamer **Fashion**, 58
steamer **Iowa**, 348
steamer **Maid of the Mist**, 299
steamer **Mary Somers**, 302
steamer **Massachusetts**, 409
steamer **Mississippi**, 352
steamer **Newsboy**, 411

steamer **Oceola**, 337
steamer **Piney Woods**, 394
steamer **Princeton**, 80
steamer **Scourge**, 243
steamer **Trent**, 232
steamer **Waterwitch**, 430
steamers **Iris & Vixen**, 195
steam-packet **America**, 223
steamship **Acadia**, 42, 139
steamship **America**, 144
steamship **Cambria**, 95
steamship **Edith**, 44, 112, 404, 412
steamship **Falcon**, 426, 451
steamship **New Orleans**, 8, 35, 62, 90, 123
steamship **Portland**, 221
steamship **Telegraph**, 8
Stebbins, 295
Stedman, 420
Steel, 64, 338
Steele, 92, 98, 187, 278, 289, 316, 320, 339, 427, 454
Steen, 8, 312, 322
Steenbergen, 197
Steener, 172
Steenrod, 70
Steer, 221
Steere, 81
Stees, 383
Steiger, 160, 201, 393
Steiner, 109
Steinmitz, 329
Stelle, 201, 393, 424
Stellwagen, 89
Stephen, 426
Stephens, 10, 38, 132, 329, 361
Stephenson, 8, 244, 245
Stephonson, 245
Stepper, 159
Steptoe, 115, 121, 313, 319
Sterling, 139, 350
Sterrett, 433
Stettinius, 140, 262, 354
Steuart, 107, 169, 217, 288
Steuben, 439

Stevens, 38, 50, 163, 164, 170, 172, 217, 284, 288, 316, 319, 347, 401, 437
Stevenson, 13, 29, 77, 79, 135, 214, 262, 430
Stever, 281
Steward, 79, 123, 130, 138, 171
Stewart, 17, 20, 42, 66, 71, 77, 84, 88, 94, 96, 118, 122, 136, 139, 141, 146, 159, 160, 165, 169, 196, 203, 210, 213, 220, 231, 232, 244, 246, 248, 253, 269, 274, 294, 300, 307, 327, 351, 353, 372, 381, 386, 423, 424, 435, 444
Steyermarkschen, 160
Stidham, 175
Stier, 126
Stiles, 50, 355
Stinchecomb, 79
Stith, 59
Stockman, 167
Stocks, 49
Stockton, 25, 26, 50, 113, 241, 326
Stockwell, 226
Stoddard, 67, 76, 109, 229, 274, 277, 322
Stoddert, 18, 394
Stodherd, 49
Stoffer, 375
Stoke, 246
Stokely, 26, 175
Stokes, 24, 26, 69, 76, 81, 92, 222, 230, 269, 291, 293, 294
Stone, 20, 80, 112, 131, 231, 232, 238, 285, 300, 319, 332, 341, 362, 387, 418
Stonestreet, 257
Stony, 211
Stony Lick, 150
Stony Ridge, 148
Stoops, 159
Storer, 76, 274
Stores, 183
storeship **Erie**, 169
storeship **Matilda**, 169
Storm, 160, 247
Storrow, 35
Story, 10, 325

Stotesbury, 8
Stott, 3, 64, 196, 199, 244, 257, 361, 364, 393
Stout, 85, 145, 278, 441
Stowell, 426
Strange, 309, 341
Strans, 94
Straub, 245
Strauss, 391
Street, 216
Stribling, 169
Strickland, 101
Strickney, 22
Stringham, 25
Stripe, 150
Stroman, 79
Strong, 44, 95, 235
Strother, 285, 406
Stroub, 307
Strutsman, 374
Stuart, 32, 124, 211, 231, 237, 246, 279, 281, 320, 407
Stubbs, 86, 103, 160, 429
Stuck, 206, 370
Stugker, 87
Stull, 198
Stunton, 30
Sturgeon, 410
Sturgis, 234, 291
Sturms, 141
Stutz, 159, 392
Suarey, 241
Sublett, 128
Subtraction, 150
Suddam, 430
Suddards, 57
Suedly, 49
Sugarland Farm, 255
Suit, 85
Sulcer, 107
Sulivan, 28
Sulivane, 1
Sullivan, 13, 108, 160, 225, 263, 342, 352, 442
Sully, 352
Summer, 341

Summer Hill, 365, 377
Summers, 3, 105, 145, 174, 395
Sumner, 25, 44, 56, 66, 97, 114, 146, 313, 318, 338
Sumpter, 21
Sumter, 8, 439
Supple, 84
Surrender of Cornwallis, 416
Suter, 19, 114, 141, 194, 341, 345
Suter's Fort, 353
Sutherland, 24, 88, 202, 212, 292
Sutter's Fort, 432
Sutton, 175, 194, 246, 250, 276, 322
Sutzens, 139
Suyder, 36
Swagart, 6
Swaggert, 245
Swan, 48, 56
Swann, 96, 120, 254, 332, 405
Swarthwout, 258
Swartzwelder, 148, 149
Swasey, 172
Sweeney, 307, 352
Sweeny, 80, 118, 159, 160, 162, 170, 196, 200, 247, 342, 393, 437
Sweet Pink, 152
Sweeting, 159, 160, 392
Sweetlin, 412
Swett, 277
Swift, 191
Swineburn, 415
Syfferly, 160, 239
Sykes, 317
Symmes, 409
Szyrma, 364

T

Taafe, 309
Taber, 359
Tabers, 164
Tabler, 438
Tabor, 432
Tait, 100, 130, 141, 228, 438
Take All, 151
Talbot, 1, 27, 71, 83, 160, 409, 429
Talbott, 141, 282

Talcott, 8, 322, 338, 343
Talfair, 57
Taliaferro, 177, 285
Talleyrand, 180
Talliaferro, 104
Tallmadge, 217, 288, 409
Talty, 393
Taney, 34, 66
Tangle, 410
Tanner, 160, 416, 432
Tanneyhill, 276, 281
Tansill, 292
Taplin, 276, 281, 321
Tarin, 162
Tarlton, 160, 215
Tastet, 160
Tate, 27, 369, 392, 438
Tatem, 290
Tatnall, 90
Taulbee, 41
Tayloe, 48, 216, 308, 447
Taylor, 3, 8, 14, 18, 20, 23, 25, 30, 33, 35, 41, 50, 54, 58, 60, 63, 73, 76, 79, 83, 90, 95, 97, 99, 102, 106, 121, 122, 125, 127, 133, 136, 140, 144, 146, 160, 169, 174, 176, 177, 181, 183, 194, 202, 213, 214, 218, 231, 232, 243, 244, 245, 254, 259, 279, 282, 285, 286, 287, 291, 293, 302, 307, 311, 313, 318, 320, 326, 329, 334, 338, 341, 349, 366, 373, 375, 391, 394, 397, 405, 406, 407, 410, 413, 415, 418, 424, 425, 426, 433, 435, 442, 447
Taylor's Addition, 152
Tazco, 194
Teackle, 272, 414, 434
Teas, 107
Tee, 135, 176, 209
telescopic comet, 425
Telfair, 22, 49, 259
Telley, 128
Temple, 71
Templeman, 96, 149, 152, 237, 266, 267
Templeton, 44, 281
Ten Broeck, 111, 278, 324, 341

Ten Eyck, 53
Tenant, 160
Tench, 160, 231
Tenney, 213
Tennille, 230
Tensfield, 73
Terrett, 109, 121, 187, 292
Terris, 263
Terry, 76, 131, 308
Test, 149
Tete, 264
Teter, 139
Tevis, 164
Thacker, 88, 139
Thatcher, 165, 171, 224
Thaw, 194, 218
Thayer, 83, 266
The Forest, 300
The Mountains, 234
The Request, 150
Thecker, 269
Thessalia, 152
Thibanden, 144
Thistle, 75, 263
Thistles, 51
Thom, 232
Thomas, 17, 65, 73, 76, 80, 86, 98, 116, 121, 139, 144, 149, 160, 171, 174, 183, 203, 219, 220, 224, 235, 239, 244, 245, 248, 286, 307, 310, 312, 340, 344, 354, 356, 368, 380, 387, 392, 394, 413, 423, 435, 444, 449, 451
Thomason, 99
Thomasson, 48
Thomear, 424
Thompson, 3, 8, 31, 58, 62, 69, 71, 79, 81, 87, 103, 109, 131, 133, 139, 140, 141, 142, 150, 158, 160, 162, 164, 166, 175, 176, 179, 182, 183, 187, 191, 194, 202, 203, 212, 224, 226, 227, 235, 248, 273, 280, 287, 300, 307, 309, 312, 328, 355, 365, 368, 375, 381, 382, 399, 400, 405, 424, 425, 426, 431, 452
Thomson, 273, 415
Thorburn, 326, 374

Thorn, 11, 79, 244, 247, 275, 277, 321, 343, 393, 447
Thornburn, 389
Thorne, 3, 59
Thornley, 80, 200, 229, 300
Thornly, 196
Thornton, 42, 44, 110, 121, 141, 209, 241, 274, 410
Thorp, 70
Thrift, 126, 257, 329, 332, 357, 388, 391, 406
Throckmorton, 16, 42, 76, 110, 269, 293
Throop, 88, 449
Thruston, 51, 307, 393
Thuckley, 97
Thurgar, 222, 294
Thurston, 218
Thyson, 153, 243, 244, 246, 393
Tibbats, 79
Tibbets, 33
Tiber creek, 362
Ticknor, 77
Tidball, 11, 217, 288, 424
Tiedger, 391
Tiernan, 31
Tifft, 71
Tiger, 6
Tilden, 203, 339, 344
Tilghman, 11, 73, 112, 160, 266, 295, 390, 426
Tillinghast, 191, 367, 424
Tillman, 33, 264
Tilson, 254
Tilton, 276
Timber Land, 151
Timon, 399
Tims, 200
Tine, 381
Tinklen, 244, 245
Tinney, 160, 189, 244, 245
Tio, 371
Tippett, 73
Tippin, 276, 278, 322
Tisseuil, 442
Titton, 56
Titus, 323

Tobey, 340, 342, 344
Tobin, 151, 431
Tochman, 91, 107, 197, 250, 365
Todd, 70, 107, 128, 278, 280, 282, 283, 285, 289, 290, 373, 382, 388, 391, 448, 450
Todschinder, 160
Toft, 381
Toler, 77, 118, 172, 416, 432
Toles, 26, 119
Tolson, 79, 104, 296, 335
Tomlinson, 149
Tompkins, 17, 42, 76, 92, 103, 124, 163, 259, 307, 419
Tonge, 137, 160
Toole, 45, 47, 75
Toorea, 137
Topham, 160, 392
Tophan, 160
Topping, 206
Torre, 264, 267
Totten, 20, 313, 339, 342, 407
Toucey, 223, 328
Toulmin, 172
Tousard, 308
Towar, 8
Tower, 314, 320
Towers, 55, 179, 182, 196, 199, 221, 229, 231
Towle, 116, 216, 306, 393
Towles, 144
Town, 163
Town Hill, 151
Town Hill Prospect, 151
Town Ridge, 151
Townsend, 7, 168, 183, 268, 307, 339, 344, 439
Towson, 172, 407
Toy, 258
Tozer, 141
Tracts United, 151
Tracy, 5, 32, 84, 259, 275, 322
transport **Dolphin**, 183
Transylvania, 152
Trapier, 338, 344
Trappist Monastery, 328

Trask, 255
Traveller's Rest, 150
Travers, 141, 160, 178, 244, 247, 290, 393
Traverse, 162
Treadway, 169
Treat, 355
Treaty of Peace, 85
Trebon, 216
Tree, 248, 318, 340
Trefry, 401
Treville, 124
Trevitt, 340, 342
Trezvant, 8
Trgy, 50
Tricou, 264
Trieou, 264
Trimble, 369
Trio, 150
Tripler, 179
Triplet, 99
Triplett, 22, 48, 160, 248, 293, 332
Trist, 58, 225
Troad, 152
Tromp, 261
Trott, 160
Trotter, 263
Trousdale, 8, 322, 407
Trowbridge, 32, 217, 288
Troxell, 216
True, 410
Truex, 278
Truman's Hope, 234
Trumbo, 107
Trumbull, 355
Trunbull, 415
Trunnell, 12
Trust, 225
Truston, 76
Truxton, 274
Tryon, 40
Tschiffely, 160
Tubbs, 250
Tuchahatchee, 175
Tuck, 54

Tucker, 20, 38, 49, 54, 71, 87, 99, 118, 125, 160, 184, 211, 232, 270, 272, 280, 283, 319, 325, 392, 394, 438, 441
Tunbridge, 38
Tunstall, 131, 430
Turnbull, 51, 108, 127, 315
Turner, 16, 50, 95, 98, 121, 125, 130, 138, 141, 146, 148, 160, 163, 167, 173, 225, 246, 259, 270, 291, 293, 298, 308, 311, 329, 338, 342, 344, 349, 352, 450
Turney, 297, 327
Turpin, 246, 324, 362
Turton, 369
Tustin, 351, 372
Tweedy, 94
Twiggs, 39, 58, 89, 107, 119, 173, 212, 283, 310, 407
Twing, 172
Twining, 327
Twomey, 334
Twomy, 227, 369
Tyler, 3, 62, 77, 79, 92, 94, 121, 130, 134, 168, 182, 217, 244, 245, 262, 283, 288, 308, 318, 382, 387, 419, 426, 434
Tyner, 102
Tyrill, 347
Tyson, 51, 160, 162, 245, 301, 324, 354, 401, 443

U

Ufford, 28
Ulrick, 400
Undergraff, 121
Underhill, 354
Underwood, 226, 249, 275, 339, 342, 355
Uniack, 244
Union Tract, 25
Unwin, 164
Updegraff, 250
Upham, 67, 180, 394
Upmann, 276
Upperman, 213, 273, 393, 438, 449
Upshur, 184

Upton, 32
Ursuline Convent, 261
Utter, 222
Uttermohle, 393

V

Vail, 28, 78, 237
Valencia, 126
Valentine, 162, 369
Vallalobos, 253
Van Aiken, 258
Van Amberg, 247
Van Benthuysen, 369
Van Bokkelen, 309
Van Brunt, 56
Van Buren, 62, 232, 315, 316, 419
Van Campen, 285
Van Cortland, 212
Van de Venter, 276
Van Dorn, 314, 316
Van Dyke, 98, 136
Van Hamm, 73
Van Horne, 315
Van Horseigh, 95
Van Horsigh, 212, 357, 367, 453
Van Ingen, 429
Van Meter, 380, 391
Van Metre, 3
Van Ness, 25, 34, 139, 205, 206, 308, 334, 345
Van Ness Mansion, 397
Van Olinda, 233
Van Olinde, 221
Van Rensselaer, 110, 326, 376, 443
Van Reswick, 179, 197, 200, 245, 246, 247
Van Riswick, 270
Van Tyne, 422
Van Winkle, 47
Van Zandt, 77, 160
Vanbibber, 148, 149
Vance, 61
VanCoble, 329
Vanderhorst, 379
Vanderlick, 160
Vandervert, 411

Vandeveer, 79
Vandiver, 148
Vandorme, 221
Vangorden, 17
Vanhook, 66
Vanhorseigh, 164, 309
Vanhorsigh, 170, 336, 442, 451
Vanmeter, 148
Vann, 410
Vansant, 151
Varden, 392
Varien, 309
Varnes, 16
Varnum, 237
Varpes, 31
Vattemare, 237, 250
Vaughan, 150, 185, 404
Veazey, 265
Veber, 258
Veitch, 411
Velmillion, 360
Venable, 160, 196, 200, 274
Vercher, 232
Vere Burn, 54
Vermillion, 139
Vernon, 279, 281, 283
vessel **Kestrie** to **Annie Lift**, 442
vessel **Lawrence**, 395
vessel **Roger Bontemps** to **Palmetto**, 80
Vetcher, 243
Vevay, 115
Via, 107, 139, 174
Vibart, 415
vice, 145
Vickenstaff, 183
Victor, 38, 107
Vigil, 249
Vigo, 46, 49
Villagrund, 43
Villalobos, 136, 221, 294
Villand, 305
Villard, 38, 400
Villiers, 151
Vincent, 118
Vineyard, 425
Vinson, 44, 400

Vinton, 291, 401
Violett, 151
Visser, 245
Vivans, 208
Vogdes, 339, 340
Vogel, 32
Vogt, 104, 140, 222
Volly, 32
Von Schmidt, 450
Vonderlher, 369
Voorhees, 426, 451
Vreeland, 430
Vyse, 106

W

Waddell, 276
Wade, 17, 25, 205, 233, 407
Wadlington, 108
Wadsworth, 67, 275, 331, 372
Wager, 169
Wagers, 240
Waggaman, 311
Waggerman, 406, 421
Waggoner, 121
Wagley, 44, 63
Wagner, 245
Wagnery, 363, 365
Wagoner, 246, 369
Wailes, 93
Wainwright, 44, 56, 77, 168, 286, 327, 340, 345
Wait, 212
Waite, 3, 44, 56, 66, 315, 318
Wakeling, 245, 369
Wakeman, 405
Walbach, 205, 212, 325, 338
Walbridge, 63, 217, 288
Waldan, 370
Waldran, 370
Waldron, 31, 41, 90, 99, 118, 448
Walker, 3, 21, 35, 56, 57, 60, 62, 70, 76, 80, 86, 89, 99, 108, 109, 119, 124, 141, 161, 179, 205, 218, 232, 244, 245, 261, 265, 274, 275, 277, 294, 318, 322, 328, 345, 369, 378, 393,

395, 398, 414, 427, 433, 437, 438, 440, 443, 445, 447, 452
Wall, 36, 85, 93, 203, 232, 243, 246, 423, 443
Wallace, 5, 41, 82, 90, 98, 99, 105, 107, 112, 161, 163, 223, 232, 285, 436, 448
Wallach, 145, 161, 165, 196, 200, 376, 393, 394, 447
Wallack, 95, 206
Wallen, 97
Waller, 194, 383
Wallis, 161, 297, 437
Waln, 16, 42, 59
Walnut Bottom, 151
Walnut Branch, 332
Walsh, 10, 24, 32, 90, 144, 147, 166, 393, 427
Walter, 121
Walters, 152
Walton, 119, 172, 219, 238
Wankowiez, 364
Wannall, 20, 160, 218, 228, 358
Wannell, 63
Warburton, 81
Warburton Manor, 426
Ward, 3, 4, 17, 20, 29, 31, 42, 44, 49, 56, 79, 85, 88, 124, 145, 147, 165, 171, 194, 195, 204, 216, 227, 232, 247, 248, 251, 255, 266, 268, 284, 286, 289, 293, 295, 308, 314, 346, 347, 354, 364, 369, 436, 439
Warder, 196, 199, 200, 201, 222, 231, 244, 247, 351
Ware, 47, 183, 405
Warfield, 151
Waring, 65, 67, 128, 267
Warner, 161, 198, 230, 311, 392
Warraner, 81
Warren, 12, 42, 71, 115, 193, 209, 234, 265, 376, 382, 424
Warrick, 50
Warriner, 401
Warring, 29, 165
Warrington, 82, 136, 161, 219
Warwick, 114
Wash Gas Light Co, 221, 284

Wash Nat'l Monument, 410
Washburn, 37, 236
Washington, 9, 20, 25, 28, 29, 30, 34, 61, 66, 68, 75, 86, 93, 121, 125, 132, 135, 146, 169, 174, 181, 182, 205, 232, 236, 237, 238, 239, 242, 246, 311, 351, 352, 356, 357, 363, 376, 380, 382, 385, 410, 413, 418, 419, 435, 438, 439
Washington Monument, 107, 167, 172, 202, 229, 234, 269
Washington Nat'l Monument, 230, 231, 236, 237
Washington National Monument, 211
Wason, 367
Water lot, 151
Waterman, 18, 42, 54, 90, 212, 223, 293, 451
Waters, 9, 46, 62, 64, 120, 147, 153, 171, 179, 187, 228, 244, 246, 247, 297, 368, 372, 399
Waterson, 232
Watkins, 29, 129, 140, 216, 308, 424, 432
Watson, 15, 22, 24, 31, 32, 42, 51, 58, 78, 90, 107, 140, 153, 161, 169, 206, 221, 223, 274, 286, 424, 433
Watt, 66
Watterston, 80, 93, 172, 237, 243, 246, 291, 293, 410, 422
Watts, 109, 161, 362
Waugh, 7, 14, 37, 70, 73, 378, 438
Waylen, 385
Wayne, 30, 172, 188, 315, 376
Weakley, 452
Wear, 79
Weatherburne, 79
Weatherby, 6
Weaver, 6, 70, 72, 141, 161, 290, 378
Webb, 149, 160, 241, 246, 247, 274, 275, 276, 308, 322, 337, 373, 437
Webber, 444
Weber, 161
Webster, 52, 63, 72, 95, 145, 147, 151, 163, 166, 238, 244, 256, 311, 331, 358, 366

Webster tract, 151
Weddell, 412
Weed, 17, 42, 445
Weeden, 162
Weedon, 133
Weems, 246
Weichman, 161
Weightman, 71, 80, 280, 414, 427
Welat, 9
Welch, 138, 163, 279, 339, 341, 345, 369
Welcker, 201, 338, 345
Weld, 340, 341
Welden, 224
Weller, 42
Welling, 43
Wellington, 379
Wells, 27, 35, 59, 69, 76, 82, 222, 378, 379
Welsh, 7, 17, 82, 161, 162, 165, 278
Welton Glade, 96
Wendall, 369
Wentworth, 300
Wentzell, 232
Werner, 161
Wert, 369
Wesley, 212
Wessells, 316
West, 79, 160, 161, 195, 290, 303, 309, 329, 350, 382, 392
Westcott, 86, 300, 320, 390
Westerfield, 161
Weston, 136, 448
Westons, 49
Wetherall, 81
Wethered, 297
Wetherell, 1
Wetheret, 182
Wetherill, 92
Wetmore, 318, 441
Wetterhurst, 101
Wever, 76
Weyrick, 161
Whalen, 378
whale-ship **Columbia**, 185
Whaley, 161, 245, 248

Wharton, 205, 233, 309, 329, 338, 345, 425, 426
What you Please, 151
What You Will, 150
Wheat, 6, 62, 161
Wheatland, 43
Wheatley, 160, 194, 200, 393
Wheatly, 187, 335, 405
Wheaton, 90
Whedbee, 344
Wheeden, 282
Wheeler, 55, 56, 59, 79, 111, 132, 161, 199, 212, 223, 228, 258, 266, 285, 354, 422, 426, 451
Wheelock, 25, 137, 230
Whelpley, 25
Wherden, 278
Whipple, 35, 44, 56, 63, 90, 281
Whistler, 318
Whitaker, 77, 128, 141
Whitall, 25, 424
Whitcher, 216
Whitcomb, 167
White, 3, 7, 18, 30, 49, 55, 64, 73, 74, 76, 80, 88, 91, 93, 97, 98, 99, 100, 114, 131, 136, 141, 180, 194, 222, 230, 232, 236, 243, 246, 259, 263, 269, 276, 293, 294, 383, 391, 418, 424, 431, 435, 445, 453
White Marsh, 145
White Mountains, 336
White Oak Plains, 151
Whitecotton, 50
Whitely, 98
Whiteside, 279
Whiting, 9, 101, 110, 166, 174, 194, 311, 312, 313, 407
Whitlock, 217, 246, 248
Whitlow, 410
Whitman, 104, 186, 420
Whitmarsh, 22, 285
Whitmen, 431
Whitmore, 84, 417
Whitner, 142
Whitney, 3, 18, 22, 38, 79, 89, 104, 108, 118, 214, 222, 232, 324, 343, 435

Whittaker, 20, 32, 210
Whittell, 140
Whitten, 189
Whittier, 112
Whittle, 212
Whittlesey, 43, 52, 160, 312, 331, 453
Whitwell, 76, 105, 161, 334
Whyley, 266
Wichelhams, 81
Wickersham, 6
Wickershan, 235
Wickes, 347
Wickham, 23
Wickliffe, 10, 276
Wicks, 130
Wiernett, 32
Wigent, 202
Wightman, 37
Wilbourn, 131
Wilcox, 56, 62, 161, 320, 327, 453
Wild, 407
Wilde, 208
Wilder, 76, 223
Wildes, 113, 240
Wilds, 221, 281
Wiley, 3, 279, 321, 325, 382, 422
Wilford Meadows, 234
Wilkerson, 51, 229, 369
Wilkes, 130, 172, 226, 295, 347, 441
Wilkeson, 261
Wilkin, 275
Wilkins, 22, 59, 141, 166, 278, 279, 281, 317, 321, 410
Wilkinson, 3, 64, 104, 141, 232, 243, 256, 263, 276, 281, 291, 293, 442
Willard, 87, 160, 182, 245, 248, 250, 298, 331, 368, 392, 399
Willes, 87
Willet, 336, 443
Willett, 149, 161
Willey, 426
Willford, 290
William, 376
William & Mary, 152
William's Discovery, 148
William's Good Luck, 150

Williams, 3, 6, 8, 15, 19, 25, 31, 32, 33, 41, 45, 47, 50, 78, 79, 96, 101, 103, 110, 111, 115, 120, 139, 141, 147, 160, 161, 167, 171, 179, 184, 186, 194, 206, 215, 236, 240, 246, 248, 252, 266, 275, 277, 285, 286, 292, 300, 303, 316, 327, 336, 337, 359, 366, 367, 369, 382, 392, 399, 410, 423, 424, 426, 439, 443, 444, 448
Williamson, 4, 26, 38, 52, 128, 136, 147, 177, 217, 244, 248, 288, 351, 385, 430, 447
Willingham, 13
Willingman, 247
Willis, 47, 55, 99, 106, 161, 269, 293, 442
Wills, 258, 264, 362, 413
Wilmer, 81
Wilmot, 129
Wilmott, 164
Wilner, 393
Wilson, 3, 4, 5, 10, 14, 18, 23, 24, 29, 31, 32, 35, 46, 74, 79, 98, 107, 119, 130, 131, 140, 141, 144, 145, 152, 160, 161, 162, 163, 165, 171, 174, 179, 191, 193, 195, 197, 199, 202, 209, 212, 213, 217, 219, 228, 229, 231, 244, 245, 246, 247, 248, 249, 254, 257, 258, 259, 271, 276, 281, 285, 293, 299, 308, 311, 328, 333, 346, 382, 398, 401, 410, 417, 422, 428, 429, 430, 436, 442
Wilson's Risk, 151
Wiltberger, 85, 117, 162, 195, 196, 199, 200, 201, 388, 452
Wimp, 32
Wimsatt, 228, 247, 394
Winans, 107, 182, 276, 277, 281, 285, 321
Winchell, 167
Winchester, 161
Winder, 148, 231, 315, 342, 389, 447
Windsor, 48
Wineberger, 79, 141
Winebury, 194
Wing, 109

Wingate, 342
Wingerd, 377
Wingfield, 258
Winship, 232, 338, 341
Winslow, 216, 380
Winster, 161
Winter, 68, 94, 195, 200, 202, 375, 393, 437
Winthrop, 236
Winthrops, 371
Wirt, 78, 104, 161
Wise, 141, 144, 194, 196, 220, 231, 245, 246, 358, 382, 410, 424
Wisely, 198
Wiseman, 72
Wislizeners, 104
Wislizenus, 221
Wister, 82, 85
Witenmyer, 25
Withers, 3, 172, 275, 280
Witmer, 124
Witty, 309
Wm & Mary College, 33
Woener, 163
Woeverman, 204
Wolcott, 216, 272
Wolfe, 447
Wolff, 414
Wolfley, 263
Wolland, 246
Wollard, 161, 228, 358, 369, 390, 410, 420, 423
Wollaston, 224
Wollinger, 373
Wolpley, 256
Womught, 62
Wood, 3, 15, 22, 33, 42, 50, 70, 79, 84, 102, 107, 123, 149, 152, 166, 176, 183, 197, 209, 244, 276, 280, 312, 316, 317, 321, 340, 342, 365, 410, 424, 453
Woodbridge, 7, 54, 212, 220, 259, 339, 408, 426, 451
Woodbury, 243
Woodcock, 35, 170
Woodey, 161

Woodhouse, 8, 275, 323
Woodhull, 428
Woodland, 248, 290, 441
Woodruff, 11, 426
Woods, 32, 88, 226, 244, 322, 343, 350, 409, 451
Woodside, 52
Woodson, 1
Woodville, 170
Woodward, 144, 194, 248, 253, 254, 257, 349, 382, 388, 424, 451
Woodworth, 30
Woody, 356
Wool, 8, 120, 173, 181, 205, 380, 407
Woolford, 277, 281
Wooseley, 355
Wooster, 248, 312
Worcester, 245
Worden, 147
Words, 248
Wormley, 174, 444
Wormly, 26, 161
Wormsby, 434
Wormstead, 87
Worth, 115, 407
Worthen, 206
Worthington, 77, 247
Wragg, 162, 203
Wren, 81
Wright, 3, 12, 38, 71, 100, 107, 109, 112, 117, 140, 144, 165, 212, 213, 228, 245, 246, 284, 315, 318, 333, 338, 340, 369, 382, 397
Wroe, 46, 118, 438
Wroth, 404
Wroughton, 415
Wunderlich, 245
Wutherland, 139
Wyatt, 1, 28
Wyle, 180
Wyman, 21, 77, 277
Wynn, 45, 114, 232, 243, 265, 285
Wynne, 109, 278
Wyse, 199, 314
Wyth, 285

Y

yacht **Brenda**, 374
Yager, 130
Yancy, 36
Yard, 278
Yarlborough, 50
Yarnall, 77, 297
Yarrington, 30, 202
Yatemen, 161
Yates, 246
Yeager, 277
Yeatman, 235
Yeaton, 334
Yell, 191, 217, 229
Yellot, 354
Yellott, 363
Yerkes, 254
Yerty, 89
Yohegany Bottom, 152
Yonge, 173
Yool, 453

Young, 18, 42, 46, 48, 77, 78, 80, 84, 90, 103, 112, 117, 132, 161, 167, 170, 186, 187, 192, 193, 217, 223, 245, 246, 247, 248, 255, 266, 279, 282, 290, 292, 300, 302, 332, 367, 369, 372, 382, 383, 393, 404, 405, 416, 424, 427, 431, 437, 440, 448, 450
Young, 109
Yulee, 445

Z

Zabriskie, 52
Zantzinger, 55, 70
Zapponne, 324
Zeilin, 292
Zeltner, 363, 364
Zenobis, 131
Zink, 31, 41, 84
Zolkowski, 363, 364
Zorriza, 203
Zouce, 275

Other Heritage Books by the author:

National Intelligencer *Newspaper Abstracts, Special Edition: The Civil War Years, 1861-1863*

National Intelligencer *Newspaper Abstracts 1848*

National Intelligencer *Newspaper Abstracts 1847*

National Intelligencer *Newspaper Abstracts 1846*

National Intelligencer *Newspaper Abstracts 1845*

National Intelligencer *Newspaper Abstracts 1844*

National Intelligencer *Newspaper Abstracts 1843*

National Intelligencer *Newspaper Abstracts 1842*

National Intelligencer *Newspaper Abstracts 1841*

National Intelligencer *Newspaper Abstracts 1840*

National Intelligencer *Newspaper Abstracts, 1838-1839*

National Intelligencer *Newspaper Abstracts, 1836-1837*

National Intelligencer *Newspaper Abstracts, 1834-1835*

National Intelligencer *Newspaper Abstracts, 1832-1833*

National Intelligencer *Newspaper Abstracts, 1830-1831*

National Intelligencer *Newspaper Abstracts, 1827-1829*

National Intelligencer *Newspaper Abstracts, 1824-1826*

National Intelligencer *Newspaper Abstracts, 1821-1823*

National Intelligencer *Newspaper Abstracts, 1818-1820*

National Intelligencer *Newspaper Abstracts, 1814-1817*

National Intelligencer *Newspaper Abstracts, 1811-1813*

National Intelligencer *Newspaper Abstracts, 1806-1810*

National Intelligencer *Newspaper Abstracts, 1800-1805*

www.ingramcontent.com/pod-product-compliance
Lightning Source LLC
Chambersburg PA
CBHW060908300426
44112CB00011B/1390